100 YEARS

SIMON &
SCHUSTER

SEVEN

PRESIDENTS

and Their

SEARCH

FOR PURPOSE

BEYOND THE

WHITE HOUSE

LIFE
AFTER
POWER

JARED
COHEN

Simon & Schuster
New York London Toronto Sydney New Delhi

100 YEARS
SIMON &
SCHUSTER

1230 Avenue of the Americas
New York, NY 10020

First Simon & Schuster hardcover edition February 2024

SIMON & SCHUSTER and colophon are registered
trademarks of Simon & Schuster, Inc.

Simon & Schuster: Celebrating 100 Years of Publishing in 2024

For information about special discounts for bulk purchases,
please contact Simon & Schuster Special Sales at
1-866-506-1949 or business@simonandschuster.com.

The Simon & Schuster Speakers Bureau can bring authors to
your live event. For more information or to book an event, contact
the Simon & Schuster Speakers Bureau at 1-866-248-3049
or visit our website at www.simonspeakers.com.

Interior design by Lewelin Polanco

Manufactured in the United States of America

3   5   7   9   10   8   6   4   2

Library of Congress Cataloging-in-Publication Data is available.

ISBN 978-1-9821-5454-7
ISBN 978-1-9821-5456-1 (ebook)

For my parents, Dee and Donald Cohen,
who have always been my North Star
for happiness and fulfillment

Would it promote the peace of the community, or the stability of the government to have half a dozen men who had had credit enough to be raised to the seat of the supreme magistracy, wandering among the people like discontented ghosts, and sighing for a place which they were destined never more to possess?

—ALEXANDER HAMILTON, "FEDERALIST 72," MARCH 21, 1788[1]

CONTENTS

PREFACE

My first work of presidential history was called *Accidental Presidents*. It was a book about the eight times a vice president has become president upon the death of his predecessor, and history was changed in a heartbeat. It answered the question of what happens when the president dies. The question I wanted to answer next was what happens when presidents survive, how they decide what to do next, and how they make history after the White House.

The answers aren't obvious, and there's a gap in most presidential histories. They focus on how their subjects climbed to the top of the mountain, not what they did when they had to come back down again. The post-presidency is an afterthought. Sometimes that's the right choice. George Washington wanted a quiet retirement at Mount Vernon, and he got it (although his debts and hordes of voyeurs made it less restful than he would have liked). But in many cases, glossing over the final years or decades of a life is a mistake. This is when presidents often reveal who they are and what they really want in life. They have power, even if they don't hold office. We've witnessed what a former president can do, for good or ill, repeatedly in the 2020s.

This book is about history and it's about life. There is no more dramatic career transition than leaving the White House. But former presidents don't lose their drive or ambition the day they leave office. In many cases, they're just getting started. They can do what they always wanted, be it founding a new university (Thomas Jefferson) or becoming chief justice of the Supreme Court (William Howard Taft). They take on new causes, like abolition (John Quincy Adams) or fighting populism and imperialism (Grover Cleveland). They challenge their successors' policies (Herbert Hoover and Jimmy Carter). One of them completely moved on from politics, and discovered a new postpresidential voice that doesn't undermine his successors (George W. Bush). They made history in the White House, and many of them want to make it after leaving. They have, for more than two hundred years.

There's a gap in presidential history when it comes to life after the White House. But there's also a more relatable part to their stories that offers lessons and warnings for everyone. Former presidents have to answer the kinds of questions that we all face in our own lives, be they about family, finances, or the future. Formerly the leaders of the government, these once-larger-than-life figures now deal with very ordinary problems that set the stage for the rest of their lives. I started to appreciate that everyone—not just aspiring future presidents—can take away life lessons about navigating our next chapters from the stories of the post-presidency.

This fact became obvious during my writing process. Thankfully, unless they were around in 1963, few of my friends and colleagues could relate to the presidential assassinations I wrote about in *Accidental Presidents*. My three young daughters thought it was a pretty morbid subject. But everyone could understand what it's like to have one role that is all-consuming and leave it all behind. For some, it's a liberating experience. For others, it can feel like there's nothing left. As the former presidents show, the next chapter is what you make of it.

American history provided plenty of material. Many of us are interested in the presidents, and we all need models to follow in our own lives. Why not look for the latter in the former? If we do, we'll understand American history and the kinds of choices we'll all make at some point a little better than we did before.

—*J.A.C., February 2024*

INTRODUCTION

K ing George III looked across the Atlantic and mourned. He was witnessing the "downfall of the lustre of [the British] empire."[2] It was September 3, 1783, and earlier that day, the king had proclaimed peace with his thirteen former colonies across the sea. The American Revolution was over. The British Empire was defeated. What came next would prove how revolutionary the war had been. General Washington would soon do something that a king would never do—give up power.

During the war, the king had asked Benjamin West, a Loyalist artist, what he thought General Washington might do in the unthinkable event of a colonial victory. West, who knew something of Washington's reputation, answered quickly that he would "return to his farm." "If he does that," the monarch replied with skeptical disbelief, "he will be the greatest man in the world."[3]

West was right; Washington resigned his commission that year. When he gave up the presidency a few years later, voluntarily bidding farewell after two terms, King George III described his former foe as "the greatest character of the age."[4]

The Washington precedent has held, and that has made all the difference. Democratic republics only work when the leaders don't cling to power after their citizens have decided to place power in other hands. But few leaders in history have had that ability. From Julius Caesar to Oliver Cromwell, revolutionary commanders throughout history held on to power until the day they died. Planning his own return to Paris while living in exile in Elba, Napoleon Bonaparte defiantly told his aides, "They wanted me to be another George Washington." To the bellicose Corsican, that would be a fate worse than Waterloo.[5]

Washington set the precedent for other presidents to follow, but his precedent hasn't taken hold around the world. In many countries, leaving from power is dangerous. That's part of why Vladimir Putin and Xi Jinping have no intention to step down. It may also be why Kim Il Sung—who died in 1994—is still honored as North Korea's "eternal ruler," making the Hermit Kingdom the world's first and only "necrocracy."[6] Even in the United States, after the terrible events of January 6, 2021, the peaceful transfer of power cannot be taken for granted.

For those leaders who do follow Washington's precedent, leaving high office means leaving behind the powers and pomp of state, and returning to everyday concerns like relevance, professional jealousy, and ego. Away from power, leaders come face-to-face with their neglected relationships, finances, legacies, and the aftereffects of a job that leaves them older, grayer, and closer than ever to their own mortality.

Life After Power tells how seven former presidents decided what to do with the rest of their lives, and how they made history in the process. The book examines these men as human beings, who searched for purpose in their final decades. They had left the most important job they'd ever had, and they had nowhere else to climb. They offer lessons—as well as cautionary tales—to anyone contemplating the next chapters of their own lives.

The post-presidency is still an undiscovered story for most presidential biographies. They often treat their subjects' final decades as little more than denouements at best, and as slow marches to the grave at worst. That's a mistake. True, the post-presidency is not an official office. Former presidents have no formal power. But they have a status in American life that never goes away. They have many of the trappings of their old office, including these days Secret Service protection, a staff, and a pension to "maintain the dignity of the office." They will also always be the people that millions or tens of millions once voted into the White House. They want to stay in the arena. And for more than two hundred years, they have.

MAKING HISTORY

The seven former presidents in this book are not the only ones who achieved something great after the White House. But they each did something that none of their predecessors or successors did. They show that America's presidents can sometimes accomplish more after the White House than in it. They demonstrate how former presidents can take on new identities and find new purposes. They allow us to rethink about how the post-presidency—an institution with no formal structure that is almost as old as the United States—has, like the presidency itself, expanded in scope and possibility. By leaving behind the title "President of the United States" and returning to life as citizens, they've continued a democratic tradition. They've also had to answer the question of what you do when there is nowhere higher to climb, and have to decide for yourself, "What next?"

Thomas Jefferson, John Quincy Adams, Grover Cleveland, William Howard Taft, Herbert Hoover, Jimmy Carter, and George W. Bush answered this question in different ways. Their lives span American history, from the founding to the present. They come from different backgrounds and different parties. They hold different places in Americans' memories.

Thomas Jefferson was the first former president to achieve something at the end of his life that was worth including on his tombstone. He set a precedent for every former president striving for one last accomplishment. He's remembered as a Founding Father for what he did in 1776, at age thirty-three. But he was a *lifelong founder*, who spent his last decade creating the University of Virginia, one of the country's top institutions of higher learning. No other former president—and few former heads of state in history—has built an institution that has thrived for more than two centuries.

John Quincy Adams's presidency was an intermission between two of the most impressive careers in public life in American history. He's the only former president to be elected to the House of Representatives, where he served nine terms and died in the Capitol in 1848. In a much lower office, he found a much higher calling. In this historic *second act*, he became a leader for the growing abolitionist movement, he launched a crusade to protect the right to petition and free speech, he represented enslaved men and women before the Supreme Court, and he passed the abolitionist torch from the founding generation to a young congressman named Abraham Lincoln.

Grover Cleveland is the only former president to run for a nonconsecutive term and win. His successful *comeback* to the White House made him America's twenty-second and twenty-fourth commander in chief. He held back a populist tide in his own party and an imperialist wave in the other. But in the process, he sacrificed his popularity and happiness, learning the hard way that the job can be harder and less forgiving the second time around. After his second presidency, he battled with future president Woodrow Wilson at Princeton University and spent years reconciling what had happened to his legacy. His story offers a cautionary tale.

William Howard Taft never really wanted to be president. He yearned for a seat on the Supreme Court. But he *deferred that dream* to accommodate the wishes of his wife, his brothers, and his friend Theodore Roosevelt. He lost the presidency in a humiliating third-place finish in 1912, and he thought his career in public service was over. But when Warren Harding named him chief justice in 1921, Taft was so delighted that he barely remembered his four years in the White House. As chief justice, he reformed the Supreme Court and the federal judiciary. On a personal level, his years on the bench—the final decade of his life—were the happiest and most fulfilling. He is the only person in American history to lead two branches of the federal government.

Herbert Hoover's one-term presidency has gone down as one of the worst in history. But his thirty-one-year post-presidency was one of the most influential. It was a journey of *recovery*. For twelve years, he railed against the New Deal, shaping the rise of the modern conservative movement. When Franklin Delano Roosevelt died in 1945, Harry Truman resurrected Hoover, enlisting his only living predecessor to lead international famine relief after World War II.[7] Once known as the "Great Humanitarian," Hoover reformed the executive branch under Presidents Truman and Eisenhower. He reconciled John F. Kennedy and Richard Nixon after the divisive 1960 election. While his name has not fully recovered, he did recover his role as a great humanitarian and man of service. He reminded Americans why they had elected him president in the first place, and at least in his lifetime, some of that gloss had been restored to his name even if it posthumously wore off.

Jimmy Carter had the longest active post-presidency in American history, at forty-two years, before entering hospice care. He left office unpopular, with a sinking economy and American hostages in Tehran. But he went on to become one of America's most beloved leaders, after having spent four decades leading humanitarian efforts around the world. He was a constant thorn in the sides of his successors, at times undermining their policies because he was convinced that he was right and they were wrong. He viewed life after the White House as an extension of his presidency. Through his activism, he redefined what it means to be a *former* and staying relevant until the very end.

These six presidents each had compelling and instructive final chapters of their life story. But what about the presidents whose chapters are still being written? In thinking about who to include, Bill Clinton, Barack Obama, and Donald Trump have each experienced a decline in their popularity since leaving office—albeit for different reasons. Only George W. Bush has managed to significantly improve his standing and experience something of a reputational renaissance.

It's fitting for Bush to be examined in sequence after Carter, since they both left office with abysmal approval ratings. But whereas Carter pursued one of the most public journeys out of the White House in history, George W. Bush's post-presidency is different. He's a return to an earlier era, the Washington precedent. For Bush, politics ended the day he left office. After a lifetime in and around public life, he moved on. He doesn't miss it. He doesn't try to reshape his legacy. He is not introspective. His party has changed, and his successors have undone much of his work. His days are spent on his faith, family, and a pastime that no one predicted—painting. And it is through painting that George W. Bush has found a postpresidential voice that allows him to express what he believes, while steering clear of politics. His work elevates people often overlooked—from veterans to immigrants—and in doing so, he raises their visibility, shares their stories, and contributes to important conversations without undermining his successors. Whether he intended to or not, his popularity has not just recovered, but soared north of 60 percent.

THE FINAL CHAPTER

Each of these seven men charted their own paths to the White House. But they each left it in the same way. There was a peaceful transfer of power to a new president. Then they had to decide what to do with the time left.

Leaders in every field face this question. When Bill Gates left Microsoft, he and his then wife, Melinda, built a world-class philanthropic organization. Steve Jobs was forced out of Apple, but he made a historic comeback and changed humanity's relationship with technology. Oprah Winfrey was fired from her first reporting job, then hosted the highest-rated daytime talk show in American history. Then she built a media empire. Basketball legend Michael Jordan retired, had a brief baseball career, returned to the sport he'd always loved, won three more championships, then turned a $275 million investment in the Charlotte Bobcats into a more than $3 billion sale.[8] Google's CEO Eric Schmidt transformed the Silicon Valley start-up into a world leader in technology. Now he's focused on public service and helps the U.S. government and other democratic nations harness the power of technology.

We can only guess what today's leaders at the top of their fields will do next. If Elon Musk doesn't spend all day tweeting, he may live out his final days (or day) on Mars. Mark Zuckerberg could decide he's had enough of the real world and head straight for the Metaverse. And the myriad next generation founders pioneering generative artificial intelligence are so young that it is impossible to speculate as to what they will do in their twilight years.

For all of us, life doesn't end with the first line of our obituaries. If we're lucky, life is long. We all move on. We make decisions about what to do next. Life is not linear, where we're set on a path of climbing higher and higher, with no peak in sight. We need not be defined by one job, no matter how powerful that job is. Studying how the most

powerful people in the world left that power behind and made decisions for themselves is a great place to start if we want to know how
to do it well.

The post-presidency is not written into the American Constitution. But its existence is assumed, and it is essential to America's form
of government. Every president knows that the White House isn't forever. They need to believe that life after power is possible.

These seven former presidents offer proof that not only is it
possible—life after power can be great.

LIFE
AFTER
POWER

The Lifelong Founder

All eyes are opened, or opening, to the rights of man. The general spread of the light of science has already laid open to every view. The palpable truth, that the mass of mankind has not been born with saddles on their backs, nor a favored few booted and spurred, ready to ride them legitimately, by the grace of god.

—THOMAS JEFFERSON, *NATIONAL INTELLIGENCER,* JULY 4, 1826

Near the end of his life, Thomas Jefferson couldn't believe what was happening. It was October 4, 1825. Forty-nine years ago, he'd drafted the Declaration of Independence. Sixteen years ago, he'd left Washington, DC, for good at the end of his two-term presidency. He was now eighty-two years old. The octogenarian stood weak and weary. And he wondered if his life's work was coming undone.

That day, the Founding Father gazed out with disgust and disappointment. He was surveying the first class of students at the University of Virginia. It was one of the worst days of his long, and illustrious life.[1]

He wasn't thinking about his declining health, or the political changes sweeping the nation. He wasn't worried about his mounting debts, which would put the fate of his beloved Monticello in doubt. Nor was he reflecting on the fact that the Virginia Dynasty was out of power, and that a man from Massachusetts was in the White House. The questions of slavery, westward expansion, and the fate of the union seemed far away, even if for a moment.

His concern was over the viability of the University of Virginia.

This was the last great triumph of his life. And everything he'd built was under threat. The school was in danger because fourteen drunk students had rioted across the campus, a place that Jefferson had lovingly designed and built himself. This was his final masterpiece. And they'd sullied it.

The details of the riot shook Jefferson. For several days, a mask-wearing mob of students had torn across the University of Virginia's Lawn, throwing bottles of smelly urine through the windows of their instructors' homes on their way across campus. All the while, they'd chanted, "Down with European professors" in an early nineteenth-century version of the cancel culture sweeping college campuses nearly two hundred years later. They assaulted the faculty Jefferson had recruited. One even beat a professor with his own cane, leaving him bloody and humiliated.[2]

The school needed to be restored to order, and it needed swift and harsh discipline of the perpetrators. The university's administrators had gathered, looking to discover which of the students had participated in the riot. But because the mob had covered their faces with masks, the identities were a mystery. No one was talking. In a twisted show of Southern honor, the students wouldn't give each other up to the disciplinary review panel.

The university's board had no other option. They called an all-school assembly to find out the "unworthy few who lurked among" the student body.[3] The board's illustrious membership included not only Thomas Jefferson, but also James Madison and James Monroe, the latter of the three having left the presidency exactly seven months prior.[4] The three Founding Fathers and former presidents, living links to the revolutionary generation, may have been the most distinguished and intimidating undergraduate disciplinary review panel in American history. As young men, they'd once rebelled against the king of England. Now they were disciplinarians scolding entitled students.[5]

The three men looked out at one hundred undergraduates, most not even nineteen years old, who were gathered in the school's not-yet-completed Rotunda.[6] For the student body—including the guilty rioters—Thomas Jefferson was more than a distant figure from the history books. He was their patron, and a part of their lives. On Sundays, the former president would host small groups of students for dinner at Monticello. He went in alphabetical order in choosing his guests so as not to show favoritism. Over dinner, he'd tell them about the Revolution and ask them about their studies.[7]

None of Monticello's warmth could be felt that chilly October day. Jefferson was far too overcome with emotion and disappointment to speak. He burst into tears, so shaken that he had to sit down.[8] This emotional display was not in character. It caught the students, and the board, off guard.

A choked-up Jefferson—barely able to string a sentence together—asked if someone else might speak, and his trusted friend James Madison obliged. But Madison didn't have to say much. The students were shocked at the sight of Jefferson, a seemingly immortal man, now aged and in failing health, crying and whimpering in front of them. As tears flowed down the octogenarian's face, the wall of silence collapsed, and the guilty confessed. It was over.

For Jefferson, however, there would be one final insult that hit even closer to home. It turned out that the mob's ringleader was Wilson Cary, Jefferson's great-nephew. This betrayal by his own flesh and blood made the former president's cold tears boil. He wrote later that it seemed that the "last ten years of his life [building the University of Virginia] had been foiled by one of his own family."[9] He was genuinely worried about what the event meant about the future of the University of Virginia, of the next generation, and of the country they were to inherit when the Founding Fathers were long gone.

The University of Virginia was the culmination of Jefferson's life's work. The former president viewed that work as a trilogy, with the university as the final volume. The first two entries were the Declaration of Independence and the Virginia Statute for Religious Freedom, drafted in 1776 and 1777, respectively.[10] Had the riot been worse, it might have threatened state funding and future enrollments. As it was, the faculty was up in arms. Two professors resigned. Three students were expelled, including young Mr. Cary. Reform was needed to prevent revolution, and the board issued new rules of student conduct, including banning masks and setting a 9:00 p.m. curfew. Christmas break was canceled.[11]

The expulsions created space for three new students to join the university's inaugural class midyear. Among those who came to campus just a few months after the riot was sixteen-year-old Edgar Allan Poe, who spent his first year living on the West Range of campus, in a group of houses called "Rowdy Row." Poe would go on to become the most famous alumnus of that crop of students, but he, too, would prove to be a disappointment for the University of Virginia.

Poe was not Virginia royalty; he couldn't afford the school's tuition. That winter, he chopped up his dorm room furniture for firewood to stay warm. While a student, he took to drinking and he gambled. He may not have been prone to the kind of activism that had put his classmates in hot water, but he had other problems. He dropped out without a degree due to his impecunious situation, voiding what had potential to be a poetic silver lining made possible by the expulsions.[12]

Thomas Jefferson left the assembly pessimistic about university life and young people.[13] To Jefferson, the unfolding of history was supposed to go hand in hand with progress. Each rising generation was meant to be better than the last. Reason, science, and rationality were the drivers of inevitable progress. But it turned out that a few drunk students armed with bricks and bags of urine could throw his plans into jeopardy.

The University of Virginia, and Thomas Jefferson's vision, survived. The riots of 1825 weren't the last word on "Mr. Jefferson's University." They were forgotten. Jefferson had lived long enough to found a great institution, one that brought together Greek and Roman ideas, Enlightenment principles, and Jefferson's distinct personality and hopes, as well as his contradictions and ideals.

For the Founding Father, it was his last founding act.

Human beings wonder how they will be remembered. Author and diplomat Clare Boothe Luce once observed on the matter that even "a great man is one sentence."[14] The men who signed the Declaration of Independence and the Constitution knew what their sentences would be long before they died. These were the "Founding Fathers."

No matter what happened, so long as the United States survived, this is how they would be remembered.

But for many of them, the founding was not the whole story—it was their last or first great act. For some, like Benjamin Franklin, seventy years old in 1776, the founding came at the close of their long lives. Most of the Founding Fathers, however, were young when they signed the Declaration. Among the youngest was the man who wrote it, Thomas Jefferson, at just thirty-three.[15] John Adams wasn't far ahead, at forty. George Washington, senior in the group, was forty-four.

Thomas Jefferson wanted to be a Founder more than he wanted to be president. He had grand ideas, took risks, and committed himself fully to whatever he did, but he was not an executive.[16] The presidency wasn't the most important part of his life—what came before and after was. His chosen epitaph reads: "Author of the Declaration of American Independence of the Statute of Virginia for religious freedom & Father of the University of Virginia."[17] Being America's first secretary of state, second vice president, and third president didn't make the cut, nor did doubling the size of the country with the Louisiana Purchase.

The reason for the University of Virginia's inclusion is that Jefferson believed that, for the country's founding to succeed, 1776 wasn't enough. The work continued, and there would need to be a continuous process of rebuilding, reinventing, and refounding. Future generations would have to carry this forward, and thus, the success of the Revolution depended on the success of places like the University of Virginia. As one of its first students, Henry Tutwiler, recalled, "[Jefferson] well knew that, without education, political and religious freedom would have no basis on which to rest."[18]

It took Thomas Jefferson's entire post-presidency, from 1809 until 1826, to make good on that vision. In those seventeen years, he became the first president to accomplish something great after the White House. That achievement, the University of Virginia, has lasted for more than two centuries.

He did more than found a new university, however. He helped found another institution: the post-presidency. America's first former

president, George Washington, set a critical precedent for day one of
the post-presidency, stepping down after two terms and allowing for a
peaceful transfer of power. Jefferson reinforced Washington's example
by stepping back after eight years in office despite his enormous popularity. But Thomas Jefferson also set the precedent for day two, living
a vibrant life and working to accomplish something great. His was the
first post-presidency of consequence.

He debated the meaning and legacy of the Declaration of Independence with John Adams. He advised his successors on everything
from the Monroe Doctrine to the Missouri Compromise. He helped
rebuild the Library of Congress after the British burned it down during
the War of 1812. He wrote the first presidential autobiography (albeit
about his pre-presidency) decades before Ulysses S. Grant put pen to
paper in what is largely considered to be the first seminal presidential
memoir. He kept copious records, a kind of early version of presidential centers or libraries. Every former president to come followed at
least some of the examples he set.

Like former presidents to follow, he encountered very typical challenges of heartache, financial difficulty, and mortality. Jefferson's wife,
Martha, had died in 1782, nearly two decades before his presidency,
and he never remarried. He'd lost five of their six children by the time
he left Washington. His own health failed over the course of several
years, and his debts only grew, until they became insurmountable. By
the time he passed away, he'd lost nearly every member of the founding generation. He was survived by James Madison, James Monroe,
and John Adams. Adams died a few hours after he did, on July 4, 1826.

The United States is no longer a young country. Americans wonder how the Founding Fathers should be remembered. Their legacy is
being debated. Many people's views of Jefferson, in particular, have
changed, and with it their understanding of American history. Jefferson wrote about the unalienable rights of every human being. Yet he
enslaved hundreds of Black people at Monticello. Even the University
of Virginia was built by enslaved laborers.[19] Two hundred years after
his death, Thomas Jefferson's one sentence is getting longer and longer, and more and more complicated. Many have turned on Jefferson,
and his statue has been removed from New York's city hall. As historian

Annette Gordon-Reed once wrote, "Jefferson's vision of equality was not all-inclusive, but it was transformative."[20]

But even these critiques of Jefferson are, in a way, Jeffersonian. To understand Thomas Jefferson requires looking at his entire life, from his boyhood to his deathbed. He believed that every generation of Americans, like every class of incoming students, would make progress. They would improve on the work of the generation that came before them. That was the way of the Enlightenment. But even he wondered and worried about his legacy. He thought future Americans would look back at his generation and say that it was barbaric, like the witch burners of old.[21]

Jefferson would have anticipated many of today's debates about the founding and its legacy—both what those debates get right, and what they get wrong. He would have hoped for such a competition of ideas. And he would have wanted that competition to unfold at America's great universities, including places like the University of Virginia.

THRICE DENIED

From boyhood, Thomas Jefferson knew how he wanted to spend his final years. He was captivated by ideas and learning. He came to believe that a university would be the ideal place to store the wisdom he'd gained over a lifetime, and to pass it on to the next generation. But that ambition would have to wait. At age thirty-three, he'd written the Declaration of Independence—which he claimed didn't have new ideas, but was rather an expression, he called it, of the "American mind."[22]

He was born not only at a time of coming political revolution, but also during the Age of Enlightenment and after the Scientific Revolution. These movements were connected. Newton, Galileo, and Copernicus had devised new theories that challenged existing notions of how the natural world worked. Jefferson would do the same for politics, and much else.

Education was his focus. He was a member of the esteemed Randolph family of Virginia, and he had the best schooling possible in colonial Virginia, culminating at William & Mary. There, he studied under teachers like George Wythe and William Small, the only member of the William & Mary faculty who was not an Anglican priest, and who taught Jefferson about the Scottish Enlightenment and provided a secular education.[23] Jefferson's interests spanned the William & Mary curriculum, from political theory and religion, to engineering and astronomy. He applied education throughout his life, using the movement of the moon to devise a new way of finding longitude, advising a change in American currencies away from English pounds and shillings to a new system using decimals, dollars, and cents. He spoke and read Latin, French, Italian, and Spanish (although John Quincy Adams later questioned Jefferson's claim that, armed with a copy of *Don Quixote*, he learned Spanish while crossing the Atlantic). Whatever his embellishments of his linguistic abilities, Jefferson is credited with inventing more than one hundred new words, among them, appropriately enough, the verb "neologize."

He was different from other presidents. A group of independent experts once took up the task of determining which president was the smartest, surveying biographies, profiles, data, and the various rankings that score presidents best to worst—an imperfect methodology, but perhaps the best available. Their verdict was clear: Thomas Jefferson.[24] On raw intelligence and openness to new experiences, he topped the list, followed by John Quincy Adams and Abraham Lincoln.

He was also different from most men of his generation. As a young Virginian, he became known as a writer. That reputation helped earn him an invitation to the Continental Congress in 1775. There, John Adams selected him to write the Declaration of Independence.[25] That act made him famous. It put him on a path that was not his own. He'd helped found the United States, and the young nation needed leadership. That meant Thomas Jefferson.

He didn't want what came next. Before he became America's third president, Jefferson tried to retire from public life at least three times. Life, politics, and other priorities got in the way.

He became the governor of Virginia in 1779, at just thirty-six years old.[26] After two years in that position, he wanted to leave public life. But after his beloved wife, Martha, died in 1782, he needed to leave their shared home. He set sail as America's minister to France, along-side John Adams and Benjamin Franklin, to make a new life in Paris.

It was in Paris that Jefferson's mind came alive. It was at the time the intellectual capital of the world. He toured the country, visited its museums, and studied its architecture, philosophy, history, and food. After four happy years, he returned home to Virginia in 1789. The French Revolution had arrived, and he couldn't stay. With France be-hind him, he was once again ready to retire. He might have started his own university then, fresh from his travels. But it wasn't meant to be.

While Jefferson was on his way home from Europe, his friend James Madison wrote him a note asking if he'd serve in President George Washington's new administration. At first, Jefferson refused, replying, "My object is to return to . . . retirement."[27] But when he arrived home in the United States, he learned that Washington had already nominated him as America's first secretary of state. The new Senate had confirmed him.[28] Retirement, and founding a new univer-sity, would have to wait.

As Washington's secretary of state, Jefferson was politically mar-ginalized by an emerging Federalist block led by Treasury Secretary Alexander Hamilton and Vice President John Adams, both of whom advocated for a strong central government and close ties to Great Brit-ain.[29] Unhappy in the role, Jefferson resigned his post in 1793. Again, he was ready for "a retirement I doat on," a chance to live as an "Ante-diluvian patriarch" in Virginia.[30] But the flood came soon enough. The Federalist Party, led by Adams, was on the ascent. Jefferson wanted to stop it.

Jefferson's first, brief retirement was cut short by politics, but it was important for what came later. Now as a private citizen, he peti-tioned his government about founding a new university. He wrote to President George Washington about the idea, thinking he'd get a sym-pathetic hearing from his fellow Virginian.[31] The president had given some shares of stock to the Virginia legislature in 1795, and Jefferson thought they could be put to good use endowing a new university mod-eled on the great universities of Europe, like those in Edinburgh and Geneva.[32] After the French Revolution, many European intellectuals and professors were fleeing the continent, and an American might be able to recruit new faculty from their ranks. There were two problems with the idea. First, Washington had little interest. Second, few of the fleeing French professors spoke English.[33]

Retirement could have lasted forever, and Washington's refusal might have been the last word on the matter. At this point, Jefferson had had a distinguished career in public service. Had he wished, he might have lived out his days quietly. But the Federalists, led by Adams and Hamilton, were in power. Jefferson hated their politics, which he viewed as monarchical and a betrayal of the Revolution. He challenged Adams for the presidency in 1796. Ironically, nearly every college president in the United States endorsed Adams, not Jefferson. The Federalist may have been a proto-monarchist. But at least he wasn't a Jacobin.[34]

The results came, and Jefferson was in second place, behind Adams. Second place was not a total loss—it made him Adams's vice president. Until the passage of the Twelfth Amendment in 1804, there was no separate selection of the president and vice president, and the offices went to the top two finishers.[35]

Though he was opposed to his own administration's policies, Jefferson served as vice president. He had few responsibilities in the role. He often wandered Philadelphia, at that time the nation's capital and its second-largest city, in search of diversions. He once paid fifty cents to see an elephant on Market Street. He was elected president of the American Philosophical Society,[36] an organization cofounded by Benjamin Franklin that at one point counted Charles Darwin as a member.[37] The group was so important to Jefferson that he led the society even during his own presidency, only stepping down in 1814.[38]

He raged against Adams's "Quasi-War" with France and the Alien and Sedition Acts. He was outraged by the Federalists' overreaches. He ran again after Adams's first term.[39] This time he won, defeating the president in what would come to be called the "Revolution of 1800," when one party handed power to another.

The ivory tower couldn't stand the idea of a Jefferson presidency. The head of Yale College, Timothy Dwight, told his students that President Thomas Jefferson would not only enact bad policies, but many of them would be blasphemous as well. Under President Jefferson, he cautioned somewhat dramatically, "the Bible would be cast into a bonfire . . . our wives and daughters dishonored, and our sons converted into the disciples of Voltaire."[40]

When it came to governing, the Jefferson administration featured fewer guillotines than Dwight had feared. There was no reign of terror. The transfer of power from Adams to Jefferson was a simple, peaceful affair. When he arrived in Washington, the fifty-seven-year-old widower didn't arrive at the head of an angry mob. He rented a room at a humble boardinghouse[41] called Conrad and McCunn's.[42] When he went to take his oath, he didn't march in a parade. He walked the two hundred paces to the U.S. Capitol, accompanied by a small group of well-wishers to a building that was still under construction.[43]

The limits of his power were clear on his first day, before he even took his oath of office. When he entered the Old Senate Chamber, he was met by Chief Justice John Marshall, one of the Federalists' so-called "Midnight Judges," whom Adams had appointed in the waning days of his administration. Marshall was one of Jefferson's chief political foes.[44] He would administer Jefferson's oath. And the judge would remain on the bench until 1835, a last vestige of the Federalist Party long after it was gone. Meanwhile, John Adams was nowhere to be found on Inauguration Day. He'd left town at 4:00 a.m., not wanting to witness the day's events. The two former friends didn't speak again for more than a decade.

The new president had other matters on his mind. But he showed limited enthusiasm about the new role. He returned to Conrad and McCunn's, where he remained for the first fifteen days of his administration, not eager to move into his new home on Pennsylvania Avenue.[45]

The Jefferson presidency was transformative. From fighting the Barbary pirates to lowering the national debt, he made his mark in his first four years. He even founded the United States Military Academy at West Point.[46] But his most consequential action, by far, was the Louisiana Purchase of 1803. Overnight, Jefferson doubled the size of the United States for the bargain price of $15 million.[47]

His second term proved more challenging. France and Britain, then at war, targeted American sailors on the high seas, taking them into their navies' service. The president retaliated with a trade war against both nations, effectively cutting off the United States from international commerce, and pushing the Embargo Act of 1807.[48] The policy was a failure, and it severely damaged the U.S. economy, lowering its GDP by perhaps as much as 5 percent.[49]

After eight years in power, Jefferson was ready to hand over the reins to James Madison. In his final days, the departing president was ecstatic to be leaving the capital, writing, "Never did [a] prisoner, released from his chains, feel such relief as I shall on shaking off the shackles of power."[50] He made no attempt to hide his joy. One attendee at Madison's inaugural ball told the president he looked "happy and satisfied" and that "a spectator might imagine that [Jefferson] were the one coming in, & [Madison] the one going out of office."[51] Meanwhile, John Quincy Adams, also in attendance, thought "the crowd was excessive, the heat oppressive, and the entertainment bad."[52]

At long last, Jefferson was done with politics. He was going back to his beloved Virginia for good.[53]

THE PERFECT SETUP

Not every former president is set up for success. Thomas Jefferson was. Though he was sixty-six years old—well above life expectancy for the time—he began his post-presidency in good health. He was popular and had founded a political dynasty, with his fellow Virginians James Madison and James Monroe succeeding him as president. This was the last time in American history that the same political party won six presidential elections in a row. He did not need to worry that his legacy would be undermined by his successors. Without professional or political obligations, he was freer to be more productive and happier than at any point in his life.[54]

Jefferson was heading home, and his table at Monticello would become one of the most sought-after invitations in the United States. Elected leaders from Washington and Richmond would come to dine with him, and scholars from around the world would seek his company. Virginia was the leading state in the United States, and it had grown from a population of 4 million in 1790 to more than 7 million in 1810.[55] The independent nation was developing its own distinct culture, grounded in, but different from, British folkways.[56] With Napoleon in France and King George III in Great Britain, the world's superpowers had their own troubles. The United States looked secure. Jefferson wanted to return to Monticello and pursue a goal he'd waited for his entire life.

Home Sweet Home

The return home is a psychologically complex part of the post-presidency. Some presidents find that it helps them remember who they were before the presidency, while others have found it disorienting. But Jefferson was exactly where he'd wanted to be. Monticello had been under construction for forty years by the time he arrived in 1809.[57] Finished at last, the house set in the Virginia foothills and surrounded by land was part of Jefferson's family's history. He described it as his "essay in architecture."[58] John Adams's great-grandson, Henry Adams, later wrote, with a mixture of admiration and jealousy, that Jefferson had "built for himself at Monticello a château above contact with man."[59]

Adams the younger was right. The three-story house is remarkable. Most homes of the era were dark, but Monticello was filled with light, as Jefferson had added floor-to-ceiling windows all around, as well as skylights. This was closer to the model of the French style that Jefferson had studied in Paris than it was to American homes. The white dome at the top was the first such structure in North America, with a glass oculus as its apex. Throughout the house, visitors could see trophies from Jefferson's life, including Native American artifacts gathered by Lewis and Clark in the east portico entrance,[60] across from portraits of Sir Francis Bacon, Sir Isaac Newton, and John Locke, men whom he called his personal trinity of great statesmen.[61] By the entrance sat two busts, one of Alexander Hamilton and the other of Jefferson himself, the latter much larger than the former. The two founders were, Jefferson joked, "Opposed in death, as in life."[62]

The former president never traveled far. In his own home, he seldom left the first floor, only climbing up the narrow staircases to the other floors, where the rest of his family lived, on rare occasions. When the house got overcrowded with guests, he'd retreat to his other home, at Poplar Forest, ninety miles away.[63] He never returned to Washington. He only visited Richmond, the state capital, once.[64]

There was a routine to this new life. He rose early, opening the curtains on both sides of his bed to let in the light. He'd positioned the bed carefully to keep in the heat in the winter and have cool breezes in the summer. Whatever the season, he dunked his feet in ice-cold water to rouse himself for the day every morning in what today we might refer to as a cold plunge.[65]

Each morning began with writing. He kept compulsive records, keeping a diligent log of the weather and climate around Monticello. He wrote to leaders, friends, and well-wishers around the world, and he worried that he spent so much time keeping up with correspondence that he'd get nothing else done.[66] He responded to as many as one thousand letters every year—1,267 in 1820 alone—many of them from strangers.[67] Responding to these letters, always in his "neat, round, and plain" penmanship, was made more difficult as the years went on by a wrist injury, but he kept it up.[68] He was writing to some of the most learned men of his day, and he knew that his responses would be part of the historical record, so he was careful and deliberate in what he said.

When he wasn't writing, he was working. He could be seen all over the estate. Monticello's overseer, Edmund Bacon, said of his employer that Jefferson was "well proportioned, and straight as a gun-barrel. He was like a fine horse."[69] He rode daily, exercising along with the more than thirty horses he owned in his life.

The image of a Founding Father trotting across his estate might sound idyllic. But Jefferson's riding served another purpose. Throughout his life, he suffered from several illnesses, including chronic diarrhea, which he called his "visceral complaint." At the time, the condition could be life-threatening, and it often left him exhausted. An amateur physician, Jefferson had scoured medical journals, stumbling across a recommendation that riding would ward off diarrhea. It would, he hoped, "strengthen the bowels."[70]

There was another chronic condition hanging over Jefferson— debt. As a rule, Virginia plantations were almost always money-losing propositions. Monticello was far from profitable, as it had poor soil quality that made growing cash crops difficult.[71] Jefferson rarely seemed to care about his debts. He spent lavishly, supported his family, hosted hundreds of visitors a year, and bought every comfort he wanted.

The former president's debts were almost as old as he was. The original source was his late slave trader father-in-law, John Wayles. When Wayles died in 1773, he passed on his debts to Jefferson. By 1809, interest had compounded, making the total come to around $11,000. That sum would be more than a quarter of a million dollars today.[72]

The fact that Jefferson allowed his debts to spiral out of control was, in some ways, out of character. As president, he'd demonstrated fiscal responsibility, lowering America's debt from $83 million to $57 million.[73] Managing his own affairs couldn't be more difficult than managing America's. But though he kept detailed records of almost every other part of his life, Jefferson stopped keeping a complete ledger of his own accounts in the 1770s. He may not have known how bad things were.

Nor did he care to. While he was president, he didn't want to appear to profit from the office. He took pride in "having added nothing to my private fortunes during my public service and of retiring with hands as clean as they are empty."[74]

He managed his debts, but only barely, until the end of his life. He was helped by his daughter Martha, who ran the estate, and by the fact that Virginia creditors were almost always willing to lend to their state's favorite son on favorable terms. Likewise, Americans did not want to see a popular former president become a pauper. No one would take Monticello from him as long as he was alive.

The War of 1812

Jefferson did get some help with his money troubles from an unlikely source—King George III. The British Crown was often at war with Napoleon's France, and it helped wage that war by seizing American ships, sailors, and cargo on the high seas. Unable to tolerate the humiliation and loss anymore, President James Madison signed a declaration of war against Great Britain on June 18, 1812.

With news of another war against Great Britain, Jefferson was elated. He welcomed the War of 1812. If America was victorious again, it might be able to expand its territory north into Canada. The British would have to leave North America once and for all.[75] But that didn't happen. Soon, America fought for its very existence in a second struggle for independence. British troops took Washington, DC, in 1814. They burned the Capitol. And President James Madison and First Lady Dolley Madison fled the scene with a full-length portrait of George Washington in tow.

The country fought for its survival, and Jefferson remained safe at home. But he was not spared. The British blockade of the Chesapeake Bay halted wheat exports from Maryland and Virginia, including those from Monticello. Between four and five hundred barrels of Jefferson's flour sat unsold in Richmond, rotting away. Desperate for his crops to go to market, Jefferson asked President Madison to build a canal to the Elizabeth River so that trade could resume.[76] But Madison had a war to fight, and there were no resources to divert from the war effort.

But some measure of relief was in sight. The British had fueled their fires over Washington, DC, with three thousand books from the congressional library. When he heard this news, Jefferson was horrified. He wrote to James Monroe, then serving as both the secretary of state and the secretary of war, that the British conduct "disgrace[s] our enemies more than us."[77]

The smoke cleared, and the British left the capital. Congress reassembled in the only remaining federal building in Washington, the Patent Office. Near the top of their agenda was rebuilding the Library of Congress. Here, Jefferson could help.

The Library of Congress served as both a place for research and the United States' de facto national library. As president, Jefferson had appointed its first two librarians, and he was very familiar with the institution.[78] He also had in his personal collection one of the most impressive libraries in North America, which he had collected over a lifetime. Before he set sail for France in 1783, he'd cataloged all of his 2,640 volumes over the course of a 246-page document.[79] Now his collection totaled 6,487 books on almost every subject.[80] Congress needed a library. Jefferson had one of the best in the country. He was ready to sell it.[81]

The logistics and the politics of making a sale to Congress weren't easy. Jefferson hadn't been in the capital in half a decade, and he didn't know who he should contact. He asked his old friend and confidant, a man named Samuel H. Smith, to send a proposal to Congress. The Senate was eager to close the deal, and offered $23,950 after a unanimous vote.[82] The House of Representatives would be a different matter. Congressmen's objections ran the gamut. Jefferson's library included too many books in foreign languages. Many seemed downright radical, even dangerous. Noting the worries about the library's contents, New Hampshire representative Daniel Webster proposed that Congress should buy the library and then return "all books of an atheistical, irreligious, and immoral tendency."[83]

Despite some resistance, the House approved the purchase by a slim majority of ten votes, agreeing to what the Senate had already approved.[84] Jefferson's library was his no more. He watched ten wagons filled with his treasured collection depart Monticello, never to be seen by him again.

The Library of Congress owed its survival to Jefferson. By selling his own collection, Jefferson had refounded it. Most of the books that he sold were destroyed in a fire in the Capitol in 1851, but some remain to this day.[85] They can be identified on the spine, or in some cases the title page, with a mark the former president added—"TJ."[86]

The proceeds did not last long. Jefferson sent $4,870 to the financier John Barnes, who'd lent him money to repay a Polish general named Thaddeus Kosciuszko, a friend from the Revolutionary War.[87] Another $10,500 went to his friend and creditor William Short.[88] The rest, he kept to support himself and his family.[89] This was a temporary reprieve.

Matters were made much worse when a severe economic panic hit in 1819, which affected every American, including Jefferson.[90] The state of Virginia was near bankruptcy.[91] Meanwhile, Jefferson cosigned a note with his grandson's father-in-law, which was forfeited when the lender called in the debt.[92] The amount that he owed only grew.[93]

Jefferson was saved from having to give up Monticello by Virginia creditors. They did not want to take it from him. He was also saved by the generosity of Americans he'd never met. After his family's attempt to organize a lottery failed, committees of citizens organized fundraising drives. They sent him nearly $16,500 in a nineteenth-century version of a GoFundMe campaign.[94]

Despite his debts, Jefferson was optimistic. Five months before his eventual death in 1826, he wrote to James Madison, "My own debts had become considerable but not beyond the effect of some lopping of property."[95] He'd leave between $1 million and $2 million in debts, measured in today's dollars, for his heirs to pay off. Unlike Jefferson, they did not have the goodwill of Virginia creditors, and they lost the estate. The sale took place on January 15, 1827, a wrenching experience, both for Jefferson's family and for the enslaved men, women, and children who lived on the estate, and who were now forcibly separated and sold. Fifty years and two generations later, one of Thomas Jefferson's grandsons, Thomas Jefferson Randolph, made the final payment on the Founding Father's obligations.[96]

The Jeffersons, and the Other Jeffersons

The future of his family, and of Monticello, were top of mind for Jefferson. He had a public legacy, but this was his personal legacy, what he'd leave to those closest to him. He'd built Monticello as a young man, and he'd imagined living there until the end of his days, accompanied by his wife, children, and grandchildren. With Martha's death in 1782, he became a widower, one of only a few presidents who entered and left office without a spouse; the others were Andrew Jackson, Martin Van Buren, and Chester Arthur—who, like Jefferson made it to the White House a widower—and James Buchanan, who never married.

Martha's loss affected her husband deeply. He promised her on her deathbed that he'd never remarry. He might have spiraled into depression, cutting short his career and his life expectancy.[97] But Jefferson was saved from that fate by his daughter Martha, a remarkable woman who went by "Patsy" and who was his closest confidant. Remembering her mother's death and the toll it took on her father, she recalled that she became Jefferson's "constant companion, a solitary witness to many a violent burst of grief."[98]

Thomas and Martha Jefferson had six children. But only Patsy and another daughter, Mary, survived to adulthood. Patsy served as Jefferson's First Lady, and Mary died tragically in 1804. Once again, Patsy saved her father, who was grieving the loss of his daughter. Thanks to her, he had plenty of grandchildren upon whom he could dote.

In total, Patsy was the mother of twelve children, eleven of whom survived to adulthood, and three of whom were born at Monticello. Her healthy brood meant that Jefferson's postpresidential home was filled with the pitter-patter of children's feet running across the floorboards. They called him "Grandpapa," and he lived as "a patriarch of old,"[99] racing his grandchildren up and down the lawn and giving them treats of dried fruit.[100] He played games with them,[101] and was involved in every part of their lives, even naming some, like Benjamin Franklin Randolph, James Madison Randolph, and George Wythe Randolph.[102] He read to his grandchildren from the Bible and from Shakespeare. He credited Patsy's children with helping to stave off the ennui that many people feel as they age, helping him to live a longer and happier life.[103]

He needed his family, and he needed Patsy, who was a remarkable woman, in her own time or any. She may have been the best-educated woman in Virginia, and Jefferson took pride in her accomplishments. He had enrolled his daughter at the best school he could find in Paris, a Catholic convent that still provided a secular education to Protestants. Patsy spoke four modern languages, knew history, geography, and science, and was more than capable of holding her own at her father's table at Monticello.[104] Guests noticed that the women of Monticello—led by Patsy—were as outspoken, if not more so, than were Jefferson and his visitors.[105] Jefferson often turned to Patsy for advice, even when she was a young girl.[106] "It is in the love of one's family only that heartfelt happiness is known," he wrote.[107] His own pursuit of happiness would have been impossible without Patsy.

But Jefferson's family life was not all happiness. Thanks to the passage of time and advances in science, it's been confirmed that he had not one, but two families at Monticello. One family was free, and the other enslaved. One was known, and the other the subject of hushed rumors.

The story was centered on a young enslaved woman named Sally Hemings. Hemings had accompanied Jefferson's daughter Mary across the Atlantic, when she joined her father during his time as the United States' minister to France. According to Sally's son, a man named Madison, it was in Paris that his "mother became Mr. Jefferson's concubine."[108] At the time, Sally was just fourteen years old. Jefferson was in his forties.

There's not much about Sally Hemings in the historical record. We do not know what she made of her situation, and there are not writings in which she tells us in her own words. But we do know a bit of her story. When she arrived in Paris, she became a free woman. Slavery was illegal in France. Because of this, Jefferson paid her and her brother, James, a cook, for their work. For a brief time in their lives, at least, they weren't slaves—they were servants.[109]

But they returned to slavery when they came back to America. When Jefferson boarded a ship home in 1789, Sally came with him. But she had a choice. She was free and didn't have to return. She chose to go back, though we don't know why. She may have feared the French Revolution. But we do know that she set conditions on her and her brother's return. The Hemings siblings insisted that they would be treated better than the other enslaved people at Monticello. They would work in the house, not in the fields. They would be given proper clothing.[110] And Sally negotiated freedom for her future children, if not for herself.[111]

Though we don't know why she did what she did, we do know that she was brave and intelligent. She negotiated with Jefferson, and for his part, he kept his promises to her. Sally's children, including those she bore with Jefferson, were freed after his death. This was the only nuclear enslaved family at Monticello that stayed together after the sale of the estate.[112]

We also know that the connection between Jefferson and Sally Hemings is even more intricate than this skeletal outline of her early story suggests. Sally Hemings was not a stranger to Jefferson, or his family. She was Thomas Jefferson's late wife's half sister, as the two shared a father in John Wayles.[113] No likenesses of Sally survive. But she likely resembled Martha Jefferson.

For her beauty, Sally Hemings caught the attention of visitors to

Monticello. The more complimentary visitors called her "Dashing Sally," while Jefferson's Federalist and racist detractors called her "Dusky Sally."[114] Guests noticed that many of the enslaved men and women serving them, Sally's children, bore a striking resemblance to their host. One visitor, Henry Randall, was particularly startled, turning to Jefferson and then the servers, unable to look away from their likenesses. That night he wrote, "The resemblance [between Jefferson and his slaves] was so close, that at some distance or in the dusk the slave, dressed in the same way, might be mistaken for Mr. Jefferson."[115]

History has proven that Randall was correct. Though the former president never revealed the truth about Sally Hemings, or her children, in 1997, Annette Gordon-Reed published *Thomas Jefferson and Sally Hemings: An American Controversy*, exploring the case for the relationship and bringing it back into the mainstream conversation. Then in 1998, a DNA study linked one of Sally Hemings's children, Eston, to the male line of Jefferson's family.[116] The genetic record shows that Jefferson and Hemings likely had at least six children, four of whom survived to adulthood.[117] Jefferson was present at Monticello on each of the dates of their conception, including during his time as president.[118] Their names were Beverly, Harriet, Madison, and Eston. Eston Hemings changed his name to Eston Hemings Jefferson in 1852.[119]

The Hemings family is very much a part of Jefferson's story, even if they were in the shadows for two hundred years. His treatment of Sally and their children, whom he kept in slavery, is a stain, a fact that he understood. In his own time, an African American mathematician named Benjamin Banneker confronted Jefferson, pointing out the contradictions in the life of a man who wrote the Declaration of Independence, but kept men and women in slavery. At the time, Jefferson didn't have a reply to Banneker. There was none.[120]

Jefferson knew that America would have a reckoning over his legacy and over slavery. As early as 1781, in his *Notes on the State of Virginia*, he wrote, "I tremble for my country when I reflect that God is just."[121] He believed future generations might look back at the era in horror.[122] Today, Jefferson is both rightly praised and rightly condemned. And Sally Hemings and their children are, at last, remembered.

SHAPING A LEGACY

Jefferson knew he would be remembered. But he wasn't certain how. He didn't want to leave history to chance, or to his political opponents. Every letter, every note, and every book he touched would shape how the next generation would understand who he was, what he did, and his place in American history. With that in mind, he set to shaping the historical record. He was the first former president to do so.

Founding Friends

The key to Jefferson's past was in faraway Quincy, Massachusetts. In 1776, Adams, already famous throughout the colonies, spotted Jefferson's talent and chose him to draft the Declaration of Independence, impressed by his writing abilities after the young man had "seized upon [his] heart."[123] But despite that bond, the two were at loggerheads throughout their lives. As historian Gordon Wood has noted, they were "divided in almost every fundamental way: in temperament, in their ideas of government, in their assumptions about human nature, in their notions of society, in their attitude toward religion, in their conception of America, indeed, in every single thing that mattered."[124]

Politics split them apart. Adams had been the leader of the Federalist Party, and Jefferson's opponent in 1796 and 1800. But he was also the key to Jefferson's story. More than anyone else, he understood his role in the American founding. But twenty years after they had signed the Declaration of Independence, they were not speaking. Their silence threatened to create space for other Founding Fathers and would-be historians of the era to craft their own narratives about American history.

Distance and pride had made reconciliation difficult. It was six hundred miles from Monticello to the Big House in Quincy, and they were too old and too stubborn to make the journey. Adams felt betrayed by Jefferson's candidacies in 1796 and 1800. He wrote bitterly to their mutual friend Benjamin Rush, "Mr Jefferson has reason to reflect upon himself. How he will get rid of his Remorse in his Retirement I know not. . . . I wish [Jefferson's] Telescopes and Mathematical Instruments, however, may secure his Felicity."[125]

But age was mellowing the partisans. Adams wanted to reconcile, perhaps more than Jefferson, who was younger, healthier, and more popular. Jefferson had work to do; he was laying the groundwork for his university. Yet Adams lived a relatively isolated life in Quincy. His favorite son, John Quincy Adams, was far away, serving as America's minister to Russia.

It was Rush, a fellow signer of the Declaration of Independence, who wanted most of all for the ice to break.[126] As early as 1809, the year Jefferson left the presidency, Rush had written to Adams about a dream he'd had. He dreamt that his son had been reading a future history of the United States detailing how the two presidents had come together later in life. To make that happen, Rush proposed that Adams send Jefferson a note, but Adams refused.[127] Then in 1811, Rush took it upon himself. Thinking of history, he pleaded with Jefferson that he contact Adams while they were both still alive. "Posterity," he said, "will revere the friendship of two Ex presidents that were once opposed to each Other."[128] But Jefferson, too, refused.

A breakthrough came thanks to two Virginians, John Coles and his son Edward, who was President Madison's private secretary.[129] These men were Jefferson's neighbors. They traveled to Quincy in the summer of 1811 to meet with John Adams.

This was the closest Adams had been to Jefferson in ten years. Not one to hide his feelings, he let the two Virginians know the source of his decade-long resentment. Jefferson was not only his political opponent, he had betrayed his old friend, not even doing him the courtesy of contacting him after winning the presidency in 1800. Here, the Coleses saw an opening. They told Adams this was a misunderstanding, and that Jefferson had wanted to get in touch, but he didn't want to appear to lord his victory over his friend and defeated opponent.[130] Upon hearing this explanation, Adams was relieved. His stated opinion changed, practically on the spot. "I always loved Jefferson," he told his guests, "and still love him."[131]

To the south, Jefferson was also ready to bury the hatchet. After hearing what Adams had said, he wrote to Rush, "This is enough for me. I only needed this knolege [sic] to revive towards him all the affections of the most cordial moments of our lives."[132] On New Year's

Day 1812, Adams sent a package to Jefferson, including two volumes of lectures that John Quincy Adams had recently given at Harvard. He also sent an update on his daughter Abigail Adams Smith, who had just undergone surgery for cancer. He included a note, recalling fondly "our revolution" in 1776.[133]

There was once again contact between Quincy and Monticello. Rush was overjoyed, telling Adams, "I consider you and [Jefferson] as the North and South poles of the American Revolution.—Some talked, some wrote—and some fought to promote & establish it, but you, and Mr Jefferson *thought* for us all."[134]

The correspondence that followed shaped their friendship and their legacies. Adams was the more eager pen pal, writing 109 letters in fourteen years, compared to Jefferson's forty-nine.[135] Adams commented, enviously, on Jefferson's "unbound popularity"[136] as the author of the Declaration of Independence, which he knew cemented his friend's place in history.[137] They debated every subject of interest—politics, literature, art, and history. They could be playful and competitive. Jefferson joked with Abigail Adams, "I have compared notes with mr [sic] Adams on the score of progeny, and find I am ahead of him, and think I am in a fair way to keep so."[138]

At one point, the reconciliation was almost derailed.[139] It came out that, in the lead-up to the 1800 election, Adams had attacked Jefferson personally, saying that "cool, dispassionate and deliberate insidiousness never arrived at greater perfection."[140] After the news broke, Adams feared that Jefferson might never speak to him again. But Jefferson urged his friend to forget that part of the past. Relieved, Adams called Jefferson's note dismissing the matter "the best letter that ever was written."[141]

They were two sides of the same coin of the American founding, committed to the spirit of 1776. But they differed on fundamental questions about the role of government, religion, and foreign policy. Despite their differences, the two needed each other. They never met in person again. But one by one, their old friends from the Revolution were dying. Adams and Jefferson kept a running list of those still living. By 1813, they were the only two left who had served on the Declaration's drafting committee.[142]

With the founding generation dying out, they wondered how that Declaration would be remembered. In one letter, Adams asked Jefferson, "Would you go back to the cradle and live over again your seventy years?"[143] Jefferson responded to the strangely framed question with a serious answer, "I think with you that it is a good world on the whole . . . and more pleasure than pain has been dealt out to us."[144]

They knew their time was limited. "When it is reasonable we should drop off," Jefferson wrote, "and make room for another growth. When we have lived our generation out, we should not wish to encroach on another."[145] For Adams, that increased the urgency of their task. It was most important that the next generation understand what the founders had envisioned. With an eye toward posterity, he told Jefferson, "You and I, ought not to die, before We have explained ourselves to each other."[146]

Writing About What Mattered

The former presidents wanted to explain themselves to each other, and to future generations. The Founders were dying, one by one. And as the first history books about the United States were being written, Adams and Jefferson worried. In 1803, during Jefferson's first term as president, Chief Justice John Marshall had published a five-volume biography of George Washington, which quickly was becoming the definitive history of the young United States.

It painted Washington as the champion of a strong central government. The account was not favorable to Jefferson. Marshall relegated Jefferson's role in writing the Declaration of Independence to a footnote, stating that "the draft reported by the committee has been generally attributed to Mr. Jefferson."[147] This was a historical understatement for the ages.

Though Adams had appointed Marshall, he was also worried about those early drafts of history. He wrote to Jefferson that he was "so little Satisfied with Histories of the American Revolution, that I have long Since, ceased to read them. The Truth is lost."[148] Though history would likely remember Jefferson fondly, Adams believed it wouldn't be so kind to him.[149]

Whatever Adams's opinions, Jefferson didn't want to take any chances. He asked former president James Madison to write a history of the United States, one more sympathetic to the views of their shared party, the Democratic-Republicans.[150] But Madison declined. That meant that Jefferson needed to take matters into his own hands. In 1818, he edited and compiled three volumes of letters and notes from his time as secretary of state and president.[151]

These volumes later came to be known as *The Anas*, or a collection of notes and gossip. This collection had "copies of the official opinions given in writing by [Jefferson] to General Washington while [he] was Secretary of State."[152] He wanted this work to offer a counter to the Federalist Marshall narrative, and to be a resource to future historians. But Jefferson didn't think they offered enough to guarantee his place in history. With that in mind, he began writing an autobiography in 1821,[153] covering his birth through the year 1790 and emphasizing his role as the author of the Declaration of Independence.[154]

The writing project of the Jefferson post-presidency was not meant for public consumption. It was for personal edification. This work, which he began as president, is what's come to be known as the "Jefferson Bible," a title he never gave it.

Jefferson's views on religion were complex. He studied Christianity and many other faiths.[155] He knew their tenets, but he was skeptical of organized religion.[156] The Jefferson Bible was meant to provide a clear guide to Jesus's teaching, stripped of miracles and what he called the "artificial vestments in which they have been muffled by priests."[157] Putting together the work was a painstaking exercise, in which he combined text from six versions of the New Testament, written in four languages. He used a razor to cut out different sections, merging them into a single volume. By 1820, he'd created a chronological version of the New Testament that fit his deist philosophy, focused on history, not on the divine, and bringing to the fore ethical teachings, not supernatural elements, from the narrative.[158]

Neither Washington nor Adams had undertaken such ambitious writing projects. Nearly every former president is now expected to write an autobiography. They tell their side of history. The presidential memoir may have taken off after Grant wrote his, and nearly every president since Harry Truman has published their own. But Jefferson did it first. And like him, every president now keeps careful records, with an eye toward releasing them to friendly historians.

FATHER OF THE UNIVERSITY OF VIRGINIA

Jefferson had helped found the United States, and he wanted to make sure it survived. The fate of slavery and westward expansion, a legacy of his own Louisiana Purchase, made him worry for the future. In 1820, following the debates over the Missouri Compromise, he lamented, "We have the wolf by the ear, and we can neither hold him, nor safely let him go."[159] He needed to do what he could with the time he had left. And, as historian Herbert Sloan wrote, the University of Virginia became Jefferson's "safe haven in the remaining years of his life, a pursuit he preferred to unpleasant reality."[160]

To Jefferson, education would save the Revolution. "If a nation expects to be ignorant & free," he wrote, "it expects what never was & never will be."[161] That required new educational institutions, a task that would take years. At age seventy-four, more than ten years past the male life expectancy in 1817, he wrote that founding the university was his "single anxiety in this world. it is a bantling of 40. years birth & nursing, & if I can once see it on it's legs, I will sing with sincerity & pleasure my nunc demittas."[162]

That dedication came from his strong belief in the Enlightenment idea of progress, that notion that future generations, through science and reason, could and would improve humanity's condition. But even with wise leaders like Cicero, Cato, and Brutus, the Roman Republic couldn't survive without an educated population. The United States needed not only enlightened leadership, but enlightened people.[163]

From his earliest days, he valued education. On his mother's side, his great-grandfather and his five brothers had all attended William & Mary.[164] As a young man, he'd drafted "A Bill for the More General Diffusion of Knowledge," calling for near-universal basic public education in Virginia, including for girls through the elementary school level.[165] As governor, he'd joined the board of his alma mater, William & Mary, where he reorganized the curriculum.[166] Education was always a part of his life. It would dominate his final chapter.

As a former president, he finally had what he needed to make the university come alive, namely time, power, and experience. Without an office, he had no more public obligations, and there was no higher office in which he could serve. He had the esteem not only of his fellow Virginians, but also of a friendly administration in Washington, led by President Madison and then Monroe.

The work began in earnest in 1810, when Jefferson wrote to John Tyler, then Virginia's governor, arguing that, without education, the state's future was in peril. Jefferson pushed for universal public education at every level, and he advocated for every county in the commonwealth to be divided into "little republics" that would put a school near every child.[167] But this was too ambitious for Richmond, and it would take many years for the Virginia legislature to fund Jefferson's ideas.

He didn't take no for an answer. Rather, he refined his ideas and his approach. He intended the University of Virginia to be more than another school. To him, it was to be "the future bulwark of the human mind" in the Western Hemisphere.[168] There was an egalitarian angle to Jefferson's vision, and he wanted to spread the benefits of education more widely.[169] At the time, just 1 percent of white males went to college, to say nothing of women and racial minorities who would not be able to enroll at institutions like the University of Virginia for more than a century.[170] Finally Jefferson wanted the university to secure his home state as the first state among equals, the leader of the rest of the states.

The College of William & Mary was not up to the task Jefferson had in mind. He viewed his alma mater as too tied to the Episcopal Church,[171] and sometimes referred to Williamsburg as "Devilsburg."[172] Meanwhile, old universities like Harvard and newer institutions like Transylvania University in Kentucky were not only led by Presbyterians and Congregationalists, they were outcompeting William & Mary. Virginia was beginning to suffer from brain drain, as its best and brightest went elsewhere for education and opportunity.[173]

Universities in other states were more than competition, they were threats. Many were run by Jefferson's political opponents, including the Federalists in the North. Most of them were religious, which he thought detracted from their educational value by emphasizing divine interpretation and doctrine over history, science, and ethics. Jefferson didn't want Virginia's best and brightest to leave the state to attend these schools, but worried that they might. As he wrote at the time, "If our legislature does not heartily push our University, we must send our children for education to Kentucky or Cambridge."[174]

Jefferson didn't wait for the state legislature to act, and he found a new avenue to pursue his ambition. In 1814, he became a trustee for the Albemarle Academy in Charlottesville, Virginia. It was a start, but the only problem for Jefferson was that this school didn't exist, would never educate a single student, and wasn't intended to be a university. The academy had a board, but no building or faculty. Still, Jefferson believed that the Albemarle Academy would serve as the "midwife" to the University of Virginia.[175]

Founding a new university required Jefferson to become an entrepreneur. He needed to articulate a vision, build a team, and finance his project. Most important, he needed a new name. The "Albemarle Academy" would not do. He renamed the school Central College, an implicit swipe at William & Mary, in the eastern part of the state. By calling the school "central" he showed his intent to serve the whole commonwealth, not just one region or sectional interest. This, he hoped, gave him buy-in from legislators across the state.[176] Next, he recruited and appointed a board of visitors. James Madison and James Monroe joined their fellow Virginian.[177]

America was not used to presidents working together—there had only been five. And by 1817, it was rare to see three Founding Fathers meet in the same place. Most were dead, and those remaining were in poor health and did not travel. But when Jefferson called, Virginians answered. President James Monroe, then in his first year in office, and James Madison traveled to Charlottesville on May 5, 1817, for the first formal meeting of the board of visitors of Central College.[178]

In preparing for the meeting, Jefferson had thought of every detail. He timed it to take place on May 5, Court Day in Charlottesville. The city's leaders would be there, and citizens would be crowding the streets.[179] As he rode into town wearing a broad-brimmed hat, a large white cravat, and a dark gray coat, Jefferson knew he had an audience he could use to build public support. At that meeting, the board approved the site of the school to be Charlottesville, and authorized the purchase of land.[180]

News of the meeting traveled far and wide. From Massachusetts, John Adams wrote to Jefferson, congratulating him on making something "very great and very new." But he warned that the university might not last long, because it wouldn't always have such distinguished patrons as three presidents.[181]

At the time, Jefferson was seventy-four years old, and knew that most men of his era were dead by forty-five. With limited opportunities left, he brought the same energy to this task as he had displayed at the start of his career. He surveyed the land for the university and laid out where the school's pavilions would be. He designed the structures and a new kind of "academical village," an architectural feature that brought professors from different disciplines together around a central Lawn, and gave each building classrooms and living areas. He borrowed designs from his time in France, modeling the five pavilions on either side of the University of Virginia's Lawn off a hospital he'd seen in Paris.[182]

"Mr. Jefferson's University" was taking shape, even if it did not yet have full funding. The vision, team, and plans were his. He budgeted for building materials and faculty costs. He guided tradespeople and builders, carpenters and masons as they began their work.[183] He designed the curriculum. The vice president of the Thomas Jefferson Foundation and University of Virginia professor Andrew O'Shaughnessy has described Jefferson's example as "a wonderful study in leadership."[184]

The work continued, and on October 6, 1817, the school's cornerstone was laid. A parade of Freemasons in full finery marched down the street for the event, pouring wine and oil over the stone, as a band played "Yankee Doodle."[185] But the occasion also showed the contradictions of the nascent university, and of its founder. Ten enslaved men leveled the ground with shovels and spades in order to lay the cornerstone. Five members of the board of visitors held more than one hundred slaves each. When the school eventually opened its doors, there were nearly two hundred enslaved persons working on campus, a larger population than the student body.[186]

As the school moved from Jefferson's designs to the building phase, he would often ride the four miles from his home to the construction site. Many of the enslaved men and women he saw working, and making as many as nine hundred thousand bricks a year, lived at Monticello.[187] Jefferson would sometimes observe their work from afar,[188] obsessively watching through a telescope placed on the North Terrace, near his dining room.[189]

The school's fate would be decided in Richmond. Jefferson still needed money. And he needed a political ally to secure those funds. The man for the job was state senator Joseph Cabell, thirty-five years Jefferson's junior.[190] Jefferson had taken a shine to Cabell as early as 1800, when he was vice president and Cabell was a newly minted graduate of William & Mary. Observing the inadequacies in Cabell's education, he sent him a lengthy reading list to fill the gaps.[191]

Though Jefferson was out of office, Cabell was in the state senate, and in a position to advance Jefferson's cause. Meanwhile, Jefferson used his status as a Founding Father and former president to build public support by writing about the university in the *Richmond Enquirer*, which he did by posing as a tourist visiting Charlottesville and enthusiastically speaking about the idea of a new university.[192]

Cabell's work looked like it would bear fruit during the 1817–1818 meeting of the House of Delegates. Jefferson sent him a draft bill he had written to fund the project. But the bill failed, and Cabell had to find a new maneuver, attaching a rider to establish the new university to a larger bill providing for the education of indigent children. He secured a small amount in funding, $15,000 a year from the state's Literary Fund, and avoided the biggest potential controversy by not naming the location of the university, even though work was already begun in Charlottesville. In 1818, the General Assembly formally approved the funds and named the school the "University of Virginia."[193]

Jefferson's university existed on paper, if not yet in reality. There were unanswered questions. Where would they recruit students and faculty? What would the school teach? How would it be governed?

And would the state formally sanction Charlottesville as the location? The board assembled at Rockfish Gap in the Blue Ridge Mountains in August 1818 to settle those questions.[194]

Twenty miles from Charlottesville, they met at the Rockfish Inn, looking out from a height of 1,900 feet onto the surrounding countryside. The small, humble inn was far away from political squabbles and interference in Richmond. Away from prying eyes, Jefferson would have total control over how the university's fate would be decided.[195]

Reaching such a remote location was not easy. Jefferson had to travel twenty-five miles on horseback over two days to get there. Even worse, he had to borrow $100 from a Charlottesville merchant in order to afford the trip, a debt that he may not have repaid.[196] But he was determined to lead the meeting, and he choreographed the whole affair to achieve his desired outcome.[197] In fact, he'd already written a draft of the board's final recommendations before the board even gathered.[198]

The board's twenty-two members assembled in a small, low-ceilinged room, around a dining table.[199] Jefferson sat silently through most of the discussion. He knew he'd have the last word and didn't need to exert himself debating the rest of the group. Better to let them think they were shaping the outcome.[200]

The location was once again an issue of contention. In addition to Charlottesville, the board proposed two other towns, Lexington and Staunton, as alternate locations. But Jefferson favored Charlottesville because it was close to his home, and also because it didn't lean in any particular sectarian direction, geographically, politically, or religiously.[201] The board agreed with him.

Also following his wishes, the board agreed the university would be a secular institution, with no professor of divinity, unlike most other universities of the time.[202] In keeping with Jefferson's vision, and reflecting the Declaration of Independence, the Rockfish Gap Report mentions happiness eight times, including the argument that "nothing, more than education, advanc[es] the prosperity, the power and the happiness of a nation."[203] This was the most important document in the founding of the University of Virginia.[204] And its text directly linked its purpose to the American Founding in 1776.

Jefferson left the Rockfish Gap happy, but exhausted. It took him longer to get home than it did to get to the meeting. He fell ill and took some time to recover.[205] But he still needed state approval, and funding. The fight was not over.

But that fight was now not Jefferson's to wage. The task fell to Cabell in Richmond. On January 25, 1819, Virginia's state senate accepted the report of the Rockfish Gap Commission.[206] The board then approved Jefferson as the logical choice for rector, at the institution's helm.[207]

The university had a leader, but not a faculty. Jefferson was thrilled by the choice of the university's first professor, Thomas Cooper, as the chemistry teacher.[208] But the choice was a political disaster that threatened the school's fate. Cabell feared that Cooper's agnostic religious views could throw the whole enterprise into chaos.[209] He was right. Under pressure from Presbyterians in the Shenandoah Valley, Jefferson rescinded Cooper's position, greatly disappointed that he had to do so.[210] Cooper went on to teach at South Carolina College, where he became the school's president.[211] But in Virginia, the Cooper incident hung over the university, and it made Jefferson even more hostile toward religious leaders in his state. He wrote to a friend, "The priests of the different religious sects . . . dread the advance of science as witches do the approach of day-light."[212]

Religion was one of the most important fault lines in the university's creation. Episcopalians made up two-thirds of the legislators,[213] and they and Presbyterians alike railed against prospective faculty members and the secular nature of the institution.[214] But Jefferson refused to allow his university to be affiliated with any church. In fact, the University of Virginia would be the future home of America's first Jewish university professor, a mathematician named J. J. Sylvester, who came to Virginia as a refugee after being blackballed by anti-Semites at the University of Cambridge.[215]

For Jefferson, secularism did not mean anti-religion or atheism.[216] He was a student of religion, and wanted different faiths to establish their own presences at the university. He believed that the moral teachings derived from faith, like those he studied in the Jefferson Bible, were important aspects of a true education and a life well lived.[217] But he objected to organized religion and to the idea that one denomination had exclusive access to truth. Faculty and students of different faiths could tend to their own beliefs, and come to worship as they chose, a reflection of the ideals in the Virginia Statute for Religious Freedom.[218] Historian Merrill Peterson said that Jefferson's ideas for the university contained "the dominant forces of his life and mind, of democracy and enlightenment and nationality."[219]

If questions of God made starting a new university difficult, questions about money might have made it impossible. As Monticello showcased, Jefferson had expensive tastes. When state legislators pored over his designs and funding requests, they wondered if the school needed to be quite so lavish. This was to be a public university, and public funds were at stake. The legislators didn't believe that a tour of campus need be a lesson in architecture, and they had a point. The plans for the school's Rotunda alone were estimated at a colossal $70,000, almost as much as Jefferson's total personal debt burden. This expenditure would take resources away from William & Mary, the alma mater of not only Jefferson, but also nearly 50 percent of the House of Delegates.[220] For Jefferson, taking funds from that school may have been part of the point.

The president turned to the state senator for help. But Cabell was ill, and he was getting worse. He was so ill that he'd coughed up blood on the senate floor and didn't think his health could survive the legislative session.[221] He told Jefferson that he planned to retire. But the former president was not sympathetic.[222] The future of the university was at stake, and Cabell's letter filled him with a terrible sense that it might all fall apart. Without funding, and without Cabell, there might not be a University of Virginia. Now Jefferson used his moral authority, exhorting Cabell with an emotional and direct plea designed to burden him with the kind of duty expected of soldiers on the battlefield. He said what Cabell was doing was "desertion," and ordered him to "stand at [his] posts in the legislature."[223]

In his last decade, Jefferson had one cause, and his friends and supporters needed to help him. "What object of our lives can we propose so important?" he asked Cabell. "Health, time, labor, on what in the single life which nature has given us, can these be better bestowed than on this immortal boon to our country?" He reminded Cabell that he was older, and in even poorer health, than his young friend. But he told him he would "die in the last ditch" to finish the job.²²⁴ Cabell admired Jefferson more than anyone else in the world, and he obliged. He stayed at his post in the legislature, working to secure funding.

With a charter and funding, by November 1821, Jefferson was ready to submit a progress report to the governor of Virginia. There were now completed buildings, and visitors could make out a new campus in Charlottesville.²²⁵ Jefferson could look out with enormous pride and see the tops of some of the structures from his home at Monticello. He wrote to an old friend from his days in Paris, Maria Cosway, that catching a glimpse of the pavilions was "a constant gratification to [his] sight."²²⁶

With the school nearing completion, Jefferson prepared the curriculum, focusing on what he knew best: law and government. Students at the university were to study the founding, the Declaration, the Federalist Papers, and Washington's Farewell Address, as well as classical texts. He established a system of electives, originally a European idea to give students more freedom to choose their own courses.²²⁷ He wanted to mold a new generation of "mini Jeffersons," men of the Enlightenment.²²⁸

This work became all-consuming. Jefferson reported to Madison that he spent four hours a day for two months putting together the curriculum, assembling a list of 6,860 volumes for the school's library. He spoke to a Boston bookseller, who agreed to sell this collection at a cost of $3.50 per book.²²⁹ The school's extensive library notably excluded abolitionist literature—an instance of Jefferson compromising with the pro-slavery element of the state in order to advance the university.²³⁰ In all its grandeur, depth, and contradictions, however, the school would be pure Jefferson.

After the disaster of recruiting a chemistry professor, Jefferson set himself to recruiting a faculty, looking once more to Europe. Bringing top professors across the ocean to a school that didn't yet exist would be a challenge. But the board believed that with the right compensation—between $1,000 and $1,500 a year—they could afford to recruit eight top professors.²³¹ For that mission, Jefferson dispatched a Virginia lawyer named Francis Gilmer across the Atlantic on May 8, 1824, giving him letters of introduction to the American minister in Great Britain and to other dignitaries across the pond.[232]

This work was more important to Jefferson than the presidency, and he always knew it would be. Before he was president, he tried to found a university; while he was president, he wanted to do that work; and after the presidency, he was at last able to pursue that goal, an ambition he'd known he held for his entire life. In his final decade, he brought all the energy and drive from his earlier years together, and combined it with the wisdom and standing he'd gained in the decades in between. The result was something better than he'd hoped for as a young man. That was what he wanted to be remembered for.

Jefferson's journey as a lifelong Founder is still instructive today. His rise was meteoric and much of his career was spent in positions of high station and influence. Yet, he held on to the idea that a new university must be created in order to carry forward and build on what he and the other Founders had started. It would have been easy for him to leave the presidency and spend his final years with his inventions, books, and grandchildren. But he always held on to his vision of founding the university of the future, and it was the pursuit of that idea that kept him going, fulfilled him until his final hours, and allowed him to die peacefully, knowing that his legacy had been institutionalized.

FOUNDER'S FAREWELL

The University of Virginia was coming to life, but its founder, Thomas Jefferson, was dying. He'd suffered for many years from various diseases, including dysentery, malaria, and possibly tuberculosis.[233] But he'd live long enough to see the school open, and now was ready to share it with one of his oldest friends from the Revolution, the Marquis de Lafayette.

Lafayette was a hero, both in the United States and in France. He'd helped the colonists win the war, and he had authored the French Declaration of the Rights of Man, with advice from Jefferson. Now an old man, he came to America in 1824 at the invitation of President Monroe for a yearlong visit and tour. This was to be a national event, and the president called him the "nation's guest."[234] Lafayette brought his son, Georges Washington Motier de Lafayette, along with him.[235]

When they arrived in Virginia, the Lafayette family received a hero's welcome. Hundreds of people turned out for a parade of four gray horses as the former general made his way to Monticello along with a military escort.[236] When he arrived on November 4, 1824, Lafayette was greeted by a large and enthusiastic crowd. This was a new generation that had only read about him in the history books. Now he was there in front of them.

The man for whom the event meant the most was Thomas Jefferson. He'd hoped to see this day. He was weak, and earlier that year he'd had a feeding tube because of an abscess on his jaw. He knew that this visit would be the last time he saw his old friend.[237]

At eighty-one years old, Jefferson at first walked slowly down the steps of Monticello to greet Lafayette. But he sped up in excitement, remembering when the two were young during the American Revolution, as well as their time in Paris together. Lafayette, suffering from gout, dismounted and left behind his escort of fifty cavalry.[238] The two embraced warmly after three decades of separation.

"My dear Jefferson!" and "My dear Lafayette!" they exclaimed as their eyes watered. Biographer Dumas Malone described the meeting as "one of the most sentimental and most dramatic events in the entire lifetime of this highly disciplined and characteristically undramatic man."[239] Jefferson introduced the general to Patsy, who'd first met him when she was a young girl in Paris. Now she was a mother of eleven, and the real hostess of Monticello.[240]

There was to be a feast that night. James Madison arrived late to dinner, and he joined the pair and the other guests in offering toasts to their late friends, including the "immortal Franklin . . . who wrested thunderbolts from the clouds," and to all "the heroes and sages of the revolution." They toasted Jefferson, cheering that he had "poured the soul of the Continent into the Declaration of Independence."[241] They drank Monticello's wine cellar dry.[242]

The next day, the group visited the University of Virginia. Dining under the stars in a not-yet-finished Rotunda, Lafayette became the university's first public guest. And again they toasted, thirteen times for each of the original colonies.[243]

Four days after Lafayette's departure, Francis Gilmer returned from his mission. He had recruited five professors from Europe, not enough to teach every subject in Jefferson's curriculum, but enough to make sure that the university would be able to begin operations in the new year.

The University of Virginia opened for its first classes on March 7, 1825. The occasion brought together a small crowd of around forty students, a number that would grow to 116 by September.[244] For his whole life, Jefferson had waited to meet these students. But he was neither impressed, nor overly sentimental. Most, he believed, showed little promise, a feeling presumably reaffirmed after the student riots. A third of the class, he complained, was "incapable of application."[245]

That first class was Jefferson's last. His doctors diagnosed him with several diseases, including dysuria, an inflamed urinary canal caused by an enlarged prostate.[246] Meanwhile, his debts climbed to almost $100,000, more than $2 million in today's dollars.[247] His family petitioned the state to authorize a lottery to sell their land. Many Virginians and people across the country raised money for the Jeffersons, totaling nearly $16,500.[248]

Indeed, Jefferson was so loved that he was nearly killed. In October 1825, the sculptor John Browere visited Monticello to make a life mask of the Founder's face. To do so, Browere placed a plastic mold over Jefferson. But the artist left the mold on for too long. The plaster hardened to the point where it was almost impossible to remove. Since he was barely able to breathe, Jefferson's granddaughters were afraid that he might suffocate. The mask was removed with a chisel.[249] After that close encounter, Jefferson informed his circles that there would be no more masks or portraits.[250]

He prepared for his end. He wrote to James Madison, asking him "to take care of me when dead."[251] He sketched the obelisk that would mark his grave site.[252] He readied his final will on March 16, 1826, at age eighty-two, dividing up his land among his family and making a few specific bequests, including to Madison, whom he gave a gold-mounted walking staff. To the University of Virginia, he gave his library. His grandchildren each got a watch.[253] His collection of forty thousand letters went to his grandson Thomas Jefferson Randolph, who preserved them until his own death in 1875.[254] Many of those documents can now be found at the Library of Congress.

To Sally Hemings and her family, Jefferson kept his promise. His will dictated that five of her children would be freed. But it didn't mention Sally. However, Patsy released Sally after her father's death.[255] Sally Hemings died in Virginia in 1835. But the other 130 enslaved people of Monticello were sold in an attempt to settle some of the estate's debts. The resulting family separation compounded the tragedy of slavery at Monticello.[256] The last survivor of the group was a man named Peter Fossett, who remembered that sale as late as 1898. He recalled, "We were scattered all over the country, never to meet each other again until we meet in another world."[257]

With his last will and testament finalized, Jefferson's final days were quiet. His doctor gave him frequent doses of opium, relieving some of his pain.[258] He wrote to Patsy just hours before he slipped into intermittent unconsciousness. It was a poem about her late mother and sister, titled "A Death-bed Adieu." Its last two lines read "Two Seraphs await me, long shrouded in death: / I will bear them your love on my last parting breath."[259]

For his part, Jefferson had one final farewell to make. On the Fourth of July, there was to be a celebration in Washington, DC. It was 1826, the fiftieth anniversary of the Declaration of Independence. The mayor of Washington invited the last three living signers of the Declaration, Jefferson, Adams, and Charles Carroll of Maryland, to be his guests of honor.[260] But none could make it, as their health was too fragile. Instead, Jefferson crafted a letter for the occasion to be published in the *National Intelligencer*.

The letter was optimistic. It was a message that captured his philosophy, and his motivation in authoring the Declaration and founding the University of Virginia: "All eyes are opened, or opening, to the rights of man. The general spread of the light of science has already laid open to every view. The palpable truth, that the mass of mankind has not been born with saddles on their backs, nor a favored few booted and spurred, ready to ride them legitimately, by the grace of god."[261]

That was his last public declaration. On July 4, 1826, at 12:50 p.m., near the exact hour at which he had signed the Declaration of Independence in 1776, he died with his eyes open. Hundreds of miles to the north, John Adams died that evening, too, at around 6:50 p.m. His final words were "Thomas Jefferson still survives." He was six hours too late.[262]

Jefferson had always wanted to die in Virginia. In 1787, he had told a friend that "all my wishes end, where I hope my days will end, at Monticello."[263] He got his wish. The students of the University of Virginia and the citizens of Charlottesville grieved. A few months prior, many of them had rioted across his campus. Now they wore black pins on their left arms for the rest of the term. One community member wrote, "I never saw young men so deeply affected by any circumstance in my life."[264]

With Thomas Jefferson's death coming just hours before John Adams's passing, there were only two former presidents still living after July 4, 1826. America's fourth president, James Madison, born in 1751, died at age eighty-five on June 28, 1836, less than a week before Independence Day that year.[265] The fifth president, James Monroe, made it to his own Fourth of July, passing away on the holiday in New York City five years to the day after the deaths of Adams and Jefferson, at age seventy-three.[266]

Meanwhile, the sitting president, John Quincy Adams, had a terrible task the day Jefferson died. He had to mourn not only the passing of America's third president, but also his father, America's second commander in chief. President Adams said that he saw the hand of "Divine Providence" in the timing. "In one day, almost in the same hour, have two of the Founders of the Republic, the Patriarchs of Liberty, closed their services to social man. . . . If Science and Philosophy lament their enthusiastic votary in the halls of Monticello, Philanthropy and Eloquence weep with no less reason in the retirement of Quincy."[267]

It was an eloquent message, and it was well received. But the country didn't stay united in mourning for long. Politics was tearing the country apart. James Monroe's "Era of Good Feelings" was gone.

There wasn't a Virginian on the ballot in 1824—a first in American history. And Jefferson hadn't wanted John Quincy Adams to be president. Instead, he backed William H. Crawford, a prominent figure in Georgia politics who served in both Madison's and Monroe's cabinets,[268] but who suffered a debilitating stroke, and came in third, behind John Quincy Adams and Andrew Jackson, but ahead of fourth-place finisher Henry Clay of Kentucky.[269]

Despite his reservations about Adams, Jefferson was still hopeful. He wrote to the president-elect's father, and predicted that, even after the acrimonious election, the country would unite, just as it had after the revolution of 1800.[270] Besides, Jefferson believed the country had dodged a bullet. "[Jackson]," he confided, "is one of the most unfit men I know of for [the presidency]. He has had very little respect for laws or constitutions."[271]

The voters disagreed with Jefferson. While John Quincy Adams's administration was a bridge between the Founders and the next generation, it was doomed from the start. It looked like his—and Jefferson's—worst fears would soon be realized. The Age of Jackson was coming.

2

A Second Act

[He is the] acutest, the astutest, the archest enemy of Southern slavery that ever existed. I mean the Old Man Eloquent, John Quincy Adams.

—HENRY WISE

March 4, 1829, looked like the end of the road for John Quincy Adams. It was Andrew Jackson's inauguration. Like his father, Adams skipped town on his successor's big day, unwilling to face the man who'd defeated him after just one term in office. Now the founding's most celebrated son was headed back home to Quincy, Massachusetts, without a position, and with few prospects.

The now former president was sixty-one years old. As a boy, his famous parents, John and Abigail Adams, had set him on the path to American greatness. Few of the Founding Fathers' children amounted to much, but Adams was the exception. He'd served the United States almost from the beginning, as an effective ambassador, senator, and then secretary of state. His presidency was a foregone conclusion. But in a democracy, not everything goes according to plan.

Things fell apart in the 1824 election, when Adams came in an unexpected second place. He'd lost the popular vote to Jackson, but neither had won a majority of votes in the Electoral College. The matter was thrown to the House of Representatives, where Speaker Henry Clay—the fourth-place finisher in that year's presidential election—awarded

Adams the presidency, not Jackson. When Clay then became Adams's secretary of state, the whole affair stank of a "Corrupt Bargain." The Adams administration was a political stillborn. Four years later, the voters sent Jackson to the White House.

Now in the seventh decade of his life, Adams might have thrown in the towel. He didn't. Instead, after eighteen months, he embarked on what became one of the greatest second acts in American history. He won a seat in Congress and, in a much lower office, found a much higher calling.

As a former president and the son of a Founding Father, he walked into the chamber as more than a freshman member of the lower house. He had standing and could command his colleagues' attention on any issue. He was not trying to move up the ladder, and so he had nothing to lose in the House. He used his position to advance a cause that he came to care about deeply: abolition.

Adams's second act would far outshine his first. As a congressman, Adams was more decisive than he had been as president. He took a stand on the most divisive issue of the day and became Washington's most influential abolitionist a generation before emancipation. Through his sixties, seventies, and early eighties, he battled his critics on the House floor. He defended escaped slaves before the Supreme Court. He held off a pro-slavery attempt to annex Texas. He even chaired a committee that almost impeached a slaveholding president.[1] And in the end, he passed the torch of abolition to a freshman member of Congress, Abraham Lincoln.

Second acts are rare, especially for presidents. No one would have suspected that a man who started his career with an appointment by George Washington in 1794 would end it in 1848, serving in Congress alongside Abraham Lincoln. His four years in the White House, from 1825 until 1829, were an intermission between two of the most remarkable careers in American public life.

When he died, Congressman Adams was not remembered for his defeat in 1828. He was remembered as "a living bond of connexion between the present and the past."[2] He'd worked for or met with every president from George Washington to James K. Polk. He'd found a higher calling in the House of Representatives than he ever had in the White House. And he'd shown that defeat is not the end of the road— it can be the beginning of a new path.

THE PRESIDENT IS DROWNING

Psychologists have a theory about dreams of being naked. Those dreams often represent deep insecurity and fear. They indicate depression and the feeling of being overwhelmed. John Quincy Adams was naked and overwhelmed a few months into his presidency. And he was drowning— literally and figuratively.

President Adams made a habit of skinny-dipping in the Tiber Creek, a tributary to the Potomac River near Washington, DC. Skinny- dipping wasn't unusual for men of this time. The early nineteenth century witnessed plenty of it. His routine was to wake up between four and five in the morning, walk to the Potomac, and take a dip for anywhere from twenty minutes to an hour.[3] As president, he often en- listed his long-time valet, Antoine Michel Giusta, to tag along.

Antoine and Adams met in Belgium. Antoine, a Frenchman, had deserted from Napoleon's army and met Adams, who was negotiating the Treaty of Ghent to bring the War of 1812 to a close. Antoine be- friended Adams, and he married Louisa Adams's maid. The two men were more than employer and servant. They were close friends.

They planned to go for their usual swim on June 13, 1825. Adams's son objected, not trusting the rickety boat they were going to take out, given the rough current that day. The president didn't care, and he and Antoine climbed aboard. Swimming suits were not commonplace, and Antoine stripped naked. Adams looked forward to an enjoyable morn- ing paddling and planned to take his clothes off once they had found the right spot to swim.

The two were barely halfway across the river before their boat sprang a leak. Just then, a breeze from the northwest came in, rocking the canoe out of control. Cold water poured in over both sides and through the hole in the hull. They couldn't bail themselves out, and the president and his valet abandoned ship.[4]

Antoine was not burdened by any clothes, and he was able to swim to shore with ease. But Adams, who was never in good shape, struggled as the water got rough around him. He gulped down water and gasped for air when he could as he floated downriver.[5] His loose shirtsleeves felt like weights dragging him down.

For nearly three hours, he struggled as he tried to stay above the waters of the Potomac River. If he'd drowned that day, he'd have been the first American president to die in office. In that event, John C. Calhoun, the vice president and pro-slavery politician, would have taken the White House. But Adams eventually made it to shore. When he was back on land, he took off his remaining clothes, and he thanked God for his survival. Antoine sent for a carriage, and the two men rode home buck naked. As Adams reported in his diary, "This incident gave me a humiliating lesson."[6] But the truth was that this wasn't his only humbling experience, even if it was uniquely embarrassing. His entire tenure in the White House offered lessons in humility, for which the near-death experience felt like an eerie metaphor.

The presidency was supposed to be the culmination of Adams's life. As a boy, he'd witnessed the Battle of Bunker Hill. He'd joined his father on a diplomatic mission to Europe, meeting with kings, queens, and the czar along the way. He was an ambassador to the Netherlands, then to Prussia, Russia, and the Court of Saint James's. He was a senator from Massachusetts. He could have joined the Supreme Court, if he had only wanted it. But a lifetime appointment wasn't for Adams. Next was secretary of state, a position he held under President James Monroe, helping to craft the Monroe Doctrine and much else to reshape American foreign policy. The White House was the next step.

The 1824 election was to be his moment. With no more Founding Fathers waiting in line, Adams was next. But unfortunately for Adams, the voters had something different in mind. General Andrew Jackson, the hero of the Battle of New Orleans, was the man the people wanted. Jackson, a military hero from the western part of the United States, was very different from Adams. And in an era of personality and populism, Adams was an East Coast patrician with little charm. Adams was described as "sober, almost to gloom or sorrow."[7] This was not the profile of a winning candidate.

Personality matters in politics. So does appearance. And we know

what Adams looked like, as he was the first president ever to be photographed, though his photo was taken years after the White House.
At five foot seven, he was overweight and round.[8] He had glaring eyes,
bushy eyebrows, and muttonchops around his face like a lion's mane.
Adams's hair was thin, and his neck disappeared into his torso, as if it
were a genetic afterthought to the rest of his body. His facial features
were pointed, even unnaturally so, and might today be mistaken for
failed plastic surgery. But the photograph doesn't capture it all. Adams's body—like many in this less hygienic age—was often covered
with pimples, boils, and scars.[9]

What Adams did have was a record of public service and brilliance.
He ran intellectual circles around his peers by proving able to out-
debate any of his contemporaries.[10] He worked hard in every post he
held.[11] The public might not have agreed with him on everything, but
he stuck by his principles. He believed in government by the best, and
that he was among the best. He was ready to be president in 1824.[12]

When Adams won the White House, despite coming in second in
the popular vote and the Electoral College, Andrew Jackson did not
take his defeat lying down. Jackson resigned his own seat in the Senate
in 1825, a move that set him in position early for the 1828 election,
still three years away. The Democratic-Republican Party nominated
him for president.[13] He became the instant front-runner, and was a
sword of Damocles over the Adams administration.

Without a mandate to govern, Adams was unable to rescue his
nascent administration. He felt impotent and was often filled with a
sense of despair, growing distracted from his official duties. He spent
much of his time helping his wife, Louisa, breed silkworms on the
front lawn of the White House. He ate unhealthily. He distracted himself by reading the Bible, strolling, and swimming. At family suppers,
he rarely showed the First Lady much affection.

When his dinners were finished, he "wasted most evenings in idle-
ness,"[14] playing billiards on his wilder nights. He usually concluded
the evening's activities by 8:00 p.m.[15] But even billiards caused him
headaches, when an overzealous congressman seized upon a White
House invoice for a $50, secondhand table. The congressman accused

the president of misusing public funds, saying the table was an extravagance. The incident was used to fuel rumors or corrupt, backroom deals in smoke-filled rooms, not to mention of gambling.[16]

Nothing was easy. Congress jammed Adams's agenda, a national program of roads and canals, land allocation for Native Americans in the Western territories, and a national university of the type once proposed by Jefferson.[17] His most consequential piece of legislation came on May 19, 1828, when he signed into law a new tax on imports. This law would come to be known as the Tariff of Abominations, and it levied a 38 percent fee on almost every good shipped to the United States. Favored by manufacturers in the North, it hurt farmers in the South and West, and the president's popularity sank further.[18]

The president was miserable, and observers knew it. White House parties were dismal affairs, and the Adamses' guests could tell they were not with a happy man. First Lady Louisa Adams was also despondent. Her marriage, never the stuff of fairy tales, was not what she wanted. She complained that the president expected "[her to] cook dinner, wash his clothes, gratify his sexual appetites . . . [and then] thank him and love him for permission to drudge through life at the mercy of his caprices."[19]

The four years in the White House were a low point in their personal lives. In 1826, when John Adams died on the same day as Thomas Jefferson, the president's depression deepened. He was now the head of the family, and nearing the end of his presidency. He'd be back to the Adams family's ninety-five-acre property in Massachusetts. There, he'd be away from public life, and he'd have to deal with his alcoholic brother, Thomas Boylston Adams. Thomas was living in the family home. According to the rumors, he was hosting bacchanals late into the night.[20]

Adams knew that, like his father, he was likely going to be a one-term president. But if he was dreading the 1828 election, he didn't show it. A disciplined diarist from the age of twelve, he barely mentioned the election in his writings. Instead, he focused on details about his daily life, like his visitors and meetings, appointments, and minor decisions. He wrote about the First Lady's silkworms, perhaps looking for a distraction from his pending defeat.[21]

The results were even more unfavorable than expected, 178 electoral votes for Jackson and only 83 for Adams.[22] If the president was
crestfallen at his rapid downfall, he didn't show it. One newspaper
described him as "uncommonly well and cheerful," and "neither morti-
fied nor disappointed."[23] But he did have a sense that this was the end.
"The sun of my political life sets in the deepest gloom," Adams wrote
morbidly in his diary.[24]

This election was nastier than the one four years prior, and neither candidate emerged unscathed. Jackson's wife, Rachel, had been
slandered as an adulterer and bigamist, as it was discovered that her
first marriage had not been legally ended when she married Andrew.
In December 1828, just a month after the election, Rachel died. She
was buried at Jackson's Tennessee estate, the Hermitage, on Christmas Eve. Jackson believed that his wife passed due to a broken heart,
after having been so maligned, and he blamed Adams and Adams's
supporters.[25]

The truth was not so clear-cut. Adams hadn't personally slandered
Rachel, but he hadn't spoken out against the attacks.[26] For Jackson,
that was enough. In his grief, he had a message carved on Rachel's
tombstone: "A being so gentle and so virtuous, slander might wound
but could not dishonor."[27]

The election hadn't been kind to Adams, either. Jackson's supporters slandered him, too, accusing the president of hiring prostitutes for
the czar while he'd been America's ambassador to Russia.[28] Adams's
reputation took a hit, not only from his defeat, but also from the rumors. His own party turned on its standard-bearer. Some old Federalists in New England alleged that he'd betrayed them as far back as
the War of 1812.[29] Jackson arrived in Washington in January, and the
president-elect refused to call on his defeated rival. The newspapers
reported on the snub.[30]

Inauguration Day was coming, and Adams faced the same question his father faced twenty-eight years prior. Would he go? He asked
his cabinet, and all but one member said he shouldn't.[31] Maybe if
Jackson had called on him and asked him to attend he would have. But
neither man wanted to be in the same room. Adams did not go.[32] He
did not want to witness the dawn of a new age in American politics.

THE INTERMISSION

John Quincy Adams began his post-presidency in a state of mourning, both over his own loss and a political shift in American politics that he did not welcome. After his defeat, he confided to his friends, "My intention [is] to go into the deepest retirement, and withdraw from all connection with public affairs."[33] When he met with his secretary of state, Henry Clay, he told the man at the center of the Corrupt Bargain, "After the 3d of March I should consider my public life as closed."[34] He had every reason to believe what he was saying.

Adams could not move on. In fact, he was stuck. Former First Lady Louisa Adams was recovering from a serious illness, and the icy roads back to Massachusetts wouldn't be dry and comfortable enough for her to travel until spring. So, instead of returning to the relative peace and isolation of Quincy, Massachusetts, they moved to Meridian Hill in Washington, DC, only a mile away from the White House.[35] No former president had ever stayed in the capital after their successor's swearing in.

The Adams family could hear the change coming. Through their windows, the sounds of parades of Jackson supporters flooding the streets came pouring in. Jackson the populist had opened up the White House to the public.[36] Partygoers, many in dirty workman's clothes, swept in to see the man they had sent to Washington. They trampled over the White House furniture in muddy boots, breaking dishes along the way. The White House staff was overwhelmed. It was so chaotic that a congressman from Georgia, a Jackson supporter, had to climb out a window to escape. Poor Antoine, still in his old job, once again saved the day, and much of the upholstery. He lured the crowd out of the house with tubs of whiskey.[37]

The former president could hear the ruckus, and he read about it all in the papers. Stuck on Meridian Hill, he got to work.[38] His early days were about defending himself and his record. He wrote an eighty-four-thousand-word rebuttal to incoming attacks from some of the Old Federalists in New England who'd turned against him. The result was a bitter, even unbecoming piece. Fortunately for Adams, it was never published.[39]

He wasn't alone. Old friends from his life in politics in and around Washington visited the family at Meridian House. But almost no one from the new administration came by. The only official from the Jackson cabinet who visited was Secretary of State Martin Van Buren. The secretary had to get Jackson's permission to pay the former president a visit, and he only came to discuss ongoing negotiations with the Ottoman Empire pending from Adams's tenure. Adams and Jackson only saw each other once during this time. It was the funeral of Virginia congressman Philip Doddridge. The two men did not shake hands.[40]

Another funeral hit the Adams family much closer to home. Two months out of office, tragedy struck. On April 30, 1829, George Washington Adams committed suicide. He was twenty-eight years old.

The Adams men were no strangers to depression, or to alcoholism. George Washington Adams was brilliant like his father, but troubled. His father was not much of a source of support.[41] George's depression had spiraled, and he mismanaged his family's finances, failed at his law practice, and even fathered a child out of wedlock with the family doctor's chambermaid. The child's mother was afraid of what George might do, and feared for her child's safety. A restraining order was put in place.[42]

George's condition did not improve. In April, after a heavy night of drinking aboard the steamboat *Benjamin Franklin*, he lost his mind. The paranoid man worried that his fellow passengers were plotting against him. He tried to escape. But when the captain refused to let him off the boat, George jumped overboard and to his death. There was no suicide note.[43]

His father was deeply affected by the loss. "My thoughts are so wandering," Adams wrote, "that I distrust the operation of my own reason."[44] Louisa, mother to twelve children, only three of whom survived past the age of two, was devasted. With only two sons left, the two Adams parents grieved, a rare moment of emotional connection.[45]

It was up to Adams to retrieve George's body, and he traveled to New York that June, accompanied by his middle son, John II. His son's body had washed ashore, and it was recovered on City Island, an area of New York that is now a part of the Bronx. Before he saw his son's body, Adams had only read about his death in the papers. When he arrived by his side, he couldn't bear to see the body and asked that his casket remain shut.[46]

In a matter of months, Adams had lost the presidency and a son. Like Jefferson, he had enormous debts, and he owed his creditors nearly $42,000.[47] His debts climbed[48] due to mismanagement of the family finances and bad investments,[49] and unlike Jefferson, there were no adoring masses to bail him out. He was unpopular, and, if his condition didn't improve, he might be close to penniless.

Shortly after, Adams arrived home to Quincy, and he saw that the Big House, where his father once lived, was in disrepair. Adams considered selling the house and buying a smaller property.[50] This wasn't Jefferson's Monticello—the Adams family purchased it in 1787, and Abigail Adams described it as looking like a "wren's nest," with all the comforts of "a barracks."[51] It was much quieter and relatively isolated. This was not a place that would attract visitors from far and wide, as Monticello did.

Home at last, Adams needed work. He tried his hand at tree farming, but lacked both a green thumb and a farmer's patience. When his crop of trees failed, he threw up his hands in frustration, and he ranted, writing in his diary that the whole affair was a metaphor for the death of his career.[52] He tried his hand at writing, and scribbled and published a poem about England's takeover of Ireland, earning him a $100 commission.[53]

He did not want a monastic or scholarly life, but he was a student of ideas and history, and Adams's personal library contained nearly six thousand volumes,[54] among them Jefferson's works. He studied Jefferson,[55] as well as the Psalms, and he read Cicero, noting parallels between his own life and that of the Roman statesman, an elitist like Adams who—rightly—worried about the death of the republic when he witnessed the rise of another general, Julius Caesar.[56] But he did not want to spend the rest of his life in contemplation, and his thoughts frequently wandered back to Washington.

For almost his entire adult life, Adams had been in public service.[57] It was the only life he knew. When he visited the capital a few months after leaving it, he remembered his old life.[58] He wanted to have a position again, and his associates in Quincy began to think for themselves about how they could engineer a second act.

While some of Adams's compatriots wanted him to return to politics, his family did not. Louisa was the most opposed, as her health was still frail, and she didn't want to return to Washington. Wondering and worrying about what the future had in store, she wrote to her son John, "There are some very silly plans going on here and God only knows in what they will end, but I fear not at all to my taste."[59]

Their other living son, Charles Francis Adams, was no more enthusiastic. Rather than return to politics, he urged his father to write a biography of his grandfather John Adams.[60] But John Quincy Adams had little interest, and it would be Charles Francis who later took up the cause of family historian, compiling a ten-volume set of his grandfather's writings over many decades, which was published in 1856.[61]

Whatever the family's reservations, a well-timed newspaper article tipped the scales in favor of Congress. On September 7, 1830, a few lines appeared in the *Boston Daily Courier* that caught Adams's interest. The piece suggested that Adams might be a good representative for the district based in Plymouth.[62] Adams had discussed the idea in private, but hadn't pursued it.[63] Now, with the notion out in the open, he was more interested, and he was glad to be back in the public conversation.

Soon after the *Courier* piece, Boston celebrated its bicentennial. Prominent citizens in attendance, among them Congressman Joseph Richardson of the very same Plymouth, asked to meet with Adams.[64] The visitors performed a rehearsed piece of political choreography, with one asking Adams if he'd heard that Richardson would not seek reelection. After his friend spoke, Richardson confirmed that the rumors were true. He wanted to return to his old life as a minister. His seat would soon be open, and Richardson told Adams that he was a shoo-in.[65] Not only that, if Adams didn't run, it would be a disaster, as there was no telling who'd get the seat.[66]

Though Adams was tempted, he didn't say yes right away.[67] He was proud, but he didn't think a role in the House was beneath a former president. Rather, as he wrote in his diary, no one "could be degraded by serving the people as a Representative in Congress."[68] What Adams wanted was not to throw his hat in the ring, but to be asked to run by others. He was, and on October 13, 1830, he got the news that the Republican convention unanimously selected him to represent Plymouth in the 22nd Congress.[69] Two months later, he won the election handily, with 1,817 of 2,565 votes.[70] President Adams would soon be Congressman Adams.

When he heard the news that he was headed back to Washington, he was uncharacteristically excited. Adams boasted in his diary, "I have received nearly three votes in four, throughout the district."[71] Though he couldn't win a national election, he was still the favorite son back home. He'd thought he was politically dead in 1828, but now he was resurrected. "Election as President of the United States was not half so gratifying to my inmost Soul," he confessed.[72] No former president had ever won a seat in Congress. None has since, save for the disgraced Andrew Johnson, who returned briefly to the Senate.

For Adams and for the United States, this was uncharted territory. He thought about his five presidential predecessors. Save for his father, four had returned home to Virginia, rarely leaving.[73] But there was a precedent for public service. George Washington accepted a military commission. Jefferson had worked with the state of Virginia to found a university, with Madison's and Monroe's assistance.[74] Monroe joined the Virginia Constitutional Convention as a delegate in 1829.[75] But this was different. None had returned to Washington. None held elected office.

The role had appeal. Not only would he be back in the capital, he'd have a new source of income, as well as a fund to cover travel expenses between Quincy and Washington.[76] Before he could make that journey, though, he'd have to wait. The election took place in November 1830, but the 22nd Congress would not begin until December 1831. He was ready to work, so Adams headed to Washington early.[77] He stopped in New York on the way, where he visited former president James Monroe.[78]

After Elizabeth, his wife, passed, James Monroe sold his plantation and left Virginia to live with his daughter Maria Hester Monroe in Manhattan. Their address was 63 Prince Street, a lovely two-story brownstone near the Bowery.[79] Adams and Monroe reunited, and the two former presidents reminisced about their time in Washington. Adams, Monroe's secretary of state, was there to pay his respects to the man who'd put him in the position that set him up for the White House. Shortly after Adams's visit, on July 4, 1831, Monroe died. He was the third of five presidents who passed away on Independence Day. None has since.

When he returned to Washington after visiting Monroe, Adams was welcomed by many as an old friend, and as something of a curiosity. This was a first, an ex-president not only back in the capital, but headed to Congress. The city was intrigued, even if the current administration still despised Adams. A few days later, on New Year's, hundreds of visitors came to see him. They told him about the town's gossip, and Adams was glad to hear about a growing feud between President Jackson, Vice President Calhoun, members of the cabinet, and their wives, which became known as the Petticoat Affair. Policy debates over tariffs and, more important, crises over slavery and westward expansion also plagued the Jackson administration.[80]

Adams was back in the city he loved. But he did not yet know what his role would be in the nation's great debates.

THE PRESIDENT RETURNS

When Adams walked into the Capitol on December 5, 1831, he was both a junior member of Congress and an elder statesman. Earlier in his career, he'd served in the Senate, on the other side of the building. But he'd never served in the lower house. Now he was one person in a sea of 213 congressmen.[81] Not only that, a supermajority of his colleagues were Jackson men. This was not a crowd that was predisposed in his favor.

Alongside Adams, there were eighty-nine freshmen entering Congress. All of them knew his name, but it's doubtful he knew many of theirs. He entered the chamber and took his assigned seat, one of the worst in the House, number 203.[82] When Henry Clay greeted the sixty-four-year-old Adams, the Kentuckian asked cheekily how the former president "felt upon turning boy again in the House of Representatives."[83]

At first Adams didn't know how to answer Clay's question. Every step in his career had led to the presidency, what he'd thought would be his professional peak. The House didn't naturally lead anywhere. He had a position, but no agenda, which made him fixate on his lower status. He had powerful friends, but also powerful enemies. His greatest foe was the president.

The long arm of Jackson extended to the House. As a former secretary of state, Adams expected to be assigned to the Committee on Foreign Affairs. Instead, the Speaker gave him the Committee on Manufactures, worrying that Jackson might punish him if he gave Adams a seat on the committee of his choosing.[84] When Adams found another member on the Foreign Affairs Committee who was willing to trade places, the Speaker, loyal to Jackson, refused. The former president was a freshman member of the House, and he had to report to the committee to which he was assigned.[85]

Not long after, Adams began to make his mark in the House. December 12 was a day for petitions, an occasion for members to present notes and letters from citizens who wrote to them wanting their elected officials to take action on issues of concern.[86] The right to petition is protected in the First Amendment, and it's an old tradition with roots in English common law. Even imperial Russia, where Adams had served as ambassador, had a history of upholding the right of serfs to directly petition the czar.[87]

Aware of that history from the Old and New Worlds, Adams rose to present a number of petitions he'd received. It was early in his tenure, and his voice shook as he did so.[88] This wasn't because he was an anxious public speaker. It was because one petition in the bunch was incendiary, and Adams knew it. The letter came from a group of Pennsylvania Quakers. And they were petitioning to end the slave trade in Washington, DC.[89]

Slavery was the most explosive topic in American politics, and it had been since the founding. The Missouri Compromise had threatened to split the country in two over the issue, and there were few members of Congress who dared speak about slavery in the open. Adams did not have such concerns.

Unlike most other members of the House, he did not have a higher

office to which he aspired, and he did not owe his position to party
leaders or political favors. He had his own standing, and he was prepared to use his position to get Congress to discuss and debate the
issue. What's more, regardless of the content of their petition, these
Quakers—though not his constituents—had written to him. They had
a right to be heard.[90]

There was a tradition of silence on the matter of slavery, but no
congressional rule against presenting petitions about it. When Adams
broke tradition by speaking up in his epic debut, members were
shocked and out for blood. The South Carolina delegation stormed
out in protest. Soon, the chamber was filled with the noise of furious
congressmen.[91]

Despite the strong reaction, Adams stood firm, he even enjoyed the
commotion. He also set two precedents for how he would conduct himself going forward. Even if he did not agree with the content of petitions
he received, he would present them. And even if the petitions sent to
him did not come from his district, he would bring them to the floor.[92]

After petition day, Adams was back at the center of the nation's debates. He'd taken a stand and felt a renewed sense of purpose. Friends
congratulated him. Louisa, now back in Washington with her husband, noticed that his spirits had improved.[93] He stood for reelection
and won in 1832. But Andrew Jackson was still the president. With
an unfriendly White House, it was not clear how much impact Adams
could have in Washington.

Jackson was a constant thorn in Adams's side, and Adams never let
go of his hatred for his successor. When Harvard University, Adams's
alma mater, offered Jackson an honorary degree in 1833, Adams re-
acted with a mixture of jealousy and rage. The president of Harvard, a
distant Adams cousin, invited him to attend the ceremony. But Adams
declined, responding that Harvard was disgracing itself by associat-
ing with "a barbarian who could not write a sentence of grammar and
hardly could spell his own name."[94]

Adams could be prone to self-pity, and still did not know what he'd
be able to accomplish in Washington. In 1833, he turned sixty-six,
and he wondered how many years he had left, writing in his diary that
his "whole life has been a succession of disappointments."[95] It was a

ridiculous sentiment coming from John Quincy Adams.[96] But it was how he felt in his private moments, as he worried about his mortality and his country, and slept less than five hours a night.[97]

He was jolted back into reality by a near-death experience. On November 8, 1833, Adams was on a train from Quincy to Washington. He'd never made the trek back to the capital by rail, and his first experience with the new technology did not go well.[98] Just as he got comfortable in the train's second car and began to relax for the journey, the train caught fire. It derailed and was hurtling forward with no safeguards in place.

The accident turned into a disaster. The train's momentum carried it nearly two hundred feet, and Adams was thrown from his seat, his body hitting the other side of the train car like a loose piece of luggage. Nearly everyone else on board was injured. The train was destroyed. As he steadied himself, Adams saw blood, broken bones, and his fellow passengers in significant pain, a level of physical suffering he hadn't seen since the Battle of Bunker Hill.[99] But Adams was unscathed, which was remarkable given his age and the fact that he had been tossed around. When the train arrived in New York at 6:30 a.m., he thanked God that he had "escaped unhurt from the most dreadful catastrophe that ever my eyes beheld!"[100] He could have died, and he remembered how lucky he was to be alive.

Tragedy struck the Adams family again, however, on October 23, 1834. John Adams II died of alcohol poising at just thirty-one years old. Like his late brother, John II had struggled in life. He'd served as his father's private secretary in the White House before running a flour mill owned by the family. He'd failed in his business ventures, which combined with mourning his brother to thrust him into an irreversible state of melancholy. This time, however, John Quincy was at his son's bedside when he died. The former president's daughter-in-law, John II's widow, Mary, and her children moved in with Adams and Louisa.[101] Now, of all the Adams children, only Charles Francis was left.[102]

Before John II's death, John Quincy had not yet settled into the House. He remained restless about the lower station and entertained the idea that the Anti-Masonic Party would nominate him for president in 1832, or maybe he would run for Massachusetts governor. He was almost appointed to the Senate.[103] But after he won a third term in the 1834 election, in which he secured 86 percent of the vote, Adams knew he was there to stay. He was about to become a master of the House.

GAGGED

Adams was secure in his position. He knew he could remain in the House as long as he desired. But while he agitated on the right to petition, he didn't yet have a cause he owned. Debates about slavery and westward expansion were the nation's most consequential main issues, yet Congress hardly debated them. John Quincy Adams had dipped his toes into these choppy waters. But he hadn't yet dived in.

Abolition was not a new issue to Adams. His family had never owned slaves, and they had always opposed slavery. John Adams, his father, had opposed immediate abolition, in favor of gradual emancipation, and had made his own views known. John Quincy shared his father's opinion, even as a young boy. He'd seen serfdom in Russia.[104] He'd witnessed plantation slavery in Virginia. And he believed that "slavery . . . is the great and foul stain upon the North American Union."[105]

While his feelings were clear, his record was not. While serving in the Senate during the Jefferson administration, a bill to ban the importation of slaves to the Louisiana Territory had come up. Adams opposed the measure, believing at the time that the benefits of slave trade outweighed the moral wrong of slavery.[106] As president, he had not championed immediate abolition or gradual emancipation.[107]

Now in Congress, Adams still did not believe that the moment called for abolition, or that the country was ready for it. But he was certain that the abolitionist petitioners had a right to be heard in Congress. Many petitioners were Quakers and Protestants from denominations gaining new prominence during the Second Great Awakening. While they spoke up, Congress was mum on slavery. In the aftermath of the Missouri Compromise, many members believed that another debate could tear the country in two.

Congress may have been silent, but members could hear the sounds of slavery when they went to work. Shackled men, women, and children were marched from one trade market to another, within sight of the Capitol. Just a half mile away, there was a slave jail called the Yellow House.[108] Lafayette Square, near the White House, was once a slave market.[109]

Congress had developed a very Washingtonian remedy to deal with petitions. They ignored them. Adams could read out as many of them as he liked, and the other members sent the petitions to die in com-mittee.[110] Besides congressional intransigence, the abolitionist move-ment was also weak because it was divided. Members of the American Colonization Society favored gradual emancipation, as Adams's father had. They pushed for a "return" of free Africans to the colony of Li-beria, established following Nat Turner's slave rebellion in 1831.[111] But a new group, the American Anti-Slavery Society, instead pushed for immediate emancipation without compensation for slaveholders. William Lloyd Garrison's newspaper the *Liberator* became the chief platform for this faction.[112]

John Quincy Adams had not planted his flag with either camp. But abolitionists understood he was sympathetic to their cause. When the Frenchman Alexis de Tocqueville asked Adams, over a dinner, "Do you regard slavery as a great evil for the United States?" Adams replied, "Yes, unquestionably. It's in slavery that are to be found almost all the embarrassments of the present and fears of the future."[113]

In this third term in Congress, Adams found a third way on slavery. In three months, more than forty thousand people had signed over three hundred petitions addressed to him. There were as many as 350 anti-slavery societies, large and small.[114] He chose not to focus on gradual or immediate emancipation, but instead on the right to peti-tion itself.

The right to petition may sound obscure today, but it wasn't then. Presenting petitions was a significant part of the congressional agenda in Adams's era. Not only is the right to petition explicitly protected in the First Amendment, but President Jackson had brought it up in his message to Congress, the equivalent of the State of the Union. Jack-son called anti-slavery petitions "repugnant to the principles of our national compact."[115] Despite the president's feelings, Congress did not have the authority to restrict petitions based on their content.[116] Such a prohibition would violate the First Amendment.[117]

With that in mind, Adams continued to read abolitionist petitions. Pro-slavery congressmen pushed back, but he enjoyed the debates. But in December 1835, South Carolina congressman James H. Hammond decided he'd had enough.[118] Hammond proposed that petitions about the question of slavery should be rejected outright, which would have effectively silenced Adams and the petitioners.[119] The measure did not pass, but Hammond kept at it. On May 18, 1836, Congressman Henry Pinckney, also of South Carolina, declared that Congress had no role in deciding the question of slavery in the states and could not even change the status of slavery in Washington, DC.[120]

The prospect of ending any debate about slavery whatsoever horrified Adams. Not only was the idea morally wrong, it was illegal. It violated the First Amendment. When the resolution came up for debate, congressmen yelled over each other. Adams struggled to be heard.[121]

Then Speaker James K. Polk, a Tennessee slaveholder and future president, ignored his protests. The outcome of the vote on the measure was a blow to Adams, abolition, and the Bill of Rights. By a margin of 95–82, the House approved the resolution to table all debate. Adams exclaimed, "Am I gagged or am I not!?" With that question, he inadvertently christened the new edict forbidding debates about slavery—the Gag Rule.[122]

ADAMS FINDS HIS VOICE

It was in being gagged that Adams found his voice, and with it a mission that had been missing in his first few terms in the House. He was almost seventy years old. He'd lost the presidency and his reputation. But he was a new man in Congress. He was in a safe seat, which allowed him to take strong positions without worrying that he'd be challenged by a Jacksonian candidate. He found that, even if one member can't move legislation on his own, he can change the national debate. He was ready to do just that.

It was well known that Adams was against slavery. But his views against slavery were hardening during his time in the House, thanks to his experience and his reading of abolitionist writers like Benjamin Lundy, a Quaker from New Jersey of the Garrisonian wing.[123] Even if Adams wasn't quite ready to make their cause his own in Congress, when the issue at hand was protecting the First Amendment, he did not compromise.

He had disdain for the opposing view. Historian Robert Remini argues that "Adams's hatred of the South and Democrats in general stemmed from his desire to punish them for having wrecked his administration." That personal hostility hardened his abolitionism. "By attacking slavery, he could inflict the revenge he so desperately sought for the role played by Democrats, north and south, in ruining his presidency."[124]

He wasn't in a position to repeal the Gag Rule. For his first few terms in Congress, the slavocracy had found Adams to be a nuisance, but little more.[125] However, they underestimated how strongly he'd react to being gagged. Adams understood the First Amendment by the plain meaning of its text, and he read in it Americans' right to petition their government. When that freedom was threatened, he fought back. It was a legal and psychological kind of "reactance," a theory by American psychologist Jack Brehm, who observed a "motivational arousal that emerges when people experience a threat to or loss of their free behaviors. It serves as a motivator to restore one's freedom." But this wasn't just about Adams's freedom to present the petitions—it was about the basic rights of Americans.[126]

To Adams, the freedoms protected in the Bill of Rights were fundamental. In turn the Gag Rule was a fundamental threat. He spent the next six weeks making that case. His passion boiled over in heated debates, and the Speaker of the House struggled to maintain order.[127]

In those days, the debates in Congress often turned violent. It was not uncommon for quarrels to draw blood. There were at least eighty violent incidents on the House floor during the 1830s and 1840s, many of them over the Gag Rule. Southern congressmen challenged Northerners to duels. One abolitionist Whig congressman from Ohio, Joshua Giddings, was attacked seven times. A colleague threatened to lynch him. A Southern congressman threatened another member that he would cut his throat "from ear to ear."[128] In such a hostile work environment, members often showed up armed and ready for a fight.[129]

Adams managed to avoid physical altercations. He was a former president, and he was in his seventies. "If the Member from Massachusetts had not been an old man, protected by the imbecility of age," barked one of his detractors, "he would not have enjoyed, as long as he has, the mercy of my mere words."[130] But it was the slaveholders in Congress who were at Adams's mercy more often than not. He loved to outwit his foes in debates. Upon reading of Adams's verbal jousts in Congress, Ralph Waldo Emerson wrote admiringly that Adams was "no literary gentleman, but a bruiser. . . . [H]e must have sulphuric acid in his tea."[131]

This stand was popular among Emerson's set and in Adams's district. But Adams believed that his positions were "suicidal" nationally.[132] If the other side wouldn't listen to reason, he'd use congressional procedure against them.

The Gag Rule was set to expire when Congress went on its holiday recess. With that in mind, the day after Christmas, Adams presented a petition from a group of abolitionists in Pennsylvania. His opponents had not noticed that the Gag Rule was no longer in effect. When he realized what had happened, Speaker Polk didn't know what to do. A panicked congressman had to reintroduce the Gag Rule, which passed again over Adams's objections. When the dust settled, an outraged Calhoun called Adams a "mischievous old man" for his maneuver.[133] But the abolitionists were delighted. More than half of Congress had tried to silence Adams, but he wouldn't stop. They cheered him in abolitionist newspapers, and though Adams had never been the head of a grassroots movement before, now he was becoming a spokesman for a national cause, even if he wasn't yet ready to commit to congressionally mandated abolition.[134]

He hadn't yet staked out his position on abolition, and the former president was walking a fine line. He believed that he was correct morally. But he also knew better than most that slavery was the most divisive issue in the country. The Founders, going back to Jefferson, had feared that it would lead to a civil war.[135] If Adams pushed Congress too hard, violence in the House chamber might not stay in the

House chamber. If the abolitionist movement looked dangerous, fewer Americans would agree with it. But if he did not stand firm, then the slaveholders in Congress would win.

The position that Adams chose was neither for gradual nor immediate emancipation. As the United States expanded westward, he opposed the spread of slavery into the new territories. This policy was later adopted by Abraham Lincoln before his presidency, and it was akin to the idea of containment, with the hope of a gradual end to the institution of slavery where it already existed.[136]

This position held as Adams's foes in Washington changed. In 1836, Andrew Jackson finished his second term. Vice President Martin Van Buren was on his way to the White House. Van Buren, a New Yorker, was a master of backroom politics and had earned the nickname "Little Magician." But he led a fractured political coalition, and he knew that the issue of slavery threatened to break his support.[137] The real action on slavery, however, wasn't in the White House—it was in Congress.

Governing happened in the legislative branch. Titans like Henry Clay and Daniel Webster ruled the Senate. Former vice president John C. Calhoun was back in the upper chamber as well, where he defended slavery as not a necessary evil, but as a "positive good."[138] With the Great Triumvirate of Clay, Webster, and Calhoun in the Senate, the House of Representatives lacked towering figures. The exception was John Quincy Adams, who though a congressman was still the most famous member of the lower house.

His stature and experiences served him well, and he enjoyed toying with his opponents. Once, he presented petitions for the abolition of slavery in the District of Columbia, only for the Speaker of the House to demand that he take his seat and be quiet once seated, as was predicted. Having a bit of fun, Adams took the Speaker at his word and moved in slow motion, continuing to speak in elongated words—"aaand . . . to . . . deeeclaaare . . . everrry . . . huuuuuuman . . . beeeing . . . freee . . . who sets . . . Foooot . . . upooooon . . . its . . . sooooil"—as his body slowly lowered to the seat.[139]

Exasperated, Adams's foes directed their ire not only at the congressman but also at the petitioners themselves. Southern congressmen accused the women's abolitionist groups writing to Adams of being prostitutes. In turn, Adams retorted that many of the slaveholders making those accusations had fathered illegitimate children, including in many cases with women they enslaved.[140] If they wanted to debate sexual propriety, he'd be more than happy to take them up on that issue.

The congressman was hitting his stride. But his next act nearly caused a riot in Congress. When Adams presented a petition from a group of Virginians, the signatories were not just any Virginians. The former president claimed the petitioners were in fact a group of twenty-two slaves. The American people had a right to present petitions, but slaves?[141]

The House was not prepared for this moment. The Speaker demanded to see the petition, but Adams didn't hand it over. A South Carolina congressman rose to his feet and called for Adams to be indicted, charging that the petition incited rebellion. One member from Georgia cried out that the petition needed to be burned on the spot. Another from Alabama, a four-hundred-pound behemoth, called for Adams's censure and expulsion from the House.[142]

Adams was amused by the onslaught he had witnessed. He'd expected the commotion. But he hadn't yet even read out the petition. The protesting members of Congress did not know what they were protesting. Not even the Speaker knew. Adams revealed that this petition was not about abolition. Instead, it called for Adams to be removed from the House—the exact objective of many of the protesting members.[143]

After the debate, it wasn't clear if the petition was actually from slaves or, more likely, a forgery. If the latter were true, whoever the sender was probably suspected Adams would not read it to the chamber. They assumed he was like most politicians and would cast aside his principles the moment it contradicted his own station. This was a miscalculation. If it was a forgery, Adams called the bluff, and used it to draw out his opponents.[144] The "Madman of Massachusetts" also raised the broader question about slaves and the right to petition.[145] Embarrassed, the objecting members accused him of "trifling with the House." Nevertheless, he spoke for two hours on the matter, asking if a petition from slaves could be read, and contending that it could.[146]

He'd gotten the better of his opponents. The Southern congressmen proved themselves politically and intellectually weaker, and he looked like a shrewd leader.[147] Back home, his constituents in New England applauded.[148] He took a victory lap and proudly drafted four letters reporting his account of the drama to be published in his hometown newspaper.[149]

When he'd arrived in Congress, Adams may not have had a cause in mind, but now a cause had found him. He'd taken a stand and gained new prominence—he'd made a difference, and he'd also made a point. The right to petition, he claimed, was not just for white Americans. It was for enslaved Black Americans as well. The law's protections extended to them.[150] Coming from the son of a Founding Father, this constitutional argument had weight. When Adams spoke, Congress listened.

ADAMS TAKES ON TEXAS

John Quincy Adams was no stranger to Texas. As president, he'd explored buying the territory from Mexico.[151] Slavery was not top of mind for him in those days, expansion was, so when the issue of Texas came up again in 1837, he was ready to fight it in a way he never would have as president.

Westward expansion was a matter of foreign policy. Throughout his career, Adams was an expansionist who had been at the forefront of these debates. As secretary of state, he'd negotiated the Adams-Onís Treaty with imperial Spain, under which the empire ceded the eastern part of Florida to the United States.[152] He'd negotiated treaties with Native American tribes to acquire their lands.[153] The Monroe Doctrine, which he'd shaped, expanded America's influence in the Western Hemisphere.[154] But now, when the issue of expanding the United States to Texas came up, Adams was against the idea.

No other issue carried such weight. Congress received nearly two hundred thousand petitions about annexation in a one-year time span, from 1837 to 1838.[155] Making the issue more complicated, Mexico had already abolished slavery in its territory, including in Texas. But when the territory declared independence in 1836, slavery was being reintroduced.[156]

President Jackson recognized the independent Republic of Texas on his second-to-last day in office in 1837, and he even nominated an American ambassador.[157] But Jackson passed the issue of annexation on to his successor, Martin Van Buren.[158] Van Buren, always worried that his political coalition might break, worried that Texas annexation could be his downfall, as he needed the votes of both Southern slaveholders and Northerners.[159] Two more pro-slavery members in the Senate from Texas would also tip the delicate balance achieved by the Missouri Compromise in favor of slavery's expansion.[160]

Texas annexation and the Gag Rule were bound to collide. It would be impossible for Congress to debate annexation without taking up the issue of slavery, frankly and in the open.[161] The battle lines were drawn in April 1838, when Congressman Ebenezer Shields of Tennessee submitted a resolution for Texas annexation[162] and Congressman George Briggs of Massachusetts challenged it.[163] Into the breach stepped Adams, who presented anti-Texas petitions from abolitionists across the country.[164] He called what the pro-annexation members were advocating "a war of conquest," and he denounced the reintroduction of slavery to a territory where it had been abolished.[165]

That Adams would be opposed was not a surprise. His opponents resorted to their old tactics, trying to dismiss his petitions because they were submitted by women's groups.[166] Then Adams shot back that women had the same right as every other American to petition their government.[167] The debates grew hotter, and Adams's stand won him death threats, including a letter threatening to lynch him and a package with a bullet placed in the palm of a glove.[168]

With the temperature rising in the House, the Tennessee congressman's annexation resolution was tabled by a vote of 122–74.[169] But Adams didn't want short-term delay—he wanted a long-term fix. He took to the floor and mounted the equivalent of a filibuster, holding his place for three weeks, from June 16 through July 7.[170]

The seventy-one-year-old congressman spoke with conviction, his hands shaking as he decried the Gag Rule, Texas annexation, and slavery. He held his ground until Congress went into recess. There was no longer any doubt where he stood. He took to his diary and confided, "If the most ardent desire, and a most vivid hope of the total extinction of Slavery on Earth, and especially at no distant day throughout this North American Union, constitutes an abolitionist, I am one."[171]

He achieved what he aimed to achieve. Congress was set to reconvene in December, and he anticipated debates would boil over again in the winter. But Texas formally withdrew its annexation proposal on October 12, 1838, over anti-slavery sentiment in the United States and fear of provoking a war with Mexico.[172] A few weeks later, Adams was reelected by a comfortable margin to a fifth term.[173] The voters would never send Adams home. If Congress wanted rid of him, they'd have to hope for some other means.

In 1839, Adams made his boldest move yet, proposing a constitutional amendment that would ensure that every child born in the United States would be free, regardless of race, beginning in 1842. This was two decades before the Emancipation Proclamation. Adams knew the amendment would go nowhere, but after the fight over Texas, he was ready for full-throated support for abolition.[174]

The slavocracy struck back. A majority of Congress made the Gag Rule permanent, even prohibiting congressmen from receiving abolitionist petitions. The vote was close, 114–108, and Adams took it to heart that it was not the end.[175] He did what he could to maneuver around House rules, defy the Gag Rule, and bait his colleagues. He was coming into his own. Ralph Waldo Emerson remarked, "Mr. Adams chose wisely and according to his constitution, when . . . he went into Congress. . . . He is like one of those old cardinals, who, as quick as he is chosen Pope, throws away his crutches and his crookedness, and is as straight as a boy."[176]

THE *AMISTAD*

The next great debate over slavery was not going to be in the halls of Congress. It would take place in the Supreme Court. And it was coming to the United States not in the form of a petition, but in the cargo hold of a ship named the *Amistad*.

It was 1839, and the schooner was sailing to a harbor in the Caribbean. On board was a cargo of enslaved men, women, and children from the west coast of Africa. Though the United States had banned the transatlantic slave trade on January 1, 1808, the earliest date allowed by the Constitution,[177] and though several nations had followed suit, including Great Britain and Portugal in 1817, the Netherlands in 1818, and Spain in 1835, the slave trade continued.[178]

The port of Havana was a hotbed for the slave trade. When the *Amistad* arrived at port, on board were fifty-three Africans, including three young girls, who were taken from the Guinean coast. They were transported there by a Portuguese slave trader. They were then purchased by sugar plantation owners named Jose Ruiz and Pedro Montez. Now bound for Camaguey, Cuba, then still a Spanish possession, their fate looked sealed.[179]

But the enslaved men and women on the *Amistad* took their fate into their own hands. A few nights into their journey from Havana, they broke free of their shackles, grabbed knives meant for cutting sugarcane, and killed the ship's captain and cook. They spared the other members of the crew on the condition that they be taken back home to West Africa, across the Atlantic.[180]

The crew betrayed them. Instead of heading east, the *Amistad* sailed north, toward the United States. On August 26, a ship from the Revenue Cutter Service, the precursor to the U.S. Coast Guard, spotted the vessel near Long Island and boarded it. The Africans were taken to Connecticut, where a New Haven judge declared they should be tried for murder and piracy for their so-called mutiny aboard the *Amistad*.[181] The captives were not able to communicate, as they couldn't speak Spanish or English. They could not explain the truth of what had happened. Still, news of the group spread across the country.

Abolitionist groups took interest in their plight and tried to open lines of communication. They sent a teacher for deaf students to New Haven, thinking that a nonverbal breakthrough would be possible.[182] But it was a Yale professor of ancient languages named Josiah Gibbs who cracked the code. Gibbs met with the slaves and learned how to count to ten in their language. With that knowledge, he wandered around the wharves of New Haven and New York, where dialects from all over the world were spoken by merchants coming to port. Gibbs counted slowly and loudly in the slaves' native tongue, hoping that someone would recognize what he was saying. He got lucky. An eighteen-year-old African sailor on Staten Island identified the language as Mende, and he volunteered to translate.[183]

The captives could now tell their story in their own words. What had happened to them was printed in newspapers across the country. John Quincy Adams learned about it from an abolitionist newspaper called the *Emancipator*.[184] When he read of their journey, he cheered the Africans' bravery, and deplored what he called their present "calamitous" condition.[185]

He was right. Their situation was dire. The group was locked in a New Haven jail in four small rooms. President Van Buren appeared likely to turn them over to the Spanish ambassador, who demanded that they be extradited to stand trial in Cuba. American slaveholders viewed the *Amistad* captives as property that must be returned. Abolitionists believed they were free men and women taken from their homes, and who should therefore be free to return to them.[186]

For Van Buren, this was a political nightmare. He did not want to risk support in the South over his handling of the *Amistad* case.[187] Extradition to Cuba seemed to be the safest bet for his survival. He wrote a letter to Judge Andrew T. Judson in Connecticut making that case.[188]

On the other side, the *Amistad* captives would get help from a new organization founded to support them called the Amistad Committee, launched by New York City merchant Lewis Tappan.[189] The committee believed this was a matter for American courts, not the Spanish justice system, and that the group should be sent back to Africa, not to Cuba. A Connecticut court agreed and ruled that the *Amistad* passengers were "born free, and still of right ought to be free and not slaves."[190] But U.S. Attorney William Holabird appealed the ruling. With the legal fight escalating, the matter seemed likely to be headed to the Supreme Court. The *Amistad* captives would need the best representation they could get.[191]

John Quincy Adams was not the abolitionists' first choice. But Daniel Webster and Rufus Choate, both from Massachusetts, declined to take the case.[192] When the abolitionists approached Adams, he also hesitated. He wanted to know more about the details of the matter, and he wrote a letter asking representatives of the Amistad

Committee to go through moral and legal questions. It was clear from his line of questioning that he was on the abolitionists' side, and the Amistad Committee leaked Adams's letters, giving the public the impression that he was already involved.[193]

The *Amistad* case would take Adams's fight to a new branch of government.[194] It also presented a new way for him to challenge the slaveholding establishment. As the *Amistad* matter made its way through the courts, Adams offered resolutions in Congress demanding the president's correspondence about the issue, including diplomatic exchanges with Spain. When the abolitionist organizer Tappan visited Adams in Quincy, he asked him to represent the *Amistad* group. But Adams still demurred, saying he was too old, too busy, and that too much time had passed since he had last argued before the Court, in 1809, for him to be the best man for the job now. After much persuading, he agreed to take the case.[195]

Adams wanted to learn more about the matter. On his way to Washington from Quincy, he stopped by New Haven to meet the captives from the *Amistad*. He was disturbed by their conditions, especially as winter was approaching. And as a man of deep Christian faith, he was moved when three of the captured Africans read to him from the New Testament.[196] He understood the gravity of the task ahead of him, and the moral wrong that would be done should the *Amistad* captives be sent to slavery in the Spanish empire.[197]

He studied every detail about the *Amistad*, worrying privately, "How shall I do justice to this case and to these men?"[198] As his expectations of himself and the public's fascination with the case grew, his concerns became more pronounced. He had time to prepare, as there were delays in starting the proceedings.[199] But the *Amistad*'s day in court finally arrived on February 22, 1841. It was George Washington's birthday.

The Supreme Court was near Adams's office. At the time, the Court and Congress were both housed in the U.S. Capitol, and the justices worked on the Senate side of the complex, down a set of stairs to a dark, intimate room in the basement. For the first part of the century, Chief Justice John Marshall had presided in this room. Now Roger Taney sat in Marshall's chair.[200]

The government made a simple case. The *Amistad* was a merchant ship, flying the Spanish flag. The slaves were cargo, with all of the necessary approvals from the government of Spain. The slaves had taken the ship by force, and so became pirates and murderers. Under the terms of a 1795 treaty with Spain, the United States had no choice but to return the "cargo" to Cuba.[201] Reflecting how the U.S. would want imperial Spain to behave were the situation reversed, Attorney General Henry Gilpin twisted the Golden Rule: "Let us do to them as we wish them to do to us."[202]

Now it was Adams's turn. Alongside Roger Baldwin, a leading abolitionist lawyer from Connecticut, he made his case. Baldwin provided a legalistic rebuttal, challenging the idea that they were pirates, as none of them had sought to steal anything from the ship. Furthermore, the *Amistad*'s documents were not in order.[203]

Baldwin's argument was correct on the merits, but it didn't move the justices. That task fell to Adams, who on February 24 rose to speak. No former president had ever argued before the Supreme Court. Future presidents James Polk, Abraham Lincoln, James Garfield, Grover Cleveland, Benjamin Harrison, William Howard Taft, and Richard Nixon would do so at points in their lives. But John Quincy Adams was the first to do it, both before and after his time in the White House.[204]

The courtroom was packed for the occasion. The audience knew they were in for a historic moment.[205] Van Buren had staked out his administration's position. Chief Justice Taney, the author of the future *Dred Scott* decision, was, to say the least, unsympathetic to the cause of abolition. Five of the justices were Southern slave owners. The odds were not in Adams's favor.

Before he came to Congress, Adams was also not known for his rhetorical abilities. As president, Adams had never been a great orator. But during his career in the House, he'd developed a powerful voice, honing his skills in combat with the slavocracy. He made an appeal to authority, pointing out that he was a former secretary of state, and he'd negotiated with Spain. He believed the 1795 treaty was irrelevant to the matter at hand. He made political attacks, calling the five-foot, six-inch Van Buren a man guilty of "Lilliputian trickery," a reference to Jonathan Swift's 1726 satire *Gulliver's Travels* and the inhabitants of a fictional land of tiny people.[206] Adams's main argument, however, was moral.

There were two copies of the Declaration of Independence hanging on the Court's walls. Adams pointed to them as he made his case, citing the Declaration explicitly eight times.[207] Its text, he argued to the justices, was "implanted in your hearts."[208] Slavery, he said, was not in keeping with the Declaration. Adams argued, "If these rights are inalienable, they are incompatible with the rights of the victor to take the life of his enemy in war, or to spare his life and make him a slave."[209] He reminded the justices that one of the Founders' grievances against King George III was that he'd sent men across the sea for trials in foreign lands, as they were planning to do with the enslaved people of the *Amistad*.[210]

There was no better messenger for this case than John Quincy Adams. No more Founding Fathers were alive; James Madison, the last of them, had died in 1836. Adams knew this generation well and had grown up with their wisdom and conversations around his dining room table. He was the closest living connection to that generation. Adams was the son of a Founder and had worked in the administrations of Washington, Madison, and Monroe. He personally knew Jefferson. He reminded the justices that he had appeared before the Court in 1804, and asked that the name of those who had been on the bench then be read. "Where are they all?" he asked. "Gone! Gone! All gone!" he answered as tears poured down his face, recalling his father's generation and what they'd left behind.[211]

Feeling the power and gravity of the moment, Adams's voice quavered. He breathed heavily. He told the justices that, when their time came, he hoped they'd be able to take their places among the "illustrious dead."[212]

He'd spoken for four and a half hours, and would again for four more. The audience couldn't look away, and the attorney general was gobsmacked, both at the stamina of the old man and his eloquence. The justices listened as John Quincy Adams made one of the most powerful, and emotional, cases the Court had ever heard.[213] When the arguments finished on March 1, the waiting began.[214]

The wait would last longer than the Van Buren presidency, which ended on March 4, 1841. While Adams anticipated the verdict, the first Whig president, William Henry Harrison, took his oath of office. But Adams skipped the inauguration. This was likely a wise idea, as it was a bitterly cold, windy day, and the seventy-three-year-old Adams might have fallen ill.[215]

Five days later, Justice Joseph Story delivered the majority opinion of the Court. The ruling was definitive: seven to one in the Africans' favor, with even Chief Justice Taney in the majority.[216] The justices wrote in the majority opinion, "There does not seem to us to be any ground for doubt . . . that these Negroes ought to be deemed free." They concluded that the Africans ought not only be freed, they now owned the *Amistad*, a major victory.[217] Adams was elated, and he gave copies of his arguments to abolitionist groups, which were then printed in newspapers across the country.[218]

It was a year and a half from the taking of the *Amistad* to the former captives' departure back home on the West African coast.[219] They sailed aboard a new ship called the *Gentleman*, which was provided by Christian abolitionist groups.[220] But before they left the New World, they signed a Bible and gave it to Adams as a sign of their thanks.[221]

The Bible was inscribed with a note. A few from the *Amistad* group had learned English and wrote to Adams: "Most Respected Sir, The Mende people give you thanks for all your kindness to them. They will never forget your defense of their rights in the great Court of Washington." They closed by quoting Psalm 124, "Our soul is escaped as a bird out of the snare of the fowlers: the snare is broken, and we are escaped."[222] In 2007, Massachusetts governor Deval Patrick, the first African American to hold the post, took his oath of office on the Mende Bible.[223]

Before *Amistad*, Adams was a champion of the abolitionist cause; now he was its hero. With a former president in their ranks, the abolitionist movement was no longer on the fringes of American life.[224] Adams had not only made a point, he'd made a difference. He was the leading abolitionist in Congress and was now willing to fully own it. With Adams leading the charge, abolition seemed like it would one day be possible.

MAN OF THE HOUSE

The balance of power had flipped in Washington, this time in Adams's favor. For the first time, in 1841, a Whig president was in office, William Henry Harrison. The Whigs also had their first majority in Congress, with 142 seats to the Democrats' 98.[225] A Whig himself, Adams was popular with abolitionists and loathed by slaveholders. He was also more powerful than ever, and he finally became the chairman of the House Foreign Affairs Committee. Emboldened after *Amistad*, he took on the Gag Rule.

His new tactic was ingenious, if risky. He presented a petition calling for his own removal from Congress due to his abolitionism. The slaveholders in Congress wanted his removal, but by tying it to abolition, Adams would have them violate their own Gag Rule by debating it. Beyond the strategy, Adams had a propensity for trolling his adversaries and wanted to have some fun at their expense, which meant triggering them, and then ogling at their escalating anger as they realized he was goading them. He was toying with them, and exasperated Southern congressmen rose to object. Five resigned from Adams's committee. Three replacements for them refused to take their seats.[226] But Adams was just warming up. He told his friends he had a resolution that would set Southern members "ablaze."[227] He made good on his word on January 25, presenting a petition calling for the peaceful dissolution of the United States over the issue of slavery.[228]

This petition came from a group of abolitionists from Haverhill, Massachusetts. They were calling for disunion because they were outraged that their taxpayer dollars were being used by the federal government in ways that supported slavery. When they heard the petition, Southern delegations called for Adams's head, to which he replied, "I am all ready for another heat."[229] More astute antagonists refrained from attacking him, however, knowing there was little they could do.

Virginia congressman and future Confederate officer Henry Wise was one of the more foolish members of Congress. He was furious, and he pushed to censure Adams for presenting such a seditious resolution, ironic given the fact that he would go on to serve in the Confederate army.[230] Adams welcomed the attack, responding, "Good!" He baited

Wise, who made Calhoun-style arguments, speaking of slavery as a positive good,[231] and calling Adams a traitor, akin to Aaron Burr and Benedict Arnold.[232] With the floodgates open, other Southern congressmen joined in, offering their own resolutions against Adams.[233]

The House was turning into a courtroom, with Adams on trial. And he was determined to win that same day.[234] But while Adams was outnumbered, his enemies felt they needed more time to prepare their political assault and moved to adjourn. After a brief adjournment, a new congressional foe emerged, this time Thomas Marshall, a freshman representative from Kentucky, and the nephew of Supreme Court Justice John Marshall.[235] Decades earlier, Adams's father had appointed Marshall's uncle to the Court, but now the two heirs of the founding squared off. Marshall was confident he had the upper hand. He called for Adams to be expelled from the House for advocating "high treason."[236]

The seventy-three-year-old Adams would have none of it. In his second act, he had all the stature he'd built up in his first, but nothing to lose. He wouldn't be bullied. He reminded his Southern colleagues that—even if some of them didn't like him—his voters did. If the House approved his removal, the 12th district of Massachusetts would just send him back, and he'd keep up the fight.[237] "I have constituents to go to that will have something to say if this House expels me," he taunted. "Nor will it be long before you gentlemen will see me again!"[238] He spoke with a level of confidence he'd never shown as president.

The House adjourned once again, but Adams continued his counterattack. He called one detractor a "beef-witted blunderhead." Others, he said, were "drunk with whiskey and drunk with slavery."[239] Wise and Marshall were his top targets, and he recalled Wise's infamous history of dueling before he entered Congress. Then, Wise had once been the subject of a censure resolution, but Adams had defended him.[240] Reminding his antagonist of that fact, Adams told the chamber, "I saved this blood-stained man from the censure of the House. . . . Although his hands were reeking with blood of murder."[241]

As for Marshall, Adams had some extra fun and was ready to enjoy himself. Marshall had accused a former president of treason.

But Adams pointed out that Article I, Section III, Clause 1 of the Constitution defines treason, and what he was advocating was far off the mark. Looking down at John Marshall's nephew, he mocked him, stating, "It is not for him, or his puny mind, to define [treason]." He suggested that Marshall should go to law school so he could "commence the study of that profession which he has so long disgraced."[242]

The fight was on, and the gallery of the House chamber was packed with spectators wanting to catch a glimpse. Marshall was so badly humiliated that his colleagues abandoned him, including Henry Wise. Supporters of censure melted away, but the defense didn't rest. For Adams, this was about honor and principle, and he kept speaking in what was his most fiery moment on the House floor yet. His opponents offered to withdraw the censure resolution, on the condition that Adams would do the same for the petition about disunion. But he wouldn't let them off the hook that easily. "No! No! I cannot do that," he yelled. "If I withdraw the petition I would consider myself as having sacrificed the right of petition."[243]

For a week he spoke, telling the story of his life before Congress and his connection with the Founders. He spoke of his own father, as well as of Washington, Jefferson, Madison, and Monroe. He said they opposed slavery, even if they had allowed it to continue and made terrible compromises over it. The Southern members invoked the Gag Rule to shut him up. But Adams persisted, knowing he could hold the floor for days and weeks, so long as his strength held.[244]

Knowing they were beaten, on February 7, his opponents folded. They withdrew the censure resolution by a margin of 106–93. But that wasn't good enough for Adams. He had momentum and responded by presenting more abolitionist petitions, suggesting that he wouldn't stop until the Gag Rule was eliminated for good.[245]

Adams was winning. And so was the cause of abolition. Theodore D. Weld, an abolitionist ally in Congress and an influential figure in Harriet Beecher Stowe's writing of *Uncle Tom's Cabin*, saw the events as pivotal. Weld called it "the first victory over the slaveholders in a body ever yet achieved since the foundation of the government."[246]

The pro-slavery faction knew that their fight against Adams was a lost cause. Marshall moaned that he "would rather die a thousand deaths than again to encounter that old man."[247] Henry Wise had a strange new respect for his foe, calling him the "acutest, the astutest, the archest enemy of Southern slavery that ever existed. I mean the Old Man Eloquent, John Quincy Adams."[248] That nickname stuck.

No one would have described John Quincy Adams as Old Man Eloquent before he entered Congress. As president, he had not inspired. But in the House, he was advocating for a cause in which he believed, and for which he was willing to fight. He had a lifetime of experience. He had a higher national stature than anyone else in the chamber. As the last great connection to America's founding, he felt a responsibility to stand up for the ideals of that time, even if those ideals had not been made real yet.

The Southern congressmen had tried to gag him. But they'd helped him discover his voice. Copies of Adams's speeches were printed across the country.[249] Speaking invitations came flooding in.[250] For the first time, he was the leader of a popular movement, and he loved it. When the British author Charles Dickens and his wife, Catherine, visited Washington, they asked to have lunch with Adams. They requested an autograph on the way out.[251] Adams wrote of this time that the fame he had achieved was "more tickling to my vanity than it was to be elected President of the United States."[252]

Not everything was perfect. The abolitionist cause was growing, but still a minority position, both in government and in the country. He'd won his rematch against the censure resolution, but lost another fight over the annexation of Texas, after President William Henry Harrison died on his thirty-second day in office and Virginian John Tyler, America's tenth president and an unrepentant slave owner, moved it forward.

Tyler was America's first accidental president. He only got the top job when his boss died.[253] He'd become a Whig only recently, and was added to the ticket merely in the hopes that Harrison would be able to carry Virginia with his help. Even in that task, Tyler failed. Adams was not pleased to see Tyler ascend. But Henry Wise was glad that Tyler was now president. Wise was soon appointed America's minister to Brazil.

However, Adams wasn't alone in objecting to President Tyler. This was the first time a president had died in office, and there was no precedent to fall back on that could offer guidance on how the succession should take place. The language of the Constitution was vague. It stated merely that the duties of the presidency would "devolve" to the vice president. But did that actually make Tyler the president of the United States? Or was he merely performing the role in a kind of acting capacity?[254]

Tyler's opponents in Congress, including the Whigs, believed he was not the president. Many said he should be called the "vice-president acting as president." Less diplomatic antagonists called Tyler "His Accidency."[255]

However he got the office, Tyler intended to use his new power. He vetoed Whig legislation that would have been signed had Harrison lived. Furious, the House authorized a thirteen-member Select Committee, headed by Adams, to investigate whether or not the president should be impeached—the first such committee in American history.[256] Voters took note of the dysfunction in Washington, and the Whigs lost control of Congress in 1842. Tyler held on to power, but he was no longer a member of the party. He was hated by Whigs who had excommunicated him, Democrats who didn't trust him, and Northerners from both parties who were repulsed by the slaveholder.

Few members of Congress loathed John Tyler more than Adams. When President Tyler visited Boston in 1843 to mark the completion of a monument at Bunker Hill, the former president did not attend, though he had witnessed the battle as a boy. He dismissed Tyler's speech that day as "the mouth-worship of liberty from the lips of the slave-breeder."[257]

But Tyler was the president, and he had the upper hand on the issue of Texas annexation.[258] The debate continued in Congress for two years, and Adams was pleased when the Senate rejected an annexation treaty in 1844.[259] He hoped his old friend Henry Clay might win the presidential election that year.[260] But instead, James K. Polk, the former Speaker and Adams's old nemesis, won the White House.[261] In the closing days of his administration, Tyler pushed Congress on annexation, "the prospect" of which, said Adams, "is death-like."[262] But Tyler got his way, and the resolution for annexation passed on March 1, 1845. This was three days before Polk's inauguration.[263]

On Texas, Adams lost. But he'd delayed annexation. The fight had galvanized the abolitionist movement. He'd added his moral authority to the debate against slavery's expansion. He'd served six terms in the House, winning reelection every two years. He outlasted four presidents—Jackson, Van Buren, Harrison, and "His Accidency" John Tyler. He'd given life to the abolitionist cause. He was proud of his work.

He was also proud of his only surviving son, Charles Francis. In 1843, Charles, then a member of the Massachusetts state legislature, introduced a resolution calling for a constitutional amendment to nullify the Three-Fifths Clause to the Constitution. His father introduced a similar amendment in Congress.[264] Charles would go on to serve as the vice presidential candidate on the Free-Soil ticket in 1848, ironically with Van Buren at the top of the ticket. He was Abraham Lincoln's ambassador to the United Kingdom.[265] He helped ensure that the crown didn't aid the Confederacy during the Civil War. The Adams line held.

THE CLOSING ACT

It would have been impossible to imagine Adams's second act when his life began. He was born in 1767, a British subject. There was no United States, no House of Representatives, and the abolitionist movement didn't exist. Now they were very real, and they owed much of their current form to him.

The United States had changed from the agrarian republic envisioned by Jefferson. Now trains and steamboats transported goods and people across the continent. Americans were corresponding with one another over great distances, almost instantaneously, by telegraph. Adams wanted to see what was out there.

It had been a long time since he'd traveled far. Before the White House, he'd been one of the most well-traveled Americans alive, serving across Europe. But almost every day of his post-presidency was in Quincy, Washington, or between the two cities. That changed in the summer of 1843, when he decided to make a national tour, crossing from Saratoga, to Montreal, to Niagara, a journey of 438 miles. Thanks to new trains and new canals, he made the journey in just two days and nine hours.[266] He found that he was known in every town, and he had supporters across the region.

At every stop, there were people to greet him. He went to church with future president Millard Fillmore in Buffalo. He then rested at the home of Abraham Lincoln's future secretary of state, the then-governor of New York, William Seward.[267] Steaming down the Erie Canal, in every town he visited, Syracuse, Utica, and more, he was welcomed by citizens and dignitaries. He traveled west, and he saw that, now in his late seventies, he had a national following he never could have imagined as a younger man. He loved it!

Ahead of his visit to Cincinnati, Ohio, to lay the cornerstone of a new observatory, word spread that he'd be coming. Anticipation grew as he slowly made his way from Cleveland to Columbus. There, he met with a group of freemen working for total and immediate emancipation. They thanked Adams for his work in Congress.[268] He replied, "The day of your redemption" is bound to come. "It may come in peace, or it may come in blood; but whether in peace or in blood, LET IT COME."[269]

The enthusiasm for Adams built into a kind of grassroots support that he'd never had in the White House. There were parades and placards along the way with words like "John Quincy Adams, Defender of the Rights of Man." Even the press loved him.[270] In Akron, Ohio, a young woman spontaneously kissed him on the cheek.

Public displays of affection were not what Adams was used to. As a young law student, he'd written against such displays, calling public kissing "a profanation, of one of the most endearing demonstrations of Love."[271] Now in his seventies, he felt the opposite. He kissed the young woman back, declaring that he "returned the salute on the lip."[272] Word spread, and kissing Adams became a trend. When he went south of the Ohio River, a young woman asked for "the first kiss in Kentucky."[273]

As president, Adams would never have been greeted so warmly. He wouldn't have returned any kisses. Maybe that kind of popular appeal could have saved his White House in 1828.[274] But a decade and a half in Congress had made him into a wise politician and a popular figure. He was a relic from a bygone era, but he was proving fit for the times.

When he returned to Washington for the 28th Congress, Adams's spirits were high, but his health had suffered during the long, cold journey. Soon after he arrived, on December 4, 1843, he submitted another resolution to repeal the Gag Rule. He lost by only four votes.[275] Undeterred, he submitted the same resolution a year later.[276] This time it passed by twenty-eight votes, including those of six Southern congressmen.[277] At long last, the Gag Rule was gone forever. This was one of the great moments of Adams's time in the House, and of his career.[278]

He might have ended his second act there, satisfied with a job well done. He had given up hope that the future of slavery could be decided peacefully in the halls of Congress, and didn't believe it would be settled in his lifetime. But he'd nurtured the abolitionist movement, and it was growing. The energy he derived from it also gave him a reason to keep defying his mortality. The slaveholders in Congress were determined to fight him until the very end and he intended to drag that out as long as possible. This would be his legacy and he knew it.

The debates on the floor didn't let up. There was a furious exchange with a congressman from Alabama, and Adams's opponent quoted his words back at him, recalling what he'd said to the freed Black men in Ohio. "The day of your redemption" is coming, whether "in peace or in blood, let it come." That statement appeared to advocate civil war. Adams, near eighty years old, rose to his feet and thundered back defiantly, "I say now, let it come. . . . Though it cost the blood of millions of white men." The chamber fell silent.[279] He had provoked his enemies and won so many times that he had become irrepressible and beyond reproach.

The town of Quincy relished in their fighting septogenarian, whose increasingly radical abolitionism didn't cost him support at home. In 1846 he won his seat for the ninth, and final, time. A few weeks later, however, Adams suffered a stroke while touring the campus of Harvard Medical School. He recovered, but he was partially paralyzed and took some time to regain his ability to speak. He wrote of that day, "From that hour I date my decease, and consider myself for every useful purpose to myself or to my fellow creatures dead." He gave his diary the morbid title of his "Posthumous Memoir."[280]

His second act had been a surprise—including to him. He'd taken on a new cause, and he'd shown how a former president can not only run for office again, but also make a real difference. His White House years seemed distant, a grim reminder of a long-gone past. His diary entries were cheerful and verbose with expressions of fulfillment, free of the kind of self-pity of 1828 and 1829. Now he was satisfied. And he'd found purpose to replace regret.

But he wasn't dead yet. His eightieth birthday came on July 11, 1847. Adams's friends and loved ones gathered to celebrate the milestone. Two weeks later, he and Louisa Adams marked their fiftieth wedding anniversary. His father was never one for sentimental gifts, so Charles Francis handed him a bracelet to give to his mother.[281] The family's last party came on New Year's Day, when they celebrated the start of 1848. The event was attended by senators, congressmen, judges, and generals back from the Mexican-American War. For many of the guests, it would be the last time that they ever saw John Quincy Adams.[282]

There was no one quite like Adams. He'd been at the forefront of American public life for nearly seven decades. Many of the Founding Fathers didn't have many, or any, children. Even fewer of those children had survived to adulthood. Those that did typically didn't amount to much. The few that had were dead by 1848. But here was a man present at the birth of the Republic. He was still helping to guide it more than half a century later.

John Quincy Adams entered the House chamber for the 30th Congress, which would be his last. The room fell silent, a nonpartisan reverence left its members unsure of what to do next for a moment. Then they applauded. Northerners and men from the West admired him. Southerners hated, but respected him. None of his contemporaries—Martin Van Buren, Andrew Jackson, Henry Clay—held such a place in American history.[283]

There was a new admirer in the back of the House chamber. It was a tall man from Illinois with a bad seat. Abraham Lincoln joined Congress in 1847 as a freshman Whig.[284] In front of Mr. Lincoln sat a man from Georgia, Alexander Stephens. Stephens was Lincoln's friend. He was also the future vice president of the Confederacy.[285]

Congressman Adams headed to work on February 21, pulling up to the Capitol in a horse-drawn carriage. The issue of the day was a debate about a peace treaty with Mexico sent to the Senate by President James K. Polk.[286] This was not Adams's concern as a member of the House. What was on his desk was a more banal issue, whether Congress should authorize medals for veterans of the Mexican-American War. Adams opposed even this routine matter, as any show of support, he thought, would signal his acquiesces to the spread of slavery in newly acquired territories. He was prepared to vote no.[287] It would have been his last act of defiance.

At half past one, the clerk began to speak.[288] Adams rose, but his body began to sag. He grabbed his desk, clutching it with frail hands. A nearby congressman from Ohio rushed over and held him up. Thanks to his intervention, Adams didn't crash to the black-and-white marble tile of the House chamber.[289] A cry went out: "Mr. Adams is dying!"[290]

The business of the House came to a halt. Members rushed over. Abraham Lincoln watched in astonishment as this immortal figure seemed to be taking his last breaths. A congressman from Massachusetts put cold water on Adams's forehead, carrying him on a box sofa to the drafty Capitol Rotunda so that he could get some air.

As he lay there, Adams was surrounded by paintings of the founding hanging on the walls. There was his father in John Trumbull's depiction of the signing of the Declaration of Independence, standing next to Jefferson. There was the surrender of General Burgoyne at Saratoga. The surrender of Lord Cornwallis at Yorktown. George Washington resigning his commission.[291] To most of his colleagues, these scenes were history. To the dying Adams, this was not art or history. This was his life.

When a cold breeze blew through the Rotunda, Adams was moved to the Speaker's private office, just off the House floor. One member sent for Louisa, who came rushing to the Capitol from their home on F Street.[292] But he was so far gone by the time she arrived he couldn't recognize her, and she cried at his side.[293]

Every branch of government ceased its operations while Adams lay in a coma for two days. He died in the Capitol at 7:20 p.m. on February 23, 1848.[294] "The glory of the family is departed," Charles Francis wrote of his father's passing. "I, a solitary and unworthy scion, remain overwhelmed with a sense of my responsibilities."[295]

The country had followed Adams's final hours, almost in real time. Reporters in Washington were able to keep the public up-to-date thanks to a telegraph line that Congress had funded from Washington to Baltimore, which shot out directly from the U.S. Capitol.[296]

No former president had ever passed away in Washington. The closest analogue was William Henry Harrison, who died in office in 1841.[297] There was a period of mourning, and Lincoln was a member of the Committee of Arrangements for Adams's funeral in Washington. He served as an honorary pallbearer, carrying the man and his ideas forward. President James K. Polk, hardly a friend of Adams, described the service as "a splendid pageant."[298]

In his second act, Adams had left a mark on Congress and Abraham Lincoln. The two likely never met beyond perhaps a handshake or superficial small talk. Adams had no reason to seek Lincoln out, or give him the time of day.[299] But Adams was a connection to the American Founders, and a connection from them to Lincoln. Congressman Adams's speeches informed future president Lincoln's actions during the Civil War, including the Emancipation Proclamation and the recruitment of Black soldiers to serve in the Union army.[300]

The fact that Adams achieved such a powerful second act in the lowest political station of his career offers a hidden message within his extraordinary legacy. With no higher ladder to climb, Adams was left to channel much of his ambition toward preserving and advancing his principles. It was in doing so that the cause of abolition found him, not the other way around. This runs contrary to how many people approach a second act, often choosing the more premeditated path. They pick a cause and chase it, and had Adams known what that cause was, he might have done the same. In truth, Adams went back to Congress because he didn't know how to live a life outside of public service and he was antsy. To subject himself to such vulnerability without a defined goal or purpose was either a great act of professional courage or an act of desperation. Either way, his story shows how sometimes the best second acts choose you rather than the other way around.

With John Quincy Adams's death on February 23, 1848, there were three former presidents still living: Martin Van Buren, John Tyler, and James K. Polk, America's eighth, tenth, and eleventh presidents, respectively. Polk died four months after leaving office, on June 15, 1849, likely of cholera.[301] Van Buren and Tyler both died in 1862, in the midst of the Civil War that American presidents from the beginning had feared, at age seventy-nine and seventy-one, respectively. Tyler died in Richmond, Virginia, the capital of the Confederacy, having been elected to the Confederate Congress, labeled a traitor to the Union, and denied a state funeral. His obituary in the *New York Times* told readers that he was "going down to death amid the ruins of his nation state. He himself was one of the architects of its ruin."[302]

Meanwhile, as John Quincy Adams passed away in the halls of Congress, ten-year-old Grover Cleveland, the fifth of nine children, was at home in the small town of Fayetteville, New York. His large family lived a simple life provided for by his father, a Presbyterian minister. Though no one could have expected that the humble Grover would one day become president, he had made a study of the former commanders in chief, writing at the age of nine, "George Washington improved his time when he was a boy and he was not sorry when he was at the head of a large army fighting for his country. . . . Jackson was a poor boy but he was placed in school and by improving his time he found himself president of the United States guiding and directing a powerful nation."[303]

Cleveland's path would take him from city hall in Buffalo to the White House in three years. He lost his bid for reelection, but then made a never-repeated comeback to the White House four years later for a second, nonconsecutive term. The story of the man who is both America's twenty-second and twenty-fourth president became newly relevant given Donald Trump's own run for a nonconsecutive term in 2024. But a deeper history reveals a man who helped bring America into the twenty-first century, and whose character stands out as an example of unexpected presidential greatness.

The Comeback

Is it ordained that I am to be the instrument through which democratic principles can be saved?

—GROVER CLEVELAND

Comebacks are easy to contemplate, but hard to execute. Presidents who lose their reelections are particularly tempted to run again, and no matter their defeat, they still have a political base on which they can build. Their followings can distort their perceptions of political reality or push reluctant ex-presidents to attempt a return. Former presidents try to make it back to the White House for many reasons. For some, it's personal. For others, it's political. There's pride, power, and prestige. A few have ideas, policies they want to execute and see through. Some want to get back the power to pardon. But no matter their reason, comebacks rarely happen in American political life.

That challenge doesn't stop former presidents from trying to get their old jobs back. Martin Van Buren was defeated for reelection in 1840, but then ran as a Free-Soiler in 1848 without winning a single electoral vote. Millard Fillmore ran as a "Know Nothing" in 1856—he got eight electoral votes.[1] Ulysses S. Grant ran for a nonconsecutive third term in 1880, but lost the Republican nomination on the thirty-fourth ballot of the GOP convention to James Garfield, who wasn't even running.[2] Theodore Roosevelt ran as a Bull Moose in 1912, but he split the Republican vote with William Howard Taft and handed the presidency to Woodrow Wilson. Even Herbert Hoover made moves again in 1936 and 1940, albeit unofficially. In our own memory, Donald Trump has attempted another run at the White House in 2024.

It turns out that former presidents are bad at running for president. But there is one exception to that rule: Grover Cleveland. Cleveland won the White House in 1884, but lost it in 1888. He then mounted a never-repeated comeback in 1892, making him both America's twenty-second and twenty-fourth president. The only Democrat to win the White House between 1856 and 1912, Cleveland made history, even if history often forgets him.

Cleveland ran again not because he wanted power, but because he believed in his principles, and worried that there was no one else to carry them forward. His Republican successor, Benjamin Harrison, was steering the country in the wrong direction. The Democratic contenders were party bosses or populists. The idea of four years of either was intolerable.

His comeback was successful, but his second presidency presented difficulties from day one. The world had changed since his first term. There were challenges at home and abroad that he did not cause but that overwhelmed his presidency. Though he held back a populist tide in his own party, he left office the second time less popular, more unhappy than when he had entered, and full of regret.

He didn't have to make a comeback to become America's twenty-fourth president. He had entered the White House the first time as a bachelor and left with a bride. He could have been happy in Manhattan with his young and growing family. Instead, his second retirement after his second term began with a cloud hanging over it. He moved to Princeton, New Jersey, in hope that he could rid himself of the melancholy. It took time, but he found peace through the adoration of the student body, while scratching his political itch by academically battling a young Princeton professor named Woodrow Wilson. These quarrels may have inadvertently set Wilson on his path to the White House.

AN UNLIKELY PRESIDENT

When the president of the United States meets a young child, he typically offers generic words of encouragement. Not Grover Cleveland, who was brutally honest and gave words of warning.

It was 1887, and New York businessman James Roosevelt was on his way to Washington. Roosevelt was bringing along his five-year-old son, Franklin.[3] James had business at the White House, and he wanted his boy to meet the president.

James Roosevelt and Grover Cleveland were friends. Like Cleveland, Roosevelt was a Bourbon Democrat, the conservative wing of the party. They were both New Yorkers. They had business that day. Decades before the Panama Canal,[4] Roosevelt was trying to build a canal through Nicaragua to connect the Atlantic and Pacific Oceans. He wanted the president's advice and support. Cleveland, who at the time was fighting with Congress, was all too happy to put those battles aside for a meeting with a friend and his son.

Cleveland knew that Franklin was bright and enjoyed Washington. When he clapped eyes on the child, he leaned over, took the young man by the hand, and gave him a piece of advice. "My boy," said Cleveland, "a great many people will probably tell you that they hope that someday you will be the President of the United States, and I want to tell you that for your own sake I hope you will never have to be President."[5]

Forty years later, Roosevelt described that meeting as "one of [his] most vivid early recollections," continuing, "I cannot help feeling that what [Grover Cleveland] said he spoke from his heart and I think he was absolutely right."[6] But Franklin Roosevelt didn't take Grover Cleveland's advice. But to be fair, neither did Grover Cleveland. He lost his bid for reelection in 1888, only to run again in 1892.

Cleveland and Roosevelt had more in common than one chance meeting. They were both Democrats. They were both governors of New York. They both went from Albany to Washington. They both won the national popular vote three times in a row, the only two presidents to do so. They both ended decades of Republican domination of the White House. And, they both achieved something electorally that is unique to them—Cleveland's nonconsecutive reelection and FDR's historic third and fourth terms.

But Roosevelt is remembered, and Cleveland is often forgotten. Though the Cleveland presidencies witnessed what one aide described as "Herculean toil," no one mythologizes the two-time president.[7] He didn't lead the nation through the Great Depression or a war. He didn't create new programs that changed Americans' relationship with their state. But he was a man who captured the spirit of a changing age. The plurality of the American people voted for him three times in a row because they trusted him. It was an age of corruption, spoils, and populism, and Cleveland's integrity made him stand out.

The fifth of nine children, Cleveland grew up poor. His father, Richard, was a Yale-educated Presbyterian minister who moved his family from place to place, and often made less than $600 a year.[8] Richard Cleveland died in 1853, not yet fifty years old. It was then-sixteen-year-old Grover who had to support the family. The future president never graduated from college, and he didn't join the ministry like his father. Even as a young man, he needed to work and provide for his family.[9]

Despite his lack of a college education, it was clear that he was intelligent and an unusually hard worker, known for putting in eighteen-hour days. He was admitted to the bar at age twenty-two, without a law degree.[10] Most people got their jobs through connections. But Cleveland earned his own seat at the table.

He was an unusual Democrat. He wasn't the product of New York machine politics or the son of Southern slaveholders. He didn't fight in the Civil War. Besides, the Democrats had fought on the losing side and the Republicans loved to wave the so-called "Bloody Shirt" every chance they got.[11]

He was a New Yorker who hadn't taken up arms for the North or South, though he was opposed to slavery, supported Lincoln, and his brothers fought for the Union. Cleveland avoided the draft[12] thanks to a law called the Enrollment Act, which allowed for the payment of $300 for a substitute.[13] A Polish immigrant named George Beniski, who survived the war, fought in Cleveland's stead.[14] Years later, an impecunious Beniski showed up at the White House seeking President Cleveland's help. He was turned away.

Cleveland's start in politics was a short stint as an assistant district attorney and then the sheriff of Erie County, home to the growing city of Buffalo.[15] Buffalo was becoming a commercial hub, thanks to the Erie Canal. Between 1830 and 1860, its population increased tenfold.[16] As the city's sheriff, Cleveland took his duties seriously—he was the local hangman, personally pulling the lever after guilty verdicts in two murder cases. He's the only president whose résumé included local executioner.[17]

Executing men made him ill, and the sheriff's life wasn't for him. He left the job in 1873 and was back behind a desk, working as a lawyer. His political career could have ended then, but the local Democratic committee tapped him to run for mayor of Buffalo in 1880, thinking he had bipartisan appeal. They were right. Cleveland won the race in what the *Buffalo Evening News* called a "day of change."[18]

Mayor Cleveland was a man who could be trusted. He promised low taxes and good government, and he delivered on both.[19] He was so focused on fiscal responsibility that he canceled Buffalo's Fourth of July celebrations. He argued that the money should go back to the citizens. Instead of asking the taxpayers to fund the festivities, he made a donation from his own accounts to fund 10 percent of the event, and then helped organize a private collection that more than covered the remaining costs.[20]

Voters appreciated his integrity. He was known as the "veto mayor," and he nixed any proposals that smelled of graft. Less than a year after he became mayor of Buffalo, he was elected governor of New York.[21] In Albany, he took on Tammany Hall and gained national prominence.[22] A year later, he was president of the United States. This was a meteoric, but unexpected, rise. In three years, he went from a Buffalo law firm to the White House.

At no other time would this rise have been possible. The Republicans, dominant since 1860, were weak after the assassination of James Garfield in 1881. It took months for Garfield to die, lying in bed with an infection from the bullet wound, likely caused by medical malpractice.[23] The loss of its champion had sent the Republican Party into a tailspin. With Garfield's death, Chester Alan Arthur was made president. He was known as a leader in Roscoe Conkling's Stalwart faction of the party, which favored patronage and the political machine, and he'd been offered the vice presidential nomination under Garfield without the candidate's knowledge.[24]

Arthur hadn't wanted the job. Upon hearing that the president had been shot, he was horrified by the idea of taking Garfield's seat. "I pray to God that the President will recover," he said. "God knows I do not want the place I was never elected to."[25] The Republican Party hadn't been sold on an Arthur presidency, either. There were bitter fights between factions called the Stalwarts and the Half-Breeds, who squabbled over the spoils system as Arthur instituted his own reforms.[26]

Meanwhile, the Democrats, out of power since the Civil War, didn't have a leader. Their candidate in 1876, Samuel Tilden, had run against corruption and only lost after a bitter dispute over the results and under a cloud of controversy that some labeled the "fraud of the century." Tilden could have run again and might have won, but he was in his seventies and declared he didn't have the physical strength in 1884.[27] Without an obvious successor, into the void stepped Grover Cleveland.

To win the White House, the Democratic Party needed a candidate that could appeal to the nation. The Democrats of this era were not so much an ideological voting bloc as a coalition of interest groups. There were Southern members, many of whom were former slaveholders. There were Northern manufacturers and party bosses. And there were populist farmers from the West. Every four years, they'd all have to vote the same way to get their candidate in the White House.[28] With the Old South and swing states like Indiana and Cleveland's home state of New York all in line, it was possible.

The Democrats needed one more factor in their favor to make it a sure bet. They needed the Republicans to nominate a weak candidate. In 1884, they did, with the selection of former secretary of state and Speaker of the House James Blaine. Blaine had a formidable résumé, but he was a flawed nominee. He beat out Arthur at the Republican convention, but had plenty of detractors, including from his own party, who saw him as the embodiment of corrupt politics. They taunted him with jeers of "Blaine, Blaine, James G. Blaine, the continental liar from the State of Maine."[29]

He also alienated key voters. At a time when the Irish-American vote in places like New York City was growing more important, Blaine had a reputation for anti-Catholic animus.[30] That reputation became an issue for the Republican Party when a prominent minister associated with Blaine decried the rise of "rum, Romanism, and rebellion"[31] in American politics, a nativist slogan that turned off new immigrants already suspicious of Blaine.[32]

Knowing that their twenty-four-year hold on the White House was in danger, the Republicans fought hard in 1884. Cleveland didn't have his party's full backing. One prominent Tammany Hall politician called his nomination "party suicide."[33] For a political faction that already looked very dead, as it hadn't won the White House since 1856, this was an unfair, if not strange, worry.

The contest turned into a nasty campaign. With the attacks coming left and right, a bombshell report in the Buffalo *Evening Telegraph* threatened to derail Cleveland's entire candidacy. The piece revealed an explosive allegation against Cleveland. Released ten days after the Democratic convention, its headline read "A Terrible Tale: A Dark Chapter in a Public Man's History, the Pitiful Story of Maria Halpin and Governor Cleveland's Son."[34]

The *Telegraph's* report alleged that, ten years earlier, while Cleveland was the sheriff of Erie County, he had fathered a boy out of wedlock with a woman he had physically abused. That woman's name was Maria Halpin.[35] Ms. Halpin had signed an affidavit testifying to that effect. If true, the story's contents could end Grover Cleveland's career. They'd send Blaine to the White House, the latest in a long line of Republican presidents.

Voters read through every detail of the report. According to the story, Ms. Halpin—then a thirty-six-year-old widow—had a consensual romantic relationship with Cleveland. But things quickly went south, and Cleveland allegedly impregnated Ms. Halpin, hired private detectives to hound her, and even tried to force her into an insane asylum.[36]

The public worried that there were two Grover Clevelands. The first was the one who'd won the nomination; he was an upstanding man of the law, someone who would take on the party bosses and put in place honest, good government. The second was a mystery. He could be found in Buffalo saloons, drinking his fellow bachelors under the table, and lusting after women late into the night.[37]

There was truth in both stories. Cleveland was a man of his word. He also was romantically involved with Ms. Halpin. Her child's parentage wasn't certain, but it was plausible (and likely) that Cleveland was the father.[38] Though he hadn't taken the child—or Ms. Halpin—under his wing, he did place the boy in an orphanage and then with a family to take care of him. He paid $5 a week to have him looked after.[39] He even helped name the boy Oscar Folsom Cleveland, after a man who could have also been the boy's father, and who was Cleveland's dear friend and late law partner.[40]

His secret was out. His aides asked how they should respond. Cleveland gave them a simple direction, "Whatever you do, tell the truth."[41] As he said, he and Ms. Halpin had been "illicitly acquainted."[42] He honestly didn't know if he was the father. The public would have to make up its mind as to whether or not this was disqualifying.

The Republicans pounced on the news of the scandal. A Baptist minister in Buffalo named George Ball accused Cleveland of being a womanizer who "foraged" for young women and who brought them up to his third-floor downtown "harem."[43] Ball claimed the election was not just between two candidates but between "the brothel and the family, between indecency and decency, between lust and law."[44]

A late-breaking story may have made the difference for Cleveland. The day before the election, Ms. Halpin issued a piece in the *Detroit Free Press* in her own words. She cleared him of all charges, declaring that she had "no fault whatever to find in Mr. Cleveland." True, she had signed an affidavit alleging horrible crimes. But it turned out she hadn't read it before putting her name to it.[45]

The election was close. It came down to New York, which Blaine lost by just one-tenth of a percentage point, or 1,246 votes calculated in a recount. That margin was enough.[46] Grover Cleveland was on his way to the White House. Behind him was a fragile coalition of Democrats whose votes carried the day thanks to a small group of anti-corruption Republicans called the Mugwumps. John Quincy Adams's grandson, Henry, was a leader of this faction.[47]

Cleveland got the last word. With news of the Halpin story,

Republicans had mocked him by chanting, "Ma, ma, where's my Pa?" Now Cleveland supporters had counter-chants of their own: "Gone to the White House, ha ha ha!"[48] and "Hurray for Maria, hurrah for the kid! We voted for Grover, and damned glad we did!"[49]

THROWING AWAY THE PRESIDENCY

Grover Cleveland was an unlikely Democratic nominee for president. A sex scandal almost cost him the election. Now a man who'd risen from obscurity to power in three years was about to take his oath of office. He did so with his hand on a Bible that his mother had given him when he was fifteen. In his inaugural address, he promised "equal and exact justice to all men."[50]

This was not a throwaway line. With the wounds of the Civil War still fresh and Jim Crow taking hold in the American South, Cleveland had to promise to be a president for all Americans. As the first Democrat in the White House since James Buchanan, this was not a given.

The inaugural crowd cheered Cleveland. It was unusually warm for early March,[51] and his supporters optimistically called the conditions "Cleveland weather."[52] They expected more sunny days to come.

Their hopes were soon dashed by Congress. The Democrats controlled the House, but the Republicans held the Senate. Facing a divided government, Cleveland pulled out his veto pen yet again. Most of his vetoes were over pensions. He couldn't stand fraudulent claims by Civil War veterans, many of whose claimed injuries happened after the fighting was over.[53] He nixed 414 bills in four years on everything from the civil service to the money supply. This was more than twice the total for every previous president combined.[54]

The Democratic Party still hadn't rallied around Cleveland, despite his having returned them to power. But while he fought Congress and his own party, his mind sometimes wandered to more pleasant matters. Cleveland was a lifelong bachelor, a fact the American public was well aware of after the Halpin scandal. Now the president was in love. He was about to get married.

At the start of the Cleveland administration, America didn't have a First Lady. Cleveland's sister Rose stepped up to perform that role.

History would later reveal that Rose Cleveland broke a glass ceiling of her own, and that she may have been America's first gay First Lady. Though she kept her personal life secret, she had a romantic partner later in her life, a wealthy widow named Ms. Evangeline Simpson Whipple, with whom she kept a detailed romantic correspondence. The two women lived out their days together in Bagni di Lucca, a small town in the Tuscany region of Italy.[55] Rose's love life was a secret, but her brother's was the talk of Washington.

Cleveland was never a handsome man. At 280 pounds or more, he was described by one British diplomat, "The President is 5 feet high and 4 feet wide: he has no neck and six chins."[56] Still, power has its romantic appeal and the single president was the most eligible man in the capital. Despite his past indiscretions, women sought his attention, and there were receptions for women at the White House, rumors at the dinner parties, and gossip mongers in the newspapers who theorized about when and with whom he'd tie the knot.[57]

It turned out he already had his eye on Frances Folsom. A young woman, Frances was his late law partner Oscar Folsom's daughter. Mr. Folsom had died in a very nineteenth-century accident when his buggy collided with a wagon that was parked in front of a saloon, throwing him from his seat and breaking his neck.[58] After his friend's death, Cleveland had been named the executor of the estate, and he and Folsom's family grew close. The then-eleven-year-old Frances sometimes called him "Uncle Cleve." He, in turn, would call her "Frank."[59]

Frances blossomed into a beautiful lady. When Cleveland was elected president of the United States, she was still an undergraduate at Wells College in upstate New York. He courted her from afar by sending flowers and love letters to campus. He asked her mother for permission to marry her in 1885, his first year in office.[60]

The age difference between the two was vast, but they were in love. Completely devoted to her, Cleveland asked in his proposal, "Would you put your life in my hands?" Frances responded simply, "Yes." She meant it.[61]

Frances Folsom was engaged, she had graduated from college, and she was about to become the First Lady. She needed to learn how to do the job, and so she set sail across the Atlantic, ready to visit Europe with her mother and learn how high society conducted itself in foreign capitals. While making her way across the sea, her fiancé sent her a love letter.

The message was intercepted along the way. An enterprising but devious Western Union operator got his hands on it and sold the telegram to the press.[62] Noting that the president of the United States—a man with a sex scandal in his past no less—was sending sweet nothings to a mysterious woman on a ship crossing the Atlantic, he knew there was money to be made.

The snoop made a mistake, however. He saw that the letter was addressed to "Ms. Folsom." Given the age difference between the president and Frances, he assumed it was to Frances's mother, Emma, not to her. When the press reported that Cleveland was sending notes to Mrs. Folsom, he complained in his diary, "I don't see why the papers keep marrying me to old ladies. I wonder why they don't say I am engaged to marry her daughter."[63]

The error was soon corrected, and the engagement to Frances became public knowledge. On June 2, 1886, at 7:30 p.m., the forty-nine-year-old Grover Cleveland married the twenty-one-year-old Frances Folsom. A president had only been married in office once before, when John and Julia Tyler wed in 1844.[64] But this would be the first White House wedding. Frances became (and still is) the youngest First Lady in American history.

The wedding was not lavish, but it was beautiful, and so was Frances. She wore a white ivory satin dress with orange blossoms and two muslin scarves over her shoulders. The groom had on a long necktie and white studs as he walked her down the western staircase of the White House.[65] It was a small affair, with just thirty-one guests gathered below a crystal chandelier casting light over the Blue Room.[66] John Philip Sousa led the Marine Band in a wedding march.[67] Frances, ahead of her time, changed the word "obey" to "keep" in her wedding vows.[68] When the ceremony concluded, guests were given a box of bonbons and handed an autographed box containing a slice of wedding cake wrapped in silver foil.[69] The New York Times described the whole thing as a "jolly, good-natured affair, and thoroughly democratic."[70]

The president and his new wife were happy. But the White House is not a place for newlyweds. They tried to get out of town quietly for their honeymoon. But the press got word of their movements, and reporters followed them in a hired train car. They hid in the trees at the resort in western Maryland where the Clevelands were to stay in order to catch a glimpse. When he saw that the reporters had tracked them down, Cleveland threw up his hands in rage and called the gaggle a group of "ghouls."[71]

It was natural for reporters to take an interest in Frances. She was young, beautiful, and charming, the Jackie Kennedy of her day. Her image was used on advertisements across the country, adorning everything from luggage to liver pills, all without her consent. When he saw his wife's likeness used in this way, the president's anger only grew.[72]

Nothing about their lives was private, but the two were content. With Frances at his side, Grover sometimes even enjoyed being president.[73] One observer remarked, "[Cleveland] seemed as happy as a man in the back country districts who had suddenly 'got religion,' and got it thoroughly."[74] The couple hosted parties and events at the White House.[75] She helped him to build valuable relationships on Capitol Hill.[76]

The president would need those relationships soon enough. Debates were heating up over one of the most contentious issues of the day, tariffs. Two decades after the Civil War, and less than a decade after the end of Reconstruction, race remained the most divisive matter in American politics. But tariffs were also a third rail. Before the income tax, they were a major source of federal revenue.[77] Minor adjustments could make or break industries. The politics of the issue divided farmers in the South and West, who favored low tariffs, against manufacturers in the Northeast, who advocated higher duties.

This was an issue on which Cleveland had a firm position, and he was ready to stick with it. He believed the government's revenues were sufficient. Manufacturers who benefited from tariffs didn't need them. He wanted to lower the rates and to allow more free trade.[78]

The president made his position clear. Against him stood a coalition of Republicans and Northern Democrats who had the most to lose from lower tariffs.[79] With even a portion of his own party opposed, Cleveland knew he had a difficult road ahead. But this is why he had run for the White House in the first place. "What is the use of being elected or re-elected," he asked, "unless you stand for something?"[80] His friend Richard W. Gilder believed he had just proudly "thrown the presidency away" for the sake of his principles.[81]

He didn't back down. Instead, he sent an extraordinarily blunt message to Congress,[82] calling the tariffs a "vicious, inequitable, and illogical source of unnecessary taxation."[83] The *Nation* described this statement as "the most courageous document that has been sent from the Executive Mansion since the close of the Civil War."[84] Members of his own party didn't see it that way. With an election coming up, some stated their position that he shouldn't run again. "Damn the nomination," he responded. "I will say what I think is right."[85]

Had the Democratic Party dropped Cleveland, it would have constituted an act of political self-immolation. Cleveland was the first Democrat to win the White House since the Civil War. No other party official had that stature.[86] Kicking him off the ticket in a corrupt backroom deal would have been an embarrassment. With that understanding, a few party bosses tried to claim that he'd promised not to run for reelection in the first place, as if to pretend that him dropping off the ticket was his idea, and not theirs.[87] His fiercest opponents published a forged letter in his name to that effect.[88]

The Democrats decided their nominee at the convention.[89] The president had made his peace with not being the party's nominee, if that was their choice. He told a friend, "I should personally like better than anything else to be let alone and let out."[90] But there was no alternative to Grover Cleveland. He won the nomination by acclamation.[91] However, the party remained divided, and his chances in November were far from certain.[92]

The campaign was just as vicious as the one four years prior. There was a new rumor that Cleveland was an abusive husband.[93] It wasn't true, and Cleveland's friends took to the *Boston Globe* to call the slander "grotesquely, outrageously, totally false in every respect."[94] Distraught, Frances wrote that the accusation was a "foolish campaign story without a shadow of foundation."[95] Cleveland, disgusted by the attacks and their effects on his wife, wrote to his friend Wilson Bissell, "I am sure of one thing. I have in [Frances] something better than the presidency. . . . I absolutely long to be able to live with her as other people do with their wives. Well! Perhaps I can after the 4th of next March."[96]

He got his wish. Republican nominee Benjamin Harrison did not have the most commanding presence. His handshake was described as being as strong as a "wilted petunia."[97] But he was a formidable candidate. A Civil War veteran and the grandson of America's ninth president, he was also the great-grandson of a man who had signed the Declaration of Independence. He had a pedigree Cleveland could only dream of. Harrison also picked Levi Morton, a wealthy New Yorker whose Rhinecliff estate in the Hudson Valley sat adjacent to many of the Gilded Age titans of industry, as his running mate in an attempt to win Cleveland's home state.

The Democratic leaders did not rally around Cleveland. David Hill, a party boss and his former lieutenant governor from New York, didn't mobilize the machine. Without Cleveland's support of the bosses, Harrison won the Empire State and his own home state of Indiana. Even though Cleveland won the national popular vote, he lost the Electoral College. When he heard the results, he accepted them and remarked simply, "Well it's all up."[98]

That didn't have to be the end of it. A few of Cleveland's aides called on him to contest the election. It was close, and they still felt wronged by the 1876 commission that had handed the White House to Republican Rutherford B. Hayes after the results of three Southern states were disputed.[99] But Cleveland had no interest in contesting the election. "One party won and the other party lost—that is all there is to it," he told the group.[100]

In a close election, his stance on the tariff made the difference. He had no regrets on that score, however. He told a group of reporters, "I would rather have my name to that tariff measure than be President."[101] He conveyed that same feeling in his final message to Congress.[102]

The president wasn't going to change his position any time soon. And he was ready to leave Washington. More than politics, Frances was the love of his life. He wanted a family. He thought about his own father, who had died when he was young. He wanted to watch his children grow up.

The president also wanted to be done with the White House. But the First Lady didn't. Frances Cleveland packed her social calendar in those final weeks.[103] She skipped the Harrison inauguration, a dismal, rainy affair,[104] and instead handed out autographed pictures of herself at the White House.[105]

The First Lady was vain, but she was kind. Her last goodbye was to Jerry Smith, an older Black man on the White House staff. He wasn't the crying type, but his eyes watered under his black rimless hat at the thought of her leaving.[106] When she saw his face, the First lady told him, "Now, Jerry, I want you to take good care of all the furniture and ornaments in the house, for I want to find everything just as it is now when we come back again." Smith was stunned. He asked what she was talking about. "We are coming back just four years from today," Frances told him confidently.[107] She was right.

THE INTERREGNUM

Grover Cleveland never expected to be president. Now that he was a former, he didn't know what to do next. He once remarked that the country "would be relieved of all uncertainty and embarrassment if every president would die at the end of his term."[108]

He had a full life ahead of him, however, with a young wife and, soon enough, a growing family. They weren't wealthy, but they had more than enough money to be comfortable. He was frugal and had saved nearly $25,000 a year in office. They sold their home in Oak View, an area of Washington, DC, that would later be named Cleveland Park after the First Family.[109]

It was certain that they'd leave Washington behind. But after the Halpin scandal, they didn't want to go anywhere near Buffalo, either. The bitter Cleveland believed his old hometown was filled with "scum."[110] Instead, the couple decided to move to New York City. As president, Cleveland had dedicated the Statue of Liberty in 1886.[111] Now that same statue welcomed them to their new home.[112]

Life in New York began at the redbrick Hotel Victoria in Midtown Manhattan. The eight-story building covered an entire city block at Fifth Avenue and Twenty-Seventh Street, but only had eighteen apartments, each with plenty of room. For six months, they lived in a spacious second-floor apartment[113] equipped with the latest technology, including a telephone.[114]

That autumn, they left the Hotel Victoria for a four-story townhouse at 816 Madison Avenue.[115] Every morning, Cleveland could be spotted strolling downtown, which appears to have been the chief form of exercise for a man who protested that "bodily movement alone, undertaken from a sense of duty or upon medical advice, is among the dreary and unsatisfying things of life."[116]

Cleveland took a job at the law firm Bangs, Stetson, Tracy & McVeigh, where a longtime friend was in charge of the business. The former president had an "of counsel" role. He had a salary, but he opted out of the partner track, and he paid one-tenth of his fee toward the office expenses. As often as he could, he made it home in time for dinner with Frances.[117]

The fifty-something Cleveland couldn't always keep up with his twenty-something wife. They wanted a family, but the socialite Frances also wanted a social life and to travel.[118] Her husband was still popular in many circles, and could have commanded the most interesting table in town. But he avoided dinner parties, and he only accompanied his wife to the theater to please her.[119] He read the Bible, but not much else. He enjoyed trips to their summer home, Gray Gables, on Buzzards Bay off the Massachusetts coast.[120] He went to Monument Beach for long fishing and hunting trips. Frances would stay home in Manhattan during most of these trips.[121]

It was a simple life, away from the prying eyes of the press that had haunted them in their White House years. For the first time since he was fifteen, Cleveland didn't need to work to make a living. He could take a breath. When Frances gave birth to their first child, a girl named Ruth, on October 3, 1891, he thought that he had everything he needed in life.[122] Well-wishes came pouring in, and he wrote to a friend, "I scarcely do anything just now but read the kindest messages of congratulation."[123] A first-time father, he could "see in a small child more of value than I have ever called my own before. . . . [It is] hardly worth a thought, all that has gone before."[124] This might have been the rest of his life, and he could have been happy.

It wasn't meant to be. Cleveland had been prepared to give up the presidency, if that's what standing on his principles would cost. But he was growing uneasy out of office. The Harrison administration was leading the country down the wrong path. The Democratic Party was going to be taken over by either the party bosses or the populists. He came to suspect that he was the only one who could hold back the worst tendencies of both sides.

Former presidents had run before, and Cleveland decided to test the political waters as early as December 16, 1889, less than a year out of office. He made a public appearance before the Merchants' Banquet in Boston, calling for "political honesty"[125] and offering his "uncompromising support . . . to ballot reform and civil service reform."[126] The real takeaway wasn't about policy, however. It was that the crowd applauded Cleveland with over-the-top enthusiasm. He still had a base. Now he'd have to decide if he'd use it.[127]

He wanted to run on policy. Tariffs were at the top of his list, as were sound money and small government. These were the issues where the Harrison administration's policies worried him most. The Sherman Silver Purchase Act of 1890 mandated the inflationary purchase of millions of ounces of silver a month, draining the nation's gold reserves.[128] Proponents of the gold standard—"Goldbugs" as they were called—worried that flooding the market with cheap money was nothing more than a populist strategy meant to win over farmers in the Midwest, even if it destroyed the economy. The issue of fiscal and monetary policy came to a head when Harrison signed the first billion-dollar federal budget, outside of the extraordinary circumstances of the Civil War.[129] Not only that, Harrison had signed the McKinley Tariff of 1890, sending rates through the roof.[130]

The voters were displeased, and they let their displeasure be known. In the 1890 midterms, the Democratic Party won a staggering comeback in Congress. The Republicans lost ninety-three seats in the House, more than half of their total number. They also lost ground in the Senate. The Democratic victory was all the more significant because Harrison had added six new states to the Union in his first two years, thinking that they'd give him a supportive buffer in Congress.[131]

With the Democrats showing signs of life, Cleveland sensed an opening. He began to explore a potential comeback. When they saw that he was interested, his allies encouraged him, but they told him to avoid controversy, including his old position on tariffs. He refused. "I am supposed to be a leader in my party," he told them. "If any word of mine can check these dangerous fallacies, it is my duty to give that word, whatever the cost may be to me."[132]

He threw away the presidency on principles in 1888. Now he was prepared to throw away his chance to get it back by sticking to the same principles. He wanted the voters to know where he stood, and in 1891 he released an open letter decrying the "dangerous and reckless experiment of free, unlimited, and independent silver coinage."[133] Democrats opposed to Cleveland thought he was digging his own political grave, but Cleveland felt he had a new lease on his political life.[134] He reported that a "weight [had] been lifted off and a cloud removed. At any rate, no one can doubt where I stand."[135]

The public found his honesty appealing. Cleveland wasn't known as a great speaker, but on October 8, 1891, before a crowd of thousands at Cooper Union, he was greeted with cries of "three cheers for Grover Cleveland!"[136] The *New York Times* reported that "such a scene as greeted his appearance is seldom seen at a political meeting or anywhere else."[137]

Audiences came to love Grover Cleveland. When he impressed four hundred guests during a dinner a few months later, steel tycoon Andrew Carnegie remarked on his popularity. It was never clear what to do with former presidents. But upon seeing Cleveland in action, Carnegie asked, "Why not run them again?"[138]

GOING FOR IT

Frances Cleveland was always ready to return to the White House. Grover wasn't so sure. What tipped him over the edge was Harrison's policies and the fact that he had no successor in the Democratic Party. When he saw the rise of David Hill of Tammany Hall, he wondered, "Is it ordained that I am to be the instrument through which democratic principles can be saved?"[139]

The decision would be made for him at the convention. But while the delegates met in Chicago, Cleveland was nowhere near. Instead, he was in his gun room at his vacation home at Gray Gables. A young man named Charles Jefferson would have to tell him if he won the nomination or not. Recalling that night, Jefferson remembered that Cleveland seemed uninterested in the news. He was busy doing laundry.[140]

Cleveland did care. If he failed to win the nomination, his reputation would suffer. If he was nominated, he'd be on the ballot in November. He might win, and then he'd be president again. He'd have to give up life in New York. He'd have to go back to dealing with the press, as would Frances. He was thinking about that fact as he folded his clothes surrounded by his guns and heard the news—the nomination was his.[141]

For him to win, he'd need the Democratic Party machine, even if he wasn't their chosen candidate. In September, Cleveland met with the bosses at his old haunt, the Hotel Victoria. Over dinner, he got straight to the point. "Well, gentlemen, what do you want?"[142]

This wasn't a real question. No matter what they wanted, he wouldn't give it to them. But Lieutenant Governor William Sheehan made the mistake of thinking Cleveland was curious. He told him, "We want pledges from you. . . . We want you to give us promises that will satisfy us that the organization will be properly recognized if you become President again." Cleveland was furious. He clenched his fists and banged the table as he barked back, "Gentlemen, I will not go into the White House pledged to you or to anyone else. I will make no secret promises. I'll be damned if I will!"[143]

They were the party machine, but he was the most powerful Democrat alive. He was an imposing figure at nearly three hundred pounds. "I'll tell you what I'm going to do," he vowed. "I intend to address a letter to the public in which I shall withdraw from the ticket. I intend to explain my situation and to report what you have said to me here."[144] He meant it. The bosses surrendered. They weren't getting any favoritism from Cleveland.[145]

Never before had a former president faced a sitting president as the nominees of one of the major parties. It could have been a brawl to put the previous elections to shame. But it wasn't. Cleveland was older, and he was dealing with gout. He did not mount an active campaign. Harrison and the Republicans were still licking their wounds from 1890. The president didn't have much fight left in him, as First Lady Caroline

Harrison had caught tuberculosis and died two weeks before the election. Both campaigns suspended operations to mourn her passing.[146]

The results handed Cleveland a mixed mandate, with 277 Electoral College votes, but once again only a plurality of the popular vote. A Populist candidate, Congressman James Weaver of Iowa, got twenty-two votes in the Electoral College, mostly in pro-silver Western states. Meanwhile, the Republicans lost both chambers of Congress for the first time since the Civil War.[147] Harrison was done after one term.

This time, Cleveland would have a one-party government behind him. He'd returned the Democrats to the White House. He was the most successful politician of his age. As future president William Howard Taft, then a judge on the Sixth Circuit in Cincinnati, remarked, "[Grover Cleveland] led his party to the greatest victory in its history."[148] But he wasn't in control of everything.

There was trouble brewing in faraway Hawaii. During Cleveland's first term, America had secured a naval base at Pearl Harbor. He worked on a treaty with King Kalakaua to set aside the area for America's use.[149] But some members of Congress didn't think that went far enough. They wanted to annex Hawaii and add its territory to the United States.

That case became stronger in 1891, when Queen Liliuokalani ascended to the Hawaiian throne. She had no intention to accommodate American settlers and sugar planters as her predecessor had. Instead, she proposed a new constitution to restore power to the Hawaiian monarchy, a move that outraged American settlers.[150] More than two thousand took up arms against the queen. On January 17, 1893, just before Cleveland's second inauguration, they overthrew her government and locked her in a jail cell.[151]

Making matters worse, they were aided by a detachment of U.S. Marines that landed on the islands. The marines didn't fire a shot, but they helped overthrow the Hawaiian monarchy by their presence alone. Even more egregious, America's minister to Hawaii, John Stevens, had declared Hawaii an American protectorate.[152] Washington hadn't ordered any of this, but the coup had American fingerprints all over it.

President Harrison was an imperialist. He called for the annexation of Hawaii. But he failed to get the Senate to approve the treaty before his administration ended. The matter would end up on Cleveland's desk.[153] And it was no secret that the new president did not see eye to eye with his predecessor.

A coup three thousand miles from Washington wasn't the only crisis Cleveland would have to deal with on day one. A bubble burst when the Philadelphia and Reading Railroad collapsed.[154] Soon other railroads and steel mills filed for bankruptcy. There was a run on gold, made all the more painful due to the Harrison administration's policies that had depleted the nation's reserves.[155]

With crises at home and abroad, Grover Cleveland became the twenty-fourth president on March 4, 1893. This time, the ceremony was bitterly cold. There was a heavy snow over Washington. The president's inaugural address was almost inaudible over the howling wind.[156] But the crowd was excited.

Never before had a former president taken the oath of office again. Cleveland was now a unique figure in American history. As Robert McElroy, one of his foremost biographers, described, Cleveland was the "first President-elect since 1840 who was manifestly a greater political figure than any man whom he could conceivably select for his Cabinet."[157]

Likewise, First Lady Frances Cleveland was in a league of her own. She'd been introduced to the public as a recent college graduate, descending a staircase at the first White House wedding. Now she was a mother and two-time First Lady. Anticipating a more exciting White House than ever before, the *New York Times* chronicled, "Mrs. Cleveland's return will be to society like the opening of a familiar book at a favorite chapter."[158]

Mrs. Cleveland was thrilled to be back. But her husband's emotions were mixed. "Every feeling of jubilation," he wrote, "and even my sense of gratitude is so tempered as to be almost entirely obscured by the realization, nearly painful, of the responsibility I have assumed."[159]

There was a moment of joy on his Inauguration Day. An excited Frances Cleveland was once again the First Lady (as she had predicted!), and she planted a big surprise kiss on her husband's fatty cheek during the ceremony. The crowd, almost entirely men in bowler hats holding umbrellas against the wind, erupted in cheers. After the ceremony, the First Lady rode happily in the inaugural parade. She was headed back to the White House.[160]

Frances entered her old, new home triumphantly. She was wearing a giant fur wrap and a matching hat.[161] But not everything was the same as it had been four years ago. Now the halls of the White House had a new source of illumination: electric light bulbs.

Frances and Grover Cleveland were used to the technology from their time in New York. But the Harrison family hadn't adapted. They were so frightened of electricity that they'd refused to flip the light switches. Every night, an engineer would come and do the honors for them.[162]

When they arrived, Mr. and Mrs. Cleveland cleaned house. They let go of most of the staff, excluding Irwin "Ike" Hoover, who knew how to work the light switches. Ike would go on to a forty-two-year career in the White House.[163] When he flipped on the lights, Frances didn't like what she saw. The Harrisons had left the house in a state of disrepair. Robert Lincoln O'Brien, the president's personal secretary, described a scene like "a Noah's Ark of every type of cockroach and waterbug known to science."[164] This was an inauspicious beginning to the second term.

"PERPLEXING DIFFICULTIES"

President Cleveland believed that the White House was a place to work, not primarily to live. He and Mrs. Cleveland purchased a house called Woodley, a white, Federal-style home set on top of a hill in the northwest of the city.[165] Except for during the social season, he and Frances could be found there, away from the Washington infighting.

But when he was at work, Cleveland was on the second floor of the White House. He was at the Resolute desk again, given to President Hayes by Queen Victoria.[166] In that seat, he faced what he called a set of "unusual and especially perplexing difficulties,"[167] beginning with Hawaii.

He had to move quickly. He withdrew the Hawaii annexation treaty from the Senate. He called for the issue to be reexamined, and he appointed former representative James H. Blount, a Democrat from Georgia who had chaired the House Committee on Foreign Affairs, as a special commissioner.[168] It was up to Blount to go to Hawaii and report back what was happening.

The president appointed Blount because he shared Cleveland's opposition to the annexation of Hawaii. But the Southern congressman did not share Cleveland's reasons. Blount was a racist. He was afraid of non-white populations being added to the United States. Hawaii, he thought, should be for the non-white Hawaiians.[169]

With Blount dispatched, Cleveland turned to another perplexing difficulty, which was the imploding economy. The stock market had crashed. Prices plummeted. Hundreds of banks failed. The government's gold reserves were disastrously low.[170] Panic was everywhere.[171] This was America's worst economic shock until the Great Depression.[172]

He was ready to act. Fearing inflation and the future of the dollar, he took on the Sherman Silver Purchase Act, which he saw as the root cause of the government's gold shortfall and much else.[173] At the time, the United States used both gold and silver to back its paper currency, but in 1834 had set the ratio of gold to silver at 16 to 1, and began a transition to the gold standard. The Sherman Silver Purchase Act had caused monetary chaos, and without a Federal Reserve to manage the money supply, Cleveland turned to Congress.

But Congress wasn't in session. The legislature wouldn't meet again until December 4, nine months after his inauguration. Cleveland worried that a delay would only make matters worse, and so he took aggressive action. He wouldn't have been as ready to do so at such an early point in his first term, but as a returning president, he had the confidence to call a special session of Congress to meet in August, four months ahead of schedule.[174]

His attention had been devoted to the economy and Hawaii. But a third crisis that could doom the Cleveland presidency was growing at home. Grover Cleveland had cancer. If he didn't do something about it, he might not make it to the end of his second term. The youngest First Lady in American history could become the youngest First Widow.

A Cancer on His Agenda

The president was sick, but he didn't know it when he entered office. A habitual cigar smoker who loved chewing tobacco, he one day massaged his tongue over the roof of his mouth. He felt a rough spot.[175]

But he didn't see a doctor about it. He only sought advice when the spot metastasized into a lump the size of a quarter.[176]

Robert M. O'Reilly, the president's physician, suspected the worst, and he advised the patient that he had "a bad looking tenant, I would have it evicted immediately."[177] O'Reilly sent a sample of tissue to a nearby lab with a note for the pathologist. He cautioned that this was "the most important specimen ever submitted." The lab confirmed: cancer.[178]

Frances was pregnant with their second child. She was alarmed about her husband's cancer and asked for a second opinion from Dr. Joseph Bryant, a family friend. But Dr. Bryant agreed with the diagnosis, and said the lump needed to be removed.[179] He warned that if there was any delay, he would refuse to perform the operation out of fear for his reputation and the fate of the patient.[180]

The president prided himself on honesty. Now he had to hide what was happening to him. With the economy on the brink and the political environment unstable, no one could know that he was sick. Earlier in his career, his aides had advised, "Whatever you do, tell the truth." Now the rule was "Whatever you do, say nothing."[181]

There were rumors. But the press—typically Cleveland's foes—put them to rest. In June, the New York Times reported that "imaginative persons . . . have been misinforming the public." Anyone who saw him at the White House, shaking hands with hundreds of visitors, would see immediately that nothing was amiss, and that he was in good health.[182]

For once, Cleveland was grateful to the media. Had the public known that he had cancer, the panic would have gotten worse. Most Americans could still remember president Ulysses S. Grant, whose long and agonizing battle with cancer had played out in public. President Garfield had suffered for months before succumbing to his gunshot wounds in 1881.[183] If another president died a painful, public death, it would be devastating. With that in mind, Cleveland advised his inner circle, "If rumor gets around that I am 'dying' then the country is dead, too. We must have secrecy."[184]

Even Cleveland's vice president was kept in the dark. Adlai E. Stevenson, grandfather of the future Democratic presidential nominee, was not a friend of Grover Cleveland. Stevenson had only been put on the

ticket to win Illinois and to appease voters looking for a soft money advocate who could appeal to both populists and party bosses.[185] Stevenson
couldn't be trusted, and he couldn't know that a slip of a surgeon's knife
might make him the next president of the United States.[186]

Hiding the tumor was made easier by the fact that it was inside
his mouth. But the surgery would be hard to keep secret. The doctors
would need to be careful and leave no visible scars on his face. Cleveland's speech would have to remain unchanged. Dr. Bryant insisted
this was all possible.[187]

To maintain secrecy, the surgery also couldn't happen in Washington. It couldn't be done at the president's summer home. Both locations were too public. So Cleveland suggested the *Oneida*, a wealthy
friend's yacht. This would provide the perfect cover. It was not unusual
for presidents to leave hot, humid Washington over the summer, and a
vacation upriver was perfectly plausible. There would also be no press
on board the boat. Everyone agreed on the plan, and they set the date
for surgery as July 1.[188]

Preparation began immediately. The *Oneida* had to be transformed
from a luxury liner into a floating hospital. The ship's saloon was to
be an operating room, lit by a single electric light bulb hooked to a
portable battery. The only remnant of the old saloon left was the ship's
organ, which was bolted to the floor and so could not be removed.[189]

The saloon of a yacht headed downriver—even with the best doctors, staff, and equipment—is not an ideal operating room. Under the
best of circumstances, it would bob in the river's current. If a strong
wind rose, the whole vessel would rock and a knife could slip. When
he boarded the *Oneida*, Dr. Bryant warned the captain, "If you hit a
rock, hit it good and hard, so that we'll all go to the bottom!"[190]

To keep up appearances, the surgeons hid belowdecks, out of the
public view. The president stepped aboard on June 30, and the *Oneida*
steamed along the East River. The press thought it was a Fourth of July
fishing expedition.[191]

The president was calm. The night before the procedure, he smoked
a cigar and stayed up late, drinking and talking about the petty annoy-
ances of his job. He complained about hordes of office seekers who
came knocking on his door, begging for work. He moaned, "They haunt

me in my dreams!" The group retired at midnight, ready for the next day, but fearful.[192]

The president's wake-up call was a surgeon's knock on his door. Dr. Bryant and a team of six were prepared. They examined the patient and put him to sleep. No president had ever submitted to anesthesia while in office. The surgery began at 12:32 p.m. with a prayer and a cocaine solution injected into Cleveland's mouth to numb the area. Managing the president's pain would be more challenging than they'd expected. The nitrous oxide gas they were using to keep him under wore off quickly, and they'd have to work fast while its effects lasted.[193]

For an hour and a half, the United States was without a conscious commander in chief. The vice president had no idea. Cutting through precedent and tissue at the same time, the surgeons removed Cleveland's two upper left bicuspids—the teeth between the molars and canines. The gas began to wear off, and the surgeons gave Cleveland another dose to keep him sedated. They cut deeper, and at 1:14 p.m., Dr. Bryant removed a large chunk of his upper left jaw, three more teeth, and a small part of the soft palate. This was the most delicate, and dangerous, part of the procedure. By 1:55 p.m., it was finished. Cleveland survived. There were no visible scars. Even his mustache was almost entirely intact.[194]

He awoke an hour after the procedure, and first saw Bryant's assistant, Dr. John Erdmann. He winced, then barked in a disoriented haze, "Who the hell are you?" His doctors saw that he was in pain and gave him more cocaine solution to help. He slowly dozed off. Half conscious, he mistook one of his staff for an office seeker, and he told him he could have whatever job he wanted. The crew carried him to bed. All aboard breathed a sigh of relief.[195]

For five days, Cleveland recovered aboard the *Oneida*. Then it was on to Buzzards Bay to rest. The public wondered why the president hadn't made a Fourth of July appearance, but he didn't arouse too much suspicion. Of Cleveland's cabinet official, only Secretary of War Daniel S. Lamont knew what had happened to him.[196]

The president wasn't out of the woods quite yet. His doctors had removed much of his jaw, and he needed to have some of it replaced.[197] This would require a second procedure. He got it on July 17, back aboard the *Oneida*. Kasson C. Gibson, a dentist, fitted Cleveland with a plaster mold to fill the cavity in his mouth and a rubber device to restore his face's shape. As clumsy as the remedy was, Cleveland would be able to speak normally.[198]

But the procedures took a toll. He lost weight and grew paler. It took time to get used to the rubber jaw, which could be painful. When Attorney General Richard Olney visited him, Cleveland exclaimed, "My God, Olney, they nearly killed me!"[199]

With his continued absence, the public began asking more questions about what was going on with Grover Cleveland. But his reputation for honesty helped cover up his subterfuge. When he told the press that he had gone fishing and had a bout of rheumatism, they believed him. A July article in the *Boston Globe* was headlined "Stories of 'Cancer' Apparently Are Fictions, Pure and Simple."[200]

The American public had no idea what happened aboard the *Oneida* until 1917. Dr. William Keen wrote about it in the *Saturday Evening Post*.[201] By then, Grover Cleveland had passed away, and America was in the midst of World War I. Few people cared that the presidency had hung on the edge of a knife.[202]

Finishing the Job at Home: Silver, the Tariff, and Labor

Cleveland's second term was not going according to plan. The president needed time to recover, but governing couldn't wait. As the scale of the nation's challenges became clearer, he waited impatiently for the August special session, when the House and Senate would convene to deal with the crises.

Voters and elected officials alike agreed: the economy was a mess. America's gold reserves were depleted, and the international silver market had deflated prices, leaving advocates in a bind.[203] Farmers wanted more coinage of silver to drive up inflation and the cost of their crops. Merchants and creditors were opposed, pushing for a stable money supply linked to gold.[204]

Cleveland sent a message to Congress calling for the repeal of the Sherman Silver Purchase Act.[205] This move split the Democratic Party between the North on the one hand and the South and West on the other, a divide between the manufacturers and the farmers. While Cleveland and his old nemesis David Hill were united, a young populist from Illinois with a fetish for silver, Congressman William Jennings Bryan, was rising in opposition.[206] He looked to be the future of the party.[207]

As debates in Congress continued, Mr. and Mrs. Cleveland welcomed their second daughter into the world. Born on September 9, 1893, Esther Cleveland was the first, and so far, only child of a sitting president born in the White House. The press dubbed her "the White House Baby," a nickname she carried into her adult life.[208]

Cleveland would have loved to spend his days with Frances, Ruth, and Esther. But he had to work with Congress to solve the economic crisis. While the House supported his position, the Senate was opposed. Democrats pushed for a compromise, but a frustrated Cleveland shouted at a cabinet meeting that there would be no middle ground on the issue of silver.[209]

It took time, but Cleveland got his way. By a vote of 43–32 in the Senate and 194–94 in the House, the Sherman Silver Purchase Act was no more.[210] America stopped buying four and a half million ounces of silver a month. But the country's gold reserves remained low. Wall Street had to bail out the government to the tune of nearly $65 million, staving off further economic collapse. The Morgan Bonds, named after financier J. P. Morgan, provided the necessary fix, but came to symbolize the cozy relationship between Wall Street and the White House. This eroded Cleveland's support among populist voters, who now looked for an anti-establishment figure to back.[211]

The silver issue continued to haunt the Cleveland administration.[212] The fighting got so intense that Cleveland's interior secretary warned him that "the [Democratic] Party will be so irreparably divided and demoralized that defeat will ensue."[213]

He wouldn't give in on silver, and he decided to take on the McKinley Tariff as well.[214] Once again, the House was with Cleveland, but the Senate was not.[215] He was politically weaker than ever. A Democratic member from Alabama denounced Cleveland on the floor, crying out, "I hate the ground that man walks on." Another compared Cleveland to Judas Iscariot.[216]

The votes were not there for Cleveland on this issue. He'd have to compromise if he wanted to preserve what little political capital he had left for the fight against silver, the primary reason he'd run for the White House. He allowed the Wilson-Gorman Tariff Act to pass in 1894, only slightly reducing the tariff.[217] He let his displeasure be known, calling the law an example of "party perfidy and party dishonor."[218] This was a remarkable indictment against his own party.

When the dust settled, Washington had acted, and Cleveland had led. The *Times* complimented a "remarkable Congress," the first controlled entirely by Democrats since the Civil War.[219] But the president was not happy. He was more isolated than ever, with opposition from Congress, his own party, and a growing segment of the American people. His administration could stem a rising populist tide, but it couldn't turn it back.[220]

It looked more certain every day that the country's dire economic straits would lead to civil unrest. After the Industrial Revolution, America was witnessing the rise of a new and expanding labor movement that had taken hold in many of the country's growing cities. That movement was beginning to flex its muscles.[221]

In its first year, Cleveland's administration witnessed an estimated 1,375 strikes put on by 287,765 strikers. The total number of strikers more than doubled the following year to 690,044—with only a slight increase in strikes to 1,404—and looked certain to increase further.[222] Most labor strikes were peaceful, but some were violent. If things continued as they were, there could be a wave of national crises. Labor was now a force and an issue in American politics.[223]

The country reached a breaking point in 1893. It came because of the Pullman Palace Car Company, a maker of luxury train cars based in Chicago, that had declining revenues and decided to lay off workers, reduce hours, and cut wages by as much as 35 percent.[224] The timing couldn't have been worse for struggling Pullman employees and their families, who were preparing for a bitterly cold winter.

Many of the Pullman workers lived in company housing, so-called pop-up Pullman villages. The company hiked prices and rents well above what was normal in Chicago. Life became unaffordable for many residents. Even necessities like water were sold at five times the price that nearby residents in Chicago who didn't work for the Pull-man company paid.[225]

Frustrated and lacking options, workers organized through the American Railway Union, led by the charismatic socialist Eugene Debs, who would go on to run for president in 1920 from his prison cell and garner around one million votes. They called for massive strikes against the Pullman Company, and even nationwide protests. Management responded by firing protesters, and the union pushed for arbitration. But the company ignored them.[226]

The American Railway Union rallied its members in support of the Pullman strikers, ordering them not to handle any Pullman train cars anywhere in the country. At the time, Chicago was the hub for rail transit in the United States. With more than two hundred thou-sand workers on strike nationwide and the city out of commission for freight, interstate commerce ground to a halt. Mail deliveries in twenty-seven states and territories all but ended overnight. Much of the nation was at a standstill.[227]

Cleveland, an advocate for limited government, had not yet weighed in. He preferred to allow labor and management to settle their own is-sues. But he began to have second thoughts and believed that he had to do something. Attorney General Olney, a corporate lawyer who'd made a name for himself working with the railroads, pushed him to intervene. With Olney's insistence and the situation in Chicago getting worse, Cleveland dropped his laissez-faire approach, opting for the use of ex-ecutive power on a scale not seen since the Civil War.[228]

He'd waited until the situation was nearly out of control. *Harper's Weekly* described the Chicago strike as a "reign of terror."[229] On July 2, Olney secured an injunction against the union, prohibiting it from "compelling or inducing" laborers to strike.[230] This effectively declared the strike illegal.[231] A furious Debs called the move "a plot to place Chicago under martial law."[232] But there were no teeth to enforce the injunction, and so the strike continued. Fearing chaos, Cleveland sent in nearly two thousand troops. He allegedly declared, "If it takes the entire army and navy of the United States to deliver a postal card in Chicago, that card will be delivered."[233]

It was at this point that the strike turned violent. As Allan Nevins wrote in his biography of Cleveland, "[T]wo distinct steps, the resort to an injunction and the use of Federal troops . . . seemed unprecedentedly bold. Court injunctions had been used before in labor troubles, but never in such sweeping form."[234]

The country was not prepared for widespread violence. Many of the striking workers could remember the Civil War. Now Debs was predicting that America would split once again, this time over class, not race. He seemed eager for it. He more than matched Cleveland's anger, and he cried out, "The first shots fired by the regular soldiers at the mobs here will be the signal for a civil war."[235]

The threat of the country splitting in two again shocked the public. Clashes between strikers and the Illinois National Guard left four dead on July 8. Cleveland issued a warning against the "public enemies" in Chicago.[236] Within days, Debs and the other Pullman strike leaders were arrested. The crisis was over. According to Debs, "As soon as the employees found that we were arrested and taken from the scene of action they became demoralized, and that ended the strike."[237]

Chaos and blood in the streets of Chicago were not what the American people had voted for when they elected Grover Cleveland, and it was certainly not what he came back to do. In the midterms in 1894, the Democrats lost 125 seats. A congressman from Missouri described the results as "the greatest slaughter of innocents since the days of King Herod."[238] A new Populist Party had turned out 1.5 million voters, delivering six senators and seven members of the House.[239] America's political landscape was changing. It was leaving Grover Cleveland behind.

American Empire

While American politics was changing, so, too, was its role in the world. The United States' interests didn't just span a continent, they spanned the Western Hemisphere.[240] It was clear that Cleveland was an anti-imperialist, along with figures as diverse as Andrew Carnegie, Samuel Gompers, and Mark Twain.[241] He did not want the country to become a colonial power. He worried that if it did it would change fundamentally, and no longer be the country he had known.

The country was different. In 1890, historian Frederick Jackson Turner declared that there was no more frontier, once a defining fact of American life.[242] Thirty-five percent of Americans lived in cities.[243] With no more land at home to settle, they were looking abroad.[244]

While the American people were eyeing the rest of the world, Grover Cleveland was not. In his first inaugural address, he had cited Washington's Farewell and called for a "policy of neutrality." He had championed a stronger American navy, however, so that the country could be defended by a force that "befits our standing among the nations of the earth."[245]

Debates about America's role in the world came to a head in Hawaii. James Blount returned with his report. He told the president about an armed revolt, a marine detachment gone rogue, and an American flag flying over foreign islands without Washington's consent.

The president was outraged. He told the truth, informing the public that it was "beyond all question that the constitutional Government of Hawaii had been subverted with the active aid of [America's] representative to that government and through the intimidation by the presence of an armed naval force of the United States."[246] Though Blount had ordered the American flag to be lowered and the marines withdrawn, the damage was done.[247]

Cleveland tried to turn back the clock, but it was impossible. He called for the restoration of the Hawaiian monarchy, but Democrats in Congress said that the United States—a democratic republic—was not in the business of restoring absolute monarchies. The queen had also made it clear that, were she reinstated, she would retaliate against American settlers.[248] When asked if she'd grant amnesty against those who'd overthrown her, she responded, "My decision would be as the law directs, that such persons should be beheaded and their property confiscated."[249]

An American president could not consent to the beheading of American citizens, much less by a foreign leader. Cleveland didn't know what to do. In a December cabinet meeting, he and his advisors decided to pass the Hawaii buck to Congress.[250] He cited the "constitutional limitations of . . . Executive power."[251]

The matter was for Congress to decide, but he let his opinion be known, defending his opposition to Hawaii annexation by calling it a matter of "right and justice." He worried that, if annexation passed, it would be a sign that the United States was no longer the country he had known, and that he had "entirely misapprehended the mission and character of our government and the behavior which the conscience of the people demands of their public servants."[252]

He was not known for his speeches, but this was a remarkable example of moral clarity and powerful rhetoric. Charles Francis Adams Jr., grandson of John Quincy Adams and keeper of the Adams family traditions, wrote admiringly of Cleveland's declaration. He told the president that he could "remember no stand taken by a government so morally sound and dignified."[253]

His words were not enough to change history. Cleveland delayed the annexation of Hawaii, but a joint resolution passed both houses of Congress on July 7, 1898, soon after he left office. He read the news in the paper, and wrote despondently, "Hawaii is ours. . . . I am ashamed of the whole affair."[254]

Cleveland lost on Hawaii. But he won elsewhere in the Western Hemisphere. There was a border dispute between Venezuela and British Guyana that had been ongoing since 1841, as there had been no formal boundary set on the British territory since it was acquired from the Netherlands.[255] Great Britain pushed its claim farther and farther into Venezuela, and the Venezuelan caudillos—who also claimed much of British Guyana as their own—pushed for American arbitration, citing the Monroe Doctrine against new European interference on the continent.[256] But Cleveland didn't want any part of this dispute at first, preferring to "avoid a doctrine which I knew to be troublesome."[257]

When British ships sailed up the Orinoco River, Venezuela's ambassador to the United States appealed to Secretary of State Richard Olney, who had left his job at the Department of Justice.[258] American public opinion favored intervention, and Cleveland asked Congress to form a commission to arbitrate the Venezuela boundary dispute, and to enforce its recommendations "by every means."[259] The British, facing pressure on the other side of the globe from the Boers in South Africa,[260] came to the table and recognized America's role.[261] Great

Britain and Venezuela signed a treaty of arbitration in Washington one month before Cleveland's second retirement.[262]

This 1895 Venezuela boundary dispute has largely been forgotten. But it was a major milestone in United States history. This was the first time that America invoked and enforced the Monroe Doctrine on its own, and the fact that Great Britain submitted to the commission's judgment remade its relationship with the United States. The American Enterprise Institute's Kori Schake describes the 1895 Venezuela Crisis as "that moment when [America] realized and asserted its power" and when "the hegemon of the international order reassessed its strategy toward a rising America." After these events, "the ground had shifted in Anglo-American relations."[263]

"Luckless Years"

The second Cleveland term did not have a happy ending for him. He'd suffered defeats on foreign policy and on the economy. He was politically isolated. He later described this time as his "luckless years." He complained of being depressed as early as 1894. In early 1895, he told one of his ambassadors that he was "dreadfully forlorn."[264] When his children were targeted by would-be kidnappers, Mrs. Cleveland had to demand increased protection.[265]

He'd defeated Harrison. He'd held back a populist tide. He'd had policy victories. The economy had not fully recovered from the Panic of 1893, but it had stabilized. But the Democratic Party had changed, and it rejected Grover Cleveland and his more conservative ideas. America was becoming an imperial power. Americans were moving to the cities and working in factories. The twentieth century was coming.

Looking back on the last twelve years, he knew that it was unlikely that a man like him would ever be elected president once, let alone twice. There would not be a third term. He believed in the two-term limit that George Washington had set.[266] Besides, he would have lost this time, and not with a plurality of the popular vote.

After Cleveland, there was a vacancy in leadership at the top of the Democratic Party. A rising populist wing was "looking for a Moses" to lead them out of the wilderness, and they found such a man, in Congressman William Jennings Bryan.[267]

The Bryan wing in the Democratic Party was a new force in American politics. The thirty-six-year-old Midwesterner was in his second term in the House. The *New York Times* described the charismatic politician as a "boy orator" and a "general demagogue."[268] In 1896, he became the youngest nominee of a major party in American history. And the Republicans nominated Cleveland's old foe from the tariff debates, William McKinley.

To the president, the election seemed like it might be a choice between the lesser of two evils. At the Democratic convention, the pro-silver Bryan gave a speech out of Cleveland's nightmares. Bryan stretched his arms out like the crucified Christ and bellowed to the hall, "You shall not crucify mankind upon a cross of gold!"[269] Those words hung in the air, and observers noted a "fearful silence."[270] But then, applause erupted for half an hour. The party was Bryan's.[271]

The Democrats explicitly denounced their own president's policies in their party platform, condemning his response to the Pullman Strike. When it was released, the Republicans labeled this the party's "anarchy plank."[272] When he read about it, Cleveland felt that "those who controlled the convention displayed their hatred of me and wholly repudiated me."[273]

There were a few Bourbon Democrats left. They tried to organize a "National Democratic Party" convention in Indianapolis that September, and they sent Cleveland an urgent message asking him to run. His supporters told him, "You will be nominated tomorrow unless you make a definite refusal." So, he refused. "I cannot for a moment entertain [the idea]," he told the group. But he also refused to campaign for Bryan. He even considered supporting McKinley, telling a friend, "I am perplexed concerning the course I should pursue."[274]

The president's endorsement would not have changed the outcome of the election in 1896. Given the economy and civil tensions, it would have been difficult for any Democrat to win, whatever their politics. But Bryan's defeat—though far from final—was almost as historic as his rise. The Republicans pulled together their old coalition, as well as rising groups like immigrants and laborers, to win California, Oregon, the upper Midwest, and all of the Northeast, including Cleveland's home state of New York.

Victory belonged to the GOP. McKinley's hometown of Canton, Ohio, was giddy on election night, with flag-waving, pistol shooting, and cheering. The president-elect stayed up almost until sunrise, celebrating with his friends, neighbors, and political allies.[275] Meanwhile, Bryan was quiet.[276] But he soon came to blame his predecessor, fuming, "I have borne the sins of Grover Cleveland."[277]

The candidate had a point. The *Baltimore Sun*, sympathetic to the outgoing president, opined, "The hero of this campaign will be that of a man who was not a candidate, not a manager, not an orator. . . . This is Cleveland's day, the vindication of his course."[278] Many Democrats likely did not approve of Cleveland. But they also didn't want to elect someone like Bryan, who would throw out every policy Cleveland had ever advocated.

The silver issue continued to hang over American politics. In 1900, four years after Bryan's first defeat, author L. Frank Baum published a fantasy novel called *The Wonderful Wizard of Oz* in which the main character, Dorothy, has a pair of slippers, which solve her problems. Though the 1939 Hollywood movie adaptation depicted the slippers as being made of rubies, in Baum's book, they were made of silver. Dorothy traveled through the land of Oz, which according to some scholars is a metaphor for the debate around currency. According to this interpretation, the silver slippers represent the argument for free silver, while following the yellow brick road is a nod to the gold standard, and the Emerald City is meant to represent a new path of greenbacks, or paper money.[279]

With American politics changing, Cleveland was in a strange position. Eight years earlier, he was a lame duck. Now he was a lame duck again. That two-time experience of powerlessness was as morose as it sounds. He wallowed in a moment of self-pity. He asked one of the staff to remove his portrait and put it in the White House attic, thinking no one would want to see his face again.[280]

But the president still had work to do. A few miles off the Florida coast, the Cuban people were rebelling against the Spanish empire. The Spaniards dealt with the unrest harshly, sending Cuban civilians to "reconcentration camps" to separate them from the rebels.[281] Under punitive Spanish rule, disease and starvation led to the deaths of more than three hundred thousand Cubans.[282] Upon hearing of the suffering, Americans sided with the rebels, and pushed for the United States to intervene.[283] Many were spoiling for a fight against the dying Spanish empire, and the "yellow press" stirred up Americans' bellicosity.

President Cleveland, along with much of the business community, did not want the United States to enter a war by choice. He believed the rebels were "the most inhuman and barbarous cutthroats in the world."[284] Had he supported them, however, and intervened and achieved battlefield victories, his popularity with the more jingoistic Bryan wing may have increased. But that wasn't what he was interested in. As University of Michigan professor David Winter has argued, presidents whose motivation is power are more likely to get America involved in wars.[285] Instead, Cleveland issued a statement of neutrality: "There will be no war with Spain over Cuba while I am President."[286]

It was clear that Congress didn't feel the need for restraint. After Cleveland's message, one senator retorted that it was the legislature, not the president, who had the power to declare war under the Constitution. Cleveland fired back, "Yes, but [the Constitution] also makes me Commander-in-Chief, and I will not mobilize the army."[287]

The president knew public opinion was against him. He explored purchasing Cuba from Spain, thinking that this course would be both more just and cheaper. But the Cuba issue went unresolved and would land on McKinley's plate. Cleveland feared the United States would be at war in a matter of months.[288]

Fearing the worst, the president arranged to meet the president-elect to discuss what to do. Cleveland's gout was getting worse, and he limped into the meeting. When they sat down, Cleveland cautioned McKinley against going to war with Spain. To his delight, McKinley agreed. McKinley had run on restoring the economy, and that's what he wanted to do. War would risk recovery. At the end of the meeting, McKinley asked, "Now, Mr. Cleveland, isn't there something you would like me to do for you?" Cleveland responded, "No, Mr. President, there is nothing that I want personally."[289]

What Grover Cleveland wanted was to leave the White House. On

McKinley's Inauguration Day, he wrote, "In a few hours I will cease to be President. The people seem to have deserted me."

He told a friend, "I envy [McKinley] today only one thing, and that was the presence of his own mother at the inauguration. I would have given anything in the world if my mother could have been at my inauguration."[290] There was one bright spot, however. In his inaugural address, McKinley declared, "Wars should never be entered upon until every agency of peace has failed," a line that pleased Cleveland.[291]

When the ceremony concluded, the two men traveled back to the White House and entered together through the front door. Later in the day, as he left for the last time, Cleveland, still using his umbrella as a cane, departed through a side door, out of public view. He boarded a train, where his wife and babies were waiting.[292]

Despite the best wishes of Grover Cleveland and William McKinley, America would be at war with Spain a year later.

Former Again

Grover Cleveland's comeback was a never-repeated triumph. But on the other side, he felt defeated. His second term had not ended with success. It had been consumed by crises. From the moment he'd set foot in the White House, events—often out of his control—determined his fate.

His second term was not without victories, and neither Harrison nor any of the other Democratic contenders would likely have been able to speed up the economic recovery. Some might have made matters worse. The Pullman Strike could have descended into more violence. And Cleveland had enacted major civil service reforms protecting civil servants from political firings and worked with a young Theodore Roosevelt, the commissioner of the U.S. Civil Service Commission and a holdover from the Harrison administration, to professionalize the workforce.[293] He'd repealed the silver purchase bill. He'd settled the Venezuela Crisis.[294] He'd kept America out of war. He'd held back the populists and party bosses while helping his party move beyond its antebellum roots. With anyone else at the helm of the Democratic Party, the nineteenth century might have ended quite differently.

He had a simpler view of his time in the White House. He had "done [his] duty as [he] saw it." But he did not feel boastful about his time, undoubtedly a consequence of having finally experienced what it was like to be unpopular. At a dinner in his honor after his second term, the host asked him, "What shall we do with our ex-Presidents?" At first, Cleveland joked that they should be taken out to a five-acre lot and shot. Then he thought better of his comment. He concluded, "A five-acre lot seems needlessly large, and in the second place an ex-President has already suffered enough."[295]

A Princeton Man

His second post-presidency would be very different from his first. The latter had lasted four years. This would be for the rest of his life.

He had a family now. The Clevelands welcomed baby Marion in 1895, and now had three young children. Manhattan would not do for the brood, and they settled in Princeton, New Jersey. They purchased a home that they dubbed "Westland," after Andrew West, the Princeton professor who convinced them to make the move.[296]

They had chosen Princeton after the president attended the 150th anniversary of the founding of the College of New Jersey, when the school changed its name to Princeton University.[297] With that visit, as Robert McElroy showed, "The President had entered Princeton as an admirer of the college. He left it a Princeton man."[298]

He arrived at his new home in time for his sixtieth birthday on March 18, 1897. Away from Washington, he breathed a sigh of relief. "I have worked hard. Now I am entitled to rest." And rest he did. He rose at eight in the morning. He read the paper, hunted ducks, fished, and walked around town. He was home most nights to play cards with his friends. By one count, he played a staggering 527 games of bridge in the first five months after the White House. He never traveled far.[299]

He'd amassed a small fortune of $350,000 and didn't need to work, and the son of a poor minister now enjoyed trading stocks as a hobby.[300] He took on a few honorary roles in the life insurance industry,[301] a part of the economy in need of better management and good governance.[302] Cleveland's proposals helped simplify communications to policyholders, and earned praise from newspapers and companies like Mutual Life and New York Life.[303]

Cleveland was not an intellectual, though he did enjoy poetry, and could quote Tennyson by heart. Andrew West wanted him to take up the pen and to write a memoir, but the former president thought it wouldn't be of much interest to the public. Grant's memoir, published in 1885, had set the bar impossibly high for the genre. He could be prone to self-pity and indulgent humility, and said, "There is no reason for my writing my autobiography. . . . What I did is done and history must judge of its value, not I." He continued, somewhat disingenuously, "My private life has been so commonplace that there is nothing to write about."[304] When a friend brought his dog over to Westland, the animal leapt into Cleveland's lap. The owner tried to pull it away, but Cleveland stopped him, saying, "No, let him stay. He at least likes me."[305]

Rather than write a memoir, he wrote essays. He could earn $2,500 a piece, and some were published in the *Saturday Evening Post*, the *Atlantic*, and *Ladies' Home Journal*.[306] In the *Home Journal*, the conservative argued against women's suffrage—a position also held by Mrs. Cleveland, which did not age well for either of them.[307]

The Ivy League was an odd fit for Cleveland, but it took. He was a man without a college degree who was often uncomfortable around intellectuals. But campus life shook Cleveland out of his melancholy. "I feel like a locomotive, hitched to a boy's express wagon," he remarked shortly after his arrival. The trustees awarded him an honorary doctorate, and over time, the former president earned the nickname "the Sage of Princeton," an echo of Thomas Jefferson, the "Sage of Monticello."[308]

Over time, the Cleveland family became happy. On October 28, 1897, Frances gave birth to their first boy. Princeton students put banners and signs across campus to mark the occasion, and one read "Grover Cleveland, Jr., arrived today at twelve o'clock. Will enter Princeton with the class of 1919, and will play center rush on the championship football teams of '16, '17, '18, and '19."[309]

The prediction was half right. The boy did graduate in the Princeton class of 1919, and he did play football. But his name wasn't Grover Cleveland Jr. The former president didn't much like his own name, and wrote, "So many people have been bothered by . . . Grover, and it has been so knocked about that I thought it ought to have a rest."[310] Instead, he named his son Richard, after his grandfather.[311] Richard Cleveland became a diplomat and distinguished lawyer. In the 1950s, he represented Whittaker Chambers in the Alger Hiss case.[312]

Cleveland became a university trustee in 1901 and delved into the school's business. He analyzed its budgets, surveyed its programs, and attended every board meeting he could. He helped to reorganize the undergraduate experience and reformed the club system.[313] Like Jefferson before him, he found that former presidents make good university administrators.

Princeton University was undergoing significant changes, some of which would reverberate on the national stage. At the time, the graduate school was expanding, thanks in no small part to Cleveland courting a donation from his friend Andrew Carnegie.[314] The school needed a new location.

This decision pitted former president Grover Cleveland against future president Woodrow Wilson, who at the time was president of Princeton University, the first in the school's history without training in theology.[315] The two weren't strangers or natural enemies. Wilson had taken to the pages of the *Atlantic* in 1897 to reflect on the second Cleveland presidency. He argued that, though Cleveland's place in American history wasn't certain, he had "rendered the country great services." Cleveland, Wilson wrote, had "been the sort of President the makers of the Constitution had vaguely in mind."[316]

Grover Cleveland and Woodrow Wilson appeared at first to be natural allies. Cleveland had given an address at a 1902 ceremony in favor of installing Wilson as Princeton's new president, a position to which he was unanimously elected.[317] At the time, Wilson's politics were close to Cleveland's, as biographer Arthur Link described Wilson then as "a foe of Bryanism, government regulation, and the restrictive practices of labor unions."[318]

But their collegial relationship would not last. Both the sons of ministers, they came to follow different political gospels. Wilson was an academic born in the Old South. Cleveland had never graduated from college, and he hailed from New York. Wilson became a progressive, and Cleveland remained conservative. When it came to the future of the campus they now shared, they had very different ideas of what kind of a school Princeton should be.

This conflict came to a head when Wilson pushed for a new graduate school to be located "at the heart of Princeton." Cleveland's friend Andrew West wanted the school to be separated from the undergraduates, away from campus life. When West, with the chairman's support and multiple six-figure bequests from the likes of William Cooper Procter, of Procter & Gamble, won out, Wilson was defeated, and he was furious.[319]

To Wilson, this dispute was about more than faculty lounge debates. It had national significance. He demanded of West, "Will America tolerate the seclusion of its graduate students?"[320] When it became clear that the United States would indeed have to make its peace with a more secluded graduate student presence at Princeton University, Wilson let his displeasure be known. He warned Grover Cleveland, "You will regret what you have said."[321]

In a strange way, Wilson was right. There was a grander significance to the location of the Princeton graduate school. Pulitzer Prize–winning columnist George Will, a Princeton man himself, contends that the decision about where to place it changed world history. In 1910, done with Princeton and with the help of New Jersey political bosses, the academic Wilson became the governor of New Jersey. From there, it was three short years to the White House—a rise almost as meteoric as that of Grover Cleveland. Surveying Wilson's career, Will has argued, "I firmly believe that the most important decision taken anywhere in the 20th century was where to locate the Princeton graduate college. When Wilson lost he had one of his characteristic tantrums, went into politics and ruined the 20th century."[322]

Grover Cleveland didn't live long enough to see the Wilson presidency. He had other matters to worry about. On January 7, 1904, twelve-year-old Ruth Cleveland died of diphtheria. This was a terrible blow, and the former president wrote in his diary, "It seems to me I mourn our darling Ruth's death more and more. So much of the time I can only think of her as dead, not joyfully living in Heaven."[323] Ruth's death brought him closer to his faith than he had been in decades. He wrote,

"God has come to my help and I am able to adjust my thoughts to dear Ruth's death with as much comfort as selfish humanity will permit."[324]

Princeton rallied around the grieving Cleveland. On Cleveland's seventieth birthday in 1907, his friends orchestrated a national letter-writing campaign to shower him with love and affection. Even Woodrow Wilson, still president of Princeton, wrote an article for the *New York Times*, stating, "It has been one of the best circumstances of my life that I have been closely associated with you in matters both large and small."[325] Cleveland, overwhelmed with gratitude, replied in the *Times*, "It seems to be impossible for me to acknowledge, except through the press of the country, the generosity and kindly consideration of my countrymen."[326]

There were opportunities to return to public life.[327] President McKinley asked him to arbitrate an international dispute over the Hague Agreement, but he said no. Likewise, he refused a chance to run for governor of New Jersey.[328] He was done with politics.

And the Democratic Party, at least for now, was done with Cleveland. It once again nominated Bryan in 1900. Throwing up his hands in resignation, Cleveland wrote to his friend Wilson Bissell, "The pending campaign has brought upon me much unhappiness."[329]

Bryan's defeat that year made some Democrats rethink their attitude about the only man who'd won them the White House since 1856. A few party leaders even considered renominating Cleveland in 1904.[330] But when he was asked by a *New York Times* reporter if he would, he replied that the idea was "perfectly absurd."[331]

Instead of Cleveland, the Democrats nominated Alton B. Parker, a conservative judge whose rise signaled a temporary repudiation of Bryan. The nomination of Parker "very much pleased" Cleveland. He intended to help Parker campaign. But his health was failing, and he only gave two speeches.[332]

Parker lost to Theodore Roosevelt in 1904, coming up more than a million votes shy of William Jennings Bryan's tally four years prior. The Democratic populists, it seemed, were willing to stay home with a conservative on the ballot.[333] But the populists still didn't have enough power within the party to win the nomination and the presidency on their own. Cleveland hoped that, with time, the Democrats might come around to his positions.[334]

In the meantime, Cleveland had made his peace having another Republican, Theodore Roosevelt, as president. Roosevelt was a fellow reformer from New York. The two respected each other from their work on the civil service together. When Cleveland congratulated him on becoming president, Roosevelt said the experience was "as if a senior had patted a freshman on the shoulder and assured him of his success."[335]

With that respect in mind, and recalling Cleveland's actions during the Pullman Strike, President Roosevelt asked him to settle a dispute with a group of striking coal miners. The president said he needed someone "whose word would have the ear of the nation, Grover Cleveland." But mentioning Cleveland's name was enough to get them to come to the table.[336]

The 1904 election was Cleveland's last. He worried that Bryan might rise again, and said that—if he lived until 1908—he'd support the Republican ticket. But he didn't give up hope for the Democrats. He wrote, "Our party, which has withstood so many clashes with our political opponents, is not doomed at this time."[337]

He was right. The party wasn't doomed, though it did run Bryan again in 1908. The next Democratic president would be Woodrow Wilson.

Grover Cleveland's last words, spoken in bed at his Princeton home on June 24, 1908, were "I have tried so hard to do right."[338] There is a tone of regret in those words. He tried, but often he did not succeed. He is remembered as the only president to mount a successful comeback. But that part of the story only captures how to get back what you've lost professionally. There's a cautionary tale on a personal level as well. He had more experience in his second term and a united government. But he faced a different set of challenges that were out of his control and that he had difficulty managing. He left office less popular and having sacrificed years with his family. He made those sacrifices because he believed it was the right thing to do.

That fact wasn't lost on the country. He had a small funeral, which was attended by President Theodore Roosevelt. The president eulogized Cleveland, recalling his predecessor as having had an "entire devotion to the country's good, and a courage that quailed before no hostility."[339] One reporter witnessed Roosevelt hold back tears.[340]

With Cleveland's passing, there were no former presidents left. McKinley had been assassinated in 1901. Benjamin Harrison died that same year. Rutherford Hayes died in 1893. Chester Alan Arthur died of Bright's disease in 1886.

The future of American government would soon fall to William Howard Taft, a man who defeated William Jennings Bryan in 1908 by 321 electoral votes to 162.[341] Though he never lived to see his run, Cleveland would have supported Taft. Likewise, Taft admired Cleveland, and he wrote to Frances that her late husband was "as completely American in his character as Abraham Lincoln."[342]

Like Cleveland, Taft was out of step with the times and destined to be a one-term president. He'd lose the White House to Woodrow Wilson. Wilson would change the party irrevocably, moving beyond the conservatism of Grover Cleveland. But for Taft, defeat opened the door to what he wanted most in the world: to become chief justice of the United States.

A Dream Deferred

The truth is, that in my present life I don't remember that I even was president.

—WILLIAM HOWARD TAFT

William Howard Taft did not want to be president. He dreamed of a seat on the U.S. Supreme Court. That dream didn't come true until 1921, when at the age of sixty-three, the Senate confirmed him as America's tenth chief justice. To get there, he had to be president of the United States first, a job he never wanted and that almost destroyed his career.

At no point in his life did Taft make any secret of his dream. He called the Supreme Court his "sacred shrine." He told friends, "I love judges and I love courts. They are my ideals on earth."[1] Even when he was in the White House, he said that he'd prefer to be on the bench. When someone asked if he'd rather be Chief Justice John Marshall than president of the United States, he replied, "I would rather have been Marshall than any other American. . . . He made this country."[2]

Both Democratic and Republican presidents considered nominating Taft to the Supreme Court. They knew he was qualified for the job. But the timing was never right. Republican Benjamin Harrison considered him in 1889, as did Democrat Grover Cleveland in 1895. William McKinley almost made the ask in 1897. But Taft was either too young or not the right nominee for the moment. As his years increased, so, too, did his worries. He began to despair and lamented that his "chances of going to the moon and of donning a silk gown [on the Supreme Court]" were one and the same.[3]

That all seemed to change on January 22, 1900. By then, Taft was a judge on the Sixth Circuit, based in Cincinnati. This position was known as a feeder for the high bench and set him up well for the Supreme Court, especially with his fellow Ohioan William McKinley in the White House. That cold January day, McKinley asked Taft to come to Washington. Taft hurried to the capital, thinking that his time had come. But he wasn't headed to the Supreme Court. The president wanted to send him halfway around the world, to Manila. "Judge," he said, "I would like to have you go to the Philippines."[4]

McKinley wanted to make Taft the governor-general of a new American possession 8,500 miles away from Washington. Taft later recalled that "[McKinley] might as well have told me that he wanted me to take a flying machine." In the meeting, he informed the president, "I am sorry you have got the Philippines, but I don't want them."[5] But McKinley saw Taft as a loyal Ohio Republican, both highly capable and knowledgeable of the law and of how to establish a new government. He ignored Taft's objections.

McKinley wasn't the only person who wanted Taft to have a new job. The most important decision-maker was Helen "Nellie" Herron, his wife, followed by Taft's brothers, who didn't think that being a judge set him up well for political office.[6] But being the governor-general of the Philippines might, especially given the visibility. With McKinley's order and his family's insistence, Taft was off to Manila.

Taft gave up a lifetime appointment when he took the job in the Philippines, but he didn't give up his dream of the Supreme Court. President McKinley saw that Taft was disappointed and assured him that when a seat on the Court opened up, Taft would be at the top of his list.[7]

That didn't happen. A few months later, Leon Czolgosz, a Polish immigrant turned anarchist, assassinated William McKinley in Buffalo, New York. Nevertheless, between 1900 and 1909, the new president, Theodore Roosevelt, offered Taft a seat on the Supreme Court three separate times. But Taft had to say no, out of a sense of responsibility to his job, because of the wishes of his family, and after it became clear that the presidency was his, even if he didn't want it.[8] He became Roosevelt's chosen successor. As president, Taft nominated six justices to the Supreme Court, including a chief justice. This was more nominations than any other president in a single term. The irony of being the nominator, and not the nominated, made him resent his new job even more.[9]

A dream deferred was not a dream denied. Taft held out hope for the Court. He played the long game and kept the door to the Court open. When the time came for him to pick a chief justice, he chose a sixty-five-year-old over a younger contender, praying that the man's passing would open up the seat for him at a later date.[10] Even after his humiliating third-place finish in the election of 1912, he stayed close with the Republican Party, and positioned himself for a future nomination, should the Roosevelt wing lose its grip. Through two terms of Democrat Woodrow Wilson, most aspirants would have given up hope. But Taft proved as persistent as he was patient.

The same man who renominated him in 1912, the dark horse Republican candidate Warren Harding, won the White House in 1920. Chief Justice Edward White—the Taft appointee—died six months later.[11] On June 30, 1921, the day he was nominated, the Senate confirmed Taft as the tenth chief justice of the United States.

Taft's life was an odyssey to the Supreme Court. He is the only person to ever lead two branches of the federal government. He upheld his family responsibilities, professional obligations, and dealt with health scares. But he made it, and those final ten years of his life were his most fulfilling. When he finally made it to the Supreme Court, he told his fellow justices, "I don't remember that I was even president."[12]

NOT HIS OWN MAN

For most of his life, William Howard Taft was not his own man. He was a people pleaser and could be a pushover. He allowed his family and friends to channel their ambitions through him, regardless of his own wishes for himself. They were the ones who wanted him to be president. He deferred his dreams to fulfill theirs.

One of the ironies of Taft's life is that it took sixty-three years for him to make it to the Supreme Court, because he was perfectly positioned for the role from birth. His father, Alphonso Taft, was the attorney general of the United States.[13] Alphonso also wanted to be on the Supreme Court. He once told Justice Salmon Chase, an Abraham Lincoln appointee, that "to be Chief Justice of the United States is more than to be President."[14]

Alphonso Taft's dream rubbed off on his son, and the Taft household was filled with legal debates and lessons about legal history. Young Will went to Yale, and then Cincinnati Law School. He graduated with high honors.[15] By age twenty-nine, he was the youngest judge in Ohio.[16] At thirty-two, he was solicitor general of the United States. His time as solicitor general convinced Taft even more that the Court was his dream. He argued eighteen cases before the Court, winning fifteen of them.[17] This was a man who could be a Supreme Court justice.

But that wasn't what his wife, Nellie, wanted. Nellie Taft was a fellow Ohioan, and she wanted power. Being the solicitor general's wife gave her a taste for Washington high society that she never lost.[18] When Taft returned to Cincinnati in 1892 for what she feared might be a lifetime appointment as a judge on the Sixth Circuit, she was unhappy. Author Charles Dickens may have described nineteenth-century Cincinnati as "a beautiful city, cheerful, thriving, and animated," but to Nellie Taft, it was provincial. Being a judge's wife was much less interesting than being a politician's wife.[19]

Nellie Taft would have been a remarkable figure in any era. But in late nineteenth- and early twentieth-century America, she was even more so. Unable to achieve her potential in a world dominated by men, she resented the role of women in a patriarchal society. She didn't have many female friends. She didn't enjoy keeping the company of "uninteresting women." Alice Roosevelt, the larger-than-life eldest daughter of Theodore Roosevelt, noted that being put in a room with other women while the men attended to business could "bore [Nellie] to death."[20]

Like William Howard Taft, the future Nellie Taft never made a secret of her dream. At age sixteen she traveled to Washington and met with President Rutherford and First Lady Lucy Hayes. Women could not vote at the time, let alone run for the White House. So young Nellie told Mr. and Mrs. Hayes that she'd do the next best thing. She would "marry a man who will be president." Amused, Hayes responded, "I hope you may, and be sure you marry an Ohio man." Nellie followed that advice in every respect—and she left nothing to chance. Her husband pledged "an equal partnership" when they married, and she made sure he meant it.[21]

The Taft family operated like a kind of court, deliberating before delivering verdicts on Taft's career. This wasn't a royal court dominated by one man. It was a judicial court, where the opinion of the majority held. Taft abided by the verdict of his brothers, half brothers, and especially his wife—Nellie was a Marie Antoinette and Count de Vergennes in one.

Nellie did not share her husband's love for courts, or his reverence for the judiciary. Her passions were politics, power, and the presidency. She feared that if the couple remained in Cincinnati due to his lifetime appointment as a judge, they would be "fixed in a groove."[22] Like Taft's brothers, she believed that her husband could make it all the way to the White House. They were the ones who pushed Taft to accept McKinley's offer to go to Manila. Nellie described her husband stepping down from a lifetime appointment as a judge as "the hardest thing he ever did."[23]

Taft had never been an executive before he governed the Philippines. He was not a charismatic leader or confident decision-maker. He was more familiar with consensus building and deliberations within a courtroom than public speaking. But now he had to administer thousands of islands with a diverse population of 7 million people. An overweight man from Ohio, he was also ill-suited to tropical climates. While overseas, he suffered heatstrokes, and on one occasion, he nearly drowned.[24]

But Taft was devoted to his work. He was appalled by the conditions on the islands, and he requested more resources from Washington. He put in place new public health measures. He instituted a civilian government and a legal system modeled on U.S. courts. The islands were making real gains under his leadership, and he was becoming popular with the local population.[25] He was occasionally spotted riding a water buffalo. At times, he enjoyed himself. After a day of recreation, he wrote to Secretary of War Elihu Root, "Stood trip well. Rode horseback twenty-five miles." "How is the horse," Root replied to the three-hundred-pound governor-general.[26]

He was doing well, but Taft wasn't going to stay in Manila forever. Whenever rumors of a Supreme Court vacancy spread, the first name on reporters' lips was Taft. When a spot did open up, with the death of associate Justice Horace Gray in 1902, it looked like his moment had come.[27]

President McKinley was no more. He'd been assassinated in September 1901, just two months after Taft went to the Philippines. The late president never got to keep his promise to put Taft on the bench. But the new president, Theodore Roosevelt, was Taft's friend. He was ready to make good on his predecessor's pledge. Roosevelt sent a telegram to Taft, informing him that he was going to nominate him to the Court. "I greatly hope you will accept," the president wrote. "Would appreciate early reply."[28]

The reply was not what Roosevelt expected. For his entire life, Taft had been waiting for such a telegram. But he'd have to wait a while longer. The timing was not right. "Great honor deeply appreciated," he told Roosevelt in what must have been a painful reply. "Look forward to time when I can accept such an offer but even if it is certain that it can never be repeated I must now decline."[29]

Taft had gone to the Philippines on the insistence of his family and the president. But the decision to stay was his. He believed that he had a job to do, and he wanted to see it done. He told Nellie that he "would not for a place on that bench give up the work in the Philippines."[30]

This was a hard choice. "All his life, [his] first ambition had been to attain the Supreme Bench. . . . [H]e wanted it as strongly as a man can ever want anything," Nellie wrote.[31] His family was surprised. Taft wrote to his half brother Charles to explain himself. He was needed abroad. From 1899 until 1902, Filipinos led by Emilio Aguinaldo had fought against the United States, preferring independence to a change in colonial rulers from the Spanish to the Americans. In those three years, more than four thousand American and twenty thousand Filipino combatants died, not to mention tens of thousands of civilians lost to disease and violence. Taft was now responsible for organizing a civilian government, and for moving the archipelago forward from the brutality it had experienced. He knew that his departure from the

Philippines would be "[c]onsidered by the Filipinos as an indication that severe and unpopular measures were about to be put in force."[32]

Theodore Roosevelt was not one to take no for an answer. When another vacancy came up on New Year's Day 1903, when Justice George Shiras, in poor health and in his seventies, announced he'd retire, Roosevelt wrote to Taft again. The president was apologetic. "I am awfully sorry, old man," he wrote, "but . . . I find that I shall have to bring you home and put you on the Supreme Court."[33]

This was Roosevelt's second time asking, and this time he'd done his homework. He'd spoken with Taft's family to ensure they'd support a decision to return to Washington. Taft wrote to his brother that he knew he would likely have to say yes this time. The *Washington Times* reported that Taft would be seated on the Court "within a few months."[34]

The news that Taft was likely leaving leaked, and it soon flooded all over Manila. This time, the Filipino people were the ones who objected, and they made their opinions known with public demonstrations calling for Taft to stay. Crowds of Filipinos gathered in the streets, imploring him not to go. One morning, he and Nellie were awakened by a band playing outside their palace window, as nearly eight thousand people held up signs in English, Spanish, and Tagalog saying "We want Taft!" Taft described watching these displays as the "proudest and happiest" of his career.[35]

The crowd in Manila could be heard all the way in Washington. Prominent Filipinos informed President Roosevelt that Taft was the only one "able to count upon the cooperation of all political parties," and they would be "deeply hurt by the departure of Taft." Meanwhile, telegrams, letters, and cables poured into the White House from politicians, political bosses, and concerned citizens who wanted Taft to remain at his post. After reading them, Roosevelt sent a note to Taft: "All right, stay where you are. . . . I shall appoint someone else to the Court." He had no other option than to let Taft stay.[36]

Taft had been offered his dream job twice. He'd said no twice. It was supremely unlikely that lightning would strike three times. But it did.

But the next job offer he got wasn't on the Supreme Court. Secretary of War Elihu Root, a critical figure at the turn of the century who was every bit as responsible for America's expanding role in the world as the commander in chief, was stepping down from his post after more than four years in the job. With such an important vacancy, Roosevelt needed a prominent figure and an ally in the position. He needed Taft. And this time, Taft had to say yes.

The Taft family was thrilled. He and Nellie would be back in Washington. And it wasn't hard to imagine a secretary of war becoming president. Roosevelt knew this wasn't what Taft wanted, and he chuckled as he called his friend back to the capital. "If only there were three of you! Then I would have put one of you on the Supreme Court . . . one of you as Secretary of War . . . and one of you permanently as governor of the Philippines."[37]

It soon became clear that Taft's tenure at the War Department was preparation for the White House. Taft's responsibilities touched every part of the federal government, and he assumed new duties every time Roosevelt left Washington, as he liked to do for long trips to the Rocky Mountains and the Southwest. When he left town, the president would ask Taft to "sit on the lid" in the capital. Historian Bill Severn describes Secretary of War Taft as the "President's executive assistant, policy adviser, legal counselor, arbitrator, trouble-fixer, political sales-man, personal diplomat, good-will ambassador, and sometimes acting Secretary of State. Sort of a substitute President."[38] When Secretary of State John Hay died in 1905, Taft assumed many of those duties as well.[39] Everything he did brought him closer to the White House— and further from the Supreme Court.

The 1908 election was the Republicans to lose. Four years prior, Roosevelt had won reelection against the Democrat Alton Parker—a judge—in a landslide. He could have won a full second term in his own right, but he pledged not to run again. It was time for his successor— Taft.[40]

There was one more chance for Taft to get off the path to the White House. With Justice Henry Brown ready to retire in 1906, he could have been the man for the hour. Senator Henry Cabot Lodge of Massachusetts, who had presidential ambitions himself, told Roosevelt that the Court needed Taft. What was required, Lodge said somewhat cheekily, given Taft's weight, was "a big man—one who would fill the public eye and one in whom the public had confidence."[41]

This was Taft's last chance not to be president. With the White House finally within reach, the Taft family court didn't want him to give it up. They rallied in opposition to Lodge. Horace Taft in particular thought that this was his brother's moment for the White House. So did Mrs. Taft.[42] It was always a bad idea to bet against the wishes of the Taft family.

There was only one other person who could save Taft from the White House: Theodore Roosevelt. He was the most powerful American alive, and he was the man who could decide the fate of any potential nominee in 1908. Taft trusted him and did what he advised. In Washington, there was a saying that "T.A.F.T." stood for "take advice from Theodore."[43]

Up until that point, Roosevelt had positioned Taft as his natural successor, but he hadn't closed the door on putting his friend on the Supreme Court. He told Taft that he didn't have to decide what he wanted immediately. The president invited the Tafts to dinner at the White House. Sensing the tension in the room, Roosevelt teased his guests. He invented a story and told them that he'd recently met a fortune teller who'd said to him, "I see a man weighing three hundred and fifty pounds. There is something hanging over his head. . . . At one time it looks like the presidency, then again it looks like the chief justiceship."[44]

"Make it the chief justiceship," begged Mr. Taft. "Make it the presidency," pleaded Mrs. Taft.[45] The dinner ended, and shortly thereafter the Tafts held what the New York Times described as a "family council" to decide William Howard Taft's fate. Would he "retire from the world" by joining the Supreme Court? Or would he be president?[46] Those who knew the family dynamics understood that Taft would be a bystander in this conversation. The public speculated. The New York Sun opined in March 1906 that it was a shame that Taft couldn't split the baby on this one, as after all, it was "impossible, under the Constitution and laws, to cut Mr. Taft in two!"[47]

As always, Nellie Taft took charge. She spoke privately to President Roosevelt and informed him in no uncertain terms that Taft was meant for the White House, not the Court. Sure enough, that August Taft wrote to Roosevelt, "I shall not accept the vacancy made by [Justice] Brown."[48]

Even though the nomination was his, Taft didn't jump into the political fray. He was not eager for the fight. He told the Republican Party leadership that he wasn't seeking the nomination, but if nominated, he would accept it.[49] He likely held out hope that Lodge or another contender would move in. But with Roosevelt backing him, there was no serious challenger to Taft.

The party rallied behind Taft. At the Republican convention in Chicago, he won the nomination to a "deafening roar" that had as much to do with Roosevelt as it did with him.[50] But in his acceptance speech, Taft did not sound triumphant. Instead of trumpeting his triumph, he spoke of the "responsibility" that the nomination "impose[d]," not the words of an enthusiastic candidate.[51] His mood did not change in the lead up to the November election. Rather, he told a friend that "the next four months are going to be kind of a nightmare for me."[52]

The nightmare ended with a Taft victory over William Jennings Bryan. Taft won nearly twice as much support in the Electoral College as did Bryan.[53] Though Taft was a Republican, Grover Cleveland would have been thrilled by the outcome.

Victory did not improve Taft's mood. After the election, one observer noted that he looked like a man "whose job had got him down even before he tackled it." The president-elect wondered if in four years his friends might not congratulate him, but instead "shake their heads and say 'poor Bill.'"[54]

Taft had said no to the Court three times. It was unlikely he'd ever be asked again. Former presidents do not become Supreme Court justices. But he wasn't in control. As his youngest son, Charles, said of his father, "Ma wants him to . . . be President."[55] That was that.

PRESIDENTIAL MISFIT

Taft was now the president. But he did not like being a politician. He'd never run for office before—he'd been appointed to every government job he'd ever held. The 1908 election was the first he'd ever run, let alone won.

He was different from a rarefied group of predecessors who'd never held elected office before the presidency. They'd all won wars, from George Washington to Zachary Taylor and Ulysses S. Grant. They were popular figures with popular followings of their own. Taft was not. Though 52 percent of the voting public had pulled the lever for him, that was as much about Theodore Roosevelt's standing and Nellie Taft's ambition as it was about Taft's charm.

Going into the job, he knew that it would not be easy, and he also didn't think it would be much fun. The night before his inauguration, the president-elect and his wife slept in the Blue Room of the White House, a rare privilege made possible by their friendship with the Roosevelts.[56] Nellie could hardly get a moment's rest as she anticipated the next day's event. While her dreams were about to come true, her husband's were not. The next day, they woke up to a terrible blizzard. When he looked out the window, Taft joked that he'd "always said it would be a cold day [in hell] when [he] got to be president of the United States."[57]

But Nellie was not bothered by the weather. She was ecstatic to have made it to exactly where she'd always wanted to be. She was the first First Lady to ride with the president in his carriage from the Capitol to the White House, a sign of her enthusiasm and the prominent role she wanted to play. To her, this moment was a kind of "secret elation."[58]

That feeling carried her right into the White House, where she said she felt "as Cinderella must have felt when her mice footmen bowed her into her coach."[59] As First Lady, she'd not only host parties and dignitaries, she'd also join policy debates and play a substantive role in her husband's administration.[60] Mrs. Taft felt at home. But Mr. Taft felt like "a fish out of water." He admitted to himself that, though he was the president, Nellie was in fact "the politician of the family."[61]

An unnatural politician, it became clear that Taft was ill-suited to life in the White House. He couldn't remember the names of the hundreds of people he met. He had thin skin, a fact noted by his aides, including Archie Butt, a holdover from Roosevelt.[62] And he always thought about his predecessor—when the White House staff beckoned him with a "Mr. President," he'd often look around the room, expecting to see TR.[63]

Taft was unlike previous presidents in how he understood his new role as well. As constitutional scholar Jeffrey Rosen notes, Taft was "the only president to approach the office in constitutional terms above all."[64] Roosevelt had tried to use the bully pulpit to push Congress in one direction or another, proposing and advocating for specific policies on everything from conservation, to antitrust, to foreign policy. Taft did not. He believed in a constitutionally limited role for his office, and that all legislative power belonged with Congress, not the president. When Congress debated tariffs, he didn't call members telling them how to vote. Instead, he issued a short, 340-word statement that simply reemphasized the importance of the matter: "The less time given to other subjects of legislation in this session," he advised, "the better for the country."[65]

Without the president telling them what to do, Congress debated and modified tariffs on their own.[66] Because Taft didn't push for their preferred outcome, his supporters grew frustrated. They wanted Roosevelt, a man who would deliver.[67] But Taft was always thinking about the limits the Constitution placed on him as president. The public saw him acting more like a jurist—deliberating, debating, and rarely deciding—than an executive.[68] This dissatisfaction with his conservative approach grew, and Roosevelt came to think that his chosen successor was "a good lieutenant, but . . . a poor captain."[69]

The Republican Party was beginning to split between two men with two different ideas of the Constitution and the role of the president. While Taft's limited approach was becoming clearer, Roosevelt made it known that he thought the commander in chief had sweeping powers, and was only forbidden to act when the Constitution explicitly said so. The split deepened, and though Taft was prepared to build on Roosevelt's legacy, he thought the main responsibility lay with Congress.[70]

When he didn't act forcefully enough, Roosevelt viewed him as weak. But when he did take action, Roosevelt grew almost as irate. This was the case when Taft took on what Roosevelt called the "Good Trusts," like U.S. Steel, but it came to a head over personnel as much as policy.[71]

When he became president, Taft kept most of Roosevelt's team, including members of the cabinet, in place. But he didn't keep the team for long. He replaced all but two Roosevelt cabinet members within a few months of taking office. Instead of Roosevelt men, Taft surrounded himself with a handpicked group of corporate lawyers.[72]

The true affront to Roosevelt was Taft's decision to replace James Garfield—the secretary of the interior and the son of the twentieth president. Taft nominated Richard Ballinger, the former mayor of Seattle and incumbent commissioner of the General Land Office. It was clear that Ballinger was no Roosevelt ally, and as he'd have significant say over a policy area that the former president had made his mark on, Roosevelt was furious about the nomination.[73]

The conservation movement owes its start to Theodore Roosevelt. He launched America's system of public lands and national parks, and he remains America's most famous conservationist. These parks and the associated legislation were a significant part of his legacy, and Garfield was his chosen steward. Taft was not the world's leading conservationist, though he was nearly as committed to the cause as his predecessor—after all, Taft set aside 8.5 million acres of land for federal protection and created ten national parks. But Roosevelt wanted his man in the job.[74]

Roosevelt wasn't the only person upset by the nomination. Gifford Pinchot, the chief forester and another Roosevelt holdover, was suspicious. An article in Collier's appeared with the headline "The White Washing of Ballinger," and the even more damaging subtitle: "Are the Guggenheims in Charge of the Department of the Interior?" Scandal was in the air, and a congressional hearing was coming.[75]

The hearing would feature a young lawyer named Louis Brandeis. Brandeis was the chief investigator, looking into alleged conflicts of interest in coal land leases in Alaska that implicated Ballinger.[76] Taft stood by him. He was glad when Congress exonerated him in a partisan vote of 7–5.[77] But Pinchot didn't let go of his anger. He set sail for the French Riviera to meet Roosevelt and tell him what had happened. Just back from a safari through Africa, Roosevelt was now ready to play a very dangerous political game.[78]

For the moment, Taft's mind was away from politics, and even the courts. He was dealing with another crisis. Nellie had fallen during a dinner party on May 17, 1909, aboard the USS Sylph, the president's yacht.[79] It turned out that she'd had a terrible stroke, and she'd lost control of the muscles in her right arm and leg. She had trouble speaking. When he saw what had happened to his wife, Taft could barely console himself. She had worked so hard for his presidency and it had nearly killed her. Archie Butt said he had "never seen greater suffering or pain on a man's face" as when William Howard Taft looked at Nellie.[80]

Two First Ladies had already died in the White House, Letitia Tyler in 1842 and Caroline Harrison in 1892. Nellie Taft might have been the third. Taft had never wanted the presidency, and the thought that he'd lost not only his path to the Court, but also perhaps his wife, was terrible. He cared for Nellie, nursing her back to health.[81] While the First Lady was recovering and Roosevelt was plotting, Taft felt more isolated and alone than ever.

Confrontation

There was no light at the end of the tunnel for Taft, or for his presidency. His predecessor was preparing to run against him. That contest between Roosevelt and Taft would not only destroy their friendship, it would also threaten the Republican Party's decades-long hold on the White House going back to the Civil War, which had only been broken by Grover Cleveland. It would usher in a new era of progressive politics. It would also witness Taft—a man who had never wanted to be president—fighting for the White House with everything he had.

Before they were presidents, Taft and Roosevelt were friends. Born a year apart, they met in Washington when they were in their thirties. Taft was the solicitor general under President Harrison, and Roosevelt served at the helm of the Civil Service Commission. At the time, Taft lived at 5 Dupont Circle, down the street from Roosevelt. Many mornings, they'd walk to work together.[82]

That was all over. It became clear that Roosevelt was displeased with Taft during the 1910 midterms, when the former president told the public that he needed to "help the Republican Party to win at the polls this Fall," so that Taft's possible renomination in 1912 might at least "be of use."[83]

Differences between Taft and Roosevelt came into public view. Roosevelt railed against Supreme Court decisions on labor rights, which

Taft thought inappropriate and called "an attack upon our system." A senator from Ohio named Warren Harding, a party man loyal to the president, wrote that Roosevelt was "utterly without conscience and regard for truth." As the 1912 election drew nearer, Roosevelt laid out his own platform, which he declared a "New Nationalism." When he read what Roosevelt had to say, Taft mourned, "I don't know whether we are drifting, but I do know where every real thinking patriot will stand in the end, and that's by the Constitution."[84]

The public was not happy. The Democrats won seats in the Senate and a majority in the House in the 1910 midterms, with 230 members to the Republicans' 162. Taft was weak and a politically carnivorous Roosevelt smelled blood in the water.[85]

The Taft presidency had brought nothing but misery. It nearly killed Nellie. Taft's friendship with Roosevelt was over. He was losing his once-sterling reputation. He had two years left in the White House. It felt like a criminal sentence.

With Taft readying for reelection, the once-unthinkable came into view—Roosevelt, the most popular Republican in America, could challenge the incumbent president and win. The idea took on, and a popular political cartoon depicted Roosevelt, dressed in his old Rough Rider uniform, carrying a Big Stick, standing near his old boxing gloves. Its caption read "The Question—Can a Champion Come Back?"[86] Another magazine asked, "Is the Republican Party Breaking Up?"[87] Even Taft wrote, "If you were to remove Roosevelt's skull you would find written on his brain '1912.'"[88]

The president was worried. He'd never been healthy, but he gained even more weight, and he tossed and turned at night, suffering from sleep apnea.[89] During the day, he played golf in an attempt to distract himself, but whenever his swing was off, he grew angry. He tried to get out of Washington as much as he could, accepting invitations whenever possible so as to leave the capital and politics behind.[90]

The lines were drawn on February 21, 1912, when Roosevelt declared to a group of reporters, "My hat is in the ring, the fight is on, and I am stripped to the buff." Knowing that he'd likely suffer a knockout blow, Taft told his brother Horace he would "accept that and go through the campaign and be beaten like a gentleman." He added,

"I can get along with one term. A second term is not essential to my happiness."[91]

The president didn't want to go gently into that good night. A second Roosevelt presidency would be very different from the first, a possibility that concerned Taft. When he gave another speech attacking the Supreme Court, even calling out Justice William Moody by name, Taft said his old friend had become "a great danger and menace to the country." In turn, Roosevelt had taken to calling Taft names of his own, labeling his old friend an "apostate" and a "floppy-souled creature."[92]

Popular figures had the potential to overwhelm parties, and Roosevelt was beloved by the public. When he showed up at the Republican convention that year, he was greeted with rapturous applause.[93] But he was not in charge. Though Taft had fewer supporters among the general public, he was still the head of the Republican Party. With Elihu Root's help, he won seventy-one contested delegates, and with them the nomination.[94] The man whom President Taft chose to nominate him at the 1912 Republican National Convention was none other than Ohio senator Warren Harding, who announced Taft's name over the "jeers, hisses, and taunts" of Roosevelt supporters.[95]

Roosevelt was defeated. But he wasn't done, and cried out to his supporters, "We have been robbed." He pledged to build his own party.[96] This would be a Progressive, or Bull Moose, party. The War of 1912 was on.

The perfect metaphor for the Taft presidency came into view in the spring of 1912. After much anticipation for its maiden voyage, the ocean liner *Titanic* crashed into an iceberg and sank to the bottom of the Atlantic. The president's aide, Archie Butt, was on board, along with many of the eminences of the day. Henry Adams captured the political mood in the White House at the time when he said, "I do not know whether Taft or the *Titanic* is likely to be the furthest reaching disaster," a far too soon comparison between a sinking ship and a soon-to-be-defeated candidate—the former having taken lives, the latter believed to be followed by the loss of livelihoods.[97]

It looked like the only thing that could save the Taft presidency was a miracle. On October 14, 1912, he almost got one. John F. Schrank, a mentally disturbed Bavarian under the impression that William

McKinley's ghost wanted him to kill Roosevelt, shot Theodore in the chest. The bullet broke through a metal case and a fifty-page speech folded inside Roosevelt's pocket before lodging in his chest. Roosevelt was wounded, but in dramatic fashion, the Bull Moose finished the speech before heading to the hospital. It was an event that became a part of Roosevelt's legend.[98]

Roosevelt continued to campaign. The *New York Times* believed that, were he to win, it would be a disaster, and the paper editorialized that it was of the utmost importance that Wilson come in first and Taft second. Otherwise, America would witness the "collapse of a great party" and the end of the GOP.[99] The idea that Taft had any chance of winning, however, looked fanciful.

The most tragic casualty of the 1912 election was Vice President James Sherman, who died on October 30, 1912. With the election just days away, there was no time to choose a new running mate for Taft or to reprint the ballots. For that reason, Sherman's name remained when voters went to the polls.[100] As the American people decided who should be in the White House, the Republican Party offered them Taft, a political dead man, and a literal corpse.

The lifeless Republican Party, headed by Taft, was up against formidable candidates. Not only was the Bull Moose Theodore Roosevelt running, but two of Grover Cleveland's old nemeses were also on the ballot. Eugene V. Debs, of the Pullman Strike, was the Socialist Party's candidate. And Woodrow Wilson, the New Jersey governor and former Princeton president, was the Democrat's nominee. Three of the candidates in 1912 won the presidency at some point in their lives. The fourth, Debs, would later be jailed by that year's victor.

The results delivered were a stunning defeat for Taft. He won 23 percent of the vote and carried only Utah and Vermont. Meanwhile, Roosevelt won six states and eighty-eight electoral votes, coming in second. Debs rallied 6 percent of the vote, a distant fourth.[101] And Woodrow Wilson, with just 42 percent of the popular vote, won forty states and 435 electoral votes. This was more than enough to make him the next president, even if the majority of the American people had voted for someone else.

The only man running who never wanted to be president took

his defeat in stride. "The vote in favor of Mr. Roosevelt was greater than I expected," Taft said, "and to that extent the result was a disappointment."[102] But he was satisfied that he'd accomplished his main objective—Roosevelt wouldn't be president, and the Republican Party might have a chance to return to its pre-progressive ideas. With that in mind, Taft was ready to leave the White House. As he told Nellie, "I have held the office of President once, and that is more than most men have. . . . I am content to retire from it with a consciousness that I have done the best I could."[103]

He was about to leave the White House, but Taft also left a mark on the federal government, in many ways more so than Roosevelt. In one term, Taft started more antitrust actions than had Roosevelt in his nearly eight years in office. He'd set aside more land for conservation. Ironically, his greatest impact may have been on the Supreme Court itself.

In his four years, Taft nominated six justices, more than any other president in a single term, before or since. He'd once jokingly told his nominees, "Damn you, if any of you die, I'll disown you!"[104] When he named Edward Douglass White chief justice, he did so almost wistfully. "It does seem strange," the president said, "that the one place in government which I would have liked to fill I am forced to give to another. . . . There is nothing I would have loved more than being chief justice."[105]

Taft may not have been an adept politician, but he was still a savvy operator. In choosing White, he hadn't given up on his dream. White was sixty-five years old. The other contender for the job was Charles Evans Hughes, an associate justice who was also the youngest on the Court, at just forty-eight.[106] Taft knew that White wouldn't be around forever. Hughes might outlast both of them. Now if there was ever a friendly Republican president in office again, Taft would have a shot.

PROFESSOR TAFT

President Taft hadn't given up hope that he'd one day become Chief Justice Taft. But for that to happen, the stars would have to align in a seemingly improbable way. He'd need another Republican in the White House—and it couldn't be Roosevelt or anyone from Roosevelt's wing of the party. He'd need Chief Justice White to step aside, or die, at just the right time. He'd need to remain in the party's good graces. It couldn't take too long—no president of either party, except for Taft, would nominate an old man to a lifetime appointment on the Supreme Court. And, never a healthy man, Taft would have to maintain physical viability.

The contest against Roosevelt had been painful, both personally and politically. But the battle had given Taft new confidence. Standing up to Roosevelt showed a political backbone that had been lacking in his career up until that point. He was defeated, but he'd fought on his own terms. He'd held back what he called the "Rooseveltian menace." As he told Nellie, after that, he was "not going to be pushed anymore."[107] He'd been president, and now Nellie couldn't push him around, either.

William Howard Taft didn't want to run for office ever again. Even if he had, he'd never make it back to the White House. When a few supporters suggested he consider running in 1916, he joked—maybe thinking of Roosevelt as well as himself—that former presidents have no place in the White House. Better that they should be given "a dose of chloroform or of the fruit of the lotus tree" to "secure the country from the troublesome fear that the occupant could ever come back."[108]

A Democrat was in the White House, but at least Roosevelt wasn't. Though Taft and Woodrow Wilson were on opposite ends of the political spectrum, he was relieved to be handing over power to someone else. He felt free as "a dead politician," even if Nellie would miss it.[109]

Taft came in third place in 1912, and he was no longer popular. But he was still respected. After the bitterness of the 1912 election, the New York *Sun* predicted that Taft's standing would recover, and that "the name of President Taft will stand in the list of those Presidents . . . who served this country far better and more wisely than the people could see." The same paper declared that Roosevelt—who was still very much in the arena—had perpetrated the "brutal wrecking of the party to which he owed all his honors in the past."[110]

While the *Sun* was wrong that Roosevelt's standing would not recover, it was right that the Republican Party was in shambles, and might stay that way for a generation. With the GOP split and the Democratic Party in charge, with control of the Senate and a commanding majority in the House, American politics was entering a new phase. Both Taft and Roosevelt were on the outs.

Wilson didn't get a majority of the vote in 1912. But despite that fact, he said that his victory was "much more than the success of a party."[111] It was a transformational moment in America, and the new president pledged "to lift everything that concerns our life as a Nation to the light that shines from the hearthfire of every man's conscience and vision of the right." With a religious zeal, he would transform the role of president into the chief executive of the modern administrative state.[112]

For now, none of that was of concern to Taft. He was on his way to Georgia for twenty-five days "of almost unalloyed sweetness" and plenty of golf. He would read the newspaper over his breakfast, and a smile would creep over his face. He told friends that he was ready to "watch the playing of the game down there in Washington, without any responsibility of my own."[113] Now that was all someone else's problem.

With a new Democratic administration in Washington, there was no clear role for Taft, and no way to the Supreme Court. But he didn't want to golf for the rest of his days. He had three objectives. First, he needed money. Second, he wanted to return to the law and study America's changing politics to push back against threats to constitutional government. And third, he wanted to restore the Republican Party to its pre-Roosevelt positions, both because he disagreed with his predecessor's more nationalist policies, and because he knew that a Republican Party dominated by Roosevelt would never nominate him to the bench.

Money came first. Taft was out of practice as a lawyer, having been a judge since his early thirties. He didn't want to join a firm. Fortunately, his alma mater, Yale, saved him from the job hunt. His $5,000 salary as a Yale professor wasn't much, especially compared to the $75,000 he'd earned as president. But he told Yale's president it would be enough. After all, without the White House kitchen staff, he'd be eating less. He lost eighty pounds in eight months and could now dress himself in the morning without a valet's help. He could also sleep peacefully through the night. Life was much better.[114]

Taft was a Yale man through and through, the first in what would become a long line of Yale alumni to become president of the United States. The son of a Yale graduate, he was a member of the class of 1878. When he visited the campus during the 1908 election, the Yale band played a new ditty called "Waltz Me Around Willie" in his honor.[115] Now he was glad to be back on campus just one month after leaving office. He was the newly minted Kent Professor of Law and Legal History. But noting his 340-pound frame, he joked that he was "afraid that a Chair would not be adequate, but that if [Yale] would provide a Sofa of Law, it might be all right."[116] During faculty meetings, he had to borrow a three-hundred-pound campus policeman's armchair because no other seat could hold him. It was clear that he didn't mind jokes about his weight. He now had a thicker skin, in addition to his large gut.

The university life suited him. He'd arrived on campus too late in the spring semester to teach, but prepared eight lectures titled "Some Questions of Modern Government" on everything from national defense to voting rights.[117] The women's suffrage movement had taken off during the Taft presidency. During his own tenure, President Roosevelt had described himself as "not an enthusiastic advocate for women's suffrage."[118] But his Progressive Party backed expanding the franchise in 1912. The winner that year, Woodrow Wilson, was opposed. He went so far as to argue that the "type of woman who took an active part in the suffrage agitation was totally abhorrent."[119] It was much to Wilson's dismay, then, that his own inauguration was overshadowed by thousands of suffragettes, who marched up Pennsylvania Avenue and braved jeers and assaults while making their "Great Demand" for a constitutional amendment for women's right to vote.[120]

Never a progressive, Taft was somewhere between Roosevelt and Wilson on women's suffrage. He believed that the Constitution left the matter up to the states, but he nevertheless spoke to the National American Woman Suffrage Association—a move that boosted the cause, even though the president was hissed during his speech because he was unsupportive of its main objective. He later explained that he was "not in favor of suffrage for women until I can be convinced that all women desire it."[121]

By 1915, despite the growing suffrage movement, he still wasn't convinced. He wrote condescendingly in the *Saturday Evening Post* that immediately giving the vote to women would "increase the proportion of the hysterical element of the electorate."[122] As would also be the case with Woodrow Wilson, World War I changed Taft's mind about women's suffrage. Taft didn't drop his attitude toward women's political participation, but he believed that, were women able to vote, his League to Enforce Peace—a progenitor of the League of Nations— might find more support than men were giving it. With that in mind, he wrote, "[M]odern progress requires that women's influence be allowed to exert itself through the ballot."[123]

His views were out of step with the progressive era, but the former president had a career as a public intellectual. He toured the country and gave lectures, sometimes earning $1,000 for each speech, the equivalent of $30,000 in today's figures. He also had a wealthy supporter in Andrew Carnegie, who offered both Taft and Roosevelt a private pension of $25,000 a year.[124] However, they both refused, thinking it would be unseemly for a former president to take the tycoon's money and that it might complicate a future Supreme Court nomination.[125]

For the Yale student body, having a former president on campus was a novelty. He graded their papers without a teaching assistant's help. He was well liked, and the student newspaper reported that "more jokes [were] told in his classroom than in any other."[126]

But the novelty wore off after a semester or two. He had experience, but Taft had never been a teacher. He was unprepared to deal with rowdy students who chewed gum and smoked in class, if they didn't skip his lectures altogether. Taft found that students didn't have to listen to him, and they didn't want to, not even in his required course on constitutional law. Some students made bets on whom he'd call on to recite a boring lecture. Many cheated on their papers and exams. Taft realized he had to change his teaching style when his top students voiced their concerns. The president needed to entertain.[127]

Teaching was a humbling experience for Taft. He wanted to be treated like any other professor, not as a former president above fair criticism. He became a part of campus life, attending football games and social events. He coached the debate team. Away from politics, he now had a chance to "take little excursions into various new fields of knowledge, and welcom[ed] the challenge of exploring new ideas."[128]

He had other pursuits as well, and became president of the American Bar Association. He used that position to fight against the recall of judges.[129] He wrote about politics and the future of the Republican Party, not with an eye toward running again, but keeping in mind that it was always possible that Roosevelt would make another try at the White House, a possibility that would doom his prospects of joining the Court.[130]

His lectures became a book that took on the progressivism of both Roosevelt and Wilson. He argued that "popular government is not an end. It is a means of enabling people to live together in communities, municipals, state and national."[131] He came out forcefully against the Wilsonian idea that the president is the "steward of the people," uniquely empowered to enact whatever policies he wants because he and the vice president were the only nationally elected leaders and so had a special kind of legitimacy. Instead, he argued for a constitutionalist vision of the separation of powers.[132] Jeffrey Rosen argues that Taft's postpresidential writings offered "an invaluable (and still relevant) primer on the constitutional scope of the president's power."[133]

Even with a Democrat in office, Taft was hopeful. He believed that Wilson had "gotten off on the right foot" in his first few months. That opinion began to change when he saw that Wilson was moving to transfer the government of the Philippines to the Filipinos, a move Taft believed was necessary and would come, but was premature.[134]

There was no clear alternative to Wilson. Taft knew he wouldn't win if he ran again, and he didn't want the job. He wondered if he could follow in John Quincy Adams's footsteps and run for Congress, maybe even one day leading the Judiciary Committee. But he dismissed that idea. It would be better, he decided, if he "serve[d] in the ranks," resurrecting the party and defending his ideas.[135]

Taft wouldn't be on the ballot in 1916, but he wanted to make sure that Roosevelt wasn't, either. His predecessor remained the most powerful figure in the GOP, even if many conservative Republicans were still bitter about 1912. In Chicago that year, both the Republican Party and Roosevelt's Progressives held conventions. The two conventions might nominate two candidates, once again handing the presidency to Wilson. Instead, the Progressives wanted unity, and proposed Roosevelt as the single candidate.

The Progressives rallied, and they cheered for Roosevelt for ninety-three minutes.[136] But when Roosevelt refused to be their candidate, the Progressives collapsed. Most came around to Charles Evans Hughes, the man that Taft had made a Supreme Court justice.[137] Senator Harding delivered a keynote speech at the Republican convention, but it received little attention. The *New York Times* dismissed the little-known politician, saying, "[I]t is not necessary to burden one's memory . . . if one is merely trying to remember the names of people likely to be president."[138]

The nomination of Hughes pleased Taft. First, Hughes wasn't Roosevelt. Second, he had the potential to bring together the conservative and progressive wings of the party. When Taft had nominated Hughes to the bench in 1910, he had done so in part to remove a potential rival from the presidential field in 1912, and to ensure that Hughes would never become chief justice. If Hughes won the White House, the man that Taft had put on the Supreme Court a few years prior might return the favor and put him on the bench.[139]

There was no guarantee the Republican Party could unite to defeat Wilson. Taft's old friend Elihu Root took up that cause, working to reconcile the only two living former Republican presidents. At first, the idea of burying the hatchet with Taft did not sit well with Roosevelt—the bitterness from 1912 was still in the air. But Roosevelt agreed to make a joint appearance, and even to shake hands. The two met at the Union League Club in New York on October 3, 1916, a month before the election. It was clear that the animosity between Roosevelt and Taft remained "unchanged and unreconciled." Far from an Adams and Jefferson rapprochement, their reunion was faux friendship that didn't fool anyone, and the *Times* described the meeting as showing "a phantasmagoria of Republican unity." Roosevelt continued to fume, and called Hughes a "whiskered Wilson."[140]

The campaign came down to a single issue: war. Wilson campaigned on a platform to keep the United States out of war in Europe.

Hughes's position on the matter was ambiguous—the voters didn't know what they would get with a man many mocked as Charles "Evasive" Hughes. But it was certain at least that he was not Wilson. For many Americans, that would be enough. But the Republican Party was fighting an uphill battle in 1916. Taft believed it would be a landslide for the Democrats.[141]

He was wrong. Wilson won 277 electoral votes to Hughes's 254. The election came down to 3,773 votes in California and the decision of one man—Governor Hiram Johnson, Theodore Roosevelt's progressive running mate in 1912—not to endorse Hughes.[142] Without Johnson's support, Hughes failed to carry California, and Wilson won reelection. The Republican Party remained in the political wilderness, and so did Taft.

A WARTIME FORMER PRESIDENT

War changed everything, for the country and for Taft. Europeans had been fighting and dying in the trenches of Europe since 1914. But the United States under Woodrow Wilson remained neutral. Wilson had won the 1916 election with the slogan "He Kept Us Out of War."[143] But it was becoming clear that he couldn't keep that up forever. A year before the election, in May 1915, German U-boats torpedoed the *Lusitania*, killing 1,200 people aboard, including 123 Americans.[144] Three days later, Wilson told the American people that they were "Too Proud to Fight."[145] But Germany resumed unrestricted submarine warfare in February 1917,[146] and the United Kingdom revealed the Zimmermann Telegram, a German scheme to invade the United States with Mexico.[147] Neutrality was no longer an option. Less than a month after his second inauguration, the first of what would become 4 million Americans were headed for Europe.[148]

Taft was now a wartime former president. He'd never approved of President Wilson's progressivism, but he believed that when the United States was at war, he owed the commander in chief his service.[149] After the *Lusitania*, he'd sent the president a letter expressing his support, noting the "heavy weight of responsibility" that the president now bore.[150]

The fact that Wilson delayed military action after the *Lusitania*, and that he had not spent the last year and a half arming and training more American soldiers for the fighting to come, disappointed Taft. In 1917, the American army stood at just 127,000 men, comparable to the armed forces of Chile.[151] By hesitating to strengthen the armed forces, Taft believed that Wilson had "exposed this country to the charge of weakness and vacillation" and "subjected the nation to additional humiliation."[152]

Whatever their past differences, Taft was ready to be of service to the wartime Wilson administration. He had his chance when more than four hundred labor strikes in the first month of the war effort threatened to cut off supplies to America's troops. Facing labor unrest, Wilson invited Taft to serve as chairman of the National War Labor Board (NWLB), an entity meant to settle disputes between management and labor.[153]

Based on his record, many suspected that the former president would be a reliable voice for business interests and work against the interest of labor. But during wartime, he wasn't focused on favoritism. His goal was to "arrange a truce between labor and capital in this country."[154] He stationed himself in Washington, worked hard, and ensured that every document put in front of him came before the panel (1,245 cases in total). He toured the country, speaking to factory workers and chairing town halls. His fourteen-month stint on the board put him in closer contact with working Americans than he'd been at any other point in his life. He helped to address labor's concerns, averting an estimated 138 strikes. And he recognized the value of labor during wartime, witnessed the often-appalling conditions in America's factories, especially in the South, and came to sympathize with calls for "a living wage."[155]

Taft had never been seen as a voice for labor. One surprised pro-Roosevelt reporter said that Taft was "rapidly becoming popular among laboring people." Taft's actions on the labor board were beginning to gain attention in the progressive wing of the party, and the reporter continued by saying that Taft had made himself a plausible nominee to the Court even by a Roosevelt-endorsed president, as "the reasons which formerly made him non-eligible will now be removed."[156]

There was another former president who wanted to serve: Theodore Roosevelt. The Rough Rider asked to be sent to the frontlines
in Europe, and he told Wilson he could raise four divisions to fight
in France. But Wilson said no to what seemed like a preposterous
request by a man stuck in another decade.[157] He may have been right
that Roosevelt had no place in combat, but he alienated a potential ally
when he could have turned a foe into a friend. The refusal likely cost
him Republican support in Congress.[158] Wilson also missed a chance
to send the most prominent Republican alive to the most dangerous
place on earth—a place from which there was no guarantee that Roosevelt would return.[159]

Political Positioning

The war that was supposed to end all wars could not last forever. Having fulfilled his duties on the NWLB, Taft turned his thoughts to the
future. If the Republican Party was going to have a say over any peace
settlement, it would have to have victory in the 1918 midterm elections.

Though Taft had worked with Wilson, it was clear that the president would never reward a Republican—even Taft—with a seat on the
bench. Taft needed a Republican majority in the Senate and a future
Republican president—he also needed to do what he could to ensure
that whoever those Republicans were, they weren't from the Roosevelt
wing.

It was 1918, and Republicans were desperate for a win. There were
rumors that Roosevelt wanted to run for president in 1920. Though
that possibility horrified Taft, he could work with his former friend in
the midterms and think about what came next later.

They came together based on their disapproval, even hatred, of
Woodrow Wilson. They believed the American Expeditionary Force
was needed in Eastern Europe, as well as in the trenches in France.
In Russia, the Bolsheviks and the White Russians were fighting a
civil war, and Taft and Roosevelt advocated for America to intervene
more in support of the White Russians, arguing that the five thousand
troops engaged in the effort were inadequate to tip the scales against
the communist revolution.[160]

Even more disturbing to Taft, who'd once hoped Wilson might put him on the Supreme Court, the president nominated his old nemesis Louis Brandeis. Taft's friend Gus Karger informed him that "the Senate simply gasped" at the nomination, which the former president called an example of Wilson's "devilish ingenuity."[161] The nomination faced opposition, and the *Boston Globe* called Brandeis "a radical, a theorist, impractical, with strong socialistic tendencies."[162] The *New York Times* said that the Court was meant to be a conservative institution, and that the nomination of a progressive like Brandeis might undo the work of Chief Justice John Marshall.[163] The Senate held its first-ever public hearings on a Supreme Court nominee. But after a four-month process, America's next Supreme Court justice, the first Jewish justice in the Court's history, was confirmed, with a vote of 47 in favor, 22 opposed, and 27 abstentions.[164]

Taft was beside himself. Not only was Brandeis anathema to his understanding of the Constitution, but the idea of ever serving with Brandeis in the future was appalling. Now he could never be an associate justice—a peer to Brandeis—he'd have to be chief. The chances of that looked slimmer than ever.[165]

He got back into politics with the help of Will Hays, the chair of the Republican National Committee, who sensed that both Taft and Roosevelt were ready to come out swinging against Wilson. Hays wanted the party to move on from 1912, and he approached Taft about a true reconciliation with Roosevelt, with whom he shared the goal of getting rid of the "miscreant in the White House."[166]

The two former presidents came together at Hays's invitation in May 1918, at the Blackstone Hotel in Chicago. There was no phantasmagoria this time—they embraced in front of a crowd, and cheers from the party faithful filled the room. With November coming, they worked together, pushing for a Republican Congress to advocate a quick and just end to the war. They reviewed and edited each other's speeches and refined their arguments, ready to take on Wilson and the Democrats. They were never going to be fast friends again—but time, ambition, and mutual antipathy toward Wilson were enough to bring them together. There were glimpses of their past selves, and one close observer described the two at the time as "like a pair of schoolboys."[167]

They got what they wanted in 1918. The midterm election—held in the midst of the deadly Spanish influenza[168]—yielded a resounding Republican victory. The party won twenty-five seats in the House and five in the Senate, giving them control of both houses of Congress for the first time since 1908. The results showed that the Republicans would have momentum heading into 1920. They also doomed what Woodrow Wilson wanted to make his greatest legacy.

Wilson wanted to change the world. His goal was to make a new global institution, the League of Nations, to end wars forever. But to succeed, he'd need Republican support, including Taft's. But asking for Republican support was far from Woodrow Wilson's mind when he made his way on a train through the Italian Alps on January 6, 1919, heading for the Peace Conference in Versailles. He intended to negotiate this new League into existence on his own.

The president's train stopped in Modena, Italy. There, an aide handed him a telegram. As he read its contents, a local journalist detected first surprise and then a smile flicker across the president's face. Woodrow Wilson had just learned that Theodore Roosevelt—heartbroken over the death of his son Quentin in Europe and suffering from jungle fever after an ill-fated trip up the Amazon—had passed away. Roosevelt died in his sleep at his home, Sagamore Hill, near Oyster Bay.[169] This was the end of Wilson's greatest rival.

If Wilson was pleased by the news of Roosevelt's passing, the public was not. The nation mourned. Charles Lee, a Roosevelt staffer from his White House days, reported, "I have lost the best friend I have ever had, and the best friend any man ever had." Americans flew flags across the country at half-mast. Five airplanes flew over Sagamore Hill, dropping laurel wreaths on his home.[170]

Two days after his death, Taft arrived at Roosevelt's funeral service at Christ Episcopal Church in Oyster Bay, but the former president didn't know his place. The funeral arrangements were not well done, and at first he sat nearer to the servants than the front with family members and close friends. He did not get up, and he still thought of

Roosevelt as senior to himself. However, Roosevelt's son Archie saw Taft in the back and motioned for him to come up, toward the front of the church, telling him, "You're a dear personal friend and you must come up farther."[171]

Moved, Taft walked between the pews with tears rolling down his cheeks. He made his way to a seat behind Vice President Thomas Marshall and in front of Republican senator Henry Cabot Lodge. This was the place where an old friend belonged.

Taft and Roosevelt did not end as enemies, much to Taft's relief. After the funeral, he wrote to Roosevelt's sister Corinne, "Had [Roosevelt] died in a hostile state of mind toward me, I would have mourned the fact all my life. I loved him always and cherish his memory."[172]

The Final Stretch

Roosevelt's death gave Wilson room to push forward the League of Nations. And it changed Taft's career prospects, as without its greatest standard-bearer, it was less likely that a progressive wing would choose the Republican nominee in 1920. Up until then a supporter of the League of Nations, Taft began to strike a delicate balance.

In May 1915, at the Willard Hotel in Washington, DC, Wilson had declared his intention to build "a feasible assembly of nations." Taft had shared Wilson's vision for a League, and of a world made "safe for democracy."[173]

The League of Nations was once a bipartisan idea. Theodore Roosevelt had declared that "it would be a master stroke if those great Powers honestly bent on peace would form a League of Peace, not only to keep the peace among themselves, but to prevent, by force if necessary, its being broken by others." Taft, a man with significant experience in foreign affairs, agreed, and two months after Wilson's speech, stated, "We think a League of Peace could be formed that would enable nations to avoid war."[174]

In January 1918, Wilson gave his Fourteen Points speech, making the League his goal in any postwar settlement by calling for a "general association of nations."[175] In February 1919, the League of Nations committee of the Peace Conference met to make that idea a reality.[176] The League of Nations became partisan at Versailles.

Wilson had traveled to Paris confident that he could make the League happen. This was the first time a sitting president ever ventured to Europe. He thought that he could do what needed to be done on his own. He did not invite Taft, or any other Republican, to come with him to negotiate the Treaty of Versailles. This was a political miscalculation noted on both sides of the aisle. Eleanor Roosevelt, who accompanied her husband, Franklin, to Paris, later wrote that Wilson "seemed to have very little interest in making himself popular with groups of people whom he touched."[177] After the negotiations, Wilson chose to sail home from France not to Washington or New York, but to Boston, a jab at Republican Massachusetts senator Henry Cabot Lodge, the Republican Senate Majority Leader and chairman of the Foreign Relations Committee, and the man who would emerge as the League's greatest foe.[178]

Even though Wilson had not asked for his help or counsel, Taft said he would still "vote for the covenant [of the League of Nations] as it is, without hesitation." But Republican senators were not as willing to ignore Wilson's slights. Lodge despised the president, saying, "I never expected to hate anyone in politics with the hatred I feel toward Wilson."[179]

He hated not only Wilson but Wilson's treaty, and was concerned about what it would do to American sovereignty and a tradition going back to Washington's Farewell Address that held that America should avoid permanent alliances.[180] Wilson recognized Lodge's position, but dismissed him, insisting that "some of our sovereignty would be surrendered for the good of the world."[181]

The text confirmed Lodge's worst fears. The treaty appeared to be "hastily drafted." The wording of its provisions was not clear. Important provisions were ambiguous and open to interpretation. Of concern was Article X, which committed signatories to protect "the territorial integrity and existing political independence of all Members of the League." The article said that the Council of the League of Nations, not the United States, would decide how that commitment would be met.[182]

This raised questions in Republican senators' minds. Did Article X mean that the Council could send Americans into combat across the globe on its own? What would be the role of Congress in declaring war, then? What did this mean for the power of future American presidents as commanders in chief? Concerned, Lodge circulated a "round-robin" resolution against ratification that was signed by thirty-seven senators. While not a majority, this was still enough to stop the Senate's two-thirds requirement to ratify the Treaty of Versailles.[183]

While Lodge voiced his opposition, Taft remained supportive of the League. But he recognized that the president needed to change course if he wanted Republican votes. Taft spoke with the Republican National Committee about possible revisions to the treaty and said that members should have the option to withdraw from the League after a certain period of time, that Article X be made nonbinding, and that the Monroe Doctrine be endorsed.[184]

These discussions didn't stay secret for long. When Taft's private letters were released, the press accused him of having "abandoned the bandwagon" of support for the League. Wilson's administration stopped engaging him altogether, and Wilson's private secretary, Joseph Tumulty, even said that Taft was no longer a "great statesman," and that his ideas showed he had "degenerated."[185] Wilson returned to Paris for the Peace Conference, but he arrived home again with a treaty that was mostly unchanged.

Despite growing opposition, Wilson was confident in his vision. With the treaty in hand, he walked into the Senate chamber on July 10, 1919, and spoke for forty minutes, calling the Treaty of Versailles "nothing less than a world settlement." No president had personally delivered a treaty to the Senate since 1789, and Wilson's message was not well received.[186]

The president stumbled and stammered while he spoke, the effects of a minor stroke.[187] He tried to be charismatic and channeled his roots as the son of a Southern Presbyterian minister, preaching to the Senate, as he finished, "The stage is set, the destiny disclosed. It has come about by no plan of our conceiving, but by the hand of God who led us into this way. We cannot turn back. . . . The light streams upon the path ahead, and nowhere else." There was only scattered applause.[188]

With Wilson's flag planted, Taft was in a bind. He still believed in the League and had offered more than fifty speeches and opinion pieces in support. As late as January 1919, he'd argued, "[T]he League of Nations is Here. . . . [I]t was up to the leaders and the people to make it a living thing."[189] When Lodge objected, Taft urged the public to ignore the Republican leader, and to discard "the narrow partisanship and the brute willingness of these little Americans in the Senate."[190]

That position was no longer tenable. With Wilson sick and unwilling to compromise, Republican opposition was growing. Taft might have been able to help, but Wilson didn't want him to. With the League's fate in doubt and the 1920 presidential election approaching amid growing Republican opposition, Taft began to abandon his old positions on the League.[191]

Public opinion began to change as Republicans made their case against the League through a series of Senate hearings. In response, Wilson launched what would become a thirty-three-stop tour across the United States to make the case for the League directly to the American people.[192] This was another mistake. Wilson was a second-term president who, though he wanted to run, was not likely to see a third. The president needed votes in the Senate, not in the states. By going around the Senate and directly to the voters, Taft believed, "Wilson [was] playing into [his opponents'] hands."[193] Meanwhile, Lodge released a report laying out his objections and proposing revisions to the Treaty of Versailles.

The League lost its most prominent spokesperson when Wilson suffered another stroke, this one debilitating. After multiple speeches across multiple states, sometimes more than one in a single day, his health failed. In September, Wilson collapsed in Pueblo, Colorado, and his staff rushed him back to Washington.[194] He was barely able to work. First Lady Edith Wilson and the president's doctor, Cary Grayson, took over much of the day-to-day functions of the presidency.

This was a terrible moment for the White House. In private, Secretary of State Robert Lansing discussed whether Wilson was still fit for office and brought up the constitutional provision about the "inability" of the president to "discharge his powers and duties." He wondered if the vice president should take over. But Thomas Marshall had no interest in taking the job, and Grayson released statements saying that the president's condition was improving. Lansing was silenced, and the public had no idea how bad things were on Pennsylvania Avenue.[195]

They did know that Wilson was unwell, however. When Senator Warren Harding saw a photograph of the president taken as he was returning to Washington, he said, "[I]t was about the most pathetic picture I have ever seen. He really looked like a perfectly helpless imbecile."[196]

Wilson looked like he was dying, and so, too, was the League of Nations. Knowing the most likely outcome, Taft criticized both Wilson and Lodge for putting their ambitions first ahead of the League.[197] Lodge submitted the Treaty of Versailles to the Senate for its consideration in November, but with what he called "reservations," reasserting American sovereignty, which Taft saw as acceptable and the last chance for the League.[198]

Wilson, though weakened, didn't want compromise. He told Democrats to vote against the treaty so long as Lodge's reservations were attached. With Wilson opposed to the Lodge version, the treaty failed by a vote of 55–39, and an unrevised version then failed 53–38.[199] The League of Nations could not pass the U.S. Senate.

Both sides pointed fingers. Lodge blamed Wilson, saying that the revised treaty could have passed. There had been "enough Democrats voting with us." America might have joined the League, but, Lodge told his supporters, the treaty "was killed by Wilson."[200]

The final nail in the coffin was hammered home on March 19. Twenty-one Democrats defied the ailing Wilson, and they supported the treaty with Lodge's reservations. This was still short of the supermajority required for passage. The *New York Times* was headlined "America Isolated without Treaty: Its Defeat, Washington Feels, Will Add to Our Unpopularity Abroad."[201] Taft was furious. He blamed both sides. "The whole world has suffered through the bitter personal antagonism, vanity and smallness of two men, Henry Cabot Lodge and Woodrow Wilson," he wrote.[202] But if this was the League's fate, so be it. In the 1920 election, Taft changed his position and rejected the idea of the United States ever joining the League of Nations.

With Roosevelt dead, no one knew whom the Republicans would

nominate in 1920, not even Taft. One of the two front-runners was Leonard Wood, a man with an incredible résumé. He was a Congressional Medal of Honor winner for his service in the 4th Cavalry Regiment's mission to capture the Apache Geronimo, Grover Cleveland's physician late in his second term, the head of the 1st Volunteer Cavalry—the Rough Riders—and the former army chief of staff. Wood was the heir apparent to the Roosevelt wing. With his nomination looking more likely, Taft thought his prospects of being nominated to the Court looked even worse, and resigned himself to defeat by saying, "It would seem as if the funeral bake meats [of Roosevelt] had furnished forth the feats for their heir."[203]

The other top contender was Frank Orren Lowden, a man from Minnesota who'd married into the Pullman Palace Car Company of the Pullman Strike fame. He was the governor of Illinois, and many thought he would be able to chart a middle path between the still-warring conservative factions. While not as compelling as Wood, Lowden had a strong case for his candidacy.

But the party remained divided when the convention began in June 1920. The progressives and conservatives could not settle on a nominee, and every possible contender had issues that raised concerns, including their health and potential scandals in their past. On the tenth ballot, dark horse candidate Republican Warren Harding of Ohio, a Taft loyalist, was chosen as the compromise.

Though he looked like a president, at six feet tall with a strong frame of 210 pounds and piercing eyes, Harding was not a known national figure. As a senator, he'd introduced 134 bills, 122 of which were about Ohio, and very few of which had any national significance. Many of his positions were unknown. But it was clear that he opposed the League of Nations.[204]

That settled the matter. If the Republican nominee was against the League, so was Taft. Earlier in the process, he'd written, "My natural affiliations are with Harding of Ohio, who is a good man and to whom I am indebted for very effective support in 1912." But it wasn't just Harding's character and loyalty that made Taft warm to his candidacy. This was a political calculation, knowing that Harding was the most likely man to put him on the bench.[205]

When Taft changed his position on the League and supported Harding, many of his former League enthusiasts were outraged. Some called him a "turncoat." He read many of their complaints. He shared some of the concerns, and believed that the choice facing voters in 1920 was between two "mediocre men." But what mattered to him was that Harding "is going to be elected and I think we must vote for him." If he became president, Taft hoped that Harding might change his position on the League. But Harding made it clear that he would not. He now spoke for the party and told the *Washington Post* that such hopes were "doomed to disappointment."[206]

With a campaign message promising a "return to normalcy," Harding won 404 electoral votes and 60.4 percent of the popular vote in 1920. Women were able to vote for president for the first time, thanks to the passage of the Nineteenth Amendment earlier that year. Both Mr. and Mrs. Taft pulled the lever for Harding.[207]

With a Republican headed to the White House, the United States would never join the League. Taft wondered if this was his last chance to join the Court. He'd gotten lucky with Harding's victory, an improbable candidate who had renominated Taft at the Republican convention in 1912. In the eight years since, Taft had shown his strengths as a scholar and as a leader. He'd repaired his relationship with Roosevelt. The Republican Party was coming together again. He'd compromised his position on the League, which made him aligned with Harding on policy. Now he'd have to see if that was enough for President Harding to make his dream come true.

A DREAM REALIZED

William Howard Taft got an early Christmas present on December 24, 1920. He was traveling to Marion, Ohio, home to president-elect Warren Gamaliel Harding, where he was about to have the most important job interview of his life.[208]

With the Wilson administration ending in a few months, Taft was pleased that Harding was on his way to the White House. He'd wired Harding to congratulate his successor and to offer his support. Harding took him up on it, inviting his predecessor to Marion to discuss potential cabinet nominees. Among the men under consideration was businessman and humanitarian Herbert Hoover, who was about to become the secretary of commerce. Hoover was a rising star who'd worked with Wilson on the Treaty of Versailles. Though he was a supporter of the League of Nations, British economist John Maynard Keynes described him as "the only man who emerged from the ordeal of Paris with an enhanced reputation."[209]

The conversation at Harding's house was friendly but serious. When Mrs. Harding asked Taft how she should behave as First Lady, he told her that she should make sure that her husband go by "Mr. President," not "Warren," in the future.

Then the former and future presidents sat down for breakfast. They munched on waffles and creamed chipped beef, a mix of salted and thinly sliced meat covered in sauce. The conversation went long, going past noon over coffee and toast. When the meal was done, the president-elect took Taft to his study. He dropped a yuletide bombshell that Taft had been waiting for since he left the White House. "By the way, I want to ask you," Harding probed somewhat casually, "would you accept a position on the Supreme Bench? Because if you would, I'll put you on that Court."[210]

Taft was trying to contain his enthusiasm, but he told Harding what the president-elect already knew, that being a justice had "always been the ambition of [his] life."[211] Every American president since Grover Cleveland had thought about nominating Taft to the Supreme Court. He'd had three chances under Roosevelt. Now it was about to happen. But he still could not say yes quite yet.

The timing was right, but the position wasn't. Taft was a former president of the United States. He'd appointed six of the current justices. Not only that, one of the associate justices was Louis Brandeis, his old nemesis. With that in mind, Taft did not want to be another associate justice among many. He wanted to be the chief.[212]

He was making one final bet after a lifetime of waiting. Harding had offered him a spot on the Court, but he didn't have the top job to offer yet. Chief Justice White, put in that position by Taft in 1910, was now seventy-five years old. But despite his age, he was still in power.

The reason that Taft was so confident in his bet was that he believed that he and White had an understanding. The chief justice, he thought, was simply "holding the office for me and that he would give it back to a Republican administration."[213] He didn't have any reason to doubt that idea, so Taft left Marion, Ohio, and went on vacation to Bermuda, thinking that his dream position was about to be his.

A few weeks later, fresh from Bermuda, Taft headed to Washington for a meeting with Harding. Harding assured him that he was still his first choice—despite the fact that he had also been talking to Utah senator George Sutherland about a spot on the Court. Then Taft met with Chief Justice White. The meeting was not what he'd expected. He saw that the chief justice was old and in poor health, nearly deaf and blind, and barely able to read legal briefs. But White did not intend to step down for Taft.[214]

The former president was crestfallen. He went home and wondered what would happen. On May 19, 1921, his most morbid wishes came true. White died after a failed operation at Garfield Hospital in Washington.[215] The timing couldn't have been better. Taft wrote, "In [White's] death the country loses one of the great men who has headed [the Supreme Court]."[216] But in White's death Taft gained what he'd always wanted. He might have been thinking then of Theodore Roosevelt, who after McKinley's assassination said, "It's a terrible thing to come into the presidency this way, but it would be far worse to be morbid about it." With his dream coming true, Taft refused to be so publicly morbid; instead, writing privately—and opportunistically—to his journalist friend Gus Karger, "The unexpected has happened. . . . And now the question is, 'What is to be done?'"[217]

There was a little bit more waiting ahead. But on June 21, Harding passed the word to Taft, informing his aide to "[t]ell the Big Chief that I am going to put that over about the first of July."[218] Moving ahead of schedule, Harding sent Taft's nomination for chief justice to the Senate on June 30. Without a confirmation hearing, the Senate moved.[219] The former president was confirmed the day he was nominated. Only four senators voted against him.

On July 11, 1921, Taft took a ceremonial oath as the tenth chief justice of the United States. The newspapers reported, "William Howard

Taft's lifetime ambition was realized to-day." He called it "the greatest day of my life."[220] This was his dream.

Hail to the Chief Justice

The Supreme Court's next term began in October, and Chief Justice Taft took his oath again, this time administered by Associate Justice Joseph McKenna, a McKinley appointee, who recited the oath from memory after a clerk forgot to bring a copy.[221]

For the first time since he'd left the Sixth Circuit, Taft's professional life was secure. He had a lifetime appointment as the chief justice, and also the authority of a former president. He'd been humiliated in 1912, but in 1921 was triumphant.[222] "The truth is," he told his fellow justices, "that in my present life I don't remember that I even was president."[223]

Being president, and an executive before that, made him a more effective chief justice. As governor-general of the Philippines, he'd gained administrative and diplomatic experience. As a law professor at Yale, he'd honed his constitutional philosophy. As president, he'd learned how to lead one of the three branches of the federal government.[224]

He didn't want this lifetime appointment to go to waste. He focused on his work and health, and as chief justice, he woke at 5:15 in the morning, and worked until breakfast at 8:00. He then walked three and a half miles from his home on Wyoming Avenue in Kalorama to the Supreme Court, then housed in the United States Capitol Building, the same room where John Quincy Adams had argued the *Amistad* case.

Once he arrived, he worked until the late afternoon, then walked home for dinner, ate with Mrs. Taft, and worked again until ten at night. He regimented his life, and he detailed his activities minute by minute, noting to his brother Horace that he allowed himself only an hour of leisure every day. The routine paid off. His weight, once 354 pounds, dropped to 259 pounds.[225]

He had reverence for the new institution he led and said that entering the Court was like walking "into a monastery."[226] He wanted to steward the Court. Once upon a time, he'd been a judicial president;

now he was a presidential judge. Historian Robert Post described how "it was Taft who, as former chief magistrate of the Executive Branch, transformed the role of Chief Justice into something analogous to a chief executive for the judicial branch of government."[227]

The Court needed new leadership. The justices were divided, with a McKinley appointee, two Roosevelt appointees, two of Taft's own appointees, and three Woodrow Wilson men. Every president of the twentieth century had a say. Taft was at loggerheads with many of his colleagues, especially Justices Holmes and Brandeis.[228]

The Taft Court was not in good shape. Justice James Clark McReynolds, a Wilson appointee, had gout. Justice Willis Van Devanter, one of Taft's judges, was losing his eyesight.[229] Justice Joseph McKenna had suffered a stroke in 1915, which left him with paralysis.[230] Once a talented jurist, his writing was deteriorating, and Taft worried about him. He wrote to his brother Horace, "I don't know what course to take with [Justice McKenna], or what cases to assign him."[231]

Taft took matters into his own hands. He polled the rest of the Court and asked what should be done. When a majority agreed it was time for McKenna to step down, the chief justice handed McKenna's son a memo outlining the Court's position. Soon after, McKenna resigned, and he died a few months later at age eighty-three.[232] In total, Taft would see four new justices join the Court, three nominated by Harding, and one a Coolidge man.[233]

He'd waited his whole life to join the Court, and he didn't want to spend the rest of his years sitting around with a lifetime appointment and nothing to show for it. He set about reforming the judiciary, creating a Conference of Senior Circuit Judges, which he led. He pushed for the Judiciary Act of 1925, which increased the jurisdiction of appeals courts and gave the Supreme Court more control over its docket.[234]

He also made sure that, at long last, the Supreme Court had its own building.[235] This may have seemed like a symbolic move—changing a building doesn't change the institution. But Taft believed the move had constitutional significance. A separate branch of government needed a separate home. The justices, he said, needed "breathing space" away from Congress.[236]

The Taft reform agenda made the Court more efficient. Since the Civil War, the number of cases before it had nearly tripled, hitting nearly two thousand in some years. There was no way the justices could give a fair hearing to such a high number. Now, with more control over what cases they took up, they could focus on issues that mattered most. Jeffrey Rosen describes this reform as "the most important change in the Court's procedures since the Judiciary Act of 1789." And it's a reform that's lasted—these days, the Court is asked to review seven thousand cases a year. It only takes up about one hundred, leaving the remainder to lower courts.[237]

With a smaller number of cases, the Taft Court made its mark. The chief justice wrote an average of 50 percent more opinions per term than his colleagues, and he was able to forge consensus among the factions.[238] He courted his fellow justices like a politician, and even warmed to Justice Brandeis, whom he "[came] to like . . . very much indeed."[239] From 1921 until 1928, the Taft Court delivered unanimous verdicts 84 percent of the time.[240]

The Taft Court ruled on the issues that defined the Roaring Twenties. Taft sided with business in 1921's *Truax v. Corrigan*, over a labor dispute in Arizona.[241] He then struck down a statute that protected labor from Pullman Strike–style injunctions, on due process and equal protection clauses grounds.[242]

He was deferential to Congress, but ready to provide a check. In *Bailey v. Drexel Furniture Co.*, the Court unanimously struck down a federal 10 percent tax on companies whose profit came in part from child labor. Though Taft's sympathies were with those "good people" who sought to limit such practices, to him the issue at hand was whether Congress had the authority to impose such a penalty in the first place.[243]

Though Taft was a limited-government conservative, he wasn't a libertarian. In *Board of Trade of City of Chicago v. Olsen*, his opinion upheld the Grain Futures Act, which regulated the trading of commodities futures.[244] According to Taft's reading of the Commerce Clause, such regulations were permitted if passed by Congress. This ruling would later provide the basis for New Deal–era regulations.[245]

Not always able to lead a consensus, his most noteworthy dissent

was *Adkins v. Children's Hospital,* a dispute over a federal law governing women's and children's minimum wages in DC. Here, Taft sided
with labor and with Congress in favor of minimum wage provisions.[246]

As a former president, he had particular interest in 1926's *Myers v.
United States,* a case about the limits of presidential power. Myers,
the former postmaster of Portland, Oregon, got the job in 1917 with
President Wilson's nomination and the consent of the Senate. But
Wilson fired Myers in 1920, before his four-year term was up. However, Myers believed that the president didn't have that authority to
fire him.[247] To Taft, the issue was whether or not the president was in
charge of the executive branch and its workforce, not about one four-
year term. Taft ruled against Myers in a 6–3 decision, explaining, "The
President," even one with whom he disagreed, like Woodrow Wilson,
"is empowered by the Constitution to remove any executive officer
appointed by him by and with the advice and consent of the Senate,
and this power is not subject in its exercise to the assent of the Senate,
nor can it be made so by an act of Congress."[248]

The most famous issue before the Taft Court was Prohibition. This
issue affected nearly every American household. The former president
was not a heavy drinker, but he did enjoy champagne. He opposed
Prohibition as a personal matter. But as the Eighteenth Amendment
had made it the law of the land, his role was to uphold it, not to dictate
based on his own preferences. This position caused friction with Nellie Taft, who was unable to persuade her husband to rule against it.[249]

Prohibition had ramifications far beyond alcohol consumption. In
Olmstead v. United States, Roy Olmstead, a Seattle police officer, was
accused of corruption and bootlegging.[250] When police wiretapped his
home without a warrant, he claimed his Fourth Amendment rights
were violated. Taft authored the 5–4 decision against Olmstead, stating
that it was up to Congress to forbid such wiretaps.[251] Justice Brandeis
authored a historic dissent. The *Olmstead* ruling was overturned by the
Warren Court in 1967, in *Katz v. United States,* and set the tone for
many of the Court's later debates about surveillance.

The ghost of Chief Justice Taft is still with us today, including in
ways that would have surprised the twenty-seventh president. Former

president Trump faced multiple legal charges after he left the White House. One of those charges was a count of conspiring to defraud the United States over his actions related to the counting of Electoral College votes in the wake of the 2020 election.[252] And it was Chief Justice Taft who defined what it means to "defraud" the government in the 1924 case *Hammerschmidt v. United States*. In the court's opinion, Taft wrote, it doesn't just mean cheating Washington out of money. It "also means to interfere with or obstruct . . . lawful governmental functions by deceit, craft or trickery, or at least by means that are dishonest."[253] A century after those words were written, Trump would have to pass the Taft test.

Taft's Roaring Twenties

As chief justice, Taft could stay above the messy politics of the Roaring Twenties. Harding had campaigned on a "return to normalcy" after war, strikes, riots, the Palmer Raids, and inflation. The Harding presidency, however, was anything but normal. It was the era of Prohibition, but booze ran freely at 1600 Pennsylvania Avenue. Twice a week, members of the Harding cabinet and their lackeys, called the "Ohio Gang," would gather around a poker table in the White House, gambling and drinking late into the night. Alice Roosevelt Longworth wrote that "no rumor could have exceeded the reality" of that debauched scene and later observed that "Harding was not a bad man, he was just a slob."[254]

This wasn't just a gentleman's gambling ring. It later came out that, while he was president, Harding fathered a child out of wedlock. The girl's mother's name was Nan Britton. Ms. Britton met Harding during the 1920 campaign, and she named their daughter Elizabeth Ann Blaesing. DNA tests administered to Blaesing's descendants in 2015 proved that Elizabeth was Harding's daughter.[255] That wasn't the only scandal of the Harding administration, however. Allegations of the Veterans' Bureau implicated its new head, Charles Forbes, who may have taken up to $200 million from the department.[256] Likewise, Secretary of the Interior Albert Fall's Teapot Dome scandal left a permanent stain on the Harding presidency.

But Harding never had to answer for the scandals of his own administration. In June 1923, he set off for a cross-country tour and then
a voyage up the Alaska coast from Washington State aboard the USS
Henderson.[257] On his way back, a naval seaplane landed alongside the
Henderson and a messenger handed Harding a note from Washington.
The note's contents remain unknown, but Harding collapsed upon
reading it. His health deteriorated all the way back to San Francisco,
where he arrived early in the morning on July 29. He got some rest at
the Palace Hotel, in room 8064.[258] He died on August 2, 1923, and
though Mrs. Harding didn't consent to an autopsy, the cause of death
was determined to be cerebral apoplexy, a stroke.[259]

Word of Harding's death shocked the nation. The Republican
Party was not prepared for what came next. Henry Cabot Lodge, then
in his seventies and still in the Senate, exclaimed, "My God! That
means [Calvin] Coolidge as president!" Indeed, Silent Cal had already
taken the oath at 2:47 a.m. on August 3 at his family home in Vermont,
where his notary public father read him the oath of office.[260] When he
was asked later what his reaction to unexpectedly becoming president
was, Calvin Coolidge replied, "I thought I could swing it."[261]

Taft was heartbroken. The man who had renominated him to
be president in 1912, and had made him chief justice in 1921, was
dead.[262] During his lifetime, Taft had seen three presidents pass away
in office, all after assassinations, first Lincoln, then Garfield, and finally McKinley. Based on that history and his own appreciation for the
system of government established by the Constitution, Taft had more
confidence than Lodge in the transition. "My feeling of deep regret is
somewhat mitigated by the confidence I have in the wisdom, conservatism and courage of [Harding's] successor," he wrote. "Of course,
[Coolidge] lacks the prestige and experience, but he is deeply imbued
with a sense of obligation to follow Mr. Harding's policies."[263]

With the rise of Calvin Coolidge, the long-promised return to normalcy happened. Coolidge was not as presidential as Harding—Alice
Longworth once commented that he looked as if he'd been "weaned
on a pickle."[264] But he made up for it in character. He'd grown up in
Plymouth Notch, Vermont, a place where he learned about morality,

frugality, and hard work. There was no scent of the Harding scandals on the vice president, and when the news of the Harding administration malfeasance broke a few months later, Coolidge remained blameless. He was a small-government conservative on the opposite side of the spectrum as the latter-day Roosevelt. But like Theodore Roosevelt, Coolidge won reelection in his own right, with the largest Republican vote total in history. Unemployment fell to historic lows, and there were plenty of jobs to go around. Scholar Frederick Allen documented, "Between 1922 and 1927, the purchasing power of American wages increased at the rate of more than two percent annually. And during the three years between 1924 and 1927 alone there was a leap from 75 to 283 in the number of Americans who paid taxes on incomes of more than a million dollars a year."[265] Coolidge was popular, but he chose not to run again in 1928.[266] The Republican Party nominated Commerce Secretary Herbert Hoover.

While Chief Justice Taft admired Hoover's accomplishments in the private and public sectors, he wasn't impressed by him as a president. He'd recommended Hoover to Harding as secretary of commerce, but described Hoover as a "curious man. He has the reputation of being anxious to absorb credit in matters in which he is interested. . . . He is not communicative, and he has a capacity for cutting off inquiry if he does not wish to be inquired of."[267] Taft wasn't the only Republican confused by Hoover. President Coolidge said that his commerce secretary had "offered [him] unsolicited advice for six years, all of it bad!"[268]

Despite the reservations of the two most prominent Republicans alive, Hoover sailed to victory in 1928 with 444 electoral votes to Democrat Al Smith's 87.[269] On Inauguration Day, the task of administering the oath of office to Herbert Hoover fell to Chief Justice William Howard Taft. Showing his age, Taft misread the oath. A schoolchild noticed the mistake and wrote to the chief justice about it. Smiling as he did so, Taft responded, "You may attribute the variation to the defect of an old man's memory."[270]

Hoover also noticed the error. However, he dutifully responded "I do" when prompted by the chief justice. It was a clumsy beginning of the Hoover presidency.[271]

THE END OF THE ROAD

Born in 1857, during the Buchanan administration, no man who became president waited so long to achieve his dream as did William
Howard Taft. On the centennial of his birth, Chief Justice Earl Warren came to Taft's alma mater, Yale University, to deliver a lecture on
his predecessor's legacy. Warren called Taft's story "an odyssey, the narrative of a long journey beset with detours, delays, distraction and a
sometimes receding destination."[272]

At the end of Taft's odyssey, he'd come home. He'd gotten his
dream job at age sixty-three. In the last decade of his life, he gave the
job everything he had. These were his happiest and most fulfilling
years. He lasted in the job despite a lifetime of unhealthy habits and
multiple heart attacks in the 1920s that sometimes made him too sick
to attend some major events, including Woodrow Wilson's funeral in
1924.[273] When that happened, he confided, "[T]ruth is I have had a
pretty close call to a breakdown. . . . I cannot do all the work there is
to do."[274] He kept working for six more years.

At the end of one of the longest careers in public life for a president since John Quincy Adams, Taft thought about returning to Manila, where his ascent to the White House began. But he worried that
the changed city "would be peopled with ghosts."[275] When his brother
Charles died, Taft traveled to Cincinnati for the funeral, against his
doctor's advice, and the journey exhausted him so much that he was
put on bed rest when he returned.

He told a classmate from Yale, "We have reached a time when
the dead among our friends are in the majority."[276] On his birthday in
1927, he remarked, "It is borrowed time beyond seventy." That didn't
matter to a man who had what he always wanted, and he continued, "I
am going to struggle and try to enjoy it."[277]

He worried about the future of the Court and if his reforms would
last after his death. To his fellow Harding appointee, Justice Pierce
Butler, he wrote, "With [Van Devanter] and Mac [McReynolds] and
Sutherland and you and Sanford, there will be five to steady the
boat. . . . Brandeis is of course hopeless."[278]

The saddest day of Taft's career wasn't Election Day in 1912, when he lost the presidency. It was February 3, 1930, when he resigned from the Court due to his failing health. No chief justice had ever wanted the position more, and none in the last century had voluntarily stepped down from the bench. He didn't live out his lifetime appointment, but he was confident in his successor, a man he'd appointed two decades prior, Charles Evans Hughes, whom he had denied the chief justice-ship two decades prior in favor of the older Chief Justice White.[279]

As he left, the departing chief justice got a proud send-off. Hoover said Taft had "given an almost unparalleled career to the highest responsibilities in the Nation."[280] Justice Oliver Wendell Holmes visited and told him, "We call you Chief Justice still, for we cannot give up the title by which we have known you all these later years and which you have made so dear to us."[281]

To be called Chief Justice was all he'd ever wanted. Taft died two weeks after the Hughes swearing-in ceremony, on March 8, at seventy-two years old.[282] Nellie Taft was by his side as he slipped into unconsciousness. President Herbert Hoover, overwhelmed by the Great Depression, visited Taft's home twice.

With Taft's passing, Calvin Coolidge was the only other living ex-president. He died three years later. The old Republican Party was gone.[283] Though Taft had left his mark on the presidency and on the Court, a more transformational president was about to make his way to the White House. Another Roosevelt, this one named Franklin, was going to make a New Deal with America.

Recovery

There is no joy to be had from retirement except by some kind of productive work. Otherwise, you degenerate into talking to everybody about your pains and pills and income tax.

—HERBERT HOOVER

Herbert Hoover lived until the age of ninety. But history remembers him for just four years of his life, from 1929 until 1933, when the Great Depression began on his watch. He never fully recovered his old place in American life after that. But when he was asked how, in his eighties, he'd dealt with his critics, he had a simple reply: "I outlived the bastards."[1]

Herbert Hoover was once a hero. He was known as the Great Humanitarian for leading famine relief in Europe during and after World War I. He kept tens of millions of people from starving to death in Europe and Russia. As secretary of commerce, he spearheaded relief efforts after the Great Mississippi Flood of 1927. He may have saved more lives than any candidate for president in history.[2]

Because of that, he was seen as above partisan politics. True, he grew up in West Branch, Iowa, a town that he said had one Democratic resident.[3] But few knew much about his politics other than that his Stanford roommate claimed Hoover voted for William McKinley in 1896.[4] Yet he'd worked for Woodrow Wilson and attended the Paris Peace Conference as a member of the Democrat's delegation. In 1920, the Democratic Party courted him as a candidate for the White House. In March of that year, he even won the New Hampshire Democratic primary.[5] Franklin Roosevelt remarked at the time: "[Hoover] is certainly a wonder and I wish we could make him President of the United States. There could not be a better one."[6]

But Hoover was a Republican. He ran as such in 1928 with the slogan "Who but Hoover?" Sixty percent of the voters said they didn't want anyone else. He won 444 electoral votes. The Republican domination of the White House continued.[7]

That all changed with the Great Depression. No one viewed the Republican Party, or Herbert Hoover, the same way after. Tens of millions of Americans were out of work. Thousands of banks closed. Gross national product shrank by a third in four years.[8] When the American economy collapsed, Hoover's good name went down with it.

The presidency was the only job he ever had in which Herbert Hoover ever failed. It was also the most important job of his life.

The American people blamed Hoover for the economic collapse. Words like "Hoovervilles" and "Hoovercarts" became part of the lexicon. Later he said, "I am the only person of distinction who's ever had a depression named after him."[9]

His defeat in 1932 was a foregone conclusion three years before voting started. But he wanted to recover what had been lost. He wanted to get the American economy back on track. He wanted to recover his good name and reputation. He yearned for his old role in American life, and maybe even his old position in the White House. More than anything, he wanted to be of service.

He couldn't recover personally as long as Franklin Delano Roosevelt was president. The two men had different values and paths to success, which made it difficult for them to relate to each other. But those divergent paths grew into a very personal hatred for one another. The Republican Party also turned on Hoover, wanting nothing to do with the man who'd lost them the White House.[10] The American people didn't stop blaming him for their misery. While other presidents had left office unpopular in the past, Herbert Hoover was in self-imposed exile from politics, since neither party wanted anything to do with him, and there didn't seem to be any path back.

Exile lasted for twelve years. He campaigned against the New Deal. He tried to run for president again. He fought to keep America out of World War II, even as he warned the American people about the evils of Adolf Hitler and all the suffering that came with his reign. He grew more conservative and more concerned about the spread of fascism and communism.[11] But given that the Roosevelt administration had no interest in engaging him and his own party feared any association would be politically immolating, Hoover had no effective platform or public mandate to share what he heard and to advocate for what he believed was the right course of action to avoid war. These were his years of endless frustration.

But Franklin Roosevelt's death in 1945 gave Hoover a chance at resurrection. The new president, Harry Truman, was hardly a Roosevelt disciple, and he had the most difficult hand dealt to him of any commander in chief since Abraham Lincoln. Truman needed Hoover's help after a world war, and he asked him to lead global relief efforts. Then Hoover helped Truman reorganize the executive branch, work that continued under President Eisenhower. Back in public life, Hoover reconciled John F. Kennedy and Richard Nixon after the bitter 1960 election. All the while, he worked, authoring dozens of books and leading countless charities and nonprofits, including the Boys & Girls Club of America and the Hoover War Library at Stanford University.

At thirty-one years long, Hoover's post-presidency was the longest yet. It was also the most productive. He never permanently recovered his good name. But he did recover some of his old place in public life, and the ability to serve others. He reminded the world why he was once known as the Great Humanitarian. He was a public servant again. At the end of his life, that's what mattered to him.

"DEMOCRACY IS A HARSH EMPLOYER"

Hoover knew what his four years in the White House had cost him. When he left the White House, he commented bitterly, "Democracy is a harsh employer."[12]

Rise and Fall

Life had never been easy for Herbert Hoover. Born in 1874 in West Branch, Iowa, he grew up in a poor Quaker household that had an ethos of "stern but kindly discipline." His father was a blacksmith. Young Bert, as he was then called, once stepped on a red-hot iron, leaving a mark that he dubbed the "brand of Iowa" and a scar that stayed with him, a constant reminder of where he came from.[13]

Tragedy struck his family when both his parents died before his ninth birthday, making him an orphan. Bert then left the Midwest for Oregon, where he lived with an aunt and uncle.

Even then, it was clear that young Hoover was bright and that he worked hard. He'd overcome adversity, and he was intensely curious. He entered Stanford University when it first opened its doors to students as a member of the "pioneer" class. There he met Lou Henry, the school's only female geology student, in a lab, and the two fell in love. They married in 1899, and with their degrees in hand set off to China, where they experienced the Boxer Rebellion firsthand. Their service-minded nature kicked in as Lou Henry tended to the wounded in the American compound while Hoover built barricades during a monthlong siege. They survived in the end at the final encampment of foreigners narrowly escaping the rebellion. Free from physical threats, they went all over Europe and made their way to Siberia. They had the kinds of adventures that few couples experienced in those days, and it deepened their love for each other.[14]

Theirs was a romantic life, filled with success. By 1914, Hoover was a self-made millionaire who'd built his fortune through engineering and mining ventures around the world.[15] But then the world was at war. Woodrow Wilson called on Hoover to help mobilize the country and conserve food. This put Hoover on what he later called the "slippery slope of public life."[16]

Hoover served his country as the chairman of the Commission for Relief in Belgium, feeding 11 million civilians.[17] President Wilson then appointed him as America's first director of the U.S. Food Administration, where he led food conservation at home and helped feed a further 83 million people, including 10 million Russians after the Bolshevik Revolution.[18] For that work, he became known as the Great Humanitarian, and had earned a reputation that transcended geographies and put him above partisanship. He then served as secretary of commerce under Presidents Warren Harding and Calvin Coolidge, a position in which he helped more than seven hundred thousand Americans displaced by the Great Mississippi Flood in 1927, many of them Black people living in poverty and segregation in the Jim Crow South.[19]

He was popular, but he had detractors. Calvin Coolidge thought Hoover was too progressive, and said that the man "has offered unsolicited advice for six years, all of it bad.!"[20] But Silent Cal was an accidental president who got the office after the death of his boss. Herbert Hoover seemed destined for the presidency. When Coolidge opted not to run in 1928, the secretary of commerce practically waltzed to the Republican Party's nomination and then to the White House.[21]

His winning campaign message was optimistic: "We in America today are nearer to the final triumph over poverty than ever before in the history of any land," he proclaimed at the Republican convention.[22] Seven months into his presidency, those words would ring hollow.

Poverty was coming for America. On October 28, 1929, the Dow Jones Industrial Average dropped 13 percent in one day. The day after, it fell again, this time by 12 percent. The stock market didn't recover its losses until 1954. Meanwhile, more than 1,350 banks suspended operation the next year. In a matter of months, 4 million Americans were out of work.[23]

The Great Depression was on. Hoover was an engineer, and he wanted to fix what ailed the economy. To create jobs, he ordered new construction projects and accelerated progress on what would become the "Hoover Dam."[24] To protect manufacturers and labor, he signed the Smoot-Hawley Tariff into law.[25] To aid the recovery, he created new agencies like the President's Emergency Committee for Employment and the Reconstruction Finance Corporation.

These actions had good intentions, but some may have made matters worse. More than one thousand economists wrote an open letter to President Hoover asking him to veto the Smoot-Hawley Tariff, but he refused.[26] Whatever the effects of his policies, Hoover's approach to the onset of the Great Depression was not laissez-faire, free-market orthodoxy. The *New York Times* commented, "No one in [Hoover's] place could have done more."[27] But Hoover's initiatives didn't work; they were too little, too late. Americans blamed Hoover, and the worse the situation grew, the faster they forgot why they had elected him in 1928.

Taking potshots at Hoover became a national pastime. When Babe Ruth signed a two-year, $160,000 contract with the New York Yankees in 1930, he became the highest-paid player in the world.[28] At that moment, 4.5 million Americans were out of work.[29] A reporter asked if that seemed fair—after all, Ruth was now making more than the president. "Why not?" Ruth retorted, having hit forty-nine home runs and batted .359 that season. "I had a better year than he did."[30] When Hoover attended the World Series, the crowd booed the president.[31]

In the 1932 election, Franklin Roosevelt carried all but six states and won the Electoral College, 472–59, the Democratic Party's largest victory yet.[32] FDR headed to the White House to the tune of his campaign song, "Happy Days Are Here Again,"[33] and *Time* magazine labeled Hoover "President Reject."[34]

Press secretary Theodore Joslin had the unfortunate task of telling the president he'd lost. When he called Hoover at his home in Palo Alto early on election night, just after 6:30 p.m. local time, he reported that Hoover "took [the news] without flinching."[35] A less sympathetic biographer declared that Hoover was left "mute." On the way to bed, the president shook his aides' hands and told them, "Goodnight, my friends, that's that!"[36]

The campaign had been vicious, and personal. A Democratic campaign operative named Charles Michelson assaulted not just Hoover's policies, but the man himself. As one contemporary writer documented, "Michelson more than any other person was responsible for creating the Depression image of the Hoover administration which plagued the

Republican Party for years afterward." It was Michelson who invented the neologism "Hooverville."[37] The president knew what Michelson was up to. He nicknamed an ugly blue dragon on a Ming vase in his office "Charlie."[38]

Hoover was a loathed lame duck. But Roosevelt wasn't going to take office until March 4, 1933, Inauguration Day. With the passage of the Twentieth Amendment, this would be the final four-month-long presidential transition in American history. And it was the worst transfer of power in American history until January 2021.

Cold Transition

Hoover's problems started with Congress, which was quick to abandon the outgoing president. A member of his own party, Republican congressman Louis McFadden, introduced a resolution of impeachment in the House of Representatives, denouncing Hoover for everything from his handling of war debts to his use of force against the Bonus Army in the summer of 1932. Hoover was spared the humiliation of a vote when the House tabled the motion.[39]

His problems continued with the media, whose attacks quickly escalated. Newspaper publisher William Randolph Hearst unleashed a series of broadsides declaring that, after such a defeat, Hoover should resign.[40] A few columnists suggested that he should appoint Roosevelt to a position in the presidential succession, and then he should resign so that the president-elect could get the job earlier. Hoover dismissed such schemes as "silly."[41]

He wanted to do as much as he could in his last four months. But he felt powerless. He tried to call on Roosevelt for help, publicly asking him to work together to address the country's economic challenges. But the president-elect had little incentive to do so.[42]

The two men knew each other from their time in Paris in 1919, but Hoover and Roosevelt could hardly have been more different. FDR was an East Coast patrician and the cousin of a former president. Hoover was an orphan from Iowa. Roosevelt was a politician. Hoover was a businessman and his first elected office was the White House. Ideologically, they were getting further and further apart.

Hoover invited Roosevelt to the White House during the transition, and the president-elect said he would "cooperate . . . in every appropriate way, subject, of course, to the requirement of my present duties as governor of [New York]."[43] But Joslin told Hoover not to trust Roosevelt, who had a reputation for backroom deals in Albany.[44]

They sat down on November 22, and Hoover was shocked at Roosevelt's physical condition. As assistant secretary of the navy, the six-foot-two, 188-pound Roosevelt had once been described as a "twentieth-century Apollo," and that was the man that Hoover had met many years ago.[45] But the president-elect had been diagnosed with polio in 1921, at the age of thirty-nine. Most Americans knew that Roosevelt was living with a disability, but he'd hidden his infirmity well. He wore a cape to cover his crutches, had his pants tailored long to cover his leg braces, and had those braces painted black so that the steel would not shine in photographs or in the sun.[46] He was helped by a willing press corps that refrained from publishing pictures that would have revealed the extent of his paralysis. Shocked by what he saw in their meeting, and bitter over his defeat, Hoover told Joslin that it was clear that Roosevelt was "both physically and mentally unable to discharge the duties of the office he must so soon assume."[47]

The meeting didn't go well for either party. Hoover spent the first hour lecturing Roosevelt, including about the economy and European countries' debts from World War I. They spoke for ten minutes alone. After the encounter FDR was even less interested in working together.[48] He found Hoover patronizing, out of touch, and pushy. He was happy to let Hoover own the Great Depression, and he would come in to lead the recovery.

President-elect Roosevelt could do as he pleased, and he chose not to help Hoover. He told the Republican, "It would be unwise for me to accept an apparent joint responsibility with you."[49] Hoover released a statement: "Governor Roosevelt apparently does not assent to my suggestion for cooperative action. I will respect his wishes."[50]

This was petulant, but Hoover was exasperated. Roosevelt also had a habit of speaking out of both sides of his mouth. While the president-elect publicly stated that the Constitution did not give him the authority to take action, privately he wielded his influence freely, coordinating with allies in Congress to block Hoover's agenda.[51]

Hoover was isolated, with few allies in or out of his administration, save his family. On January 5, 1933, Calvin Coolidge died at his home in Northampton, Massachusetts, creating a dark and melancholy vacancy for Hoover, who would soon be the only living former president, and very much alone.[52] Two weeks later, Roosevelt stopped in Washington on his way to Warm Springs, Georgia. Once again, he refused to cooperate.[53]

While Hoover scrambled and the country was in a Depression, the president-elect continued on to Miami to celebrate his win with his Harvard pals and friends like Vincent Astor, whose heated pool in Rhinebeck, New York, Roosevelt used for physical therapy.[54] The party arrived in Miami on February 15, and Roosevelt—though campaign season was long over—stopped in front of a cheering crowd at Bayfront Park near downtown. He wanted to give a short speech from the backseat of his green Buick.[55]

The president-elect was charismatic, and the press snapped hundreds of pictures of him, with light bulbs flashing and popping like pistols. Seeing the huge crowd, Columbia professor and Roosevelt aide Raymond Moley started to get nervous. This was an uncertain time, and the prospect of political violence was very real.[56]

Moley was right to be nervous. The mayor of Chicago, Tony Cermak, walked over to shake Roosevelt's hand. As he did so, a bricklayer named Giuseppe Zangara opened fire on the Buick. "Too many people are starving!" Zangara cried out as the sparks leapt from his .32 caliber double-action revolver.[57]

In total, Zangara fired five shots from thirty-five feet away. When the smoke cleared, he'd missed his primary target. Instead, he wounded multiple bystanders and hit Mayor Cermak. As the mayor struggled through the cars, heading toward Roosevelt's Buick, a small, dark red spot grew slowly on his chest until it covered his shirt.[58] When he made it to the Buick, the president-elect and his driver raced toward Jackson Memorial Hospital, with Roosevelt feeling his bleeding companion's neck for a pulse as his heartbeat slowly faded and he coughed up blood.[59]

All the while, Roosevelt remained calm. He visited Cermak's hospital bed, and the mayor reportedly told him, "I'm glad it was me instead of you."[60] Cermak died three weeks later. Those words were carved on his tombstone.

At the time, presidential assassinations were more common than they are today. Hoover was seven years old when James Garfield was assassinated.[61] He was twenty-six when William McKinley was gunned down. That a politician would be killed in 1933 was widely expected, and Joslin commented that "the marvel is that this was the first attempted assassination" of the Depression. He was surprised that Hoover was not the target.[62] But Roosevelt's survival made him even more popular than he was before.

The worst crisis at the end of the Hoover presidency was a series of bank failures that swept the nation. In 1929, there were twenty-four thousand banks operating in the United States. Four years later, ten thousand had closed and their deposits evaporated.[63] Hoover called the banking system "the weakest link" in the American economy. It looked like that link was about to break.[64]

This crisis demanded a response, but at first Hoover wanted the banks to stay open and for the market to determine which ones survived before he came around to the idea of a "banking moratorium." Roosevelt wanted them all closed, in what he called instead a "banking holiday." Under the plan, depositors would not be allowed to withdraw their funds, and the hope was that the economic panic would dissipate before the banks reopened. But the American public wasn't waiting for Washington to figure it out—ordinary citizens were going to the remaining banks and exchanging dollars for gold, draining the Federal Reserve.[65]

The president made one humiliating, last-ditch appeal for Roosevelt's help. After Michigan shuttered its banks and other states followed suit, Hoover called on Roosevelt to support closing the banks. "You are the only one," the president told the president-elect, "who can stave off disaster."[66]

Hoover was still the president, with legal authorities, but he hesitated without the support of his successor. Roosevelt had nothing to gain from rescuing Hoover. He once again refused. Adding insult to injury, he didn't acknowledge Hoover's message for nearly two weeks.[67]

The last three weeks of the Hoover administration saw more chaos, both domestically and abroad. Adolf Hitler took power in Germany after the Reichstag Fire on February 27, 1933. Japan had already invaded Manchuria and was about to leave the League of Nations.[68] But Americans were focused on matters closer to home, and Hoover—unable to end the crisis—blamed Roosevelt, theorizing through the escalating banking disaster, "The public is filled with fear and apprehension over the policies of the new administration. . . . The people are acting in self-protection before March 4."[69]

The public didn't share Hoover's assessment. They'd chosen Roosevelt to be the next president, and the country was, as historian David Kennedy has written, "numb and nearly broken, anxiously awaiting deliverance."[70] Hoover vowed to fight and to keep working "until 10:49 AM March fourth, when I leave for the Capitol. We must try everything, not once, but a dozen times." He made one last request for Roosevelt to call a special session of Congress to solve the banking crisis as soon as he took office. The president-elect wouldn't budge.[71]

Inauguration Day was as dramatic as any since the Civil War. With the economy collapsed, more than a hundred thousand spectators gathered to cheer Roosevelt and say good riddance to Hoover. The crowd witnessed the president and president-elect riding in the same car, an open convertible, despite the dangers, to the Capitol. They shared a blanket to stay warm, but after the terrible transition, there was no love lost between them. While Roosevelt waved his silk hat at the crowd, neither he nor Hoover looked at one another. Hoover's expression was set in a grim stare. He had been awake late into the night working until the very end, as he'd promised.[72]

When they got to the Capitol, Hoover signed a few last-minute documents while he still could. Meanwhile, Roosevelt prepared to deliver his inaugural address. Chief Justice Charles Evans Hughes was nearby, preparing to administer the oath of office.[73]

Four months after his election, Roosevelt walked thirty-five yards on the steps of the East Portico of the Capitol, supported by his steel leg braces and the arm of his son James. He delivered his inaugural address at the podium and spoke solemnly and clearly. Onlookers who might have been worried about his disability were impressed by his strength. In what felt like a "beleaguered capital in wartime," Roosevelt looked every bit the commander in chief, and victory finally seemed possible.[74]

The press described Roosevelt's address as a "Jacksonian speech," laced with criticisms of Herbert Hoover, and the crowd loved it.[75] "The only thing we have to fear is fear itself," the president declared to a cheering crowd. The famous line communicated confidence that the public hadn't heard yet from Herbert Hoover, a sense that they had the power to end the Depression. But whatever Roosevelt's rhetoric, Hoover remained very much afraid. The Depression was far from over, and he feared what Roosevelt might do.

The former president's long train of humiliations was only beginning. Even before he took his oath, the Marine Band had played "Hail to the Chief" for Roosevelt, rather than for Hoover. The Secret Service did not escort Hoover out of Washington, though his staff had requested the customary guard and there were real threats on his life. Instead of the Secret Service, railroad police officers joined Hoover on his way to New York. There, he was met by the chief of police.[76]

President Roosevelt wasted no time. He declared the "banking holiday," closing every bank in the United States, including the Federal Reserve, for a four-day period, beginning at 1:00 a.m. on March 6.[77] That period was extended, and the banks reopened in stages, according to terms set in the new Emergency Banking Act.[78] Disappointed, Hoover issued a statement that FDR's action should "receive the wholehearted support and co-operation of every citizen."[79] But few people were listening to Herbert Hoover anymore.

THE EXILE

The 1932 election was the first of four that Roosevelt won. He would go on to lead the United States through the Great Depression and World War II. Meanwhile, Herbert Hoover was a pariah in self-imposed exile for as long as Roosevelt was president. He was not welcome in Washington. During those twelve years, he returned to the capital twice. Once, he rode in on a midnight train for a quick breakfast at 9:00 a.m., and he left the city immediately after. The second time, Roosevelt was out of town. They never saw each other again.[80]

Hoover began his post-presidency in New York City, but he might as well have been on Elba. He did not know if he'd recover his old place in American life, or if the American economy would make it. He agonized over both, and the emotional anxiety only became more pronounced after he left office. During his time in the White House, he'd become increasingly isolated, shouldering a burden that no one else understood. He may have developed what Fiona Lee, a psychologist at the University of Michigan, would describe as a "subjective sense of distinctiveness from others," a sense that he was removed from those around him. In other words, it's lonely at the top, and this makes the fall that much more painful.[81] For Hoover, now more loathed than any of his predecessors since Andrew Johnson, the isolation was terrible.

The former president took walks around the city, greeting surprised pedestrians with an awkward hello. He reengaged with humanitarian organizations, many of which were focused on aid to children. But he didn't want to stay in Manhattan. He left New York on March 16 on an afternoon train, with no fanfare.[82]

Five days later, he arrived home in Palo Alto, back to his "own gadgets and gardens," in a place as familiar and comforting to him as Monticello was to Jefferson. But unlike Jefferson, Hoover, with the rest of his life ahead of him, had no idea what would come next. And he was a political pariah.[83]

When he arrived in California, he told a gaggle of reporters that he was "entitled to a long, long rest."[84] But he was uneasy, and he spent many hours in his Buick driving on California highways, thinking about the country's troubles and what he could do.[85] These drives were not meditative. He stewed over his thoughts and worked his mind into overdrive. These weren't reflections about the past, either, but rather musings over the present and the future. In isolation, he began to form a narrative of what was going on that was a blend of truth, opinion, and his own feelings about Roosevelt. He didn't regret his policies as president, but he did regret that he hadn't been a more effective communicator.

Though he may have been far away from the halls of power, the American people hadn't forgotten their feelings about Herbert Hoover. His name remained synonymous with the Depression. Many psychologists explained that the song "Who's Afraid of the Big Bad Wolf?," one of the most popular of 1933, was an allegory about Hoover.[86] The early textbooks and histories of the Depression were being written, and they portrayed him as a villain, responsible for all of capitalism's excesses.

Hoover wanted to tell his side of the story, to correct the record, and to speak out against his successor. He believed that the public's view was all wrong. The Depression had started not in America, but in the economic chaos of post–World War I Europe. The U.S. Federal Reserve had made matters worse, he claimed.[87] Nearly a century later, historians are still debating, with few of them siding with Hoover.

He could not believe that he was being portrayed as a villain. The American people, it seemed, had forgotten his good works. In one day, he had lost the presidency, his name, and his record before the White House. Now he wasn't the Great Humanitarian. He was "the associate and tool of Wall Street and organized wealth," quite an evolution from once being a Quaker orphan in Iowa.[88]

The American people hadn't forgotten the Hoover administration, and neither had the Roosevelt White House. Anyone associated with him had a target on their back. Hoover's former treasury secretary, the aging tycoon Andrew Mellon, was under FBI investigation.[89] When the FBI failed to prove any wrongdoing, Roosevelt's lieutenants turned to the IRS to indict the former treasury secretary on tax charges. This was political. "The Roosevelt administration made me go after Andy Mellon," reported Tax Commissioner Elmer Irey. But a grand jury in Pittsburg cleared Mellon.[90] That wasn't the end of it, however. Hoover's tax returns were being audited, and he even suspected Roosevelt's aides were opening his mail. He wrote a postscript in one letter with a cheeky message: "If the gentleman who opens this letter could please transmit a copy of it to the President I should be greatly obliged."[91]

Herbert Hoover had few friends in Washington, but he at least had the company of Lou Henry and their two sons, who were relieved to be away from politics. Herbert Jr. described the presidency as "the worst thing that ever happened to the family."[92] Now the couple could eat breakfast together and listen to the radio in peace, with no responsibilities. Hoover felt that "for the first time in long memory, neither Mrs. Hoover nor I had to get up in the morning at the summons of a human or mechanical alarm clock with its shock into reality."[93]

They lived in what was known as the Lou Henry and Herbert

Hoover House—no more creative name was given to the sprawling property that looked like blocks stacked on top of each other. Perched on San Juan Hill, it overlooks the Stanford campus, where they met. Lou Henry designed it, and Hoover used his engineering skills to ensure that it was fireproof. His study on the second floor had a view of the San Francisco Bay and Mount Tamalpais. It was home.[94]

The one other good fortune that Hoover had was money. He'd entered public service after a successful career as a self-made business-man. He was proud of the fact that he'd earned his wealth. And he pointed out that his "net assets even at their top were never one-half the inherited fortune of Mr. Roosevelt."[95] When he was offered a position giving a weekly radio address, to be sponsored by the Old Guard Tobacco Company at $3,000 per appearance, he turned it down, thinking former presidents shouldn't sell their services like that.[96]

He didn't have a position, but he did want to do something. One of his secretaries once remarked that "[t]he Chief's idea of a vacation is to work eight hours a day instead of sixteen."[97] But in those early days, his schedule was usually blank.

He began to fill it with work on charitable and nonprofit organizations, what he called "benevolent institutions." He served as the chairman of the Boy's Club of America, which saw 1.5 million young men pass through during his tenure. He sponsored educational organizations and humanitarian work in Europe, usually with a focus on children. He built up the Hoover War Library, founded in 1919, which would later become the Hoover Institution on War, Revolution and Peace and a leading think tank and archive at Stanford University.[98]

While Hoover settled into California, Roosevelt was hard at work in Washington. Even once settled into the White House, the president was not yet done pummeling Hoover's reputation. Roosevelt continuously invoked the bogeyman of his predecessor in public speeches, leading Hoover to start thinking more about politics. During Roosevelt's first one hundred days, Hoover read the paper and learned about new government programs the president was launching on everything from financial reform, to employment, to rural infrastructure.[99] Roosevelt pulled the United States off the gold standard in April, and he launched a program requiring Americans to sell most of the gold in their possession to the government at a price that was set by the president and his aides.[100] That November, Roosevelt recognized Joseph Stalin's Soviet Union. Prohibition was repealed by the end of the year.[101]

Roosevelt continued to enjoy widespread support. As president, he had the biggest platform in the world, and 54 million people—out of an estimated 82 million American adults—tuned into his "Fireside Chats," broadcast on the radio across the country. These chats made many Americans feel like they had a personal relationship with Roosevelt. Few, if any, had ever felt such a connection with President Hoover.[102]

Recovering His Voice and "Raising Hell"

Herbert Hoover didn't want to remain in exile. More than any former president before him, save perhaps John Quincy Adams, he opposed his successor's administration, both in terms of policy and personality. He saw the New Deal as not just a matter of policy disagreement, but as an attempt to break with American tradition, and with what Hoover believed made America exceptional. Roosevelt had told the country the only thing it had to fear was fear itself, but Hoover was very much afraid of Roosevelt.

Hoover wanted to speak out against the New Deal, but he was committed to a year of silence, during which time he would determine what he wanted to say and how to use his voice. He began writing and studied political thought, fearing that Roosevelt's programs were doing away with "American Individualism" and ushering in socialism. He began to develop a thesis that would launch his postpresidential political crusade, arguing that "the freedom of men's minds and spirits . . . born with the Renaissance . . . reinforced with the Reformation, [and] . . . brought to reality by the American revolution" was at stake.[103] With the New Deal, he claimed, "we are engaged in creating regimented men, not free men, both in spirit and in economic life."[104]

Hoover had once been closer to the progressive wing of the Republican Party—beloved by Democrats and Republicans alike. His conservative predecessors, Harding and Coolidge, saw him as a figure to their left. Now he was growing more conservative. He spoke of the American founding and of the virtues of free-market capitalism, while decrying "collectivism." If Americans' way of life was to change, it should be through a gradual process of reformation, not Rooseveltian revolution. As his arguments persisted, the more he came to use the word "conservative" to describe his ideology.[105]

With every new Roosevelt program, Hoover grew more alarmed. He decided to break his silence. "Here's what I am going to do," he told Joslin. "I'm going to lay off for six or eight months and then I'm going to start in raising hell. . . . I've caught a lot of it in the last four years; now I'm going to give a lot of it. I'm going to talk and write and do any damn thing I want to do."[106]

Despite the fact that he'd lost his reelection by a historic margin, he predicted confidently, "When the American people realize some ten years hence that it was on November 8, 1932, that they surrendered the freedom . . . they will, I hope, recollect that I at least tried to save them."[107] It was a moment of self-righteousness, but it also showed no introspection. Hoover began to rally surrogates to assault the New Deal.[108] Raymond Clapper, a notable *Washington Post* columnist and Hoover ally, visited the former president in Palo Alto in July 1934. The outside world might have thought that Hoover would live out his days in quiet retirement, but Clapper found that Hoover was spending his time thinking about his next step.[109]

That next step came on September 28, 1934, when Hoover's book *The Challenge to Liberty* hit the shelves. The challenge, he believed, was the New Deal. He laid out a polemic against Roosevelt. Many of his closest associates had advised him not to write the book. The New Deal was popular, and they feared the book would make him seem partisan and petty. Even Robert Taft, a rising conservative star, a Hoover protégé, and William Howard Taft's son, called *The Challenge to Liberty* "extreme."[110]

Hoover didn't pay much heed to such criticisms. He wondered if the book would be his "last shot at public service," and he wanted to say his piece.[111] "For the first time in two generations," he warned, "the American people are faced with the primary issue of humanity and all government—the issue of human liberty."[112]

It was no wonder that Taft worried that the book was extreme. The critics thought so, too. The book was not well received, and one critic claimed that Hoover believed in "freedom for the few and bondage for the many."[113] Despite such reviews, *The Challenge to Liberty* was a best-seller. By March 1935, it sold more than one hundred thousand copies, thanks in large part to a deal with the Book of the Month Club.[114]

The former president was now one of the New Deal's most outspoken critics. The press speculated that Hoover might be interested in more than selling books, and might still have political aspirations. This suited Roosevelt fine, who preferred having Hoover as a foil. The Republican Party wasn't eager to see Hoover reenter politics, however.[115]

In the 1934 midterm, Hoover didn't campaign for Republican candidates.[116] The Democrats made a killing at the ballot box, and now there were only twenty-five Republicans left in the Senate, making for a veto-proof Democratic supermajority for Roosevelt.[117] If the first two years of the Roosevelt presidency worried Hoover, the next two would make him despair. Roosevelt pushed a slew of new programs, including the Banking Act and the Social Security Act. This was such a sweeping set of proposals that it's since been called the Second New Deal.[118]

Roosevelt's programs grew in scope and ambition, and Hoover's attacks grew in volume and invective. He believed that Social Security had merits, but that its financing was destined to fail.[119] More than that, he told an audience at Stanford University, "the first of social securities is freedom," and Roosevelt's programs constituted what he later described as a "New Deal Apocalypse."[120]

To make his case, Hoover toured the country. He spoke before a crowd of ten thousand in Philadelphia, warning that President Roosevelt "recently in addressing the youth of our nation advised them 'to dream dreams and see visions.' I have advised them to wake up."[121] Though they weren't as concerned, even some Democrats objected to Roosevelt's actions. They worried that the president was running roughshod over the Constitution. Al Smith, the Democrat from New York who ran against Hoover in 1928, asked, "In the name of Heaven, where is the independence of Congress?"[122]

There were critics to Roosevelt's left as well. Upton Sinclair, the muckraking journalist, believed the New Deal didn't go far enough. He proclaimed, "the Communist road . . . happens to be the only road that leads to the new world." He won the Democratic nomination for governor in Hoover's home state of California, though he lost with less than 40 percent of the vote.[123] Meanwhile, other left-wing populists like Father Coughlin and Louisiana governor Huey Long were ready to challenge Roosevelt directly. Long would have run against Roosevelt in 1936 had he not been felled by an assassin's bullet in Baton Rouge.[124]

In Search of a Platform

More confident in his political ideology, Herbert Hoover had developed a postpresidential voice. He was waging what he called a "crusade against collectivism." But while speeches and articles provided a path back into the public conversation, he hadn't recovered his place in American life. For that, he'd need to get back into public service.

The next chance to challenge Roosevelt came in 1936. Hoover understood that he would not have a clear path to the Republican nomination. His preferred candidate was former Illinois governor Frank Lowden. But Lowden, at one time a front-runner for the 1920 Republican nomination, was now seventy-three years old. Lowden had no chance, and Hoover had no successor.[125] He was still the leader of the Republican Party, even if the majority didn't want him.

That Hoover could have been the Republican nominee that year was not impossible. Roosevelt's vice president, John Nance Garner, believed "Hoover couldn't win, but he would carry more states than anyone else [the Republicans] can put up."[126] Perhaps hoping for a rematch and another chance to defeat Hoover, Roosevelt made a bet with his aides that his former rival would get the Republican nomination.[127]

But Hoover didn't have a chance and he grossly underestimated how toxic he had become even within his own Republican Party, which blamed him for the Great Depression and the crushing defeat in 1932. The few supporters he had were disorganized and confused as to why their champion wasn't trying to get the nomination.[128] Early polling in February showed a mere 4 percent in favor of Hoover on the low end, and 17 percent on the high end.[129] When the time for the convention came, a few supporters chanted, "We want four more years of Hoover."[130] But the convention managers worked to give him a speaking slot when the radio audience would be at its lowest so as to marginalize the only living former Republican president.[131]

In 1936, the Republican party nominated Kansas governor Alfred Landon. On the campaign trail, however, Roosevelt ignored his actual opponent, and instead attacked Hoover by name. Hoover was better known than the GOP nominee, and a much easier scapegoat.[132] That November, Landon lost by even more than Hoover had four years prior, carrying only Vermont and Maine, and losing even his home state of Pennsylvania to Roosevelt in a blowout.

Roosevelt had proven that he was in the White House to stay. But Hoover's resolve to fight back grew stronger. Landon, he believed, had lost because he had tried to "out–New Deal the New Deal."[133] The conservative Hoover believed voters wanted a true alternative to Roosevelt. He also believed that Roosevelt's personal attacks against him were uncalled for, and he resented having to relive the character assaults from four years prior. He wanted to recover his good name.

Hoover did not attend Roosevelt's second inauguration in 1937. Roosevelt acknowledged that America had not yet recovered from the Depression, and that "millions of families [were still] trying to live on incomes so meager that the pall of family disaster hangs over them day by day."[134] But the results gave him a mandate to lead. An emboldened Roosevelt decided to make his most aggressive move yet, against the Supreme Court.[135]

A few members of the old Taft majority were still on the bench. They acted as a legal bulwark against New Deal excesses. They'd overturned National Recovery Administration and the Agricultural Adjustment Act, and Justices George Sutherland, Pierce Butler, Willis Van Devanter, and James McReynolds earned the nickname the "four horsemen," forming a bloc against the White House.[136]

Furious at the check the Court was providing, Roosevelt told his friend, New Deal advisor and future Supreme Court justice Felix Frankfurter, "Very confidentially, I may give you an awful shock in about two weeks." The president made good on his word in February. He introduced the Judicial Procedures Reform Bill, which would have allowed him to pack the Court with up to six new justices.[137]

There was a political firestorm. The outraged Hoover phoned Republican senator Arthur Vandenberg, who said after that it was clear that the former president was "eager to jump into the fray."[138] Hoover was on the side of the majority of the American people on the matter of court packing. Even Frankfurter's wife, Marion, told her husband, "I hate the whole bill so thoroughly. . . . I can't bear to have you accused of being in any way responsible for it."[139]

Hoover spoke out, and in a speech in Chicago, he declared, "Hands off the Supreme Court!"[140] Roosevelt responded in March, defending his proposal by saying that America's government was a "three horse team," with each horse representing one branch. "Two of the horses are pulling in unison today," the president said. "The third is not."[141] But Congress disagreed. The Senate Judiciary Committee unanimously recommended that the judicial reform bill be rejected. The committee's statement, Hoover said, was "a great American historical document."[142]

That wasn't the end of it, however. Justice Van Devanter, a Taft appointee, soon announced that he would be retiring. That gave Roosevelt the chance to nominate his replacement. Meanwhile, Justice Owen Roberts, a Hoover appointee, started to side with the more liberal justices. This was a move that historians have since dubbed "the switch in time that saved nine."[143]

With a more compliant Supreme Court and Democratic majorities, Roosevelt's power had few checks. If the Democrats did well in the 1938 midterms, Hoover feared the Republican Party would be done for.[144] To Hoover's relief, the Democrats stumbled in 1938. Roosevelt's court-packing plan had been unpopular. A deep recession in 1937 bled over into 1938, lowering the nation's GDP by 10 percent and costing millions more Americans their jobs.[145] Unemployment, already high at 15.1 percent, rose to 20 percent.[146] When the stock market crashed again in October 1938, Adolf Berle, a Columbia professor and former member of Roosevelt's brain trust, called the disaster a repeat of 1929. The New Deal hadn't yet ended the Depression, and things could always get worse.

The Democrats lost seventy-two seats in the House and eight in the Senate in the midterms.[147] Sensing an opening, Hoover began to sketch out a more affirmative vision, rather than only criticizing the

Roosevelt administration. "American young men and women should have the right to plan, to live their own lives with the limitation that they shall not injure their neighbors," he said.[148] There was some life left in the Grand Old Party. Hoover wanted to bring it back.

HOOVER'S CRUSADE

The United States was not the only country experiencing the Great Depression. It was a global phenomenon with global consequences. Terrible economic conditions in Weimar Germany contributed to the rise of Adolf Hitler. It was clear that war was coming for Europe. Hoover turned his gaze across the Atlantic, and he set sail for Europe in 1938, crossing on an ocean liner called the *Washington*. When he arrived, he got something he'd been missing for a decade: a hero's welcome.

In Europe, Hoover was beloved. Streets were named for him in Brussels and Prague, tributes to his work during and after World War I. During this trip, he visited fifteen countries and met with twenty-two heads of state and the leading lights on the continent. Europeans didn't blame Herbert Hoover for the Depression. Most blamed the Treaty of Versailles.[149]

It was a momentous journey. On February 16, he was given the title "Friend of the Belgian People" by King Leopold.[150] After a stop in Estonia, he crossed the Gulf of Finland and landed in Helsinki, where he was greeted as a "special favorite of the Finnish nation."[151] He met the Finnish foreign minister, who'd read Hoover's 1922 book, *American Individualism*. Were he the sitting president of the United States, he hardly could have asked for a warmer welcome.

In Europe, he was still the Great Humanitarian. While he was there, he thought about trying to run for president again in 1940, believing that this mission would leave him "better equipped for continued battle against New Deal collectivism." More than that, he wanted to understand what was happening on the continent, and he asked his hosts in Belgium when they thought war would come. "Who knows?" they said. "Perhaps a year, perhaps two years, perhaps never."[152]

He was about to get a better idea than most what was coming for Europe. On March 7, Hoover entered Germany. This was first time he'd crossed its border since the end of World War I. He made his way to Berlin on a brand-new highway built by the fascist government.[153] He didn't know it, but the Anschluss was five days away. He was about to meet Adolf Hitler.

When he arrived in Europe, Hoover hadn't planned on meeting Hitler. He had what he described as "long since formed a great prejudice against the whole Nazi faith."[154] He even declined an honorary degree from the University of Berlin, protesting the regime.[155] But Hitler invited him, and Hoover agreed to meet at the German Chancellery. He was accompanied by Hugh Wilson, America's ambassador to Germany, who earlier had complimented Hitler as a man who "pulled his people from moral and economic despair" into a "state of pride."[156] The two men walked together to meet the Führer under a marble archway carved with the initials "AH."[157]

Hoover had expected the meeting to last twenty minutes, but it went on for more than an hour.[158] He went in under the impression that Hitler was not the real power in Germany, and instead that he was controlled by "some group of unknown geniuses." But though he saw that Hitler was "a great deal of an exhibitionist" with "strange hair," he noticed that he was "forceful, highly intelligent, and had a remarkably accurate memory." Hitler, Hoover saw, was "the boss himself."[159]

Hitler was not subtle. He said that democracy was doomed to failure, and Hoover disagreed. The Führer exploded, and Hoover observed that Hitler "seemed to have trigger spots in his mind which set him off when touched like a man in furious anger." He left the meeting disturbed, and the *New York Times* ran a story reporting, "Hoover Blunt to Hitler on Nazism; Says Progress Demands Liberty."[160]

Hoover didn't know what Hitler was planning, but he had no illusions about the man he'd just met. Most of the world had up to that point ignored Hitler's repression of German Jews. But Hoover saw what was happening in Germany. He was an early Zionist who had supported the Balfour Declaration, which called for a national homeland for the Jewish people in what would become Mandatory Palestine.[161] He went on to denounce the Nazis' "concentration camps, persecutions of Jews, political trials, and bombing of civilian populations."[162]

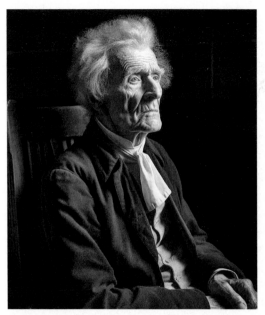

An 82-year-old Thomas Jefferson created using generative AI.
Photo credit: Frank Long

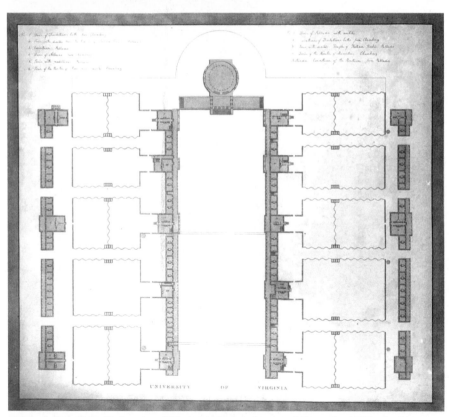

Original plan of the University of Virginia's famous lawn and Rotunda, 1825, also known as the "Maverick Plan" after its engraver, Peter Maverick. *Photo credit: Accession #3313, Special Collections, University of Virginia Library, Charlottesville, Va.*

Portrait of 75-year-old Congressman John Quincy Adams captured by Philip Haas in 1843, marking the earliest photograph of a U.S. president through a daguerreotype. *Photo credit: IanDagnall Computing / Alamy*

Death of John Quincy Adams at the U.S. Capitol, February 23, 1848. *Photo credit: WDC/Alamy*

President Grover Cleveland, 49, married Frances Folsom, 21, in the Blue Room of the White House, June 2, 1886. *Photo credit: Ivy Close Images / Alamy*

Ex-President Grover Cleveland with his son Richard, taken around 1901–1902. *Photo credit: CBW / Alamy*

President William
Howard Taft and
First Lady Helen
Herron Taft attending
a baseball game in
1910. *Photo credit: Niday
Picture Library / Alamy*

Former President William Howard Taft (center) with the League to Enforce Peace group,
1916. *Photo credit: Heritage Image Partnership Ltd / Alamy*

United States
Supreme Court
group portrait, 1925.
Center front is Chief
Justice William
Howard Taft.
*Photo credit: Everett
Collection/Shutterstock*

President Herbert Hoover and President-elect Franklin Roosevelt barely speak as they take an uncomfortable ride to the latter's inauguration on March 4, 1933. *Photo credit: Library of Congress Prints and Photographs Division*

Former U.S. President Herbert Hoover, on a visit to Germany, received an unexpected invitation from Adolf Hitler himself to the Reich Chancellery. Pictured from left to right: Herbert Hoover, Adolf Hitler, accompanied by interpreter Councilor Paul Schmidt, and the American ambassador in Berlin, Hugh Wilson. This historic moment unfolded on March 8, 1938, just four days before the Anschluss. *Photo credit: AP Images*

Herbert Hoover receives a key from 12-year-old Kevin Lovelle, as he opens the Boys Club building in New York City on October 18, 1960. *Photo credit: Phyllis Twachtman/World Telegraph Photo/ Library of Congress Prints and Photographs Division*

Two days after leaving office, former US-President Jimmy Carter (left) and former Vice President Walter Mondale (right) arrive in Weisbeden, Germany, to greet fifty-two American hostages who were freed from Iran after 444 days in captivity. *Photo credit: Keystone Pictures USA/ZUMAPRESS.com/ Alamy Live News*

Ex-President Jimmy Carter at a Habitat for Humanity building project in Charlotte, North Carolina. *Photo credit: Stock Connection Blue / Alamy*

Ex-President Bush dancing with a group of women during a Bush Center visit to Africa. *Photo credit: Paul Morse/ George W. Bush Presidential Center*

George W. Bush doing his famous "Bush push" with a veteran participating in the Bush Center's W100K bike race. *Photo credit: Layne Murdoch/ George W. Bush Presidential Center*

George W. Bush (right) demonstrating his "cold wax" technique to the author at his art studio in Kennebunkport, Maine. August 11, 2020. *Photo credit: Freddie Ford*

After the meeting with Hitler, Hoover headed to Carinhall, Field Marshal Hermann Göring's hunting lodge, which had been designed by the same architect who'd planned Berlin's 1936 Olympic stadium.[163] Göring knew of Hoover's dislike for Roosevelt, and pushed to see if he could exploit American political division, beginning the meeting by thanking Hoover for his relief work in Germany two decades prior and then criticizing Roosevelt.

Despite his differences with the president, Hoover didn't engage. He told Göring that, as an American, he wasn't going to denounce his own government while traveling abroad. The Nazi leader then grew more aggressive, vowing that the Third Reich would never find itself in such a vulnerable position as had been the case after Germany's defeat in World War I. He laughed and pointed at a map of Czechoslovakia. "What does the shape of that country remind you of?" he asked. Before Hoover could respond, Göring answered his own question: "That is a spearhead. It is a spearhead plunged into the German body." Hoover later made a note about the meeting at Carinhall. Göring, he observed, was "far more agreeable than Hitler; probably had a clever mind." But he was "utterly ruthless, utterly selfish and probably utterly cruel."[164]

When he left Europe, Hoover was more worried than when he had arrived. The continent's democracies were weak, and their leaders inexperienced. Meanwhile, Germany's leaders were strong, terrifying, filled with vengeful fantasies of a greater Germany, and preparing for war. He worried about the absence of checks on their growing power. The leaders from the First World War were long gone. Hoover believed that Winston Churchill, one of the last remaining leaders from the previous era, was "no real exception" to the dearth of European leadership. His friend, Ambassador Joseph Kennedy, agreed, telling Hoover, "Something, somewhere, had gone out of [Europe]. The last war wiped out its best manhood. No new man of great consequence had come up."[165]

The former president was wrong about Churchill. But he had a clearer idea of the dangerous situation in Europe than almost any other American. Roosevelt had never traveled to the continent as president—indeed, most of his international trips up to that point were fishing expeditions to the Bahamas or Newfoundland. Hoover's insights could have been valuable, but neither the White House nor the State Department requested a briefing. He didn't offer one.

Had he met with Roosevelt, Hoover would have articulated his theory of the case. Already, FDR was bringing the United States closer to its European allies, and slowly in the direction of intervention. As repugnant as Hoover found Hitler, he would have advocated against American military intervention. He didn't want the United States to get involved militarily, and joined the leading anti-interventionist group, the America First Committee, which included the now-infamous Charles Lindbergh, as well as Frank Lloyd Wright and future president Gerald Ford.[166] John F. Kennedy, then an undergraduate at Harvard, sent the committee a $100 check.[167]

But Hoover wasn't an isolationist. He was a humanitarian who remembered the carnage of World War I. Before he was president, he spent more time abroad than any of his predecessors. He was an internationalist who believed that America could be a powerful force for good in the world. But the United States did not need to get involved in wars. It was "surrounded by a great moat" of the Atlantic and Pacific.[168] America's proper role was to remain a beacon of democracy and lead the recovery once the war was over.

Hitler had made it clear that he wanted *Lebensraum*, more land and living space for Germans and for Germany. Hoover believed that meant that the war would happen in Eastern Europe, sparing America's democratic allies France and the United Kingdom, as the Soviet Union was where the open land was. For that reason, Hoover believed that Germany "had no desire for war with the democracies; they saw no profit in it."[169] War would come, but it would see the fascists and the communists destroy each other.

Hoover was right about Hitler's push for *Lebensraum* in Eastern Europe, particularly in Ukraine. But he didn't anticipate that Poland would fight as it did. And he didn't see that the United Kingdom and France would join the fight as they would, with Hitler marching west thanks to a free hand in the east due to the Molotov-Ribbentrop Pact, a short-lived nonaggression pact with Joseph Stalin.[170] Reflecting later on his visit's terrible timing, "I of course did not then know that Hitler had already determined upon his barbarous invasion of Austria to take place a few days later. He certainly did not confide in me."[171]

Launching His Crusade

War was coming for Europe. Hoover didn't want Roosevelt to lead America into it. With the 1938 midterms behind them, the Republicans looked like they might have a chance in 1940. The freshmen Republican senators included Ohioan Robert Taft, the son of former president William Howard Taft and a rising star. His nickname was "Mr. Republican." And with a new generation coming to power, the Grand Old Party might have some life in it yet.[172]

Hoover took credit for the GOP's newfound relevance. The Quaker allowed himself a moment of uncharacteristic vanity, telling a friend, "I am getting an enormous amount of mail insisting that I carried the [1938] election." But, he remarked, "I haven't seen any account of that in the newspapers."[173]

Back from Europe and thinking this might be his moment, Hoover contemplated his most serious potential run for a nonconsecutive term yet. Foreign policy was on the ballot, and he had both experience and international standing. Hitler had invaded Czechoslovakia and Poland, and Great Britain had declared war on Germany. Imperial Japan was marching through Asia. "We can make war," the noninterventionist Hoover warned, "but we do not and cannot make peace in Europe."[174]

He did not want to throw his hat into the ring unless he was asked. That strategy may have been appropriate for 1936, but it was a miscalculation now. A small group of supporters called the Republican Circles tried to lay the groundwork for a Hoover run, with some support in the West.[175] But there was no grassroots movement. Alfred Landon, the failed Republican nominee of 1936, said the idea of either of them running would be like "two undertakers fighting over the corpse" of the Republican Party.[176]

Hoover intended to fight, and positioned himself as a leader of the noninterventionist camp. In February 1939, he spoke at the Council

on Foreign Relations, telling the audience that waging war would require the United States to transform itself "into practically a Fascist
state."[177] With most Americans wanting to avoid another war in Europe, the Los Angeles Times described Hoover's remarks as "the most
illuminating and penetrating analysis of our mis-called foreign policy
yet made by anyone."[178] The former president made his case in col-
umns with titles like "Shall We Send Our Youth to War?" which reminded readers of the terrible toll of World War I.[179]

For the first time since 1928, the American people sided with
Hoover. Even after Hitler invaded Poland, 48 percent held that the
United States should not get involved. That number climbed to 71
percent after Poland surrendered.[180]

Even if Hoover shared that sentiment against military involvement, he saw the suffering in Europe and favored humanitarian relief.
He helped establish the Polish Relief Commission to feed Polish children under German occupation. When the Soviet Union, an empire
with 170 million people, invaded Finland, a nation of 4 million, on
November 30, 1939, he raised nearly $4 million. He sent food, medi-
cines, and other supplies to the besieged Finns.[181]

To the world's surprise, Finland fought bravely and made the Soviets pay a heavy price for every inch of Finnish soil. When the 105-day
assault was done, Helsinki's losses would stand at twenty-five thousand, while Moscow's were closer to two hundred thousand, and many
more Soviets succumbed to frostbite.[182] Soviet propaganda had called
the invasion a humanitarian intervention. In response, the plucky Finns
dubbed the bombs being dropped on their cities "Molotov's breadbas-
kets," after the Soviet foreign minister Vyacheslav Molotov. They then
christened their new weapon of choice, the "Molotov cocktail."[183]

While the West did not send troops or weapons, Hoover's humanitarian work did not go unnoticed. First Lady Eleanor Roosevelt advised her husband to explore whether he could work with Hoover on
relief, but both men were mutually suspicious and neither wanted it.
Hoover refused to interact with Roosevelt through an intermediary. He
worried that FDR would use him for political advantage in the 1940
election.[184] President Roosevelt decried the Soviet's "dreadful rape of
Finland," but he did not want to work with his defeated rival.[185]

Hoover's humanitarian work also got in the way of his political ambitions. Finland had taken his attention away from the race for the Republican nomination. Any momentum for his candidacy was fading. Other candidates were gaining steam.

With the Winter War in Finland over, Hoover closed his relief mission and hired a pollster.[186] But it was too late for him. Candidates like Robert Taft, Thomas Dewey, and the dark horse Wendell Wilkie were on the ascent. Hoover's only hope was a deadlocked convention that would make him the compromise candidate, or the candidate of last resort.[187]

The Republican convention commenced in June. It was the first convention ever broadcast on television.[188] When it began, the former president languished at 2 percent in the polls. But with a national audience watching, he hoped a speech at the convention would improve his standing. With the right message, he might be drafted as the nominee.[189]

But there was one big problem with this plan. When he rose to speak, no one knew what he was saying. His microphone malfunctioned. The audience shouted, "We can't hear you! Louder!" Hoover's presidential hopes went out with an inaudible whimper.[190]

He was stunned by what had happened, and believed his opponents, possibly a mechanic under orders of a Wilkie staffer, sabotaged his microphone.[191] Whatever the case, Hoover received just seventeen votes on the first ballot, the lowest of any contender.[192] Indiana businessman Wendell Wilkie and Senator Robert Taft battled it out. Wilkie, the more interventionist candidate, won on the sixth ballot. The *New York Times* called this outcome "one of the greatest upsets in the history of the convention system in America."[193]

Wilkie was an odd pick for the Republicans. He'd never held elected office. He'd never worked in government. And he'd never served in the military. Not only that, as a younger man, he was a socialist who voted for William Jennings Bryan. He'd only recently become a Republican. A Republican leader commented of the Wilkie nomination, "I don't mind the Church converting a whore, but I don't like her to lead the choir on the first night."[194]

It wasn't clear what role, if any, Hoover could play. He wanted Roosevelt to lose. But he also worried that Wilkie was an interventionist.

However, Wilkie told reporters that he wanted Hoover to campaign for him, and the former president did give a few major addresses. Hoover even encouraged Chief Justice Charles Evans Hughes to resign from the bench and campaign for Wilkie in hope that such a prominent Republican voice could help deny FDR a third term. Hughes declined the request and Hoover came to regret making it.[195]

Another Roosevelt victory wasn't guaranteed. His vice president, John Nance Garner, thought his boss wasn't going to run, and attempted to secure the nomination himself. The fact that Roosevelt was running for an unprecedented third term caused alarm in many circles. Grover Cleveland's widow, Frances, now in her seventies, told her children not to vote for Roosevelt in 1940. She remined them, "Your father never approved of a third term." Four years later, when they asked why they were now allowed to vote for Roosevelt, she responded, "Your father never said anything about a fourth."[196]

When all the votes were tallied, Roosevelt won a third term. Hoover was disappointed, but he didn't despair. The results in 1940 were closer than they'd been in either 1936 or 1932. Wilkie was a liberal Republican. The increasingly conservative Hoover believed that his defeat was further evidence that voters wanted a real contrast with Roosevelt.[197]

Herbert Hoover turned sixty-seven years old in 1941. He knew he wasn't going to be president again. It may have been a relief. He would not seek public office again. Instead, he'd focus on advocating his ideas through writing what would become a six-volume memoir, speaking, and working to correct what he saw as mistakes in the historical record about his presidency.[198] Meanwhile, the Battle of Britain was fought throughout the 1940 campaign season. And though Britain had survived this onslaught, it couldn't hold on for much longer without American intervention. Hoover wanted to be heard, but he also yearned to serve.

"YEARS OF FRUSTRATION"

As the 1940 election approached, Hoover's energy, work ethic, and desire to serve the public intensified. A big part of this was his hope that, if Wendell Wilkie won, he could move to Washington and take a position in the new administration. Instead, after the Republican's defeat, Hoover took his crusade north of the capital to Manhattan. He and Lou Henry settled into the four-bedroom suite 31-A at the Waldorf Astoria. With a view overlooking Park Avenue, the orphan from Iowa had neighbors like Cole Porter and the Shah of Iran.[199] He paid for the company—$32,000 a year in rent. But despite the lavish setting, these were years of frustration for Hoover.

While the United States was neutral, the world was at war. Witnessing the destruction in Europe and Asia, Hoover wanted to lead a new humanitarian mission to help those living under Nazi occupation. But America was on the sidelines, and he desperately asked a friend, "Can you believe the spiritual leadership of America has so lost its bearings as to be opposed even to an effort to help those who lie in the ditch?"[200]

He blamed Roosevelt, telling Secretary of State Cordell Hull, "I know tens of millions of Americans would also be shocked. . . . History will never justify the government of the United States siding with the starvation for these millions."[201] The Roosevelt administration aided Britain militarily through the Lend-Lease Act, but the humanitarian mission Hoover wanted didn't happen.

What Hoover feared most was that the United States would have to fight Germany and Japan.[202] That fear was soon realized, not due to any policy of the Roosevelt administration, but by Japan's decision to launch a surprise attack against the U.S. naval base at Pearl Harbor on December 7, 1941. When the smoke cleared, 2,403 Americans were dead. The U.S. Pacific fleet was crippled. America would soon be at war on two continents.[203]

The attack on Pearl Harbor took Washington by surprise. Hoover didn't hear about it for hours. He and Lou Henry were in Bucks County, Pennsylvania, having lunch with friends. As the Japanese fighters left behind their smoldering targets, Mr. and Mrs. Hoover were headed home for New York. Enjoying himself, he'd asked her not to turn on the radio. It was such "a peaceful and happy weekend," he later recalled.[204]

When they returned to Manhattan, the quiet was over. They were greeted by a gaggle of reporters at the Waldorf. Cameras flashed and the journalists asked the former president a slew of questions for which he was unprepared. "What do you think of the war?" one asked.

"What war?" Hoover replied, not knowing that the USS *Arizona* lay at the bottom of Pearl Harbor.[205] When he learned what had happened, he issued a statement in support of the president. He concluded, "We will have victory."[206]

The anti-interventionist cause died at Pearl Harbor. But the America First crowd's words lived on. Hoover had already turned in the manuscript for his next book, *America's First Crusade*, before Pearl Harbor. The book examined the history of World War I and the Treaty of Versailles, making the case against military intervention. Two months earlier, the argument might have been well received. Now the message landed with a thud.[207] The *New York Times* critic wrote scathingly, "From our only living ex-president we might well expect in this grim hour some words that would help awaken the country to the gravity of its danger . . . and that would bind us closer to our democratic Allies. We have instead a volume that will make judicious friends of Mr. Hoover grieve."[208]

The book's timing could not have been worse. But once the United States was at war, Hoover wanted victory, and to be of service. Bernard Baruch, a Roosevelt appointee, was tasked with leading the office of war mobilization. He advised the president that Hoover had assisted with mobilizations during World War I. He said that enlisting a prominent Republican could be a powerful show of unity.[209] But Roosevelt would not budge. When Baruch presented his idea, the commander in chief snapped at him, "I'm not Jesus Christ. I'm not raising Hoover from the dead." That was the end of the discussion.[210] Hoover might have been able to do some good. But Roosevelt had no interest in putting politics aside, even then.

Millions of Americans were fighting on three continents. Hoover watched on the sidelines in horror. He saw the combat losses, as well as the untold millions of civilian men, women, and children who were dying or suffering in Europe, Africa, and Asia. The Great Humanitarian had no role to play. He despaired and wrote to a friend, "I am convinced that you and I are not going to be allowed to take any part in this war whatever."[211]

Where he could, he contributed. He wrote articles and worked on his memoirs. With the assistance of Hugh Gibson, a former Charles

Evans Hughes clerk, he drafted *The Problems of a Lasting Peace*, a work of applied history that examined what it would take to prevent a new war after the defeat of Germany and Japan. He supported humanitarian works where he could.[212]

His life changed on a chilly January day in 1944 when Lou Henry returned home late to the Waldorf Astoria after a concert featuring harpist Mildred Dilling. That evening, Mrs. Hoover's husband found her on the floor of their suite, barely registering a faint pulse. She had collapsed and died of a heart attack on January 7.[213] In a rare communication, Franklin Roosevelt sent his predecessor a message: "To you and all who mourn with you the passing of a devoted wife and Mother, I offer the assurance of heartfelt sympathy in which Mrs. Roosevelt joins me."[214]

This was the end of a forty-four-year marriage. Even after she passed, Hoover learned something new about the woman he'd met in a geology lab back at Stanford.[215] After her funeral he sorted through Mrs. Hoover's belongings and found a drawer filled with checks written out to her, totaling several thousand dollars. Over the years, she'd lent friends money. Whenever they'd tried to pay her back, she'd accepted their checks so as not to embarrass them. But she didn't cash them. She turned her loans into gifts.[216]

There was an election ten months away, and Hoover, still mourning, issued a statement that he was not seeking the nomination. He did not plan to advise any candidates.[217] His life as a politician was over. He did speak at the Republican convention a few weeks after the D-Day invasion,[218] but his remarks were less partisan, and he reminded the audience that "millions of sons of both Republicans and Democrats are fighting and dying side by side. . . . They want to be free Americans again."[219]

The governor of New York, Thomas Dewey, was the Republican nominee that year. Dewey, fearing any public association with the former president, asked Hoover not to campaign for him, and his team didn't even allow Hoover's sons to take a photo with the Republican nominee at the convention.[220] Hoover had been out of office for twelve years, but he was still a political liability. When he dedicated a memorial in Charleston, West Virginia, and received a twenty-one-gun salute, one man commented, "By gum, they missed him."[221]

Dewey's assessment was cruel, but correct. Roosevelt loved invoking Hoover's name, and still spoke as if he were running against his rival from 1932. In his own acceptance speech at the Democratic convention, Roosevelt spoke about Hooverism, and when Hoover read the president's remarks, the former president commented, "Apparently I was still as important as in 1932, 1936 and 1940."[222]

Roosevelt's playbook worked in the last three elections, and it worked a fourth time. Hoover gave two friends sealed envelopes with his prediction about what would happen in November: "This election is lost. It could have been won."[223] It was the closest yet for Roosevelt, but Dewey won just under 46 percent of the vote, not enough to carry the day.

Once again, the public did not know how sick the president was, and he was rarely photographed. He had new heart ailments and bronchitis. He was sixty-three years old and dying. A few months before the election, he had to be carried into Bethesda Naval Hospital, where a doctor examined him and heard fluid building up in his lungs. The doctor recommended bed rest, but a Roosevelt aide ignored the suggestion, "due to the exigencies and demands on the president."[224] The ailing president's inauguration did not take place at the East Portico of the Capitol, in public view, but was rather a private, "homey little ceremony on the back porch of the White House," in which he gave a five-minute address, the shortest since George Washington.[225] He knew he was dying, but he'd run again to finish what he started, telling his son James, "I don't dare shake the faith of the people that's why I ran again. . . . The People elected me their leader and I can't quit in the middle of the war."[226]

Hoover knew the president was not well, even if the White House hid the extent of his condition. He wrote to his friend Felix Morley, the president of Haverford College, that he hoped Roosevelt "would live long enough to reap where he had sown."[227] That wish did not come true. Roosevelt suffered a stroke and died of a cerebral hemorrhage on April 12, 1945, at 3:35 p.m.

Herbert Hoover was seventy years old, and when he heard the news, he issued a short statement: "Whatever differences there may have been, they end in the regrets of death."[228] There was sadness, but also relief that he'd outlived Roosevelt. He didn't know what would come next, but he believed that Roosevelt's passing would be "a severe blow to the collectivists—for a while."[229] He anticipated that his life might be about to be very different from what it had been for the last twelve years. "Now that there has been a change in Washington," he told his sister, "I may be on the move often."[230]

RESSURECTION

Harry Truman never expected to be president. When he had the number two job, he referred to himself as a "political eunuch." Now that the top position was his, however, he reported that he "felt as though the moon and the stars and all the planets fell on me last night when I got the news. I have the most terribly responsible job any man ever had."[231]

Roosevelt also never prepared Truman to be president. "I hardly know Truman," Roosevelt had told an aide, just before adding him to the ticket. "He has been over here a few times, but made no particular impression on me."[232] With Roosevelt's death, a parochial politician from Missouri with no national name recognition was now tasked with winning the Second World War and picking up the pieces when the fighting was done. There was only one man on earth who could empathize about what Truman was getting into—Herbert Hoover.

Hoover was skeptical of Truman. He was a political unknown, and Hoover assessed him to be a "dual personality," with both "amiability and goodwill" and "little ideological conviction."[233] But it was a positive development for Hoover that Truman was not Roosevelt, and that the two had never been close. In fact, Truman had only served as vice president for eighty-two days. He'd never had a single one-on-one meeting with his boss.[234] That daylight made Truman's new responsibilities much more difficult, but it was welcome news to Hoover.

His old foe was dead, but Hoover didn't expect to return to Washington. He'd sold his home at 2300 S Street NW, where he'd lived when he'd served as commerce secretary.[235] Nevertheless, Hoover sent President Truman a note: "All Americans will wish you strength for your gigantic task. . . . You have the right to call for any service in aid of the country."[236] He had opened the door, and Truman made the call. With the battle against Japan still raging, Truman understood that he needed to prepare for peace before the war was over. Hoover could help.

Europe lay in ruins. Much of East Asia was destroyed. It was clear that the recovery would be a daunting task and that global famine was a real possibility. Meanwhile, the United States was protected by the Atlantic and Pacific Oceans, and it was one of the few countries in the world that had a food surplus.[237]

Truman was from Missouri, an agricultural state, and he had served as an artillery officer during World War I. Like so many Americans, he remembered how Hoover had led famine relief in the aftermath of the First World War, and what he had done on the home front to enlist the help of everyday Americans.[238] With that history in mind, the president asked Secretary of War Henry Stimson to phone Hoover and ask him to come to Washington. Though Hoover had been waiting for such a call for twelve years, he said no. He needed the president to ask.[239]

Hoover's insistence could be seen as standing on ceremony, or even vanity or childishness. It certainly didn't reflect Quaker values of humility. But there was more to it. Truman had inherited Roosevelt's staff, and like their old boss, they despised Hoover.[240] Hoover was wary of any contact from a Democratic administration. For twelve years, he'd been the White House's punching bag, and he was skeptical that was going to change so quickly. He didn't want to be humiliated, and he believed that he was owed the courtesy of direct contact as the only living former president.

He soon learned that Truman was not Roosevelt, and that this new president didn't have hostility toward him. They had a great deal in common. They'd both grown up in Midwestern farming communities. They'd both seen the devastation of World War I, Hoover in his relief work and Truman as a young artillery officer. They'd both lived in FDR's shadow. Neither enjoyed that experience.[241]

On May 24, Truman drafted a note to his only living predecessor:[242] "If you should be in Washington I would be most happy to talk over the European food situation with you. Also it would be a pleasure to me to become acquainted with you."[243] The note was simple, direct, and from the president. It was what Hoover needed. He accepted the invitation and returned to the White House on May 28, 1945, for the first time since Franklin Roosevelt's inauguration in 1933.[244]

Though it was the same building, the world was different. The Nazis had surrendered to the Allies. Now the job in Europe was what one American general called the "logistics of peace,"[245] a subject that Truman and Hoover spoke about for nearly an hour. Though they'd never met, and the conversation was all business, it went well. The former president came prepared and made recommendations about how to prioritize food aid to Europe.[246]

Both Truman and Hoover saw the outlines of the coming of the Cold War, and it was clear that Europe would be divided between the democratic West and the communist East. If the United States got the recovery wrong, the Soviet Union would take advantage. "Bare subsistence meant hunger," Hoover warned Truman, "and hunger meant communism."[247]

After the meeting, Truman described his encounter with Hoover as "most pleasant and satisfactory." Hoover followed up with an eighteen-page memo summarizing his ideas, but he didn't expect much follow-up, and he believed that Truman "was simply endeavoring to establish a feeling of good will in the country." What he'd missed was how valuable the meeting was for Truman, who later recalled, "[Hoover] helped me to review the world food-distribution problem, which he knew from one end to the other."[248]

Before he could focus on winning the peace, Truman had to win the war in the Pacific. Victory came faster than many had expected, after August 6, when the United States dropped an atomic bomb on Hiroshima. After that, Stalin declared war on Japan on August 8. The day after, a second atomic bomb fell on Nagasaki. Japan surrendered on August 15. World War II concluded with Allied victory, and General Yoshijiro Umezu and Foreign Minister Mamoru Shigemitsu of imperial Japan signed the document, making their capitulation official on September 2, all within the first five months of the Truman presidency.[249]

Herbert Hoover had prayed for the war to end, but not like this. He wanted total military victory, but when he saw the use of nuclear weapons, he was horrified, writing that the "indiscriminate killing of women and children, revolts my soul." He warned of a world that saw the proliferation of the bomb: "If it comes into general use, we may see all civilization destroyed."[250]

The Humanitarian Statesman

No matter how it ended, the war was over, and the postwar world was coming into view. In February 1946, Secretary of Agriculture Clinton Anderson called Hoover to tell him that the president wanted to make him the honorary chairman of the new Famine Emergency Committee. Truman followed up, promising Hoover that this would not be a sinecure—there was real work to do, and Hoover could lead it.[251]

The seventy-two-year-old Hoover traveled to Washington. He was coming off of a fishing trip, and he looked "tanned and fit" when he met with Truman on March 1, with the energy and hope of a younger man on a new assignment.[252] There was a group of outside experts who advised that food crises in Europe and Asia could lead to more than a million deaths if America did not take action. To Truman, this was "the most important meeting we had held in the White House since I had become president."[253]

If Hoover was going to take the job, he wanted to be empowered, not subject to vetoes from agencies like the State Department. He wanted a line to Truman, and Truman was ready to give Hoover the lead, telling him, "You know more about feeding nations and people than anybody in the world."[254]

It's what Hoover wanted to hear, both because he knew he could deliver and because it coddled a badly bruised ego. Two weeks later, with the president's mandate in hand, he boarded the "Faithful Cow," a U.S. Army C-54 transport plane, headed for Europe. For the next fifty-seven days, he traveled the world, traversing thirty-five thousand miles and twenty-two countries on three continents. His goal was to understand the needs and to rally support for famine relief, both at home and abroad. He gave speeches, hosted press briefings, and met with seven kings and thirty-nine prime ministers. Some of the people he met along the way were the children or grandchildren of people he'd helped feed during World War I.[255] A quarter of a century after he'd earned the nickname the Great Humanitarian, Hoover emerged from his exile and returned to the work he loved.

The conditions on the ground varied from country to country. Much of Western and Northern Europe, including Belgium, Denmark, and Sweden, was well on the way to recovery. But the situation elsewhere was more dire, and infant mortality rates ranged from twenty per one thousand in central Europe, to as high as fifty per one thousand in the east.[256] Hungry men lined up for blocks in Paris, waiting for beans and gruel. When Hoover witnessed a food riot in Italy, he persuaded the pope to make an address urging Catholics to restore calm.[257] In Germany, he visited the chancellery, the site of his meeting with the Führer eight years prior, which now was bombed to smithereens, and which Hoover called "as ersatz as Hitler himself."[258]

He was seeing a Europe that most Americans did not know, and he wanted the American people to understand why their support was needed, and in their interest. On Good Friday, President Truman gave a radio address explaining that "America cannot remain healthy and happy in the same world where millions of human beings are starving."[259] Hoover followed up with a speech from Cairo, after having persuaded Egypt to export three hundred thousand tons of grain to needy countries. In his radio address, Hoover was specific, noting the exact number of calories being consumed in different parts of the world, and outlining which countries, including the United States, had the capacity to meet the demand.[260]

None of this was new to Hoover. During World War I, Americans had answered Hoover's calls for "Meatless Mondays" and "Wheatless Wednesdays," in order to have a surplus to ship to Europe. But the public was less receptive in 1946. Now Hoover was not the trusted messenger he once was, and after fifteen years of the Depression and war, they were not as willing to make sacrifices.[261]

In need of more public support, the president asked Hoover to come home and speak directly to the American people, to rally support.[262] But Hoover was full of humanitarian zealotry and didn't want to cut his mission short. He believed that the task of seeing what was happening in Asia was as important as Europe.[263] With Truman's permission, he continued to India, where he met with Mahatma Gandhi and Jawaharlal Nehru.[264] When he visited China, then engaged in a civil war between the Communists and the Nationalists, he sat down with Generalissimo Chiang Kai-shek and General George Marshall. He closed the Asian portion of his trip in Korea and Japan, where he met with General Douglas MacArthur, who had served Hoover as the chief of staff of the U.S. Army, and who—under Hoover's direction— had forced the Bonus Army out of its camps in Washington.[265]

The world after the war would look very different if the relief mission failed. As Hoover told Marshall, "It is useless to build a democracy over a cesspool of poverty, starvation and its consequent breeding of hate and antagonisms."[266] He continued home to San Francisco, and then to the White House to tell Truman what he'd seen of the post–World War II world.[267]

When Hoover entered the Oval Office, he had a better understanding of what was happening on the ground around the world than the commander in chief, or any of his top advisors. Truman had only traveled outside of the United States once as president, for the Potsdam Conference in May.[268] His predecessor's firsthand accounts were all the more important. As he later recalled, "Mr. Hoover's report outlined a country-by-country, month-by-month minimum program," which was "invaluable . . . in planning the measures that had to be taken for the months ahead."[269]

Hoover's report made it clear that the United States could not prevent global famine alone. With that in mind, Hoover boarded a plane bound for Argentina, another one of the few countries with a food surplus.[270] He touched down in Buenos Aires on June 6, forty-eight hours after dictator Juan Perón had taken power. The president had sent Hoover to Argentina, but the State Department wanted him nowhere near what could easily become a diplomatic crisis due to an unfavorable new government. True to his word, Truman vetoed Foggy Bottom's objections and endorsed Hoover's visit.[271]

The State Department tried to sabotage Hoover's mission. He may have been a former president and the emissary of the current president, but the U.S. ambassador did not meet him at the airport, instead dispatching a low-level staffer in what must have been the highlight of the lucky young foreign service officer's career. When Hoover asked the ambassador for help arranging a meeting with Perón, he was told it could take a few days to set up and might not even be possible. Frustrated but undaunted, Hoover instead called Mexico's ambassador to Argentina, who arranged the meeting with Perón in twenty minutes.[272]

The Argentine dictator didn't impress Hoover. But his wife, Eva Perón, did. Mrs. Perón struck Hoover as "an intelligent woman and very cordial." But her husband had the power, and Hoover worked to ingratiate himself at a formal dinner, where he was given the 196th spot out of 216 seats. Hoover didn't mind the slight, writing that he would have "eat[en] even Argentine dirt if I could get the 1,600,000 tons" of grain that was needed. It worked, and Argentina agreed to export grain, in exchange for the United States unfreezing gold deposits.[273]

Hoover returned to Washington pleased. He proved that former presidents—even unpopular ones—can be effective public servants. He also set a precedent that would later be adopted by Jimmy Carter, of former presidents meeting with American foes in the name of humanitarianism. Countries with food surpluses, including Canada, Argentina, and Australia, exported to needy countries. The United States alone shipped over 6 million tons of grain overseas. "Yours was a real service for humanity," Truman told Hoover. "Without your efforts . . . the suffering abroad would have been much greater."[274]

Much of the world still suffered. In Stalin's Soviet Union, large numbers of civilians were starving, and the post–World War II death toll from famine in Eastern-bloc countries like Moldova, Ukraine, and Russia may have exceeded 1 million lives.[275] Meanwhile in China, the bloody civil war raged, and the communists under Mao used hunger as a weapon. In the city of Changchun alone, as many as 160,000 civilians starved to death during a five-month-long siege against the Nationalist-held city.[276]

Famine relief was also just one piece of the postwar reconstruction, and Hoover believed that the U.S. needed to help rebuild Europe so that it could be "a dam against Russian aggression."[277] Aid to Europe wasn't just charity—it was an investment in security. Together with Senator Robert Taft, Hoover advocated for postwar reconstruction efforts. As Raymond Moley recalled, "It was Hoover's report on his survey of the food situation in Europe for Truman, plus confidential information he gave Truman and Marshall, that formed the basis" for what became known as the Marshall Plan.[278]

Hoover could take some satisfaction in his work—the Great Humanitarian was not lost to the history books. No former president had ever acted as the global envoy for the White House, and he'd broken new ground, and done so in a bipartisan spirit. But the effort had taken a toll. He'd spent much of the winter in unheated hotels, shivering in bombed-out European cities.[279] He was no longer the young man who'd traveled the world with Lou Henry. He'd flown through a blizzard over Newfoundland, which forced his pilot to make a speedy descent. The rapid change in air pressure burst Hoover's eardrums, and he had to wear a hearing aid from then on.[280]

A Political Odd Couple

Truman and Hoover weren't done with each other yet. The president called on Hoover to help reorganize a rapidly expanded executive branch, whose powers had expanded greatly, along with an ever-increasing number of agencies and executive branch personnel under Roosevelt.[281] Recognizing the strain on the small White House staff even then, Roosevelt had convened a group of advisors called the Brownlow Committee, which summed up its findings clearly: "The president needs help."[282]

Nearly a decade later, the president still needed help. Hoover was doubtful that the commission could be successful, but he obliged, telling reporters that this would be his last public service.[283] But the work continued in one form or another until 1955. Their partnership was becoming a lasting friendship. They were one of the oddest couples in Washington, but Truman told a skeptical friend that, though Hoover may be "to the right of Louis the Fourteenth . . . he deserves to be treated with respect as an ex-President."[284]

Truman even undid some of Roosevelt's more excessive slights against Hoover. Early in his administration, Roosevelt's interior secretary, Harold Ickes, had changed the Hoover Dam's name to the

Boulder Dam, despite the fact that Hoover had served as chairman of the Colorado River Commission and played a key role in the dam's construction, which began during his administration in 1931, finished in 1935, and came online the following year. In a show of appreciation and respect, Truman restored its old name in April 1947.[285] The president's gesture didn't go unnoticed. At the annual Gridiron Dinner, a high-profile event for Washington journalists, Hoover told the audience, "Amid the thousand crises which sweep upon us from abroad, [Truman] has . . . brought to the White House new impulses of good will toward men." The president, also in attendance, scribbled a note to Hoover: "With esteem and keen appreciation to a great man."[286]

Politics tested their friendship. When the Republicans won control of the House and Senate in 1946, it was clear that Truman couldn't take his reelection in 1948 for granted.[287] Hoover spoke at the Republican convention, but his remarks weren't partisan, and Truman sent him a cable telling him that his speech "was the utterance of a statesman."[288] In public, however, Truman was still willing to go after the Democratic Party's favorite bogeyman, and he repeatedly invoked the memory of "Hoover carts" in his stump speech, reminding his audience of the Great Depression and the former president's role.[289]

This became a pattern, and Truman attacked Hoover on the campaign trail, describing him as "one engineer who really did a job of running things backward."[290] Hoover didn't know what to make of these assaults, and came to think that Truman was a man who just couldn't resist playing the politics. "One day I find Truman, a devoted public servant who really comes from the people," he mused. "The next time I find him to be a Pendergast-machine politician who will do anything for a vote."[291]

That Hoover's name was still a partisan cudgel sixteen years after he left the White House, after a Great Depression and a world war and a major humanitarian effort, was a source of great sorrow and disappointment. But Truman was Hoover's friend now, and besides, he thought the president wasn't going to be reelected anyway. He had become less partisan in his old age, even though he had become more conservative. His skin had thickened, and even if at times old age offset that with a bit of crotchety snark, he seemed more able to roll with the punches.

Hoover wasn't alone in that prediction. The *Chicago Tribune* pre-printed its election coverage before the 1948 results were in, giving the story the infamous headline "Dewey Defeats Truman." But Truman proved the naysayers wrong. Holding the *Tribune* aloft in unabashed triumph, he celebrated his 303 electoral votes to Thomas Dewey's 189, while the Democrats retook the House and Senate.[292]

In victory Truman was ready to forget what he had done, and he wrote to Hoover as if he hadn't bad-mouthed him on the campaign trail, telling him, "I believe we can really accomplish some good re-sults."[293] Hoover confronted Truman about his campaign rhetoric, and the president apologized, making the excuse that he'd been reading from prepared scripts.[294]

Because he had been anticipating a Republican White House, the Hoover commission on reorganizing the executive branch had not yet released its first report. But with Truman back in for four more years, it published its findings that June, including 273 recommendations, 72 percent of which were implemented, including an aggregate of $7 billion worth of budget cuts and the creation of a new Depart-ment of Health, Education, and Welfare and the General Services Ad-ministration.[295] This built on his postwar humanitarian work, which reminded the world of Hoover the Great Humanitarian, and the com-mission was now offering a reminder that he had been a successful business executive as well. Deep down, he hoped that by sandwiching his presidency in between great deeds, the world might forget about President Hoover and just remember Herbert Hoover.

Hoover had broken new ground for former presidents as public servants. Even though he was a Republican, he'd worked for a Dem-ocratic administration. Just as he hit his stride, Hoover found his ego once more tested with a chance to enter politics in 1949, when Sena-tor Robert Wagner of New York retired and Governor Thomas Dewey offered to appoint him in Wagner's place. The move would not have been unprecedented. Andrew Johnson had been elected to the Senate in his post-presidency. But Hoover turned it down, thinking it should go to a younger man, and John Foster Dulles got the seat, which he lost in the next election before becoming an influential secretary of state.[296]

Hoover was glad to be back in public service, but this didn't mean he would become a desperate yes-man, either. He was prepared to say no, even to the president. During the Red Scare in the 1950s, Truman asked him to lead another bipartisan commission, this one tasked with looking into Wisconsin senator Joseph McCarthy's allegations that there were communists at the State Department.[297] Hoover, an anti-communist, declined to get involved, due to his worries about the civil rights implications and the politicization of the issue.[298]

The McCarthy hearings were important for another California Republican Quaker, a young congressman named Richard M. Nixon, who played a prominent role in the trial of Soviet spy Alger Hiss. In contrast to the bombastic and paranoid McCarthy, Nixon seemed serious and effective. The future president gained many admirers, including Hoover. When the guilty verdict against Hiss was announced, Hoover sent Nixon a telegram: "At last the stream of treason that has existed in our government has been exposed in a fashion all may believe."[299]

With events like the Hiss trial and the vindication of Hiss's accuser, Whittaker Chambers, a communist defector and an editor at *Time*, the modern conservative movement was taking shape as both a force for anti-communism and resistance to the New Deal. For two decades, Hoover had played a role in midwifing the movement. But it still didn't have a leader.

THE GRAND NEW PARTY

Dwight D. Eisenhower was not the conservatives' first choice for president, or Hoover's. The general's victory in the 1952 election was bittersweet. Hoover had hoped for a Republican president for twenty years, but he'd wanted Robert Taft, "Mr. Republican,"[300] not the moderate Eisenhower. President Eisenhower would make peace with the New Deal. He also showed the Republicans how to compete and win.

During the 1952 primaries, Hoover had pushed hard for Taft. The

Ohio senator entered the nomination contest with a strong chance, and he was aligned with Hoover on policy issues. Eisenhower entered the contest late, on June 4. And it soon became clear that Taft wouldn't win the nomination, though Hoover scrambled with a group of GOP leaders in suite 31-A at the Waldorf to try for their second choice, General Douglas MacArthur, a neighbor in suite 37-A.[301]

Eisenhower was not a politician, but he had political cunning, defeating all comers and selecting the conservative Nixon as his running mate in order to gain support from Western delegates and to shore up his base among the anti-communist bloc. Hoover, used to being disappointed at Republican conventions, gritted his teeth and threw his support behind Eisenhower. He may not have liked Ike, but, "Being a Republican," he stated, "I shall vote for the Republican ticket."[302]

The 1952 election was a story of rising and falling political dynasties. Robert Taft, William Howard Taft's son, failed to gain the Republican nomination. Henry Cabot Lodge Jr., who had sponsored the bill for the Hoover Commission and managed Eisenhower's campaign, lost his Massachusetts Senate seat to John F. Kennedy. Eisenhower's opponent, Democrat Adlai Stevenson III, the grandson of Grover Cleveland's vice president, went down to defeat. When the votes were in, American politics were remade.

Eisenhower won 55 percent of the popular vote and 442 votes in the Electoral College, making him the first Republican president since Hoover, and with a comfortable margin.[303] Massachusetts congressman Joseph Martin, soon to be Speaker of the House, credited Hoover with making that victory possible. He argued that Hoover had kept the Republican Party alive during its wilderness years. "No one has contributed more to the upbuilding of the Republican Party than you have. . . . Tuesday was a great vindication to you," Martin told him.[304]

The former president hadn't played a prominent role on the campaign trail, but author Clare Boothe Luce noted that one Republican had been waiting twenty years for a Republican victory and suggested Eisenhower phone Hoover on election night. Eisenhower obliged and the president-elect told Hoover that he'd be calling him in the future for advice.[305] He later tapped Hoover to lead another commission that built on his Truman-era work to reorganize the executive branch. The second Hoover Commission, though less successful than the first, published two volumes with recommendations on everything from civilian control of the military to the budget process.[306] While 64 percent of the recommendations became law and resulted in $3 billion of budget cuts, the vast majority of those savings were later repurposed to fight the Korean War, which was an unwelcome outcome for a man who was all too familiar with the cost of war. When the work was nearly done, the now eighty-one-year-old Hoover breathed a sigh of relief. He was exhausted, and told the world, "I have never worked harder, nor longer hours than on the present job."[307]

"Exclusive Trade Unionists"

There were two firsts for Hoover during the Eisenhower presidency. For the first time since 1933, there was a Republican in the White House. And also for the first time since that same year, Hoover was no longer the sole living ex-president. Harry Truman was now also a member of what Hoover called "that most exclusive trade union."[308]

They'd lost touch, but two acts of Congress brought Truman and Hoover together again. As president, Truman had decided to build a library for his papers on his own. In 1955, Congress passed the Presidential Libraries Act, a new law that established a system of public and private support for presidential libraries that every president since has followed. Hoover had his archive on Stanford's campus, but he helped Truman—who'd left office with a sub-30 percent approval rating—raise $200,000 for his own.[309]

The second law was the Former Presidents Act, which passed in 1958. For the first time, former presidents were provided pensions, starting at $25,000 a year.[310] As the only two living former presidents, only Hoover and Truman were eligible. Hoover was much wealthier than Truman, a haberdasher before he entered politics, and he didn't need the pension. But he accepted the money so as not to embarrass his friend or set unrealistic precedents, writing, "My case is not a precedent for public officials. No man can make any substantial savings from being President of the United States."[311]

Famous Last Words

Both former presidents were showing signs of their age. When he heard that Harry Truman had recently broken two ribs while trying to get out of his bathtub, Hoover wrote him a humorous note, observing that "bathtubs are a menace to ex-Presidents." He recalled his own experience falling into a tub during a relief mission to Venezuela, where he'd sustained several injuries at the time, including cracked vertebrae.[312]

Life without politics was simpler for Hoover. In the summers, he was in California, where he attended meetings of the Bohemian Grove, the men's club in the Redwoods that had been a refuge and a place of annual pilgrimage. There he set up his Caveman Camp, named after a nearby statue of a prehistoric man. In this bucolic setting, he spent his days fishing and waxing philosophic with like-minded men, including many from his class at Stanford. During the winters, he could often be found likewise fishing in Florida, away from Washington. The rest of the year, he was in Manhattan, at home at the Waldorf in 31-A.[313]

He didn't waste time. At age eighty-two, he told a young woman, "There is no joy to be had from retirement except by some kind of productive work. Otherwise, you degenerate into talking to everybody about your pains and pills and income tax."[314] He was at his desk most days by 6:00 a.m., and he wore a three-piece suit and hosted dignitaries visiting New York, now home to the United Nations. He often worked for twelve hours a day, reading papers and writing. Children wrote to him, and he'd reply to almost all with the same advice: "Work hard, study, and go fishing." He smoked constantly, and the International Association of Pipe Smokers offered him the Pipe Smoker of the Year award.[315]

His real task was writing. He published a landmark book, *The Ordeal of Woodrow Wilson*, in 1958, the first time that one former president wrote a book about another, although John Quincy Adams tried. Wilson was a progressive icon and Hoover's conservatism had hardened, but he said his Democratic predecessor was "the only enduring leader of those statesmen who conducted the First World War and its aftermath of peacemaking." Edith Wilson, then eighty-six years old, wrote to Hoover, "You seem to have really understood [my husband]."[316]

He kept writing his last words for two decades after the war. He published seven more books by 1964, including *An American Epic*, a four-volume set covering 1913 to 1963 in minute detail.[317] His magnum opus, *Freedom Betrayed: Herbert Hoover's Secret History of the Second World War*, remained unpublished until 2011, when it saw the light of day thanks to the work of historian George Nash.[318] He was incredibly productive, and one of his research assistants from that time, Mary Louise, says that he was so prolific because he wanted to "set the record straight."[319]

Hoover's Last Election

By 1960, a new generation that didn't remember the Great Depression had come of age. Historians were starting to revisit Hoover and his legacy. While most still blamed Hoover, a few were breaking ranks, including Harris Gaylord Warren and his work *Herbert Hoover and the Great Depression*.[320]

The 1960 presidential election would be Hoover's last. He knew both candidates well, as he was a friend of Joseph Kennedy, and once called his son, John F. Kennedy, his "favorite senator."[321] Hoover admired Nixon's anti-communism, and the former president spoke in favor of his nomination at the Republican convention, but that speech was more a swan song than a rallying cry, as Hoover told the audience, "In each of your last three Conventions I bade you an affectionate good-bye. Unless some miracle comes to me from the Good Lord this is finally it."[322]

There was no conservative standard-bearer in the 1960 election, as there hadn't been one in 1952 or 1956. In the weeks before the election, Hoover joined a dinner at the Plaza Hotel hosted by a new magazine called the *National Review* and its young editor, William F. Buckley, who addressed the group and bemoaned the fact that there was no clear conservative candidate in the race. "We are all of us," Buckley reported to the assembled conservatives, "in one sense out of spirit with history."[323]

Neither candidate won a majority of the popular vote that November, and the electorate delivered the narrowest margin since Grover

Cleveland's victory over James Blaine in 1888. Razor-thin margins in places like Illinois, with a strong Democratic political machine, led to allegations of wrongdoing. When Kennedy was declared the winner, many Nixon supporters urged their candidate to challenge the results, but Nixon conceded to Kennedy early in the morning.[324]

Despite Nixon's concession, the country remained divided, giving Hoover one last public role to play. Vice President Nixon was in Florida for a vacation and to lick his wounds. By coincidence, John F. Kennedy was vacationing nearby, and so, too, was Herbert Hoover. Ambassador Kennedy phoned Hoover to ask if he might arrange for Nixon to meet publicly with his son, in order to show the nation a display of friendship.[325]

More than willing to do so, Hoover called Nixon and practically ordered him, "I think we are in enough trouble in the world today; some indication of national unity are not only desirable but essential." Nixon agreed, and the two candidates met in Key Biscayne, Florida, on November 14. The story was front-page news.[326]

As Eisenhower's vice president, Richard Nixon presided over the Senate chamber during the counting of electoral votes on January 6, 1961. It was a painful moment, and he told the Senate, "In our campaigns, no matter how hard they may be, no matter how close the election may turn out to be, those who lose accept the verdict and support those who win."[327] Hoover admired Nixon, but thought his political career was over, and told him that he would "discover that elder statesmen are little regarded by the opposition party until they get over 80 years of age, and are harmless."[328]

Hoover had gone from political pariah to national unifier and he had recovered the self-confidence to do it in the shadows. President Kennedy invited Hoover to be his guest at the inauguration, but bad weather forced his plane to turn back to Miami, and he sent his regrets: "I do wish you every blessing of the Almighty, and I am confident of your great success as our President."[329] When Kennedy offered Hoover a position as the honorary chairman of the newly created Peace Corps,[330] he sent his regrets again—he was eighty-six, and he didn't have another act of public service in him.[331]

The only thing that could make Hoover change his mind about not serving his country happened in Dallas, Texas, on November 22, 1963. When John F. Kennedy was assassinated and Lyndon Johnson became the president, the then eighty-nine-year-old Herbert Hoover wrote in distress to the White House: "I am ready to serve our government in any capacity, from office boy up."[332]

The Chief's End

Throughout his life, few things gave Hoover more satisfaction than being of service. He had what Harvard professor and social scientist Arthur Brooks has described as the "need to be needed . . . the essence of being alive . . . and a question of human dignity."[333] The thought of not having a purpose or meaningful work, as had often been the case for the twelve years of the Roosevelt presidency, was terrible.

When he couldn't travel the world anymore, his home at suite 31-A was a place where presidents and would-be presidents came to seek advice and pay their respects. President Johnson visited in December 1963, along with Chief Justice Earl Warren. During the 1964 election, Richard Nixon visited to talk politics. Republican candidate Arizona senator Barry Goldwater—a conservative, like Hoover—called to keep him up-to-date.[334]

Hoover couldn't make the 1964 Republican convention due to his health, but he sent a message to be read by Senator Everett Dirksen, who called Hoover "the grand old man of the grand old party." Thirty years after his presidency, the delegates gave Hoover an ovation in absentia.[335]

Three months later, news of Hoover's passing came in the form of a short note from his doctor. It included only his name, the date, and the time of death: "President Hoover. Oct. 20, 1964. Time: 11:35 A.M." Hoover had slipped into a coma in his suite. His two sons were by his side. The Goldwater and Johnson campaigns suspended operations to mourn his passing, and both attended his funeral at St. Bartholomew's in New York. His body was then transported to Washington, DC, where it was greeted by a twenty-one-gun salute and carried by a military escort to Capitol Hill, where he lay in state. He was laid to rest in West Branch, Iowa, at a gravesite he chose that over-looked the cottage in which he was born.[336]

After such a long and varied life, the country didn't know what to make of Herbert Hoover at his passing. The *New York Times* remembered what had been called the "'Hoover Depression' by [Hoover's] political opponents." But, the obituary continued, "later judgments . . . have suggested that he was the victim of events that coincided with his tenure." The paper noted what the thirty-first president had accomplished in his thirty-one years after the White House, and reported that his service to Truman and Eisenhower had "restored him in the affection of millions."[337]

There is a powerful lesson in Herbert Hoover's story. He learned how quickly a life's reputation can be destroyed, and while he never fully understood how it happened, he focused on the forward. He was determined to once again serve the world, the country, and his party, but recognized that he'd have to work harder than what would be ex-pected of someone at his stage of life. Hoover had an almost dogmatic sense of purpose and view about what needed to be done and what role he could play. The closer he got to recovering what he had lost, the harder he worked. And, as mortality approached, he worked even harder.

Two weeks after Hoover's death, the 1964 election was over. Barry Goldwater carried only six states, the same number that Hoover had won in his matchup against FDR in 1932.[338] Running on its most con-servative platform since the 1920s, the Republican Party again looked as dead as it had been the day Hoover left office.

One of the states Goldwater did win was Georgia, with its twelve electoral votes.[339] While Goldwater wouldn't go on to the White House, the voters of Georgia's 14th district that year sent Hoover's fellow engineer Jimmy Carter back to Atlanta for a second term in the state senate.[340]

Twelve years later, the peanut farmer from Plains, Georgia, was headed to the White House with a story as improbable as the story of the orphan son of a blacksmith who became a multimillionaire globe-trotting humanitarian and president.

Jimmy Carter began his presidency in much the same way that Herbert Hoover did—after one term, unpopular, and with the dawn of a new political age unfolding after him, be it the Age of Roosevelt or the Age of Reagan. Carter's active post-presidency, at more than forty-two years, was also the only one longer than Herbert Hoover's. In that time, he'd transform how America understood his legacy, and what is possible in the post-presidency.

The Former

My faith demands that I do whatever I can, wherever I can, whenever I can, for as long as I can.

—JIMMY CARTER

Former presidents have a lot in common with former astronauts. They've both had an otherworldly experience. After occupying the Oval Office or orbiting the earth, few other jobs or experiences can measure up.

Philosopher Frank White theorized about what happens to former astronauts in his 1987 book, *The Overview Effect*. White described how, when astronauts finish their missions, they experience a "cognitive shift in awareness that results from the experience of viewing Earth from orbit or the moon."[1] After orbiting the earth from space, daily life back on the ground seems mundane by comparison. Their concerns become larger than life—world peace, global hunger, climate change, and other world-changing causes.

Presidents tend to experience a reverse overview effect when they leave office. For four or eight years, presidents' agendas are filled with the issues that occupy the minds of former astronauts. They return to normal life on their successor's Inauguration Day. However, there's one major difference between the two trajectories. Astronauts return to earth with newfound fame and a platform they've never had before. Former presidents reenter civilian life with less, not more, fame than they had in office. Their platform shrinks, along with their influence.

They no longer have the bully pulpit of the presidency, they don't command the military anymore, and they don't decide the fate and outcomes for billions of people. Instead, their days are filled with the more mundane daily tasks, and the problems they encounter are far from those that landed on the Resolute desk. This transition can be a downer for many presidents and some can't let go of their time in the White House.

Jimmy Carter certainly couldn't. He was young when he left office, at just fifty-six years old. But he was unpopular, with a conservative successor who'd run against nearly every one of his policies. Carter was not about to make a comeback, and there was no position to which he wanted to be appointed.

The White House was out of reach, as well as any national elected office. He had few connections in the business world. So Carter decided to do something different. He turned the post-presidency into a lifetime appointment with power of its own. For more than four decades, he used his status as a "former" to continue the work he began in the White House. As Emory University president James Laney once said, Jimmy Carter was "the only president who ever used the White House as a stepping-stone."[2] Carter himself told a group of alumni from his administration, "What we're doing at the Carter Center," his postpresidential home base, "is an extension of what we were doing in the White House."[3]

After his single term, he had unfinished business. As unpopular as he was, he also had a platform and connections that he intended to use. He turned his unpopularity into an asset that freed him from partisan or institutional constraints. He became an activist, a humanitarian, a global health advocate, a human rights defender, and a democracy promoter. He worked with, criticized, and undermined his successors, regardless of party.

Jimmy Carter's forty-two-year active post-presidency was the longest in American history.[4] His more than seventy-eight-year marriage to Rosalynn Carter is the longest presidential marriage to date. Together, they traveled to more than 145 countries after the White House.[5] They worked with leaders as diverse as Archbishop Desmond Tutu and Yasser Arafat. Carter negotiated with Syria's Hafez al-Assad and North Korea's Kim Il Sung. He led global health campaigns and eradicated diseases. He built hundreds of homes through Habitat for Humanity. He transformed the post-presidency and gave the status "former" a power of its own.

By the time Jimmy Carter entered hospice care in February 2023, his presidency had faded into memory. Two generations had come of age. They couldn't remember the Soviet Union, the Iran hostage crisis, stagflation, and gas lines. What they remembered was former president Carter. Though he'd left the White House with a 34 percent approval rating, by the time his active post-presidency ended, he was the second-most popular Democratic politician alive, behind only Barack Obama.[6] The post-presidency would never be the same.

CRASH LANDING

Jimmy Carter's presidency reached its climax less than an hour after it was all over.[7] Ronald Reagan had taken his oath of office, and the former president and vice president, Walter Mondale, were in a car headed for Andrews Air Force Base, leaving Washington behind.

At 12:38 p.m., 9:08 p.m. in Tehran, the car phone rang. Knowing what he was about to hear, Carter picked up the receiver and listened for a moment. He put down the phone and turned to Mondale to utter the words he'd been waiting to say for 444 days: "They're out."[8] As of that moment, fifty-two Americans held captive during the Iran Hostage Crisis were safe. It was over. But so was the Carter presidency.

Downward Spiral

The last eighteen months of the Carter administration were the worst, and everyone knew it. Former Hubert Humphrey advisor Jeane Kirkpatrick summed up the feeling neatly in a 1979 article for *Commentary* magazine titled "Dictatorships and Double Standards," in which she stated bluntly, "The failure of the Carter administration's foreign policy is now clear to everyone except its architects."[9]

Kirkpatrick was right. In its foreign policy, the United States began the decade with a loss in Vietnam, followed by the fall of Saigon in 1975. Things didn't get better—during the Carter administration, the USSR made gains from Angola, to Mozambique, to Nicaragua.[10] There were new communist regimes all over the world that had taken over not through democratic elections, but through force and with the military aid and support of the Soviet Union.[11] On February 14, 1979, America's ambassador to Afghanistan, Adolph Dubs, was kidnapped and murdered in Kabul. Then Moscow invaded Afghanistan on Christmas Day. It looked like the Soviet Union might win the Cold War.

Nothing was going according to plan for Carter. He'd entered office a foreign-policy dove, but by the end of his term, he'd been mugged by reality. He began a defense buildup that would accelerate under his successor, Ronald Reagan.[12] He'd wanted to advance landmark arms-control agreements, but he'd had to shelve a proposed second Strategic Arms Limitation Treaty (SALT II). He'd started arming Afghan rebels, but it was too little, too late.

He wasn't without foreign-policy accomplishments. Jimmy Carter delivered the Camp David Accords, conceived by Richard Nixon and Henry Kissinger,[13] which culminated in a ceremony on the South Lawn of the White House in 1978 in which Israel and Egypt signed a historic peace agreement.[14] The previous year, he'd transformed American diplomacy in Latin America, working with Congress to pass the Panama Canal Treaty in 1977. He recognized the People's Republic of China in 1979.

Most important, he'd promised to deliver "a government that is as honest and decent and fair and competent and truthful and idealistic as are the American people."[15] After Vietnam and Watergate, that's what America wanted, and the plainspoken, uncorrupt Jimmy Carter had seemed like a breath of fresh air. He'd deregulated the airline industry and with the Environmental Protect Agency—established in 1970—up and running, he had climate change on the national agenda, the first time an American president had done so.[16]

None of that seemed to matter on November 4, 1979, however. An Iranian mob stormed the American embassy in Tehran, taking fifty-two Americans hostage for 444 days.[17] The American public followed the story every night on a new ABC program called *The Iran Crisis:*

America Held Hostage, which later became *Nightline*. In 1979, Iran
cut oil production by 4.8 million barrels a day,[18] and prices went up
400 percent.[19] The mixture of low growth, high unemployment, and
double-digit inflation and interest rates popularized a new term: "stagflation."[20]

The American people now believed that an honest peanut farmer
from Plains, Georgia, was not up to the challenge of being president of
the United States. Carter—despite his humble background and lack
of DC connections—seemed out of touch with the concerns of everyday Americans. In one of his most ill-fated speeches, he told the American people that they were experiencing a "crisis of confidence" and
needed to "stop crying and start sweating." While he may have been
right, the message of malaise landed with a thud.[21]

His own party turned on him. A young senator named Joe Biden
warned Carter that Senator Ted Kennedy would challenge him in
1980.[22] After a bitter fight, Kennedy failed to win the nomination, embarrassing himself in an interview with CBS journalist Roger Mudd
when he could not explain why he was running for president in the first
place.[23] But Massachusetts's favorite son did real damage to Carter and
gave him a run for his money. He then delivered a rousing speech at the
Democratic convention that overshadowed the incumbent president.

It was clear that after four years of Carter, Americans wanted
change. They got it in Ronald Reagan, who had mounted his third
bid for the White House after failed attempts in 1968 and 1976. The
former movie star and two-term governor of California asked voters a
simple question: "Are you better off than you were four years ago?"[24]
In 1980, even for moderate voters and some Democrats who were
turned off by Reagan's conservatism, the answer was no. They gave
Reagan 489 Electoral College votes to a paltry 49 for Carter.[25]

A Carter loss was predictable, but not preordained. Earlier in the
fall of 1980, the polls had shown that Carter had a chance against
Reagan. But by the time of the election, Carter's pollster Pat Caddell
informed him that he'd fallen ten points behind Reagan. This was an
insurmountable lead.[26] Anticipating his defeat, Carter watched the results come in at home in Plains, Georgia, where he'd held a rally to
close out his campaign. He carried his home state, but even before

the networks started to call the election, at around 8:00 p.m. Eastern, Carter knew it was over.[27]

He did not want his presidency to end. But there was no point in delaying the inevitable. At 9:01 p.m. on election night, before the polls had closed on the West Coast, Carter phoned Ronald Reagan. The Republican candidate was taking a shower at his home in Palisades, California, anticipating a longer night. But Carter didn't want to lead on his supporters anymore. He told his wife, Rosalynn, that he just wanted to "get it over with."[28]

He was defeated, but he wasn't done being president. He had work to do. As George Packer wrote, Carter "finish[ed] his term like a man staring under the hood of his car in the middle of a mudslide."[29] The president worked as if his last hundred days were his first, and he signed legislation on everything from mental health to land conservation in Alaska.

But the most critical matter of the Carter presidency remained unresolved until the bitter end. He'd called the Iran Hostage Crisis the most "gripping and politically important [issue]" facing the American people.[30] He worked on that issue every day, personally negotiating for the American hostages' release from at least September 9, 1980, onward.[31] His negotiations concluded at 6:30 a.m. on the day of Ronald Reagan's inauguration. It was January 20, 1981, and the clock was running out.

That morning, Carter was bleary-eyed and exhausted. He rode in the presidential limousine from the White House to the Capitol, accompanied by Ronald Reagan. Earlier in the day, the president had received a call from National Security Agency director Admiral Bobby Ray Inman. Inman told him that his negotiations had worked and that the hostages were going to be allowed to board a plane out of Tehran. But there was a catch—Ayatollah Khomeini would not let them depart until Reagan was sworn in. Carter could not take any credit. This was one last humiliation.[32]

It was also a terrible way to begin a post-presidency. But in many ways, this didn't feel like the end of the White House years. True, Carter was no longer the president. But he still had much of the pomp and circumstance of the office around him. When he got to Andrews

Air Force Base, he stepped out of a limousine decked out in American flags. He boarded the president's plane, on loan from Ronald Reagan. The plane had the seal of the president of the United States on its side. He was accompanied by his former vice president, his chief of staff, and his domestic policy advisor. Many members of the Carter administration brought their families along after his young daughter, Amy Carter, had looked upset at leaving her friends behind, and Carter invited everyone to join them, calling out, "Come on, everybody, this is a time to be happy. Get on board."[33]

The former president had one last mission, an encore before his band broke up. He and his aides were leaving Washington and headed for a stop in Georgia. But their real destination was West Germany. They were going to meet fifty-two former hostages, soon to be free on American soil.[34]

This was not freelance diplomacy. President Reagan loaned Carter his plane and asked his defeated foe to go to West Germany. To Reagan's secretary of state, Alexander Haig, sending Carter to the American base in Wiesbaden had two benefits. First, it "had the virtue of giving Carter public credit for the deliverance of the hostages," a gracious gesture from the new administration. Second, it "separat[ed] [Carter] from the nearest media center by the width of the Atlantic and the Rhine." There were reporters on the plane, but meeting freed American hostages beyond the water's edge would be an opportunity for the former president to rise above politics.[35] There was little risk of Carter grandstanding on other matters.

Few members of Carter's team knew what their next jobs would be. They had been working to the last minute, with little time to think about what would come. Carter gave a farewell address, but there the end was abrupt, and there was no "organizational death ritual" of the type that Stanford University professor Bob Sutton finds helps teams move on.[36] The Carter administration had been working until the last minute to free the American hostages—they hadn't had time for rituals.

There were mixed feelings aboard the plane. White House appointments secretary Phil Wise felt a sense of joy, and he wandered up and down the aisle chanting, "We're free, we're free, thank God Almighty, we're free at last." Aide Anne Wexler sang a different tune. She reminded the reporters that the 1984 Iowa Caucuses were "exactly three years from today."[37]

They didn't have much time to think, as it was a short flight from Andrews to Warner Robins Air Force Base in Georgia. When they landed, they got in a motorcade to Plains, where the Carters were greeted by three thousand supporters on Main Street. The former president delivered brief remarks, and then he and his wife danced a polka as a local band played "Dixie."[38]

The party was most welcome, and the Carters returned home tired afterward, but hardly able to sleep. They were too busy thinking about West Germany and the freed Americans. The sun rose a little before 8:00 a.m., and they reboarded the plane. The exhausted former president had a rare chance for some rest as he crossed the Atlantic.

At 8:30 p.m. that night, the former president and his team landed in West Germany. They were greeted like Jimmy Carter was still president. Carter met with German chancellor Helmut Schmidt, then traveled via motorcade with his aides to the military hospital where the freed hostages were being examined. The fifty-two Americans had suffered terrible physical and mental abuse for more than a year.[39]

When Carter walked into a conference room with the group, he tried to break the ice with a joke. He congratulated them that their release had finally knocked Ronald Reagan off the front pages. It was a political remark that fell flat. Many members of the group resented Carter. They believed that he'd failed them. The former president could sense the tension, and he changed his tone. He spoke with them for an hour. They explained their 444-day trial, and he listened. He told them how his administration had acted during the crisis. He was approachable, and it became clear how personally invested he had been in their fates. One freed hostage recalled, "He knew all of us by name, knew our backgrounds, our families."[40]

This wasn't an easy conversation, however. The freed hostages asked Carter pointed questions, including about his decision to allow the Shah into the United States to seek medical treatment, a decision that had immediately preceded the storming of the embassy. They asked him about Operation Eagle Claw, the ill-fated rescue mission Carter had authorized that not only failed but also had resulted in the deaths of eight American service members. There was a moment of relief when Carter told them that the U.S. had not paid a ransom for their release and the group cheered.[41]

The meeting ended, and the former president was even more exhausted. But he was determined. He went to tell a group of reporters about the conversation. Standing in front of a flag-waving crowd, he said that the encounter with the fifty-two Americans was one of the "most moving and gratifying" moments in his life. He condemned the Islamic Republic of Iran, which he said had perpetrated a "despicable act of savagery."[42]

Then it was all over. On the way home, Carter turned to his former chief of staff, a Georgian named Hamilton Jordan, and whispered, "You know, Ham, if we had had a little luck back in March or April and gotten 'em out then, we might be flying back to Washington instead of Plains."[43]

The former president may have been right. Had Operation Eagle Claw succeeded, it would have been a triumph. Carter would have looked tough, and he might have won the election triumphant. But the counterfactual didn't matter. The Carter team had had one last great day together. But they'd lost. When they landed in Georgia, this time they went their separate ways. Ronald Reagan was in the White House. Jimmy Carter was back on his peanut farm.

BACK TO EARTH

Before 1976, few people on earth knew who James Earl Carter Jr. was. When he told his mother, Lillian, that he intended to run for president, she replied, "President of what?"[44] Expressing a similar sentiment after he announced, Carter's hometown paper, the *Atlanta Journal Constitution*, ran a story headlined "Jimmy Who Is Running for What!?"[45]

There was even more confusion outside of Georgia. The *New York Times* didn't know what to make of the one-term governor. The paper called him either a "Southern-style Kennedy" or "just another Democratic dark horse." When Gallup commissioned a survey for a list of possible presidential candidates for 1976, respondents came up with thirty-one ideas. Carter's name wasn't on the list.[46]

He was a mystery even to many of those who ended up working in the Carter administration. His future labor secretary, Ray Marshall, said, "[Carter] was a liberal. He was a conservative. He was a centrist. It depended on the issue."[47] His one-time chief speechwriter, James Fallows, recalled, "I came to think that Carter believed fifty things, but no one thing."[48]

Likewise, the American people didn't know what they were getting with Carter. But they'd long believed they could trust him. His breakout happened in the Iowa Caucuses when he came in a surprise second place, albeit behind "Uncommitted." From there, he defeated more than sixteen candidates in the 1976 Democratic nomination contest.[49] He defeated Republican president Gerald Ford, the man who had pardoned Richard Nixon after Watergate.

The American people elected Jimmy Carter because they believed in him. This was a time of political instability. No president of either party since Dwight Eisenhower had completed two terms. A Southern governor with a portrait of Martin Luther King Jr. hanging in his Atlanta office, a man who was an evangelical Christian with a charming smile, and who, most important, had spent his career faraway from Washington and Watergate could be trusted.

In 1976, voters liked what they'd learned about Carter. Shortly after his inauguration, his approval rating hit a high of nearly 75 percent.[50] Watching the polls, one envious Republican National Committee operative commented, "[Carter] was folks, and folks was in."[51] But the honeymoon didn't last long. When Reagan took office, Carter's approval rating sank to 34 percent.[52] Everyone in America knew who Jimmy Carter was. By 1981, they wanted to forget all about him.

Carter couldn't forget about the last four years. He wanted them to continue. He'd outlined some of his coming priorities in his farewell address, when he'd used Thomas Jefferson's famous phrase "life, liberty, and the pursuit of happiness" to tell his audience that "for this generation, ours, life is nuclear survival; liberty is human rights; the pursuit of happiness is a planet whose resources are devoted to the physical and spiritual nourishment of its inhabitants."[53] Even former Nixon speechwriter William Safire grudgingly called this turn of phrase the "most skillful line of the Carter presidency."[54]

The Oval Office is far away from Plains, the Carters' hometown of roughly five hundred inhabitants. The White House seemed like another world. They moved back into a home that had been in the family since 1961. It was the only one the former first couple had ever owned, but they hadn't lived there full-time for nearly a decade.[55] They were young, just fifty-six and fifty-three years old. At what might have been the peak of their professional careers, they were back where they started, without a clue about what came next.

The ranch-style home at 209 Woodland Drive, surrounded by woods of oak and hickory trees, was no longer big enough for the Carters. During their first week back, they put in a new pine floor in the attic in an attempt to give themselves more storage space.[56] Every day, they woke up in the small, quiet house. It was eerie after the noise and staff at 1600 Pennsylvania Avenue. Jimmy and Rosalynn Carter were unsettled. They feared that all that awaited now was an "altogether new, unwanted, and potentially empty life."[57]

Carter called January 21, 1981, his "involuntary retirement."[58] The fact that he'd lost to a man like Ronald Reagan made the experience even more unbearable. Before he was governor of California, Reagan was a B-list movie star. To Carter, his telegenic successor was both shallow and extreme. On the campaign trail, he'd described Reagan as the second coming of conservative firebrand Barry Goldwater, a man who'd won only six states, saying that Reagan was as "different from me in almost every basic element of commitment and experience and promise to the American people."[59]

After the election, Carter never lost his animosity toward Reagan, or his bitterness at his defeat. As late as 1995, in an interview with historian Douglas Brinkley, he was asked what he thought his biggest failure in office was. To Carter, it wasn't the Iran Hostage Crisis or stagflation. It was "allowing Ronald Reagan to become president."[60]

Rosalynn Carter felt the same as her husband. She was Jimmy Carter's partner in all things, and the love of his life. During their four years in office, she'd led many White House initiatives, including groundbreaking work on mental health. On the national stage, she'd earned a reputation as the "steel magnolia" for her Southern toughness.[61] But after the loss in 1980, she was not quite so steely. In defeat,

she admitted that she "was bitter enough for both of us."[62] She later
wrote that she threw up her hands in those early days and wondered,
"How could the press have been so bad?" and "How could God have
let this happen?"[63]

The Carters were also broke, which made matters worse. In truth,
Jimmy Carter had never been rich. While he was president, he'd put
what assets he had, including the family peanut farm, into a blind trust
in order to avoid even the appearance of conflicts of interest. His principles were noble, but they cost him. The farm did not do well in those
four years. It was mismanaged, and it suffered from a terrible drought
that hit Sumter County hard. While he was in the Oval Office, he
hadn't known how bad it was getting down in Plains. But just after his
defeat in 1980, his lawyer and trustee, Charlie Kirbo, came by to tell
him, "You're a million in debt."[64]

Debt is a problem that plagues many Southern presidents. George
Washington, Thomas Jefferson, James Madison, and James Monroe,
all Virginians, suffered the same fate. After he died, Jefferson's family
had to sell Monticello. However, Carter had no Monticello to fall back
on. The only help that he had was that, since Truman, former presidents have had pensions.

They also typically have plenty of opportunities for sinecures in
the business world. The first former president to cash in big on that
status was Gerald Ford, Carter's predecessor. Ford pioneered the practice of former presidents joining corporate boards and attracting large
speaking fees. Ford joined the leadership teams of several Fortune 500
companies, including 20th Century Fox,[65] and was an honorary director at Citigroup.[66] After Carter, Ronald Reagan earned $2 million on
a single tour through Japan.[67] From 2001 until 2016, Bill and Hillary
Clinton earned a staggering sum of a reported $153 million in speak-
ing fees.[68] Even George W. Bush, who left office as unpopular as Carter, can command $250,000 for a single speech, and Barack Obama
often gets between $500,000 to $1 million.[69]

No one would pay that kind of money to hear Jimmy Carter speak
in 1981. He had few connections to join the business world, and
even less desire to make them. But he did need to make a living. His
$69,630 a year pension was not enough.[70]

Fortunately, Carter got a lifeline from Archer-Daniels-Midland Company, a Chicago firm that was looking to break into the peanut industry. The company offered to buy Carter's warehouse for nearly as much as he owed. Overnight, his debts were gone, and he no longer had to think about selling the farm. He then started to tap into what would become the main source of his postpresidential income, writing books.

Before he left the White House, Carter had been offered a $900,000 advance for a memoir. Now that he was out of office, he exchanged his typewriter for a word processor, and he got to work.[71] He was the last presidential memoirist to have an advantage that every other modern president has lacked. Carter got to keep many of his papers from his time in the White House, as he was not yet bound by the recently passed Presidential Records Act of 1978, a post-Watergate law.[72] Because that statute was not retroactive, Carter arrived in Plains with dozens of boxes with papers from his White House years. In total, he had twenty-one volumes and a million words' worth of notes written on five thousand pages. These documents would be the basis for his first book, *Keeping Faith: Memoirs of a President*. It was published in 1982.

Carter told his readers that his goal with the book was to provide "a highly personal report of [his] own experiences" as president.[73] As such, the writing process was often reflective, and a chance to relive his four years. His real goal was more straightforward, however. He later told a journalist that, in writing the book, he just wanted to "redeem our family finances."[74]

The critics were not impressed, and *Keeping Faith* got mixed reviews. The *New York Times* described it as "vintage Jimmy Carter, a mirror, in fact, of its author: honest, sincere, intelligent, dry, humorless and impersonal."[75] Only slightly kinder, the reviewer at *Foreign Affairs* pithily said the book had "no great literary distinction, but it is short, sincere and straightforward."[76]

The president wasn't the only member of the Carter family with a book deal. Mrs. Carter received much better reviews with her own, more popular memoir, *First Lady from Plains*. Her book came out in 1984, and she chose to detail her entire life up until the end of the

White House years. The *Times* noted the contrast with Mr. Carter, and said that "as a writer, [Mrs. Carter] is better (and franker) hands down" than her husband.[77] This was a comparison she loved, and she relished the positive attention she got next to her husband's work.

The two Carters would go on to long, and profitable, writing careers. In the next four decades, Mr. Carter wrote thirty-two books on everything from fly-fishing and faith to the Middle East.[78] His 2001 work, *An Hour Before Daylight: Memories of a Rural Boyhood*, was a story of growing up in Jim Crow Georgia during the Great Depression. It was a Pulitzer Prize finalist that year, but Carter lost out to historian David McCullough's *John Adams*.[79] He and his daughter, Amy, cowrote a children's book with the ridiculous but charming name *The Little Baby Snoogle-Fleejer*. For her part, Mrs. Carter wrote five books, well received and mainly about caregiving and mental health.

The two authors tried to work together, but it was a disaster that nearly ended their relationship. Jimmy recalled the process of writing 1987's *Everything to Gain: Making the Most of the Rest of Your Life* with Rosalynn as "the worst threat we ever experienced in our marriage."[80] The two were both protective, stubborn, and competitive. Frustrated with her husband and coauthor, Mrs. Carter would often hang up a "Do Not Disturb" sign on her door so that she could have peace to edit her husband's work. She'd cross out entire pages that she didn't like. Unable to agree, they compromised by writing different sections of the book. The sections ended with a tag of "J" or an "R," so that the readers could tell who was responsible for what on any given page.[81] Mr. and Mrs. Carter never coauthored a book again.

Their shared Christian faith was a much more fruitful area of collaboration. Jimmy Carter, a born-again Christian, was the most publicly devout president of modern times. During his time in the White House, he'd taught Sunday school. The Carters were members of the Maranatha Baptist Church in Plains, a redbrick house of worship with a white steeple and a few dozen parishioners to which they returned in 1981. The former president went back to teaching Sunday school, sometimes attracting up to one thousand people from around the world to the church's small sanctuary. This was an integral part of their life together, and to the Carters, Maranatha Baptist was more than

"the center of [their] social life." To them, church was "like breathing."[82] He only stopped teaching Sunday school due to old age and the
COVID-19 pandemic in 2020, at age ninety-five.[83]

Writing and teaching Sunday school classes didn't fill his days.
Carter's old White House staff knew he was bored—they sent him
a Sears, Roebuck order for power tools so that he'd have a hobby.[84]
Though he spent countless hours making everything from cradles for
his grandchildren to railings for the elevator at the Plains Historic Inn,
carpentry wasn't for him.[85]

The Carters never wanted to stay in Georgia forever. In her memoir, Rosalynn said that, even as a young girl, she had "always secretly
wanted to get out of Plains."[86] Now in their fifties, she and her husband had seen the world. They wanted to get out again. Plains was
home, but it felt smaller than ever.

SHOTS FIRED

Jimmy Carter reentered public life thanks to the assassination of a
dear friend. On October 6, 1981, members of the terrorist organization Egyptian Islamic Jihad shot and killed Egyptian president Anwar
Sadat during a military parade in Cairo. The extremist group believed
that Sadat had betrayed the faith by making peace with Israel through
the Carter-brokered Camp David Accords.[87] It was a devastating blow
to the region, and to Carter personally.

The former president was shocked. He and Sadat were close. They
were bonded by the Camp David Accords, of course, but they also had
similar backgrounds as farmers, veterans, and men of faith, even if one
was a Christian and the other a Muslim. Their families were close.
In August 1981, seven months after the Carters had left the White
House, President Sadat and his wife, Jehan, visited them in Plains.
During that visit, the two families prayed together and they shared a
home-cooked meal in the Carter home.[88] After Sadat's murder, Carter
told the press, "I have never had a better and closer personal friend
than Anwar Sadat."[89]

Sadat's funeral was to take place four days after his assassination,
and the United States needed to send representation. It was out of

the question for President Reagan to go. That March, he'd survived an attempt on his own life at the hands of John Hinckley Jr., a deranged gunman trying to impress the young actress Jodie Foster. Instead, Reagan chose to send a delegation including Secretary of State Alexander Haig and former secretary of state Henry Kissinger. He also selected his three living predecessors, Richard Nixon, Gerald Ford, and Jimmy Carter. When a reporter asked why it was too dangerous for Reagan to go to Cairo for the funeral but not for Nixon, Ford, and Carter to attend, a Reagan aide responded, "One is the president of the United States, and the others are former presidents."[90]

The three made for a powerful, but odd, trio. When he heard that they were being sent to Cairo, Republican senator Bob Dole described the throuple as "see no evil, hear no evil, and evil."[91] They each had a strange relationship with the office they shared—Nixon had resigned in disgrace, Ford became president without winning an election, and Carter left after one term without wanting to. Carter and Nixon certainly were not close, though Carter had invited the California Republican to attend his inauguration in 1977. However, Nixon had declined the invitation to avoid press attention. Nixon's participation was important, however, and Carter welcomed it. Not only was Nixon a foreign-policy expert, he respected Carter for his work on the Camp David Accords. As one of Nixon's research assistants later wrote, "Carter attracted a curious blend of Nixon's admiration and aversion."[92]

But the real surprise of the trip wasn't Richard Nixon. It was Gerald Ford. Carter had defeated Ford in 1976, and the two weren't allies. But while Nixon stayed after the funeral and toured the Middle East, Carter and Ford returned to the United States together. The two navy veterans were crammed in the small cabin of the same plane for hours. The former foes became fast friends, as did their wives, Betty and Rosalynn. They began a partnership that would last for decades.[93]

The friendship with Ford did not mean that Carter was going to put aside his old partisan animosities. Shortly after he returned to the United States, Carter headed to Washington for his first private meeting with President Reagan. He was going to debrief his successor about what he had seen in Egypt. But Carter tanked the meeting before it started.

As he entered the White House, Carter spoke to the press. On his way to the Oval Office, he explicitly criticized Reagan on everything from his economic to his defense policies. He called the Reagan presidency "an aberration on the political scene," and he said that Reagan's "false and erroneous promises [were] now being realized."[94]

This was not a productive way to engage the president, but Carter was correct that the first year of the Reagan administration was not going well. The economy was still in recession, with interest rates and inflation still high, and the Soviet Union continued to make gains. And former presidents have made a habit of criticizing their successors in the twentieth century—Herbert Hoover, after all, was the most prominent critic of both Franklin Delano Roosevelt and the New Deal. Even the more sober William Howard Taft, once a Wilson ally on the League of Nations, teamed up with Theodore Roosevelt to campaign for Republicans in 1918. In the early republic, Congressman John Quincy Adams tried to impeach President John Tyler.

There was something different about Carter's attacks, however. Hoover went after Roosevelt from exile; Carter did so on his way to the Oval Office, after having been invited by Reagan to represent the United States abroad. Taft waited a few years to go after Wilson; Carter waited a few months. John Quincy Adams laid into John Tyler from his position in the House of Representatives; Carter had no position.

It was clear that Carter resented his "involuntary retirement," and he seldom passed up an opportunity to lambaste Ronald Reagan. When Reagan stopped having staff provide former presidents with national-security briefings, Carter complained, though neither Nixon nor Ford were bothered by the end of the informal practice. Instead, Carter threatened to go to the press if the briefings didn't resume. It was a childish move, but he got his way. Reagan relaunched the briefings for former presidents. Carter got back a small part of the privileges of the presidency.[95]

Carter went after Reagan in part because he hated being powerless. He was still unpopular, and he had no platform of his own. So he decided to build one.

In 1982, Emory University in Atlanta appointed Carter as a professor. But he didn't intend this to be a quiet academic position to lecture, grade papers, and attend faculty meetings, as Taft had done at Yale.[96] Instead, Emory would become the home base for the Carter Center, a new kind of institution that he envisioned as giving new power to the post-presidency.

When Carter thought about what he wanted his Center to do, he wasn't returning to an idea from before his presidency, or starting a new chapter. He wanted to continue the kind of work he'd started in the White House. The Carter Center would be a place to which he could "invite people to come like Anwar Sadat and Menachem Begin came to Camp David." He would be able to continue the work of his presidency and focus on his chosen projects, free from institutional responsibilities or political constraints.[97]

None of this would happen without money. Carter calculated that he would need $25 million to launch the Center, a tall order for a man who's never been great at fundraising, and who'd left the White House with few friends in the business world. But he was determined. From his office at Emory, he spent much of the next five years fundraising for the Carter Center.[98]

There were a few easy wins. CNN founder Ted Turner gave $100,000 to the Center, at the time "the most money [he] had ever donated to a single cause."[99] The Turner donation was the beginning of an important relationship for Carter, who would appear regularly on CNN, an Atlanta-based network that in 1980 became the first twenty-four-hour cable news network.[100]

There were some donations that came from unexpected places. Ryoichi Sasakawa was a Japanese billionaire who had served in the Diet, or parliament, during World War II. After the fighting was over and Japan was defeated, he was imprisoned by General Douglas MacArthur for alleged war crimes. He later made his fortune in the shipping and gambling industries. Carter didn't know Sasakawa well before the businessman visited Plains in 1981. Sasakawa was amazed by what he saw, and by the fact that the former president was "living in such a humble cottage."

After seeing how Carter was living, he gave the former president $1.7 million for his Center before dinnertime.[101] Carter was grateful, but he wasn't sure if he could take his money. He did a background check on his would-be benefactor, and his concerns were allayed when he learned that Sasakawa also supported the World Health Organization and Harvard University. If those august organizations would take his money, then Carter could, too.[102] Over time, Sasakawa became one of the Carter Center's most reliable longtime benefactors and partners.[103]

But not every high-net-worth individual was as ready to open their checkbooks as Turner and Sasakawa were. When Carter traveled to New York to meet with businessman Donald Trump, he asked for $5 million. Trump said no immediately, a decision that, while aggravating at the time, likely spared the Center plenty of grief decades later. But the meeting left an impression on the future president. Trump wrote in his upcoming book, *The Art of the Deal*, that before that meeting he had "never understood how Jimmy Carter became president." But after, he did. The answer, Trump believed, "[was] that as poorly qualified as he was for the job, Jimmy Carter had the nerve, the guts, the balls, to ask for something extraordinary. That ability above all helped him get elected president."[104]

Getting the Carter Center started wasn't easy. But it has since grown into a global behemoth. As of 2021, contributions came to $292 million from 117,423 donors. Major sponsors included the Coca-Cola Foundation, Home Depot, and Freedom House. It also has support from governments, including from countries as diverse as Canada and the Kingdom of Saudi Arabia.[105]

The former president didn't wait for construction to end for his work to begin. As president, he had focused on the Middle East, and that's where he wanted to put his effort. The region became an obsession in his post-presidency, particularly the Arab-Israeli conflict. He wrote about it in February 1983 with former president Ford, who shared with him the "painful conclusion" that Israel was "not living up" to its Camp David commitments, and that it had "shown little inclination to grant real autonomy to the Palestinians in the West Bank and Gaza areas."[106]

To continue their work, Ford and Carter hosted a two-day conference at the Ford Library, where they discussed how to bring peace to the region. Ford described the conference as "the first time two former presidents ever cooperated in such a tandem fashion,"[107] perhaps forgetting former presidents James Madison and Thomas Jefferson's collaboration founding the University of Virginia.[108]

In the first few years of his post-presidency, Carter established partnerships that would last for decades, including with President Ford. Another important early partnership was with Habitat for Humanity. Over the years, Carter would become synonymous with the organization in many people's minds, with photographs of the former president, in his fifties, sixties, seventies, eighties, and even nineties, rolling up his shirtsleeves and hammering in a nail to a new Habitat for Humanity project, changing the public's perception of him.

The Carters started their Habitat partnership work at 742 East Sixth Street in Manhattan, in the East Village. Back then, as historian Douglas Brinkley observed, the notion of a former president "doing menial labor of the most unpleasant and backbreaking kind seized the public's imagination." For his part, Carter thought that Rosalynn—whom he'd met in 1945 on summer break from the U.S. Naval Academy[109]—was a more striking figure. He remarked at the time, "My wife has never been more beautiful than when her face was covered with black smut from scraping burning ceiling joists."[110]

Over time, Carter became such a prominent spokesman for Habitat for Humanity that some observers thought he had founded it. But that wasn't the case. Habitat for Humanity was founded in 1976 by a Georgia couple named Millard and Linda Fuller. It's a Christian charity to which the Carters gave an enormous amount of their time, beginning in 1984. For one week every year, they'd volunteer to build a home for people in need, in the U.S. or abroad.[111]

But Jimmy Carter didn't want to spend the rest of his life working on charitable projects and launching a Center, and neither did Mrs. Carter. When journalist Helen Thomas interviewed her in 1984, the former First Lady said, "the most important thing [to do] is to beat Reagan."[112] Her memoir, published that year, concluded, "I would be out there campaigning right now if Jimmy would run again. I miss the world of politics. . . . I'd like to be back in the White House. I don't like to lose."[113]

Her husband didn't like to lose, either. He knew he had no chance of winning in 1984, and so didn't run, but Carter waited until after Iowa and New Hampshire to endorse Walter Mondale,[114] who was at one point afraid that his old boss's hesitation meant that he would try to get his old job back.[115] Mondale wanted the still-unpopular Carter to be a nonentity on the campaign trail, but it was impossible for the party to ignore its only living former president altogether.

Leading up to the 1984 Democratic convention in San Francisco, party leaders debated whether or not they should even invite Carter to speak. If he appeared, he'd be a reminder of his failed presidency, and of Reagan's victory. Before Carter, no Democratic president had lost his reelection bid since Grover Cleveland in 1888. But unlike Cleveland, Carter lost in a landslide. He knew that many party leaders viewed him as a liability. Aware of that fact, he told a reporter, "I would hope I would not be a detriment to anybody, particularly the ticket."[116]

The nomination of Walter Mondale—his vice president—meant that Carter had to have some role at the convention. He was given a speaking slot, but the organizers tried to relegate him to a time that wouldn't be broadcast live.[117] When Carter aides protested, they relented and gave him a better slot. But even then, the former president's remarks went largely unnoticed by the national press.

The Democrats gave Carter much the same treatment that the Republicans once gave to Herbert Hoover. Mondale distanced himself from his old boss. In his acceptance speech, he mentioned Carter only once. He said that the party was now "wiser, stronger, and focused on the future," unlike in 1980.[118] Democratic vice presidential nominee Geraldine Ferraro—the first woman in American history to be nominated by a major party—went further, calling any comparisons of her ticket to Carter-Mondale "odious." And like Mondale, she reminded reporters, "It's not 1980."[119]

Ferraro was right. For the Democrats, 1984 was worse than 1980. Jimmy Carter carried six states back then. Now Walter Mondale had just one in his column, his home state of Minnesota. Jimmy Carter didn't like the outcome, but he wasn't surprised. Perhaps most disturbingly, though, Ronald Reagan received 60 percent of the vote in Georgia. The Republican even won Sumter County, home to Plains. That had to hurt.[120]

With four more years of Reagan, Carter had little hope of having much influence in Washington. He wasn't in exile, as Herbert Hoover had been. Reagan had invited him into the fold multiple times, sending him to meet the freed Americans after the Iran Hostage Crisis, and dispatching him to represent the United States at Anwar Sadat's funeral. They'd met in the Oval Office. But Carter and Reagan would not warm to each other, and Carter chose to focus on building his Center in Atlanta, rather than on cultivating connections in Washington.

He wanted the Center to have an impact on the Global South, a catch-all phrase for the developing world. Carter was the first American president to visit sub-Saharan Africa in office, when he traveled to Nigeria in 1978.[121] He continued that work alongside leaders like Norman Borlaug, the Nobel Prize–winning agronomist who previously brought the Green Revolution to the Indian subcontinent. Borlaug's high-yield, disease-resistant crops are credited with changing agricultural practices and saving hundreds of millions of lives on the subcontinent.[122] Knowing that track record, Carter wanted to bring the Green Revolution to Africa.

This task would not be easy. In 1984, Borlaug, then in his seventies, noted that much of Africa is more prone to drought than India. There was more environmental degradation. But as a farmer, Carter wanted to try. In 1985, he used his presidential clout to bring together the Sasakawa Africa Association and the Nippon Foundation to apply the techniques that Borlaug had so successfully brought to India. They created a program called SG 2000, which began in Ghana, Sudan, Zimbabwe, and Zambia.[123] This effort helped feed millions of people in fourteen countries, and it helped establish the Carter Center as a global humanitarian organization.[124]

When the Center opened in 1986, Carter had established a strong reputation for himself as a former president. President Reagan came to Atlanta for the occasion, and he told his old rival, "You gave yourself to your country, gracing the White House with your passion and intellect and commitment."[125]

That year, the Carter Center began perhaps its most impactful program, an effort to eradicate a disease called Guinea worm. Jimmy Carter saw the devastating effects of this disease during a visit to

Accra, Ghana, where he witnessed a young woman whose face was contorted in pain, and who had an abscess on her chest. There was a Guinea worm about to burst from the woman's body. At the time, nearly 3.5 million people suffered from this condition.[126]

Guinea worm was a relatively unknown, and neglected, disease. The World Health Organization still calls it "an affliction of poverty," as it affects people who lack access to clean water.[127] Individuals become sick after drinking from contaminated water that can harbor hundreds of thousands of Guinea worm larvae. Though they may not show symptoms for a year, they later develop blisters that swell and burst, exposing the worm. While Guinea worm isn't fatal, like Ebola or AIDS, it is excruciating. Open wounds can become infected, sometimes leading to severe disabilities.[128]

For four decades, the Carter Center has led the global campaign against Guinea worm, improving the lives of millions of people. While there is no vaccine to prevent Guinea worm, and antibiotics don't treat it, its transmission can be stopped through better surveillance, containment, and treatment. With partners like Dr. Bill Foege, the man who helped to eradicate smallpox, and in collaboration with national ministries of health, and philanthropies like the Bill & Melinda Gates Foundation, the Carter Center and the World Health Organization have had a real impact. Between 1986 and 2018, the prevalence of Guinea worm declined from 3.5 million cases a year to a mere twenty-eight. This was a historic humanitarian accomplishment.[129] No other former president has matched it.

THE DIPLOMAT

An American president is called the "leader of the free world." Not having that status can be jarring. As president, Jimmy Carter had always focused on foreign policy, from peace in the Middle East to his recognition of the People's Republic of China. Though he lost that office, he never lost his desire to lead.

The former president had to conceive of his role after the White House in a new way, and underwent a kind of "cognitive reappraisal" in how he would engage with the world. This is a concept made famous by psychology professor Richard Lazarus, who posited a two-step process of assessing what is at stake and evaluating methods of coping in changed circumstances.[130] Carter didn't want to end the work he'd begun in the White House, and he'd now turn his status as a former president into a method to continue the work.

To be effective, former presidents need political support, even if not a political office. Carter left the White House with a 34 percent approval rating. But thanks to his humanitarian work and the passage of time, he was enjoying a political rebirth. His standing was improving, which became evident in the 1988 presidential election. He would have endorsed his fellow Georgian, Senator Sam Nunn, in the race, but when Nunn didn't run, Carter stayed above the fray, and he declined to endorse any candidate. But he was looked to as an elder statesman, and during the primary campaign, Jesse Jackson asked him to mediate a dispute with the eventual Democratic nominee, Massachusetts governor Michael Dukakis, over his selection of Lloyd Bentsen of Texas as his vice presidential candidate.[131]

Jimmy Carter's relationship with the Democratic Party in the 1980s is a tale of two conventions. In 1984, when Carter's own former vice president was the Democratic nominee, he was shunned at the San Francisco convention. But in 1988, the Democratic convention was in Atlanta. This was Carter's home turf, and he had a supportive crowd waiting to greet him. While Carter remained unpopular nationally, eight years of Reagan had aged his legacy well and Democrats now approved of the Carter presidency by a margin of 2 to 1.[132]

When Carter took the stage for a twenty-minute prime-time address, a jazz band played as he approached the podium to a standing ovation. He knew that the Republican nominee, Vice President George H. W. Bush, would go after him on the campaign trail that year.[133] With that in mind, Carter opened his speech by declaring, "My name is Jimmy Carter, and I am not running for president! Did you hear that George?"[134]

It was a well-received line, and Carter's speech made it clear that, though he was a partisan, he was not interested in returning to politics. What he was attempting to do was to deprive George H. W. Bush of ammunition. It took Herbert Hoover twelve years to make that kind of statement—Carter did it in eight. But at a national level the party was still reeling from the legacy of Carter's administration, and Dukakis— aided by a seemingly inhuman debate answer on the topic of rape and an awkward photo in a tank—failed to convince the voters otherwise. While he managed to improve on both Carter's and Mondale's performances in 1980 and 1984, he still lost the 1988 election with just 45.7 percent of the popular vote.

George H. W. Bush may have been Ronald Reagan's vice president, but his administration brought Jimmy Carter back into the fold. The man most responsible for Carter's return to Washington was James A. Baker III, the new president's choice to serve as secretary of state.

It would take a man of Baker's diplomatic and managerial skills to engage Carter. If there was one thing that Carter's supporters and antagonists both agreed on, it was that he was difficult to work with. The *Los Angeles Times* had opined that "the fatal flaw of [Carter's] presidency" was his "unwillingness to delegate authority on small matters."[135] To illustrate that point, his former speechwriter, James Fallows, wrote a piece called "The Passionless Presidency," in which he alleged that the micromanaging President Carter personally reviewed every request to use the White House tennis court.[136] Even Democratic leaders like Speaker of the House Tip O'Neill found Carter to be impossible. When Carter's aides gave O'Neill and his family seats in the second-to-last row at the president's inaugural gala in 1977, the irate Speaker yelled at Hamilton Jordan, the president's chief of staff, "When a guy is Speaker of the House and gets tickets like this, he figures there's a reason behind it. . . . I'll ream you out, you son of a bitch!"[137] President Carter's relationship with Congress did not improve.

But James Baker believed he could do better. Baker believed that "[Carter] just wants to be useful. . . . He never complains. But if you don't clearly spell out his assignment, and then ride herd over him, then he can get in your way."[138]

The Bush administration needed help in Panama, and Carter was the perfect man for the job. The strategically located Latin American country, which had been ruled by two strongmen for two decades, was scheduled to hold a democratic election in May 1989. Baker believed that Manuel Noriega, then the military leader of Panama, was "up to his epaulets in drug trafficking."[139] He and Carter both suspected that the upcoming vote would be rife with fraud in favor of military leader and Noriega's narco-partner, henchman, and chosen successor, Carlos Duque.[140]

Former presidents can be powerful diplomatic allies, and Jimmy Carter was uniquely well suited for a mission to Panama. He was widely respected throughout Latin America, and especially in that country. One of Carter's signature accomplishments as president was a series of treaties that transferred control of the strategically significant Canal Zone from the United States to Panama.[141] Because of that work, Panamanians trusted him, and they would listen to him. This was also an important opportunity for Carter. It was a chance for him to prove himself again as a global leader.

He shared the same objective with the White House to promote democracy in Panama and worked closely with the Bush administration. The president dispatched him to monitor the upcoming elections as the head of a delegation sent by the National Democratic Institute.[142] And as National Security Advisor Brent Scowcroft advised him before he left, "Your prestige and reputation in Panama are such that the Noriega regime cannot but take notice of your views."[143]

The former president had affection for Panama, but he had no illusions about Noriega. He'd written in April to the strongman, telling him in no uncertain terms, "Unless there is clear and concrete evidence that efforts are being made to restore confidence in the process and to ensure free and fair elections, I must assume that the commitment of your government as expressed to me will not have been fulfilled."[144] The offended Noriega called Carter's message "a letter of threats and lies." But despite the bluster, Carter was able to negotiate visas for himself, former president Ford, and a delegation of twenty election monitors to travel unrestricted throughout Panama. They arrived at Omar Torrijos Airport on May 5 aboard a U.S. government plane, ready to see if the election would be free and fair.[145]

It was not. The former president appeared on local radio stations, encouraging Panamanians to head to the polls. When voting began, he saw that turnout was high, higher even than either Noriega or the U.S. intelligence community had anticipated. As many as 800,000 Panamanians voted, out of a population of around 2.4 million.[146]

There was record turnout, but voters had to overcome significant barriers to get to the polls. Many local media outlets were closed or censored in the lead-up to election day. There were rolling blackouts. While Carter traveled to different polling locations, he could hear gunfire in the background.

The early results indicated a landslide in opposition to Noriega's candidate, Carlos Duque. Observers from the Catholic Church evaluated 115 polling places, and they determined that the margin against Duque looked to be as high as 3 to 1, with a margin of error of 10 percent. There was no way that Duque would win.[147]

Fearing that Noriega would not accept defeat, no matter how wide the margin, Carter headed to the National Counting Center in Panama City. There, his worst fears were confirmed. He saw legitimate votes being counted, but also witnessed ballot stuffing and other forms of outright fraud.[148] Outraged, he stepped up on top of a platform in the middle of the room and yelled to the fraudulent vote counters. His Spanish was halting, but his message was clear: "Are you honest or are you thieves?"[149]

That stand for democracy in Panama may have been the single finest moment of his post-presidency. After leaving the center, Carter held an evening press conference in the lobby of his hotel. "The government is taking the election by fraud," he told the world. "It's robbing the people of their legitimate rights."[150] Former president Gerald Ford followed Carter and described the situation on the ground succinctly: "I never thought the fraud would be this blatant. These people are absolutely shameless."[151] They weren't only among friends, however. Also in the room was one of Noriega's henchmen, who told a Carter aide that the delegation needed to leave the country by 5:00 a.m. the next day, or else.[152]

The Panamanian dictator had sent his message, but he didn't wait for Carter to get out of town to turn up the screws on his people. He had eleven thousand troops at his command, and he sent tanks and soldiers into the streets. Fearing that vote stuffing wasn't enough to tip the scales, his gunmen stole ballots in the open. He then declared martial law and nullified the election.[153]

The election-monitoring delegation returned to Washington, and Carter and Ford met with President Bush. After speaking with his predecessors in the Oval Office, the president held his own press conference. He told the assembled reporters, "I call on all foreign leaders to urge General Noriega to honor the clear results of the election."[154]

Every option was on the table when it came to Panama, including the use of military force. This was where Carter began to disagree with the president. He favored diplomacy and a multilateral response. As he told the public, "Obviously unilateral action is much weaker than action in concert with other democratic countries. I think these are more fruitful."[155]

Not one to let events take care of themselves, Carter set to work, lobbying Latin American governments and the Organization of American States to speak out about the fraud in Panama. He faxed leaders his own report of what he saw. Shortly after, the Organization of American States condemned Noriega and designated its secretary-general and the foreign ministers of three Latin American countries to resolve the situation.[156] With that accomplished, Carter hoped Noriega would step down on his own.[157]

But Noriega had no intention of bowing to outside pressure, and President Bush continued to explore every option available.[158] He was worried about the thirty-five thousand American citizens in Panama, as well as the need to "defend democracy in Panama, to combat drug trafficking and to protect the integrity of the Panama Canal Treaty." President Bush ordered the invasion of the country on December 21, 1989.[159] Soon after, opposition leader Guillermo Endara—who had been attacked by Noriega's forces during the vote count—became Panama's president.[160]

This was not how Carter had hoped the Panama crisis would end. But he had played an important role in protecting the country's democracy. The American people saw that, and though they still did not approve of his presidency, they did start to approve of him and of his post-presidency. ABC newsman Peter Jennings said shortly after the

Panama invasion that Carter had shown he had a "strong commitment to peace and justice."[161] And the *New York Times* ran a story with the headline "Carter Begins to Shed Negative Public Image."[162]

This was a turning point in the Carter post-presidency. Not only did his image improve, he began a new line of effort at the Carter Center, which would go on to perform election-monitoring missions around the world. Jimmy Carter became one of the most prominent faces of this effort, and working with international organizations like the National Endowment for Democracy, he and his staff monitored more than one hundred elections, with a focus on Africa, Latin America, and Asia.[163]

Carter had proven that former presidents can be capable diplomats. And he wanted to do more. When he agreed with the White House, he would work with them. But if he disagreed, he would do so vocally, and he would freelance his own diplomacy. Every year that passed after his presidency, he became more willing to speak his mind on the issues of the day.

Going Rogue

The end of the Cold War marked the dawn of a new era in international relations. The Soviet Union was breaking up. The Unipolar Moment had begun. And the world was changing.

It was not inevitable that the Cold War would end peacefully, or at all. Early in his presidency, Carter had warned against an "inordinate fear of communism," believing in never-ending peaceful coexistence with the Soviet Union.[164] He only changed his mind after the Soviet invasion of Afghanistan, when he admitted, "[My] opinion of the Russians has changed more drastically in the last week than even the previous two and a half years."[165]

It took Ronald Reagan, a man very different from Jimmy Carter, to imagine that the Cold War could end, and to put that idea at the center of American diplomacy by stating his theory of the case: "We win, they lose."[166] The Berlin Wall had come down in 1989. The Soviet Union collapsed in 1991. Newly independent states, from Ukraine, to Poland, to Kazakhstan, were emerging. Now it was time for the Bush

administration to focus on the new world, and issues like German re-
unification and the fate of the former Warsaw Pact. While the White
House turned its gaze to Europe, Carter once again zeroed in on the
Middle East.

After Carter's performance in Panama, the administration was
ready and willing to work with him on foreign policy, including Middle
Eastern issues. There didn't seem to be much of a problem with the
idea. James Baker wrote, "Just as long as [Carter] reported to us, which
he did, I had no problems with him talking with Assad or Arafat. I
frankly saw the Arab-Israeli dispute as a pitfall to be avoided."[167]

But Carter never had any intention of avoiding the "Arab-Israeli
dispute"—it was an obsession. He believed that, as the man who had
delivered the Camp David Accords, he could uniquely make peace
between Israel and the Palestinians.[168]

He also believed that, of all of America's presidents, he had a special connection to the region. In May 1973, just a few months before the Yom Kippur War, Jimmy Carter, then the governor of Georgia,
traveled to Israel with Mrs. Carter at the invitation of Prime Minister
Golda Meir. For their entire lives, they'd read about Israel in church
and in Bible study.[169] Because of that history, Carter said he had "attachment to Israel as the land of the Bible."[170] Now, after the White
House, he wanted to turn that attachment into policy. In his 1985
book, *The Blood of Abraham*, Carter described the Middle East as the
most important region in the world.

The modern Israel-Palestinian conflict was beginning to come to
the fore. After the First Intifada, which began in 1987, the Palestinian Liberation Organization took on new prominence under its leader,
Yasser Arafat. The Hashemite Kingdom of Jordan dropped its claims to
the West Bank in 1988.[171] With these changes, Carter believed there
was an opening for a deal, and he met with Arafat in Paris in April
1990. After that meeting, he stated his belief that "obviously Chairman Arafat is one of the key leaders who has done everything he can
in recent months to promote the peace process."[172]

This was a sincere statement, but it was ill-timed. Just a few days
before that encounter, Arafat had been in Baghdad. In Iraq, he'd

attended a rally with President Saddam Hussein. He had pledged to fight Israel "with stones, with rifles."[173]

The prospects for any kind of Middle East peace changed on August 2, 1990, when Saddam Hussein invaded Kuwait.[174] The Arab League condemned Iraq's aggression, but Arafat supported Saddam as a champion of the Arab people.[175] It was a diplomatic mistake on his part that alienated the PLO from its Gulf backers, including the all-important Saudi Arabia.[176]

There was a new war in the Middle East, and Carter reversed some of his old positions. As president, he articulated what became known as the Carter Doctrine, following the Soviet invasion of Afghanistan.[177] The Carter Doctrine supported American military intervention in the event of any outside power attempting to take control of the Persian Gulf. In 1990, Saddam Hussein was attempting to do just that. But Carter advocated against the use of American military force. He wanted to create a diplomatic solution.[178]

Carter had an idea, but it wasn't his. The idea came from Yasser Arafat, who proposed what became known as the "linkage solution."[179] Under the Arafat plan, Iraq would withdraw from Kuwait in exchange for Israel's withdrawal from the West Bank, home to many Palestinians. Carter was taken with the notion, and he sent the proposal to President Bush and his team. But the White House was not interested. Frustrated, Carter took to *Time* magazine, arguing that "an attack on Iraq without further provocation from Saddam will erode U.S. support in the Middle East."[180]

Iraq may have pushed past Kuwait and taken more of the Gulf, but many believed that invading one country was provocation enough. American military intervention looked more likely every day. Faced with the possibility of America sending troops to the Middle East, Carter took matters into his own hands that November.

The former president went rogue. Unbeknownst to the U.S. government, he wrote to the leaders of the permanent members of the UN Security Council, urging them not to endorse Bush's "line in the sand rhetoric," and to oppose any military intervention.[181] He sent the letter to every member except the United Kingdom's Margaret Thatcher. As he later reported, he believed that trying to convince Thatcher would be a "waste of a stamp."[182]

He'd started his rogue diplomacy in secret, but it didn't stay secret for long. President Bush heard about what Carter was doing from Canadian prime minister Brian Mulroney. The president and his team were furious.[183] National Security Advisor Brent Scowcroft later wrote of Carter's attempt to go around the White House, "It seemed to me that if there was ever a violation of the Logan Act prohibiting diplomacy by private citizens, this was it." Secretary of Defense Dick Cheney compared it to treason.[184]

But Carter didn't care. He believed in what he was doing, the Logan Act hadn't been used to prosecute someone since Malcolm X, and the ends would justify the means. Furthermore, former presidents are private citizens with agency and power of their own. Carter intended to take advantage of that fact.

He was unsuccessful. President Bush gave Saddam Hussein a deadline of January 15 to withdraw from Kuwait, a last chance for diplomacy.[185] Feeling the clock running out, five days before the start of Operation Desert Storm, Carter made one last attempt to stop the military intervention. He wrote to King Fahd of Saudi Arabia, Hafez al-Assad of Syria, and Hosni Mubarak of Egypt, imploring them not to support the U.S. position. But those Arab leaders ignored him.[186] The UN Security Council voted to authorize the use of military force against Iraq, with twelve in favor and two against. The only countries that took Carter's position against intervention were Cuba and Yemen.[187]

The United States waged the First Gulf War at the head of a coalition, joined by Arab countries like Saudi Arabia, Egypt, and Kuwait, as well as permanent members of the UN Security Council, France and the United Kingdom. The campaign was more successful more quickly than many had expected. As early as February 28, Bush announced, "Iraq's army is defeated, and Kuwait is liberated."[188] In the meantime, Saddam had linked the war to Israel, but not in the way that Carter had intended. During the Gulf War, Iraq launched thirty-nine Scud missiles at nonbelligerent Israel, primarily hitting civilians in cities like Haifa and Tel Aviv.[189]

The episode did not reflect well on Carter. A *Washington Post* columnist sympathetic to the former president described his anti–Gulf War efforts as "breathtakingly brazen, not to mention in bad taste and confusing to other governments." The writer continued, "Former presidents, of all people, do not have their own foreign policies." Carter admitted that his actions were "not appropriate perhaps."[190] But he disagreed—former presidents can have their own foreign policies, and there's little that the White House can do to stop them.

From then on, Carter got the cold shoulder from the Bush White House.[191] The sitting president's approval rating climbed to 89 percent after the Gulf War.[192] But that high did not last long. With a recession and an ill-advised pledge not to raise taxes that he later reversed, Bush was vulnerable leading up to the 1992 election. That year, he lost to Bill Clinton in a three-way race among himself, Clinton, the governor of Arkansas and a man the president's son's age, and Ross Perot, a billionaire populist businessman. Twelve years after the Carter presidency, America had once again elected a young, Southern Baptist, outsider Democratic governor to the White House.

Going Nuclear

William Jefferson Clinton was the first Democratic president that Jimmy Carter ever met.[193] It was January 20, 1993, and it might have been a great day for Carter. He was Clinton's only living Democratic predecessor. They had similar stories, and they might have been natural partners. Not only that, many former Carter officials now worked for Clinton, including Warren Christopher, Clinton's secretary of state, who'd served as deputy secretary during the Carter administration.

But Clinton and Carter were not natural partners. During the Democratic primaries, Carter came close to supporting Clinton's rival, Massachusetts senator Paul Tsongas. When Tsongas visited Plains alongside his wife, Niki, and described the Carter home as "one of the Mecca stops along the way to the White House," Carter was both flattered and impressed. He reported that "the South is quite receptive to the kind of message that Senator Tsongas brought."[194]

Courting Jimmy Carter did not make a Tsongas presidency. On the advice of political advisor James Carville, Clinton avoided Carter and believed that the Democrat was still a liability with the wider public, even if the Democratic base had come around to him.[195] The governor of Arkansas made his position clear: "Jimmy Carter and I are as different as daylight and dark."[196]

It took North Korean dictator Kim Il Sung to bring Jimmy Carter and Bill Clinton together. The Hermit Kingdom's "Great Leader" had led the country as its totalitarian ruler since the Truman administration. Four decades later, by 1994, Kim was developing and accelerating North Korea's nuclear weapons program. He'd blocked inspectors from the International Atomic Energy Agency.[197] With a belligerent Kim and a growing North Korean nuclear threat, war on the Korean Peninsula could turn hot again. Clinton was prepared to send in troops. He might have even ordered a tactical military strike on one of the North's nuclear facilities.[198]

Fearing the worst, the eighty-two-year-old Kim invited Carter to come to North Korea and negotiate a settlement. When the U.S. State Department objected, Carter telephoned the White House directly and asked for permission.[199] He got the green light with help from Vice President Al Gore, who told him that the president would support his mission. With that endorsement, Jimmy and Rosalynn Carter headed to Pyongyang.

They crossed the Demilitarized Zone at Panmunjom from South Korea to North Korea on June 15, 1994.[200] Kim was still refusing to allow IAEA inspectors to inspect his plutonium sites. More Western sanctions were likely, and war was possible. As National Security Advisor Anthony Lake observed, "Carter's role was to offer a way out."[201]

Clinton had made it clear that the former president was there with his blessing, but he was not a U.S. diplomat. Carter was a private citizen. He had no authority to make a deal or set policy. Rather, he was a messenger. That's what the White House wanted him to be, at least.[202]

But Carter wanted to play a bigger role. When he met with Kim, he told the "Dear Leader" that the Clinton administration would drop its push for UN sanctions under the right conditions. He agreed with North Korea's position that it had a right to process nuclear fuel rods.

Without the U.S. government's endorsement, Carter and Kim negotiated the outlines of a new framework for North Korea's nuclear program.[203]

The White House staff waited for Carter to come back from North
Korea and brief them. Instead, they were shocked to turn on their television and see, on Ted Turner's Atlanta-based CNN—Carter's favorite
network—the former president telling the world that he had reached a
"new breakthrough" with North Korea.[204] In a wide-ranging interview,
Carter described his talks with Kim and urged the United States not
to pursue sanctions.

This went well beyond his mandate, and he knew it. He later admitted that he never intended to abide by the White House's conditions for his trip. His goal had rather been to settle the nuclear issue.
As he said on PBS: "I can't deny that I hoped that it would consum-
mate a resolution of what I considered to be a very serious crisis."[205]

This was a pattern in keeping with his view of his actions in the
First Gulf War. He couldn't stand the idea of American military intervention, and he believed that he was correct. He took action—no
matter the views of the sitting president. Like the Bush administration
before it, the Clinton White House was furious. President Clinton
had been prepared to send ten thousand American troops to South
Korea.[206] A Clinton official commented, "We have no way of knowing why [Carter] thought what he thought, or why he said what he
said."[207] The White House disavowed Carter's freelance diplomacy.[208]

The American people didn't know what to make of Carter's actions. A New York Times reporter accused the former president of having "lent Mr. Kim the respectability he has craved."[209] Thought leaders
including George Will, Henry Kissinger, Rush Limbaugh, and Robert
Gates denounced what he'd done.[210]

But Carter had changed the dynamics on the Korean Peninsula.
He'd set the stage for renewed diplomacy between the United States
and North Korea. The North Koreans were back at the table. When
Kim Il Sung died on July 8, his son, Kim Jong Il, took over the Hermit
Kingdom. The country was facing a man-made famine that may have
cost the lives of between 5 and 10 percent of North Koreans, and

the new Kim was desperate.[211] To push a deal forward, the Clinton administration offered financial and humanitarian aid, in exchange for North Korea's submitting to international inspections and a freeze on the construction of nuclear reactors.[212]

This outcome pleased Carter, but South Korean president Kim Young-sam objected to what became known as the Agreed Framework. He warned, "If the United States wants to settle with a half-baked compromise and the media wants to describe it as a good agreement, they can."[213] But the Agreed Framework was successful, if only for a few years. It ended the eighteen-month showdown on the Korean Peninsula. There was no war on the Korean Peninsula in 1994.[214]

It did not end the nuclear crisis, however. The Dear Leader's son Kim Jong Un later rebuilt North Korea's nuclear program. The program remains a threat to the region and the world.

Pariah Diplomacy

Carter and Clinton never repaired their relationship after North Korea. Things got even worse for Carter with the election of George W. Bush, who remembered when Carter went rogue and undermined his father during the First Gulf War. Likewise, Carter took a special dislike for the new Bush, at a level unseen since the days of Reagan.

Though he didn't have access to the White House, Carter didn't stop his own diplomatic efforts. If anything, having an administration to oppose seemed to motivate him even more. He believed that the Bush administration wasn't only wrongheaded, but possibly dangerous, and Carter saw himself as an unelected check and balance on the sitting president.

With another Bush in the White House, Carter once again directed his focus at the Middle East. However, whereas he was widely condemned for his maneuvering a decade earlier, this time his actions won him praise, and even a Nobel Peace Prize in 2002.[215]

The Nobel Committee awarded the prize to Carter for his lifetime achievements, from the Camp David Accords on through his humanitarian and democratic work throughout his post-presidency. But the committee's citation included a thinly veiled reference to debates about Bush administration policy as well, including, "In a situation currently marked by threats of the use of power, Carter has stood by the principles that conflicts must as far as possible be resolved through mediation and international cooperation based on international law, respect for human rights and economic development."[216] Everyone at the time knew what this was really about—Global War on Terror and the coming Iraq War. As if to make it painfully clear to everyone, the *New York Times* described the Nobel citation as "a sharp rebuke to the Bush administration for its aggressive policy toward Iraq."[217]

With the Nobel in hand, Carter didn't let up. Before the March 2003 U.S.-led invasion of Iraq, he argued that, according to his understanding of the Christian just war theory, Bush's "determination to launch a war against Iraq" did not meet the required standard, and that the only Christian leaders who disagreed with it were members of the "Southern Baptist Convention who are greatly influenced by their commitment to Israel based on eschatological, or final days, theology."[218] In an interview with the *Arkansas Democrat-Gazette*, he went further still, arguing, "[A]s far as the adverse impact [of the war] on the nation around the world, [the Bush] administration has been the worst in history." He later called these remarks "careless" and "misinterpreted."[219]

It's not the norm for a former president to criticize the sitting president's wartime policies, especially early in the war. Even Herbert Hoover was measured in this regard. Understanding that what he was doing was unusual, in a 2008 *New York Times* op-ed, Carter described his approach to foreign affairs during the George W. Bush administration as "Pariah Diplomacy."[220] He called out what he described as "a counterproductive Washington policy in recent years . . . to boycott and punish political factions or governments that refuse to accept United States mandates."

The war in Iraq didn't take Carter's attention away from his main obsession: Israel and the Palestinian people. In 2006, he published *Palestine: Peace Not Apartheid*, making the case, "It will be a tragedy—for the Israelis, the Palestinians, and the world—if peace is rejected and a system of oppression, apartheid, and sustained violence is permitted to prevail."[221]

The word "apartheid" caused an explosive reaction against the book. That reaction was not limited to Israelis or to the American Jewish community—it spread to the policy world and to many ordinary Americans who were and remain largely pro-Israel. A few critics saw Carter as having crossed the line, not only pushing policies that they viewed as counterproductive, but of engaging in outright anti-Semitism.[222] Carter dismissed such criticisms, however. He said they were upset "not because of [the book's] content but because of its title."[223]

It wasn't just that Carter called attention to the plight of the Palestinian people, as he had throughout his career. It was also that there seemed to be a particular bias against Israel, a democracy, and its elected leaders that was lacking in comparison to his treatment of other countries.

For the four decades of his post-presidency, Carter's freelance diplomacy often seemed inconsistent, and at times contradictory, particularly when it came to Israel and the Arab world. He held the view that Israel was driving the problems in the Middle East, and much of the regional turmoil. During his post-presidency, he met with leaders from all over the world. When he did so, he often called out human rights abuses. But he rarely did so after meeting with Arab leaders like Hafez al-Assad in Syria and Hosni Mubarak in Egypt. When he did call attention to their abuses, his criticisms were muted.

There was never such silence about perceived Israeli abuses. In particular, members of the Israeli right and its Likud Party, going back to Prime Minister Menachem Begin, who had signed the Camp David Accords, were singled out for special condemnation. Early in his post-presidency, in a speech to the Council on Foreign Relations, Carter stated his position candidly: "Israel is the problem toward peace."[224]

He almost never put responsibility on any other country, or terrorist group. Worried about how one-sided that critique was, and what effect it might have, Carter Center Middle East fellow Kenneth Stein wrote to Carter: "I believe not only is it wrong to set a double standard for Israel; but your willingness to be harsher on Israel in public does not help or create confidence in your ability to be that sought-after mediator."[225]

Palestine: Peace Not Apartheid crossed a line for many, even some

Carter loyalists. Fourteen members of the advisory board to the Carter Center resigned in protest over the book.[226] Their joint letter said they could "no longer in good conscience continue to serve. . . . It seems that you have turned to a world of advocacy . . . including even malicious advocacy."[227]

For twenty-five years, Carter had cultivated his image as a peacemaker, and his good works had improved his standing the world over, including in the United States. But now the criticisms piled up, and Carter headed to Brandeis University in 2007 to discuss and defend the work and his positions. There, he stood his ground, but he did apologize for one sentence in his book that implied that Palestinian suicide bombings would not end until Israel withdrew from the West Bank. He called the choice of words "completely improper and stupid," and said that he'd "written [his] publisher to change that sentence immediately."[228]

The most substantive critique of the book wasn't about the title or one sentence. It came from Kenneth Stein, who by then had risen to the position of executive director of the Carter Center. Stein wrote a nearly six-thousand-word appraisal of the entire book's background and arguments. Not only was Carter's case flawed, he believed, but the former president's research was shoddy. The book had "no footnotes, citations, or source[s]" and "[used] accurate information but [omitted] part of the story to bolster [Carter's] presentation."[229]

The book made important points—and once again highlighted the needs of the Palestinian people. But whatever the merits of demerits in his case, Carter's writing made it less likely that any administration would call on him for advice. He knew his positions cost him influence, and said that he understood the "sensitivity" of his work on Middle East issues made it less likely that the White House or Congress would ask for his advice.[230] It also lost him a certain amount of support that he would never gain back and for some it means an asterisk next to his name when lauding all of his good works.

Being on the inside didn't matter to him. He remained outspoken because he believed he was right. Throughout the War on Terror, he spoke out against the Bush administration. During the Obama administrations, he beat his drum, writing in the *New York Times* in 2012 that the United States was "abandoning its role as the global champion of human rights" under President Obama. In particular, he was disturbed by the president's use of drones to target and kill overseas and by the government's domestic surveillance programs.[231]

Ex-presidents don't have to make enemies, and they don't have to engage as Carter did. It would have been easy for him to live a quiet life in Plains. But he did not believe that that was an option. As he told one interviewer, "My faith demands that I do whatever I can, wherever I can, whenever I can, for as long as I can."[232] From the day he entered public life until the end of his active post-presidency, that ethos guided Jimmy Carter, whether or not the rest of the world agreed with what he was doing.

THE NEVER-ENDING PRESIDENCY

For half a century, Carter turned his defeat in 1980 into a strength. He was no longer the president, and did not have to work with Congress or run for reelection. He was no longer the leader of the Democratic Party, and he didn't need to play politics. But he would always be a former president, and he did have a platform all of his own that he built. Many believed that his presidency was a failure. But Carter could not have disagreed more—it was the beginning of a much more meaningful time in his life.

He didn't believe that his presidency's work ended on January 20, 1981. During a reunion of 750 Carter-Mondale alumni gathered in Atlanta in 1997, he told the group, "What we're doing at the Carter Center is an extension of what we were doing in the White House."[233] More than forty years as a former was better than four more years in the White House. Historian Douglas Brinkley commented on that fact, "Cynics who claimed that Carter's postpresidential flurry of activities was designed to redeem his White House tenure overlooked a crucial factor: he did not believe his presidency needed redemption."[234]

More than any of his predecessors, Carter realized former presidents have power all of their own. He told anyone who would listen that he "intended [his] former position to enhance everything [he] did in [his] later years."[235]

It did. Many Americans—and people around the world—came to admire Carter's tenacity and commitment to good works, demonstrated for four decades after the White House. In particular, his work on global public health earned him praise. During his battle with cancer in 2015, Carter joked, "I'd like for the last Guinea worm to die before I do," a statement that captured his determination.[236]

For older Americans, Carter's name still evokes images of long gas lines and Americans held hostage in Iran, but that depiction is withering away as the generation who lived through his presidency dies out. But younger Americans juxtapose Jimmy Carter with having grown up in a time of war and democratic crisis in American institutions. They think of a man who once lived in the White House who loathed war, ran around the world promoting peace, and built homes through Habitat for Humanity for forty years, sweating under the sun as he did so. He was a pariah on the world stage for many. But he was also a humble, servant leader.

He never forgot what he'd lost in 1980, or his resentment at being sent into involuntary retirement by Ronald Reagan. "If I had to choose between four more years and the Carter Center, I think I would choose the Carter Center," he once remarked. But, after pausing, he smiled and continued, "It could have been both."[237]

His name still carried weight, even after the end of his active post-presidency. Every four years, Republicans warn that the Democratic Party is nominating the second coming of Jimmy Carter for president. But those lines don't strike the same chords as they once did. Future generations may remember him more for his post-presidency than for anything he did, or didn't do, in the White House. Even many older Americans admired a man they voted against in 1980. When Jimmy and Rosalynn Carter returned to Maranatha Baptist Church in February 2021, after being vaccinated against COVID-19, their return was greeted with cheers around the world.[238]

His never-ending post-presidency had to end someday. The end began on February 18, 2023, when the Carter Center announced that the former president had "decided to spend his remaining time at home with his family and receive hospice care instead of additional medical intervention."[239] His time in hospice marked the end of an active post-presidency at ninety-eight years old and the beginning of a celebration of a man who had redefined life after power.

It is impossible to sum up that long, active life in a sentence, or even a chapter. But a good place to start might be writer F. Scott Fitzgerald's ideal "The test of a first-rate intelligence is the ability to hold two opposing ideas in mind at the same time and still retain the ability to function." When it came to Jimmy Carter, the man who showed that ability best was George H. W. Bush.

Bush had more reason than most to dislike Jimmy Carter. He ran against the Carter-Mondale ticket in 1980. They worked together on democracy in Panama, but Carter tried to undermine Bush on the Gulf War. The former president was among the most vocal critics of Bush's son.[240] He said that George W. Bush's presidency was the "worst in history."[241]

But George H. W. Bush could hold two opposing ideas in mind at the same time about Jimmy Carter. He looked at the totality of Carter's former rivals, from his childhood in Plains, to his four years in the White House, to his work in support of democracy, human rights, and public health around the world. He appreciated that Jimmy Carter's legacy as president is distinct from his legacy as a person and as a former. Near the end of his own life, George H. W. Bush singled Carter out for praise, and said, "I respect this good man."[242]

Moving On

Historians are still writing books about the other George [Washington]. . . . By the time they get around to me I'll be long gone.

—GEORGE W. BUSH

A ticking clock looms over every post-presidency. Between their last day in office and their last day on earth, former presidents have a finite amount of time to make their marks upon the world. Had Thomas Jefferson died sixteen months earlier, he never would have met the first class of students at the University of Virginia. Had John Quincy Adams not lasted nine terms in the House, the abolitionist movement might have taken decades to find its champion and Adams never would have met Abraham Lincoln. Grover Cleveland's comeback as the twenty-fourth president positioned him to keep America on the gold standard. Had William Howard Taft not lived to see another Republican elected president, he would have missed his dream of becoming chief justice. Had Herbert Hoover not persisted and outlasted his critics, he never would have recovered his role as a public servant. Jimmy Carter transformed being a former into a platform, but his forty-two-year active post-presidency made it possible for him to have multiple world-changing achievements such as ensuring that 3.5 million people a year would no longer suffer from Guinea worm. In the previous chapters, we explored six examples of how very different presidents spent their active years after the White House. They each raced against their mortality to accomplish something that they never could have done as president, or in Grover Cleveland's case, in his first term. We know how their stories ended.

The stories of today's active presidents are still being written. Bill Clinton, George W. Bush, Barack Obama, and Donald Trump are very different men. They represent very different philosophies and even eras in today's fast-changing politics. Their post-presidencies are historic. We've seen global humanitarian missions and political scandal and controversy amid a former First Lady's failed presidential campaign. We've witnessed a new kind of post–White House celebrity in Barack Obama, with Netflix and Spotify deals and mixed leadership in the Democratic Party coming from a man who may one day eclipse even Jimmy Carter for the longest active post-presidency in history. And we've watched a post-presidency unlike any other with Donald Trump, one that began after a second impeachment and continued with indictments and an attempt at a comeback to the White House, while facing primary challenges from his own vice president and UN ambassador.

George W. Bush stands out from this group. He left office with the lowest approval rating of any president since Jimmy Carter, at 34 percent.[1] But in less than a decade, faster than the pace set by Carter, his popularity has more than doubled. It is now more than 60 percent.[2] That rise has been possible despite the fact that much of the Republican Party—and his Republican successor, Donald Trump—rejected his policies, and despite the fact that many Democrats have never approved of him.

How did the quiet return of George W. Bush's popularity happen? A comparison with Jimmy Carter is instructive. Whereas Carter viewed his presidency as never-ending, George W. Bush closed the book on his last day and never looked back. He moved on. In that regard at least, he is the anti-Carter.

Bush has shown there's still an appetite for the George Washington precedent. It's a quiet post-presidency, with respect for institutions. His time in the public eye was over, and he walked away. He didn't seek fame or public office. In an age with historically low trust in institutions, no matter one's political or policy disagreements, that display of character counts for something. Former president Carter's popularity returned thanks to his good works. Bush's returned because of his example, and because of the passage of time. He moved on from politics, and in an age when everything is political, that's earned him respect.

That context of respect is part of what has created a path for George W. Bush to find a postpresidential voice that the public welcomes, albeit through the unexpected mode of painting. He chooses to paint the people who represent America, but who are often overlooked—veterans and immigrants, and presumably more subjects to come—and in doing so, elevates their stories and their issues without politicizing the issues or undermining his successors.[3] It's a unique presidential voice, made more authentic by the fact that the public has seen him fade away from politics.

When Bush left office, he didn't anticipate this turnaround in public opinion. Nor did he seek it. Painting was certainly not on his mind, nor was it initially intended to be anything more than a new challenge for him to take on. What he wanted was to make a clean break from decades in the spotlight. He didn't have an axe to grind, nor did he see himself as the leader of the opposition. He didn't have one last act in public life he'd dreamed of since boyhood, nor was he interested in countering his critics. This was it.

A decade after the White House, I spoke with President Bush about his time out of office. The conversation took place over the course of two days at his family compound at Walker's Point, a jut of land sticking out into the Atlantic Ocean in beautiful southern Maine. It was the summer of 2020, the sun was shining, and we could hear the waves hit the rocky coastline. George W. Bush greeted me outside with a surgical mask hanging down below his face, and as we entered the main house and walked into a room, I was reminded of a different time; he's still the same man—with all the energy and eccentricities we all saw from 2001 until 2009. But the White House could not have felt further away.

This was the time of the COVID-19 pandemic, and we sat at a

distance with the windows open. Like everyone else in America, we were uneasy. Life was uncertain. But despite how surreal that moment was, the most normal thing about it was George W. Bush. He seemed perfectly himself, and at ease. These days, it's hard to imagine the former leader of the free world in anything but quiet retirement. As we sat down, he didn't wait for my first question. Perhaps after months of social distancing, he was eager to get to the punch line. He leaned forward, grinned, and with a Texas accent and a glint from the Maine sun in his eyes, made his point: "When it's over, it's over. I don't miss it."[4]

I believe him. Still, moving on isn't normal for former presidents. Bush is the grandson of a senator, the son of a president, a twice-elected governor, and a two-term president himself. He'd spent his life in and around the White House, and is now the patriarch of one of the most well-known political families in American history. He displays none of what philosopher and psychologist William James once described in a letter to H. G. Wells as America's "national disease . . . the moral flabbiness born of the exclusive worship of the bitch-goddess Success."[5] He's no longer interested in it.

Most people who desire or have held power don't have an easy time letting go. For Bush, it looks like second nature. When he left office, he was both unpopular and unemployed. But unlike Hoover or Carter, he didn't focus on the past. He doesn't look back. He might be what Northwestern University psychology professor Dan McAdams describes as a "chunker," people who live their lives in chapters, or "chunks." "Each chapter," McAdams explains, is "like a full-fledged, coherent story with its own build-up and climax." The climax of Bush's public life was the presidency. That's over. This new chapter is longer than his presidency. It's real life.[6]

Bush doesn't try to shape his legacy, a term he disdains. He doesn't push a political agenda. Even when his brother ran for president in 2016, he was rarely seen on the campaign trail. He doesn't want a second act. Whatever unfinished business he had now belongs to someone else. The rest is history.

In the meantime, George W. Bush's post-presidency is an ongoing experiment. And at least so far, it's working.

"AN UGLY WAY TO END THE PRESIDENCY"

Most Americans remember George W. Bush's presidency, and they remember its conclusion. Bush himself can't forget. "This was one ugly way to end the presidency," he tells me.

The Great Recession was on. In March 2008, the Fed bailed out Bear Stearns. In July, IndyMac failed. In September, the U.S. Treasury took over Fannie Mae and Freddie Mac. Lehman Brothers filed for bankruptcy in September. The next day, the government bailed out American International Group (AIG). Gross domestic product dropped by 4.3 percent and unemployment rose to 10 percent. This was the worst economic collapse since the Great Depression.[7]

World affairs were just as parlous. Russia invaded and occupied Georgia in August that year, taking over the territories of South Ossetia and Abkhazia and almost making it to the capital, Tbilisi, before the United States sent aid and Secretary of State Condoleezza Rice to intervene.[8] A month later, Islamic Jihad of Yemen carried out a terrorist attack against the U.S. embassy in Sanaa. With the War on Terror at its height, the U.S. had more than 160,000 troops in Iraq and nearly 40,000 in Afghanistan.[9]

The American people were not optimistic. The Bush administration, and George W. Bush, had hit a low point in every poll. His approval rating, once as high as 90 percent in the weeks after 9/11, stood at 34 percent. This was Jimmy Carter territory.[10]

Into the vacuum stepped Democratic presidential candidate Barack Obama, a young, first-term senator from Illinois, who promised hope and change. Obama had exploded onto the national stage with a rousing speech during the 2004 Democratic convention in support of Bush's then-challenger, Massachusetts senator John Kerry.[11] From the beginning of his national career, Obama had opposed the war in Iraq, a stance that set him apart from his primary opponent, New York senator and former First Lady Hillary Clinton.[12] Obama's popular positions, charisma, and personal story won the voters' support, the Iowa Caucuses, and eventually the Democratic nomination in 2008. From there, the White House was within his grasp.

George W. Bush was unpopular and term-limited, and it wasn't clear that any Republican could have won the White House in 2008. When Arizona senator John McCain and his running mate, Alaska governor Sarah Palin, challenged Barack Obama and Delaware senator Joe Biden, they were behind in almost every poll for the entire campaign season, save for a brief surge around the GOP convention.[13] As most pundits predicted, in an election with almost 10 million more voters than four years before, McCain-Palin went down in defeat.[14] They received 2 million fewer votes than Bush had in 2004. America had decisively elected its first Black president, and Obama would have Democratic supermajorities in the House and Senate. Change was coming.

There had been many racist attacks against candidate Obama, including conspiracy theories about his birth.[15] But most of the country—both right and left—had enormous hope for the future, and for the Obama presidency. The new president entered office with a 69 percent approval rating. Shortly after he was elected, he won a Nobel Peace Prize, despite the fact that he did not yet have any major accomplishments in the White House.[16] But Barack Obama was not George W. Bush. Facing the most popular Democrat in a generation, both at home and abroad, and an emerging Democratic majority of young people and racial minorities, the Republican Party looked like it might be finished for a generation.

President Bush hadn't been on the ballot in 2008, but his record was. Obama spent much of the campaign attacking the president, tying John McCain to what he called the "failed policies" of the Bush administration.[17] He accused them both of "hypocrisy, fear peddling, and fear mongering."[18] To the outgoing president, none of that mattered on January 20, 2009. A chapter in American politics, and in Bush's life, was over. He had one last job—hand over power to Barack Obama.

The new president's Inauguration Day was freezing, with temperatures hovering around twenty-eight degrees. With bitterly cold winds cutting through even thick winter coats, the inaugural crowd shivered as they waited on the National Mall. But to them, the weather was low on their list of priorities. They were buzzing with excitement, as more than a million people waited to see Obama sworn in as the forty-fourth president of the United States, a record turnout for an inauguration.[19]

Bush remembers the event and the crowd clearly, and what that day meant. He recalls how abrupt it all felt. He had hoped for a different result at the ballot box, though McCain was an old political rival from 2000. But Bush shared some of the crowd's excitement, if not about the president-elect, then about what that day meant. "Having . . . dealt with countries where [the peaceful transfer of power] doesn't happen . . . witnessing the swearing in of the first African American president was a big deal."[20]

When the ceremony was done, Bush boarded Marine One and said goodbye to the White House staff. "It's peaceful. . . . That in and of itself is so heartening. It is a beautiful experience."[21] Bush had been in and around official Washington his entire life. His father had been elected to Congress in 1966, when George W. Bush was twenty years old. But with Barack Obama now in the White House, for the first time in decades, he no longer had any reason to come back to the capital. His life would never be the same. But he didn't think much about what that meant for him personally. "He's not an introspective guy," Karl Rove, Bush's political advisor and the architect of his victories in 2000 and 2004, told me.[22]

He also hadn't spent much time thinking about the "afterlife," as Laura Bush calls it. For more than a decade, his life had been planned to the minute, including his time with family. Now his schedule was his own. He didn't have a plan for the next thirty days, let alone the next thirty years. He hadn't laid out a postpresidential agenda in his farewell address. Instead, he'd used the occasion to express a sense of gratitude and optimism about the United States.[23]

What he did want to do was prepare the country for the future. That meant that the transition had to go as smoothly as possible. Barack Obama was not inheriting an easy job. Bush was passing on a global war on terror to his successor. To prepare for the handoff, the outgoing president had met with the president-elect at the White House on November 10—the first time that Obama had ever been to the Oval Office.[24] The National Security Council prepared transition memoranda for Obama and his team, detailing the national-security challenges that would land on their desks on day one.[25]

Outgoing presidents have to prepare for and execute a transition, but they are not required to do much. Bill Clinton's team had certainly not been as accommodating. After the Clinton transition, the Government Accountability Office reported "damage, theft, vandalism, and pranks" in the White House. Those pranks included many White House computer keyboards with missing "W" keys. There would be no such antics in 2009.[26]

The Bush policies were still playing out, and it was too soon to tell how initiatives like the Troubled Asset Relief Program, or TARP, initially authorized at $700 billion to save the economy, would work.[27] "Because the [financial] crisis arose so late in my administration," Bush later wrote in his memoir, "I wouldn't be in the White House to see the impact of most of the decisions I made."[28] There was no time for on-the-job training for Barack Obama—the job was his now.

When George W. Bush left office, he was sixty-two, and he looked more like his father than ever before. His once-dark hair was grayer and longer. His eyes looked darker. He was tired, and he showed it.

He took a moment to reflect. Before the president headed to the president-elect's inauguration, White House press secretary Dana Perino entered the door to the Oval Office for a final meeting with her boss. As she did so, Bush straightened his tie and he looked in the mirror. Behind him, there was a letter on the Resolute desk addressed to "44." With his tie in place, he took one last look around the room, and he turned to Perino: "You know, when I first got here . . . I said I want to be able to look at myself on the day I leave office and like what I see, and to have been honorable. I can still look myself in the eye."[29]

History would be the judge of Bush's presidency. He was confident that history's final verdict might take decades to come in, and he might not be around by then. The president felt at peace with that. In the meantime, America had a new president. And George W. Bush was moving on. When it's over, it's over.

THE AFTERLIFE

"You can't long for what you don't have."[30] That's Bush's attitude about fame, power, and the White House. That proposition is up for debate. But on the last day of his presidency and every day after, it's what he's felt.

Actioning that sentiment was a different task altogether, and he didn't yet have a plan. But he did have a life to return to. He was close with his family, including a rock-solid marriage to First Lady Laura Bush, and their two daughters, Barbara and Jenna. Both his parents, George H. W. Bush and Barbara Bush, were still alive, a first in presidential history. Many of his closest friends and aides were still around him. As had been the case with his predecessor Jimmy Carter, Bush's Christian faith had deepened in the White House, and that faith would help him find a soft landing into civilian life and let go of the presidency.

He was heading to Texas. He didn't want to be someone who professes to "love Arkansas, or . . . Illinois, and then they go to New York or DC," he tells me, alluding to his predecessor and successor.[31] The Bush family was going home.

If the president was unpopular in Washington, Midland, Texas, was still Bush country. In a city of just over one hundred thousand people,[32] twenty thousand showed up to greet a Boeing 747, dubbed Special Air Mission 28000, that landed with the former president.[33] Eight years earlier, this had been the spot where he'd held a rally in Centennial Plaza before heading to the White House. "I made a lot of controversial decisions," he told the crowd two terms later. "But my values haven't changed."[34]

His values hadn't changed, but things were different and how to express those values out of politics remained an open question. He left the governor's mansion in Austin on December 21, 2000, and took the oath of office in Washington, DC, as president a month later. These were the two most important public roles in his life. Now he was back at the ranch in Crawford, and it was quiet at the dinner table that first night. Laura and their daughter Barbara were there.[35] No one else. The next morning, Bush woke up early, as usual, and he asked Laura who was going to make the coffee. "You are," she told him.[36]

With a bad cup of coffee in hand as he sat down for breakfast, there was no President's Daily Briefing waiting for him, just the morning paper.[37] "I would read the news and instinctively think about how we would have to respond," he recalls of this time in his life. "Then I remembered that decision was on someone else's desk."[38] This had less to do with going in reverse, and more to do with figuring out how to find the brakes. "I felt like I had gone from a hundred miles an hour to about 10. I had to force myself to relax."[39]

That adjustment was harder than it sounded. He was grasping at straws. One day, he asked his daughters, "I wonder if there is a group in Waco I could go talk to?" They teased that he was "going to get a fez and go join a gentleman's club."[40]

Laura had purchased the house without him having seen it, so he had a new home that he'd never been to in North Dallas, in a neighborhood called Preston Hollow. The Bushes' new neighbors had to get used to the Secret Service moving in and installing a gate where people coming and going had to show identification cards. Meanwhile, Bush was on duty walking his dog, Barney. In his memoir, he described the experience of taking out his own dog after the White House as "picking up that which I had been dodging for the past eight years."[41]

It was clear that the former president needed a project. That project turned into his memoir, *Decision Points*, which he wrote on the suggestion of Karl Rove and historians like Jay Winik. By this time, every former president wrote a memoir a few years after they left office. It wasn't required, but there was a general expectation, not to mention a financial reason. But even with this very normal ritual, Bush faced critics.

Many former presidents write memoirs for their own reasons. They want to correct the record as they see it, or to secure their legacies. These works are self-congratulatory. That wasn't what Bush wanted. "I think it is foolish to try to shape your legacy," he told me.[42] It's "an exhausting word, *legacy*," he says with disparaging emphasis. "It's a self-centered word." A person's record "is not what people think of you the day you leave."[43] He's confident in that prediction for himself. "Historians are still writing books about the other George," he tells me, referencing America's first president. "By the time they get around to me I'll be long gone."

This may be wishful thinking. But he may have a point. Gerald Ford pardoned Nixon after Watergate, to the public's outrage. The decision may have cost him the White House in 1976. But thirty years later, Democratic senator Ted Kennedy praised Ford's decision as a portrait in courage.[44] Illustrating that legacies experience ups and downs, Ford's decision underwent further reassessment amid multiple indictments against Donald Trump in the lead-up to the 2024 presidential election. The outcome of that reassessment is mixed. Some historians and scholars note that Ford's precedent set the expectations that it is a bad look for the country to have a president arraigned and fingerprinted, creating a dangerous perception that presidents get a free pass. Others draw a comparison between the alleged crimes of Nixon and Trump, and observe that Ford's decision helps set a marker that distinguishes pardonable crimes from those that should be prosecuted.

There's also Ronald Reagan, who Bush recalls was once labeled a "dunce and a warmonger."[45] His reputation has experienced a posthumous, albeit largely partisan renaissance. Now he's known as the Great Communicator, and every Republican presidential candidate positions themselves as the next incarnation of Ronald Reagan.[46]

History, of course, isn't kind to every former president. Bill Clinton remained a powerful figure in the Democratic Party for years. He delivered one of the most important speeches at the 2012 Democratic convention that renominated Barack Obama, and of course aided his wife Hillary Clinton's run in 2016. But with the rise of the #MeToo movement, his past indiscretions have come back to haunt him.[47] Woodrow Wilson's name no longer adorns Princeton University's graduate school of public policy.[48] At least ten former presidents owned slaves, including Founding Fathers, which raises questions about their place in history.[49]

The goal of *Decision Points* was not to change minds, at least in the short term. It was to give a clearer picture. Historians convinced Bush that he had what he called an "obligation to write." They "felt it was important that [he] record [his] perspective on the presidency, in [his] own words."[50]

Like Carter, Bush decided to write a memoir before he left office, even if the writing didn't begin in earnest until he returned to Texas. The president and his team spoke with Crown Publishing, which had published Barack Obama's memoir, *The Audacity of Hope*. That book, written before its subject's White House years, had been one of the most successful political memoirs in history.[51]

That's because even before he was president, Obama was a celebrity. *The Audacity of Hope* had not only sold well, it won a Grammy for Best Spoken Word Album—edging out Bill Clinton's *Giving*.[52] The book had helped convince Obama's fellow Chicagoan Oprah Winfrey to endorse him over the much-better-known Hillary Clinton in 2007.[53] Bush didn't have anywhere near the same star power as his successor.

Nevertheless, any presidential memoir is a hot commodity. In a meeting with Bob Barnett, the famed literary agent who can charge his clients $1,000 an hour, Crown pushed its own idea for what the book should be about, and what form it should take.[54] The publisher thought it should be short, uncontroversial, and readable. Maybe there should be more pictures than is typical for the genre.

Bush had something else in mind. After listening, he pitched the book he wanted to write, a book that would detail how he made his most controversial decisions as president, what he got right, and what he got wrong, from his own perspective. To explain what he meant, he started with one of the most consequential decisions of his administration: the Iraq War surge.

The Iraq War was unpopular, and it remains so. The public's support had dropped dramatically after Bush's ill-fated "Mission Accomplished" speech in May 2003.[55] Though dictator Saddam Hussein was no longer in power, and there were elections that had established a fragile new government in Baghdad, the situation on the ground was awful, both for Iraqis and for U.S. military personnel. Iraq had descended into a sectarian civil war. American casualties were mounting.

It wasn't just Democrats who were calling for America to exit Iraq. Some Republicans were, too. In 2006, ahead of the midterm election, Senate Majority Whip Mitch McConnell told Bush, "Mr. President, your unpopularity is going to cost us control of the Congress."[56] He advised the president to bring down troop levels.

McConnell's political instincts were spot-on. The Democrats picked up thirty-one seats in the House in 2006, winning a majority for the first time since Newt Gingrich's Republican Revolution in 1994. They also won the Senate with a five-seat gain.[57] Bush called the results a "thumpin'."[58]

But Bush didn't change course. He doubled down on the unpopular Iraq War, not only refusing to announce a timeline for withdrawal, despite calls from the new House Speaker Nancy Pelosi to do so, but instead switched to a counterinsurgency strategy.[59] The strategy, executed by General David Petraeus, required some twenty thousand more American troops.[60]

This was not a popular decision. A columnist at the *Washington Post* described the surge as "a fantasy-based escalation of the war in Iraq."[61] The Beltway wisdom, and in much of the country, held that the strategy would not work. For a time, the naysayers seemed right. American combat deaths in Iraq rose after the announcement and reached their peak in 2007, when 904 soldiers were killed.[62]

But over time, the situation on the ground changed. Combat losses fell. Violence subsided. American troops were making security and governance gains, both for themselves and Iraqis. Bush wanted to tell that story and how he made that decision, and the publisher wanted to hear more. Crown gave him the green light and a hefty advance.[63]

There was a challenge, however. Bush was not an author. Aware of his own reputation, he later joked that it would "come as a shock to people that I can write a book, much less read one."[64] He started by studying Ulysses Grant's two-volume memoir, the revered model for presidential memoirs, and decided that he would follow that example, not providing an account of his life or his entire time in the White House. The planning began while he was in the White House, but Bush wouldn't take pen to paper himself in any serious way until later. He was busy. "You gotta remember," he tells me, "2008 was a pretty consequential year."[65] Instead, he enlisted one of his aides, Chris Michel, to get started on it. The twenty-something Yale graduate had risen quickly through the White House ranks to become deputy director of speechwriting.[66] He was well positioned to help, based on his own experience and knowledge of the president.

Published in November 2010, *Decision Points* was an instant bestseller. It provided details about key moments in the Bush presidency, and it came out while the public's memory was still relatively fresh. Some parts of the book are personal, including its first chapter,

"Quitting," about Bush's decision to give up drinking. His history with alcohol had been a prominent issue in the 2000 election.[67]

Alcoholism once threatened to derail his entire career. In the memoir, he recalls a conversation with Laura early in their marriage in which she asked if he could remember the last day he hadn't had a drink. He couldn't. He'd once attended a dinner party at his parents' house in Maine where he'd been seated next to a beautiful older woman. He was drunk and asked her, "What is sex like after 50?"[68] That type of anecdote sells books, but it does not make a president. He gave up drinking in 1986, at age forty, crediting that decision with making it possible for him to become governor of Texas and later president of the United States.

The book detailed issues that remain controversial today. His handling of Hurricane Katrina. The Freedom Agenda in Iraq, Afghanistan, and around the world. The 2008 Financial Crisis and his policy response, which he describes as "the most drastic intervention in the free market since the presidency of Franklin Roosevelt."[69] These events continue to shape American politics. Readers, he said, "can draw whatever conclusion they want."

For his part, Bush had his own conclusion. He closed the book with these lines: "I knew some of the decisions I had made were not popular with many of my fellow citizens. But I felt satisfied that I had been willing to make the hard decisions, and I had always done what I believed was right. . . . Whatever the verdict on my presidency, I'm comfortable with the fact that I won't be around to hear it. That's a decision point only history will reach."[70]

Paying the Bills

It's not cheap to be a former president. Hillary Clinton once infamously remarked that she and Bill Clinton were "dead broke" when they left the White House, a comment that made her seem out of touch to most people, since the Clintons—headed to New York—could still afford a very comfortable lifestyle.[71] But the Bush family is also relatively wealthy, even for former presidents. After graduating from Yale University and Harvard Business School, George W. Bush entered the

Texas oil business, and a large portion of his net worth came from his former ownership stake in the Texas Rangers.[72]

He exited the White House with much of that wealth intact, but he was worried that it might not last given some hefty carrying costs and the unexpected bills associated with getting older. Bush recalls being "a little concerned about how I was going to make a living. . . . I watched Mother and Dad spend eighty percent of their health care bills in their last two years of their life."[73] As a former president, he had a small staff, the ranch in Crawford, and soon he would be in charge of the Bush family compound at Walker's Point, as well as his home in Dallas. With all that in mind, two months after he left office, Bush hit the paid speaking circuit, as former presidents have since Ulysses S. Grant.[74]

Former presidents are highly paid speakers, but the practice of raking in lucrative fees is often seen as distasteful. George H. W. Bush, who also hit the circuit after the White House, once joked that the practice was akin to "white-collar crime."[75] But Bush the younger doesn't see a conflict of interest. As a former president, he does not have a political agenda, and he's clear about his intentions. "I just want to make sure I have enough to leg it out," he tells me, reflecting on his need to earn money after the White House.[76]

He has occasionally joined up with former president Clinton, who'd been giving paid speeches since shortly after he left office. Usually, Clinton did most of the talking. Bush pointed this out to him, commenting, "You know, I get paid more than you do for these things." Clinton, confused, competitive, and wondering for a moment if he was being shortchanged, responded, "No, no I think we get paid the same." His successor grinned and replied, "Not per word."[77]

After that, Clinton didn't let Bush off the hook. "I want to hear what George has to say," he'd often remark at the start of an event.

Faith and Family

Bush relied on his faith to help him move on. The last few decades of his life had played out publicly. Now, as a former president, he could focus on the private aspects of his life.

Faith plays a different role in Bush's understanding of the post-presidency than it did for Jimmy Carter. Carter, the first born-again Christian elected to the White House, said his "faith demand[ed] that [he does] whatever [he] can, wherever [he] can, whenever [he] can, for as long as [he can]."[78] That meant a focus on the here and now, and continuing the work of his presidency. His faith often drove him to work on matters as controversial as the Israel-Palestinian conflict, and it gave him a sense of righteousness when he challenged his successors' policies. Bush, also a devout Christian, has a different view. He is not as vocal about his faith, even if he had been as a politician. He has instead leaned on it in his own life in ways that his best friend and former secretary of commerce, Don Evans, believes has helped him to move on from politics. "[My friend] worships a much higher power than the presidency," he says.[79] Whether one believes this or not, faith and politics are separate matters for Bush, and that separation helped him fill the presidential void more quickly.

There hadn't always been such a separation. Bush's faith helped get him elected president. He credits it with helping him to quit drinking and to build closer bonds with his family. Voters saw that in a 1999 Republican debate leading up to the Iowa Caucuses, when the GOP candidates had been asked who their favorite political philosopher was. Businessman Steve Forbes answered John Locke. Alan Keyes chose the Founding Fathers.[80] Bush responded, "Christ, because he changed my heart."[81]

That response got some pushback from the moderator, and won him a few raised eyebrows from more secular audiences. But what became known as the "Christ moment" resonated at the time and place.[82] After the scandal-plagued Clinton years, the statement struck a chord.[83] It was just what evangelical voters in Iowa wanted to hear.

More than any other president since Jimmy Carter, Bush was open about his faith. He read the Bible every day in the White House at 5:30 in the morning.[84] But he hadn't always been religious. The Reverend Billy Graham influenced him as an adult. But it was businessman Don Evans, then Bush's best friend from their days as young men in the oil fields of Midland, who gave him a Daily Bible in the 1980s. The book was split into 365 readings, and he went through one each day.[85]

These days, Bush reads the works of faith leaders like the late Tim Keller, whom he describes as the "only guy who can take a cynical, overeducated mind, and logically explain Christ."[86] Keller's *Counterfeit Gods: The Empty Promises of Money, Sex, and Power, and the Only Hope That Matters* helped him make peace with having no power after the White House.[87]

During that first year out of office, many presidents struggle with the extra time they have on their hands. But Bush had an easier time than most, mainly because his strong sense of faith and closeness with family offered an immediate and purposeful answer to how he would spend all the extra hours.[88] When he was elected president, his twin daughters, Barbara and Jenna, were high school age. In those crucial years, his official duties often prevented him from being present for them.[89] But now, as a former, he has time. He wants to be more present.[90] He sends text messages each morning, often with scripture verses or meditations from books like Sarah Young's *Jesus Calling*, along with a string of emojis that capture how he feels about it. It's his way of "letting my little girls know that I'm there if they need me."[91]

It works. "I have that waiting for me every morning," Barbara tells me.[92] When he was president, her father "wouldn't have done that before, but we just got to know each other a lot better both as adults."[93] Jenna has similar stories. "He senses when we really need somebody to listen and when we need a reminder of why we do what we do, who we are," she tells me.[94]

This isn't how the history books will remember him. But it's what he is focused on, and what he cares about most while he is alive. "What's your biggest legacy?" he asks me rhetorically. "I didn't lie, cheat or steal. . . . My girls call me Dad, and my family still loves me."[95] This has been the exception, far more than the norm for most presidents after they leave office.

Not every former president is so fortunate. And no other former president has had what Bush had on day one after the White House— two living parents. Not only that, he shared something unusual with them, as he's the second president whose father was also president, after John Quincy Adams, whose father died in 1826.

The two Bush presidents were close, but their relationship was mysterious and the subject of the public's armchair psychology. George W. Bush followed his father's example, and sometimes his literal footsteps. Both Bushes went to Phillips Academy in Andover, Massachusetts. They both graduated from Yale. They both served in the U.S. military. They both lived in Texas. And they both made it to the White House.

They also both had strained relationships with the press. In particular, the younger Bush thinks about 1984, when George H. W. Bush was the Republican vice presidential nominee, and his Democratic counterpart was Geraldine Ferraro. The first woman on a major-party ticket, Ferraro's candidacy attracted many sexist attacks, but she also garnered puff pieces from reporters overly interested in her appearance, who wrote about the latest "Ferraro look," as well as more substantive accolades.[96] *Newsweek* put her on its cover with the headline "Making History."

George H. W. Bush got no such treatment. In 1987, *Newsweek* described him as a "wimp."[97] He was often portrayed as an out-of-touch elitist. During the Reagan reelection, Barbara Bush once exploded at the disparate treatment of the two candidates, pointing out that Ferraro's net worth was higher than that of the Bush family. Mrs. Bush called Ferraro a "four-million-dollar—I can't say it, but it rhymes with rich." She regretted that statement and apologized.[98]

George H. W. Bush was not so vocal about his own critics, despite the fact that he had been defeated in his reelection bid to Bill Clinton, a man his son's age.[99] But for the rest of his life, according to his son, there was a "sting of defeat [that] lingered long past Bill Clinton's inauguration."[100] No matter that feeling, the two did not discuss the loss much. Bush describes his father as a member of the World War II generation, one who seldom talked about his experience in the war, or other challenges throughout his life.[101]

But this was still a historic moment. As John Adams had died during his son's presidency, there had never been a father-son pair of former presidents in American history before 2009. But it didn't result in new public revelations. The two seldom spoke to each other about their time in the White House publicly or privately. They didn't come together to advance some shared cause.

Occasionally, the two would be invited to speak together at a public event. It was a unique opportunity to have two former presidents from the same family, but organizers were more interested in the novelty of their pairing than either Bush was. Though these events did occur, there would be no tour where they talked about their perspectives on their presidencies or their unique place in American history as father and son. When I asked why, Bush tells me with some degree of neutrality that his father "just wasn't interested in it."[102] Some of this may have had to do with the fact that during 43's term, the two had spent eight years creating that separation. Some kind of emotional transition driven by one, or both, of them could have created this dynamic, but since neither of them are particularly reflective, it never happened.

The one exception to this was George W. Bush's next book, *41: A Portrait of My Father*. It was Dorie Lawson, daughter of the late American historian David McCullough, who gave him the idea to write it. She told Bush what a shame it was that John Quincy Adams never wrote a biography of his father. Adams missed his chance. Bush didn't have to.[103]

Bush was used to comparisons with the Adams family. During his White House years, Bush had a portrait of John Quincy Adams hanging over a dining room table, and when his father came for a meal, the elder Bush sometimes remarked, "It's great to be having lunch with Q and W."[104] Now the idea of doing something John Quincy Adams hadn't done appealed to Bush. John Quincy Adams had tried, but in addition to his own mental meandering, he had nine terms in the House that got in the way of writing a biography of his father. Bush had no intention of running for office. He had time, but not much left with 41.

Though George W. Bush does not have much interest in shaping his own legacy, he *is* interested in shaping his father's.[105] His father's presidency is often overshadowed by the charismatic two-term leaders Ronald Reagan and Bill Clinton who bookended it. Bush believes this is a mistake. His father had a consequential presidency, guiding the United States and much of the free world through the end of the Cold War. Now Bush wanted to give his father the credit he believed he was due, to put his views in the public record, and to perhaps find a new way to communicate with his father.[106] If he was going to correct the record, however, he would have to drive that agenda himself.

There was another reason to write *41*. Bush knew that he would be compared to John Quincy Adams, and to his own father. But he wanted to contribute to a separate history for George H. W. that would stand on its own. He wanted his eight years and his father's four to be judged independently—more for his dad's benefit than his own.

This was a time-sensitive issue for 43, as historian Jon Meacham was writing his own book about George H. W. Bush, 2016's bestselling *Destiny and Power*. This book was scheduled to come out after Bush's own biography. "I like Jon a lot," Bush told me. "I think he is a very good historian. But I was a little bit concerned about a '41 was good, 43 was bad' kind of book," in the sense that his father's legacy would be colored by the recent bias of his own unpopularity.[107] The Meacham book aside, he wanted to help his father by creating the separation that would have occurred if they didn't have the same last name. His own book was meant to avoid such presentism. Meacham's book came out afterward and, while it was fair and didn't pursue this gimmick, comparisons were still made.

Bush set to work, conscious of the fact that his father's health was failing, and that there wasn't much time left to write *41* if he wanted his father to see it. The book came out in 2014, when George H. W. Bush was wheelchair-bound and suffering from a condition similar to Parkinson's disease. But he was still able to read his son's work.

For the general public, the book had some new stories. Bush described how his father almost didn't run for reelection in 1992 because of the pressure it was putting on one of his other sons, Neil, whose business dealings were coming under scrutiny.[108] He also detailed how Pat Buchanan's primary challenge to his father in 1992 made him realize in 2004 that he needed to consolidate his conservative base early on to avoid a similar fate.[109] But Bush didn't pretend to provide an objective history of his father, and the book received mixed reviews. In the *New York Times*, Peter Baker called it "more Hallmark card than biography."[110] That's in part because it wasn't just meant for the public or the historical record—it was a kind of card, a note to his father that may have taken the place of conversations they never had.

George H. W. Bush passed away in 2018. His son was pleased by how his father was remembered. More than 3,000 people attended the memorial service at the National Cathedral and 17.5 million viewed it on television and online.[111] "When Dad died," Bush recalls, "all of the sudden there was a reappraisal. It took his death for people to realize what a good man he is or was." This made him proud. "I wasn't consoling a country. I was honoring a man," he recalls of his eulogy.[112]

Choosing His Moments

The Bush family is political. Since 1967, a Bush has almost always held public office. But that changed in 2009, the day W. left the White House. There were no Bushes at the national level. America was moving on, too.

Still, former presidents can be powerful political voices, and Bush had to decide how he wanted to use his. He didn't want to be the next Jimmy Carter, whom he recalled as having "made [his father's] life miserable,"[113] particularly when it came to the First Gulf War.[114] And as his father advised him, "Second-guessing your successors weakens the institution of the presidency."[115]

But politics is personal, and the Bush family wasn't quite done with politics yet. In 2016, Jeb Bush, the former governor of Florida, and George W. Bush's younger brother, ran for president. He was the early front-runner and built up a massive campaign war chest with Republican donor support. But their mother, Barbara, wasn't pleased by her son's run, at least not at first. "We've had enough Bushes," she lamented.[116] That less-than-enthusiastic assessment turned out to be prophetic.

Jeb's run for president provided one of the most difficult challenges to date for President Bush's desire to steer clear of the political life. As the 2016 Republican field took shape, Jeb's standing in the polls faded and brotherly instincts kicked in. George tried to rally support, albeit mostly behind closed doors with elected leaders and supporters. But despite a lifetime in politics, being back in the partisan fights made him uncomfortable, even if he wanted to help his sibling's campaign. There were missteps. In October 2015, W. told a group of Republican donors gathered in Denver that he "just [didn't] like" Ted Cruz, a fellow conservative Republican from Texas. Bush said this despite the fact that Cruz had worked on his legal team during the 2000 Florida recount and he even served as a staffer in his administration.[117] When the comment leaked, Bush called it "cringeworthy."[118]

By the time voting started in the Republican primaries in early 2016, Jeb Bush was a second-tier candidate. In February of that year, Cruz won the Iowa Caucuses. But then businessman Donald Trump, by then the clear front-runner, won the New Hampshire Primary. The plausible third contender was Florida senator Marco Rubio. Jeb's campaign was about to make its last stand in South Carolina, and George W. Bush headed to the Palmetto State to stump for his brother.

At first, Bush thought he could make a difference. He'd been popular in the state. When he won the South Carolina Primary in 2000, it turned the tide of his campaign against John McCain. But Jeb's campaign sank in South Carolina in 2016. The results had Jeb in fourth place, with just 7.8 percent of the vote.[119] Meanwhile, Trump came in first, handily beating both Cruz and Marco Rubio. After South Carolina, Jeb dropped out of the race. The field narrowed. There was no Bush.[120]

Jeb's defeat made it clear that the GOP was no longer the party of the Bushes. The rise of populist Donald Trump was a repudiation of the Republican establishment that their family once led. The new Republican nominee disowned his predecessor's legacy on everything from the Iraq War to immigration.[121] His attacks on Jeb Bush, whom he called "Low Energy," were insulting.[122]

The field came down to Donald Trump and Ted Cruz. Throwing up his hands, Bush told a group of alumni from his administration that he was "worried that [he would] be the last Republican president."[123] It turned out that he was wrong about that. Though Trump lost the popular vote—capturing a smaller percentage than Mitt Romney had in 2012—he won 306 votes in the Electoral College, well above the 270 needed to win.[124] The results came as a surprise not only to Bush, but to much of the country.[125]

Even if he was wrong about Trump's electoral prospects, Bush was onto something. George W. Bush was the last of a kind of Republican president, one from a previous era, as Grover Cleveland was the last conservative Democrat in his own time. The party was moving on from the Bush family, and much of its past. In 2016, no former Republican nominees for president attended their party's convention.[126] Of the four living GOP presidential candidates, only Bob Dole endorsed Trump.[127]

George W. Bush wasn't the last Republican president. But he'd have to decide if he'd be the only Republican president to attend Trump's inauguration. His father—both for health and personal reasons—was not going to make it.

Former presidents don't have to go to these events. Not every former, or incumbent, president attends every inauguration. John Adams left town and missed Jefferson's. John Quincy Adams skipped Andrew Jackson's. Martin Van Buren ducked out before William Henry Harrison's. Andrew Johnson—the first president to be impeached—refused to witness Ulysses S. Grant's swearing in. Though he's attended many since 1981, Bush missed some. He'd skipped Barack Obama's second inauguration in 2013, due to his father's health, and he'd opted out of Clinton's in 1997. He was gearing up for his own run and he had no desire to cheer on the man who'd defeated his father and won a decisive second term.[128]

Despite Trump's attacks on his family, Bush decided to attend. "The whole thing is full of majesty," he explains of his feeling about presidential inaugurations. As a former, he also enjoys the perks. "You get a really good seat," he jokes.[129]

Because of his prominent placement, he was visible to everyone watching Trump's inauguration. It was raining, and as he struggled to get his poncho on, it got caught. The television cameras turned to him. "I looked like a condom trying to get it on," he recalls with his vintage, albeit unfiltered sense of humor.[130] The audience watched his every move, not only because of who he is, but because he was sitting next to Hillary Clinton, the former First Lady, whom Trump had defeated that November. Together, Bush and Clinton made more news. As Trump spoke about "American carnage," Bush allegedly turned to Clinton and whispered, "That was some weird shit."[131]

There were many strange aspects of Trump's victory, and of the

American public's views of their new president. Trump was elected in part because he ran against the legacy of Bush. That stance won his support in the Republican base, which was growing more working class and populist. But on Trump's Inauguration Day, Bush had a higher approval rating than Trump. Trump's approval was around 50 percent,[132] while Bush was at 60 percent.[133] That meant that many people who voted for Trump—and even a large number of Clinton supporters—approved of Bush, even if they voted for candidates who rejected his policies.

In eight years, Bush's standing had risen dramatically. That rise continued during the Trump presidency. There were viral moments that helped his popular image, like when he handed former First Lady Michelle Obama a cough drop at Senator John McCain's funeral in 2018. Bush handed the former First Lady another mint at his father's funeral. For reasons that remain difficult to explain, the video of the sweet exchange got more than 7 million views on YouTube and the image of the Altoid exchange made its way around the world before the service was over. Michelle Obama was interviewed about it on the *Today* show.[134]

Puffy viral moments didn't mean he was well liked by everyone. When Bush appeared in a box at a Dallas Cowboys game with Ellen DeGeneres, a friend and also a leading voice for gay rights in America, there was outrage from many of the talk show host's fans. A writer in *Vanity Fair* called the two watching a football game together "a simulated apolitical utopia" that was "out of touch with reality."[135] The passage of time had not healed all wounds.

These episodes reflected a new dynamic in American politics. When Bush left office in 2009, 150 million people around the world were on Facebook. This number more than doubled by the end of that year, and was soon in the billions.[136] That made him the first former president who left the White House in the age of social media. In a world where his every move is watched and can go viral, he's careful about his conduct. Small gestures can have outsized positive impact, if used appropriately.[137]

Modern former presidents like Herbert Hoover and Jimmy Carter didn't shy away from giving their opinions on the issues of the day.

But Bush is far more cautious. He tries to choose these moments. He spoke at Congressman John Lewis's funeral in 2020, a chance to honor a man with whom he had disagreed frequently, but whose example as a leader of the civil rights movement he admired.[138] The moment was a chance to speak about race relations in the United States, which had deteriorated in Bush's post-presidency. One of the worst moments in race relations had come in 2018, when white supremacists rioted in Charlottesville, Virginia, after which Bush and his father issued a rare joint statement condemning "racial bigotry, anti-Semitism, and hatred in all its forms."[139]

After George Floyd's murder in 2020, Bush and Laura issued a statement again, acknowledging the importance of seeing America through the lens of the disenfranchised and sharing that they were "anguished by the brutal suffocation of George Floyd and disturbed by the injustice and fear that suffocate our country."[140] Bush's critics point out that there are many critical issues on which he has been silent. But he believes, "You can be a healing voice if you pick and choose your moments."[141] He'll continue choosing the moments on his own terms, not because of any kind of popular demand. That's for politicians.

There's another rule for him about these statements—differently from predecessors like Hoover or Carter, Bush doesn't criticize his successors by name. Even on January 6, 2021, when a pro-Trump mob stormed the Capitol in a violent attempt to stop the electoral process and Bush called this attack an "insurrection," he did not name Trump. Rather, he said, "[T]his is how election results are disputed in a banana republic—not our democratic republic."[142] He called out the "reckless behavior of some political leaders," a nonspecific statement that implicated both the president and some of his supporters.[143] Later, in a show of support for President Biden and for the institutions of democracy, Bush, Clinton, and Obama made a joint video on Inauguration Day 2021 in which they spoke about the critical importance of the peaceful transfer of power.[144]

He continues to pick his battles. When President Biden withdrew American troops from Afghanistan—ending a twenty-year war that began under Bush—the former president didn't undermine a decision to which he objected, but he did call for the administration to "cut red tape for refugees."[145] After Russia launched its invasion of Ukraine on February 24, 2022, he advocated U.S. support for the besieged nation.[146]

These statements do not move the needle on policy. But they do convey Bush's opinions. They're reminders of a man who has left the arena, and of the era that he represented before such divisive politics reached a boiling point.

FULFILLING PROMISES

The Former Presidents Club rarely gets together. But on April 25, 2013, Jimmy Carter, George H. W. Bush, Bill Clinton, George W. Bush, and President Barack Obama and First Lady Michelle Obama made a joint appearance for an important occasion. It was a sunny, hot afternoon in Dallas, Texas, and the group had assembled for the dedication ceremony for the President George W. Bush Presidential Center. It was a historic event. As Bush the younger remarked with some self deprecating levity, "There was a time in my life when I wasn't likely to be found at a library, much less found one."[147]

Getting Started

Every former president, except Donald Trump, begins building a presidential library soon after they leave office. Building them takes years. It's a very involved process, and the Presidential Libraries Act of 1955 requires the transfer of presidential papers to the federal government. The legislation was updated in 1986 to require private endowments, which transfers much of the burden of building and maintaining these libraries to the former presidents.

The work of building George W. Bush's institution began during his presidency, when six universities and one city, all in Texas, submitted bids to host it. The logical choice, however, was Southern Methodist University, Laura Bush's alma mater and the site of Bush's final campaign rally in 2004, close to their home in Dallas.[148]

Building the Bush Center would be expensive. But unlike Carter, Bush left office with strong ties to the business community, particularly

in Texas. Knowing that a former president's ability to fundraise dimin-
ishes every day after the White House, he set to work early. Once
again, his old friend Don Evans was a help. Evans aimed to raise a
massive $300 million for the project. He succeeded by 2011, in time
for Bush's sixty-fifth birthday.[149]

By this time, Bush had learned lessons from the example of his
father's institution, the George H. W. Bush Library at Texas A&M
University, in College Station. As governor, George W. Bush had visited his father's library. He didn't like some of what he saw. One professor affiliated with the library said that George H. W. Bush would
go down in history as a mediocre president, at best. Bush thought it
improper for a person paid by the George H. W. Bush Library to deni-
grate George H. W. Bush. To make sure that didn't happen to him, 43
would have to get the institution's governance right.

Bush wanted his center to be very much a part of, but independent from, SMU. Campus politics were challenging, and a group of
professors objected to the center. A faction worried that the institute
would be overtly political.[150] About a quarter of the faculty attended
a meeting to air these concerns.[151] Bush set out to win hearts and
minds. It was like a small political campaign, as he wandered into
classes at SMU, took pictures with students and faculty, and spoke on
campus. It worked.

SMU provided a twenty-three-acre plot for the center on the east
side of the campus, and three consecutive ninety-nine-year leases.[152]
The president of SMU was given a permanent seat on the center's
governing board. But there is no requirement to confer with the university's faculty senate. And the Bush Center has a high degree of autonomy in determining what content it develops and how it engages
with the campus and policy issues.[153]

The Agenda

Bush didn't want the Center to serve as a shrine to his presidency and
he had no interest in using it as a way to settle old scores or backfill unfinished business. Part of building an institution that reflects his values meant keeping promises that he had made on behalf of America,

most notably to people across Africa in the fight against HIV/AIDS, and to the veterans who he had asked to defend the country against terrorism. He'd start there and build on it over time, and like the presidency, there would eventually come a time for him to step back.

To do this, the former president needed to assemble a new team. It took some convincing to get Dallas businessman Ken Hersh on board as the CEO of the George W. Bush Presidential Center. Hersh didn't have much interest in heading a quiet archive or a sleepy family office. But Bush convinced him by talking about the institute as a "think and do tank."

The agenda took shape around a Bush initiative called the President's Emergency Plan for AIDS Relief (PEPFAR), which launched in 2003, as well as the President's Malaria Initiative, which began in 2005.[154] The impact of these programs is still felt around the world. The Irish singer-songwriter and humanitarian Bono once called PEPFAR a "genius plan, pretty crappy acronym."[155] In what he called a "tough column for a liberal to write," New York Times writer Nicholas Kristof described it as "the single best policy of any president in [his] lifetime." Its programs to fight HIV and AIDS have saved an estimated 25 million lives—equal to the population of Taiwan.[156] But there is still more to do, and the Bush Center aimed to be a part of it.

The Center chose to focus much of its global health work on preventing cervical cancer, including through its roughly $40 million Go Further campaign and its partnerships with governments and pharmaceutical companies.[157] "We get out of the presidency and it turns out women are dying because [of] cervical cancer and nobody is really focused on it," he explains as context.[158] He was eager to use the Bush Center's platform to shine a spotlight on the problem and then, in his words, get after it. The Center sponsors screenings and HPV vaccines to HIV-positive women who are alive thanks to PEPFAR, but who are now up to six times more likely to contract cervical cancer as a result of the disease.[159]

To Bush, PEPFAR is guided by faith. It took shape during his administration with the help of an evangelical Christian who worked for him, his speechwriter Michael Gerson.[160] Bush argues that "faith says every life matters. All life is precious. In other words, we are all God's

children. It doesn't say only white Christians."[161] For this reason, the
United States has a role to play in global public health. Laura Bush
says, quoting from the book of Luke, "To whom much is given, much
is required."[162] While the Bush and Carter centers are different, the
same faith-based lessons guided both of their work to improve global
public health.

And like Carter, Bush has undertaken multiple missions to sub-
Saharan Africa, from Zambia to Tanzania. As president, he traveled to
this part of the world to see these programs take shape. Now he could
see their impact. He's met children named "George" and "Laura,"
whose parents are alive because of PEPFAR programs.[163] Many of
the beneficiaries of these programs share Bush's faith. "God is good,"
he remembers telling a group of children. The kids replied, almost in
unison, "All the time." The response surprised and inspired him. Back
in Dallas, he recounted the story and told his senior staff that this is
how they need to be thinking every day.

After seeing the impact of these programs on so many lives, Bush
does try to move the needle to support them, even out of office. In
2017, when its budget was threatened, Bush penned an op-ed in defense of the program.[164] PEPFAR's budget remained intact—a rare
bipartisan foreign-policy success.[165]

A Lifelong Commitment

The Bush Center's work also supports veterans of the Global War on
Terror. Since 1973, the U.S. has had an all-volunteer military. After
9/11 and the start of the Global War on Terror, many young Americans
volunteered to fight in places like Afghanistan and Iraq, and many
carry wounds from those battlefields with them. As their former commander in chief, Bush believes that he owes this community his lifelong support.[166]

He wanted the center to do more than offer rhetorical support.
And he wanted the Center to be a supportive part of veterans' lives.
Center initiatives like the Veterans and Military Families program
conduct research into the challenges faced by veterans and are home
to leadership programs that help veterans overcome post-traumatic

stress, integrate back into civilian life, and find community. Team 43 Sports is one such program, through which the Center hosts events for injured service members and their families, like the W100K, a high-endurance three-day bike ride, and the Warrior Open golf tournament.[167]

He also wants to be a part of their lives. Bush often bikes with the veterans. Far from podiums and teleprompters that made real connections difficult while he was president, this is a competitive environment where hierarchies like the chain of command fade pretty quickly. Along with the veterans, he sweats, jokes, and engages in trash talk. Some with prosthetic arms and legs can be seen speeding along the trails at Center events and have inspired other wounded warriors in their recoveries. Bush is a part of that community, and intimately so. One participant recalled when Bush "pick[ed] cactus thorns out of my butt at Palo Duro Canyon."[168]

The events are reminders of the human costs of the Global War on Terror. Many of the disabled veterans who come are exceptional athletes in their own right who suffered injuries in combat. They did so following orders that came from Bush's desk as president. That's why he does this work.

Though he doesn't second-guess his decisions to invade Iraq and Afghanistan, he does recognize that the military was unprepared to support veterans of those theaters of war. Fighting in the streets of Baghdad and in Kandahar left physical injuries and invisible wounds like post-traumatic stress that continue to affect thousands of veterans. Despite the fact that the invisible wounds of war have been documented since at least the age of shell shock in World War I, many of these veterans were provided inadequate care, especially in the early days of the war. "There was no baseline measurement," Bush remembers. "There was no understanding. It was like, 'Soldier, get back in!'"[169] This widely held mentality perpetuated a stigma around post-traumatic stress that made it difficult for many soldiers to acknowledge what they were experiencing.

With that in mind, the Bush Center runs programs to help veterans transition to civilian life and deal with traumatic brain injury, or PTS. The Center raises awareness about an issue that still carries a great deal of stigma. Bush dropped the "D" in PTSD, emphasizing that it is a combat injury, not a disorder.[170]

The hardships that many of these veterans faced in places like Iraq and Afghanistan are difficult to imagine for those who did not serve during the War on Terror. Though Bush was a member of the Texas Air National Guard, he never saw combat. But some of what he's seen in this group reminds him of parts of his own life. He thinks about his mother, Barbara, who grieved when she lost her daughter, Robin, to leukemia when she was twenty-eight and Robin was just three. He also thinks of his old business partner Rusty Rose, a former co-owner of the Texas Rangers. Rusty battled depression and died at age seventy-four. Remembering his friend, Bush tells me, "I didn't really understand the extent of [depression] being an illness, and Rusty really educated me. I have never been in the dungeon, but I have friends who have been."[171]

FINDING A NEW VOICE

Former presidents have always had powerful platforms, even if they are not official. That's especially true for today's former presidents, who can reach audiences of hundreds of millions of people around the world in an instant. They also have libraries, centers, foundations, pensions, and Secret Service details. They have standing in the public eye. But it's still not clear how they should use that platform and, at least among today's living presidents, there is very little consistency. Bush is the quiet president, and while he still has more to say, he will only do so if he can communicate outside of the political fray. This is a tall order, but when he took on a new challenge of painting, that new-found skill helped him discover his postpresidential voice.

Bush never intended to become a painter. He wasn't grasping for a new medium or form of communication. But he had done what he was expected to do in the first chapter of his post-presidency. He wrote a memoir, built a center, and he gives speeches. What next?

Bush was bored when Yale historian John Lewis Gaddis visited him in Dallas in March 2012, and the professor could sense the former president's agitation. At the time, the Republican primaries were going on, but it was becoming clear that former Massachusetts governor Mitt Romney would be the nominee.[172] Bush had no role on the campaign trail. He was out of politics, and not a sought-after surrogate. With the nation's attentions on the primaries, Bush was glad to take the time to meet with a scholar he knew from Yale and whom he had called on for advice when he was president.

It was Chris Michel, who'd helped Bush with *Decision Points* and was a former Gaddis student, who had arranged the meeting.[173] Professor Gaddis and Bush sat down at 7:30 a.m. one day. The professor could tell the president needed work to satisfy his nervous energy.[174] Out of the blue, Gaddis told him, "You should take up painting. This is what Churchill did when he was out of power."[175]

It was an unexpected suggestion. Gaddis isn't an artist, but he assigns students in his Grand Strategy course a two-part Churchill essay, published in 1921 and 1922 in *Strand Magazine*, called "Painting as a Pastime." The essay makes the point that even the most powerful figures need time for other pursuits that allow them to "recharge their batteries."[176]

Churchill took up painting after he left the admiralty in disgrace in 1915, a low point in his career. The future prime minister described how "painting came to [his] rescue in a most trying time." In typical fashion, Churchill was dramatic in his description of the art form: "Painting is a companion with whom one may hope to walk a great part of life's journey. . . . My hand seemed arrested by a silent veto," he says of his first encounter with a blank canvas. But as he "splashed" paint all over it, "anyone could see that it could not hit back. No evil fate avenged the jaunty violence. The canvas grinned in helplessness before me. The spell was broken. . . . I have never felt any awe of a canvas since."[177]

During the meeting with Gaddis, the rest of Bush's life seemed like a blank canvas. Painting may have been out of character for a conservative Republican politician from Texas, but Bush delved into the Churchill essay and decided to give painting a try.[178] Maybe, he thought, he'd be better than the Brit.[179] "If Churchill can do it, I can do it," he joked to Laura with a competitive swagger.[180]

For Churchill, painting was a pastime that came at low points in his career. He painted most after the failure of the Gallipoli Campaign, when he lost the admiralty. He also painted when he left Number 10. But when he had power again, he stopped painting. "Power was central to [Churchill], which is a flaw in my judgment," Bush says. "If power becomes central in your life, and then you don't have it, your life becomes miserable."[181]

There was one obvious problem with Bush's plan. He didn't know how to paint. He hadn't picked up a paintbrush since high school, and he had no friends in the art world. "If he had ever taken an art class, it was at Yale when it was supposed to be an easy A. . . . He never looked at art at all," Laura says. There was a major art collection hanging around him in the White House, but the most he ever looked at artwork was during the "cultural niceties of being president" like "pop[ping] into the Louvre with the French president."[182] And, even then, his interest was less in the art than in engaging his host.

Painting is not easy, and Bush kept his new interest a secret. Karl Rove later described how he "went about it in a typical Bush way and didn't tell anyone about it until he was sure he wanted to do it, whether he wanted to continue to do it, and if he had any skill at doing it."[183]

He relied on technology to get him started. He paid three dollars for an iPhone app called Penultimate, which allowed him to draw and send simple images to his family. If he was giving a speech, he'd send a stick figure at a big rectangular podium, with a couple of hairs poking up. Laura Bush liked this game of Pictionary, saying the sketches "had a lot of personality and a lot of action."[184] The kids were confused. When her father responded to a text with a sketch of a plane with a stick figure on board, Barbara asked, "Is Dad okay?"[185]

"He was just desperate for a pastime," Laura recalls. So, she decided to help, setting up a conversation with her high school friend-turned-artist, Pamela Nelson. Nelson enlisted a local instructor named Gail Norfleet. "Gail, I have a student for you," she promised cryptically. But Norfleet didn't want to take on another student. She typically taught young kids or students at community colleges, and the idea of doing private lessons wasn't appealing. But when she heard it was George W. Bush calling, Gail said, "This would be too interesting to pass up."[186]

With a teacher on board, Bush grabbed his daughter Barbara's easel, left over from her high school art classes. Under Gail's instruction, he got to work. The artist taught the president about perspective. His first task was to paint a cube. Then it was a watermelon.[187] Every Monday they met for three hours in a studio that Laura Bush started to call the "the man cave."[188]

He needed some practice as a painter, and he needed to study. But a former president can't just visit a museum—the Secret Service and security concerns get in the way. So Gail brought the art world to him, telling him to take an online course offered by the Museum of Modern Art. Bush's longtime assistant Logan Garner signed him up under a pseudonym, and he studied art history online.

News quickly spread around the Bush family circles. His mother, Barbara, confronted him about his new hobby. "I hear you finally quit smoking cigars," she quipped, "and you're a painter?!" "Yes, Mother," he confessed. "If you are a painter," she demanded, "paint my dogs!"

Pets are a good place to start for would-be portrait artists. If the painting doesn't turn out well, pets don't complain. When her son was finished, Barbara liked the result. She proudly displayed the work. His father was less interested. "Dad was kind of interested in the fact that I was painting," Bush recalls. "I remember painting a lot [up in Maine] and I came with paint all over me and he asked, 'Do those shorts come in clean?'" George H. W. Bush never visited the studio. Even if he'd wanted to, he was too fragile to climb the narrow wooden stairs.[189]

A few friends were slowly let in on the secret. Over dinner one night, Bush offered to paint Karl Rove's dogs. The former president asked for a photograph of the animals, and Rove sent a few. Once he started working, Bush asked for more, demanding every angle of the canines. When Bush explained to a puzzled Rove that he'd been inspired by Winston Churchill, Rove said he was relieved he'd chosen painting instead of bricklaying.

The rest of the world found out soon enough, and well before Bush wanted anyone else to know. The beans were spilled by a Romanian hacker named Marcel Lehel Lazar, also known as Guccifer, who broke the news in April 2014. Guccifer had hacked Bush's sister Dorothy's email account, which had email attachments of some of the paintings. A few made headlines, including self-portraits of Bush in the bathtub and the shower.

These weren't explicit, but they were embarrassing. There were also private family pictures, including of George H. W. Bush recovering in the hospital. The Bush family wasn't Guccifer's only target. He'd also hacked a former U.S. Cabinet member, a former member of the U.S. Joint Chiefs of Staff, and a former presidential advisor.[190] He was indicted by a Romanian court, extradited to the U.S., and sentenced to fifty-two months in prison.[191]

The bathtub portrait was surprising to most people, both because of its subject and its creator. When I asked Bush why he'd chosen such an image, he said he was interested in learning how to paint water—plus he wanted to surprise his teacher, Gail. He thought his long, extended legs in the tub would do the trick. He chuckled and then made an odd comment about the incident: "I'm kind of a precocious dude and I guess it was my view of funny," he told me with a swaggering confidence.[192] This wasn't the only time he surprised Gail. On one occasion, frustrated by his lack of progress, Bush took his shirt off and asked her to photograph his back so that he could be more precise in what he was painting and capture the anatomic form. He proceeded to paint it on the spot.

After the Guccifer hack, the world knew that Bush was painting. Gail notified him that the *New York Times* critic had seen his work. Not a stranger to negative press, Bush responded, "I don't really want the *New York Times* to review me." Frustrated, Gail told him, "You've got potential. This is a big moment. I have been painting all my life, and the *New York Times* has never paid attention to me."[193]

People were paying attention, and he wanted a challenge; Bush is competitive, even with himself. Gail introduced him to Roger Winter, a friend and instructor at SMU. Winter came to Bush's studio and took a look at the former president's work. If Bush was going to be a painter, Winter said, he needed to do more. He should experiment beyond family portraits, dogs, and shower scenes.

When Bush asked what his next subject should be, Winter advised him to paint what he knows. For a former president, that meant world leaders. At first, Bush was uncertain, and a little insecure as a novice painter. "You think I can do that?" he asked.[194] Heads of state don't take kindly to unflattering portraits, no matter who paints them.

The answer to Bush's question was yes. He painted twenty-four portraits, culminating in his first public art show, *The Art of Leadership: A President's Personal Diplomacy*, on April 5, 2014.[195] The show featured many visitors from his eight years in the White House. There was the widow's-peaked UK prime minister Tony Blair. France's Nicolas Sarkozy had a flat lip and a dour expression, and his portrait hung near Rwanda's Paul Kagame and the Dalai Lama. Pakistan's Pervez Musharraf and Afghanistan's Hamid Karzai weren't far away.

Many of the reactions from his subjects were positive, even if they didn't think that Bush's work was particularly flattering. When I asked Karzai about his painting, he jokingly complained, "[Bush] didn't make me look a bit old, he made me look quite old. . . . I should look like that in my eighties." But he was glad to be a part of the show. "[Bush] still remembered me as someone that he had to paint and as a friend. That was a good sign, and I appreciate him. . . . If I could paint, I would paint him, too."[196]

The portrait of Vladimir Putin took the spotlight. Bush and Putin had met in Slovenia in 2001. After that encounter, Bush told the press, "I looked the man in the eye. I was able to get a sense of his soul." This comment didn't age well, and Condoleezza Rice later wrote that the phrasing was "a serious mistake."[197] Bush's painting reflects that mistake. Putin's expression is grim, and his face off-color. Karl Rove says there's a deadness to it that reflects something deeper. Bush isn't as interested in the psychoanalysis. To him, it just wasn't a very good painting.

The art world gave Bush mixed reviews. The *Guardian* panned the paintings as "art that tells us nothing at all."[198] The *New York Times* said Bush appeared to be "something of a natural when it comes to oil paintings, a decent amateur."[199] Bush's opinion of his works was more straightforward: "They're okay."[200]

He was a work in progress as an artist. The reviews didn't matter to him. He'd had his first show. It was becoming clear to his family and friends that there would be more to come, and that this was not a hobby. Bush had found a new voice.

With the world leaders in the rearview mirror, Gail thought Bush needed a new instructor. "I've taught you all I can teach you," she told him. It was a generous gesture, as she was getting noticed as the president's art instructor.

His next teacher was Jim Woodson, a fellow Texan and a long-time professor at Texas Christian University. Though the Bush family hadn't met him, they did have some of Woodson's work hanging on their walls. Bush had no idea until he took up painting.[201]

The two were an odd couple. "Woodson and I don't share the same values," an amused Bush tells me frankly, and with a good-natured smirk. "He's a Bernie Sanders man."[202] Laura adds, smiling as well, "He has a ponytail."[203] But the pairing worked.

Woodson coached Bush on how to experiment with new colors and styles, as opposed to painting with colors as they come from a tube. Bush kept reading about the art world, and he studied the work of artists like Lucian Freud, the British painter and grandson of Sigmund Freud. "It's appalling that [Freud] had thirteen or fourteen children out of wedlock," Bush commented, "and he painted his daughter buck naked, spread-eagle." But the former president separates the art from the artist.[204]

The next big project came from another instructor, Sedrick Huckaby. By this point, Bush had painted world leaders, people who everyone knows. Huckaby challenged him to paint the people he knows, but who are unknown to the rest of the world.[205] With that in mind, Bush decided his next subject would be veterans.[206]

This work would take Bush into a new kind of setting. Painting someone's portrait is a very intensive, personal experience. No former president had spent this much time, one on one, with men and women he'd sent into combat. Prior to painting these veterans, Bush would spend hours learning their stories and getting to know them as people. Only then would he sit with a photograph and paint them. "When you paint [these veterans] and you start thinking about the depth of their agony," Bush tells me, "it gives you a much better sense of what they're dealing with."[207]

Many are alumni of Team 43 programs or other Bush Center initiatives. There was Saul Martinez, a U.S. Army sergeant who lost both his legs in Iraq in an IED explosion, and who had a difficult recovery. Martinez and Bush had played golf together through the Warrior Open. Martinez recalls, "I think [Bush] found a lot of joy in seeing this double amputee tee off and hit a good golf shot."[208] Martinez talks about how he struggles with "survivor's guilt." He survived, but two of his close friends died in the blast, a story that is one of many that the president has depicted, explaining, "I painted each one of these veterans because they impacted me."[209] To Martinez, the painting emphasized his growth, not his struggles, and was a "warm hug" from the president.

The story of Staff Sergeant Alvis "Todd" Domerese also affected Bush. Domerese's vehicle was hit by two IEDs on patrol in Iraq, and he later redeployed to Afghanistan. After those experiences, he had PTS that gave him night sweats. Bush tried to capture that, noting that "the painting has a lot of heavy, dark purple."[210]

There's one veteran Bush painted twice, Major Chris Turner. Turner joined the army in 2005, straight out of Clemson University's ROTC program.[211] On October 5, 2013, Turner was hit by a bullet fired at him by an Afghan security guard. The assailant fatally shot one of Turner's troops, which Turner witnessed. "He saw someone get killed," Bush told the *Dallas Morning News*, "and so I got home . . . and I was just thinking about what it must be like to have imprinted in your memory an event that just keeps with you."[212]

Through painting these veterans, Bush got to know more about what they'd experienced on the battlefield and after. "I don't think we really understood the stigma [of PTS]," he says. "Turner taught me about that." The next time Bush painted him, the image was lighter, showing some indication of Turner's recovery.[213]

Corporal David Smith, from Akron, Ohio, served in the Alpha Company "Raiders" of the 1st Battalion, 4th Marines in Iraq. Smith accidentally shot a fellow soldier, severely wounding him in 2004. Bush got to know Smith through Team 43 Sports, and learned about his challenging transition to civilian life. Smith now speaks publicly about how he had contemplated suicide. He put a shotgun in his mouth one day, which Smith's mother told Bush about. Smith is now an advocate for veterans getting greater support and attention from both the military and the Department of Veterans Affairs.[214]

This series of portraits culminated in Bush's next book, *Portraits of Courage: A Commander in Chief's Tribute to America's Warriors*. Its ninety-eight subjects "opened my eyes," he tells me. The work "enabled not only me, but also people around me to better understand post-traumatic stress."[215] *Portraits of Courage* came out in 2018. It was a number one *New York Times* bestseller.

At a time when the share of the U.S. population that are veterans has declined by more than half since 1980, Bush believes that the book can help raise awareness about the community and its needs.[216] But his work has drawn criticism, including accusations that he does it to "atone" or because of his "guilt" from the War on Terror.[217]

I asked him about that critique, and he cut me off before I could finish, fully aware of this psychoanalysis. "Yeah, the guilt. 'Is this a way for you to get over your guilt?'" He shakes his head. He doesn't feel guilt, although he acknowledges his mistakes. Again, history will be the judge.[218] Meanwhile, the veterans of an all-volunteer military who signed up to defend their country inspire him. He believes that "people will understand why the sacrifice was necessary over time." In the meantime, their government owes them care, and Bush uses his influence to support them. That includes bringing attention to their personal stories, through whatever medium he can.[219]

History's final verdict on his presidency isn't in, but neither war turned out as Bush had hoped. President Obama pulled America's combat troops out of Iraq in 2013, only to send thousands back after the rise of ISIS. President Trump brought down troop levels in Afghanistan, and President Biden withdrew completely in August 2021, to chaos on the ground as the Taliban retook Kabul.

On the twentieth anniversary of 9/11, Bush spoke in Shanksville, Pennsylvania, the site of the downed airliner, United 93, whose cockpit passengers stormed the hijackers in order to prevent it from reaching its target.[220] In recounting the event from that terrible day, he remembered, "The terrorists soon discovered that a random group of Americans is an exceptional group of people. Facing an impossible circumstance, they comforted their loved ones by phone, braced each other for action, and defeated the designs of evil."[221]

The Global War on Terror, especially the Afghanistan theater, once had popular support. President Obama had called Afghanistan the "good war," in contrast to the "bad war" in Iraq, when he was on the campaign trail in 2008.[222] But most Americans on both sides of the aisle now believe the wars lasted too long. Terms like "regime change," "nation-building," and "freedom agenda" no longer rally support; far from it.

But we still don't know how history will unfold. For those wondering about Bush's own view, he points to a speech he gave to an assembly of Christians in South Korea. He delivered it in a stadium built for the Seoul Olympics in 1988. Now, decades later, there was a massive audience waiting to hear him speak. The introduction went on too long, and Bush thought back to Harry Truman, America's president during most of the Korean War, which lasted from 1950 until 1953.

When Truman left office, South Korea was a dictatorship. Truman's own approval rating was at a low of 32 percent.[223] The Korean War had a lot to do with that fact. But Truman stayed the course, increasing defense spending, and held back the North's advance along the 38th parallel. Though Truman never saw a democratic South Korea, more than seventy years later, South Korean people vote in free and fair elections. Seoul is a strong American ally. And today, Truman ranks near the top in presidential rankings.[224]

That history was on Bush's mind when he spoke to fifty thousand people in the stadium in Seoul that day. They are the beneficiaries of that legacy. "People are able to assemble, freely and without fear. And they could worship freely without fear," he says of South Korea. Truman had left office "deeply unpopular, and here I was, watching the beliefs of Harry Truman play out right before my very eyes."[225]

The other example he recalls is Japan. Bush remembers working with Junichiro Koizumi, who served as prime minister of Japan from 2001 through 2006. The two leaders became friends. But their fathers had fought each other during World War II in the Pacific. Bush asks, "How did that happen? How does that happen? It's not fate. It's one of the effects and by-products of free societies. . . . The question facing America is 'Do we believe that still, and do we believe freedom can bring peace?' I say we do."[226]

The Korean War and World War II weren't only about democracy, and neither was the war in Afghanistan. "Time dulls the memory of the post-9/11 period," Bush cautions. "The lesson of 9/11 is that the human condition elsewhere matters to the security at home. That lesson is fading rapidly."[227]

When I asked again, knowing the history that we do now, if he feels guilt about the Global War on Terror, his answer remains the same. "No, I don't. I didn't paint out of guilt. I painted out of wanting to honor sacrifice, service, duty, recovery. . . . I painted with pride."[228]

He was proud of his work, but there wasn't a clear next step for him as a painter. "George likes to have a project, he likes to have a job, he likes to have a direction," Laura Bush says of her husband. He asked his friends for ideas. One suggested painting people no one knows, and that are too often ignored—the homeless.[229] He contemplated the idea, but it didn't stick.

Instead, he decided to paint immigrants. As governor of Texas, immigration was one of the most important issues on his desk. During his two terms in office, he tried and failed to get comprehensive immigration reform passed. That failure is one of his few regrets from his eight years in the White House.

The idea came from former Republican National Committee chair Ken Mehlman, who suggested Bush return to the issue by painting immigrants in 2018. In the 2016 election, immigration had been front and center, and it was a toxic issue for many in American politics. With so much rancor in the air, Mehlman wanted the former president to "get back in the conversation." He could use his voice to showcase the positive contributions immigrants make to America's way of life.[230]

This issue followed Bush wherever he went. The work of the Bush ranch in Crawford depends on immigrants. The ranch is a 1,600-acre plot of land twenty-five miles west of Waco. Ninety acres of that land is devoted to tree farming, another thing that John Quincy Adams and George W. Bush have in common. It was unprofitable business for them both. The farmhands that help tend the ranch and native grow oaks, cypresses, and other tough trees that can handle the dry, hot Texas climate[231] are mostly from Mexico.

They've come to the United States legally on H2A visas, a category that enables American farmers to hire foreign workers temporarily when there is a lack of domestic labor. Bush admires the immigrants who work his land. "These guys are incredibly hard workers. They go home every year for two months. They send money home to their families. . . . And our tree farm would fold if it wasn't for them. We can't find people that are willing to work in June when it is a hundred and four degrees," he says.[232] Given the country's demographic headwinds, immigration also plays a vital role in keeping the workforce young and dynamic. With that background, Ken's suggestion turned into another book, *Out of Many, One: Portraits of America's Immigrants.*

The most famous subject isn't a farm hand, it's Arnold Schwarzenegger, the Austrian immigrant, bodybuilder, movie star, and former Republican governor of California. There are also portraits of former secretaries of state Madeleine Albright and Henry Kissinger, born in Czechoslovakia and Germany, respectively. His former staffer, Dina Powell McCormick, born in Egypt, is included. There are alumni of the Presidential Leadership Scholars Program, a joint initiative of the George W. Bush, Bill Clinton, George H. W. Bush, and Lyndon B. Johnson presidential centers.

There are lesser-known subjects with equally inspiring stories. Lev Sviridov was born in Russia, the grandson of a Holocaust survivor. His mother—whom Bush calls a "ball of fire"—launched a TV program after the collapse of the Soviet Union. She exposed corruption, and had to flee Russia for her safety. Once financially secure, Lev and his mother were now homeless, and he was beaten up as a young boy because he is Jewish. Sviridov then became a Rhodes Scholar. He's now a prominent professor and chemist at Hunter College in New York.[233]

There's also Jose Mallea. He was an engineer who'd worked at Cervecería Regional, Venezuela's second-largest brewing company. Because of Hugo Chavez and later Nicolas Maduro's socialist policies, he and his family fled their home in 2016. He took a low-paying job at the Biscayne Bay Brewing Company, owned by an alumnus of the Bush administration, and became one of its most valuable employees.[234] "The fact that he was willing to risk everything to leave, and he was living in a country with some of the biggest thugs," impressed Bush. "I wanted a guy that was happy to get away from his country's situation."[235]

Out of Many, One: Portraits of America's Immigrants came out on April 20, 2021, during the COVID-19 pandemic, a few months after the first Americans received their vaccines. The conversation about work had changed in the last year. Many white-collar workers were now at home. But many blue-collar workers, dubbed "essential," had to show up, physically, despite the pandemic. They were the grocery store clerks, truck drivers, and the men and women staffing critical facilities, including hospitals. Many of them are immigrants. Mehlman thought that a former president highlighting the contributions of immigrants at such a time would be valuable.[236]

There was another important aspect of the timing of the book's release. April 2021 was three months into the new Biden administration, after a divisive election in which immigration had been front and center once again. With a new administration, there was a chance for new initiatives. In a *Washington Post* op-ed, Bush made clear that the book was "not a brief for any set of policies." Rather, his goal was "to humanize the debate on immigration and reform" and share "principles."[237]

By now, Bush had been a painter longer than he'd been president. He knew how to use his voice in this new role. Unlike the White House, this role would last for the rest of his life. Whether he's in Texas or Maine, he spends hours in the studio each day painting. Among his favorite subjects to paint are the grandkids, nieces, and nephews. He can be seen listening to seventies and eighties rock, songs like "Centerfield" by John Fogerty. His gray hair is covered with flecks of blue, red, and green paint.

Studio 43, as he calls it, is where he spends countless hours these days. There are versions of his studio in Crawford, Walker's Point, and Dallas. The setup in each studio is as close to identical as possible. Each is a mess, cluttered with dozens of paintings on clotheslines. The floor and the furniture are covered with paint. There are dirty smocks on easels and a massive table where he mixes paint.

It's hard to imagine any of Bush's predecessors in such a setting.

Observing him in his studio, one could forget that this man was once the president of the United States, leader of the free world. It's like a different part of his brain turns on. When he's around other artists, he says it "opens up my mind and their mind." As president, you're "surrounded by the Condi Rices, who are telling you, 'Here are your options.' . . . [But] this is fundamentally different."[238]

He painted even more during the social isolation of COVID-19, when the country was locked down, heading to his studio from early in the morning until late at night. Over time, his style has changed, as has his technique. He uses beeswax, resin, and solvent, mixed with oil paint. Once he's done painting, he moves quickly. The Bush Center describes how he lays "a clean sheet of paper over the new painting and uses a roller to imprint the top sheet onto the bottom sheet. Once separated, the original bottom sheet is largely left in its original condition while the new top sheet is imprinted with a replica of the original."[239] "You have no idea what it's going to look like," he says when describing the result.[240]

He signs each piece "43" on the front, and "George Bush" on the back. His collection of paintings made with his new technique came out in April 2022. Its title? *Waxing Poetic.*[241]

Becoming an artist won't be the first line of Bush's obituary. "The interesting thing about art is that the definition of achievement is ill-defined," he says. "It really becomes not what other people think of your art, but what you think of your art. Only you know whether or not you are making progress. . . . The goal is to be as good an artist as you can be."[242] He's doing what economist and historian David Galenson calls "experimental innovation," switching styles and iterating without a clear vision.

Though painting was a surprise to those who know him, his passion about it isn't. "My dad has insane amounts of energy and is very fast paced," Barbara says. "So when he started painting, it was so interesting to me because it is sort of antithetical to his nature." She observes that he focuses and slows down, as he does in Bible study. "It's changed his personality, and he looks up more and points out objects in nature that he thinks would be worth painting."[243]

Bush will never sell a painting directly, or indirectly. This would become a slippery slope. Books and speeches are one thing, but the paintings are his voice and he won't commercialize that or turn this journey into a commodity.

"Painting is an unbelievably interesting learning experience for me," Bush tells me softly, but with firm conviction. He notes with almost stoic objectivity that when it comes to his passion as a painter, everyone around him missed it as something that would drive him. They get it now and so does he. This is part of why Bush will never sell a painting, nor will he donate one to be auctioned for charity. To do so would open doors that cannot be shut and undermine the new voice that he has created. "It has become an integral part of the last part of my life. . . . It's also proof that an old dog can learn new tricks."[244]

CONFRONTING MORTALITY

Nowadays, there's a routine to the quiet Bush post-presidency. He wakes up early, around 4:45 or 5:00 a.m. He reads scripture, then the news and opinion pieces, usually a mix of the *Dallas Morning News*, the *Wall Street Journal*, *Axios*, and sometimes *Drudge*. In his inbox there's a newsletter by his relative John Ellis, and conservative opinion writers like David French and Jonah Goldberg.

Every morning, he sends his messages to his family and then reaches out to a group he calls the "shut-ins." These are people from all parts of his life who are going through difficult times, some he knows well, others a mutual friend has added to his list. He has call sheets, just like when he was president.[245]

From September to June, he's in Texas, shuttling between Dallas and the ranch at Crawford. When he goes to the Bush Center, he has meetings and calls, he golfs and he goes to public events and private dinners organized by his colleagues and friends.

When Texas gets hot in the summers, he heads to the Bush compound in Kennebunkport, Maine. When they're together, the Bush family has dinner as often as they can. After a walk, it's early to bed, around 9:15 or 9:30 p.m. And wherever he is, he paints. He's often in the studio by 7:30 a.m. He stays there for three or four hours, taking breaks from painting to exercise on the elliptical or Peloton.

His father is gone, and he's the patriarch of the Bush family. That's a fact that he's very conscious of at Walker's Point, land that has been in the family for more than a century. "Watching your parents die is obviously an opportunity to think about death," he tells me. "I had a very frank discussion with Mom," and asked her, "Do you fear death?" She said, "Not at all. She was ready to die." His father was a closed book. "My dad didn't want to talk about it. . . . I think he might have mentioned . . . 'I'm looking forward to seeing Robin.'"[246]

With Barbara Bush and George H. W. Bush gone, George and Laura moved into the main house on the compound. They were hesitant at first, this was his parents' home, not theirs.[247] And he thinks about what will inevitably come. "After my mother and father died, I feel like I'm next."[248]

The political world that Bush and his family once dominated is behind him. That doesn't mean he's forgotten it. He worries about people losing belief in "America's goodness and the fairness [of] a democratic system."[249] He sees a young generation that doesn't believe in capitalism, and rising populism on the right and left, but thinks it will pass like the Know Nothings from the nineteenth century.

Part of his faith is based on his respect for institutions, and the belief that a former president needs to step away from the spotlight and move on. Now there's something very normal, even boring to some outside observers, about this final chapter of Bush's life. What's extraordinary, though, is how ordinary it is. Bush hasn't sought elected office. He hasn't led his party or a faction of it in exile. He doesn't want to be back in the public eye, and he rarely opines. But of all the living former presidents, Americans' opinions of him may have changed the most. His approval rating is in the 60s, higher than any American leader in national elected office.[250]

That's worth pondering. Power is often sought out as an end in itself. The idea of losing it is intolerable to many, who wonder if life would be worth living without it. Many on both sides of the aisle believe that politics is only about power, and they discount the importance of character and the idea that political institutions exist to secure rights and freedoms that come before politics, and that every human being is owed by nature of their humanity. Bush has no interest in getting back into the arena. There's more to life than politics. And there's only one president at a time.

What's next for George W. Bush? "I don't plan for decades out," he tells me, looking out the window at Walker's Point. "I plan for the next day. The only thing you plan for decades out is where you are going to be buried."[251] He means that literally, and by all accounts has the question answered. For 43, it's never going to be about looking backward or projecting forward. It's all about the present, and even he doesn't know what the next day will bring. He prefers it that way.

CONCLUSION

The Founding Fathers worried about former presidents. In *Federalist* 72, Alexander Hamilton wondered, "Would it promote the peace of the community or the stability of the government to have half a dozen men who had had credit enough to be raised to the seat of the supreme magistracy, wandering among the people like discontented ghosts, and sighing for a place which they were destined never more to possess?"[1]

Hamilton's musing is representative of how the Founders wrestled with the idea of ex-presidents. They had good reason to be concerned. With few exceptions in history, leaders did not give up power of their own accord—they held it until their last breath. But America's system of government depends on the existence of formers, people who step aside. The fact that there are so many former heads of state and heads of government around the world today, flying from city to city, speaking at conferences, and collecting enormous fees for doing so, is in many ways a legacy of Washington's Farewell.

But as this book and history show, that story isn't the end. Former presidents retain a kind of power. And the ambition of a former president can still be made to counteract the ambition of their successors and to carry on their own agenda. These ambitions rarely dissipate with the loss of one office.

But former presidents are a feature of democracies, not a bug, and their presence in American life is an unstated assumption of our system of government. With the passage of a Twenty-Second Amendment in 1951, which enshrined the two-term limit, it was made more likely that presidents would have to move on at some point. The presidency isn't for life.

For most of American history, former presidents have been charting their own way forward, left to manage their own affairs out of office. There is no playbook, path, or position, and the outcomes vary more dramatically now than ever before. Today's active ex-presidents are testaments to that fact. Bill Clinton, George W. Bush, Barack Obama, and Donald Trump could not be more different in how they have, and are approaching, their time out of office.

Not every president has a chance to accomplish something great after the White House. Eight of them died in office, and another three died shortly thereafter. James K. Polk died of cholera just 103 days after his presidency, buried in a mass grave at fifty-three years old. Chester Arthur lived for two years as a former president, before succumbing to Bright's disease. Lyndon Johnson had four years after his presidency, with the cloud of the Vietnam War hanging over him.

Not every former president uses their position for good. Franklin Pierce, a Northerner who favored popular sovereignty—the idea that democracy allowed citizens, and not the federal government, to decide if the territory in which they lived would allow slavery—tried to rally the living ex-presidents in 1861 to resolve the Civil War. But his efforts were torpedoed by Martin Van Buren, and Pierce became a vocal critic of Lincoln, a sympathizer for the South, and a correspondent of Confederate president Jefferson Davis. Worse still, Pierce's predecessor, the Virginian John Tyler, defected from the Union and won a seat in the Confederate House of Representatives. He died a traitor in January 1862, and President Lincoln denied his predecessor a state funeral. Instead, Tyler was honored in Richmond, the Confederate capital.

And not every former president gets the results they wanted. Andrew Johnson failed to win a Senate seat in 1868, then fell short in securing a seat in the House in 1872, and he only returned to public office in 1875, five months before his death. Ulysses Grant left office a war hero, but with a reputation for scandal that contributed to his failure to win the Republican nomination for president in 1880.

Theodore Roosevelt's split from the Republican Party in 1912, and his subsequent run for the White House as a Bull Moose, handed the presidency to Woodrow Wilson, a man he despised. TR might have won the White House eight years later, had he not died of strains of malaria picked up in the Amazon and from a broken heart after his son Quentin's death in battle during World War I.

Life After Power tells the stories of what's possible in the next chapter, and how to get it right. The seven presidents featured in this book breathed life into the post-presidency.

Thomas Jefferson, John Quincy Adams, Grover Cleveland, William Howard Taft, Herbert Hoover, Jimmy Carter, and George W. Bush broke new ground. They showed how to reenter the arena and have marked out potential paths for their successors in the process, widening the possibilities for those to come. They've shown how former presidents can lead in every branch of the federal government, sometimes twice. They've played their parts in war and peace. They've built new institutions, led humanitarian causes on a global scale, and shaped their legacies both through loud action and quiet restraint. Far from becoming ghosts of their former selves, they've demonstrated that life doesn't end with the job that will be the first line of their obituaries.

The post-presidencies of these men showcase the story of America. The terrible compromises made by the Founding Fathers and the heated debates over westward expansion are captured in Thomas Jefferson's anguish over the Missouri Compromise of 1820, and his hopes for his new university. The growth and power of the abolitionist movement was made possible by John Quincy Adams's speeches on the floor of the House of Representatives and before the Supreme Court. American politics and America's role in the world at the end of the nineteenth century were changed by Grover Cleveland, a man who never thought he'd be president once, let alone twice. We can come to a deeper understanding of the debates about American involvement in World War I and II, and of the hopes for the world after the wars, through the post-presidencies of William Howard Taft and Herbert Hoover. Jimmy Carter and George W. Bush not only reminded the

American people of the importance of character in the White House but they also showed how public opinion changes over time, and how Americans constantly reassess themselves and their history.

The philosopher Carl Jung once wrote about what he called the "afternoon of life." He observed, "Thoroughly unprepared, we take the step into the afternoon of life. Worse still, we take this step with the false presupposition that our truths and our ideals will serve us as they have in the past. But we cannot live the afternoon of life according to the program of life's morning, for what was great in the morning will be little at evening and what in the morning was true, at evening will have become a lie."[2] In many ways, the afternoon of life is the story of how the men who were once president took their own steps into whatever came next.

They found that leaving power is never easy. Presidents who lose elections are rejected by the people and lament being deprived of the time they felt necessary to finish the job. But some find defeat to be motivating. They have something left to prove, which is why some of the most consequential post-presidencies began after a loss. Of the seven case studies in this book, only Thomas Jefferson and George W. Bush won reelection, although Cleveland never lost the popular vote and later secured another presidency. One-term presidents also typically leave office younger than their two-term counterparts, and so have longer for whatever comes next. I doubt that John Quincy Adams would have run for Congress had he defeated Andrew Jackson in 1828. Without Congressman Adams, the abolition movement would have been denied one of its greatest champions.

Many successful former presidents didn't want to be president above all else. Thomas Jefferson tried to retire three times before he became president. William Howard Taft was pushed into the White House by Nellie Taft, his brothers, and Theodore Roosevelt. Each of these men returned to the arena for their own reasons, and they had convictions that predated and outlasted their four or eight years in office.

The most successful former presidents learn to put politics behind them. They can still campaign for their fellow partisans, but they don't view bipartisanship as a dirty word. For twelve years, Herbert Hoover was one of Franklin Delano Roosevelt's fiercest critics. But he became one of Harry Truman's most trusted advisors. William Howard Taft served on Woodrow Wilson's National War Labor Board, and he might have been able to help Wilson get the Treaty of Versailles through the Senate, had Wilson shown some bipartisanship and engaged his predecessor in a cause they both shared. Jimmy Carter, though he never put politics behind him, was in some ways post-partisan. He saved his harshest criticisms for Ronald Reagan and George W. Bush. But he never shied away from criticizing the policies of his fellow Democrats Bill Clinton and Barack Obama.

Their decisions and actions offer examples for anyone contemplating the next chapters of their own lives.

For the founders among us, Thomas Jefferson's story showed that our early ideas may be some of our best, and what we do at the end of our lives can build on the work we did at the start. The University of Virginia has lasted for more than two hundred years, and it was a dream he had as a young man to which he returned as an elder statesman. The desire to live to see the university open its doors probably helped perpetuate his long life.

For those who worry that that defeat is final, John Quincy Adams offers a powerful rebuttal. Before his presidency, he was one of the most celebrated men in the United States. He lost his standing, and his position, after four years in the White House. But that was not the end. Adams shows that a title does not make a leader. As a member of the House of Representatives, he was in a lower position than he'd once held as a younger man, when he'd served as a senator, secretary of state, and president. But he took on a cause, and he worked to build an entirely different political life than the one that made him president. His second act is one of the main reasons he is still admired and where he likely had an even greater impact. Like Jefferson, his active role in the House probably contributed to a longer life.

Grover Cleveland's life offers a different lesson for how to handle defeat. For anyone forced out of a job, it is tempting to want to get back what you once had. Cleveland made a comeback to the highest office in the land after a defeat in the Electoral College, but a victory in the popular vote. But his experience offers a cautionary tale that even for those who achieve that elusive goal, the job is rarely as sweet the second time around and it comes with a different set of risks and challenges.

Cleveland could have lived his days quietly with his wife and family. He was neither bored nor unfulfilled, and his instincts told him to enjoy a life he'd always wanted. But those same instincts told him to stick by his principles, to run again and to serve. His comeback was a gamble, not only on one election, but on his standing and the rest of his life. He inherited problems not of his own making that burdened and distracted him from the very causes that had motivated him to come back. He left office less popular and less satisfied. But he kept America on the gold standard and tempered the imperialist tide. On his deathbed, he knew that he hadn't always succeeded, but could still say, "I have tried so hard to do right."

For those of us who turn down opportunities and dreams because the timing isn't right, or who think our day will never come, William Howard Taft offers an inspirational tale of persistence and perseverance. All he ever wanted was to be on the Supreme Court. He knew the White House, and everything before it, was preparation for that post. He observed that "presidents come and go, but the Supreme Court is forever." His four years in the White House were among his least happy. He was humiliated in 1912, when he came in third place in his bid for reelection. But he didn't give up hope, despite his age and possible political irrelevance. Instead, he waited and worked, and in 1921, Warren Harding—the man who'd nominated him to be president at the Republican convention nine years earlier—then made him chief justice of the Supreme Court. In Taft's last decade, he reshaped an institution he'd admired his whole life. He died happier and more fulfilled than he had been before.

A good name takes a lifetime to earn, but it can be lost overnight. Herbert Hoover understood that better than anyone. The Great Humanitarian won the White House in a landslide. He lost it four years later because his name had become synonymous with the Great Depression. He wanted to recover what he'd lost, and to help the country recover from calamity. He outlived his worst critics, and he reentered public service. Four years in office didn't define the life of a man who died at ninety.

Moving on from a dream job is a challenging task. Jimmy Carter proves that the work doesn't need to end when the job does. As his single term in office wound down, Carter feared an "altogether new, unwanted, and potentially empty life." He turned the former presidency into an office of its own, and used his experience, status, expertise, and connections to build an independent platform away from politics that none of his predecessors could have imagined. His active post-presidency lasted ten times longer than his presidency, and America's longest-lasting former continued to fight for global health, democracy, and peace. Today, he is remembered more for his time as a former than his tenure as president.

If Jimmy Carter offers a prescriptive path for those who want to hold on to key elements of what they once had, George W. Bush shows how to leave it all behind. He had no interest in getting back in the political arena. Instead, he brought back the George Washington precedent of a quiet post-presidency, away from politics. That example may seem like an anachronism, but the American people respect him for his own respect of institutions. Like Carter, his popularity has undergone a remarkable resurgence since he left office, and in much less time.

Bush's example shows that a quiet exit still leaves room for an influential voice, albeit one that looks very different. His separation from politics proved usefully constraining as it pushed him to take up fresh challenges, develop new skills and, in the process, discover a powerful postpresidential voice that he can articulate through painting.

So many presidents try to play a heavy hand in shaping their legacy. Bush has not, and yet his quiet, restrained approach has doubled his favorability, even as the Republican Party's policies and politics have become much more populist than they were during the Bush years. The evolution of his party has undoubtedly created a favorable context for his reputational rehabilitation. It is a reminder that sometimes less is more.

We may be entering the golden age of former presidents, with more of them than we've ever had before. At six points in American history, there have been no living former presidents. There will not be a seventh. The four longest active post-presidencies have all happened in the last century: Jimmy Carter (forty-two years), Herbert Hoover (thirty-one years), Gerald Ford (twenty-nine years), and George H. W. Bush (twenty-five years). There has been a record five living former presidents at the same time in the last hundred years. With longer life spans and advances in life sciences, that record won't last for long. We will soon have more former presidents than ever before.

The post-presidency is a fact of American life. The presidents we think we know still changed history after the job for which they're best known. And they did so in a chapter of life we all eventually have to confront.

Today, the world is seeing why Hamilton worried about former presidents. Donald Trump chose to begin his post-presidency in a way that none of his predecessors did. Following his loss to Joe Biden, he denied the results of an election with historic turnout in which he was defeated. Two weeks before leaving office, he spoke at a rally that led to a riot at the U.S. Capitol, a violent attempt to halt the counting of votes. He was impeached for it. He then ran for the office he lost, still perpetuating the same false narrative about the 2020 election and did so in the unprecedented situation of having been indicted in multiple jurisdictions on an assortment of legal violations.

The presidency has guardrails against excess and egregious behavior, a system of checks and balances and of the separation of powers that is meant to limit what one person can do in office. There are no such guardrails on former presidents, other than the two-term limit. What power they have relies on the consent of other people, not on the power of any office. Citizens give former presidents power by listening to what they say, by paying to support whatever they do next, and by voting.

For those wondering where the institution of the post-presidency goes from here, that's up to the American people to decide. It's up to them to choose wisely.

ACKNOWLEDGMENTS

This book would not have been possible without my loving parents, Dee and Donald. They are responsible for igniting my interest in presidents and, as I state in my dedication, showing me what is important in the later chapters of life. I also want to thank my sister, Emily, who is as vocal as she is dogmatic about what matters in life, but who is right more often than she is wrong.

I owe the greatest debt of gratitude to my wife, Rebecca, and my three daughters, Zelda, Annabel, and Iggy, whose love and support during the lengthy book writing process did not go unnoticed. There were countless afternoons and evenings where my kids colored alongside me while I typed away on this book. Rebecca tolerated the late nights and long car rides, where I worked to meet my deadlines, and graciously listened to me connect everything around us to the illustrious lives of obscure former presidents. My mother-in-law, Audrey Bear, also deserves a note of gratitude, as she was kind enough to read early chapters and offer feedback.

Alice Mayhew, my esteemed editor on *Accidental Presidents*, took a chance on me as an aspiring presidential historian and took another chance on me by purchasing this book. I only wish she had lived long enough to see the original vision unfold, having passed before I began writing. She was a legend.

My editor, Eamon Dolan, was an incredible partner in shaping this book. The topic and approach was very different from my previous books and Eamon patiently helped me hone in on a narrative that fit the topic. He pushed me when I got stuck, brought clarity to parts of the book that felt adrift, and helped me discover aspects of this story that even I didn't quite appreciate when I first embarked on the project.

Wilson Shirley, a rising star in foreign policy, was instrumental in helping research and draft this manuscript. He really was my thought partner on this project and so much of what unfolds in these pages is a testament to how much of his time and energy he devoted to working with me on this project. We had fun learning about these presidents together, debating how and why they did certain things, and even had a good laugh or two over some of the more amusing stories we found.

My interest in behavioral psychology is part of what drove me to write this book, and appreciating the scholarly foundation that defines the field helped shape this book's thesis. I'd like to again thank my dad, but this time as a psychologist, whose expertise and perspective I so admire and relied on heavily for this book. Dad, thanks for the tip on Carl Jung's "afternoon of life." Samantha Boardman and Adam Grant both offered me extensive takes on the key behavioral psychology perspectives that I might want to draw on in the manuscript. I never would have been able to navigate this vast field had it not been for them.

While most of the research for this book relied on primary and secondary sources, I was also able to draw from the living from time to time, particularly for the George W. Bush chapter. I owe a huge debt of gratitude to President Bush for so graciously giving me two days of his time in August 2020. Freddy Ford, Bush's trusted chief of staff and aide, is the man who makes the magic happen, and in addition to helping facilitate everything, he also shared his perspective. There are a number of others—Dana Perino, Karl Rove, Don Evans, Margaret Spellings, Ken Hersch, Laura Bush, Barbara Bush, Jenna Bush Hager, Hamid Karzai, John Gaddis, Ken Mehlman, and several subjects of president Bush's paintings—all of whose insights helped enrich and round out the manuscript.

Margaret Hoover deserves a special note of thanks for helping me so much on the Herbert Hoover chapter. She cares so deeply about her great-grandfather's legacy, and spent countless hours with me talking through my assessment and sharing her own perspective. Margaret gave me countless leads and the incredible treat of even interviewing one of Herbert Hoover's living research assistants. She also introduced me to George Nash, the seminal scholar on Hoover, and George's feedback and perspective proved incredibly valuable.

Eric Schmidt deserves a special appreciation from me. He is my longtime partner and friend, but more important, we went on a journey together as he transitioned from CEO of Google to executive chairman, and then to one of the great public intellectuals of our time. Having a front-row seat for his evolution is an experience that I will continue to learn from for the rest of my life. Eric, thank you for letting me in and allowing me to be part of your journey. I'm certain it is part of the inspiration for this book.

I want to thank some of my dear friends who offered early feedback and useful critique, beginning with my trusted historian friends and mentors like David Kennedy and Walter Isaacson. Trevor Thompson, Jeff McLean, Alex Pollen, Dov Fox, Pete Blaustein, Dina Powell, Dave McCormick, Yasmin Green, John Avlon, Dan Senor, Reid Hoffman, Jason Liebman, Michael Davidson, Marc Andreessen, and Fareed Zakaria all offered such useful insights.

The team at Simon & Schuster has been incredible, beginning with Jonathan Karp, who with all three of my books with the publisher, has made me feel supported and like part of the family. I've already given a shout out to my editor, Eamon Dolan, but he is so good that I'm going to offer another thanks. Stephen Bedford, Elizabeth Herman, and the entire Simon & Schuster PR team have been great partners in helping get the story out.

Special thanks to Julia Bialek, a star graduate from Yale University who I enlisted to help me with fact-checking toward the end.

My literary agent, Andrew Wylie, and the whole Wylie Agency family continue to provide encouragement and guidance with each successive book and I'm appreciative for their support.

Special thanks to my newish professional family at Goldman Sachs, beginning with David Solomon, John Waldron, John Rogers, my cohead George Lee, and the rest of the firm's management committee and partnership. I want to thank my team in the office of applied innovation for the support I have had along the way, not to mention the space to maintain my side gig as a historian while meeting the demands of a busy job.

Finally, I want to offer a broad appreciation to the many historians who have written extensively about each of these presidents. I fully recognize the genius and labor that has gone into their collective works, more often than not, in the pre-digital age, and under much more trying circumstances. I write this book humbly and with full recognition that I'm doing so on the heels of giants.

A NOTE ON SOURCES

This book builds upon the contributions of esteemed American historians who laid the groundwork for this narrative through their written works. Their diligent efforts encompassed interviews, archival research, and the careful validation of diverse accounts during a time predating the widespread use of the internet. Over the course of numerous years, they paved the way for this project. Without access to their invaluable work, composing this book would have been an insurmountable task. I approached this undertaking with profound acknowledgment and admiration for their invaluable contributions.

To ensure transparency and accuracy, I provide endnotes for factual information drawn from other sources. Additionally, when relying on another's analysis or comprehensive factual description, I diligently acknowledge the source in the bibliography, manuscript text, and provide proper citation.

NOTES

ABBREVIATIONS

CR—*Congressional Record*
GC—Grover Cleveland
HH—Herbert Hoover
HHT—Helen Herron Taft
HT—Harry Truman
JQAD—Charles Francis Adams, ed., *Memoirs of John Quincy Adams, Comprising Portions of his Diary from 1795 to 1848*, 12 vols. (Freeport, NY: Books for Libraries Press, 1969).
TJ—Thomas Jefferson
WHT—William Howard Taft

PREFACE

1. *"The Federalist* No. 72, [19 March 1788]," Founders Online, National Archives, https://founders.archives.gov/documents/Hamilton/01-04-02-0223.

INTRODUCTION

2. Sir John Fortescue, ed., *The Correspondence of King George the Third*, vol. 16. (London: Taylor & Francis, 2012), 443.
3. Joseph J. Ellis, *American Sphinx: The Character of Thomas Jefferson* (New York: Vintage, 1998), 139.
4. Ron Chernow, *Washington: A Life* (New York: Penguin Books, 2011), 757.
5. Richard Brookhiser, *Founding Father: Rediscovering George Washington* (New York: Free Press, 1997), 103.
6. Christopher Hitchens, "Visit to a Small Planet," *Vanity Fair*, June 2001, https://www.vanityfair.com/news/2001/01/hitchens-200101.

7. Dr. Lisa Payne Ossian, "The Grimmest Spectre," *Tru Blog*, Truman Library Institute, September 8, 2017, https://www.trumanlibraryinstitute.org/grimmest -spectre/.

8. Chloe Berger, "Michael Jordan Remains the GOAT—of Athletes Turned Businessmen," *Fortune*, June 21, 2023, https://fortune.com/2023/06/21 /michael-jordan-net-worth-selling-majority-stake-hornets/.

CHAPTER 1: THE LIFELONG FOUNDER

1. "Minutes of the Board of Visitors of the University of Virginia, 4 October 1825," Founders Online, National Archives, https://founders.archives.gov /documents/Madison/04-03-02-0633.

2. "The 1825 Riots at the University of Virginia," Monticello, https://www .monticello.org/exhibits-events/livestreams-videos-and-podcasts/uva -riots-ichepod/.

3. "Minutes of the Board of Visitors of the University of Virginia, 4 October 1825."

4. Cameron Addis, *Jefferson's Vision for Education, 1760–1845* (New York: Peter Lange, 2003), 119, http://ndl.ethernet.edu.et/bitstream/123456789 /30362/1/6..pdf; Dumas Malone, *Jefferson and His Time, Vol. 6: The Sage of Monticello* (Charlottesville: University of Virginia Press, 2006), 465–68.

5. "Minutes of the Board of Visitors of the University of Virginia, 4 October 1825."

6. "From Thomas Jefferson to Robert Greenhow, 24 July 1825," Founders On-line, National Archives, https://founders.archives.gov/documents/Jeffer son/98-01-02-5403. This wasn't the first such incident on campus. In June 1825, two of the American professors—John Patten Emmet and George Tucker—tried to break up a fast-forming riot, pulling the shirts of several students, only to be met with bricks and canes. Sixty-five students signed a resolution denouncing the faculty. See Addis, *Jefferson's Vision for Education*, 120.

7. Andrew J. O'Shaughnessy, *The Illimitable Freedom of the Human Mind: Thomas Jefferson's Idea of a University* (Charlottesville: University of Virginia Press, 2021), 11.

8. Malone, *The Sage of Monticello*, 463–68; James Morton Smith, ed., *The Republic of Letters: The Correspondence between Thomas Jefferson and James Madison 1776–1826*, vol. 3 (New York: W. W. Norton, 1995), 1920, as cited in Joseph J. Ellis, *American Sphinx* (New York: Vintage, 1998), 739.

9. O'Shaughnessy, *The Illimitable Freedom of the Human Mind*, 211.

10. It wasn't until 1786 that the Virginia legislature formally adopted the latter document.

11. "Minutes of the Board of Visitors of the University of Virginia, 5 October 1825," Founders Online, National Archives, https://founders.archives.gov /documents/Madison/04-03-02-0634.

12. O'Shaughnessy, *The Illimitable Freedom of the Human Mind*, 233–34; "Poe as a Student," Raven Society, University of Virginia Alumni Association, https://aig.alumni.virginia.edu/raven/poe-resources/poe-as-a-student/.

13. Maurizio Valsania, *Limits of Optimism: Thomas Jefferson's Dualistic Enlightenment* (Charlottesville: University of Virginia Press, 2012), 18, 17, cited in Gordon S. Wood, *Friends Divided: John Adams and Thomas Jefferson* (New York: Penguin Books, 2017), 525.

14. Charles Krauthammer, "The Bush Legacy," *Washington Post*, May 18, 2023, https://www.washingtonpost.com/opinions/charles-krauthammer-the-bush -legacy/2013/04/25/b6de6efa-add8-11e2-8bf6-e70cb6ae066e_story.html.

15. Edward Rutledge was the youngest signer of the Declaration, at twenty-six years old.

16. Lydia Dishman, "The Science and Psychology behind What Drives Serial Entrepreneurs," Fast Company, July 10, 2013, https://www.fastcompany .com/3019350/the-science-and-psychology-behind-what-drives-serial-entre preneurs.

17. "Jefferson's Gravestone," Monticello, https://www.monticello.org/research -education/thomas-jefferson-encyclopedia/jeffersons-gravestone/.

18. Henry Tutwiler, *Early Years of the University of Virginia: Address of H. Tutweiler, . . . of Alabama, before the Alumni Society of the University of Virginia, Thursday, June 29th, 1882* (Charlottesville, VA: Charlottesville Chronicle Book and Job Office, 1882), 5.

19. "Report to President Teresa A. Sullivan," President's Commission on Slavery and the University, 2018, https://slavery.virginia.edu/wp-content/uploads /2021/03/PCSU-Report-FINAL_July-2018.pdf.

20. Annette Gordon-Reed, "What Thomas Jefferson Really Believed about Equality," *Time*, February 20, 2020, https://time.com/5783989/thomas-jeff erson-all-men-created-equal/.

21. Andrew O'Shaughnessy, author interview by phone, May 3, 2022.

22. "From Thomas Jefferson to Henry Lee, 8 May 1825," Founders Online, National Archives, https://founders.archives.gov/documents/Jefferson/98-01 -02-5212.

23. Alan Pell Crawford, *Twilight at Monticello: The Final Years of Thomas Jefferson* (New York: Random House, 2008), 15.

24. Dean Keith Simonton, "Presidential IQ, Openness, Intellectual Brilliance, and Leadership: Estimates and Correlations for 42 U.S. Chief Executives," *Political Psychology* 27, no. 4 (August 2006): 511–26.

25. Garry Wills, *Inventing America: Jefferson's Declaration of Independence* (New York: Knopf Doubleday, 2018), 15.

26. "From Thomas Jefferson to Richard Henry Lee, 13 September 1780," Founders Online, National Archives, https://founders.archives.gov/documents/Jefferson/01-03-02-0730.

27. "From Thomas Jefferson to James Madison, 28 August 1789," Founders Online, National Archives, https://founders.archives.gov/documents/Jefferson/01-15-02-0354.

28. Lynne Cheney, *The Virginia Dynasty: Four Presidents and the Creation of the American Nation* (New York: Penguin Books, 2021), 191.

29. "From Alexander Hamilton to Edward Carrington, 26 May 1792," Founders Online, National Archives, https://founders.archives.gov/documents/Hamilton/01-11-02-0349.

30. "From Thomas Jefferson to Edward Rutledge, 30 November 1795," Founders Online, National Archives, https://founders.archives.gov/documents/Jefferson/01-28-02-0419.

31. O'Shaughnessy, *The Illimitable Freedom of the Human Mind*, 51.

32. "From Thomas Jefferson to George Washington, 23 February 1795," Founders Online, National Archives, https://founders.archives.gov/documents/Jefferson/01-28-02-0209.

33. Henry Adams, *History of the United States during the Administrations of Thomas Jefferson and James Madison* (1889), 45; O'Shaughnessy, *The Illimitable Freedom of the Human Mind*, 51.

34. O'Shaughnessy, *The Illimitable Freedom of the Human Mind*, 55.

35. In 1864, Abraham Lincoln, a Republican, and Andrew Johnson, a Democrat, temporarily abandoned their parties to form a National Union Party ticket.

36. Patrick Spero, Abigail Shelton, and John Kenney, "The Other Presidency: Thomas Jefferson and the American Philosophical Society," *Proceedings of the American Philosophical Society* 162, no. 4 (December 2018): 321–60.

37. Ibid.

38. O'Shaughnessy, *The Illimitable Freedom of the Human Mind*, 20.

39. Cheney, *The Virginia Dynasty*, 311.

40. "Federalists and Jeffersonians," Digital History, University of Houston, https://www.digitalhistory.uh.edu/disp_textbook.cfm?smtID=11&psid=3799.

41. Jack Eisen, "A Washington First," *Washington Post*, January 22, 1985, https://www.washingtonpost.com/archive/local/1985/01/22/a-washington-first/b83cf8d4-a164-4510-a361-05b21a55d4e0/.

42. "The *National Intelligencer and Washington Advertiser* (Washington City [DC]), November 24, 1802," Library of Congress, https://www.loc.gov/item/sn83045242/1802-11-24/ed-1/.

43. "Capitol Dome," Architect of the Capitol, https://www.aoc.gov/explore
    -capitol-campus/buildings-grounds/capitol-building/capitol-dome; "History
    of the U.S. Capitol Building," Architect of the Capitol, https://www.aoc
    .gov/explore-capitol-campus/buildings-grounds/capitol-building/history.

44. "From Thomas Jefferson to George Washington, 25 May 1791," Founders
    Online, National Archives, https://founders.archives.gov/documents/Jeffer
    son/01-43-02-0472.

45. Sarah Booth Conroy, "Not First Place but Honorable Mansion," *Washing-
    ton Post*, November 22, 1992, https://www.washingtonpost.com/archive/life
    style/1992/11/22/not-first-place-but-honorable-mansion/02fae28c-de9a
    -4dd1-aaa8-79b6abc2c210/.

46. For details of the founding, see Theodore Joseph Crackel, "The Founding of
    West Point: Jefferson and the Politics of Security," *Armed Forces & Society*
    7, no. 4 (Summer 1981): 529–43.

47. Jon Meacham, *Thomas Jefferson: The Art of Power* (New York: Random
    House, 2013), 644.

48. Ibid., 611.

49. Douglas Irwin, "The Welfare Cost of Autark: Evidence from the Jeffer-
    sonian Trade Embargo, 1807–09," *Review of International Economics* 13,
    no. 4 (September 2005): 631–45.

50. "From Thomas Jefferson to Pierre Samuel Du Pont de Nemours, 2 March
    1809," Founders Online, National Archives, https://founders.archives.gov
    /documents/Jefferson/99-01-02-9936.

51. "Margaret Bayard Smith's Account of Madison's Inauguration and Ball,
    [4 March 1809]," Founders Online, National Archives, https://founders
    .archives.gov/documents/Jefferson/03-01-02-0004.

52. Kevin J. Hayes, *Jefferson in His Own Time: A Biographical Chronicle of His
    Life, Drawn from Recollections, Interviews, and Memoirs by Family, Friends,
    and Associates* (Iowa City: University of Iowa Press, 2012), 40.

53. "A Presidential Transition," Monticello, https://www.monticello.org/research
    -education/for-scholars/papers-of-thomas-jefferson/featured-letters/a-pres
    idential-transition/.

54. Arthur C. Brooks, "The Seven Habits That Lead to Happiness in Old Age,"
    Atlantic, April 7, 2022, https://www.theatlantic.com/family/archive/2022
    /02/happiness-age-investment/622818/.

55. "ICONS: George Washington, 1790 Census," U.S. Census Bureau, https://
    www.census.gov/history/www/through_the_decades/fast_facts/1790_fast
    _facts.html; "ICONS: Chief Tecumseh, War of 1812, Erie Canal," U.S.
    Census Bureau, https://www.census.gov/history/www/through_the_decades
    /fast_facts/1810_fast_facts.html.

56. David Hackett Fischer, *Albion's Seed: Four British Folkways in America* (Oxford, UK: Oxford University Press, 1989); Andrew Burstein and Nancy Isenberg, *Madison and Jefferson* (New York: Random House, 2010), 56.

57. Malone, *The Sage of Monticello*, 4.

58. "Thomas Jefferson to Benjamin Henry Latrobe, 10 October 1809," Founders Online, National Archives, https://founders.archives.gov/documents/Jefferson/03-01-02-0468.

59. Adams, *History of the United States*, 99.

60. O'Shaughnessy, *The Illimitable Freedom of the Human Mind*, 16; "Building Monticello," Monticello, https://www.monticello.org/thomas-jefferson/a-day-in-the-life-of-jefferson/a-delightful-recreation/building-monticello/.

61. "Thomas Jefferson to Benjamin Rush, 16 January 1811," Founders Online, National Archives, https://founders.archives.gov/documents/Jefferson/03-03-02-0231.

62. "Alexander Hamilton Bust (Sculpture)," Monticello, https://www.monticello.org/site/research-and-collections/alexander-hamilton-bust-sculpture; Wilson Shirley tour of Monticello, May 30, 2022.

63. "Thomas Moore," Monticello, https://www.monticello.org/site/research-and-collections/thomas-moore.

64. Malone, *The Sage of Monticello*, 14.

65. Oral History of Monticello, captured by Wilson Shirley, May 30, 2022.

66. Malone, *The Sage of Monticello*, 16.

67. Ellis, *American Sphinx*, 277.

68. Burnstein, *Madison and Jefferson*, 10.

69. "'Mr. Jefferson's Personal Appearance and Habits,' an Excerpt from *The Private Life of Thomas Jefferson* by Hamilton W. Pierson (1862)," Encyclopedia Virginia, https://encyclopediavirginia.org/entries/mr-jeffersons-personal-appearance-and-habits-an-excerpt-from-the-private-life-of-thomas-jefferson-by-hamilton-w-pierson-1862/.

70. Dr. Thomas Sydenham, *The Whole Works of That Excellent Practical Physician*, 4th ed. (London, 1705), 145–46; Burnstein, *Madison and Jefferson*, 266; "Jefferson's Cause of Death," Monticello, https://www.monticello.org/research-education/thomas-jefferson-encyclopedia/jeffersons-cause-death/.

71. O'Shaughnessy, *The Illimitable Freedom of the Human Mind*, 32.

72. Malone, *The Sage of Monticello*, 4.

73. Meacham, *Jefferson: The Art of Power*, 352.

74. Burton I. Kaufman, *The Post-Presidency from Washington to Clinton* (Lawrence: University Press of Kansas, 2012), 29.

75. "Thomas Jefferson to Benjamin Rush, 16 January 1811"; "Thomas Jefferson

to James Madison, 29 June 1812," Founders Online, National Archives, https://founders.archives.gov/documents/Jefferson/03-05-02-0155.

76. Malone, *The Sage of Monticello*, 114.

77. Thomas Jefferson, *The Writings of Thomas Jefferson, Volume IX, 1809–1815*, ed. Paul Leicester Ford (New York: G. P. Putnam's Sons, 1898), 488.

78. John Y. Cole, "The Library's Jeffersonian Legacy: Bicentennial Background," Library of Congress, https://www.loc.gov/loc/lcib/9906/jeff.html.

79. "Book Lists," Thomas Jefferson's Libraries, Monticello, http://tjlibraries .monticello.org/about/lists.html.

80. O'Shaughnessy, *The Illimitable Freedom of the Human Mind*, 116; Cole, "The Library's Jeffersonian Legacy."

81. Malone, *The Sage of Monticello*, 176.

82. "Editorial Note," Founders Online, National Archives, https://founders .archives.gov/documents/Jefferson/03-07-02-0484-0001.

83. Ibid.; "The Senate Buys a Library," United States Senate, https://www.senate .gov/about/historic-buildings-spaces/capitol/senate-buys-library.htm.

84. "The 'Golden Age' of the Senate: 1801–1850," GovInfo, https://www.gov info.gov/content/pkg/GPO-200NOTABLEDAYS/pdf/GPO-200NOTA BLEDAYS-6.pdf.

85. Ashley Luthern, "On the Hunt for Jefferson's Lost Books: A Library of Congress Curator Is on a Worldwide Mission to Find Exact Copies of the Books That Belonged to Thomas Jefferson," *Smithsonian*, August 10, 2009, https://www.smithsonianmag.com/history/on-the-hunt-for-jeffersons-lost -books-38566672/.

86. Malone, *The Sage of Monticello*, 184.

87. Erick Trickey, "The Polish Patriot Who Helped Americans Beat the British," *Smithsonian*, https://www.smithsonianmag.com/history/polish-patriot -who-helped-americans-beat-british-180962430/.

88. "Sale of Books to the Library of Congress," Monticello, https://www.mon ticello.org/research-education/thomas-jefferson-encyclopedia/sale-books -library-congress-1815/.

89. Malone, *The Sage of Monticello*, 181.

90. Clyde A. Haulman, "The Panic of 1819: America's First Great Depression," *Financial History*, Winter 2010, https://www.moaf.org/exhibits/checks_bal ances/andrew-jackson/materials/Panic_of_1819.pdf.

91. O'Shaughnessy, author interview.

92. Addis, *Jefferson's Vision for Education*, 96.

93. O'Shaughnessy, author interview.

94. Gaye Wilson, "Monticello was among the Prizes in a Lottery for a Ruined Jefferson's Relief," *Colonial Williamsburg Journal*, Winter 2010; "Martha

Jefferson Randolph to Ellen W. Randolph Coolidge, [ca. 22 October, 1826],"
Monticello, http://tjrs.monticello.org/letter/1058?_ga=2.141998448.3914
86821.1641310500-1127887884.1638396416.

95. "From Thomas Jefferson to James Madison, 17 February 1826," Founders
Online, National Archives, https://founders.archives.gov/documents/Jeffer
son/98-01-02-5912.

96. Meacham, *Jefferson: The Art of Power*, 496. For more specifics, see "Debt,"
Monticello, https://www.monticello.org/research-education/thomas-jeffer
son-encyclopedia/debt/.

97. R. L. Leavy, "Social Support and Psychological Disorder: A Review," *Journal
of Community* Psychology 11, no. 1 (January 1983): 3–21; Sally C. Cur-
tin, "Mortality among Adults Aged 25 and Over by Marital Status: United
States, 2010–2017," CDC, https://www.cdc.gov/nchs/data/hestat/mortal
ity/mortality_marital_status_10_17.htm.

98. "From Thomas Jefferson to Elizabeth Wayles Eppes, [3? October 1782],"
Founders Online, National Archives, https://founders.archives.gov/docu
ments/Jefferson/01-06-02-0188.

99. Randolph, *The Domestic Life of Thomas Jefferson,* as cited in Meacham, *The
Art of Power,* 449.

100. Henry S. Randall, *The Life of Thomas Jefferson: In Three Volumes*, vol. 1
(Charleston, SC: BiblioLife, 2013), 243; "Our Earliest Amusements,"
Monticello, https://www.monticello.org/thomas-jefferson/a-day-in-the-life
-of-jefferson/when-the-flowers-were-in-bloom/our-earliest-amusements/.

101. Randall, *The Life of Thomas Jefferson*, 243.

102. Malone, *The Sage of Monticello*, 156.

103. "Thomas Jefferson to Martha Jefferson Randolph, 3 December 1816,"
Founders Online, National Archives, https://founders.archives.gov/docu
ments/Jefferson/03-10-02-0431.

104. Cynthia A. Kierner, *Martha Jefferson Randloph: Daughter of Monticello*
(Chapel Hill: University of North Carolina Press, 2012), 47, 53–54, 69.

105. Crawford, *Twilight at Monticello*, 138.

106. "From Thomas Jefferson to Elizabeth Wayles Eppes, [3? October 1782]."

107. "From Thomas Jefferson to Mary Jefferson Eppes, 26 October 1801,"
Founders Online, National Archives, https://founders.archives.gov/docu
ments/Jefferson/01-35-02-0423.

108. "Madison Hemmings Comments on the Thomas Jefferson–Sally Hemings
Relationship, March 13, 1873," Digital History, University of Houston,
https://www.digitalhistory.uh.edu/disp_textbook.cfm?smtID=3&psid=1070.

109. "The Life of Sally Hemings: Drawn from the Words of Her Son Madison
Hemmings," Monticello, https://www.monticello.org/sallyhemings/.

110. "Recollections of Peter Fossett," Monticello, https://www.monticello.org /slavery/slave-memoirs-oral-histories/recollections-of-peter-fossett/.

111. "The Life of Sally Hemings."

112. Annette Gordon-Reed, *The Hemingses of Monticello: An American Family* (New York: Norton, 2008).

113. Annette Gordon-Reed, "Sally Hemings, Thomas Jefferson and the Ways We Talk about Our Past," *New York Times*, https://www.nytimes.com/2017/08/24 /books/review/sally-hemings-thomas-jefferson-annette-gordon-reed.html.

114. Mark Silk, "Did John Adams Out Thomas Jefferson and Sally Hemings?," *Smithsonian*, November 2016, https://www.smithsonianmag.com/history /john-adams-out-thomas-jefferson-sally-hemings-180960789/.

115. "Letter from Henry S. Randall to James Parton, June 1, 1868," Encyclopedia Virginia, https://encyclopediavirginia.org/entries/letter-from-henry-s -randall-to-james-parton-june-1-1868/.

116. E. A. Foster, et al., "Jefferson Fathered Slave's Last Child," *Nature* 396, no. 6706 (November 1998): 27–28; Dinitia Smith and Nicholas Wade, "DNA Test Finds Evidence of Jefferson Child by Slave," *New York Times*, November 1, 1998, https://www.nytimes.com/1998/11/01/us/dna-test-finds -evidence-of-jefferson-child-by-slave.html/.

117. Gordon-Reed, *The Hemingses of Monticello*.

118. O'Shaughnessy, *The Illimitable Freedom of the Human Mind*, 31.

119. Foster et al., "Jefferson Fathered Slave's Last Child."

120. "To Thomas Jefferson from Benjamin Banneker, 19 August 1791," Founders Online, National Archives, https://founders.archives.gov/documents/Jeff erson/01-22-02-0049.

121. Thomas Jefferson, *Notes on the State of Virginia* (Philadelphia: Pritchard and Hall, 1781), https://docsouth.unc.edu/southlit/jefferson/jefferson.html.

122. O'Shaughnessy, author interview.

123. "From John Adams to Timothy Pickering, 6 August 1822," Founders Online, National Archives, https://founders.archives.gov/documents/Adams/99-02 -02-7674.

124. Wood, *Friends Divided*, 6.

125. "From John Adams to Benjamin Rush, 18 April 1808," Founders Online, National Archives, https://founders.archives.gov/documents/Adams/99-02 -02-5238.

126. "John Adams," Monticello, https://www.monticello.org/research-education /thomas-jefferson-encyclopedia/john-adams/.

127. "To John Adams from Benjamin Rush, 17 October 1809," Founders Online, National Archives, https://founders.archives.gov/documents/Adams/99-02 -02-5450.

128. "Benjamin Rush to Thomas Jefferson, 2 January 1811," Founders Online, National Archives, https://founders.archives.gov/documents/Jefferson/03-03 -02-0203.

129. Crawford, *Twilight at Monticello*, 84.

130. Randall, *The Life of Thomas Jefferson*, 639–40.

131. Lyman H. Butterfield, "The Dream of Benjamin Rush: The Reconciliation of John Adams and Thomas Jefferson," *Yale Review* 40 (1950): 297–319.

132. "Thomas Jefferson to Benjamin Rush, 5 December 1811," Founders Online, National Archives, https://founders.archives.gov/documents/Jefferson /03-04-02-0248.

133. "Resumption of Correspondence with John Adams, Followed by John Adams to Thomas Jefferson, 1 January 1812," Founders Online, National Archives, https://founders.archives.gov/documents/Jefferson/03-04-02-0296-0002.

134. "To John Adams from Benjamin Rush, 17 February 1812," Founders Online, National Archives, https://founders.archives.gov/documents/Adams/99-02 -02-5758.

135. John Ferling, *John Adams: A Life* (Oxford, UK: Oxford University Press, 2010).

136. "John Adams to Thomas Jefferson, 13 July 1813," Founders Online, National Archives, https://founders.archives.gov/documents/Jefferson/03-06-02-0238.

137. O'Shaughnessy, *The Illimitable Freedom of the Human Mind*, 38.

138. "Thomas Jefferson to Abigail Adams, 22 August 1813," Founders Online, National Archives, https://founders.archives.gov/documents/Jefferson/03 -06-02-0350.

139. Wood, *Friends Divided*, 508.

140. "From John Adams to William Cunningham, 24 February 1804," Founders Online, National Archives, https://founders.archives.gov/documents/Adams /99-02-02-5035.

141. "From John Adams to Thomas Jefferson, 10 November 1823," Founders Online, National Archives, https://founders.archives.gov/documents/Adams /99-02-02-7849.

142. Wood, *Friends Divided*, 398.

143. "John Adams to Thomas Jefferson, 2 March 1816," Founders Online, National Archives, https://founders.archives.gov/documents/Jefferson/03-09 -02-0362.

144. "Thomas Jefferson to John Adams, 8 April 1816," Founders Online, National Archives, https://founders.archives.gov/documents/Jefferson/03-09 -02-0446.

145. "To John Adams from Thomas Jefferson, 1 August 1816," Founders Online, National Archives, https://founders.archives.gov/documents/Adams/99-02 -02-6618.

146. "John Adams to Thomas Jefferson, 15 July 1813, with Postscript from Abigail Adams to Thomas Jefferson, [ca. 15 July 1813]," Founders Online, National Archives, https://founders.archives.gov/documents/Jefferson/03-06-02-0247.

147. John Marshall, *The Life of George Washington*, vol. 2 (New York: Derby & Jackson, 1857), 411.

148. "John Adams to Thomas Jefferson, 18 May 1817," Founders Online, National Archives, https://founders.archives.gov/documents/Jefferson/03-11-02-0303.

149. "From John Adams to Thomas Jefferson, 5 July 1813," Founders Online, National Archives, https://founders.archives.gov/documents/Adams/99-02-02-6092.

150. "To James Madison from Thomas Jefferson, 22 June 1817," Founders Online, National Archives, https://founders.archives.gov/documents/Madison/04-01-02-0067; Ellis, *American Sphinx*, 274.

151. Ellis, *American Sphinx*, 275.

152. Charles T. Cullen, ed., *The Papers of Thomas Jefferson, Volume 22: 6 August 1791 to 31 December 1791* (Princeton, NJ: Princeton University Press, 2018), 34.

153. "Jefferson's Autobiography," Avalon Project, Yale Law School, https://avalon.law.yale.edu/19th_century/jeffauto.asp.

154. Ellis, *American Sphinx*, 278.

155. "Qur'an," Monticello, https://www.monticello.org/site/research-and-collections/quran#footnote1_ilplofb.

156. Addis, *Jefferson's Vision for Education*, 59–60.

157. "Thomas Jefferson to John Adams, October 12, 1813," in *The Papers of Thomas Jefferson: Retirement Series*, vol. 6, ed. J. Jefferson Looney (Princeton, NJ: Princeton University Press), 548–51, https://encyclopediavirginia.org/entries/letter-from-thomas-jefferson-to-john-adams-october-12-1813/.

158. O'Shaughnessy, *The Illimitable Freedom of the Human Mind*, 158.

159. "Thomas Jefferson to John Holmes," Library of Congress, April 22, 1820, https://www.loc.gov/exhibits/jefferson/159.html#:~:text=I%20can%20say%20with%20conscious%20truth%20that%20there,they%20shall%20not%20emigrate%20into%20any%20other%20state%3F.

160. Addis, *Jefferson's Vision for Education*, 96–97; Adams, *History of the United States*, 20.

161. "From Thomas Jefferson to George Washington, 23 February 1795."

162. "Thomas Jefferson to Joseph C. Cabell, 18 December 1817," Founders Online, National Archives, https://founders.archives.gov/documents/Jefferson/03-12-02-0212.

163. "Thomas Jefferson to John Adams, 10 December 1819," Founders Online,

National Archives, https://founders.archives.gov/documents/Jefferson/03-15 -02-0240; Kaufman, *The Post-Presidency from Washington to Clinton*, 31.

164. Wood, *Friends Divided*, 55.

165. "79. A Bill for the More General Diffusion of Knowledge, 18 June 1779," Founders Online, National Archives, https://founders.archives.gov/docu ments/Jefferson/01-02-02-0132-0004-0079; O'Shaughnessy, *The Illimitable Freedom of the Human Mind*, 47.

166. Davison M. Douglas, "Jefferson's Vision Fulfilled," *William & Mary Alumni Magazine*, Winter 2010, https://law.wm.edu/about/ourhistory/index.php.

167. "Thomas Jefferson to John Tyler, 26 May 1810," Founders Online, National Archives, https://founders.archives.gov/documents/Jefferson/03-02 -02-0365.

168. "Thomas Jefferson to Thomas Cooper, 14 August 1820," Founders Online, National Archives, https://founders.archives.gov/documents/Jefferson/03-16-02-0147.

169. Addis, *Jefferson's Vision for Education*, 32.

170. Ibid., 13.

171. O'Shaughnessy, *The Illimitable Freedom of the Human Mind*, 7.

172. Ibid., 23.

173. "Our History," Transylvania University, https://www.transy.edu/about/who -we-are/our-history/.

174. "Thomas Jefferson to Joseph C. Cabell, 22 January 1820," Founders Online, National Archives, https://founders.archives.gov/documents/Jeffer son/03-15-02-0315.

175. "Central College," Monticello, https://www.monticello.org/site/research-and -collections/central-college#footnote8_cacigyg.

176. Malone, *The Sage of Monticello*, 365.

177. Ibid., 250.

178. Ibid., 255.

179. Addis, *Jefferson's Vision for Education*, 40.

180. O'Shaughnessy, *The Illimitable Freedom of the Human Mind*, 66.

181. "John Adams to Thomas Jefferson, 26 May 1817," Founders Online, National Archives, https://founders.archives.gov/documents/Jefferson/03-11 -02-0320; Addis, *Jefferson's Vision for Education*, 40.

182. Burnstein, *Madison and Jefferson*, 59.

183. Adams, *History of the United States*, 100.

184. O'Shaughnessy, author interview.

185. O'Shaughnessy, *The Illimitable Freedom of the Human Mind*, 86.

186. Ibid., 87, 187–88.

187. Ibid., 125.

188. Adams, *History of the United States*, 147–48.

189. O'Shaughnessy, *The Illimitable Freedom of the Human Mind*, 250.

190. Addis, *Jefferson's Vision for Education*, 41.

191. "A Course of Reading for Joseph C. Cabell, September 1800," Founders Online, National Archives, https://founders.archives.gov/documents/Jefferson/01-32-02-0110.

192. O'Shaughnessy, *The Illimitable Freedom of the Human Mind*, 87.

193. "Virginia General Assembly's Act Appropriating Part of the Literary Fund Revenue for the Creation of a Board of Commissioners for Education and for the Establishment of a University, February 21, 1818," Monticello, https://tjrs.monticello.org/letter/2315.

194. Adams, *History of the United States*, 85.

195. O'Shaughnessy, *The Illimitable Freedom of the Human Mind*, 60.

196. Ibid., 64.

197. Addis, *Jefferson's Vision for Education*, 49.

198. O'Shaughnessy, author interview.

199. Adams, *History of the United States*, 86–87.

200. O'Shaughnessy, *The Illimitable Freedom of the Human Mind*, 61.

201. Ibid., 95.

202. "Report of the Board of Commissioners for the University of Virginia to the Virginia General Assembly, [4 August] 1818," Founders Online, National Archives, https://founders.archives.gov/documents/Madison/04-01-02-0289; "From Thomas Jefferson to Thomas Cooper, 2 November 1822," Founders Online, National Archives, https://founders.archives.gov/documents/Jefferson/98-01-02-3137.

203. "Rockfish Gap Report of the University of Virginia Commissioners, 4 August 1818," Founders Online, National Archives, https://founders.archives.gov/documents/Jefferson/03-13-02-0197-0006.

204. Addis, *Jefferson's Vision for Education*, 49. For a summary of the report, see Adams, *History of the United States*, 95.

205. Adams, *History of the United States*, 97.

206. "Timeline of the Founding of the University of Virginia," Monticello, https://www.monticello.org/site/research-and-collections/timeline-founding-university-virginia.

207. O'Shaughnessy, *The Illimitable Freedom of the Human Mind*, 80.

208. "Thomas Jefferson to Thomas Cooper, 1 September 1817," Founders Online, National Archives, https://founders.archives.gov/documents/Jefferson/03-12-02-0001; O'Shaughnessy, *The Illimitable Freedom of the Human Mind*, 90.

209. O'Shaughnessy, *The Illimitable Freedom of the Human Mind*, 92.

210. Adams, *History of the United States*, 107.

211. Malone, *The Sage of Monticello*, 380.

212. "Thomas Jefferson to José Corrêa da Serra, 11 April 1820," Founders Online, National Archives, https://founders.archives.gov/documents/Jefferson/03 -15-02-0494.

213. O'Shaughnessy, *The Illimitable Freedom of the Human Mind*, 97.

214. Addis, *Jefferson's Vision for Education*, 68.

215. Lewis S. Feuer, "America's First Jewish Professor: James Joseph Sylvester at the University of Virginia," *American Jewish Archives* 36, no. 2 (1984): 152– 201; Minutes of the Board of Visitors 1841–1842, Special Collections, University of Virginia Alderman Library.

216. Adams, *History of the United States*, 127.

217. O'Shaughnessy, *The Illimitable Freedom of the Human Mind*, 161.

218. "Report of the Board of Commissioners for the University of Virginia to the Virginia General Assembly, [4 August] 1818"; Adams, *History of the United States*, 90–91; Addis, *Jefferson's Vision for Education*, 106.

219. Addis, *Jefferson's Vision for Education*, 121, 143.

220. O'Shaughnessy, *The Illimitable Freedom of the Human Mind*, 97, 119, 127.

221. Ibid., 100.

222. Malone, *The Sage of Monticello*, 383.

223. "Thomas Jefferson to Joseph C. Cabell, 31 January 1821," Founders Online, National Archives, https://founders.archives.gov/documents/Jefferson /03-16-02-0491.

224. Ibid.

225. Addis, *Jefferson's Vision for Education*, 95.

226. "From Thomas Jefferson to Maria Hadfield Cosway, 24 October 1822," Founders Online, National Archives, https://founders.archives.gov/docu ments/Jefferson/98-01-02-3111; Addis, *Jefferson's Vision for Education*, 104.

227. O'Shaughnessy, *The Illimitable Freedom of the Human Mind*, 226.

228. O'Shaughnessy, author interview.

229. "From Thomas Jefferson to James Madison, 24 September 1824," Founders Online, National Archives, https://founders.archives.gov/documents/Jeffer son/98-01-02-4565.

230. O'Shaughnessy, *The Illimitable Freedom of the Human Mind*, 157.

231. "Meeting Minutes of University of Virginia Board of Visitors, 5–7 Apr. 1824, 5 April 1824," Founders Online, National Archives, https://founders .archives.gov/documents/Jefferson/98-01-02-4171.

232. Malone, *The Sage of Monticello*, 399.

233. Norman G. Schneeberg, "The Medical History of Thomas Jefferson," *Journal of Medical Biographies* 16, no. 2 (May 2008): 118–25.

234. "An Account of General La Fayette's Visit to Virginia, in the Years 1824–'25," Internet Archive, https://archive.org/stream/accountofgeneral01ward/account ofgeneral01ward_djvu.txt.

235. Malone, *The Sage of Monticello*, 403.

236. Crawford, *Twilight at Monticello*, 201.

237. Malone, *The Sage of Monticello*, 403.

238. O'Shaughnessy, *The Illimitable Freedom of the Human Mind*, 130.

239. Malone, *The Sage of Monticello*, 404.

240. James Gambler, *Dine with Thomas Jefferson and Fascinating Guests* (Emeryville, CA: Bacchus Press, 2015), 182.

241. "Toasts for Lafayette's Dinner, [ante-5 November 1824]," Founders Online, National Archives, https://founders.archives.gov/documents/Madison/04-03-02-0417.

242. Gambler, *Dining with Thomas Jefferson and Fascinating Guests*, 184.

243. Malone, *The Sage of Monticello*, 408.

244. Adams, *History of the United States*, 120.

245. "From Thomas Jefferson to Robert Greenhow, 24 July 1825," Founders Online, National Archives, https://founders.archives.gov/documents/Jefferson/98-01-02-5403.

246. Malone, *The Sage of Monticello*, 408.

247. Steven Ha Hochman, "Thomas Jefferson: A Personal Financial Biography," PhD diss., University of Virginia, 1987, 235. Conversion made with data from the Reserve Bank of Minneapolis Inflation Rate.

248. "Jefferson Lottery," Monticello, https://www.monticello.org/site/research-and-collections/jefferson-lottery.

249. Malone, *The Sage of Monticello*, 469.

250. "From Thomas Jefferson to James Madison, 18 October 1825," Founders Online, National Archives, https://founders.archives.gov/documents/Jefferson/98-01-02-5602.

251. "From Thomas Jefferson to James Madison, 17 February 1826."

252. Malone, *The Sage of Monticello*, 431–32.

253. "Last Will and Testament," Monticello, https://www.monticello.org/site/research-and-collections/last-will-and-testament.

254. Malone, *The Sage of Monticello*, 489.

255. "The Life of Sally Hemings."

256. O'Shaughnessy, *The Illimitable Freedom of the Human Mind*, 187.

257. "Recollections of Peter Fossett."

258. Burnstein, *Madison and Jefferson*, 268.

259. "Extract from Thomas Jefferson to Martha Jefferson Randolph, July 2, 1826," Monticello, https://tjrs.monticello.org/letter/1558.

260. Gregory S. Schneider, "Jefferson's Powerful Last Public Letter Reminds Us What Independence Day Is About," *Washington Post*, https://www.washingtonpost.com/news/retropolis/wp/2017/07/03/jeffersons-last-public-letter-reminds-us-what-independence-day-is-all-about/.

261. "Thomas Jefferson to Roger Weightman, June 24, 1826," Library of Congress, https://www.loc.gov/exhibits/jefferson/214.html.

262. James Piereson, "Founding Friendship," *New Criterion*, November 2017, https://newcriterion.com/issues/2017/11/founding-friendship.

263. "From Thomas Jefferson to George Gilmer, 12 August 1787," Founders Online, National Archives, https://founders.archives.gov/documents/Jefferson/01-12-02-0029.

264. "Henry H. Worthington to Reuben B. Hicks, July 5, 1826," Monticello, https://tjrs.monticello.org/letter/456.

265. J. C. A. Stagg, "James Madison: Life After the Presidency," Miller Center, University of Virginia, https://millercenter.org/president/madison/life-after-the-presidency.

266. Daniel Preston, "James Monroe: Life After the Presidency," Miller Center, University of Virginia, https://millercenter.org/president/monroe/life-after-the-presidency.

267. "Executive Order [on the Deaths of Thomas Jefferson and John Adams], July 11, 1826," American Presidency Project, UC Santa Barbara, https://www.presidency.ucsb.edu/documents/executive-order-the-deaths-thomas-jefferson-and-john-adams.

268. "From Thomas Jefferson to Marie-Joseph-Paul-Yves-Roch-Gilbert du Motier, Marquis de Lafayette, 28 October 1822," Founders Online, National Archives, https://founders.archives.gov/documents/Jefferson/98-01-02-3120.

269. Malone, *The Sage of Monticello*, 454.

270. "From Thomas Jefferson to John Adams, 15 February 1825," Founders Online, National Archives, https://founders.archives.gov/documents/Jefferson/98-01-02-4962; "To John Adams from Thomas Jefferson, 15 February 1825," Founders Online, National Archives, https://founders.archives.gov/documents/Adams/99-02-02-7950.

271. "Daniel Webster's Interview with Jefferson," 1824, in *The Constitution in Congress: Democrats and Whigs, 1829–1861*, David P. Currie (Chicago: University of Chicago Press, 2005), 4.

CHAPTER 2: A SECOND ACT

1. Ronald G. Shafer, "'He Lies like a Dog': The First Effort to Impeach a President Was Led by His Own Party," *Washington Post*, September 23, 2019, https://www.washingtonpost.com/history/2019/09/23/he-lies-like-dog-first -effort-impeach-president-was-led-by-his-own-party/.

2. "Token of a Nation's Sorrow, 1848-02-28," Papers of Abraham Lincoln Digital Library, https://papersofabrahamlincoln.org/documents/D294541.

3. John Quincy Adams Digital Diary, vol. 30, June 1, 1816–December 31, 1818.

4. John Quincy Adams Digital Diary, vol. 33, June 13, 1825, https://www .masshist.org/publications/jqadiaries/index.php/document/jqadiaries-v33 -1825-06-13-p173#sn=1.

5. "June 13, 1925: President John Quincy Adams Nearly Drowns in Tiber Creek," New England Historical Society, https://newenglandhistoricalsociety .com/june-13-1825-president-john-quincy-adams-nearly-drowns-tiber -creek/.

6. JQAD, June 13, 1825, 7:28.

7. James Traub, *John Quincy Adams: Militant Spirit* (New York: Basic Books, 2016), 398.

8. Samuel Flagg Bemis, *John Quincy Adams and the Union*, vol. 2 (New York: Knopf, 1956), 8.

9. William W. Freehling, *Prelude to Civil War: The Nullification Controversy in South Carolina, 1816–1836* (Oxford, UK: Oxford University Press, 1992), 342.

10. Edward Everett, *A Eulogy on the Life and Character of John Quincy Adams: Delivered at the Request of the Legislature of Massachusetts, in Faneuil Hall, April 15, 1848* (Boston: Dutton and Wentworth, 1848), 56–57.

11. Ibid., 49–50.

12. William J. Cooper, *The Lost Founding Father: John Quincy Adams and the Transformation of American Politics* (New York: W. W. Norton, 2017), 195–96; Harlow G. Unger, *John Quincy Adams* (New York: Liveright, 2012), 223.

13. Sean Wilentz, *Andrew Jackson: The American Presidents Series: The 7th President, 1829–1837* (New York: Henry Holt), 50–51.

14. JQAD, June 1, 1825, 7:22.

15. Unger, *John Quincy Adams*, 247.

16. Edwin A. Miles, "President Adams' Billiard Table," *New England Quarterly* 45, no. 1 (March 1972): 31–43; William Seale, *President's House* (New York: Harry N. Abrams, 1986), 168–69.

17. Unger, *John Quincy Adams*, 248.

18. Madsen Pirie, "The Tariff of Abominations," Adam Smith Institute, May 19, 2019, https://www.adamsmith.org/blog/the-tariff-of-abominations.

19. Charles Francis Adams, ed., *Memoris of John Quincy Adams, Compromising Portions of His Diary from 1795 to 1848,* 12 vols. (Philadelphia: J. B. Lippincott, 1874), 4:531, in Unger, *John Quincy Adams,* 247.

20. Ibid., 252.

21. JQAD, July 11, 1828, 8:55.

22. Bemis, *John Quincy Adams and the Union,* 2:151.

23. "*Delaware Journal,* December 9, 1828," Chronicling America, Library of Congress, https://chroniclingamerica.loc.gov/lccn/sn83025530/1828-10-10/ed-1/seq-2/.

24. JQAD, December 3, 1828, 8:78.

25. Lorraine Boissoneault, "Rachel Jackson, the Scandalous Divorcee Who Almost Became First Lady," *Smithsonian,* June 15, 2017, https://www.smithsonianmag.com/history/rachel-jackson-was-original-monica-lewinsky-180963713/.

26. Bemis, *John Quincy Adams and the Union,* 2:154.

27. Boissoneault, "Rachel Jackson, the Scandalous Divorcee Who Almost Became First Lady."

28. Jon Meacham, *American Lion: Andrew Jackson in the White House* (New York: Random House, 2009), 3.

29. Bemis, *John Quincy Adams and the Union,* 2:161, 2:165–66; Traub, *John Quincy Adams,* 373–74; Cooper, *The Lost Founding Father,* 265, 267.

30. JQAD, February 11, 1829, 8:102.

31. Ibid., 8:100; Bemis, *John Quincy Adams and the Union,* 2:153–54.

32. John Adams, John Quincy Adams, Martin Van Buren, Andrew Johnson, and Donald Trump all skipped their successors' inaugurations. Some accounts suggest that this had as much to do with wanting to avoid Henry Clay as it did John Quincy Adams. See Lynn H. Parsons, *John Quincy Adams* (Lanham, MD: Rowman & Littlefield, 1999), 426.

33. JQAD, December 8, 1828, 8:80–81.

34. JQAD, December 31, 1828, 8:87–88.

35. Cooper, *The Lost Founding Father,* 262.

36. David S. Heidler and Jeanne T. Heidler, "Not a Ragged Mob; the Inauguration of 1829," White House Historical Association, https://www.whitehousehistory.org/not-a-ragged-mob-the-inauguration-of-1829.

37. Ibid.

38. JQAD Digital Diary, Volume 23, March 5, 1829, https://www.masshist

.org/publications/jqadiaries/index.php/document/jqadiaries-v36i-1829-03
-05-p161.

39. Joseph Wheelan, *Mr. Adams's Last Crusade: John Quincy Adams's Extraordinary Post-Presidential Life in Congress* (New York: PublicAffairs, 2009), xv.

40. Bemis, *John Quincy Adams and the Union*, 2:157–58; see also JQAD,
April 5, 1829, 8:129.

41. Wheelan, *Mr. Adams's Last Crusade*, 60.

42. Cooper, *The Lost Founding Father*, 264–65; Bemis, *John Quincy Adams and
the Union*, 2:179–80; Traub, *John Quincy Adams*, 380–81.

43. Bemis, *John Quincy Adams and the Union*, 2:180–81; Traub, *John Quincy
Adams*, 380–81; Unger, *John Quincy Adams*, 259; Cooper, *The Lost Founding Father*, 264–65.

44. John Adams Digital Diary, vol. 36, May 6, 1829, https://www.masshist.org
/publications/jqadiaries/index.php/document/jqadiaries-v36-1829-05-06
-p174#sn=2.

45. Notebook of Louisa Adams, n.d.; Adams MSS in Bemis, *John Quincy Adams
and the Union*, 2:181; Traub, *John Quincy Adams*, 382.

46. Traub, *John Quincy Adams*, 382–83.

47. Wheelan, *Mr. Adams's Last Crusade*, 65.

48. Ibid., xvii.

49. Memorandum book, with drafts of will in JQA's handwriting, and statements of his estate, 1829–32; Adams MSS in Bemis, *John Quincy Adams
and the Union*, 2:197; Freehling, *Prelude to Civil War*, 342; Traub, *John
Quincy Adams*, 374.

50. Bemis, *John Quincy Adams and the Union*, 2:187.

51. Natalie S. Bober, *Abigail Adams: Witness to a Revolution* (New York: Atheneum Books for Young Readers, 2010), 155.

52. JQAD, scattered entries from May 4 to September 6, 1831; Traub, *John
Quincy Adams*, 388–89; Cooper, *The Lost Founding Father*, 273.

53. John Quincy Adams, *Dermot MacMorrogh; or, The Conquest of Ireland: An
Historical Tale of the Twelfth Century in Four Cantos* (Boston: Carter, Hen-
dee, 1832), in Cooper, *The Lost Founding Father*, 271; Traub, *John Quincy
Adams*, 393.

54. Wheelan, *Mr. Adams's Last Crusade*, 61.

55. John Quincy Adams was atuned to Jefferson's exaggerations. See Bemis,
John Quincy Adams and the Union, 2:216.

56. Wheelan, *Mr. Adams's Last Crusade*, 6; Bemis, *John Quincy Adams and the
Union*, 2:193–94, 2:203; Cooper, *The Lost Founding Father*, 272.

57. JQAD, July 11, 1829, 8:154–155; Cooper, *The Lost Founding Father*, 261.

58. Traub, *John Quincy Adams*, 380, 387; Bemis, *John Quincy Adams and the Union*, 193.

59. Letter from Louisa Adams to John Adams II, October 1, 1830, in Adams Papers.

60. William H. Seward, *Life and Public Services of John Quincy Adams* (Scotts Valley, CA.: CreateSpace, 2013), 239.

61. John Adams, "The Works of John Adams, vol. 1 (Life of the Author)," Online Library of Liberty, 1856, https://oll.libertyfund.org/title/adams-the -works-of-john-adams-vol-1-life-of-the-author.

62. Bemis, *John Quincy Adams and the Union*, 206; Seward, *Life and Public Services of John Quincy Adams*, 244–45.

63. Seward, *Life and Public Services of John Quincy Adams*, 245.

64. JQAD, September 17, 1830, 8:238; Bemis, *John Quincy Adams and the Union*, 206–7, Unger, *John Quincy Adams*, 261.

65. JQAD, September 18, 1830, 8:239.

66. Traub, *John Quincy Adams*, 389–90.

67. Seward, *Life and Public Services of John Quincy Adams*, 246; Traub, *John Quincy Adams*, 390; Bemis, *John Quincy Adams and the Union*, 2:209.

68. JQAD, September 22, 1830, 8:240; see also Bemis, *John Quincy Adams and the Union*, 209.

69. JQAD, October 13, 1830, 8:242; JQAD, October 14, 1830, 8:243.

70. JQAD, November 6, 1830, 8:245.

71. John Quincy Adams Digital Diary, vol. 38, November 7, 1830, https://www .masshist.org/publications/jqadiaries/index.php/document/jqadiaries-v38 -1830-11-07-p022#sn=3.

72. Ibid.

73. JQAD, November 7, 1830, 8:245–46.

74. John Quincy Adams draws on Jefferson's precedent in a letter to Samuel L. Southard, Quincy, December 6, 1830; Adams MSS found in Bemis, *John Quincy Adams and the Union*, 2:210–11.

75. David Loyd Pullman, *The Constitutional Conventions of Virginia from the Foundation of the Commonwealth to the Present Time* (Charleston, SC: Nabu Press, 2010), 68, 80.

76. Impecunious situation captured in Louisa Adams letter to John Adams II, Quincy, August 29, 1832, that John Quincy Adams had tax bills exceeding his income; found in Bemis, *John Quincy Adams and the Union*, 2:211; see also Freehling, *Prelude to Civil War*, 342.

77. JQAD, November 7, 1830, 8:245–46.

78. JQAD, April 27, 1831, 8:360; Bemis, *John Quincy Adams and the Union*, 212.

79. "James Monroe's House," *New York Times*, October 25, 1919, https://times

machine.nytimes.com/timesmachine/1919/10/25/118171187.pdf?pdf_re
direct=true&ip=0.

80. Bemis, *John Quincy Adams and the Union*, 212.

81. There were forty-eight senators and three nonvoting delegates.

82. Traub, *John Quincy Adams*, 398; Cooper, *The Lost Founding Father*, 286.

83. JQAD, December 26, 1831, 8:443.

84. Bemis, *John Quincy Adams and the Union*, 2:240.

85. JQAD, December 13, 1831, 8:436–37.

86. Unger, *John Quincy Adams*, 266.

87. Orlando Figes, *The Story of Russia* (New York: Henry Holt, 2022), 87.

88. Register of Debates, VIII, Pt. II, 1426, in Bemis, *John Quincy Adams and the Union*, 2:331; JQAD, December 12, 1831, 433–44.

89. John Quincy Adams, letter to Friend Moses Brown of Providence, Rhode Island, Washington, December 9, 1833; Adams MSS in Bemis, *John Quincy Adams and the Union*, 2:331; Unger, *John Quincy Adams*, 266; David C. Frederick, "John Quincy Adams, Slavery, and the Disappearance of the Right of Petition," Law and History Review 9, no. 1 (Spring 1991): 121; Cooper, *The Lost Founding Father*, 321.

90. Bemis, *John Quincy Adams and the Union*, 2:331, 2:336.

91. JQ Adams Digital Diary, December 12, 1831, found in Unger, *John Quincy Adams*, 266.

92. Frederick, "John Quincy Adams, Slavery," 121–22.

93. Letter from Louisa Adams to John Adams II, Quincy, August 22, 1832; Adams MSS in Bemis, *John Quincy Adams and the Union*, 2:258.

94. JQAD, June 18, 1833, 8:546; Cooper, *The Lost Founding Father*, 313; Robert V. Remini, *John Quincy Adams: The American Presidents Series: The 6th President, 1825–1829* (New York: Henry Holt, 2014), 135; Letter from JQ Adams to Charles Francis Adams, no. 14, Washington, January 18, 1843; Adams MSS in Bemis, *John Quincy Adams and the Union*, 2:250.

95. JQAD, September 9, 1833, 9:14.

96. JQAD, October 7, 1833, 9:21.

97. JQAD, November 5, 1833, 9:28.

98. Traub, *John Quincy Adams*, 413–14.

99. JQAD, November 8, 1833, 9:29–30.

100. Ibid.

101. Wheelan, *Mr. Adams's Last Crusade*, 89.

102. Remini, *John Quincy Adams*, 135.

103. Cooper, *The Lost Founding Father*, 310–11.

104. Sidney Blumenthal, *A Self Made Man: The Political Life of Abraham Lincoln* (New York: Simon & Schuster, 2017), 145.

105. JQAD, February 24, 1820, 4:531.

106. JQAD, July 11, 1787, in Cooper, *The Lost Founding Father*, 70.

107. Bemis, *John Quincy Adams and the Union*, 2:328.

108. Jeff Forret, "The Notorious 'Yellow House' That Made Washington, D.C. a Slavery Capital," *Smithsonian*, July 22, 2020, https://www.smithsonianmag.com/history/how-yellow-house-helped-make-washington-dc-slavery-capital-180975378/.

109. "Lafayette Square, Washington, DC," U.S. General Services Administration, https://www.gsa.gov/real-estate/historic-preservation/explore-historic-buildings/heritage-tourism/our-capital/lafayette-square-washington-dc.

110. Frederick, "John Quincy Adams, Slavery," 119.

111. Wheelan, *Mr. Adams's Last Crusade*, 101.

112. "William Lloyd Garrison, American Anti-Slavery Society Declaration of Sentiments, 1833," Bill of Rights Institute, https://billofrightsinstitute.org/activities/william-lloyd-garrison-american-anti-slavery-society-declaration-of-sentiments-1833.

113. Pierson, *Tocqueville and Beaumont in America*, 418–20, in Bemis, *John Quincy Adams and the Union*, 2:329–30; Cooper, *The Lost Founding Father*, 304.

114. Frederick, "John Quincy Adams, Slavery," 129.

115. "Andrew Jackson: Seventh Annual Message, December 8, 1835," American Presidency Project, https://www.presidency.ucsb.edu/documents/seventh-annual-message-2.

116. Frederick, "John Quincy Adams, Slavery," 127.

117. Ibid., 129.

118. Remini, *John Quincy Adams*, 139–40.

119. Cooper, *The Lost Founding Father*, 328–29; Remini, *John Quincy Adams*, 139–40; William W. Freehling, *The Road to Disunion: Secessionists at Bay, 1776–1854* (New York: Oxford University Press, 1990); William Lee Miller, *Arguing about Slavery: John Quincy Adams and the Great Battle in the United States Congress* (New York: Vintage, 1998), 139–53; George C. Rable, "Slavery, Politics, and the South: The Gag Rule as a Case Study," *Capitol Studies* 3 (Fall 1975): 69–87.

120. Frederick, "John Quincy Adams, Slavery," 130; Unger, *John Quincy Adams*, 274.

121. Cooper, *The Lost Founding Father*, 331–32.

122. Register of Debates, XII, Pt. III, May 18, 19, 1836, 3758–78. Found in various sources: Unger, *John Quincy Adams*, 274; Remini, *John Quincy Adams*, 139–40; Cooper, *The Lost Founding Father*, 331–32; Bemis, *John Quincy Adams and the Union*, 2:337.

123. Bemis, *John Quincy Adams and the Union*, 2:354–55.

124. Remini, *John Quincy Adams*, 138–39.

125. "The Antislavery Views of President John Quincy Adams," *Journal of Blacks in Higher Education*, no. 18 (Winter 1997–98): 102.

126. C. Steindl et al., "Understanding Psychological Reactance: New Developments and Findings," *Zeitschrift für Psychologie* 223, no. 4 (October 2015): 205–14.

127. Charles Sellers, *James K. Polk*, 2 vols. (Easton, CT: Easton Press, 1987), 1:315.

128. For a detailed account see Joanne B. Freeman, *The Field of Blood: Violence in Congress and the Road to Civil War* (New York: Farrar, Straus and Giroux, 2018). See also Andrew Delbanco, "A Den of Braggarts and Brawlers: Politics on Capitol Hill was Never Civil," *The Nation*, October 25, 2018, https://www.thenation.com/article/archive/the-history-of-congressional-mayhem/.

129. Remini, *John Quincy Adams*, 139–40.

130. Joanne B. Freeman, "The Long History of Political Idiocy," *New York Times*, August 4, 2015, https://www.nytimes.com/2015/08/04/opinion/the-long-history-of-political-idiocy.html.

131. Ralph Waldo Emerson, *A Year with Emerson: A Daybook* (Boston: David R. Godine, 2003), 27.

132. JQAD, March 18, 1835, 9:220-21 in Unger, *John Quincy Adams*, 275.

133. Frederick, "John Quincy Adams, Slavery," 133–34.

134. Unger, *John Quincy Adams*, 280; Frederick, "John Quincy Adams, Slavery," 132.

135. JQAD, April 2, 1837, 9:344; JQAD, September 1, 1837, 9:365.

136. *Congressional Globe* Debates and Proceedings, 25th Congress, 3rd Session, January 22, 1839, in Traub, *John Quincy Adams*, 465.

137. Traub, *John Quincy Adams*, 442.

138. Traub, *John Quincy Adams*, 442–43; "John C. Calhoun, 'Slavery as a Positive Good,' 1837," Bill of Rights Institute, https://billofrightsinstitute.org/activities/john-c-calhoun-slavery-as-a-positive-good-1837.

139. *Register of Debates*, XIII, Pt. I, Monday (petition day), January 9, 1837, 1314–39, in Bemis, *John Quincy Adams and the Union*, 2:341–42; Unger, *John Quincy Adams*, 276–77; Cooper, *The Lost Founding Father*, 377.

140. Remini, *John Quincy Adams*, 143; Miller, *Arguing about Slavery*, 229–30.

141. Frederick, "John Quincy Adams, Slavery," 134; Cooper, *The Lost Founding Father*, 338; Traub, *John Quincy Adams*, 443; Bemis, *John Quincy Adams and the Union*, 343; Miller, *Arguing about Slavery*, 230.

142. *Register of Debates*, House of Representatives, 24th Congress, 2nd Session, February 6, 1837, in Traub, *John Quincy Adams*, 443; Miller, *Arguing about Slavery*, 231–32; Bemis, *John Quincy Adams and the Union*, 2:344; Cooper, *The Lost Founding Father*, 338.

143. Miller, *Arguing about Slavery*, 233.

144. Frederick, "John Quincy Adams, Slavery," 135.

145. "Am I Gagged or Am I Not? May 25, 1836," Government Archives, https://www.archives.gov/exhibits/treasures_of_congress/text/page10_text.html. "Madman of Massachusetts" was a flattering label given to JQ Adams in a letter from Buddey Taylowe to JQ Adams, Virginia, February 1, 1837, "On behalf of the petitioners" in Bemis, *John Quincy Adams and the Union*, 2:344. For a broader description of the event, see Bemis, *John Quincy Adams and the Union*, 2:344–45.

146. *Register of Debates*, XIII, Pt. I, Monday (petition day), January 9, 1837, 1314–39, in Bemis, *John Quincy Adams and the Union*, 2:345, 2:348; Frederick, "John Quincy Adams, Slavery," 137.

147. Bemis, 2:349.

148. Miller, *Arguing about Slavery*, 255; Traub, *John Quincy Adams*, 445.

149. "Letters from John Quincy Adams to His Constituents of the Twelfth Congressional District of Massachusetts; To Which Is Added His Speech in Congress, Delivered Feb. 9, 1837," *Quincy Patriot*, March 6–20, 1837, in Traub, *John Quincy Adams*, 446.

150. Frederick, "John Quincy Adams, Slavery," 138.

151. Bemis, *John Quincy Adams and the Union*, 2:354.

152. "Acquisition of Florida: Treaty of Adams-Onís (1819) and Transcontinental Treaty (1821)," Office of the Historian, U.S. State Department, https://history.state.gov/milestones/1801-1829/florida.

153. Hal Brands, "John Quincy Adams Isn't Who You Think He Is," American Enterprise Institute, February 8, 2020, https://www.aei.org/op-eds/john-quincy-adams-isnt-who-you-think-he-is/.

154. Richard Dunham, "Today in Texas History: Andrew Jackson Tries to Buy Texas from Mexico," *Texas on the Potomac* blog, *Houston Chronicle*, August 25, 2010, https://blog.chron.com/txpotomac/2010/08/today-in-texas-history-andrew-jackson-tries-to-buy-texas-from-mexico/.

155. Unger, *John Quincy Adams*, 283; Traub, *John Quincy Adams*, 450; Cooper, *The Lost Founding Father*, 324; Frederick, "John Quincy Adams, Slavery," 132.

156. Alwyn Barr, *Black Texans: A History of African Americans in Texas, 1528–1995* (Norman: University of Oklahoma Press, 1996), 15; Cooper, *The Lost Founding Father*, 372.

157. "A Guide to the United States' History of Recognition, Diplomatic, and Consular Relations, by Country, since 1776: Texas," Office of the Historian, U.S. State Department, https://history.state.gov/countries/texas.

158. Cooper, *The Lost Founding Father*, 370.

159. Bemis, *John Quincy Adams and the Union*, 2:359.

160. Miller, *Arguing about Slavery*, 284; see also Bemis, *John Quincy Adams and the Union*, 360.

161. *Speech of John Quincy Adams, of Massachusetts, upon the Right of the People, Men and Women, to Petition; on the Freedom of Speech and of Debate in the House of Representatives . . . ; on the Resolutions of Seven State Legislatures, and the Petitions of More than One Hundred Thousand Petitioners, Relating to the Annexation of Texas to This Union. Delivered in the House of Representatives in fragments of the morning hour, from the 16th of June to the 7th of July 1838* (Washington, DC: Gales and Seaton, 1838), in Bemis, *John Quincy Adams and the Union*, 2:366.

162. "John Quincy Adams against Annexation of Texas," Jamail Center for Legal Research, Tarlton Law Library, University of Texas School of Law, https://tarltonapps.law.utexas.edu/exhibits/republic/adams.html.

163. *Speech of John Quincy Adams, of Massachusetts*, in Bemis, *John Quincy Adams and the Union*, 2:366.

164. Ibid., 2:362.

165. "Speech of John Quincy Adams on the Joint Resolutions for Distributing Rations to the Distressed Fugitives from Indian Hostilities in the States of Alabama and Georgia, 1836 May 25," Digital Library of Georgia, https://dlg.usg.edu/record/dlg_zlna_krc027?canvas=0&x=997&y=1602&w=14929.

166. Unger, *John Quincy Adams*, 276.

167. JQ Adams to the Inhabitants of the Twelfth Congressional District of Massachusetts, Quincy, August 13, 1838, *Quincy Patriot*, August 13, 1838, in Bemis, *John Quincy Adams and the Union*, 2:369; Unger, *John Quincy Adams*, 276.

168. Original threatening letters, Microfilm Edition of JQ Adams correspondence found in Traub, *John Quincy Adams*, 462.

169. *Congressional Globe* VI, in Bemis, *John Quincy Adams and the Union*, 2:366.

170. "'This Whole Horrible Transaction,'" Story of the Week, Library of America, https://storyoftheweek.loa.org/2017/06/the-whole-horrible-transaction.html.

171. Holograph notes for speech on Texas and the right of petition; Adams MSS in Bemis, *John Quincy Adams and the Union*, 2:370.

172. "Annexation Process: 1836–1845: A Summary Timeline," Texas State Library and Archives Commission, https://www.tsl.texas.gov/ref/abouttx/annexation/timeline.html.

173. Cooper, *The Lost Founding Father*, 352.

174. *Congressional Globe* Debates and Proceedings, in Traub, *John Quincy Adams*, 465; Miller, *Arguing about Slavery*, 353–54; Bemis, *John Quincy Adams and the Union*, 2:381.

175. Bemis, *John Quincy Adams and the Union*, 340; Cooper, *The Lost Founding Father*, 355; Frederick, "John Quincy Adams, Slavery," 140; "The Antislavery Views of President John Quincy Adams"; Miller, *Arguing about Slavery*, 362–72; "John Quincy Adams and the Gag Rule," Bill of Rights Institute, https://billofrightsinstitute.org/essays/john-quincy-adams-and-the-gag-rule.

176. Miller, *Arguing about Slavery*, 297.

177. Article 1, Section 9, Clause 1 of the Constitution.

178. Bemis, *John Quincy Adams and the Union*, 2:385.

179. *U.S. v. The Amistad* (40 U.S. 518) in Traub, *John Quincy Adams*, 467; Bemis, *John Quincy Adams and the Union*, 2:385; Benjamin P. Thomas, *Abraham Lincoln: A Biography* (Carbondale: Southern Illinois University Press, 2008), 718.

180. Bemis, *John Quincy Adams and the Union*, 2:386; Traub, *John Quincy Adams*, 467; Thomas, *Abraham Lincoln*, 718.

181. Howard Jones, *Mutiny on the "Amistad"* (New York: Oxford University Press, 1987), 41, in Traub, *John Quincy Adams*, 468.

182. Bemis, *John Quincy Adams and the Union*, 2:390.

183. Mike Cummings, "175 Years Later, the *Amistad* Affair Lives On in the Yale Library's Collections," *YaleNews*, March 7, 2016, https://news.yale.edu/2016/03/07/175-years-later-amistad-affair-lives-yale-library-s-collections.

184. The specifics came in a letter from William Jay, dated Bedford, September 7, 1839, and published in the *Emancipator*. See Bemis, *John Quincy Adams and the Union*, 2:394; Miller, *Arguing about Slavery*, 399; Richards, *Life and Times*, 135–39.

185. John Quincy Adams, *Journal of Commerce* (New York), November 19, 1839, in Traub, *John Quincy Adams*, 466; also in Bemis, *John Quincy Adams and the Union*, 394.

186. Bemis, *John Quincy Adams and the Union*, 2:395; Traub, *John Quincy Adams*, 470.

187. Wheelan, *Mr. Adams's Last Crusade*, 165.

188. *Hartford Courant*, February 10, 1840, cited in Christopher Martin, *The Amistad Affair* (New York: Abelard-Schuman, 1970), 233.

189. "The Amistad Committee," National Park Service, https://www.nps.gov/people/the-amistad-committee.htm.

190. *The United States, Appellants, v. The Libellants and Claimants of the Schooner Amistad* . . . , Supreme Court of the United States, 40 U.S. 518; 10 L. Ed. 826, January 1841 term, Cornell Law School, https://www.law.cornell.edu/background/amistad/opinion.html.

191. Wheelan, *Mr. Adams's Last Crusade*, 172.

192. Ibid., 163, 175.

193. Bemis, *John Quincy Adams and the Union*, 2:396; Traub, *John Quincy Adams*, 469.

194. Traub, *John Quincy Adams*, 468–69; Bemis, *John Quincy Adams and the Union*, 392.

195. Bemis, *John Quincy Adams and the Union*, 2:398–400; Traub, *John Quincy Adams*, 472–23; Cooper, *The Lost Founding Father*, 364; Miller, *Arguing about Slavery*, 401.

196. Traub, *John Quincy Adams*, 474.

197. John Quincy Adams, *Memoirs of John Quincy Adams, Comprising Portions of His Diary from 1795 to 1848*, X:373, X:383, X:387, X:410, in Bemis, *John Quincy Adams and the Union*, 2:404–5.

198. Ibid., X:383.

199. Bemis, *John Quincy Adams and the Union*, 2:405.

200. Traub, *John Quincy Adams*, 476–77; Unger, *John Quincy Adams*, 291; Miller, *Arguing about Slavery*, 402. For more detail, see "Old Supreme Court Chamber," Architect of the Capitol, https://www.aoc.gov/explore-capitol-campus/buildings-grounds/capitol-building/senate-wing/old-supreme-court-chamber.

201. "Treaty Friendship, Limits, and Navigation between Spain and the United States, October 27, 1795," Avalon Project, Yale Law School, https://avalon.law.yale.edu/18th_century/sp1795.asp; Traub, *John Quincy Adams*, 475.

202. "The United States v. The Amistad: Attorney-General Reply," Cornell Law School, https://www.law.cornell.edu/background/amistad/reply.html.

203. "Argument of Roger S. Baldwin, of New Haven, before the Supreme Court of the United States," Smithsonian Institution, https://transcription.si.edu/project/38319#:~:text=Baldwin%2C%20however%2C%20did%20argue%20that,cause%2C%20but%20it%20was%20Baldwin's; Traub, *John Quincy Adams*, 476.

204. Norman Gross, "Presidential Bar Leaders: Fascinating Facts about America's Lawyer-Presidents," *Bar Leader* 34, no. 3 (January–February 2010): https://www.americanbar.org/groups/bar_services/publications/bar_leader/2009_10/january_february/presidential/.

205. Traub, *John Quincy Adams*, 476–77.

206. "Argument of John Quincy Adams, before the Supreme Court of the United States: In the Case of the United States, Appellants, vs. Cinque, and Others, Africans, Captured in the schooner Amistad, by Lieut. Gedney; 1841," Avalon Project, Yale Law School, https://avalon.law.yale.edu/19th_century/amistad_002.asp.

207. Traub, *John Quincy Adams*, 479; Blumenthal, *A Self Made Man*, 148.

208. "Argument of John Quincy Adams, before the Supreme Court of the United States."

209. Ibid.

210. Ibid.

211. Traub, *John Quincy Adams*, 479.

212. "Argument of John Quincy Adams, before the Supreme Court of the United States."

213. Unger, *John Quincy Adams*, 293.

214. "Argument of John Quincy Adams, before the Supreme Court of the United States."

215. Bemis, *John Quincy Adams and the Union*, 2:418.

216. Traub, *John Quincy Adams*, 480.

217. 15 Peters *U.S. Reports*, 587–98, in Bemis, *John Quincy Adams and the Union*, 2:410; Traub, *John Quincy Adams*, 480.

218. *Argument of John Quincy Adams, before the Supreme Court of the United States, in the Case of the United States, Appellants vs. Cinque, and Others, Africans, Captured in the Schooner Amistad, by Lieut. Gedney, Delivered on the 24th of February and 1st of March, 1841. With a Review of the Case of the Antelope, Reported in the 10th, 11th, and 12th Volumes of Wheaton's Reports* (New York: S. W. Benedict, 1841), in Bemis, *John Quincy Adams and the Union*, 2:414.

219. Traub, *John Quincy Adams*, 481.

220. Wheelan, *Mr. Adams's Last Crusade*, 185.

221. Remini, *John Quincy Adams*, 149.

222. John W. Blassingame, ed., *Slave Testimony: Two Centuries of Letters, Speeches, Interviews, and Autobiographies* (Baton Rouge: Louisiana State University Press, 1977), 43.

223. David Kibbe, "State Makes History as Patrick Takes Oath," *Cape Cod Times*, January 5, 2007, https://www.capecodtimes.com/story/news/2007/01/05/state-makes-history-as-patrick/50851875007/.

224. Bemis, *John Quincy Adams and the Union*, 2:411; Traub, *John Quincy Adams*, 480.

225. "Congress Profiles: 27th Congress," History, Art & Archives, United States House of Representatives, https://history.house.gov/Congressional-Overview/Profiles/27th/.

226. *Congressional Globe*, 27th Congress, 2nd Session, 158, in Cooper, *The Lost Founding Father*, 397–98; JQAD, January 22, 24, 1842, 11:68-70.

227. Unger, *John Quincy Adams*, 298; Remini, *John Quincy Adams*, 150.

228. *Congressional Globe* XI, January 25, 1842, 168, in Bemis, *John Quincy Adams and the Union*, 2:427; Miller, *Arguing about Slavery*, 430; Cooper, *The Lost Founding Father*, 398; Traub, *John Quincy Adams*, 488.

229. Adams made this comment to Theodore Dwight Weld. Theodore D. Weld to Angelina Weld, February 6, 1842, Gilbert H. Barnes and Dwight L.

Dumond, ed., *Letters of Theodore Dwight Weld, Angelina Grimké Weld and Sarah Grimké, 1822-1844* (New York: D. Appleton-Century Company, Incorporated, 1934), 2:911, found in Cooper, *The Lost Founding Father*, 399–400.

230. Major Peter G. Kucera, *Brigadier General Henry A. Wise, C.S.A. and the Western Virginia Campaign of 1861* (London: Golden Springs, 2014); Traub, *John Quincy Adams*, 489.

231. Miller, *Arguing about Slavery*, 439.

232. Charles M. Wiltse, *John C. Calhoun: Sectionalist: 1840–1850* (Indianapolis, IN: Bobbs-Merrill, 1944), 150, in Bemis, *John Quincy Adams and the Union*, 2:432.

233. Traub, *John Quincy Adams*, 489.

234. Miller, *Arguing about Slavery*, 434.

235. Traub, *John Quincy Adams*, 489; Miller, *Arguing about Slavery*, 434–36.

236. "Punishment and Expulsion of Members," U.S. Government Publishing Office, https://www.govinfo.gov/content/pkg/GPO-HPREC-HINDS-V2/html/GPO-HPREC-HINDS-V2-16.htm; Traub, *John Quincy Adams*, 489.

237. Bemis, *John Quincy Adams and the Union*, 2:434–35; Unger, *John Quincy Adams*, 300.

238. *Congressional Globe* 27, January 29, 1842.

239. Remini, *John Quincy Adams*, 150; Cooper, *The Lost Founding Father*, 400.

240. Traub, *John Quincy Adams*, 491; Unger, *John Quincy Adams*, 300.

241. Bemis, *John Quincy Adams and the Union*, 2:434.

242. William Smith Henry, *A Political History of Slavery: Being an Account of the Slavery Controversy from the Earliest Agitation in the 18th Century to the Close of the Reconstruction Period in America* (New York: Ungar, 1966); Bemis, *John Quincy Adams and the Union*, 434; Traub, *John Quincy Adams*, 491.

243. *Congressional Globe* XI, 208, in Bemis, *John Quincy Adams and the Union*, 2:435; Miller, *Arguing about Slavery*, 443; Traub, *John Quincy Adams*, 492–93; Cooper, *The Lost Founding Father*, 342; Unger, *John Quincy Adams*, 300–301.

244. Miller, *Arguing about Slavery*, 441–44; Unger, *John Quincy Adams*, 302.

245. William M. Wiecek, *The Sources of Anti-Slavery Constitutionalism in America, 1760–1848*, in Miller, *Arguing about Slavery*, 444; Traub, *John Quincy Adams*, 493; Bemis, *John Quincy Adams and the Union*, 436.

246. Barnes and Dumond, ed., *Letters of Weld*, February 7, 1842, in Traub, *John Quincy Adams*, 494.

247. Joshua R. Giddings, *The History of the Rebellion: Its Authors and Causes* (New York: Follet, Foster, 1864), 15–67, in Blumenthal, *A Self Made Man*, 150–151.

248. Statement made by Henry A. Wise as candidate for governor of Virginia in 1855. Barton H. Wise, *The Life of Henry A. Wise of Virginia, 1806–1876* (New York: Macmillan, 1899), 61–62, in Bemis, *John Quincy Adams and the Union*, 2:436–37; see also Unger, *John Quincy Adams*, 302; Miller, *Arguing about Slavery*, 357; Traub, *John Quincy Adams*, 495.

249. Bemis, *John Quincy Adams and the Union*, 2:438.

250. Traub, *John Quincy Adams*, 502; Cooper, *The Lost Founding Father*, 356.

251. Unger, *John Quincy Adams*, 302–3.

252. JQAD, October 6, 1839, 10:137–38.

253. Robert Seager, *And Tyler Too: A Biography of John and Julia Gardiner Tyler* (Sacramento, CA: Creative Media Partners, 2015), 162.

254. Jared Cohen, *Accidental Presidents: Eight Men Who Changed America* (New York: Simon & Schuster, 2019), 7.

255. Ibid, 11; Cooper, *The Lost Founding Father*, 379.

256. Ronald G. Shafer, "'He Lies like a Dog': The First Effort to Impeach a President Was Led by His Own Party," *Washington Post*, September 23, 2019, https://www.washingtonpost.com/history/2019/09/23/he-lies-like-dog-first -effort-impeach-president-was-led-by-his-own-party/; Cohen, *Accidental Presidents*, 25.

257. JQAD, April 4, 1841, 10:462–63; Cooper, *The Lost Founding Father*, 380.

258. Cooper, *The Lost Founding Father*, 402; Traub, *John Quincy Adams*, 499.

259. Cooper, *The Lost Founding Father*, 403.

260. Diary of Elise C. Otté, recounting a conversation between JQ Adams and his fellow grandfather Peter C. Brooks in the stage en route from Saratoga to Glens Falls, New York. Adams MSS in Bemis, *John Quincy Adams and the Union*, 2:473.

261. Sellers, *James K. Polk*, 2:159.

262. Bemis, *John Quincy Adams and the Union*, 476.

263. "Joint Resolution for Annexing Texas to the United States, March 1, 1845," Texas State Library and Archives Commission, https://www.tsl.texas.gov /ref/abouttx/annexation/march1845.html.

264. Unger, *John Quincy Adams*, 303; Traub, *John Quincy Adams*, 507; Bemis, *John Quincy Adams and the Union*, 446.

265. "Adams National Historical Park," National Park Service, http://npshistory .com/brochures/trading-cards/adam/charles-francis-adams-ambassador -during-the-civil-war.pdf.

266. Traub, *John Quincy Adams*, 502.

267. Seward, *Life and Public Services of John Quincy Adams*, 322.

268. *Weekly Herald*, November 15–22, 1843, in Traub, *John Quincy Adams*, 505.

269. Ibid., 508.

270. Jeremiah Chaplin and J. D. Chaplin, *Life of Charles Sumner* (Ann Arbor: Scholarly Publishing Office, University of Michigan Library, 1874), 92.

271. Massachusetts Historical Proceedings, 1902, in *Social Life in Old New England*, Mary Caroline Crawford (New York: Little, Brown, 1914), 448.

272. JQAD, November 2, 1843, 11:418–19; Traub, *John Quincy Adams*, 503; Miller, *Arguing about Slavery*, 464.

273. Miller, *Arguing about Slavery*, 464–65.

274. Unger, *John Quincy Adams*, 305.

275. Traub, *John Quincy Adams*, 507.

276. Ibid., 509; Cooper, *The Lost Founding Father*, 409.

277. Gilbert H. Barnes, *Anti-Slavery Impulse: 1830–1844* (New York: Harcourt, Brace & World, 1964), 193; Frederick, "John Quincy Adams, Slavery," 139; Bemis, *John Quincy Adams and the Union*, 2:447; Traub, *John Quincy Adams*, 509.

278. Leonard L. Richards, *The Life and Times of Congressman John Quincy Adams* (New York: Oxford University Press, 1986), 175–79; Cooper, *The Lost Founding Father*, 409.

279. Chaplin and Chaplin, *Life of Charles Sumner*, 93.

280. Everett, *A Eulogy on the Life and Character of John Quincy Adams*, 53–54.

281. Unger, *John Quincy Adams*, 306–7.

282. Traub, *John Quincy Adams*, 523; Remini, *John Quincy Adams*, 154; Albert J. Beveridge, *Abraham Lincoln, 1809–1858* (London: Victor Gollancz, 1928), 2:102.

283. Unger, *John Quincy Adams*, 306; Traub, *John Quincy Adams*, 522.

284. Thomas, *Abraham Lincoln*, 117.

285. Beveridge, *Abraham Lincoln, 1809–1858*, 108–9.

286. Unger, *John Quincy Adams*, 308.

287. *Congressional Globe*, 30th Congress, 1st Session, 380–81, in Cooper, *The Lost Founding Father*, 433–34; Miller, *Arguing about Slavery*, 459.

288. Wheelan, *Mr. Adams's Last Crusade*, 147.

289. Cooper, *The Lost Founding Father*, 434.

290. Nathan Sargent, *Public Men and Events from the Comencement of Mr. Monroe's Administration, in 1817, to the Close of Mr. Fillmore's Administration in 1853* (Philadelphia: J. P. Lippincott, 1875), 2:331–2; Wheelan, *Mr. Adams's Last Crusade*, 246–48, in Blumenthal, *A Self Made Man*, 372; Remini, *John Quincy Adams*, 154.

291. "Capitol Rotunda," Architect of the Capitol, https://www.aoc.gov/explore-capitol-campus/buildings-grounds/capitol-building/rotunda.

292. Accounts from the *Journal of Commerce* and the *National Intelligencer* in Traub, *John Quincy Adams*, 526; Unger, *John Quincy Adams*, 309.

293. Wheelan, *Mr. Adams's Last Crusade*, 248.

294. Unger, *John Quincy Adams*, 310; Potter, *The Impending Crisis*, 5.

295. Diary of Charles Francis Adams, February 22–25, 1848, in Traub, *John Quincy Adams*, 527.

296. "Whereas: Stories from the People's House: The Last Hours of John Quincy Adams," History, Art & Archives, United States House of Representatives, February 26, 2019, https://history.house.gov/Blog/2019/February/2-26_JQA _lasthours/.

297. Traub, *John Quincy Adams*, 529.

298. Milo Milton Quaife, ed., *The Diary of James K. Polk during His Presidency, 1845–1849*, vol. 3 (Chicago: A. C. McClurg, 1910), 362–63, in Cooper, *The Lost Founding Father*, 438.

299. Blumenthal, *A Self Made Man*, 153.

300. James Oakes, *The Crooked Path to Abolition: Abraham Lincoln and the Anti-slavery Constitution* (New York: W. W. Norton, 2021), 37; Blumenthal, *A Self Made Man*, 152.

301. John C. Pinheiro, "James K. Polk: Life after the Presidency," Miller Center, University of Virginia, https://millercenter.org/president/polk/life-after -the-presidency.

302. "Death of Ex-President Tyler," *New York Times*, January 22, 1862, https:// timesmachine.nytimes.com/timesmachine/1862/01/22/78676355.pdf?pdf _redirect=true&ip=0.

303. Henry Franklin Graff, *Grover Cleveland* (New York: Henry Holt, 2002), 7.

CHAPTER 3: THE COMEBACK

1. "Basic Principles of the American Party of Virginia, 1856," Digital Public Library of America, https://dp.la/exhibitions/outsiders-president-elections /anti-outsider-platforms/know-nothing-party-1856.

2. Cohen, *Accidental Presidents*, 139–141.

3. John M. Pafford, *Cleveland: The Forgotten Conservative* (Washington, DC: Regnery, 2015), 63.

4. "Building the Panama Canal, 1903–1914," Office of the Historian, U.S. State Department, https://history.state.gov/milestones/1899-1913/panama-canal.

5. "Letter from FDR to Frances Cleveland Preston, November 28, 1928," Warm Springs, Georgia. See also Ted Morgan, *FDR: A Biography* (New York: Simon & Schuster, 1985), 43, for a slight variation in the language.

6. "FDR letter to Mrs. Preston, November 28, 1928." Found at RR Auction.

7. Charles Lachman, *A Secret Life: The Sex, Lies, and Scandals of President Grover Cleveland* (New York: Skyhorse, 2011), 415–16.

8. Troy Senik, *A Man of Iron: The Turbulent Life and Improbable Presidency of Grover Cleveland* (New York: Threshold, 2022), 18.

9. Rexford Guy Tugwell, *Grover Cleveland* (New York: Macmillan, 1968), 7.

10. Ibid., 27.

11. Reinhard H. Luthin, "Waving the Bloody Shirt: Northern Political Tactics in Post-Civil War Times," *Georgia Review* 14, no. 1 (Spring 1960): 64–71.

12. "The Conscription Act of 1863," Internet Archive, https://archive.org/stream /conscriptionacto00unit/conscriptionacto00unit_djvu.txt.

13. "The Mob in New York," *New York Times*, July 14, 1863, https://www.nytimes .com/1863/07/14/archives/the-mob-in-newyork-resistance-to-the-draftriot ing-and-bloodshed.html. For details of the Enrollment Act, see "Enrollment Act: March 3, 1863," Omeka Virtual Exhibits, https://omeka.hrvh.org/exhib its/show/new-paltz-in-the-civil-war/laws/enrollment-act—march-3—1863.

14. Michael T. Meier, "Civil War Draft Records: Exemptions and Enrollments," National Archives, https://www.archives.gov/publications/prologue/1994 /winter/civil-war-draft-records.html.

15. Senik, *A Man of Iron*, 26.

16. "Population History of Buffalo from 1830–1990," Physics, Buffalo University, http://physics.bu.edu/~redner/projects/population/cities/buffalo.html.

17. "The Execution of John Gaffney at Buffalo, NY, 1873," *Buffalonian*, https:// web.archive.org/web/20171006162510/http://www.buffalonian.com/his tory/articles/1851-1900/gaffneyhanging/gaffneyhanging.html.

18. Ellen Prezepaskian, "January 2, 1882: Grover Cleveland Begins His Brief Term as Mayor," *Buffalo News*, January 2, 2019, https://buffalonews.com /news/local/history/jan-2-1882-grover-cleveland-begins-brief-term-as-may or-of-buffalo/article_8bebff94-baa6-5cf0-82fc-0d4b658c2352.html.

19. Grover Cleveland Address before City Convention, Buffalo, New York, October 25, 1881.

20. Senik, *A Man of Iron*, 65.

21. Tugwell, *Grover Cleveland*, 82; Senik, *A Man of Iron*, 61.

22. Robert McNutt McElroy, *Grover Cleveland, the Man and the Statesman: An Authorized Biography*, 2 vols. (New York: Harper & Brothers, 1923), 1:62.

23. Candice Millard's *Destiny of the Republic* (New York: Doubleday, 2011) offers a detailed account of Garfield's doctors and the folly that killed him.

24. "Garfield and Arthur," *New York Times*, June 9, 1880. Found in Reeves, Thomas C., *Gentleman Boss: The Life of Chester Alan Arthur* (Newtown, CT: American Political Biography Press, 1991), 181.

25. "Evening Star, July 4, 1881," in Ackerman, *Dark Horse*, 358.

26. Reeves, *Gentleman Boss*, 3; Allan Peskin, *Garfield: A Biography* (Kent, OH: Kent State University Press, 1978), 599.

27. *Marysville Daily Appeal* XLIX, no. 141, June 13, 1884.

28. Michael Barone, *How America's Political Parties Change (and How They Don't)* (New York: Encounter Books, 2019).

29. "Blaine, Blaine, James G. Blaine, the continental liar from the State of Maine," quoted in Mark Wahlgren Summers, *Rum, Romanism, and Rebellion: The Making of a President, 1884* (Chapel Hill: Univeristy of North Carolina Press, 2000), xi.

30. "1884: *Cleveland v. Blaine*," Explore History, Harp Week, http://elections .harpweek.com/1884/Overview-1884-3.htm.

31. Scott J. Hammond, Valerie A. Sulfaro, and Robert N. Roberts, *Presidential Campaigns, Slogans, Issues, and Platforms: The Complete Encyclopedia* (Westport, CT: Greenwood, 2012). For a full discussion, see Summers, *Rum, Romanism, and Rebellion.*

32. Diane Winston, ed., *The Oxford Handbook of Religion and the American News Media* (New York: Oxford University Press, 2012), 321.

33. "Talks with Boss Kelly," *New York Times,* July 8, 1884.

34. Tugwell, *Grover Cleveland,* 90–91.

35. Lachman, *A Secret Life,* 214–15.

36. Allan Nevins, ed., *Letters of Grover Cleveland, 1850–1908* (Boston: Houghton Mifflin, 1933), 98; Angela Serratore, "President Cleveland's Problem Child," *Smithsonian,* September 26, 2013, https://www.smithsonianmag .com/history/president-clevelands-problem-child-100800/.

37. Tugwell, *Grover Cleveland,* 42.

38. Senik, *A Man of Iron,* 91.

39. Matthew Algeo, *The President Is a Sick Man: Wherein the Supposedly Virtuous Grover Cleveland Survives a Secret Surgery at Sea and Vilifies the Courageous Newspaperman Who Dared Expose the Truth* (Chicago: Chicago Review Press, 2011), 27–28.

40. Serratore, "President Cleveland's Problem Child."

41. Lillian Cunningham, "What We Can Learn from Grover Cleveland's Distrust of the Press," *Washington Post,* June 5, 2016, https://www.wash ingtonpost.com/news/on-leadership/wp/2016/06/05/what-we-can-learn -from-grover-clevelands-distrust-of-the-press/.

42. J. M. Martinez, *Libertines: American Political Sex Scandals from Alexander Hamilton to Donald Trump* (Lanham, MD: Rowman & Littlefield, 2022), 76.

43. *Indianapolis Journal,* Indianapolis, Marion County, September 19, 1884.

44. Richard E. Welch, *The Presidencies of Grover Cleveland* (Lawrence: University Press of Kansas, 1988), 37.

45. *Detroit Free Press,* November 3, 1884.

46. Nicholas D. Sawicki, "How James G. Blaine Became the Face of Anti-Catholicism in Education," *America Jesuit Review*, January 20, 2020, https://www.americamagazine.org/politics-society/2020/01/30/how-james-g-blaine-became-face-anti-catholicism-education.

47. Pafford, *Cleveland: The Forgotten Conservative*, 31.

48. Serratore, "President Cleveland's Problem Child"; Lachman, *A Secret Life*, 308.

49. Lachman, *A Secret Life*, 308.

50. "March 4, 1885: First Inaugural Address," Miller Center, University of Virginia, https://millercenter.org/the-presidency/presidential-speeches/march-4-1885-first-inaugural-address.

51. "25th Inaugural Ceremonies," Joint Congressional Committee on Inaugural Ceremonies, https://www.inaugural.senate.gov/25th-inaugural-ceremonies/.

52. George Frederick Parker, *A Life of Grover Cleveland: With a Sketch of Adlai E. Stevenson* (London: Cassell, 1892), 141.

53. Welch, *The Presidencies of Grover Cleveland*, 62.

54. Burton Folsom, "Grover Cleveland: The Veto President," Our Economic Past, April 2004, https://fee-misc.s3.amazonaws.com/files/docLib/folsom0404.pdf.

55. For an exploration of Rose Cleveland's relationship with Evangeline Whipple, see their love letters, collected in *Precious and Adored: The Love Letters of Rose Cleveland and Evangeline Simpson Whipple, 1890–1918* (St. Paul: Minnesota Historical Society Press, 2019).

56. Stephen Gwynn, *The Letters and Friendships of Sir Cecil Spring-Rice, A Record*, vol. 1 (Boston: Houghton Mifflin, 1929), 63.

57. Annette Dunlap, *Frank: The Story of Frances Folsom Cleveland, America's Youngest First Lady* (Albany: State University of New York Press, 2010), 1.

58. "Oscar Folsom Death Notice," Newspapers.com, https://www.newspapers.com/clip/4247043/oscar-folsom-death-notice/.

59. Algeo, *The President Is a Sick Man*, 29, 46; Pafford, *Cleveland: The Forgotten Conservative*, 49.

60. Lachman, *A Secret Life*, 299; Algeo, *The President Is a Sick Man*, 29; Pafford, *Cleveland: The Forgotten Conservative*, 49.

61. Dunlap, *Frank*, 3; Lachman, *A Secret Life*, 332.

62. Lachman, *A Secret Life*, 333.

63. Alyn Brodsky, *Grover Cleveland: A Study in Character* (New York: St. Martin's Press, 2000), 163; Lachman, *A Secret Life*, 333–34.

64. "When New York Saw a Presidential Wedding: John Tyler's Romance with Miss Julia Gardiner Culminated in Their Marriage at the Church of the

Ascension in This City Seventy-One Years Ago," *New York Times*, October 17, 1915; Cohen, *Accidental Presidents*, 40.

65. "The President's Wedding," *Idaho Spring News*, June 11, 1886, https://www .coloradohistoricnewspapers.org/?a=d&d=ISN18860611-01.2.11&e=------ -en-20--1--img-txIN%7ctxCO%7ctxTA--------0------.

66. Pafford, *Cleveland: The Forgotten Conservative*, 50–51.

67. "Frances Cleveland: Topics in Chronicling America," Library of Congress, https://guides.loc.gov/chronicling-america-frances-cleveland.

68. Ronald G. Shafer, "When Presidents Fall in Love," *Washington Post*, February 14, 2019, https://www.washingtonpost.com/history/2019/02/14/when -presidents-fall-love/.

69. Lachman, *A Secret Life*, 354–55.

70. "The Nation's First Lady," *New York Times*, June 3, 1886.

71. Brodsky, *Grover Cleveland: A Study in Character*, 171; Tugwell, *Grover Cleveland*, 144.

72. Lachman, *A Secret Life*, 363; Pafford, *Cleveland: The Forgotten Conservative*, 51.

73. Pafford, *Cleveland: The Forgotten Conservative*, 51.

74. Colonel W. H. Crook, *Memories of the White House* (Boston: Little, Brown, 1911), 185.

75. Dunlap, *Frank*, 37.

76. Tugwell, *Grover Cleveland*, 147.

77. Ajay K. Mehrotra, "'More Mighty than the Waves of the Sea': Toilers, Tariffs, and the Income Tax Movement, 1880–1913," Labor History 45, no. 2 (August 2005): 165–98.

78. McElroy, *Grover Cleveland, the Man and the Statesman*, 1:269; Tugwell, *Grover Cleveland*, 158.

79. Ibid; Nevins, *Letters of Grover Cleveland*, 365.

80. McElroy, *Grover Cleveland, the Man and the Statesman*, 1:271; Nevins, *Letters of Grover Cleveland*, 377.

81. Nevins, *Letters of Grover Cleveland*, 468.

82. McElroy, *Grover Cleveland, the Man and the Statesman*, 1:272.

83. "December 6, 1887: Third Annual Message," Miller Center, University of Virginia, https://millercenter.org/the-presidency/presidential-speeches/dec ember-6-1887-third-annual-message. For more context, see Nevins, *Letters of Grover Cleveland*, 378.

84. McElroy, *Grover Cleveland, the Man and the Statesman*, 1:272.

85. Ibid., 1:310.

86. Ibid., 1:289.

87. Ibid., 1:274, 1:275, 1:277–78.

88. Senik, *A Man of Iron*, 185.

89. "The Democratic Convention," *New York Times*, February 24, 1888, https:// timesmachine.nytimes.com/timesmachine/1888/02/24/103162981.pdf ?pdf_redirect=true&ip=0.

90. McElroy, *Grover Cleveland, the Man and the Statesman*, 1:282.

91. Ibid., 1:290.

92. Tugwell, *Grover Cleveland*, 165.

93. "No White House Scandal," *Chicago Tribune*, December 7, 1888; Lachman, *A Secret Life*, 364.

94. "The Stories about the President," *New York Times*, June 11, 1888, https:// timesmachine.nytimes.com/timesmachine/1888/06/11/106325038.html ?pageNumber=4.

95. Note written on letter of Frances F. Cleveland to Mrs. Maggie Nicodemus, June 3, 1888, Grover Cleveland Papers, in *The Campaign Text Book of the Democratic Party of the United States for the Presidential Election of 1888* (New York: Brentanos, 1888), 157–58.

96. Letter from Cleveland to Wilson Bissell, June 17, 1888, Grover Cleveland Papers, in Nevins, *Letters of Grover Cleveland*, 402–3.

97. Paul F. Boller Jr., *Presidential Anecdotes* (New York: Oxford University Press, 1996), 183.

98. McElroy, *Grover Cleveland, the Man and the Statesman*, 1:297–98; Nevins, *Letters of Grover Cleveland*, 439; Lachman, *A Secret Life*, 366; Pafford, *Cleveland: The Forgotten Conservative*, 67–68; Paul F. Boller, Jr., *Presidential Campaigns* (New York: Oxford University Press, 1996) 158; Nevins, *Letters of Grover Cleveland*, 427; *The Campaign Text Book of the Democratic Party of the United States*, 158–59; Algeo, *The President Is a Sick Man*, 49.

99. Troy Senik, "Can Trump Follow in Cleveland's Footsteps?," *Wall Street Journal*, September 15, 2022, https://www.wsj.com/articles/can-trump-fol low-clevelands-footsteps-re-election-presidency-1892-2024-national ism-populism-classical-liberalism-democrat-fraud-11663263947.

100. R. J. Markel, *Grover Cleveland* (Minneapolis: Twenty-First Century Books, 2006), 76; Lachman, *A Secret Life*, 366–67.

101. McElroy, *Grover Cleveland, the Man and the Statesman*, 1:299.

102. "December 3, 1888: Fourth Annual Message," Miller Center, University of Virginia, https://millercenter.org/the-presidency/presidential-speeches /december-3-1888-fourth-annual-message.

103. William Seale, *The President's House: A History*, 2 vols. (Baltimore: Johns Hopkins University Press, 2008), 1:549.

104. "Inauguration Weather," National Weather Service, https://www.weather .gov/lwx/events_Inauguration.

105. Seale, *The President's House*, 1:549.

106. Ibid., photo.

107. Nevins, *Letters of Grover Cleveland*, 448; Algeo, *The President Is a Sick Man*, 49; Tugwell, *Grover Cleveland*, 197; Lachman, *A Secret Life*, 368.

108. Grover Cleveland, *Addresses, State Papers and Letters*, ed. Albert Ellery Bergh (New York: Sun Dial Classics, 1908), 324.

109. Graff, *Grover Cleveland*, 99.

110. Lachman, *A Secret Life*, 310.

111. Grover Cleveland Papers, Series V: Speeches, 1883–1907, October 28, 1886.

112. "May 11, 1886: Message on the Statue of Liberty," Miller Center, University of Virginia, https://millercenter.org/the-presidency/presidential-speeches/may-11-1886-message-statue-liberty.

113. McElory, 1:306.

114. *Pittsburgh Post Gazette*, June 13, 1907.

115. Nevins, *Letters of Grover Cleveland*, 449; McElroy, *Grover Cleveland, the Man and the Statesman*, 1:309; Pafford, *Cleveland: The Forgotten Conservative*, 70–71.

116. Grover Cleveland, *Fishing and Shooting Sketches* (Outlook Verlag, 2018), 74; McElory, 308.

117. Tugwell, *Grover Cleveland*, 172, 174–75; Senik, "Can Trump Follow in Cleveland's Footsteps?," 196; Nevins, *Letters of Grover Cleveland*, 443, 450; Pafford, *Cleveland: The Forgotten Conservative*, 70.

118. "Plan of the Clevelands," *Chicago Tribune*, December 1, 1889.

119. McElroy, *Grover Cleveland, the Man and the Statesman*, 1:308.

120. Pafford, *Cleveland: The Forgotten Conservative*, 70–71.

121. "Grover Cleveland Letter to Frances F. Cleveland, 18 June 1889, 20 June 1889," Grover Cleveland Papers, in Tugwell, *Grover Cleveland*, 175.

122. The Curtiss Candy Company would later claim that "Baby Ruth" candy bars were named after the child. This retroactive decision might seem odd given that she died in 1904 and the candy made its debut in 1921, but it proved an effective way to sue Babe Ruth for copyright infringement. Christopher Klein, "Babe Ruth or Baby Ruth: Who Was the Candy Bar Named After?," History, June 1, 2023, https://www.history.com/news/babe-ruth-v-baby-ruth.

123. "Letter from Grover Cleveland to George S. Hornblower, New York, October 6, 1891," in Nevins, *Letters of Grover Cleveland*, 268.

124. "Letter from Grover Cleveland to Wilson S. Bissell, New York, October 21, 1891," in Nevins, *Letters of Grover Cleveland*, 269; see also Nevins, 450.

125. *Public Opinion* VIII, no. 11 (United States: Public Opinion, 1890), December 21, 1889

126. The *Nation*, quoted in John Spencer Bassett et al., eds., *South Atlantic Quarterly* 8. Durham, NC, 1909.

127. See *Harper's Weekly*, December 21, 1889, in Nevins, *Letters of Grover Cleveland*, 461.

128. Pafford, *Cleveland: The Forgotten Conservative*, 72; Nevins, *Letters of Grover Cleveland*, 466.

129. Algeo, *The President Is a Sick Man*, 53.

130. "Tariff of 1890 (McKinley Tariff)," Federal Reserve Bank of St. Louis, https://fraser.stlouisfed.org/title/tariff-1890-mckinley-tariff-5869.

131. Nevins, *Letters of Grover Cleveland*, 463.

132. See stories in the *N.Y. Commercial Advertiser* and *Boston Post*, January and February 1891, in Nevins, *Letters of Grover Cleveland*, 467; McElroy, 1:319.

133. "Silver Letter" (Grover Cleveland to E. Ellery Anderson, New York, February 10, 1891), in Nevins, *Letters of Grover Cleveland*, 246; For a more detailed description, see Nevins, *Letters of Grover Cleveland*, 466–68; McElory, 1:320; Algeo, *The President Is a Sick Man*, 50–51.

134. McElroy, *Grover Cleveland, the Man and the Statesman*, 1:320; Algeo, *The President Is a Sick Man*, 50–51.

135. Sorrento, Maine, July 27, 1891, Grover Cleveland Papers, in Nevins, *Letters of Grover Cleveland*, 468; Algeo, *The President Is a Sick Man*, 50–51.

136. McElroy, *Grover Cleveland, the Man and the Statesman*, 1:322–23.

137. *New York Times*, October 9, 1981, https://timesmachine.nytimes.com/times machine/1891/10/09/issue.html.

138. McElroy, *Grover Cleveland, the Man and the Statesman*, 1:311–13.

139. "Grover Cleveland Letter to Shan Bissell, November 8, 1890," Grover Cleveland Papers; McElroy, 1:335.

140. Nevins, *Letters of Grover Cleveland*, 491; McElroy, *Grover Cleveland, the Man and the Statesman*, 1:356; *The Campaign Text Book of the Democratic Party of the United States*, 165.

141. Edward B. Dickinson, "Official Proceedings of the National Democratic Convention," Internet Archive, June 1892, https://archive.org/details/official proceedi00demoiala.

142. McElroy, *Grover Cleveland, the Man and the Statesman*, 1:352.

143. Ibid., 1:353.

144. Ibid., 1:353.

145. Ibid, 1:354; Nevins, *Letters of Grover Cleveland*, 497; Pafford, *Cleveland: The Forgotten Conservative*, 78–79.

146. "Mrs. Mary Lord Dimmick," *Los Angeles Herald*, April 7, 1896, https://cdnc .ucr.edu/?a=d&d=LAH18960407.2.3&e=-------en--20--1--txt-txIN-------; *The Campaign Text Book of the Democratic Party of the United States*, 162;

Pafford, *Cleveland: The Forgotten Conservative*, 83; Algeo, *The President Is a Sick Man*, 52; Nevins, *Letters of Grover Cleveland*, 504.

147. McElroy, *Grover Cleveland, the Man and the Statesman*, 1:357; Nevins, *Letters of Grover Cleveland*, 507; Algeo, *The President Is a Sick Man*, 52; "Presidential Election of 1892: A Resource Guide," Library of Congress, https://www.loc.gov/rr/program/bib/elections/election1892.html.

148. William Howard Taft, *Presidential Addresses and State Papers of William Howard Taft, from March 4, 1909, to March 4, 1910* (New York: Doubleday, 1910), 73.

149. McElroy, *Grover Cleveland, the Man and the Statesman*, 2:47.

150. McElroy, *Grover Cleveland, the Man and the Statesman*, 2:49–50; Nevins, *Letters of Grover Cleveland*, 551.

151. Pafford, *Cleveland: The Forgotten Conservative*, 111.

152. "Hawaii under Our Flag," *New York Times*, February 10, 1893, https://timesmachine.nytimes.com/timesmachine/1893/02/10/106813421.pdf?pdf_redirect=true&ip=0.

153. "February 15, 1893: Message Regarding Hawaiian Annexation," Miller Center, University of Virginia, https://millercenter.org/the-presidency/presidential-speeches/february-15-1893-message-regarding-hawaiian-annexation; Nevins, *Letters of Grover Cleveland*, 551–52; Tugwell, *Grover Cleveland*, 244–45; McElory, 2:52.

154. Algeo, *The President Is a Sick Man*, 12; Nevins, *Letters of Grover Cleveland*, 523.

155. Pafford, *Cleveland: The Forgotten Conservative*, 89.

156. "When New York Saw a Presidential Wedding: John Tyler's Romance with Miss Julia Gardiner Culminated in Their Marriage at the Church of the Ascension in This City Seventy-One Years Ago," *New York Times*, October 17, 1915; "Inauguration Weather," National Weather Service, https://www.weather.gov/lwx/events_Inauguration; Algeo, *The President Is a Sick Man*, 8; Nevins, *Letters of Grover Cleveland*, 515.

157. McElroy, *Grover Cleveland, the Man and the Statesman*, 2:1–2.

158. "Cabinet Officers' Wives," *New York Times*, February 26, 1893.

159. McElroy, *Grover Cleveland, the Man and the Statesman*, 2:7.

160. Dunlap, *Frank*, 81; Algeo, *The President Is a Sick Man*, 9–10; "Washington, DC, 1893—Crowd in Front of Capitol—Cleveland's 2nd Inauguration," Library of Congress, https://www.loc.gov/resource/ppmsc.02915/.

161. Seale, *The President's House*, 1:577.

162. Graff, *Grover Cleveland*, 179.

163. Irwin (Ike) Hoover, "Mrs. Cleveland Weeps," *Saturday Evening Post*,

March 10, 1934; For full history see I. H. Hoover, *Forty-Two Years in the White House* (Boston: Houghton Mifflin, 1934).

164. Algeo, *The President Is a Sick Man*, 13.

165. "Woodley Mansion," DC Historic Sites, https://historicsites.dcpreservation .org/items/show/46.

166. Betty C. Monkman, *The White House: Its Historic Furnishings and First Families* (New York: Abbeville Press, 2000), 169–70.

167. Grover Cleveland, *Presidential Problems* (New York: Centuary Co., 1904), 38.

168. "Cleveland: Special Message, March 9, 1893," American Presidency Project, https://www.presidency.ucsb.edu/node/206153; see also McElroy, 2:53.

169. McElory, 2:55; Tennant S. McWilliams, "James H. Blount, the South, and Hawaiian Annexation," *Pacific Historical Review* 57, no. 1 (February 1988): 25–46.

170. Lawrence W. Reed, *A Lesson from the Past: The Silver Panic of 1893* (New York: Foundation for Economic Education, 1993), 57–59, in Pafford, *Cleveland: The Forgotten Conservative*, 92.

171. Tugwell, *Grover Cleveland*, 193.

172. Algeo, *The President Is a Sick Man*, 5–6.

173. Tugwell, *Grover Cleveland*, 255–56; McElroy, 2:75; Nevins, *Letters of Grover Cleveland*, 524–25.

174. *Harper's Weekly*, July 29, 1893, in Nevins, *Letters of Grover Cleveland*, 527; Algeo, *The President Is a Sick Man*, 13.

175. Kenneth R. Crispell and Carlos Gomez, *Hidden Illness in the White House* (Durham, NC: Duke University Press, 1988), 204.

176. Algeo, *The President Is a Sick Man*, 15–16; Pafford, *Cleveland: The Forgotten Conservative*, 90–91.

177. "President Cleveland Had a Deadly Secret," Columbia Surgery, https:// columbiasurgery.org/news/2015/12/10/president-grover-cleveland-had -deadly-secret; Lachman, *A Secret Life*, 406.

178. Algeo, *The President Is a Sick Man*, 17; Pafford, *Cleveland: The Forgotten Conservative*, 90–91.

179. Algeo, *The President Is a Sick Man*, 16–17, 53; McElroy, 2:27; Nevins, *Letters of Grover Cleveland*, 529. Just three years earlier, he had authored a paper on the removal of oral tumors and reported a mortality rate of 14 percent.

180. Lachman, *A Secret Life*, 406.

181. McElroy, 2:27; Nevins, *Letters of Grover Cleveland*, 529; Algeo, *The President Is a Sick Man*, 42.

182. "The President's Vacation," *New York Times*, June 20, 1893.

183. "Gen. Arthur in Washington," *New York Times*, July 4, 1881; Lachman, *A Secret Life*, 407.

184. Wilbur Cross and John Moses, "My God, Sir, I Think the President Is Doomed," *American History Illustrated* 17 (November 1982): 41; Lachman, *A Secret Life*, 406–7.

185. Nevins, *Letters of Grover Cleveland*, 528.

186. Algeo, *The President Is a Sick Man*, 54.

187. Letters in the possession of Miss Lamont, June 20, 1893. Miss Lamont's Letters in Nevins, *Letters of Grover Cleveland*, 529. See also Algeo, *The President Is a Sick Man*, 54.

188. Senik, "Can Trump Follow in Cleveland's Footsteps?," 252; see also Algeo, *The President Is a Sick Man*, 55.

189. Algeo, *The President Is a Sick Man*, 79; Lachman, *A Secret Life*, 409.

190. Conversation between Dr. Erdmann and Allan Nevins, November 14, 16, 1931, in Nevins, *Letters of Grover Cleveland*, 530; Algeo, *The President Is a Sick Man*, 95.

191. Pafford, *Cleveland: The Forgotten Conservative*, 91; McElroy, 2:28; Algeo, *The President Is a Sick Man*, 84, 88.

192. McElroy, 2:28; Lachman, *A Secret Life*, 408; Algeo, *The President Is a Sick Man*, 86.

193. Algeo, *The President Is a Sick Man*, 86.

194. "A Yacht, a Mustache: How a President Hid His Tumor," NPR, July 6, 2011, https://www.npr.org/2011/07/06/137621988/a-yacht-a-mustache-how-a-president-hid-his-tumor; Tugwell, *Grover Cleveland*, 209; McElroy, 2:28–29; Algeo, *The President Is a Sick Man*, 91–93.

195. Dr. Erdmann to Allan Nevins, November 14, 16, 1931, in Nevins, *Letters of Grover Cleveland*, 531; Lachman, *A Secret Life*, 411.

196. Nevins, *Letters of Grover Cleveland*, 532.

197. Nevins, *Letters of Grover Cleveland*, 531–52; Lachman, *A Secret Life*, 412. Lachman writes of a second procedure focused on getting a part of the cancer the doctors missed.

198. Margaret Murray et al., "Maxillary Prosthetics, Speech Impairment, and Presidential Politics: How Grover Cleveland Was Able to Speak Normally after His 'Secret' Operation," *Surgery Journal* 6, no. 1 (January 2020): e1–e6, https://www.ncbi.nlm.nih.gov/pmc/articles/PMC6887570/; McElroy, 2:29.

199. Olney Papers in McElroy, 2:31; Nevins, *Letters of Grover Cleveland*, 532; Lachman, *A Secret Life*, 413; Tugwell, *Grover Cleveland*, 210.

200. "Thinking of Fishing," *Boston Daily Globe*, July 8, 1893.

201. Dr. W. W. Keen, M.D. L.L.D., "The Surgical Operations on President Cleveland in 1893," *Saturday Evening Post*, September 22, 1917.

202. Pafford, *Cleveland: The Forgotten Conservative*, 91.

203. "Movement of the Price of Silver," Federal Reserve Bulletin, November 1917, https://fraser.stlouisfed.org/files/docs/publications/FRB/pages/1915 -1919/24568_1915-1919.pdf; *Washington Post*, August 23, 1893, in Nevins, *Letters of Grover Cleveland*, 536; Tugwell, *Grover Cleveland*, 200.

204. Robert F. Hoxie, "The Silver Debate of 1890," *Journal of Political Economy* 1, no. 4 (September 1893): 535–87.

205. "August 8, 1893: Special Session Message," Miller Center, University of Virginia, https://millercenter.org/the-presidency/presidential-speeches/august -8-1893-special-session-message; McElroy, 2:32.

206. "Speech of Hon. David B. Hill of New York, in the Senate of the United States, Friday, August 25, 1803," https://fraser.stlouisfed.org/files/docs/pub lications/mq53c/mq53c_v1sen_0034.pdf.

207. McElroy, 2:33; Nevins, *Letters of Grover Cleveland*, 538.

208. "Baby Esther Cleveland's Name Announced," Newspapers.com, https://www .newspapers.com/clip/2437059/baby-esther-clevelands-name-announced/; Nevins, *Letters of Grover Cleveland*, 522; Tugwell, *Grover Cleveland*, 198.

209. Nevins, *Letters of Grover Cleveland*, 538, 545–46.

210. Richard H. Timberlake Jr., "Repeal of Silver Monetization in the Late Nine- teenth Century," *Journal of Money, Credit and Banking* 10, no. 1 (February 1978): 27–45; Pafford, *Cleveland: The Forgotten Conservative*, 94 puts the count at 239–108 in the house and 48–37 in the Senate. See also Jeannette Paddock Nichols, "The Politics and Personalities of Silver Repeal in the United States Senate," *American Historical Review* 41, no. 1 (October 1935): 26–53.

211. Senik, "Can Trump Follow in Cleveland's Footsteps?," 286–87; McElroy, 2:43, 2:78–79; Pafford, *Cleveland: The Forgotten Conservative*, 94; Nev- ins, *Letters of Grover Cleveland*, 546; Gary Richardson and Tim Sablik, "Banking Panics of the Gilded Age, 1863–1913," Federal Reserve History, December 4, 2015, https://www.federalreservehistory.org/essays/banking -panics-of-the-gilded-age.

212. "Profits of the Seigniorage: The Coinage of Silver Dollars Not Yet Begun," *New York Times*, November 15, 1893, https://timesmachine.nytimes.com /timesmachine/1893/11/15/109269757.pdf?pdf_redirect=true&ip=0; Nev- ins, *Letters of Grover Cleveland*, 600; Tugwell, *Grover Cleveland*, 229.

213. McElroy, 2:80; Nevins, *Letters of Grover Cleveland*, 601; Tugwell, *Grover Cleveland*, 229.

214. Nevins, *Letters of Grover Cleveland*, 563.

215. Tugwell, *Grover Cleveland*, 214; Nevins, *Letters of Grover Cleveland*, 563.

216. Edward L. Ayers, *The Promise of the New South: Life After Reconstruction*, 15th ed. (New York: Oxford University Press, 2007), 295.

217. "Tariff of 1894 (Wilson-Gorman Tariff)," Federal Reserve Bank of St. Louis, https://fraser.stlouisfed.org/title/tariff-1894-wilson-gorman-tariff-5901/full text; Nevins, *Letters of Grover Cleveland*, 568.

218. *Congressional Record* 26, pt. 8 (July 19, 1894): 7713, in Nevins, *Letters of Grover Cleveland*, 581; *Indianapolis Journal*, Indianapolis, Marion County, August 17, 1894; Tugwell, *Grover Cleveland*, 220.

219. "A Remarkable Congress: The Longest Session but Two in the Nation's History," *New York Times*, August 19, 1894, https://timesmachine.nytimes .com/timesmachine/1894/08/19/106913988.pdf?pdf_redirect=true&ip=0.

220. Tugwell, *Grover Cleveland*, 251.

221. Philip Taft, "Chapter 4: Workers of a New Century," U.S. Department of Labor, https://www.dol.gov/general/aboutdol/history/chapter4.

222. "Strikes in the United States: 1880–1936," United States Department of Labor, 1938, https://fraser.stlouisfed.org/files/docs/publications/bls/bls_06 51_1938.pdf., 29.

223. Tugwell, *Grover Cleveland*, 230–32.

224. Nevins, *Letters of Grover Cleveland*, 611; Pafford, *Cleveland: The Forgotten Conservative*, 99; McElroy, 2:144.

225. Jack Kelly, *The Edge of Anarchy: The Railroad Barons, the Gilded Age, and the Greatest Labor Uprising in America* (New York: St. Martin's, 2019), 101; Graff, *Grover Cleveland*, 187; Nevins, *Letters of Grover Cleveland*, 612; Tugwell, *Grover Cleveland*, 236.

226. Tugwell, *Grover Cleveland*, 231; Nevins, *Letters of Grover Cleveland*, 612.

227. Nevins, *Letters of Grover Cleveland*, 613–14; McElroy, 2:146; Senik, "Can Trump Follow in Cleveland's Footsteps?," 239.

228. Nevins, *Letters of Grover Cleveland*, 611; McElroy, 2:166.

229. *Harper's Weekly* editorial, July 14, 1894.

230. Re Debs, 158 U.S. 594 (1895), U.S. Supreme Court, https://www.law.cor nell.edu/supremecourt/text/158/564.

231. Nevins, *Letters of Grover Cleveland*, 618, 628.

232. McElroy, 2:165–66.

233. Nevins, *Letters of Grover Cleveland*, 628; Tugwell, *Grover Cleveland*, 238–39. The quote may not be precise and historians have had a difficult time attributing it to a specific speech or document, but the spirit of what he allegedly said is largely accepted as fact.

234. Nevins, *Letters of Grover Cleveland*, 611; McElroy, 2:166.

235. Nevins, *Letters of Grover Cleveland*, 622–23.

236. "July 8, 1894: Proclamation Regarding Railroad Strike," Miller Center, University of Virginia, https://millercenter.org/the-presidency/presidential -speeches/july-8-1894-proclamation-regarding-railroad-strike.

237. Cleveland, *Presidential Problems*, 108; McElroy, 2:166.

238. "Historical Highlights: The Historic 54th Congress, December 2, 1895," History, Art & Archives, U.S. House of Representatives, https://history.house.gov/Historical-Highlights/1851-1900/The-historic-54th-Congress/.

239. Tugwell, *Grover Cleveland*, 251–53.

240. Colin Dueck, "Henry Cabot Lodge, Hawaii, and the Shift from Continental to Hemispheric Defense," *Orbis* 66, no. 3 (July 2022): 320–33.

241. Warren Zimmerman, *First Great Triumph: How Five Americans Made Their Country a World Power* (New York: Farrar, Straus and Giroux, 2004), 11.

242. For analysis of Turner's theory, see Tiziano Bonazzi, "Frederick Jackson Turner's Frontier Thesis and the Self-Consciousness of America," *Journal of American Studies* 27, no. 2 (August 1993): 149–71.

243. "Increasing Urbanization," U.S. Census Bureau, https://www.census.gov/dataviz/visualizations/005/.

244. Bob Buyer, "Grover Cleveland Tried to Save Hawaii's Queen from U.S. Imperialists," *Buffalo News*, July 22, 2020, https://buffalonews.com/news/grover-cleveland-tried-to-save-hawaiis-queen-from-u-s-imperialists/article_186a6ff0-5110-520e-90fc-0cba904ac856.html.

245. "December 8, 1885: First Annual Message," Miller Center, University of Virginia, https://millercenter.org/the-presidency/presidential-speeches/december-8-1885-first-annual-message.

246. *Sonoma Democrat* XXXVII, no. 9, December 9, 1893.

247. Nevins, *Letters of Grover Cleveland*, 554.

248. McElroy, 2:60–61.

249. "Letter from Mr. Willis to Mr. Gresham, November 16, 1893," Office of the Historian, U.S. State Department, https://history.state.gov/historicaldocuments/frus1894app2/d459.

250. *New York Times*, December 8, 1893, in Nevins, *Letters of Grover Cleveland*, 559.

251. *Congressional Record: Containing the Proceedings and Debates of the . . . Congress* (Washington, DC: U.S. Government Printing Office, 1895), 1207.

252. "December 18, 1893: Message Regarding Hawaii Annexation," Miller Center, University of Virginia, https://millercenter.org/the-presidency/presidential-speeches/december-18-1893-message-regarding-hawaiian-annexation.

253. Ryan S. Walters, *The Last Jeffersonian: Grover Cleveland and the Path to Restoring the Republic* (Bloomington, IN: Westbow Press, 2012), 113; Nevins, *Letters of Grover Cleveland*, 562.

254. McElroy, 2:72–73.

255. Nevins, *Letters of Grover Cleveland*, 630; Tugwell, *Grover Cleveland*, 246.

256. Nevins, *Letters of Grover Cleveland*, 631.

257. Kori Schake, *Safe Passage: The Transition from British to American Hegemony* (Cambridge, MA: Harvard University Press, 2017), 149.

258. *Papers Relating to the Foreign Relations of the United States* (Washington, DC: U.S. Government Printing Office, 1895), 817.

259. McElroy, 2:182–83; Pafford, *Cleveland: The Forgotten Conservative*, 114; Nevins, *Letters of Grover Cleveland*, 639, 641; Tugwell, *Grover Cleveland*, 246.

260. "Letter from Lord Salisbury to Sir Julian Pauncefote, November 26, 1895," Office of the Historian, U.S. State Department, https://history.state.gov /historicaldocuments/frus1895p1/d529.

261. Nevins, *Letters of Grover Cleveland*, 647–48.

262. Olney, Richard, and Julian Pauncefote, "Text of the Arbitration Treaty between the United States and Great Britain," *Advocate of Peace (1894–1920)* 59, no. 2 (1897): 37–39; "December 7, 1896: Fourth Annual Message (Second Term)," Miller Center, University of Virginia, https://millercenter .org/the-presidency/presidential-speeches/december-7-1896-fourth-annual -message-second-term; McElroy, 2:201; Tugwell, *Grover Cleveland*, 249; Pafford, *Cleveland: The Forgotten Conservative*, 127–28.

263. Schake, *Safe Passage*, 149.

264. Tugwell, *Grover Cleveland*, 266.

265. "*Bisbee Daily Review* (Ariz.), December 21, 1901," Chronicling America: Historic American Newspapers, Library of Congress, http://chronicling america.loc.gov/lccn/sn84024827/1901-12-21/ed-1/seq-3/.

266. See Nevins, *Letters of Grover Cleveland*, 696–98.

267. *Republican Journal*, Digital Maine, October 22, 1896, https://digitalmaine .com/cgi/viewcontent.cgi?article=1042&context=rj_1896.

268. "Bryan's Bid for First Place," *New York Times*, July 10, 1896, https://www .nytimes.com/1896/07/10/archives/bryans-bid-for-first-place-the-silver -men-swept-away-by-a-flood-of.html.

269. Nevins, *Letters of Grover Cleveland*, 702.

270. "Words That Thrilled," *Atlanta Constitution*, July 11, 1896; *Official Proceedings of the DNC*, 234.

271. Robert Cherny, "'Cross of Gold'—William Jennings Bryan (1921)," National Registry, 2003, https://www.loc.gov/static/programs/national-recording-pres ervation-board/documents/WilliamJenningsBryan.pdf.

272. "1896 Democratic Party Platform, July 7, 1896," American Presidency Project, UC Santa Barbara, https://www.presidency.ucsb.edu/documents /1896-democratic-party-platform.

273. McElroy, 2:225–26.

274. McElroy, 2:224–25; *Campaign Text Book of the National Democratic Party*

1896, 2nd ed. (Chicago: National Democratic Committee, 1896); Tugwell, *Grover Cleveland*, 274.

275. Karl Rove, *The Triumph of William McKinley: Why the Election of 1896 Still Matters* (New York: Simon & Schuster, 2015), 364.

276. James Creelman, "Bryan Silent under Defeat," *World* (New York), November 4, 1896; "Refuses to Talk or Be Seen," *Chicago Tribune*, November 4, 1896.

277. Williams R. Hal, *Realigning America: McKinley, Bryan and the Remarkable Election of 1896* (Lawrence: University Press of Kansas, 2010), 154; McElroy, 2:237.

278. McElroy, 2:237; Tugwell, *Grover Cleveland*, 276.

279. William L. Silber, *The Story of Silver: How the White Metal Shapes America and the Modern World* (Princeton, NJ: Princeton University Press, 2019), 25–26.

280. McElroy, 2:253.

281. Louis A. Pérez, *Cuba between Reform and Revolution* (New York: Oxford University Press, 1988), 164–65.

282. John L. Offner, *An Unwanted War: The Diplomacy of the United States and Spain over Cuba, 1895–1989* (Chapel Hill: University of North Carolina Press, 1992), 46–47, 80–81, 112.

283. McElroy, 2:245.

284. Eric Foner, *The Spanish-Cuban-American War and the Birth of American Imperialism* (New York: Monthly Review Press, 1972), 1:181fn.

285. David Winter, "Why Achievement Motivation Predicts Success in Business but Failure in Politics: The Importance of Personal Control," *Special Issue: Personality and Politics* 78, no. 6 (December 2010): 1637–68.

286. "June 12, 1895: Declaration of US Neutrality," Miller Center, University of Virginia, https://millercenter.org/the-presidency/presidential-speeches /june-12-1895-declaration-us-neutrality.

287. McElroy, 2:249–50; Nevins, *Letters of Grover Cleveland*, 719.

288. Robert Kagan, *Dangerous Nation: America's Place in the World, from Its Earliest Days to the Dawn of the Twentieth Century* (New York: Knopf, 2006), 381, 395; Offner, An Unwanted War, 41, 54–55.

289. Graff, *Grover Cleveland*, 207; Nevins, *Letters of Grover Cleveland*, 727; McElroy, 2:254; "Republican Party Platform of 1896, June 18, 1896," American Presidency Project, UC Santa Barbara, https://www.presidency .ucsb.edu/documents/republican-party-platform-1896.

290. Nevins, *Letters of Grover Cleveland*, 727–28; McElroy, 2:254–55; Tugwell, *Grover Cleveland*, 284–86.

291. "The First Inaugural Address of William McKinley, March 4, 1897," Avalon

Project, Yale Law School, https://avalon.law.yale.edu/19th_century/mckin
1.asp.

292. Lachman, *A Secret Life*, 415.

293. Carl Russell Fish, *Civil Service and the Patronage* (New York: Longmans, Green & Co, 1904), 225, in Nevins, *Letters of Grover Cleveland*, 519.

294. "Inauguration Day, 1897—a Good Beginning/Dalrymple," Library of Congress, https://www.loc.gov/resource/ppmsca.28784/.

295. McElroy, 2:377.

296. Graff, *Grover Cleveland*, 208; "Grover Cleveland Home: Westland, New Jersey," National Parks Service, https://www.nps.gov/nr/travel/presidents/grover_cleveland_home.html.

297. "When Did the College of New Jersey Change to Princeton University?," Princeton University Archives blog, https://blogs.princeton.edu/mudd/2015/07/when-did-the-college-of-new-jersey-change-to-princeton-university/; McElroy, 2:234.

298. McElroy, 2:236.

299. Tugwell, *Grover Cleveland*, 287; Pafford, *Cleveland: The Forgotten Conservative*, 131–32; Nevins, *Letters of Grover Cleveland*, 730, 739; McElroy, 2:236, 2:256, 2:260.

300. Henry F. Graff, "Grover Cleveland: Life after the Presidency," Miller Center, University of Virginia, https://millercenter.org/president/cleveland/life-after-the-presidency.

301. "Too Much Reform Insurance Men Say," *New York Times*, December 7, 1907, https://timesmachine.nytimes.com/timesmachine/1907/12/07/106770147.html?pageNumber=6.

302. Pafford, *Cleveland: The Forgotten Conservative*, 144. The other two men were George Westinghouse and New York Appeals Court judge Morgan O'Brien.

303. "Too Much Reform Insurance Men Say"; Nevins, *Letters of Grover Cleveland*, 758; McElroy, 2:360–62.

304. Michael B. Costanzo, *Author in Chief: The Presidents as Writers from Washington to Trump* (Jefferson, NC: McFarland, 2019), 68–69.

305. McElroy, 2:258–59.

306. Nevins, *Letters of Grover Cleveland*, 737.

307. Grover Cleveland, "Would Woman Suffrage Be Unwise?," in *Up From the Pedestal*, ed. Aileen Kraditor (Chicago: Quadrangle Books, 1970), 200.

308. McElroy, 2:269; Pafford, *Cleveland: The Forgotten Conservative*, 132; Nevins, *Letters of Grover Cleveland*, 730; Tugwell, *Grover Cleveland*, 286; "Cleveland Speaks Out on Third Term," *New York Times*, June 19, 1903, https://timesmachine.nytimes.com/timesmachine/1903/06/19/102008730.pdf?pdf_redirecte=true&ip=0.

309. McElroy, 2:268.
310. R. J. Davis, *The Boys' Life of Grover Cleveland* (New York: Harper & Brothers, 1925), 369.
311. "Richard Folsom Cleveland," *New York Times*, November 11, 1897, https://timesmachine.nytimes.com/timesmachine/1897/11/11/100432177.html.
312. Whittaker Chambers, *Witness* (New York: Random House, 1952), 728–30.
313. Pafford, *Cleveland: The Forgotten Conservative*, 134; Nevins, *Letters of Grover Cleveland*, 732; McElroy, 2:270; Tugwell, *Grover Cleveland*, 289.
314. Joseph Frazier Wall, *Andrew Carnegie* (Oxford, UK: Oxford University Press, 1970), 897.
315. David Pietrusza, *1920: The Year of Six Presidents* (New York: Basic Books, 2008), 11.
316. Woodrow Wilson, "Mr. Cleveland as President," *Atlantic*, March 1897, https://www.theatlantic.com/magazine/archive/1897/03/mr-cleveland-as-president/519858/.
317. Pafford, *Cleveland: The Forgotten Conservative*, 134.
318. Arthur Stanley Link, *Woodrow Wilson and the Progressive Era, 1910–1917* (New York: Harper, 1972), 8–9.
319. Pietrusza, *1920: The Year of Six Presidents*, 12.
320. William Bayard Hale, *Woodrow Wilson: The Story of His Life* (Cambridge, MA: Harvard University Press, 1912), 153.
321. Lucian Lamar Knight, *Woodrow Wilson, the Dreamer and the Dream* (Atlanta, GA: Johnson-Dallis, 1924), 57.
322. George F. Will, "Not a State-Broken People," CATO Institute, July/August 2010, https://www.cato.org/policy-report/july/august-2010/not-state-broken-people.
323. McElroy, 2:328; Tugwell, *Grover Cleveland*, 287.
324. McElroy, 2:328.
325. James Kerney, *The Political Education of Woodrow Wilson* (New York: Century Co., 1926), 7.
326. McElroy, 2:381.
327. Graff, *Grover Cleveland*, 134.
328. McElroy, 2:344.
329. Ibid., 2:293.
330. Ibid., 2:315.
331. "Cleveland Speaks Out on Third Term."
332. "Cleveland Letter to Hamlin," in Nevins, *Letters of Grover Cleveland*, 757; Pafford, *Cleveland: The Forgotten Conservative*, 143.
333. "A Landslide for Roosevelt!," *Weekly Arizona Journal-Miner*, November 9, 1904, https://chroniclingamerica.loc.gov/lccn/sn85032920/1904-11-09/ed-1/seq-1/.

334. McElroy, 2:318–20.

335. *Century Illustrated Monthly Magazine* 78, 850.

336. McElroy, 2:313.

337. Ibid., 2:383.

338. Ibid., 2:384–85; Pafford, *Cleveland: The Forgotten Conservative,* 148; Tugwell, *Grover Cleveland,* 290.

339. Cleveland, *Addresses, State Papers and Letters,* 461, in Pafford, *Cleveland: The Forgotten Conservative,* 148–49.

340. *Mariposa Gazette* LIV, no. 7, July 11, 1908, California Digital Newspaper Collection, https://cdnc.ucr.edu/?a=d&d=MG19080711.2.32&e=-------en --20--1--txt-txIN--------1.

341. "1908 Presidential Election," 270 to Win, https://www.270towin.com /1908_Election/.

342. "President William Howard Taft Praises President Cleveland to Mrs. Cleveland," Shapell Manuscript Foundation, March 23, 1909, https://www.sha pell.org/manuscript/w-htaft-eulogizes-grover-cleveland/.

CHAPTER 4: A DREAM DEFERRED

1. "Mr. Taft's Idea of Heaven," *Saturday Evening Post,* Vol. 184, Issue 26, October 28, 1911.

2. Alpheus Thomas Mason, "Taft, William Howard (1857–1930)," *Encyclopedia of the American Constitution,* 2633–37, https://law-journals-books.vlex .com/vid/taft-william-howard-51715611.

3. David Henry Burton, *William Howard Taft: Confident Peacemaker* (Philadelphia: St. Joseph's University Press, 2004), 17; Henry Fowles Pringle, *William Howard Taft: The Life and Times,* 2 vols. (Newtown, CT: American Political Biography Press, 1998), 1:107–9; William Severn, *William Howard Taft, the President Who Became Chief Justice* (Philadelphia: McKay, 1970), 47; Jonathan Lurie, *William Howard Taft: The Travails of a Progressive Conservative* (New York: Cambridge University Press, 2011), 38.

4. Pringle, *William Howard Taft,* 1:159; Severn, *William Howard Taft,* 48; Lurie, *William Howard Taft,* 38.

5. *Addresses* XXXI, 70, in Pringle, *William Howard Taft,* 1:160; Severn, *William Howard Taft,* 48–49.

6. Taft to H. W. and Horace D. Taft, January 28, 1900, in Pringle, *William Howard Taft,* 1:161.

7. Franklin Matthews, "The President's Last Days," *Harper's Weekly* 45, no. 2335 (September 21, 1901): 943, in Scott Miller, *The President and*

the Assassin (New York: Random House, 2011), 319–20; Severn, *William Howard Taft*, 47.

8. Paul T. Heffron, "Theodore Roosevelt and the Appointment of Mr. Justice Moody," *Vanderbilt Law Review* 18, no. 2 (March 1965): 545–68, https://scholarship.law.vanderbilt.edu/cgi/viewcontent.cgi?article=3654&context=vlr;%20see%20also%20Pringle%201:237-247.%20https://constitutioncenter.org/blog/william-howard-tafts-truly-historic-double-double; Pringle, *William Howard Taft*, 1:237–47.

9. "William Howard Taft's Truly Historic 'Double-Double,'" National Constitution Center, June 30, 2023, https://constitutioncenter.org/blog/william-howard-tafts-truly-historic-double-double#:~:text=%E2%80%9CHe%20made%20six%20appointments%20in,Lamar%2C%20Van%20Devanter%20and%20Pitney.

10. Daniel S. McHargue, "President Taft's Appointments to the Supreme Court," *Journal of Politics* 12, no. 3 (August, 1950): 478–510, https://www.journals.uchicago.edu/doi/abs/10.2307/2126298?journalCode=jop.

11. "Executive Order 366—Death of Chief Justice White, May 19, 1921," American Presidency Project, UC Santa Barbara, https://www.presidency.ucsb.edu/documents/executive-order-3466-death-chief-justice-white.

12. Judith Icke Anderson, *William Howard Taft: An Intimate History* (New York: W. W. Norton, 1981), 259.

13. Lurie, *William Howard Taft*, 4; Severn, *William Howard Taft*, 6.

14. Ishbel Ross, *An American Family: The Tafts, 1678 to 1964* (New York: World Publishing, 1977), 47, in Doris Kearns Goodwin, *The Bully Pulpit: Theodore Roosevelt, William Howard Taft, and the Golden Age of Journalism* (New York: Simon & Schuster, 2013), 26.

15. Severn, *William Howard Taft*, 18, 30–31.

16. Taft, *Recollections of Full Years*, 22, in Goodwin, *The Bully Pulpit*, 63.

17. "William Howard Taft," Supreme Court of Ohio & the Ohio Judicial System, https://www.supremecourt.ohio.gov/courts/judicial-system/supreme-court-of-ohio/mjc/interest/grand-concourse/william-howard-taft/.

18. Anderson, *William Howard Taft*, 49.

19. Kevin Grace, "Charles Dickens in Cincinnati," University of Cincinnati Libraries, February 9, 2012, https://libapps.libraries.uc.edu/liblog/2012/02/charles-dickens-in-cincinnati/; Pringle, *William Howard Taft*, 1:108.

20. Anderson, *William Howard Taft*, 153–54, 159.

21. For Hayes anecdote, see *Alton* [IL] *Evening Telegraph*, December 2, 1908, in Goodwin, *The Bully Pulpit*, 89. For reference for "equal partnership," see WHT to Helen Heron Taft, July 15, 1885, WHTP, in Goodwin, *The Bully Pulpit*, 98.

22. Severn, *William Howard Taft*, 41.

23. Pringle, *William Howard Taft*, 1:162; Severn, *William Howard Taft*, 51; Lurie, *William Howard Taft*, 40.

24. Severn, *William Howard Taft*, 57, 61–62.

25. Peri E. Arnold, *Remaking the Presidency: Roosevelt, Taft, and Wilson, 1901–1916* (Lawrence: University Press of Kansas, 2009), 83; Kaufman, *The Post-Presidency from Washington to Clinton*, 244; Anderson, *William Howard Taft*, 82.

26. Quoted in "William Howard Taft," by Mark C. Carnes, in "To the Best of My Ability": *The American Presidents*, ed. James M. McPherson and David Rubel (New York: DK, 2000), 188, in James Chace, *1912: Wilson, Roosevelt, Taft & Debs—The Election That Changed the Country* (New York: Simon & Schuster, 1912), 24.

27. "Chief Justice to Retire," *New York Times*, June 10, 1903, https://timesmachine.nytimes.com/timesmachine/1903/06/10/102006202.pdf?pdf_redirect=true&ip=0; Pringle, *William Howard Taft*, 1:239.

28. Pringle, *William Howard Taft*, 1:240; Goodwin, *The Bully Pulpit*, 386; Severn, *William Howard Taft*, 66.

29. Severn, *William Howard Taft*, 67; Goodwin, *The Bully Pulpit*, 387.

30. Pringle Papers, February 6, 1902, in Lurie, *William Howard Taft*, 56.

31. Taft, *Recollections of Full*, 263.

32. John Whiteclay Chambers II, ed., *The Oxford Companion to American Military History* (New York: Oxford University Press, 1999), 548; Anderson, *William Howard Taft*, 82.

33. "TR to WHT, Nov. 26, 1902," in Lurie, *William Howard Taft*, 59; also in Goodwin, *The Bully Pulpit*, 386–87.

34. *Washington Times*, December 9, 1902, in Goodwin, *The Bully Pulpit*, 88.

35. *Literary Digest*, January 24, 1903, in Pringle, *William Howard Taft*, 1:246.

36. TR to WHT, Jan. 13, 1903, in Taft, *Recollections of Full Years*, 269, in Goodwin, *The Bully Pulpit*, 389; Pringle, *William Howard Taft*, 1:246–47; Anderson, *William Howard Taft*, 83; Severn, *William Howard Taft*, 67–68.

37. TR to WHT, February 14, 1903, in Theodore Roosevelt et al., ed., *The Letters of Theodore Roosevelt, Volume 3: The Square Deal, 1951–1954* (Cambridge, MA: Harvard University Press), 426, in Goodwin, *The Bully Pulpit*, 391; Severn, *William Howard Taft*, 68–69.

38. Severn, *William Howard Taft*, 70.

39. Goodwin, *The Bully Pulpit*, 425; Severn, *William Howard Taft*, 70.

40. E. Stanwood, *A History of the Presidency, from 1897 to 1909* (Boston: Houghton Mifflin, 1912), 109; Pringle, *William Howard Taft*, 1:312.

41. William Howard Taft Diaries, March 10, 1906, WHTP, in Goodwin, *The Bully Pulpit*, 498–99.

42. Arnold, *Remaking the Presidency*, 91; Goodwin, *The Bully Pulpit*, 391.

43. Lurie, *William Howard Taft*, 136.

44. H. H. Kohlsaat, *From McKinley to Harding: Personal Recollections of Our Presidents* (New York: Charles Scribner's Sons, 1923), 161–62, in Pringle, William Howard Taft, 1:313.

45. Ibid.; Severn, *William Howard Taft*, 81.

46. "Taft Family Council: Secretary to Wire His Decision on Supreme Bench Offer," *New York Times*, March 14, 1906, https://timesmachine.nytimes .com/timesmachine/1906/03/14/101836218.pdf?pdf_redirect=true&ip=0.

47. New York *Sun*, March 17, 1906, in William Howard Taft Diaries, WHTP, in Goodwin, *The Bully Pulpit*, 501.

48. Severn, *William Howard Taft*, 82; Goodwin, *The Bully Pulpit*, 499.

49. *Roswell Daily Record*, December 29, 1906, NewspaperArchive, https:// newspaperarchive.com/roswell-daily-record-dec-29-1906-p-1/.

50. "Taft Named; First Ballot," *New York Times*, June 19, 1908, https://archive .nytimes.com/www.nytimes.com/library/politics/camp/080619convention -gop-ra.html.

51. "Address Accepting the Republican Presidential Nomination, July 28, 1908," American Presidency Project, UC Santa Barbara, https://www.pres idency.ucsb.edu/documents/address-accepting-the-republican-presidential -nomination-0.

52. WHT to Charles E. Magoon, July 10, 1908, WHTP, in Goodwin, *The Bully Pulpit*, 547.

53. "1908 Presidential Election," 270 to Win, https://www.270towin.com/1908 _Election/.

54. *Syracuse* [NY] *Herald*, November 6, 1908, in Goodwin, *The Bully Pulpit*, 558.

55. Kaufman, *The Post-Presidency from Washington to Clinton*, 244.

56. Taft, *Recollections of Full Years*, 326–27.

57. Margaret Truman, *First Ladies: An Intimate Group Portrait of White House Wives* (New York: Fawcett, 2009), 105.

58. Taft, *Recollections of Full Years*, 332.

59. Ibid., 332–33.

60. Anderson, *William Howard Taft*, 161–62; Lurie, *William Howard Taft*, 15.

61. WHT to Henry A. Morrill, December 2, 1908, Pringle Papers, in Goodwin, *The Bully Pulpit*, 575.

62. Anderson, *William Howard Taft*, 24–25.

63. Lawrence F. Abbott, ed., *Taft and Roosevelt: The Intimate Letters of Archie Butt, Military Aide*, vol. 1 (Garden City, NY: Doubleday, Doran, 1930), 9.

64. Jeffrey Rosen, *William Howard Taft: The American Presidents Series: The 27th President, 1909–1913* (New York: Henry Holt, 2018), 15.

65. "March 16, 1909: Message Regarding Tariff Legislation," Miller Center, University of Virginia, https://millercenter.org/the-presidency/presidential-speeches/march-16-1909-message-regarding-tariff-legislation.

66. "Tariff of 1909 (Payne-Aldrich Tariff)," Federal Reserve Bank of St. Louis, https://fraser.stlouisfed.org/title/tariff-1909-payne-aldrich-tariff-5874/fulltext.

67. Lewis L. Gould, *Chief Executive to Chief Justice: Taft Betwixt the White House and Supreme Court* (Lawrence: University Press of Kansas, 2014), 9.

68. Alexander Hamilton, "The Federalist Papers: No. 70, March 18, 1788," Avalon Project, Yale Law School, https://avalon.law.yale.edu/18th_century/fed70.asp; Anderson, *William Howard Taft*, 125.

69. Anderson, *William Howard Taft*, 127.

70. Rosen, *William Howard Taft*, 2.

71. William Kolasky, "Theodore Roosevelt and William Howard Taft: Marching Toward Armageddon," *Antitrust* 25, no. 2 (Spring 2011): 97.

72. Anderson, *William Howard Taft*, 132.

73. Rosen, *William Howard Taft*, 55.

74. Sidney M. Milkis, "William Howard Taft and the Struggle for the Soul of the Constitution," in *Toward an American Conservatism*, ed. Joseph W. Postell and Johnathan O'Neill (London: Palgrave MacMillan, 2013), 70.

75. *Collier's Weekly*, November 13, 1909, in Pringle, *William Howard Taft*, 1:472; Gould, *Chief Executive to Chief Justice*, 62; Severn, *William Howard Taft*, 96.

76. Gould, *Chief Executive to Chief Justice*, 64; Arnold, *Remaking the Presidency*, 126.

77. Melvin I. Urofsky, *Louis D. Brandeis: A Life* (New York: Schocken Books, 2012), 270.

78. Rosen, *William Howard Taft*, 79.

79. "Sylph III (Converted Yacht)," Naval History and Heritage Command, https://www.history.navy.mil/research/histories/ship-histories/danfs/s/sylph-iii.html; Goodwin, *The Bully Pulpit*, 580.

80. Archie Butt to Clara, May 17, 1909, in *Taft and Roosevelt*, 1:89–90, in Goodwin, *The Bully Pulpit*, 580; Severn, *William Howard Taft*, 106.

81. Anderson, *William Howard Taft*, 167.

82. Robert W. Merry, "Teddy Roosevelt and Taft: The Odd Couple," *National Interest*, January 6, 2014, https://nationalinterest.org/bookreview/teddy-roosevelt-taft-the-odd-couple-9648; Goodwin, *The Bully Pulpit*, 11.

83. Henry Cabot Lodge and Theodore Lodge, *Selections from the Correspondence of Theodore Roosevelt and Henry Cabot Lodge, 1884–1918* (New York: C. Scribner's Sons, 1925), 386.

84. Theodore Roosevelt, "Address to the Colorado Legislature," *Los Angeles Herald*, August 30, 1910, 3; "Letter from Taft to Root," Taft Papers, Series 6, Reel 356 (October 15, 1910). Notably, Taft's correspondence reveals that he agreed with Roosevelt that Lochner had been wrongly decided. See also "Theodore Roosevelt on 'The New Nationalism' (1910)," *American Yawp Reader*, https://www.americanyawp.com/reader/20-the-progressive-era/theodore-roosevelt-on-the-new-nationalism-1910/; Pringle, *William Howard Taft*, 2:572.

85. "62nd Congress," History, Art & Archives, United States House of Representatives, https://history.house.gov/Congressional-Overview/Profiles/62nd/; Anderson, *William Howard Taft*, 188.

86. "The question—can a champion come back?" Political cartoon, Theodore Roosevelt Center, August 6, 1910, https://www.theodorerooseveltcenter.org/Research/Digital-Library/Record?libID=o286785&from=https%3A%2F%2Fwww.theodorerooseveltcenter.org%2FAdvanced-Search%3Fr%3D1%26st1%3D5%26t1%3D%2522Bryan%252C%2520William%2520Jennings%252C%25201860-1925%2522%26v%3Dexpanded.

87. Ray Stannard Baker, "Is the Republican Party Breaking Up? The Story of the Insurgent West," *American Magazine* (February 1910): 435–39, in Goodwin, *The Bully Pulpit*, 627.

88. Severn, *William Howard Taft*, 112.

89. John G. Sotos, "Taft and Pickwick: Sleep Apnea in the White House," *Chest* 124, no. 3 (September 2003): 1133–42, https://pubmed.ncbi.nlm.nih.gov/12970047/.

90. Anderson, *William Howard Taft*, 32–33, 253.

91. Anderson, *William Howard Taft*, 224–25; *Helena Independent Record*, May 24, 1912, NewspaperArchive, https://newspaperarchive.com/helena-independent-record-may-24-1912-p-1/.

92. Philip Weaks, ed., *Buckeye Presidents: Ohioans in the White House* (Kent, OH: Kent State University Press, 2003), 235; Anderson, *William Howard Taft*, 227, 231.

93. Lurie, *William Howard Taft*, 165.

94. Chace, *1912: Wilson, Roosevelt, Taft and Debs*, 121–22; "Taft 566–Roosevelt 466: Present Line-Up of Instructed and Pledged Delegates with All the Contests Decided," *New York Times*, June 16, 1912, https://timesmachine.nytimes.com/timesmachine/1912/06/16/100586218.pdf.

95. "Taft Renominated by the Republican Convention; Roosevelt Named as Candidate by Bolters," *New York Times*, June 23, 1912, https://archive

.nytimes.com/www.nytimes.com/library/politics/camp/120623convention -gop-ra.html.

96. "Convention Will Nominate Taft; Roosevelt Fails in Plan to Bolt; Hopes Third Party Will Call Him," *New York Times*, June 21, 1912, https://archive .nytimes.com/www.nytimes.com/library/politics/camp/120621convention -gop-ra.html.

97. Anderson, *William Howard Taft*, 233.

98. *Time*, September 27, 1943, Internet Archive, https://web.archive.org/web /20081214171539/http://www.time.com/time/magazine/article/0,9171 ,850367,00.html.

99. "Wilson First, Taft Second," *New York Times*, November 5, 1912, https:// timesmachine.nytimes.com/timesmachine/1912/11/05/100554789.pdf ?pdf_redirect=true&ip=0.

100. "James S. Sherman," *New York Times*, October 31, 1912, https://timesma chine.nytimes.com/timesmachine/1912/10/31/104909675.pdf?pdf_redi rect=true&ip=0.

101. "1912 Electoral Vote Tally, February 12, 1912," National Archives, https:// www.archives.gov/legislative/features/1912-election.

102. WHT to Charles Hopkins Clark, 8 November 1912, Hilles Papers, in Lewis L. Gould, *The William Howard Taft Presidency* (Lawrence: University of Kansas Press, 2009), 197.

103. WHT to Horace D. Taft, December 12 and 25, 1910, in Pringle, *William Howard Taft*, 2:603.

104. Bernard Schwartz, *A History of the Supreme Court* (New York: Oxford University Press, 1995), 207.

105. Anderson, *William Howard Taft*, 191.

106. "White, Not Hughes, for Chief Justice," *New York Times*, December 12, 1910, https://timesmachine.nytimes.com/timesmachine/1910/12/12/105103593 .pdf?pdf_redirect=true&ip=0.

107. Pringle Papers, November 5, 1912, in Lurie, *William Howard Taft*, 172; Anderson, *William Howard Taft*, 22, 136.

108. "William Howard Taft Remarks to the Lotos Club in New York City, November 16, 1912," American Presidency Project, UC Santa Barbara, https:// www.presidency.ucsb.edu/documents/remarks-the-lotos-club-new-york-city.

109. Severn, *William Howard Taft*, 128. Anderson, *William Howard Taft*, 251.

110. Lurie, *William Howard Taft*, 171.

111. "March 4, 1913: First Inaugural Address," Miller Center, University of Virginia, https://millercenter.org/the-presidency/presidential-speeches/march -4-1913-first-inaugural-address.

112. Saladin Ambar, "Woodrow Wilson: Domestic Affairs," Miller Center,

University of Virginia, https://millercenter.org/president/wilson/domestic
-affairs.

113. WHT to Mrs. Eugene Stafford, July 9, 1914, in Pringle, 2:857. See also
Gould, 6. See also Anderson, 255.

114. WHT to C. P. Taft, to Horace D. Taft, November 20, 1912, in Pringle, *William Howard Taft*, 2:849–50; Anderson, *William Howard Taft*, 256; Severn,
William Howard Taft, 129; "President's Salary $75,000," *New York Times*,
February 25, 1909, https://www.nytimes.com/1909/02/25/archives/presi
dents-salary-75000-house-votes-proposed-increase-to-100000.html.

115. Judith Ann Schiff, "Life after the White House: Far from Retiring, William
Howard Taft Took on the Law School," *Yale Alumni Magazine*, April 1993,
http://archives.yalealumnimagazine.com/issues/93_04/oldyale.html.

116. Mark Alden Branch, "Big Man on Campus," *Yale Alumni Magazine*, March/
April 2013, https://yalealumnimagazine.org/articles/3632-big-man-on
-campus.

117. William Howard Taft, *Popular Government: Its Essence, Its Permanence and
Its Perils* (Hartford, CT: Yale University Press, 1913), vii.

118. Katie Marsico, *Women's Right to Vote: America's Suffrage Movement* (Tarry-
town, NY: Marshall Cavendish, 2011), 34.

119. M. L. Keene and K. H. Adams, *Alice Paul and the American Suffrage Campaign* (Champaign: University of Illinois Press, 2010), 126.

120. "Crowd Converging on Marchers during Inaugural Suffrage Procession,
March 3, 1913," U.S. Senate, https://www.senate.gov/artandhistory/history
/common/image/March1913ParadeLOC.htm.

121. "President Taft Hissed by Woman Suffragists," news clipping, Ann Lewis
Woman's Suffrage Collection, April 15, 1910, https://lewissuffragecollec
tion.omeka.net/items/show/1313; "Taft for Suffrage If Women Want It,"
New York Times, November 3, 1909, https://timesmachine.nytimes.com
/timesmachine/1909/11/03/101903247.pdf?pdf_redirect=true&ip=0.

122. G. Graham, *Saturday Evening Post*, 1915, 5.

123. "Taft to Henry C. Coe, 14 November 1916," WHT; "Taft to Gus Karger, 22
February 1919," WHTP.

124. Pringle, *William Howard Taft*, 2:856; Anderson, *William Howard Taft*, 256;
"Did You Know That Presidents Receive a Pension?," National Public Pension Coalition, January 20, 2021, https://protectpensions.org/2021/01/20
/know-presidents-receive-pension-2/.

125. Kaufman, *The Post-Presidency from Washington to Clinton*, 247.

126. WHT to Mabel Boardman, 10 February 1914, WHTP, in Gould, *Chief
Execuive to Chief Justice*, 29; *The Law Student's Helper* (New York: Little,
Brown, 1914).

127. Gould, *Chief Executive to Chief Justice*, 29; Severn, *William Howard Taft*, 129–30; Kaufman, *The Post-Presidency from Washington to Clinton*, 247–48.

128. James McMurtry Longo, *From Classroom to White House: The Presidents and First Ladies as Students and Teachers* (Jefferson, NC: McFarland, 2011); Boardman Papers, January 6, 1914, in Lurie, *William Howard Taft*, 174–75; Severn, *William Howard Taft*, 130–311.

129. Norman Gross, "Presidential Bar Leaders: Fascinating Facts about America's Lawyer-Presidents," *Bar Leader* 34, no. 3 (January–February, 2010), https://www.americanbar.org/groups/bar_services/publications/bar_leader /2009_10/january_february/presidential/.

130. William Howard Taft, "The Future of the Republican Party," *Saturday Evening Post*, February 14, 1914; Gould, *Chief Executive to Chief Justice*, 33.

131. William Howard Taft, *Popular Government: Its Essence, Its Permanence and Its Perils*, 9.

132. McWilliams and Gerrity, *The President and His Powers*, 6:104.

133. Jeffrey Rosen, "Five Best: Jeffrey Rosen," *Wall Street Journal*, March 6, 2018, https://www.wsj.com/articles/jeffrey-rosen-1521234932.

134. Gould, *Chief Executive to Chief Justice*, 15–26.

135. Taft to Mabel Boardman, June 27, 1914, in Pringle, *William Howard Taft*, 2:852–53.

136. "Cheer Roosevelt for 93 Minutes," *New York Times*, June 8, 1916, https://www.nytimes.com/1916/06/08/archives/cheer-roosevelt-for-93-minutes -the-progressive-demonstration-breaks.html.

137. "Moose Angry and Bitter: Convention Ends in Gloom after Long Fight for Roosevelt," *New York Times*, June 11, 1916, https://timesmachine.ny times.com/timesmachine/1916/06/11/101573453.pdf; "Charles E. Hughes Telegram Accepting the Republican Nomination for President, June 10, 1916," American Presidency Project, UC Santa Barbara, https://www.pres idency.ucsb.edu/documents/telegram-accepting-the-republican-nomina tion-for-president.

138. Pietrusza, *1920: The Year of the Six Presidents*, 78.

139. Pringle, *William Howard Taft*, 2:892; Rosen, *William Howard Taft*, 11.

140. Gould, *Chief Executive to Chief Justice*, 80; Pringle, *William Howard Taft*, 2:897; "The Party That Merely Wants Control," *New York Times*, October 3, 1916, https://timesmachine.nytimes.com/timesmachine/1916/10/03/3019 04572.pdf?pdf_redirect=true&ip=0; David M. Kennedy and Lizabeth Cohen, *The American Pageant*, vol. 2 (Boston: Cengage Learning, 2012), 674.

141. William H. Taft to Helen H. Taft, October 31, 1916, in Pringle, *William Howard Taft*, 2:899.

142. "1916 Presidential Election," 270 to Win, https://www.270towin.com

/1916_Election/; Spencer C. Olin, *California's Prodigal Sons: Hiram Johnson and the Progressives, 1911–1917* (Berkeley: University of California Press, 1968), 152–55.

143. "Votes of Women and Bull Moose Elected Wilson," *New York Times*, November 12, 1916, https://timesmachine.nytimes.com/timesmachine/1916/11/12/100340355.html.

144. "Great Liner Is Sunk in 15 Minutes," *Pittsburgh Post*, May 8, 1915, https://www.newspapers.com/clip/25025499/us-paper-reports-sinking-of/.

145. "Woodrow Wilson Address to Naturalized Citizens at Convention Hall, Philadelphia, May 10, 1915," American Presidency Project, UC Santa Barbara, https://www.presidency.ucsb.edu/documents/address-naturalized-citizens-convention-hall-philadelphia.

146. Charles F. Horne, ed., *Source Records of the Great War*, vol. 5 (New York: National Alumni, 1923).

147. "Zimmermann Telegram as Received by the German Ambassador to Mexico; 1/16/1917; 862.20212/57 through 862.20212/311; Central Decimal Files, 1910–1963," General Records of the Department of State, Record Group 59, National Archives at College Park, College Park, MD. Online version: https://www.docsteach.org/documents/document/zimmermann-telegram-as-received, July 29, 2022.

148. "April 2, 1917: Address to Congress Requesting a Declaration of War against Germany," Miller Center, Univerity of Virginia, https://millercenter.org/the-presidency/presidential-speeches/april-2-1917-address-congress-requesting-declaration-war.

149. William H. Taft to Horace Taft, April 18, 1913, describing Wilson "as much of an opportunist as anybody we have had in the White House," in Pringle, *William Howard Taft*, 2:867.

150. Gould, *Chief Executive to Chief Justice*, 48; Pringle, *William Howard Taft*, 2:876.

151. P. C. Cohen et al., *The American Promise, Combined Volume: A History of the United States* (New York: Bedford/St. Martin's, 2012), 719.

152. *Yale Review* (Hoboken, NJ: Blackwell, 1917), 2.

153. Wendi Maloney, "World War I: Workers Greet Labor Day 1918 with Optimism," *Timeless* blog, Library of Congress, August 30, 2017, https://blogs.loc.gov/loc/2017/08/world-war-i-workers-greet-labor-day-1918-with-optimism/; Anderson, *William Howard Taft*, 256–57; Severn, *William Howard Taft*, 140–41.

154. Gould, *Chief Executive to Chief Justice*, 103; Pringle, *William Howard Taft*, 2:917; Lurie, *William Howard Taft*, 184.

155. Lauck to Pringle, October 5, 1937, in Pringle, *William Howard Taft*, 2:919,

2:915, 2:924; Severn, *William Howard Taft*, 142; Kaufman, *The Post-Presidency from Washington to Clinton*, 251.

156. Gilson Gardner, "Laboring People Now for Ex-President Taft," *Dallas Dispatch*, September 6, 1918, clipping in WHTP.

157. Michael E. Ruane, "A Glimpse into the Heartache and High Jinks in Theodore Roosevelt's Life," *Washington Post*, October 18, 2018, https://www.washingtonpost.com/history/2018/10/18/glimpse-into-heartache-hijinks-life-president-theodore-roosevelt/.

158. Richard Striner, *Woodrow Wilson and World War I: A Burden Too Great to Bear* (Lanham, MD: Rowman & Littlefield, 2014), 100.

159. Professor Richard Stiner makes this argument, saying, "Wilson missed a priceless opportunity to turn an enemy into a friend."

160. Roosevelt to Taft, June 5, 1918, in Pringle, *William Howard Taft*, 2:909.

161. Taft to Karger, January 31, 1916, Taft-Karger Correspondence, Folder 22, Cincinnati Museum Center, in Lurie, *William Howard Taft*, 181; Kaufman, *The Post-Presidency from Washington to Clinton*, 250; Gould, *Chief Executive to Chief Justice*, 68.

162. Ronald G. Shafer, "The First Jewish Justice Was Also the First to Face Confirmation Hearings," *Washington Post*, April 4, 2022, https://www.washingtonpost.com/history/2022/04/04/louis-brandeis-jewish-confirmation-hearings/.

163. Alden L. Todd, *Justice on Trial: The Case of Louis D. Brandeis* (New York: McGraw Hill, 1964), 73.

164. "To Confirm the Nomination of Louis D. Brandeis, to Be an Associate Justice of the Supreme Court of the U.S," GovTrack, June 1, 1916, https://www.govtrack.us/congress/votes/64-1/s147.

165. Gould, *Chief Executive to Chief Justice*, 69.

166. Pringle, *William Howard Taft*, 2:911.

167. *New-York Tribune*, May 27, 1918, in Goodwin, *The Bully Pulpit*, 744–45; Gould, *Chief Executive to Chief Justice*, 109.

168. Dartunorro Clark, "America Pulled Off an Election during the Spanish Flu, but Not without Paying a Price," NBC News, June 1, 2020, https://www.nbcnews.com/politics/politics-news/america-pulled-election-during-spanish-flu-not-without-paying-price-n1218286.

169. James Chace, "Excerpt: '1912,'" *New York Times*, May 9, 2004, https://www.nytimes.com/2004/05/09/books/chapters/1912.html; Benjamin Shapell and Sara Willen, "The 100th Commemoration of the Death of Theodore Roosevelt," Shapell Manuscript Foundation, January 13, 2019, https://www.shapell.org/historical-perspectives/between-the-lines/the-100th-commemoration-of-the-death-of-theodore-roosevelt-a-final-roar/.

170. "Theodore Roosevelt Dies Suddenly at Oyster Bay Home; Nation Shocked, Pays Tribute to Former President; Our Flag on All Seas and in All Lands at Half Mast," *New York Times*, January 6, 1919, https://archive.nytimes.com /www.nytimes.com/learning/general/onthisday/big/0106.html.

171. Taft to Helen Taft, January 9, 1919, quoted in Pringle, *William Howard Taft*, 2:914 in Chace, *1912: Wilson, Roosevelt, Taft and Debs*, 5.

172. Taft to Mrs. William Cowles, July 26, 1921 in Pringle, *William Howard Taft*, 2:913; Anderson, *William Howard Taft*, 258.

173. Adam Tooze, *The Deluge: The Great War, America and the Remaking of the Global Order, 1916–1931* (New York: Penguin Books, 2014), 45.

174. *New York Times Current History of the European War* 2, no. 4 (July 1915): 667–70; Burton, *William Howard Taft*, 27, 90.

175. "President Woodrow Wilson's 14 Points," National Archives, https://www .archives.gov/milestone-documents/president-woodrow-wilsons-14-points.

176. Taft and Lowell to Wickersham, December 11, 1918, in Pringle, *William Howard Taft*, 2:942.

177. Jean Edward Smith, *FDR* (New York: Random House, 2008), 169.

178. David Pietrusza, *1920: The Year of Six Presidents* (New York: Basic Books, 2008), 37.

179. Pringle, *William Howard Taft*, 2:944.

180. Thomas Knock, *To End All Wars* (Princeton, NJ: Princeton University Press, 1995), 229.

181. Stewart Patrick, *The Best Laid Plans: The Origins of Multilateralism and the Dawn of the Cold War* (New York: Rowman & Littlefield, 2009), 23.

182. *Senate, 1789–1989, V. 3: Classic Speeches, 1830–1993* (Washington, DC: U.S. Government Printing Office), 547; "The Covenant of the League of Nations, December, 1924," Avalon Project, Yale Law School, https://avalon .law.yale.edu/20th_century/leagcov.asp.

183. Sheldon M. Stern, "Henry Cabot Lodge and Louis A. Coolidge in Defense of American Sovereignty, 1898–1920," *Massachusetts Historical Society* 87 (1975): 118–34; E. M. Bennett and N. A. Graebner, *The Versailles Treaty and Its Legacy: The Failure of the Wilsonian Vision* (New York: Cambridge University Press, 2011), 44.

184. Gould, *Chief Executive to Chief Justice*, 127, 131.

185. "Taft, Urging Interpretations to Insure Ratification," in ibid., 132, 136.

186. "Woodrow Wilson Address to the Senate on the Versailles Peace Treaty, July 10, 1919," American Presidency Project, UC Santa Barbara, https://www .presidency.ucsb.edu/documents/address-the-senate-the-versailles-peace -treaty.

187. Ibid.

188. Ibid.; Woodrow Wilson, *The Papers of Woodrow Wilson*, 68 vols., ed. Arthur Stanley Link (Princeton, NJ: Princeton University Press, 1966), 61:445–46.

189. Kaufman, *The Post-Presidency from Washington to Clinton*, 253; Burton, *William Howard Taft*, 92, 99.

190. Taft to Karger, February 19 and 22, 1919, Taft-Karger Correspondence, Folder 48, Cincinnati Museum Center, in Lurie, *William Howard Taft*, 185.

191. Gould, *Chief Executive to Chief Justice*, 99.

192. Gene Smith, *When the Cheering Stopped* (New York: William Morrow, 1964), 56.

193. Taft to E. E. Whiting, September 12, 1919, in Pringle, *William Howard Taft*, 2:948.

194. August Heckscher, *Woodrow Wilson: A Biography* (New York: Scribner, 1993), 609.

195. Edwin Weinstein, *Woodrow Wilson: A Medical and Psychological Biography* (Princeton, NJ: Princeton University Press, 1981), 357, in Crispell and Gomez, *Hidden Illness in the White House*, 70.

196. Carl S. Anthony, *Florence Harding: The First Lady, the Jazz Age, and the Death of America's Most Scandalous President* (New York: William Morrow, 1998), 161.

197. Taft to Mrs. Strong, December 17, 1919, in Pringle, *William Howard Taft*, 2:949. In the letter he accuses Lodge of "exalt[ing] personal prestige and the saving of [his] ugly faces above the welfare of the country and the world."

198. Lurie, *William Howard Taft*, 189.

199. New York *Sun*, front page, November 20, 1919.

200. Henry Cabot Lodge, *The Senate and the League of Nations* (New York: Charles Scribner's Sons, 1925), 215–16.

201. "America Isolated without Treaty," *New York Times*, March 20, 1920, https://timesmachine.nytimes.com/timesmachine/1920/03/20/118311737.pdf?pdf_redirect=true&ip=0.

202. Taft to Karger, Taft-Karger Correspondence, November 3, 1919, Folder 58, Cincinnati Museum Center, in Lurie, *William Howard Taft*, 189.

203. Herbert Eaton, *Presidential Timber: A History of Nominating Conventions, 1868–1960* (Glencoe, IL: Free Press, 1964), 260.

204. Charles L. Mee Jr., *The Ohio Gang: The World of Warren G. Harding—An Historical Entertainment* (Lanham, MD: M. Evans, 2014), 70; "June 12, 1920: Speech Accepting the Republican Nomination," Miller Center, University of Virginia, https://millercenter.org/the-presidency/presidential-speeches/june-12-1920-speech-accepting-republican-nomination; "Republican Party Platform of 1920, June 8, 1920," American Presidency

Project, UC Santa Barbara, https://www.presidency.ucsb.edu/documents
/republican-party-platform-1920.

205. Gould, *Chief Executive to Chief Justice*, 72, 129; Pietrusza, *1920: The Year of the Six Presidents*, 84.

206. Severn, *William Howard Taft*, 153; Pringle, *William Howard Taft*, 2:950; Jonathan Lurie, "Chief Justice Taft and Dissents: Down with Brandeis Briefs!," *Journal of Supreme Court History*, https://supremecourthistory.org /assets/schs-journal/pub_journal_2007_vol_2.pdf; "Taft Clashes with Harding on League," *New York Times*, August 7, 1920, https://timesmachine.ny times.com/timesmachine/1920/08/07/102883427.html?pageNumber=3; Gould, *Chief Executive to Chief Justice*, 159.

207. "Presidential Election of 1920," 270 to Win, https://www.270towin.com /1920_Election/; "19th Amendment to the U.S. Constitution (1920)," National Archives, https://www.archives.gov/milestone-documents/19th-amendment.

208. "Taft Sees Harding, Indorses Program for Bringing Peace," *New York Times*, December 25, 1920, https://www.nytimes.com/1920/12/25/archives/taft -sees-harding-indorses-program-for-bringing-peace-says-senator.html.

209. John Maynard Keynes, *The Economic Consequences of the Peace* (San Diego, CA: Harcourt, Brace & Howe, 1920), 274.

210. Pringle, *William Howard Taft*, 2:954–55.

211. WHT to HHT, December 26, 1920, WHTP, in Gould, *Chief Executive to Chief Justice*, 167; Pringle, *William Howard Taft*, 2:955.

212. Pringle, *William Howard Taft*, 2:955.

213. WHT to HHT, December 26, 1920, WHTP.

214. Taft to Karger, March 26, 1921, in Pringle, *William Howard Taft*, 2:956; Severn, *William Howard Taft*, 156.

215. Pringle, *William Howard Taft*, 2:957.

216. *Green Bay Press-Gazette*, May 20, 1921, 1.

217. Pringle, *William Howard Taft*, 2:957, for Taft quote; John D. Feerick, *From Failing Hands: The Story of Presidential Succession* (New York: Fordham University Press, 1965), 158, for Roosevelt quote.

218. Frank Brandegee to WHT, June 14, 1921, WHTP, and Karger to WHT, June 14, 1921, June 21, 1921, WHTP, in Gould, *Chief Executive to Chief Justice*, 170.

219. "First Supreme Court Nominee Appears before the Judiciary Committee, January 28, 1925," U.S. Senate, https://www.senate.gov/about/powers-pro cedures/nominations/first-supreme-court-nominee-appears-judiciary-com mittee.htm.

220. *Sweetwater [TX] Daily Reporter*, October 24, 1921, in Goodwin, *The Bully Pulpit*, 748; "William Howard Taft Sworn in as Chief Justice 100 Years

Ago," Cincinnati.com, https://www.cincinnati.com/story/news/2021/07/11
/william-howard-taft-sworn-chief-justice-100-years-ago/7880969002/.

221. Taft to Horace Taft, October 6, 1921, in Pringle, *William Howard Taft*,
2:965–66.

222. Goodwin, *The Bully Pulpit*, 748–49.

223. Anderson, *William Howard Taft*, 259.

224. John E. Noyes, "William Howard Taft and the Taft Arbitration Treaties," *Villanova Law Review* 56, no. 3 (2011): https://digitalcommons.law.villanova
.edu/cgi/viewcontent.cgi?article=1017&context=vlr; Burton, *William Howard Taft*, 115.

225. Pringle, *William Howard Taft*, 2:962; Gina Kolata, "In Struggle with Weight,
Taft Used a Modern Diet," *New York Times*, October 14, 2013, https://www
.nytimes.com/2013/10/15/health/in-struggle-with-weight-william-howard
-taft-used-a-modern-diet.html.

226. Anderson, *William Howard Taft*, 259.

227. Robert Post, "The Supreme Court Opinion as Institutional Practice: Dissent, Legal Scholarship, and Decisionmaking in the Taft Court," *Minnesota Law Review* 85, no. 5 (April 2001): 1267, 1271.

228. Anderson, *William Howard Taft*, 260.

229. Severn, *William Howard Taft*, 168.

230. *American Journal of Legal History* 4, no. 2 (April 1960), 104.

231. Artemus Ward, *Deciding to Leave: The Politics of Retirement from the United States Supreme Court* (Albany: State University of New York Press, 2012), 117.

232. David J. Garrow, "Mental Decrepitude on the U.S. Supreme Court: The
Historical Case for the 28th Amendment," *University of Chicago Law Review*, 2000, https://chicagounbound.uchicago.edu/cgi/viewcontent.cgi?article=5893&context=uclrev.

233. Severn, *William Howard Taft*, 168.

234. "The Evarts Act: Creating the Modern Appellate Courts," United States
Courts, https://www.uscourts.gov/educational-resources/educational-activities/evarts-act-creating-modern-appellate-courts.

235. Rosen, *William Howard Taft*, 114.

236. Anderson, *William Howard Taft*, 261; Severn, *William Howard Taft*, 181.

237. Pringle, *William Howard Taft*, 2:996; Severn, *William Howard Taft*, 177;
Rosen, *William Howard Taft*, 116.

238. Alpheus Thomas Mason, *William Howard Taft, Chief Justice* (New York:
Simon & Schuster, 1965), 231.

239. Taft to Helen Manning, June 11, 1923, in Pringle, *William Howard Taft*,
2:970.

240. Pringle, *William Howard Taft*, 2:1051.

241. *Truax et al. v. Corrigan et al.*, 257 U.S. 312 (1921), Legal Information Institute, Cornell Law School, https://www.law.cornell.edu/supremecourt/text /257/312.

242. Pringle, *William Howard Taft*, 2:1035.

243. Taft to Horace Taft, May 15, 1922, in Pringle, *William Howard Taft*, 2:1014.

244. *Board of Trade of City of Chicago et al. v. Olsen U. et al.*, 262 U.S. 1 (1923), Legal Information Institute, Cornell Law School, https://www.law.cornell .edu/supremecourt/text/262/1.

245. Severn, *William Howard Taft*, 190.

246. *Adkins et al., Minimum Wage Board of District of Columbia v. Children's Hospital of the District of Columbia. Same v. Lyons*, 261 U.S. 525 (1923), Legal Information Institute, Cornell Law School, https://www.law.cornell .edu/supremecourt/text/261/525.

247. *Myers v. United States*, 272 U.S., at 59 (1923), Legal Information Institute, Cornell Law School, https://www.law.cornell.edu/supremecourt/text /272/52.

248. Ibid.

249. Taft to Horace Taft, October 3, 1929, in Pringle, *William Howard Taft*, 2:981–83.

250. *Olmstead et al. v. United States*, 277 U.S. 438 (1928), Legal Information Institute, Cornell Law School, https://www.law.cornell.edu/supremecourt /text/277/438.

251. Severn, *William Howard Taft*, 206–7.

252. *United States v. Donald Trump*, United States District Court, Washington, DC, filed August 1, 2023, https://storage.courtlistener.com/recap/gov.us courts.dcd.258149/gov.uscourts.dcd.258149.1.0_1.pdf.

253. *Hammerschmidt v. United States*, United States Supreme Court, https:// www.law.cornell.edu/supremecourt/text/265/182.

254. William Seale, *The President's House*, vol. 2 (New York: Harry N. Abrams, 1968), 96; Katharine Graham, *Katharine Graham's Washington* (New York: Vintage Books, 2003).

255. Peter Baker, "DNA Is Said to Solve a Mystery of Warren Harding's Love Life," *New York Times*, August 12, 2015, https://www.nytimes.com/2015/08/13 /us/dna-is-said-to-solve-a-mystery-of-warren-hardings-love-life.html.

256. Rosemary Stevens, "A Time of Scandal: Charles R. Forbes, Warren G. Harding, and the Making of the Veterans Bureau," *American Historical Review* 124, no. 1 (February 2019): 274–75.

257. Joe Mitchell Chapple, *Life and Times of Warren G. Harding: Our After-War President* (Boston: Chapple, 1924), 326–75, in John Dean, *Warren G. Harding* (New York: Times Books, 2004), 148.

258. Edward B. MacMahon and Leonard Curry, *Medical Cover-Ups in the White House* (Washington, DC: Farragut, 1987), 83.

259. Ibid., 87.

260. Cohen, *Accidental Presidents*, 242–43; Amity Shlaes, *The Forgotten Man: A New History of the Great Depression* (New York: HarperCollins, 2014), 251–52; Ruth Silva, *Presidential Succession* (New York: Greenwood Press, 1968), 28; Jules Witcover, *The American Vice Presidency: From Irrelevance to Power* (Washington, DC: Smithsonian Books, 2014), 275.

261. Charles C. Johnson, *Why Coolidge Matters: Leadership Lessons from America's Most Underrated President* (New York: Encounter Books, 2013), 113; David Greenberg, *Calvin Coolidge: The American Presidents Series: The 30th President, 1923–1929* (New York: Henry Holt, 2006), 44; Witcover, *The American Vice Presidency*, 275;

262. Pringle, *William Howard Taft,* 2:1018.

263. "Letter from Willian H. Taft to St. G.R. Fitzhugh, August 14, 1923," WHTP.

264. Alice Roosevelt Longworth, *Crowded Hours* (New York: Charles Scribner's Sons, 1933), 337.

265. Frederick Lewis Allen, *Only Yesterday: An Informal History of the 1920s* (New York: Open Road Media, 2015), 144.

266. *New York Times*, August 3, 1927, 1.

267. Taft to Horace Taft, October 11, 1925, in Pringle, *William Howard Taft*, 2:1063.

268. Lewis L. Gould, *Grand Old Party: A History of the Republicans* (New York: Oxford University Press, 2012), xlix.

269. "Presidential Election of 1928," 270 to Win, https://www.270towin.com /1928_Election/.

270. Taft to Helen Terwilliger, March 18, 1929, in Pringle, *William Howard Taft*, 2:1074.

271. Matthew Schaefer, "Herbert Hoover and American Presidents of the 20th Century," National Archives, September 12, 2018, https://hoover.blogs .archives.gov/2018/09/12/herbert-hoover-and-american-presidents-of-the -20th-century-2.

272. Earl Warren, "Chief Justice William Howard Taft," *Yale Law Journal* 67, no. 3 (January 1958): 353–62.

273. Severn, *William Howard Taft,* 169.

274. Taft to H. W. Taft, February 6, 1924, in Pringle, *William Howard Taft*, 2:1073.

275. Taft to S. H. Wilder, January 28, 1929, in Pringle, *William Howard Taft*, 2:1071.

276. Taft to G. W. Burton, February 21, 1926, in Pringle, *William Howard Taft*, 2:1070.

277. Psalm 90:10, King James Version.

278. Taft to Horace Taft, December 1, 1929, in Pringle, *William Howard Taft*, 2:1044.

279. Severn, *William Howard Taft*, 211.

280. "Herbert Hoover Statement on the Resignation of Chief Justice William Howard Taft, February 4, 1930," American Presidency Project, UC Santa Barbara, https://www.presidency.ucsb.edu/documents/statement-the-resig nation-chief-justice-william-howard-taft.

281. Oliver Wendell Holmes et al., to WHT, February 10, 1930, in Pringle, *William Howard Taft*, 2:1079; Goodwin, *The Bully Pulpit*, 749.

282. "Herbert Hoover Proclamation 1901—Announcing the Death of William Howard Taft, March 8, 1930," American Presidency Project, UC Santa Barbara, https://www.presidency.ucsb.edu/documents/proclamation-1901-an nouncing-the-death-william-howard-taft.

283. Matthew Continetti, *The Right: The Hundred-Year War for American Conservatism* (New York: Basic Books, 2022), 31.

CHAPTER 5: RECOVERY

1. Chalmers M. Roberts, "The Wrong Man for the Times," *Washington Post*, July 29, 1984, https://www.washingtonpost.com/archive/entertainment/books /1984/07/29/the-wrong-man-for-the-times/69850233-7a34-468b-871b-87 9a03c869c6.

2. "A Man Who Saved the Lives of Millions," *Zoom in on America* 14, no. 155 (July/August 2018), https://pl.usembassy.gov/wp-content/uploads/sites/23 /Zoom-in-on-America-July-August-2018.pdf.

3. Herbert Hoover, *The Memoirs of Herbert Hoover: Years of Adventure, 1874–1920* (New York: Macmillan, 1957), 9.

4. David Pietrusza, *1920: The Year of Six Presidents* (New York: Basic Books, 2008), 112.

5. "Wood Victorious in New Hampshire Primary Content," *New York Times*, March 10, 1920, https://timesmachine.nytimes.com/timesmachine/1920 /03/10/118305722.pdf?pdf_redirect=true&ip=0.

6. "The Emergence of the Great Humanitarian," National Parks Service, https://www.nps.gov/articles/emergence-of-the-great-humanitarian.htm.

7. 444 electoral votes, forty states, 58.2 percent of the popular vote.

8. "How Bad was the Great Depression? Gauging the Economic Impact,"

Federal Reserve Bank of St. Louis, https://www.stlouisfed.org/en/the-great
-depression/curriculum/economic-episodes-in-american-history-part-3.

9. Kenneth Whyte, *Hoover: An Extraordinary Life in Extraordinary Times* (New York: Vintage, 2017), 592.

10. David E. Hamilton, "Herbert Hoover: Campaigns and Elections," Miller Center, University of Virginia, https://millercenter.org/president/hoover/campaigns-and-elections.

11. "When Hoover Met Hitler, a Lesson in Media Literacy," National Archives, https://education.blogs.archives.gov/2022/01/27/when-hoover-met-hitler/.

12. Eugene Lyons, *Herbert Hoover: A Biography* (New York: Doubleday, 1964), 325; Eric Rauchway, *Winter War: Hoover, Roosevelt, and the First Clash over the New Deal* (New York: Basic Books, 2018), 29.

13. Hoover, *Memoirs: Years of Adventure*, 1, 3.

14. "Years of Adventure, 1874–1914," Herbert Hoover Presidential Library and Museum, https://hoover.archives.gov/exhibits/years-adventure-1874-1914.

15. "Huntsman, Hoover Speak the Same Language," *Chicago Tribune*, January 10, 2012, https://www.chicagotribune.com/news/ct-xpm-2012-01-10-ct-talk-huntsman-chinese-0110-20120110-story.html.

16. "Herbert Hoover," Philanthropy Roundtable, https://www.philanthropyroundtable.org/hall-of-fame/herbert-hoover/.

17. George I. Gay, *Public Relations of the Commission for Relief in Belgium*, vol. 2 (Stanford, CA: Stanford University Press, 1929).

18. Herbert Hoover, *The Crusade Years, 1933–1955: Herbert Hoover's Lost Memoir of the New Deal Era and Its Aftermath* (Stanford, CA: Hoover Institution Press, 2013), xii.

19. "The Great Mississippi River Flood of 1927," National Museum of African American History and Culture, https://nmaahc.si.edu/explore/stories/great-mississippi-river-flood-1927#:~:text=The%20flood%20inundated%2016%20million,swelled%20to%2080%20miles%20wide%20.&text=Map%20of%20the%20Mississippi%20River,Geodetic%20Survey%2C%20RG%2023); George Nash, author interview by phone, January 17, 2022.

20. R. H. Ferrell, *American Diplomacy in the Great Depression: Hoover-Stimson Foreign Policy, 1929–1933* (Hartford, CT: Yale University Press, 1957), 195.

21. Robert Sobel, *Coolidge: An American Enigma* (Washington, DC: Regnery, 2015), 368.

22. Shanon Fitzpatrick, "The Great Depression and the Macfadden Market," in *True Story: How a Pulp Empire Remade Mass Media* (Cambridge. MA: Harvard University Press, 2022), 147–83.

23. "Managing the Crisis: The FDIC and RTC Experience," FDIC, https://

www.fdic.gov/bank/historical/managing/chronological/pre-fdic.html; "The
Great Depression," Federal Reserve History, https://www.federalreserve
history.org/essays/great-depression; "Stock Market Crash of 1929," Federal
Reserve History, https://www.federalreservehistory.org/essays/stock-market
-crash-of-1929.

24. "President Visits Dam," *Los Angeles Times*, November 13, 1932, and "Wilbur Renames Boulder Dam for Hoover," *New York Times*, September 18,
1930, in Rauchway, *Winter War*, 47.

25. For a critique, see "Economists against Smoot-Hawley," *Econ Journal Watch*
4, no. 3 (September 2007): 345–58, https://econjwatch.org/file_download
/162/2007-09-editorsfetter-char_issue.pdf.

26. "1,028 Economists Ask Hoover to Veto Pending Tariff Bill," *New York Times*,
May 4, 1930, https://web.archive.org/web/20080227204101/http://www
.clubforgrowth.org/media/uploads/smooth%20hawley%20ny%20times%20
05%2005%2030.pdf.

27. Timothy Walch and Richard Norton Smith, "The Ordeal of Herbert Hoover,"
Prologue Magazine 36, no. 2 (Summer 2004): https://www.archives.gov/pub
lications/prologue/2004/summer/hoover-1.html.

28. William E. Brandt, "BABE RUTH ACCEPTS $160,000 FOR 2 YEARS;
Quickly Settles Salary Differences with Yanks in Conference with Ruppert.
STAR WILL SIGN TOMORROW. New Contract Likely to Make Slug-
ger's Earnings from Game Reach $750,000. YANKEES SUBDUE BRAVES
Take First Contest of Series by 12–9 before Record Crowd of 6,000—
Homer for Gehrig. Action Follows Rapidly. Hopes for Great Year. BABE
RUTH ACCEPTS $160,000 FOR 2 YEARS," *New York Times*, March 9,
1930, https://www.nytimes.com/1930/03/09/archives/babe-ruth-accepts-16
0000-for-2-years-quickly-settles-salary.html.

29. "Labor Force, Employment, and Unemployment, 1929–39: Estimating Methods," U.S. Bureau of Labor Statistics, https://www.bls.gov/opub
/mlr/1948/article/pdf/labor-force-employment-and-unemployment
-1929-39-estimating-methods.pdf.

30. Wilborn Hampton, *Babe Ruth: A Twentieth Century Life* (New York: Viking,
2009), 162; "Babe Ruth 1930 Game by Game Batting Logs," Baseball Al-
manac, https://www.baseball-almanac.com/players/hittinglogs.php?p=ruth
ba01&y=1930.

31. Paul Dickson, and William B. Mead, *Baseball: The Presidents' Game* (New
York: Walker, 1997), 57.

32. Michael Barone, *How America's Political Parties Change (And How They
Don't)* (New York: Encounter Books, 2019), 41.

33. John J. Tierney, "'Happy Days Are Here Again,'" Institute of World Politics,

October 1, 2019, https://www.iwp.edu/articles/2019/10/01/happy-days-are
-here-again/.

34. Lyons, *Herbert Hoover*, 317–18; Walch and Smith, "The Ordeal of Herbert
Hoover"; Donald A. Ritchie, *Electing FDR: The New Deal Campaign of
1932* (Lawrence: University Press of Kansas, 2007), 161.

35. Index cards in Raymond Moley Papers, b. 282 f. 15, in Rauchway, *Winter
War*, 43.

36. Lyons, *Herbert Hoover*, 308.

37. Thomas Schwartz, "Charles Michelson's Campaign against Herbert
Hoover," *Hoover Heads* blog, National Archives, August 4, 2021, https://
hoover.blogs.archives.gov/2021/08/04/charles-michelsons-campaign
-against-herbert-hoover/.

38. Mary Louise Parker, author interview, New York, NY, December 3, 2021.

39. Howard Space, "The Impeachment of Herbert Hoover," *Hoover Heads*
blog, National Archives, October 30, 2019, https://hoover.blogs.archives
.gov/2019/10/30/the-impeachment-of-herbert-hoover/; Stephen W. Stathis
and David C. Huckabee, *Congressional Resolutions on Presidential Impeachment: A Historical Overview* (Washington, DC: Congressional Research
Service, Library of Congress, 1998), 9; Lyons, *Herbert Hoover*, 318.

40. Robert Jackson Diary, Rauner Manuscript Collection, Dartmouth College,
Hanover, New Hampshire, November 23 and 27, 1932, in Rauchway, *Winter
War*, 46.

41. Rauchway, *Winter War*, 64–65.

42. Lyons, *Herbert Hoover*, 311; Rauchway, *Winter War*, 35.

43. FDR to Herbert Hoover, November 14, 1932, President's Individual file on
FDR, in Rauchway, *Winter War*, 58.

44. Theodore Joslin Diary, November 16, 1932, in Rauchway, *Winter War*, 59.

45. Thomas Parrish, *Roosevelt and Marshall: The War They Fought, the Change
They Wrought* (New York: HarperCollins, 1991), 27.

46. Christopher Clausen, "FDR's Hidden Handicap," *Wilson Quarterly Archives*, Summer 2005, http://archive.wilsonquarterly.com/essays/fdrs-hidden
-handicap.

47. Raymond Moley, *The First New Deal* (New York: Harcourt, Brace & World,
1966), 29, in Rauchway, *Winter War*, 67.

48. Lyons, *Herbert Hoover*, 320; Rauchway, *Winter War*, 67–69.

49. "Franklin D. Roosevelt: Exchange of Letters between President Hoover
and President-Elect Roosevelt, December 17, 1932," American Presidency
Project, UC Santa Barbara, https://www.presidency.ucsb.edu/documents
/exchange-letters-between-president-hoover-and-president-elect-roosevelt.

50. Herbert Hoover to FDR and statement, December 22, 1932, Pres. Indiv. File on FDR and FDR to Herbert Hoover, December 22, 1932, in Rauchway, *Winter War*, 71.

51. Lyons, *Herbert Hoover*, 312.

52. "Death of Coolidge Shocks Washington," United Press, January 5, 1933, https://www.upi.com/Archives/1933/01/05/Death-of-Coolidge-shocks-Washington/6011515040932/.

53. Lyons, *Herbert Hoover*, 321.

54. Steven Lomazow and Eric Fettman, *FDR's Deadly Secret* (New York: Public Affairs, 2009), 49.

55. "The Hinge of Fate: The Attempted Assassination of FDR in Miami," US Caribbean and Florida Digital Newspaper Project, https://ufndnp.domains .uflib.ufl.edu/the-hinge-of-fate-the-attempted-assassination-of-fdr-in-miami -ufndnp/.

56. Vincent Astor, interview, FDR Presidential Library.

57. Blaise Picchi, *The Five Weeks of Giuseppe Zangara: The Man Who Would Assassinate FDR* (Chicago: Academy Chicago, 1998), 20–29, in Mel Ayton, *Hunting the President: Threats, Plots and Assassination Attempts—From FDR to Obama* (Washington, DC: Regnery, 2014), 8.

58. Vincent Astor, interview.

59. Picchi, *The Five Weeks of Giuseppe Zangara*, 19–20; Theodore N. Pappas, "The Assassination of Anton Cermak, Mayor of Chicago: A Review of his Postinjury Medical Care," *Surgery Journal* (New York) 6, no. 2 (June, 2020): e105–e111, https://www.ncbi.nlm.nih.gov/pmc/articles/PMC7297642/.

60. Stephan Benzkofer, "'Tell Chicago I'll Pull Through,'" *Chicago Tribune*, February 10, 2013, https://www.chicagotribune.com/news/ct-xpm-2013-02 -10-ct-per-flash-cermak-shot-0210-20130210-story.html.

61. Hoover, *Memoirs: Years of Adventure*, 9.

62. Elmer Always to Ray Lyman Wilbur, October 15, 1932, in Rauchway, *Winter War*, 10.

63. Rauchway, *Winter War*, 199.

64. Herbert Hoover, *The Memoirs of Herbert Hoover: The Great Depression, 192–1941* (Redditch, UK: Read Books, 2015), 21.

65. Rauchway, *Winter War*, 197–99.

66. Herbert Hoover to FDR, February 18, 1933, Pres. Indiv., f. "Roosevelt, Franklin D.," in Rauchway, *Winter War*, 215–16. For Michigan context, see "Cash Rushed to Relieve Michigan," *New York Times*, February 15, 1933, https://www.nytimes.com/1933/02/15/archives/cash-rushed-to-relieve -michigan-banks-may-reopen-within-a-week.html.

67. Lyons, *Herbert Hoover*, 316.
68. "Japan Quits League to 'Insure Peace,'" *New York Times*, March 29, 1933, https://www.nytimes.com/1933/03/28/archives/japan-quits-league-to-insure-peace-says-differences-as-to-the.html.
69. Lyons, *Herbert Hoover*, 322; *Public Papers of the Presidents of the United States* (Cambridge, MA: Harvard University Press, 2020), 1042.
70. David M. Kennedy, *The American People in the Great Depression: Freedom from Fear, Part 1* (New York: Oxford University Press, 2003), 110.
71. Lyons, *Herbert Hoover*, 317.
72. Gary Dean Best, *Herbert Hoover, the Postpresidential Years, 1933–1964, Volume One: 1933–1945* (Stanford, CT: Hoover Institution Press, 1983), 1.
73. Edward G. Lengel, "Franklin Delano Roosevelt's Historic First Inauguration, March 4, 1933," White House Historical Association, https://www.whitehousehistory.org/franklin-roosevelts-historic-first-inauguration.
74. Edgar Rickard Diary, February 26, 1933, in Rauchway, *Winter War*, 226; Jonathan Alter, "'The Defining Moment,'" *New York Times*, March 7, 2006, https://www.nytimes.com/2006/05/07/books/chapters/0507-1st-alter.html.
75. "100,000 at Inauguration," *New York Times*, March 5, 1933, https://timesmachine.nytimes.com/timesmachine/1933/03/05/99296765.pdf?pdf_redirect=true&ip=0.
76. Lyons, *Herbert Hoover*, 321.
77. "Franklin Delano Roosevelt Proclamation 2039—Bank Holiday, March 6–9, 1933, Inclusive," American Presidency Project, UC Santa Barbara, https://www.presidency.ucsb.edu/documents/proclamation-2039-bank-holiday-march-6-9-1933-inclusive.
78. Milton Meltzer, *Brother, Can You Spare a Dime? The Great Depression, 1929–1933* (New York: New American Library, 1977), 422.
79. Titusville Herald Newspaper Archives, March 7, 1933.
80. Nash, author interview; Lyons, *Herbert Hoover*, 321.
81. Fiona Lee and Larissa Z. Tiedens, "Is It Lonely at the Top?: The Independence and Interdependence of Power Holders," *Organizational Behavior* 23 (2001): 43–91.
82. "Hoover to Leave for Home Today," *New York Times*, March 16, 1933, https://timesmachine.nytimes.com/timesmachine/1933/03/16/99298656.pdf?pdf_redirect=true&ip=0.
83. Hoover, *The Crusade Years*, 7.
84. *Daily Banner*, Greencastle, Putnam County, March 22, 1933.
85. Whyte, *Hoover: An Extraordinary Life*, 540.
86. "Ask the White House," White House of President George W. Bush, https://georgewbush-whitehouse.archives.gov/ask/20040119.html.

87. In 2002, Federal Reserve chairman Ben Bernanke said Hoover's assessment was actually correct, which at least introduces the idea that the prevailing narrative has some nuance to it. "Remarks by Governor Ben S. Bernanke," Federal Reserve Board, November 8, 2002, https://www.federalreserve.gov/boarddocs/speeches/2002/20021108/default.htm.

88. Best, *Herbert Hoover*, 1:129.

89. Richard Norton Smith, *An Uncommon Man: The Triumph of Herbert Hoover* (New York: Simon & Schuster, 1989), 189.

90. Amity Shlaes, *The Forgotten Man Graphic Edition: A New History of the Great Depression* (New York: HarperCollins, 2014), 207.

91. Castle to Hoover, April 30, 1934, and Hoover to Castle, May 8, 1934, in Best, *Herbert Hoover*, 1:19; Smith, *An Uncommon Man*, 187.

92. Hoover, *The Crusade Years*, xv; Whyte, *Hoover: An Extraordinary Life*, 534.

93. Hoover, *The Crusade Years*, 9.

94. Smith, *An Uncommon Man*, 172.

95. Hoover, *America's First Crusade* (New York: C. Scribner's Sons, 1942), 10.

96. Rauchway, *Winter War*, 282.

97. Lyons, *Herbert Hoover*, 419.

98. Hoover, *The Crusade Years*, 37–39.

99. "Action, and Action Now: FDR's First 100 Days," Franklin D. Roosevelt Presidential Library & Museum, https://www.fdrlibrary.org/documents/356632/390886/actionguide.pdf/07370301-a5c1-4a08-aa63-e611f9d12c34.

100. "Franklin D. Roosevelt Executive Order 6514, December 19, 1933," American Presidency Project, UC Santa Barbara, https://www.presidency.ucsb.edu/documents/executive-order-6102-requiring-gold-coin-gold-bullion-and-gold-certificates-be-delivered; Smith, *An Uncommon Man*, 181.

101. Michael Munger and Thomas Schaller, "The Prohibition-Repeal Amendments: A Natural Experiment in Interest Group Influence," *Public Choice* 90, no. 1/4 (March 1997): 139–63.

102. Christopher H. Sterling, "'The Fireside Chats'—Franklin D. Roosevelt (1933–1944)," National Registry, 2002, https://www.loc.gov/static/programs/national-recording-preservation-board/documents/FiresideChats.pdf.

103. George H. Nash, "Hoover's Forgotten Manifesto," Law and Liberty, October 2, 2014, https://lawliberty.org/hoovers-forgotten-manifesto/.

104. Hoover, *The Crusade Years*, xvi.

105. Gary Dean Best, *Herbert Hoover, the Postpresidential Years, 1933–1964*, Volume Two: 1946–1964 (Stanford, CA: Hoover Institution Press, 1983), 279.

106. Henry Stimson Diary, December 22 and 23, 1932, in Rauchway, *Winter War*, 72.

107. Hoover quoted in Smith, *An Uncommon Man*, 195.

108. Best, *Herbert Hoover*, 1:9.

109. *Washington Post*, July 29, 1934, in Best, *Herbert Hoover*, 1:27–28.

110. Whyte, *Hoover: An Extraordinary Life*, 542; Ritchie, *Electing FDR*, 186.

111. Hoover, *The Crusade Years*, xviii.

112. Herbert Hoover, *The Challenge to Liberty* (New York: Charles Scribner's Sons, 1934), 1–2.

113. *Indianapolis Times*, September 5, 1934, 8.

114. Hoover, *The Crusade Years*, cxx; Smith, *An Uncommon Man*, 202.

115. Best, *Herbert Hoover*, 1:33-44.

116. Hoover, *The Crusade Years*, 57.

117. Barone, *How America's Political Parties Change*, 41; "Tide Sweeps Nation; Democrats Clinch Two-Thirds Rule of the Senate," *New York Times*, November 7, 1934, https://www.nytimes.com/1934/11/07/archives/tide-sweeps-nation-democrats-clinch-twothirds-rule-of-the-senate.html. The senate had fifty-nine Democrats, one Farmer-Laborer, and one Progressive. See also "Party Division," U.S. Senate, https://www.senate.gov/history/partydiv.htm.

118. "President Franklin Delano Roosevelt and the New Deal," Library of Congress, https://www.loc.gov/classroom-materials/united-states-history -primary-source-timeline/great-depression-and-world-war-ii-1929-1945 /franklin-delano-roosevelt-and-the-new-deal/.

119. Hoover, *Memoirs: The Great Depression*, 460.

120. *Indianapolis Times* 48, no. 56, May 15, 1936, in Best, 1:59.

121. Hoover, *The Crusade Years*, 88.

122. *New York Times*, January 26, 1936.

123. David Pietrusza, *Roosevelt Sweeps Nation: FDR's 1936 Landslide and the Triumph of the Liberal Ideal* (New York: Diversion Books, 2022), 31.

124. Matthew Continetti, *The Right: The Hundred-Year War for American Conservatism* (New York: Basic Books, 2022), 48; Smith, *An Uncommon Man*, 176.

125. Smith, *An Uncommon Man*, 221.

126. Pietrusza, *Roosevelt Sweeps the Nation*, 185–87.

127. Nash, author interview.

128. Hoover, *The Crusade Years*, xiv; D. M. Reynolds to Hoover, May 1, 1935, in Best, *Herbert Hoover*, 1:42.

129. Pietrusza, *Roosevelt Sweeps the Nation*, 239.

130. "Boston Globe Newspaper Clipping, June 10, 1936," *Boston Globe*, https:// www.newspapers.com/newspage/431583801/.

131. "Book Manuscript Material—MEMOIRS V. III The Aftermath—1950 Printed Edition," 262, Hoover Papers, in Best, *Herbert Hoover*, 1:60.

132. Hoover, *The Crusade Years*, 106.

133. Spangler to Hoover, November 19, 1936, and John D. M. Hamilton oral history, Hoover Presidential Library, in Best, *Herbert Hoover*, 1:74.

134. "Second Inaugural Address of Franklin D. Roosevelt, January 20, 1937," Avalon Project, Yale Law School, https://avalon.law.yale.edu/20th_century /froos2.asp.

135. Best, *Herbert Hoover*, 1:76.

136. Continetti, *The Right*, 50.

137. Smith, *An Uncommon Man*, 24; "How FDR Lost His Brief War on the Supreme Court," National Constitution Center, February 5, 2023, https:// constitutioncenter.org/blog/how-fdr-lost-his-brief-war-on-the-supreme -court-2.

138. Michael Hiltzik, *The New Deal* (New York: Free Press, 2011), 364.

139. Shlaes, *The Forgotten Man*, 303.

140. "'Hands off Court,' Hoover Says, Warning of 'Road to Suicide,'" *New York Times*, February 21, 1937, https://timesmachine.nytimes.com/timesmachine /1937/02/21/118955836.html.

141. "Franklin D. Roosevelt Fireside Chat, March 9, 1937," American Presidency Project, UC Santa Barbara, https://www.presidency.ucsb.edu/docu ments/fireside-chat-17.

142. Hoover, *Memoirs: The Great Depression*, 337.

143. Richard Brust, "1925–1944: A New Deal," *ABA Journal*, January 2, 2015, https://www.abajournal.com/magazine/article/1935_1944_a_new_deal; "When a Switch in Time Saved Nine," *New York Times*, November 10, 1985, https://www.nytimes.com/1985/11/10/opinion/l-when-a-switch-in-time -saved-nine-143165.html.

144. Will Irwin, "Herbert Hoover Tells 'What America Must Do Next,'" *American Magazine*, July 16, 1938, in Best, *Herbert Hoover*, 1:112.

145. Jonathan M. Finegold Catalan, "Dangerous Lessons of 1937," Mises Institute, February 2, 2010, https://mises.org/library/dangerous-lessons-1937.

146. Michael D. Bordo and Joseph G. Haubrich, *Deep Recessions, Fast Recoveries, and Financial Crises: Evidence from the American Record* (Washington, DC: National Bureau of Economic Research, 2012); "Recession of 1937–38," Federal Reserve History, https://www.federalreservehistory.org /essays/recession-of-1937-38.

147. "Seats in Congress Gained/Lost by the President's Party in Mid-Term Elections," American Presidency Project, UC Santa Barbara, https://www .presidency.ucsb.edu/statistics/data/seats-congress-gainedlost-the-presidents -party-mid-term-elections.

148. "Herbert Hoover Speeches: Economic Club of Chicago, December 16, 1937," Pepperdine School of Public Policy, https://publicpolicy.pepper

dine.edu/academics/research/faculty-research/new-deal/hoover-speeches /hh121637.htm.

149. Nash, author interview; Hoover, *Memoirs: The Great Depression*, 2; Hoover, *The Crusade Years*, 3, 120; Lyons, *Herbert Hoover*, 356–57.

150. Smith, *An Uncommon Man*, 251.

151. "Hoover Is Welcomed by Crowd in Finland," *New York Times*, March 15, 1938, https://timesmachine.nytimes.com/timesmachine/1938/03/15/9811 1269.pdf?pdf_redirect=true&.

152. Hoover, *The Crusade Years*, 112, 116.

153. "Hoover Reaches Berlin," *New York Times*, March 8, 1938, https://times machine.nytimes.com/timesmachine/1938/03/08/98108379.pdf?pdf_redi rect=true&ip=0.

154. Louis Paul Lochne, *Herbert Hoover and Germany* (London: Macmillan, 1960), 134.

155. Lyons, *Herbert Hoover*, 357.

156. Erik Larson, *In the Garden of Beasts: Love, Terror, and an American Family in Hitler's Berlin* (New York: Crown, 2011), 355.

157. John Lukacs, "HISTORY: Herbert Hoover Meets Adolph Hitler," *American Scholar* 62, no. 2 (Spring 1993): 235–38.

158. Smith, *An Uncommon Man*, 254.

159. Herbert Hoover, *Freedom Betrayed: Herbert Hoover's Secret History of the Second World War and Its Aftermath*, ed. George Nash (Stanford, CA: Hoover Institution Press, 2011), 124–25.

160. Hoover, *The Crusade Years*, 121–22; "Herbert Hoover Speeches: October 26, 1937," Pepperdine School of Public Policy, https://publicpolicy.pepper dine.edu/academics/research/faculty-research/new-deal/hoover-speeches /hh102637.htm; Lyons, *Herbert Hoover*, 357; "Hoover Blunt to Hitler on Nazism; Says Progress Demands Liberty," *New York Times*, March 9, 1938, https://timesmachine.nytimes.com/timesmachine/1938/03/09/96804902 .pdf?pdf_redirect=true&ip=0.

161. Walter Russell Mead, *Arc of a Covenant* (New York: Borzoi, 2022), 184.

162. *Representative American Speeches 1937-1938*, vol. II, no. 10, Internet Archive, https://archive.org/stream/representativeam009611mbp/representativeam 009611mbp_djvu.txt.

163. Hoover, *The Crusade Years*, 125; Lyons, *Herbert Hoover*, 358.

164. Hoover, *The Crusade Years*, 126.

165. Ibid., 141, 310.

166. "Charles Lindbergh Makes 'Un-American' Speech," History Unfolded, September 11, 1941, https://newspapers.ushmm.org/events/charles-lindbergh -makes-un-american-speech.

167. Matthew Continetti, "The Return of the Old American Right," *Wall Street Journal*, April 8, 2022, https://www.wsj.com/articles/the-return-of-the-old-american-right-11649430434.

168. "Isolationism—The End of America's Isolation," American Foreign Relations, https://www.americanforeignrelations.com/E-N/Isolationism-The-end-of-america-s-isolationism.html.

169. Hoover, *The Crusade Years*, 129.

170. Tony Wesolowsky and Matthew Luxmoore, "Molotov-Ribbentrip What? Do Russians Know of Key World War II Pact?" Radio Free Europe Radio Liberty, August 22, 2019, https://www.rferl.org/a/molotov-ribbentrop-what-do-russians-know-of-key-wwii-pact/30123950.html.

171. Hoover, *The Crusade Years*, 125.

172. "Robert A. Taft: A Featured Biography," U.S. Senate, https://www.senate.gov/senators/FeaturedBios/Featured_Bio_Taft.htm.

173. Herbert Hoover to Will Irwin, November 16, 1938, Irwin Papers, in Best, *Herbert Hoover*, 1:117.

174. Lyons, *Herbert Hoover*, 359.

175. Joseph Allen to Ben Allen, January 22, 1939, in Best, *Herbert Hoover*, 1:121.

176. Smith, *An Uncommon Man*, 263.

177. "Hoover's Address on 'New Departure' in Our Foreign Policy," *New York Times*, February 2, 1939, https://timesmachine.nytimes.com/timesmachine/1939/02/02/94673711.html?pageNumber=6.

178. Chandler to Hoover, February 7, 1939, Herbert Hoover Papers, Post-Presidential Individual Files, in Best, *Herbert Hoover*, 1:119.

179. "*Fredericksburg News*, July 13, 1939 Issue," NewspaperArchive, https://newspaperarchive.com/fredericksburg-news-jul-13-1939-p-4/.

180. "How Did Public Opinion about Entering World War II Change between 1939 and 1941?" Americans and the Holocaust, https://exhibitions.ushmm.org/americans-and-the-holocaust/us-public-opinion-world-war-II-1939-1941.

181. Lyons, *Herbert Hoover*, 359–60.

182. Iskander Rehman, "Lessons from the Winter War: Frozen Grit and Finland Fabian's Defense," War on the Rocks, July 20, 2016, https://warontherocks.com/2016/07/lessons-from-the-winter-war-frozen-grit-and-finlands-fabian-defense/.

183. Caleb Larson, "The Molotov Cocktail: A Short History," *National Interest*, July 27, 2020, https://nationalinterest.org/blog/buzz/molotov-cocktail-short-history-163649.

184. Nash, author interview.

185. Richard Overy, *Blood and Ruins: The Last Imperial War, 1931–1945* (New York: Penguin Books, 2022), 611.

186. Nash, author interview.

187. Best, *Herbert Hoover*, 1:151–52.

188. William A. Harris, "Television, FDR and the 1940 Presidential Conventions," *Forward with Roosevelt* blog, National Archives, July 28, 2020, https://fdr.blogs.archives.gov/2020/07/28/television-fdr-and-the-1940-presidential-conventions/.

189. For poll numbers see Pamphlet, "Political Outlook for 1940," Opinion Research Corporation, May 21, 1940, in "Campaign 1940" (Hoover Papers, Post Presidential Subject Files), in Best, *Herbert Hoover*, 1:154–55; *Liberty Magazine* article referenced in Best, *Herbert Hoover*, 1:155–56.

190. *New York Times*, June 26, 1940, in Best, *Herbert Hoover*, 1:162.

191. Hoover, *The Crusade Years*, 212.

192. Richard C. Bain and Judith H. Parris, *Convention Decisions and Voting Records* (Washington, DC: Brookings Institution, 1973), 254–256; Best, *Herbert Hoover*, 1:164–65.

193. Turner Catledge, "Republicans Nominate Wendell Willkie for the Presidency on the 6th Ballot," *New York Times*, June 28, 1940, https://archive.nytimes.com/www.nytimes.com/library/politics/camp/400628convention-gop-ra.html.

194. Tevi Troy, "The Evolution of Party Conventions," National Affairs, Summer 2016, https://www.nationalaffairs.com/publications/detail/the-evolution-of-party-conventions.

195. Hoover, *The Crusade Years*, 210, 445–47, 454; Glen Jeansonne and David Luhrssen, *Herbert Hoover: A Life* (New York: New American Library, 2016), 335.

196. "Son Keeps President's Name on Stage," *Chicago Tribune*, June 28, 1984.

197. Best, *Herbert Hoover*, 1:173.

198. Nash, author interview; Hoover, *The Crusade Years*, xxv.

199. Michael Schuman, "Hoover's Legacy," *Chicago Tribune*, January 9, 1994, https://www.chicagotribune.com/news/ct-xpm-1994-01-09-9401090148-story.html.

200. Lyons, *Herbert Hoover*, 361.

201. Herbert Hoover to Hull, June 3, 1941, National Committee, Food for the Small Democracies Papers, Hoover Institution, in Best, *Herbert Hoover*, 1:189.

202. On September 4, 1941, Hoover wrote that FDR was trying to "get us into war through the Japanese back door." Herbert Hoover to Castle, September 4, 1941, Hoover Papers, Post-Presidential Initiative, in Best, *Herbert Hoover*, 1:200.

203. "FDR's 'Day of Infamy' Speech," *Prologue Magazine* 33, no. 4 (Winter 2001):

https://www.archives.gov/publications/prologue/2001/winter/crafting-day-of
-infamy-speech.html.

204. Smith, *An Uncommon Man*, 305.

205. J. Garry Clifford and Masako R. Okura, ed., *The Desperate Diplomat: Saburo Kurusu's Memoir of the Weeks before Pearl Harbor* (Columbia: University of Missouri Press, 2016), 17.

206. Best, *Herbert Hoover*, 1:204–5; Matthew Schaefer, "Hoover and the 20th Century Presidents: Franklin Roosevelt," *Hoover Heads* blog, National Archives, April 8, 2020, https://hoover.blogs.archives.gov/2020/04/08/hoover -and-20th-century-presidents-franklin-roosevelt/.

207. Herbert Hoover, *America's First Crusade* (New York: C. Scribner's Sons, 1942); Best, *Herbert Hoover*, 1:206.

208. Allan Nevins, "Mr. Hoover Looks Back on Our Part in the Last Peace," *New York Times*, February 1, 1942, https://timesmachine.nytimes.com/timesmachine /1942/02/01/85513666.pdf?pdf_redirect=true&ip=0.

209. Thomas Schwartz, "Respectful Partisans: Herbert Hoover and Bernard Baruch," *Hoover Heads* blog, National Archives, December 30, 2020, https:// hoover.blogs.archives.gov/2020/12/30/respectful-partisans-herbert-hoover -and-bernard-baruch/; Lyons, *Herbert Hoover*, 371.

210. Schaefer, "Hoover and the 20th Century Presidents"; Charles Rappleye, *Herbert Hoover in the White House: The Ordeal of the Presidency* (New York: Simon & Schuster, 2016), xiv; Timothy Walch and Dwight M. Miller, *Herbert Hoover and Harry S. Truman: A Documentary History* (Worland, WY: High Plains Publishing company, 1992), 3.

211. Herbert Hoover to Ruth Simms, December 18, 1941.

212. Herbert Hoover, *Addresses upon the American Road: World War II, 1941– 1945* (New York: D. Van Nostrand, 1946), 5–13, https://hoover.archives.gov /sites/default/files/research/ebooks/b3v4_full.pdf; William Henry Chamberlin, "The Problems of Lasting Peace," *Atlantic*, September 1942, https://www .theatlantic.com/magazine/archive/1942/09/the-problems-of-lasting-peace /657216/.

213. Edgar Rickard Diary, January 7, 1944, in Best, *Herbert Hoover*, 1:251; Lyons, *Herbert Hoover*, 334, 372.

214. Franklin D. Roosevelt to Herbert Hoover, January 7, 1944; Herbert Hoover reply, January 28, 1944. See also "On the Passing of Lou Henry Hoover," *Hoover Heads* blog, National Archives, https://hoover.blogs.archives.gov/2018 /01/10/on-the-passing-of-lou-henry-hoover/.

215. Lyons, *Herbert Hoover*, 373.

216. Hoover, *The Crusade Years*, 33–34.

217. "Letter to John Hamilton," in Best, *Herbert Hoover*, 1:256–59; "Hoover

Disclaims Link to any Aspirant," *New York Times*, May 26, 1944, https://timesmachine.nytimes.com/timesmachine/1944/05/26/85156107.html?pageNumber=34.

218. "Night Address of Ex-President Hoover before the Republican Convention," *New York Times*, June 28, 1944, https://timesmachine.nytimes.com/timesmachine/1944/06/28/86865722.html.

219. Hoover, *Addresses upon the American Road.*

220. Smith, *An Uncommon Man*, 333.

221. William K. Klingaman, *1929: The Year of the Great Crash* (New York: Harper & Row, 1989), 340.

222. Ibid. For Hoover's reaction, see Hoover, *The Crusade Years*, 256.

223. Hoover, *The Crusade Years*, 252.

224. H. G. Bruenn, "Clinical Notes on the Illness and Death of President Franklin D. Roosevelt," *Annals of Internal Medicine* 72, no. 4 (April 1970): 578–91.

225. "From the Archives: FDR Started Fourth Term 75 Years Ago," *San Diego Tribune*, January 21, 1945, https://www.sandiegouniontribune.com/news/local-history/story/2020-01-20/from-the-archives-fdr-started-fourth-term-75-years-ago.

226. Resa Willis, *FDR and Lucy: Lovers and Friends* (New York: Routledge, 2004), 139; Harry S. Goldsmith, *A Conspiracy of Silence: FDR Impact on History* (Bloomington, IN: iUniverse, 2007), 43.

227. Felix Morley, *For the Record* (South Bend, IN: Gateway, 1979), 416, in Best, *Herbert Hoover*, 1:263.

228. Ibid.

229. Hoover, *The Crusade Years*, 253; Lyons, *Herbert Hoover*, 335.

230. Best, *Herbert Hoover*, 1:264.

231. Jeffrey Frank, "How FDR's Death Changed the Vice Presidency," *New Yorker*, April 17, 2015, https://www.newyorker.com/news/daily-comment/how-f-d-r-s-death-changed-the-vice-presidency.

232. A. J. Baime, *The Accidental President: Harry S. Truman and the Four Months That Changed the World* (Boston: Houghton Mifflin Harcourt, 2017), 91; James F. Byrnes, *All in One Lifetime* (New York: HarperCollins, 1958), 224; Robert H. Ferrell, *Choosing Truman: The Democratic Convention of 1944* (Columbia: University of Missouri Press, 2013), 7.

233. Hoover, *The Crusade Years*, 253.

234. "Oral History Interview with Harry Easley," interviewed by J. R. Fuchs, August 24, 1967, Harry S. Truman Presidential Library, https://www.trumanlibrary.org/oralhist/easleyh.htm.

235. Smith, *An Uncommon Man*, 335.

236. "Herbert Hoover to Harry S. Truman, April 12, 1945," in Walch and Miller, 28.

237. Walch and Miller, 5.

238. Harry Truman, *Year of Decisions*, vol. 1 (Old Saybrook, CT: Konecky & Konecky, 1955), 465.

239. "Hoover Notes of Phone Call with Stimson, May 17, 1945," in Walch and Miller, 34.

240. "Rickard Diary, May 13–14, 1945," in Walch and Miller, 32; W. E. Leuchtenburg, *In the Shadow of FDR: From Harry Truman to George W. Bush* (Ithaca, NY: Cornell University Press, 2001), 13.

241. Walch and Miller, 27.

242. "Diary of Eben A. Ayers, May 24, 1945," in Walch and Miller, 35.

243. "Truman to Hoover, May 24, 1945," in Walch and Miller, 35.

244. "Rickard Diary, May 27," in Walch and Miller. 36–37; Best, *Herbert Hoover*, 1:269; Schaefer, "Hoover and the 20th Century Presidents."

245. Anne O'Hare McCormick, "The Logistics of Peace are Also a Problem," *New York Times*, May 28, 1945, https://timesmachine.nytimes.com/timesmachine/1945/05/28/305336142.pdf?pdf_redirect=true&ip=0.

246. "HH Notes of Meeting with Truman, May 28, 1945," in Walch and Miller, 37–38.

247. Kaete M. O'Connell, "Weapon of War, Tool of Peace: U.S. Food Diplomacy in Postwar Germany," Dissertation (August, 2019), https://scholarshare.temple.edu/bitstream/handle/20.500.12613/507/680714_pdf_791075_E9E0695C-ACB9-11E9-B0C5-299A4D662D30.pdf?sequence=1&isAllowed=y.

248. Truman, *Year of Decisions*, 1:309–10. Truman's diary at the time was less effusive, simply stating, "Saw Herbert Hoover day before yesterday and had a pleasant and constructive conversation on food and the general troubles of US Presidents—two in particular." "Truman Diary, June 1, 1945," in Walch and Miller, 53. Walch and Miller, 40, 43.

249. "Truman Will Proclaim V-J Day as Surrender Ceremonies Are Held," *New York Times*, September 1, 1945, https://www.nytimes.com/1945/09/01/archives/truman-will-proclaim-vj-day-as-surrender-ceremonies-are-held.html.

250. Walch and Miller, 8–9; Best, *Herbert Hoover*, 1:277.

251. "Notes of a phone call from Clinton P. Anderson to HH, February 25, 1946," in Walch and Miller, 63; Best, *Herbert Hoover*, 2:286.

252. *New York Times*, March 1, 1946, in Best, *Herbert Hoover*, 2:286; Walch and Miller, 66.

253. Truman, *Year of Decisions*, 1:472; Smith, *An Uncommon Man*, 352.

254. Best, *Herbert Hoover*, 2:287; Smith, *An Uncommon Man*, 352.

255. Walch and Miller, 11; Ossian, "The Grimmest Spectre."

256. Hoover, *The Crusade Years*, 258; Lyons, *Herbert Hoover*, 387.

257. "HH Diary, Undated Entry on Rome Portion of Journey."

258. Smith, *An Uncommon Man*, 354.

259. "Harry Truman Radio Appeal to the Nation for Food Conservation to Relieve Hunger Abroad, April 19, 1946," American Presidency Project, UC Santa Barbara, https://www.presidency.ucsb.edu/documents/radio-appeal -the-nation-for-food-conservation-relieve-hunger-abroad.

260. "Hoover Address, April 19, 1946, Delivered from Cairo via Radio," in Walch and Miller, 76–77; Truman, *Year of Decisions*, 1:473; Hoover, *Addresses upon the American Road*, 193–98. For specific numbers, see Smith, *An Uncommon Man*, 356.

261. Lyons, *Herbert Hoover*, 387.

262. "Truman to Hoover, April 18, 1946," in Walch and Miller, 73; Best, *Herbert Hoover*, 2:290.

263. "Hoover to Truman, April 19, 1946," in Walch and Miller, 73; Best, *Herbert Hoover*, 2:290.

264. Lyons, *Herbert Hoover*, 389.

265. "Food Need Enormous in China, Hoover Says," *New York Times*, May 4, 1946, https://timesmachine.nytimes.com/timesmachine/1946/05/04/1216 23178.pdf?pdf_redirect=true&ip=0.

266. "HH Memos on Macarthur and Japanese Occupation," n.d., in Smith, *An Uncommon Man*, 357.

267. Hoover, *Addresses upon the American Road*, 209; Walch and Miller, 12.

268. "Harry S. Truman," Office of the Historian, U.S. State Department, https:// history.state.gov/departmenthistory/travels/president/truman-harry-s.

269. Truman, *Year of Decisions*, 1:474; Walch and Miller, 12–13.

270. Truman, *Year of Decisions*, 1:474.

271. "Hoover Diary, June 6–10, 1946," in Walch and Miller, 89.

272. Jared Cohen, "What Herbert Hoover Can Teach Joe Biden," Politico, June 10, 2021, https://www.politico.com/news/magazine/2021/06/10/biden -world-covid-vaccines-hoover-famine-relief-493228.

273. Ibid.; Herbert Hoover Diary, June 20, 1946, in Walch and Miller, 88.

274. Reprinted in Herbert Hoover, *Addresses upon the American Road, 1945–48* (New York, 1948), 259–66, in Best, *Herbert Hoover*, 2:293; Truman, *Year of Decisions*, 357; "Harry Truman Letter to Members of the National Famine Emergency Committee, November 29, 1946," American Presidency Project, UC Santa Barbara, https://www.presidency.ucsb.edu/documents/letter -members-the-national-famine-emergency-committee; Walch and Miller, 12–13.

275. Ellman 2000: 611–17, Vallin et al., 2012: 70. Ellman 2000: 611-17. See also Vallin et al., 2012: 70.

276. Frank Dikkoter, *The Tragedy of Liberation* (London: Bloomsbury, 2013), 3.

277. Ben Steil, *The Marshall Plan: Dawn of the Cold War* (Oxford, UK: Oxford University Press, 2018), 215.

278. Walch and Miller, 97; Lyons, *Herbert Hoover*, 393.

279. Edgar Rickard Diary, February 23, 1947, in Best, *Herbert Hoover*, 2:299.

280. Frank E. Mason Oral History, Hoover Presidential Library, in Best, *Herbert Hoover*, 2:299.

281. John Dickerson, "The Hardest Job in the World," *Atlantic*, May 2018, https://www.theatlantic.com/magazine/archive/2018/05/a-broken-office/556883/.

282. "Papers of President's Committee on Administrative Management, 1936–1939," FDR Presidential Library & Museum, https://www.fdrlibrary.org/documents/356632/390886/findingaid_pcomm_admin_man.pdf/352fed92-f896-4c6b-ab65-3fb77246affe.

283. Walch and Miller, 129; *New York Times*, September 30, 1947, in Best, *Herbert Hoover*, 2:317.

284. Rappleye, *Herbert Hoover in the White House*, 467.

285. Walch and Miller, 182; "Hoover Dam," Bureau of Reclamation, https://www.usbr.gov/lc/hooverdam/history/articles/naming.html.

286. Hoover, *Addresses upon the American Road*, 155; Walch and Miller, 14.

287. Best, *Herbert Hoover*, 2:312; Walch and Miller, 129.

288. "Harry S. Truman to Herbert Hoover, June 23, 1948," Post-Presidential Individual Correspondence File (hereinafter PPI), Herbert Hoover Papers, Herbert Hoover Presidential Library, West Branch, Iowa. Truman's letter was handwritten. Three days later, Hoover warmly thanked Truman for his "touching note." Hoover to Truman, June 26, 1948. See also Hoover, *The Crusade Years*, 273.

289. "HT address, October 19, 1948," in Walch and Miller, 185.

290. Ibid., 187–88.

291. Ibid., 8.

292. "1948 Presidential Election," 270 to Win, https://www.270towin.com/1948_Election.

293. "HT to HH November 12 and 26," in Walch and Miller, 141.

294. Nash, author interview.

295. "Truman to Congress, June 20, 1949," in Walch and Miller, 168; Walch and Miller, 20; Lyons, *Herbert Hoover*, 402; Luke A. Nichter, *The Last Brahmin: Henry Cabot Lodge, Jr. and the Making of the Cold War* (New Haven: Yale Universitiy Press, 2020), 81–82.

296. Dewey to Hoover, July 18, 1949, and Hoover to Dewey, July 26, 1949, in HP-PII, in Best, *Herbert Hoover*, 2:332–33.

297. "HT to HH, November 25, 1950," in Walch and Miller, 199; Best, *Herbert Hoover*, 2:340.

298. "HH to HT, November 26, 1950," in Walch and Miller, 201; Lyons, *Herbert Hoover*, 335; Best, *Herbert Hoover*, 2:341.

299. Richard Nixon, *The Memoirs of Richard Nixon* (New York: Simon & Schuster, 2013); see also Richard Nixon, *Six Crises* (New York: Simon & Schuster, 2013), 67.

300. Mary Louise Parker, author interview, New York, NY, December 3, 2021.

301. Smith, *An Uncommon Man*, 398.

302. Parker, author interview; Donald W. Whisenhunt, *President Herbert Hoover* (New York: Nova Science, 2007), 141.

303. "1952 Presidential Election," 270 to Win, https://www.270towin.com/1952 _Election/.

304. Martin to Hoover, November 7, 1952, Herbert Hoover Papers—Post-Presidential Initiative, in Best, *Herbert Hoover*, 2:366.

305. Clare Boothe Luce, interviewed by Gary Dean Best, August 12, 1980, in Best, *Herbert Hoover*, 2:364.

306. Records of the Commissions on Organization of the Executive Branch of the Government [Hover Commission]," National Archives, https://www .archives.gov/research/guide-fed-records/groups/264.html#264.3; "Herbert Hoover at the National Press Club, March 10, 1954," Library of Congress, https://www.loc.gov/rr/record/pressclub/pdf/HerbertHoover.pdf.

307. Herbert Hoover to Klarence Kelland, March 7, 1955, Hoover Papers– Post-Presidential Initiative, in Best, *Herbert Hoover*, 2:387. See also Nichter, *The Last Brahmin*.

308. Timothy Walch, "Putting Ex-Presidents Back to Work," Origins, Ohio State University, https://origins.osu.edu/history-news/putting-ex-presidents-back -work?language_content_entity=en.

309. Walch and Miller, 211; Jeffrey M. Jones, "Who Had the Lowest Gallup Presidential Job Approval Rating?" Gallup, December 26, 2019, https://news.gallup .com/poll/272765/lowest-gallup-presidential-job-approval-rating.aspx; *New York Times*, October 14, 1955, and November 1, 1955, in Best, *Herbert Hoover*, 2:396.

310. "Former Presidents: Pensions, Office Allowances, and Other Federal Benefits," Congressional Research Service, March 16, 2016, https://www.every crsreport.com/files/20160316_RL34631_784f168c65ce8eec7fe3a9e0c afd57496443432e.pdf.

311. Hoover, *Addresses upon the American Road*, 127.

312. "Herbert Hoover to Harry Truman, October 14, 1964," in Walch and Miller, 12–13, 238; Best, *Herbert Hoover*, 2:292.

313. Lyons, *Herbert Hoover*, 433.

314. *People*, August 20, 1956.

315. Hoover, *The Crusade Years*, xxx; Parker, author interview; Michael Schaefer, "I Might As Well Finish My Smoke . . . ," *Hoover Heads* blog, National Archives, February 6, 2019, https://hoover.blogs.archives.gov/2019/02/06/i-might -as-well-finish-my-smoke/; Best, *Herbert Hoover*, 2:400.

316. Herbert Hoover, *The Ordeal of Woodrow Wilson* (Baltimore, MD: Johns Hopkins University Press, 1958), ix, xxiv; Best, *Herbert Hoover*, 2:404.

317. Herbert Hoover, *An American Epic* (Washington, DC: Regnery, 1959).

318. Spencer Howard, "Freedom Betrayed," *Hoover Heads* blog, National Archives, September 8, 2021, https://hoover.blogs.archives.gov/2021/09/08 /freedom-betrayed/.

319. Parker, author interview.

320. Harris Gaylor Warren, *Herbert Hoover and the Great Depression* (New York: Oxford University Press, 1959); Patrick G. O'Brien and and Philip T. Rosen, "Hoover and the Historians: The Resurrection of a President," 36, University of Iowa Libraries, https://pubs.lib.uiowa.edu/annals-of-iowa/article /4449/galley/113326/view/.

321. Parker, author interview.

322. Hoover, *Addresses upon the American Road, 1955–60*, 156–61 in Best, *Herbert Hoover*, 2:415.

323. Continetti, *The Right*, 162; William F. Buckley, *Rumbles Left and Right: A Book about Troublesome People and Ideas* (New York: G. P. Putnam's and Sons, 1963), 67.

324. Scott Bomboy, "The Drama behind President Kennedy's 1960 Election Win," National Constitution Center, November 7, 2017, https://constitution center.org/blog/the-drama-behind-president-kennedys-1960-election-win/; Best, *Herbert Hoover*, 2:418.

325. Neil McNeil Oral History, Hoover Presidential Library, in Best, *Herbert Hoover*, 2:418–19.

326. Lyons, *Herbert Hoover*, 434.

327. Evan Thomas, *Being Nixon: A Man Divided* (New York: Random House, 2015), 128–29.

328. Smith, *An Uncommon Man*, 22.

329. Hoover Library (@HooverPresLib), "Telegram and letter between Herbert Hoover and John F. Kennedy when weather prevented Hoover from attending Kennedy's inauguration, Jan. 1961," Twitter, April 3, 2020, https://twitter .com/HooverPresLib/status/1246100047974019072/photo/1.

330. "Western Union Telegram, March 2, 1945," Facebook, March 2, 2021, https:// www.facebook.com/HerbertHooverNHS/photos/pcb.5440240776016467 /5440231399350738/.

331. "Hoover Declines Peace Corps Post," *New York Times*, March 10, 1961, https://timesmachine.nytimes.com/timesmachine/1961/03/11/98539247 .pdf?pdf_redirect=true&ip=0.

332. Luhrssen and Jeansonne, *Herbert Hoover: A Life*, 397.

333. Arthur C. Brooks, "The Dignity Deficit," *National Review*, January 27, 2018, https://www.nationalreview.com/2018/01/american-poverty-root-cause-dignity -deficit/.

334. Luhrssen and Jeansonne, *Herbert Hoover: A Life*, 397.

335. "Absent Hoover Is Given Ovation by Convention," *New York Times*, July 14, 1964, https://timesmachine.nytimes.com/timesmachine/1964/07/14/9763 2873.pdf?pdf_redirect=true&ip=0.

336. "Herbert Hoover Is Dead; Ex-President, 90, Served Country in Varied Fields; Flags Lowered," *New York Times*, October 21, 1964, https://www.nytimes.com /1964/10/21/archives/herbert-hoover-is-dead-expresident-90-served-country-in -varied.html; Lyons, *Herbert Hoover*, 338.

337. Lyons, *Herbert Hoover*, 338.

338. "1932 Presidential Election," 270 to Win, https://www.270towin.com/1932 _Election/.

339. "1964 Presidential Election," 270 to Win, https://www.270towin.com/1964 _Election/.

340. "Members of the General Assembly of Georgia, 1965–1966," Digital Library of Georgia, February 1965, http://dlg.galileo.usg.edu/cgi-bin/govdimag.cgi ?path=dbs/1965/ga/s700/_ps1/g4/1965_h66/sess_p1_sno_p1.con/&user=ga lileo&sessionid=637f8586-1547653717-5036&serverid=DU&instcode =afpl&return=ggpd%3fuserid%3dgalileo%26dbs%3dggpd%26action% 3dretrieve%26recno%3d70%26numrecs%3d100%26__rtype%3drecno%26 key%3dy-ga-bs700-b-ps1-bg4-b1965-h66-bsess-p1-sno-p1.

CHAPTER 6: THE FORMER

1. For complete study on the "overview effect" see Frank White, *The Overview Effect: Space Exploration and Human Evolution*, 3rd ed. (Reston, VA: American Institute of Aeronautics & Astronautics, 2014).

2. Jonathan Alter, *His Very Best: Jimmy Carter, a Life* (New York: Simon & Schuster, 2021), 613.

3. Douglas Brinkley, *The Unfinished Presidency: Jimmy Carter's Journey to the Nobel Peace Prize* (New York: Penguin Books, 1999).

4. Until Jimmy Carter, his fellow engineer Herbert Hoover held the record for the longest post-presidency, at thirty-one years and 230 days. Carter beat that record on September 8, 2012, and continued his work until

February 18, 2023, when it was announced that the president would enter hospice care, effectively ending his active post-presidency.

5. Jimmy Carter, *A Full Life: Reflections at Ninety* (New York: Simon & Schuster, 2016), 238.

6. "YouGov Public Opinion Polling," YouGov, https://today.yougov.com/ratings/politics/popularity/Democrats/al.

7. Steven R. Weisman, "Reagan Takes Oath as 40th President; Promises an 'Era of National Renewal'; Minutes Later, 52 U.S. Hostages in Iran Fly to Freedom after 444-Day Ordeal," *New York Times*, January 21, 1981, https://www.nytimes.com/1981/01/21/us/reagan-takes-oath-40-th-president-promises-era-national-renewal-minutes-later-52.html.

8. David Harris, *The Crisis: The President, the Prophet, and the Shah—1979 and the Coming of Militant Islam* (New York: Little, Brown, 2004), 424.

9. Jeane J. Kirkpatrick, "Dictatorships and Double Standards." *Commentary*, November 1979, https://www.commentary.org/articles/jeane-kirkpatrick/dictatorships-double-standards/.

10. Hal Brands, *Making the Unipolar Moment: US Foreign Policy and the Rise of the Post–Cold War Order* (Ithaca, NY: Cornell University Press, 2016), 26.

11. Karen DeYoung, "Sandinistas Enter Managua, Ending Civil War," *Washington Post*, July 20, 1979, https://www.washingtonpost.com/archive/politics/1979/07/20/sandinistas-enter-managua-ending-civil-war/993c08bb-2a14-43cd-9227-d86054b2e03d/.

12. George C. Wilson, "Carter Is Converted to a Big Spender on Defense Projects," *Washington Post*, January 29, 1980, https://www.washingtonpost.com/archive/politics/1980/01/29/carter-is-converted-to-a-big-spender-on-defense-projects/6a04fed3-ca48-433e-a972-cca13bdf83a0/.

13. Henry Kissinger, *Leadership: Six Studies in World Strategy* (New York: Penguin Press, 2022), 191.

14. "Camp David Accords and the Arab-Israeil Peace Process," Office of the Historian, U.S. State Department, https://history.state.gov/milestones/1977-1980/camp-david.

15. Robert A. Strong, "Jimmy Carter: Campaigns and Elections," Miller Center, University of Virginia, https://millercenter.org/president/carter/campaigns-and-elections.

16. "Jimmy Carter Address to the Nation on Energy, April 18, 1977," American Presidency Project, UC Santa Barbara, https://www.presidency.ucsb.edu/documents/address-the-nation-energy.

17. Jessie Kratz, "The Iranian Hostage Crisis," *Pieces of History* blog, National Archives, November 29, 2021, https://prologue.blogs.archives.gov/2021/11/29/the-iran-hostage-crisis/.

18. "Oil Shock of 1978–79," Federal Reserve History, https://www.federalreserve history.org/essays/oil-shock-of-1978-79.

19. Frank A. Verrastro and Guy Caruso, "The Arab Oil Embargo—40 Years Later," Center for Strategic and International Studies, October 16, 2013; "Oil Dependence and U.S. Foreign Policy: 1850–2022," Council on Foreign Relations, https://www.cfr.org/timeline/oil-dependence-and-us-foreign-policy.

20. Alan S. Blinder, "The Anatomy of Double-Digit Inflation in the 1970s," University of Chicago Press, https://www.nber.org/system/files/chapters/c11462 /c11462.pdf.

21. Peggy Noonan, "Jimmy Carter's 'Malaise' Speech Aged Well," *Wall Street Journal*, February 23, 2023, https://www.wsj.com/articles/jimmy-carters-malaise -speech-aged-well-ex-president-citizen-habitat-for-humanity-address-white -house-polarization-3db889d1; "Jimmy Carter Energy and the National Goals: A Crisis of Confidence, July 15, 1979," American Rhetoric, https://www .americanrhetoric.com/speeches/jimmycartercrisisofconfidence.htm.

22. Alter, *His Very Best*, 499.

23. Chris Whipple, "Ted Kennedy: The Day the Presidency Was Lost," ABC News, August 28, 2009, https://abcnews.go.com/Politics/TedKennedy/story ?id=8436488.

24. "Jimmy Carter Presidential Debate in Cleveland," American Presidency Project, UC Santa Barbara, https://www.presidency.ucsb.edu/documents /presidential-debate-cleveland.

25. "1980 Presidential Election," 270 to Win, https://www.270towin.com/1980 _Election/.

26. "Nation: When Jimmy Knew," *Time*, November 17, 1980, https://content .time.com/time/subscriber/article/0,33009,950484,00.html.

27. Alter, *His Very Best*, 594.

28. Brinkley, *The Unfinished Presidency*, 1–2.

29. George Packer, *Our Man: Richard Holbrooke and the End of the American Century* (New York: Knopf, 2020), 207.

30. Jimmy Carter, *Keeping Faith* (Fayetteville: University of Arkansas Press, 1995), 566.

31. Harris, *The Crisis*, 390.

32. William Inboden, *The Peacemaker: Ronald Reagan, the Cold War, and the World on the Brink* (New York: Dutton, 2022), 55–56.

33. Terrence Smith, "A Weary Carter Returns to Plains," *New York Times*, January 21, 1981, https://www.nytimes.com/1981/01/21/us/a-weary-carter -returns-to-plains.html.

34. Smith, "A Weary Carter Returns to Plains"; Richard Harwood, "Freed Americans Land in W. Germany," *Washington Post*, January 21, 1981, https://

www.washingtonpost.com/archive/politics/1981/01/21/freed-americans
-land-in-w-germany/5fed6d76-d572-4c10-8c34-66caf64c830a/.

35. Alexander Meigs Haig, *Caveat: Realism, Reagan, and Foreign Policy* (London: Macmillan, 1984), 77.

36. Stanley G. Harris and Robert I. Sutton, "Functions of Parting Ceremonies in Dying Organizations," *Academy of Management Journal* 29, no. 1 (March 1986): 5–30.

37. Smith, "A Weary Carter Returns to Plains."

38. Ibid.; Harwood, "Freed Americans Land in W. Germany."

39. Brinkley, *The Unfinished Presidency*, 41.

40. Ibid.

41. Ibid., 42.

42. "Transcript of Carter's Remarks in West Germany," *New York Times*, January 22, 1981, https://www.nytimes.com/1981/01/22/world/transcript-of -carter-s-remarks-in-west-germany-after-talking-to.html.

43. David Farber, *Taken Hostage: The Iran Hostage Crisis and America's First Encounter with Radical Islam* (Princeton, NJ: Princeton University Press, 2006), 183.

44. Alter, *His Very Best*, 199.

45. Ellen Weiss and Mel Friedman, *Jimmy Carter: Champion of Peace* (New York: Aladdin Paperbacks, 2003), 48.

46. Wayne King, "Georgia's Gov. Carter Enters Democratic Race for President," *New York Times*, December 12, 1974, https://timesmachine.nytimes.com /timesmachine/1974/12/13/79883508.pdf?pdf_redirect=true&ip=0.

47. Alter, *His Very Best*, 286.

48. James Fallows, "The Passionless Presidency," *Atlantic*, May 1979, https:// www.theatlantic.com/magazine/archive/1979/05/the-passionless-presidency /308516/.

49. Julian E. Zelizer, "17 Democrats Ran for President in 1976. Can Today's GOP Learn Anything from What Happened?" Politico, September 7, 2015, https:// www.politico.com/magazine/story/2015/09/2016-election-1976-democratic -primary-213125/.

50. "Jimmy Carter Public Approval," American Presidency Project, UC Santa Barbara, https://www.presidency.ucsb.edu/statistics/data/jimmy-carter-public -approval.

51. "The Administration: Warm Words from Jimmy Cardigan," *Time*, February 14, 1977, https://content.time.com/time/subscriber/article/0,33009,914 802,00.html.

52. "Presidential Job Approval Center," Gallup, https://news.gallup.com/inter actives/185273/presidential-job-approval-center.aspx.

53. "Jimmy Carter Farewell Address to the Nation, January 14, 1981," American

Presidency Project, UC Santa Barbara, https://www.presidency.ucsb.edu /documents/farewell-address-the-nation-0.

54. "On Language," *New York Times Magazine*, February 1, 1981, https://www .nytimes.com/1981/02/01/magazine/on-language-by-william-safire.html.

55. "Photos: Jimmy Carter House, 209 Woodland Drive, Plains, Sumter County, GA," Library of Congress, https://www.loc.gov/resource/hhh.ga0438.photos ?st=gallery.

56. Carter, *A Full Life*, 206.

57. Jimmy Carter, *Everything to Gain: Making the Most of the Rest of Your Life* (Fayetteville: University of Arkansas Press, 1995), 2.

58. "Remarks of Former U.S. President Jimmy Carter at the Dedication of the Clinton Presidential Library," Carter Center, November 17, 2004, https:// www.cartercenter.org/news/documents/doc1897.html.

59. "Jimmy Carter: Independence, Missouri Remarks and a Question-and-Answer Session at a Townhall Meeting, September 2, 1980," American Presidency Project, UC Santa Barbara, https://www.presidency.ucsb.edu/documents /independence-missouri-remarks-and-question-and-answer-session-townhall -meeting.

60. Brinkley, *The Unfinished Presidency*, 3.

61. Wayne King, "Rosalynn Carter, a Tough, Tireless Campaigner, Displays Same Driving Quality as Her Husband," *New York Times*, October 18, 1976, https://www.nytimes.com/1976/10/18/archives/rosalynn-carter-a-tough -tireless-campaigner-displays-same-driving.html.

62. Rosalynn Carter, *First Lady from Plains* (Fayatteville: University of Arkansas Press, 1994), 367.

63. Carter, *Everything to Gain*, 5.

64. Alter, *His Very Best*, 617.

65. John Crudele, "Board Games," Bottom Line, *New York*, January 25, 1988, https://books.google.com/books?id=VeUCAAAAMBAJ&pg=PA19#v=one page&q&f=false.

66. "Ford's Citigroup Connection," *Wall Street Journal*, December 27, 2006, https://www.wsj.com/articles/BL-WB-1698.

67. Elisabeth Bumiller, "Ronald Reagan, Toast of Tokyo but Controversy Mars His Symbolic Trip," *Washington Post*, October 28, 1989, https://www.wash ingtonpost.com/archive/lifestyle/1989/10/28/ronald-reagan-toast-of-tokyo -but-controversy-mars-his-symbolic-trip/11cdc265-ee18-4682-8e1f-5de18 8dc3ee8/.

68. Robert Yoon, "$153 Million in Bill and Hillary Clinton Speaking Fees, Doc- umented," CNN, February 6, 2016, https://www.cnn.com/2016/02/05/pol itics/hillary-clinton-bill-clinton-paid-speeches.

69. "On Talk Circuit, George W. Bush Makes Millions but Few Waves," Politico, June 7, 2015, https://www.politico.com/story/2015/06/on-talk-circuit-george -bush-makes-millions-but-few-waves-118697; Tony Owusu, "Barack Obama Is Now Among 10 Highest Paid Public Speakers," The Street, September 25, 2017, https://www.thestreet.com/investing/highest-paid-public-speakers-143 15669.

70. Richard L. Strout, "Carter Farewell—Bowing Out with Quiet Dignity," *Christian Science Monitor*, January 16, 1981, https://www.csmonitor.com/1981 /0116/011637.html.

71. Kai Bird, *The Outlier: The Unfinished Presidency of Jimmy Carter* (New York: Crown, 2021), 604.

72. Brinkley, *The Unfinished Presidency*, 49.

73. Carter, *Keeping Faith*, xiii.

74. Paul Hendrickson, "Jimmy Carter, Casting Back," *Washington Post*, May 22, 1988, https://www.washingtonpost.com/archive/lifestyle/1988/05/22/jimmy -carter-casting-back/e835ba44-9d15-4b0c-b086-21d4c08e6312/.

75. Terence Smith, "Keeping the Faith," *New York Times*, November 7, 1982, https://www.nytimes.com/1982/11/07/books/keeping-the-faith.html.

76. Gaddis Smith, "Keeping Faith: Memoirs of a President," *Foreign Affairs*, December 1, 1982, https://www.foreignaffairs.com/reviews/capsule-review /1982-12-01/keeping-faith-memoirs-president?gad=1&gclid=CjwKCAj wwb6lBhBJEiwAbuVUSvo9K3WN727cNII8JPC-Ib-lb4C1PDqWXDO 4D8iD1h8xIHivQyKJzhoC5JEQAvD_BwE.

77. Phil Gailey, "Memoirs of a Political Partner," *New York Times*, April 15, 1984, https://www.nytimes.com/1984/04/15/books/memoirs-of-a-political -partner.html.

78. "Jimmy Carter: Biography of the 39th President of the United States," Jimmy Carter Presidential Library and Museum, https://www.jimmycarter library.gov/about_us/biography_of_jimmy_carter.

79. "Finalist: *An Hour Before Daylight: Memoirs of a Rural Boyhood*," Pulitzer Prizes, https://www.pulitzer.org/finalists/jimmy-carter.

80. Carter, *A Full Life*, 226.

81. Alter, *His Very Best*, 619.

82. Wayne King, "Carter Redux," *New York Times Magazine*, December 10, 1989, https://www.nytimes.com/1989/12/10/magazine/carter-redux.html.

83. Jeff Hullinger, "Jimmy Carter's Sunday School Teaching Days Appear to Be Over—a Hard Thing to Fathom in Georgia," 11 Alive, July 24, 2020, https://www.11alive.com/article/news/politics/jimmy-carter/jimmy-carter -sunday-school-lessons-etched-in-georgia-lore/85-abd45d9f-c8eb-49f4-ad 34-5906d674b640.

84. Carter, *A Full Life*, 230.

85. Alter, *His Very Best*, 624.

86. Carter, *First Lady from Plains*, 18.

87. David B. Ottaway, "Sadat Assassinated at Military Show," *Washington Post*, October 7, 1981, https://www.washingtonpost.com/archive/politics/1981/10/07/sadat-assassinated-at-military-show/604a2b32-408f-4e99-972d-ad6379c880c2/.

88. Leslie Phillips, "Former President Carter Welcomed Egyptian President Anwar Sadat," United Press, August 9, 1981, https://www.upi.com/Archives/1981/08/09/Former-President-Carter-welcomed-Egyptian-President-Anwar-Sadat-to/2494366177600/.

89. Art Harris, "Jimmy Carter: 'I Have Never Had a Better, Closer Personal Friend,'" *Washington Post*, October 7, 1981, https://www.washingtonpost.com/archive/politics/1981/10/07/jimmy-carter-i-have-never-had-a-better-closer-personal-friend/fc571145-4c51-4246-81f4-b41a0cff3cf8/.

90. "Ronald Reagan Remarks on the Departure of the United States Delegation to Funeral Services in Cairo for President Anwar el-Sadat of Egypt, October 8, 1981," American Presidency Project, UC Santa Barbara, https://www.presidency.ucsb.edu/documents/remarks-the-departure-the-united-states-delegation-funeral-services-cairo-for-president; Lee Lescaze, "The Funeral," *Washington Post*, October 8, 1981, https://www.washingtonpost.com/archive/politics/1981/10/08/the-funeral/ded16caf-6c4c-423f-b1ef-e01682c42bf5/.

91. Barbara Gamarekian, "Humor Tailored to Fit the Capital's Political Needs," *New York Times*, January 31, 1985, https://www.nytimes.com/1985/01/31/us/humor-tailored-to-fit-the-capital-s-political-needs.html.

92. Monica Crowley, *Nixon Off the Record* (New York: Random House, 1996), 23.

93. Carter, *A Full Life*, 234.

94. Phil Gailey, "Carter Is Critical of Reagan Policies," *New York Times*, October 14, 1981, https://www.nytimes.com/1981/10/14/us/carter-is-critical-of-reagan-policies.html.

95. Brinkley, *The Unfinished Presidency*, 58–59.

96. "President Jimmy Carter," Emory News Center, https://news.emory.edu/tags/topic/president_jimmy_carter/index.html.

97. Carter, *A Full Life*, 208.

98. Ibid., 207–8.

99. Brinkley, *The Unfinished Presidency*, 96.

100. Lucy Küng-Shankleman, *Inside the BBC and CNN: Managing Media Organisations* (London: Routledge, 2000), 80.

101. Brinkley, *The Unfinished Presidency*, 187.

102. Ibid., 186–87.

103. "Former President Jimmy Carter to Visit Africa," Carter Center, October 5, 1999, https://www.cartercenter.org/news/documents/doc918.html.

104. Donald J. Trump, *Trump: The Art of the Deal* (New York: Random House, 2009), 60.

105. "The Carter Center Annual Report, 2021," Carter Center, https://www.cartercenter.org/resources/pdfs/news/annual_reports/annual-report-21.pdf.

106. "Carter and Ford Criticize Israelis," *New York Times*, January 18, 1983, https://www.nytimes.com/1983/01/18/world/carter-and-ford-criticize-israelis.html.

107. Brinkley, *The Unfinished Presidency*, 103.

108. Iver Peterson, "Ford and Carter Tell of Difficult Communications in Government," *New York Times*, February 11, 1983, https://www.nytimes.com/1983/02/11/us/ford-and-carter-tell-of-difficult-communications-in-government.html.

109. Alter, *His Very Best*, 65.

110. Brinkley, *The Unfinished Presidency*, 154.

111. "Carter Work Projects through the Years," Habitat for Humanity, https://www.habitat.org/volunteer/build-events/carter-work-project/carter-work-projects-through-years.

112. Helen Thomas, "Rosalynn Carter: Bitter at 1980 Loss: Wishes Her Husband Would Run Again," United Press, April 25, 1984, https://www.upi.com/Archives/1984/04/25/Rosalynn-Carter-Bitter-at-1980-loss-Wishes-her-husband-would-run-again/7363451717200/.

113. Carter, *First Lady from Plains*, 383.

114. "Carter Backs Mondale for Presidency in 1984," *New York Times*, May 11, 1982, https://www.nytimes.com/1982/05/11/us/carter-backs-mondale-for-presidency-in-1984.html.

115. Godfrey Sperling Jr., "Mondale in '84: He May Run If Jimmy Carter Doesn't," *Christian Science Monitor*, March 10, 1981, https://www.csmonitor.com/1981/0310/031029.html.

116. Jack Nelson, "1988 Democratic National Convention: Once Virtual Outcast, Ex-President Plays Big Role in Atlanta: Carter Making Public Opinion Comeback," *Los Angeles Times*, July 18, 1988, https://www.latimes.com/archives/la-xpm-1988-07-18-mn-4470-story.html.

117. Brinkley, *The Unfinished Presidency*, 130.

118. "Walter F. Mondale: Address Accepting the Presidential Nomination at the Democratic National Convention in San Francisco, July 19, 1984," American Presidency Project, UC Santa Barbara, https://www.presidency.ucsb

.edu/documents/address-accepting-the-presidential-nomination-the-demo
cratic-national-convention-san.

119. Maureen Dowd, "Ferraro Sharpens Criticism of Reagan's Foreign Policy,"
     New York Times, September 30, 1984, https://www.nytimes.com/1984/09/30
     /us/ferraro-sharpens-criticism-of-reagan-s-foreign-policy.html.

120. "1984 Presidential General Election Results—Georgia," USA Election Atlas,
     https://uselectionatlas.org/RESULTS/state.php?year=1984&fips=13&f=0
     &off=0&elect=0.

121. "Jimmy Carter," Office of the Historian, U.S. Department of State, https://
     history.state.gov/departmenthistory/travels/president/carter-jimmy.

122. Scott Kilman and Roger Thurow, "Father of 'Green Revolution' Dies," *Wall
     Street Journal*, September 13, 2009, https://www.wsj.com/articles/SB12528
     1643150406425.

123. Carter, *A Full Life*, 211.

124. Alter, *His Very Best*, 630.

125. William E. Schmidt, "President Praises Carter at Library," *New York Times*,
     October 2, 1986, https://www.nytimes.com/1986/10/02/us/president-praises
     -carter-at-library.html.

126. Alter, *His Very Best*, 630.

127. "Eradication of Guinea Worm Disease," Carter Center and World Health
     Organization, https://www.who.int/docs/default-source/ntds/dracunculiasis
     /center-who-gw-case-statement2020.pdf?sfvrsn=5c00d407_4.

128. "Parasites—Guinea Worm," Centers for Disease Control and Prevention,
     https://www.cdc.gov/parasites/guineaworm/index.html.

129. "Guinea Worm Morbidity and Mortality Weekly Report," Centers for Disease
     Control and Prevention, cdc.gov/mmwr/volumes/68/wr/mm6843a5.htm#:
     ~:text=The%20number%20of%20cases%20of,dogs%20has%20compli
     cated%20eradication%20efforts; "Disease Eradication," Carter Center, https://
     www.cartercenter.org/health/itfde/index.html.

130. For full theory and explanation of "cognitive reappraisal" see Richard S.
     Lazarus and Susan Folkman, *Stress, Appraisal and Coping* (New York:
     Springer, 1984).

131. Ronald Smothers, "Carter Sidesteps Mediating Dispute," *New York Times*,
     July 16, 1988, https://www.nytimes.com/1988/07/16/us/carter-sidesteps-med
     iating-dispute.html?searchResultPosition=22.

132. Jack Nelson, "1988 Democratic National Convention: Once Virtual Out-
     cast, Ex-President Plays Big Role in Atlanta: Carter Making Public Opin-
     ion Comeback," *Los Angeles Times*, July 18, 1988, https://www.latimes.com
     /archives/la-xpm-1988-07-18-mn-4470-story.html.

133. Bernard Weintraub, "Campaign Trail; A Tempting Target, Even after 7

Years," *New York Times*, September 21, 1988, https://www.nytimes.com/19
88/09/21/us/campaign-trail-a-tempting-target-even-after-7-years.html?
searchResultPosition=13.

134. Joseph Mianowany, "Former President Jimmy Carter, Long Ignored by
Many Democrats," United Press, July 18, 1988, https://www.upi.com/Ar
chives/1988/07/18/Former-President-Jimmy-Carter-long-ignored-by-many
-Democrats/4922585201600/.

135. Betty Cuniberti, "Stars, Athletes, Politicians to Boost Drug Abuse Fund,"
Los Angeles Times, May 23, 1985, https://www.latimes.com/archives/la-xpm
-1985-05-23-vw-8291-story.html; Stephen Hess, "Jimmy Carter: Why He Failed,"
Brookings Institution, January 21, 2000, https://www.brookings.edu/articles
/jimmy-carter-why-he-failed.

136. Fallows, "The Passionless Presidency."

137. Martin Tolchin, "An Old Pol Takes on the New President," *New York Times*,
July 24, 1977, https://www.nytimes.com/1977/07/24/archives/an-old-pol-takes
-on-the-new-president-oneill.html.

138. Brinkley, *The Unfinished Presidency*, 270.

139. Thomas M. Baker, *The Politics of Diplomacy: Revolution, War, and Peace,
1989–1992* (New York: G. P. Putnam's Sons, 1995), 180.

140. Lindsey Gruson, "Charges of Fraud Mar Panama Vote," *New York Times*,
May 8, 1989, https://www.nytimes.com/1989/05/08/world/charges-of-fraud
-mar-panama-vote.html.

141. Ibid.

142. "The May 7, 1989 Panamanian Elections: International Delegation Report,"
Carter Center, https://www.cartercenter.org/documents/electionreport
/democracy/FinalReportPanama1989.pdf.

143. "Scowcroft to Carter, March 28, 1989."

144. "Jimmy Carter to Manuel Antonio Noriega, April 24, 1989," Pastor Personal
Papers.

145. Brinkley, *The Unfinished Presidency*, 279–80.

146. "Population Total—Panama," World Bank Data, https://data.worldbank.org
/indicator/SP.POP.TOTL?locations=PA; "Latin American Leaders Meet to
Examine Hemispheric Agenda," Carter Center News, Spring 1989, https://www
.cartercenter.org/resources/pdfs/news/carter_center_news/spring1989.pdf.

147. "Latin American Leaders Meet to Examine Hemispheric Agenda."

148. "The May 7, 1989 Panamanian Elections: International Delegation Report."

149. Brinkley, *The Unfinished Presidency*, 284; "Jimmy Carter: I Fear for Our Democracy, January 5, 2022," Carter Center, https://www.cartercenter.org/news
/editorials_speeches/jimmy-carter-nyt-op-ed-010522.html.

150. Lindsey Gruson, "Noriega Stealing Election, Carter Says," *New York Times*,

May 9, 1989, https://www.nytimes.com/1989/05/09/world/noriega-stealing
-election-carter-says.html.

151. Ibid.

152. Brinkley, *The Unfinished Presidency*, 285.

153. Ibid., 281–84.

154. Bernard Weintraub, "Bush Urges Efforts to Press Noriega to Quit as Leader,"
New York Times, May 10, 1989, https://www.nytimes.com/1989/05/10/world
/bush-urges-effort-to-press-noriega-to-quit-as-leader.html.

155. Ibid.

156. Brinkley, *The Unfinished Presidency*, 286.

157. "Latin American Leaders Meet to Examine Hemispheric Agenda," Carter
Center News, Spring 1989, https://www.cartercenter.org/resources/pdfs/news
/carter_center_news/spring1989.pdf.

158. Brinkley, *The Unfinished Presidency*, 287.

159. "Fighting in Panama: The President; a Transcript of Bush's Address on the
Decision to Use Force in Panama," *New York Times*, December 21, 1989,
https://www.nytimes.com/1989/12/21/world/fighting-panama-president
-transcript-bush-s-address-decision-use-force-panama.html.

160. Ibid.

161. E. J. Dionne Jr., "Washington Talk; Carter Begins to Shed Negative Public
Image," *New York Times*, May 18, 1989, https://www.nytimes.com/1989/05
/18/us/washington-talk-carter-begins-to-shed-negative-public-image.html.

162. Ibid.

163. "Democracy Program," Carter Center, https://www.cartercenter.org/peace
/democracy/index.html.

164. "Jimmy Carter Address at Commencement Exercises at the University
of Notre Dame, May 22, 1977," American Presidency Project, UC Santa
Barbara, https://www.presidency.ucsb.edu/documents/address-commencement
-exercises-the-university-notre-dame.

165. "Foreign Relations of the United States, 1977–1980, Volume I, Foundations of Foreign Policy, 133. Editorial Note," Office of the Historian, U.S.
State Department, https://history.state.gov/historicaldocuments/frus1977-80
v01/d133#:~:text=would%20reciprocate%20it.-,%E2%80%9CThe%20
President.,in%20invading%20Afghanistan.%20.%20.%20.

166. Hal Brands, "The Vision Thing," Miller Center, University of Virginia, January 14, 2016, https://millercenter.org/issues-policy/foreign-policy/the-vi
sion-thing.

167. Baker, *The Politics of Diplomacy*, 115–19, cited in Brinkley, *The Unfinished
Presidency*, 318.

168. Brinkley, *The Unfinished Presidency*, 318.

169. Jimmy Carter, *The Blood of Abraham: Insights into the Middle East* (Fayatteville: University of Arkansas Press, 2007), 21.

170. Zbigniew Brzezinski, *Power and Principle: Memoirs of the National Security Adviser, 1977–1981* (New York: Farrar, Straus and Giroux, 1983), 83.

171. Joe Macaron, "The Israeli Annexation Plan and Jordan's West Bank Moment," Arab Center Washington DC, June 3, 2020, https://arabcenterdc.org/resource /the-israeli-annexation-plan-and-jordans-west-bank-moment/.

172. Sharon Waxman, "Carter, Arafat Meet on Middle East Peace Plan," *Washington Post*, April 6, 1990, https://www.washingtonpost.com/archive/politics /1990/04/05/carter-arafat-meet-on-middle-east-peace-plan/472999e6-5b49 -4122-9c7f-d5b483b0e2c0/.

173. Barry Rubin, *Yasir Arafat: A Political Biography* (New York: Oxford University Press, 2004), 122.

174. "The Gulf War, 1991," Office of the Historian, U.S. State Department, https://history.state.gov/milestones/1989-1992/gulf-war.

175. William Drozdiak, "Arab Nations Break Silence, Condemn Iraq," *Washington Post*, August 4, 1990, https://www.washingtonpost.com/archive/politics/1990 /08/04/arab-nations-break-silence-condemn-iraq/e47cea4e-756d-453c-8622 -49e17340c808/.

176. Youssef M. Ibrahim, "Confrontation in the Gulf; Arafat's Support of Iraq Creates Rift in P.L.O," *New York Times*, August 14, 1990, https://www.ny times.com/1990/08/14/world/confrontation-in-the-gulf-arafat-s-support-of -iraq-creates-rift-in-plo.html.

177. "Foreign Relations of the United States, 1977–1980, Volume XVIII, Middle East Region, Arabian Peninsula, 45. Editorial Note," Office of the Historian, U.S. State Department, https://history.state.gov/historicaldocuments/frus1977 -80v18/d45.

178. Brinkley, *The Unfinished Presidency*, 339.

179. Youssef M. Ibrahim, "Mideast Tensions; Arafat Stresses Linkage in Settling Gulf Crisis," *New York Times*, November 26, 1980, https://www.nytimes .com/1990/11/26/world/mideast-tensions-arafat-stresses-linkage-in-settling -gulf-crisis.html; Brinkley, *The Unfinished Presidency*, 334–36.

180. "The Need to Negotiate, October 21, 1990," Carter Center, https://www. cartercenter.org/news/editorials_speeches/jc-need-to-negotiate-timemag -102290.html.

181. Brinkley, *The Unfinished Presidency*, 339.

182. Maureen Dowd, "Mission to Haiti: The Diplomat; Despite Role as Negotiator, Carter Feels Unappreciated," *New York Times*, September 21, 1994,

https://www.nytimes.com/1994/09/21/world/mission-haiti-diplomat-despite
-role-negotiator-carter-feels-unappreciated.html.

183. Brinkley, *The Unfinished Presidency*, 336–39.

184. Brent Scowcroft and George H. W. Bush, *A World Transformed* (New York: Vintage, 1999), 414; Brinkley, *The Unfinished Presidency*, 339.

185. Elaine Sciolino, "Confrontation in the Gulf: The Deadline; An Arbitrary Diplomatic Deal becomes an Imminent Threat," *New York Times*, January 15, 1991, https://www.nytimes.com/1991/01/15/world/confrontation -gulf-deadline-arbitrary-diplomatic-deal-becomes-imminent-threat.html.

186. Brinkley, *The Unfinished Presidency*, 340–42.

187. Thomas L. Friedman, "Mideast Tensions; How U.S. Won Support to Use Mideast Forces," *New York Times*, December 2, 1990, https://www.nytimes .com/1990/12/02/world/mideast-tensions-us-won-support-use-mideast -forces-iraq-resolution-us-soviet.html.

188. Andrew Rosenthal, "War in the Gulf: Bush Halts Offensive Combat; Ku-wait Freed, Iraqis Crushed," *New York Times*, February 28, 1991, https:// www.nytimes.com/1991/02/28/world/war-in-the-gulf-bush-halts-offensive -combat-kuwait-freed-iraqis.html.

189. "Part III: Iraq's Missile Attacks against the Gulf States," Human Rights Watch, https://www.hrw.org/reports/1991/gulfwar/CHAP6.htm.

190. Richard Cohen, "In Defense of the Carter Post-Presidency," *Washington Post*, December 27, 1994, https://www.washingtonpost.com/archive/opin ions/1994/12/27/in-defense-of-the-carter-post-presidency/6e091280-a9a2 -43a4-9d1f-a1865064da82/.

191. Brinkley, *The Unfinished Presidency*, 377.

192. R. J. Reinhart, "George H. W. Bush Retrospective," Gallup, December 1, 2018, https://news.gallup.com/opinion/gallup/234971/george-bush-retro spective.aspx.

193. Carter, *A Full Life*, 236.

194. Karen De Witt, "The 1992 Campaign: Georgia; Carter Welcomes Tsongas to Plains," *New York Times*, February 23, 1992, https://www.nytimes.com /1992/02/23/us/the-1992-campaign-georgia-carter-welcomes-tsongas-to -plains.html.

195. Brinkley, *The Unfinished Presidency*, 351.

196. Peter Applebome, "The 1992 Campaign: Political Memo; Misleading Echoes of Carter in Clinton," *New York Times*, July 19, 1992, https://www.nytimes .com/1992/07/19/us/the-1992-campaign-political-memo-misleading-echoes -of-carter-in-clinton.html.

197. David E. Sanger, "North Korea Said to Block Taking of Radioactive Samples from Site," *New York Times*, March 16, 1994, https://www.nytimes.com

/1994/03/16/world/north-korea-said-to-block-taking-of-radioactive-samples
-from-site.html.

198. Derek Chollet and James Goldgeier, *America between the Wars: From 11/9 to 9/11: The Misunderstood Years between the Fall of the Berlin Wall and the Start of the War on Terror* (New York: PublicAffairs, 2008), 93-95.

199. Brinkley, *The Unfinished Presidency*, 398.

200. T. R. Reid, "In Seoul, War Said to Be Unlikely," *Washington Post*, June 15, 1994, https://www.washingtonpost.com/archive/politics/1994/06/15/in-seoul
-war-said-to-be-unlikely/c8f2b9db-acfb-4917-8f8c-fde84b6d17bc/.

201. Leon Sigal, *Disarming Strangers: Nuclear Diplomacy with North Korea* (Princeton, NJ: Princeton University Press, 1999), 152.

202. Brinkley, *The Unfinished Presidency*, 402.

203. Robert L. Gallucci, Daniel B. Poneman, and Joel S. Wit, *Going Critical: The First North Korean Nuclear Crisis* (Washington, DC: Brookings Institution Press, 2004), 225.

204. Robert Gallucci, Press Briefing, White House, June 19, 1994.

205. "*Frontline* Interview with Jimmy Carter," PBS, https://www.pbs.org/wgbh
/pages/frontline/shows/kim/interviews/carter.html.

206. Bird, *The Outlier*, 616.

207. R. Jeffrey Smith and Bradley Graham, "White House Disputes Carter on North Korea," *Washington Post*, June 18, 1994, https://www.washingtonpost
.com/archive/politics/1994/06/18/white-house-disputes-carter-on-north-korea
/ca1511d4-4fd3-401e-b199-57267cf7f447/.

208. Smith and Graham, "White House Disputes Carter on North Korea."

209. David E. Sanger, "THE WORLD; Surprise! Kim Il Sung Smiles for the Camera," *New York Times*, June 19, 1994, https://www.nytimes.com/1994
/06/19/weekinreview/the-world-surprise-kim-il-sung-smiles-for-the-cam
era.html.

210. Brinkley, *The Unfinished Presidency*, 409.

211. Mark E. Manyin and Ryun Jun, "U.S. Assistance to North Korea," CRS Report for Congress, March 17, 2003, 2.

212. "The U.S.–North Korean Agreed Framework at a Glance," Arms Control Association, https://www.armscontrol.org/factsheets/agreedframework.

213. James Sterngold, "South Korea President Lashes Out at U.S.," *New York Times*, October 8, 1994.

214. "Statement of DPRK Government on Its Withdrawal from NPT," Internet Archive, https://web.archive.org/web/20090920185607/http://www.kcna.co.jp
/item/2003/200301/news01/11.htm.

215. "Jimmy Carter: Facts," Nobel Prize, https://www.nobelprize.org/prizes/peace
/2002/carter/facts/.

216. "Press Release," Nobel Prize, October 11, 2002, https://www.nobelprize.org /prizes/peace/2002/press-release/.

217. Jeffrey Gettleman, "Nobel Peace Prize Awarded to Carter with Criticism of Bush," *New York Times*, October 11, 2002, https://www.nytimes.com/2002 /10/11/international/nobel-peace-prize-awarded-to-carter-with-criticism-of -bush.html#:~:text=11%20%2D%20For%20his%20peacemaking%20and ,its%20aggressive%20policy%20toward%20Iraq.

218. Jimmy Carter, "Just War—or a Just War?" *New York Times*, March 9, 2003, https://www.nytimes.com/2003/03/09/opinion/just-war-or-a-just-war.html.

219. "Remarks on Bush Foreign Policy Were 'Careless or Misinterpreted,' Carter Says," *Orlando Sentinel*, May 22, 2007, https://www.orlandosentinel.com /news/os-xpm-2007-05-22-carter22-story.html.

220. Jimmy Carter, "Pariah Diplomacy," *New York Times*, April 28, 2008, https:// www.nytimes.com/2008/04/28/opinion/28carter.html.

221. Jimmy Carter, *Palestine: Peace Not Apartheid* (New York: Simon & Schuster, 2006), 216.

222. "Jewish Criticism of Carter Intensifies," *Jewish Week*, December 15, 2006, https://web.archive.org/web/20070613195955/http:/www.thejewish week.com/news/newscontent.php3?artid=13420.

223. Carter, *A Full Life*, 228.

224. Brinkley, *The Unfinished Presidency*, 116.

225. Ibid., 318–20.

226. "14 Carter Center Board Members Resign," CBS News, January 12, 2007, https://www.cbsnews.com/news/14-carter-center-board-members-resign/.

227. Ibid.

228. Pam Belluck, "At Brandeis, Carter Responds to Critics," *New York Times*, January 24, 2007, https://www.nytimes.com/2007/01/24/us/24carter.html.

229. Kenneth W. Stein, "My Problem with Jimmy Carter's Book," *Middle East Quarterly* (Spring 2007): 3–15, https://www.meforum.org/1633/my-problem -with-jimmy-carters-book#_ftnref8.

230. "Carter Says Obama Doesn't Call Him for Advice," NBC News, March 21, 2014, https://www.nbcnews.com/politics/politics-news/carter-says-obama -doesnt-call-him-advice-n58991.

231. Jimmy Carter, "A Cruel and Unusual Record," *New York Times*, June 24, 2012, https://www.nytimes.com/2012/06/25/opinion/americas-shameful-human -rights-record.html?_r=2.

232. *New York Times Magazine* (New York: New York Times, 1995), 28.

233. Brinkley, 478.

234. Ibid., 477.

235. Carter, *A Full Life*, 238; see also "FOX Facts: Carter Board of Councilors

Resignation Letter," Fox News, January 13, 2015, https://www.foxnews
.com/story/fox-facts-carter-board-of-councilors-resignation-letter.

236. Scott Simon, "Jimmy Carter Remains Stalwart in Vow to Eradicate Guinea
Worm," NPR, August 22, 2015, https://www.npr.org/2015/08/22/433569465
/jimmy-carter-remains-stalwart-in-vow-to-eradicate-guinea-worm#:~:text=Jimmy
%20Carter%20told%20a%20press,to%20die%20before%20I%20do.%22.

237. Stephen Collinson, "Jimmy Carter's Rewarding Post-Presidency," CNN,
August 20, 2015, https://www.cnn.com/2015/08/20/politics/jimmy-carter
-cancer-retirement-post-presidency.

238. "Vaccinated for Virus, Jimmy Carter and Wife Back in Church," AP News,
February 24, 2021, https://apnews.com/article/baptist-coronavirus-pandemic
-jimmy-carter-rosalynn-carter-5d40e69bfc2a317faad05993f1be55bd.

239. "Statement on President Carter's Health," Carter Center, February 18, 2023,
https://www.cartercenter.org/news/pr/2023/statement-on-president-carters
-health.html.

240. "Carter Says Gore Won in 2000," Democracy Now, September 23, 2005,
https://www.democracynow.org/2005/9/23/headlines/carter_says_gore_won
_in_2000.

241. "Carter Says Bush's Presidency Has Been 'Worst in History' for U.S. Impact around the World," *Seattle Times*, March 19, 2007, https://www.seattle
times.com/nation-world/carter-says-bushs-presidency-has-been-worst-in
-history-for-us-impact-around-the-world/.

242. Alter, *His Very Best*, 643.

CHAPTER 7: MOVING ON

1. "Final Presidential Job Approval Ratings," American Presidency Project,
UC Santa Barbara, https://www.presidency.ucsb.edu/statistics/data/final
-presidential-job-approval-ratings.

2. "George W. Bush's Favorable Rating Has Pulled a Complete 180," CNN,
January 22, 2018, https://www.cnn.com/2018/01/22/politics/george-w-bush
-favorable-poll/index.html.

3. "Portraits of Courage," Bush Center, https://www.bushcenter.org/events-and
-exhibits/portraits-of-courage.

4. George W. Bush, author interview, Kennebunkport, Maine, August 10–11,
2020.

5. William James to H. G. Wells, September 11, 1906, in *The Letters of William James*, ed. Henry James (Boston: Atlantic Monthly Press, 1920), 230.

6. Dan McAdams, author interview by phone, September 21, 2020.

7. "The Great Recession," Federal Reserve History, https://www.federalreserve

history.org/essays/great-recession-of-200709#:~:text=December%202007%E2%80%93June%202009,longest%20since%20World%20War%20II.&text=The%20Great%20Recession%20began%20in,recession%20since%20World%20War%20II.

8. Tabassum Zakaria, "Bush Orders Aid to Georgia, Rice to Visit Tbilisi," Reuters, August 13, 2008, https://www.reuters.com/article/us-usa-russia-bush/bush-orders-aid-to-georgia-rice-to-visit-tbilisi-idUSWBT00955720080813.

9. Amy Belasco, "Troop Levels in the Afghan and Iraq Wars, FY 2001–FY2012: Cost and Other Potential Issues," Congressional Research Service, July 2, 2009, https://sgp.fas.org/crs/natsec/R40682.pdf.

10. Lydia Saad, "Bush Presidency Closes with 34% Approval, 61% Disapproval," Gallup, January 14, 2009, https://news.gallup.com/poll/113770/bush-presidency-closes-34-approval-61-disapproval.aspx.

11. "Barack Obama Keynote Address at the 2004 Democratic National Convention, July 27, 2004," American Presidency Project, UC Santa Barbara, https://www.presidency.ucsb.edu/documents/keynote-address-the-2004-democratic-national-convention.

12. "Transcript: Obama's Speech against the Iraq War," NPR, January 20, 2009, https://www.npr.org/templates/story/story.php?storyId=99591469; Michael Kranish, "Hillary Clinton Regrets Her Iraq Vote. But Opting for Intervention Was a Pattern," *Washington Post*, September 15, 2016, https://www.washingtonpost.com/politics/hillary-clinton-regrets-her-iraq-vote-but-opting-for-intervention-was-a-pattern/2016/09/15/760c23d0-6645-11e6-96c0-37533479f3f5_story.html.

13. "General Election: McCain vs. Obama," RealClear Politics, https://www.realclearpolitics.com/epolls/2008/president/us/general_election_mccain_vs_obama-225.html.

14. "2008 Election Turnout Hit 40-Year High," CBS News, December 15, 2008, https://www.cbsnews.com/news/2008-election-turnout-hit-40-year-high/.

15. Ben Smith and Byron Tau, "Birtherism: Where It All Began," Politico, April 22, 2011, https://www.politico.com/story/2011/04/birtherism-where-it-all-began-053563.

16. "Presidential Approval Ratings—Barack Obama," Gallup, https://news.gallup.com/poll/116479/barack-obama-presidential-job-approval.aspx; "Barack H. Obama: Facts," Nobel Prize, https://www.nobelprize.org/prizes/peace/2009/obama/facts/.

17. "Obama Blasts Bush, McCain Over 'Attacks,'" CNN, 2008, https://www.cnn.com/2008/POLITICS/05/16/obama.bush.mccain/index.html.

18. Larry Rohter, "Obama Says Bush and McCain Are 'Fear Mongering' in

Attacks," *New York Times*, May 17, 2008, https://www.nytimes.com/2008/05/17/us/politics/17obama.html.

19. Carl Hulse, "Obama Is Sworn in as the 44th President," *New York Times*, January 20, 2009, https://www.nytimes.com/2009/01/21/us/politics/20web-inaug2.html; Morgan Winsor, "2009 vs. 2017: Comparing Trump's and Obama's Inauguration Crowds," ABC News, January 25, 2017, https://abcnews.go.com/Politics/2009-2017-comparing-trumps-obamas-inauguration-crowds/story?id=44927217#:~:text=There%20were%201.8%20million%20people,people%20would%20attend%20Trump%27s%20inauguration.

20. Bush, author interview.

21. Ibid.

22. Karl Rove, author interview via Zoom, July 27, 2020.

23. "President Bush Delivers Farewell Address to the Nation," White House, January 15, 2009, https://georgewbush-whitehouse.archives.gov/news/releases/2009/01/20090115-17.html.

24. Linton Weeks, "Bush, Obama Meet at White House," NPR, November 10, 2008, https://www.npr.org/2008/11/10/96811035/bush-obama-meet-at-white-house.

25. For a full discussion of these memoranda, see Condoleezza Rice, *Hand-Off: The Foreign Policy George W. Bush Passed to Barack Obama* (Washington, DC: Brookings Institution Press, 2023).

26. "White House: Allegations of Damage during the 2001 Presidential Transition," GAO, https://www.govinfo.gov/content/pkg/GAOREPORTS-GAO-02-360/html/GAOREPORTS-GAO-02-360.htm.

27. "Troubled Asset Relief Program (TARP)," U.S. Department of Treasury, https://home.treasury.gov/data/troubled-assets-relief-program.

28. George W. Bush, *Decision Points*, enhanced ed. (New York: Crown, 2010), 470.

29. Dana Perino, author interview via Zoom, July 30, 2020.

30. Bush, author interview.

31. Ibid.

32. "Midland City, Texas," U.S. Census Bureau, https://www.census.gov/quickfacts/fact/table/midlandcitytexas/PST045221.

33. "Bush Flies to Texas to Begin Post-Presidential Life," *New York Times*, January 20, 2009, https://www.nytimes.com/2009/01/20/world/americas/20iht-bush.4.19537115.html.

34. Bush, author interview.

35. Barbara Bush, author interview, Kennebunkport, Maine, August 10, 2020.

36. Bush, author interview.

37. Bush, *Decision Points*, 475.

38. Ibid.

39. Ibid.

40. Barbara Bush, author interview.

41. Bush, *Decision Points*, 476.

42. Bush, author interview.

43. Ibid.

44. "Sen. Kennedy on Ford's Courageous Decision," NPR, December 27, 2006, https://www.npr.org/2006/12/27/6685819/sen-kennedy-on-fords-courageous -decision.

45. Charles Krauthammer, "Reagan Revisionism," *Washington Post*, June 11, 2004, https://www.washingtonpost.com/archive/opinions/2004/06/11/reagan-rev isionism/449b5cc4-3605-451f-bca2-dcc174bdc0ce/; Bush, *Decision Points*, 476.

46. Bush, *Decision Points*, 476.

47. "Bill Clinton in the Era of #MeToo," NPR, October 19, 2018, https://www .npr.org/2018/10/19/658962064/the-bill-clinton-question.

48. Jason Slotkin, "Princeton to Remove Woodrow Wilson's Name from Public Policy School," NPR, June 27, 2020, https://www.npr.org/sections/live-updates -protests-for-racial-justice/2020/06/27/884310403/princeton-to-remove -woodrow-wilsons-name-from-public-policy-school#:~:text=Princeton%20 University%20will%20remove%20Woodrow,the%20name%20change%20 on%20Friday.

49. "Slavery in the President's Neighborhood. FAQ," White House Historical Association, https://www.whitehousehistory.org/slavery-in-the-presidents -neighborhood-faq.

50. Bush, *Decision Points*, xi.

51. "Obama's Books Out-Selling McCain Titles in 2008," Nielsen, October, 2008, https://www.nielsen.com/insights/2008/obama-books-out-sell-mccain-titles-in -2008.

52. Dean Goodman, "Obama or Clinton? Grammys Go for Obama," Reuters, February 10, 2008, https://www.reuters.com/article/us-grammys-obama/obama -or-clinton-grammys-go-for-obama-idUSN0852813420080210.

53. Lynn Neary, "What Oprah's Endorsement Means for Obama," NPR, December 9, 2007, https://www.npr.org/templates/story/story.php?storyId=17055698.

54. "Bob Barnett, '71: Washington Superlawyer Is the 'Doorman to the Revolving Door,'" *University of Chicago Law School News*, https://www.law.uchicago .edu/news/bob-barnett-71-washington-superlawyer-doorman-revolving-door.

55. Carroll Doherty and Jocelyn Kiley, "A Look Back at How Fear and False Beliefs Bolstered US Public Support for War in Iraq," Pew Research Center, March 14, 2023, https://www.pewresearch.org/politics/2023/03/14/a-look-back-at-how -fear-and-false-beliefs-bolstered-u-s-public-support-for-war-in-iraq/.

56. Bush, *Decision Points*, 355.
57. "America Votes 2006," CNN, https://www.cnn.com/ELECTION/2006/.
58. "Bush: 'It Was a Thumpin'," *Chicago Tribune*, November 8, 2006, https://www.chicagotribune.com/chinews-mtblog-2006-11-bush_it_was_a_thumpin-story.html.
59. Robin Toner and Kate Zernike, "House Rejects Timetable for Iraq Pullout," *New York Times*, June 16, 2006, https://www.nytimes.com/2006/06/16/washington/16cnd-cong.html.
60. Bruce R. Pirnie and Edward O'Connell, *Counterinsurgency in Iraq (2003–2006): RAND Counterinsurgency Study—Volume 2*, RAND Corporation, 2008, http://www.jstor.org/stable/10.7249/mg595-3osd.
61. Eugene Robinson, "Thinking War-War Again," *Washington Post*, January 12, 2007, https://www.washingtonpost.com/archive/opinions/2007/01/12/thinking-war-war-again/4b52782c-c429-4c1e-a278-bd6fc112d3bd/.
62. "Number of US Soldiers Killed in the Iraq War from 2003 to 2020," Statistica, https://www.statista.com/statistics/263798/american-soldiers-killed-in-iraq/.
63. Rove, author interview.
64. Mary Katharine Ham, "Quote of the Day (So Far!)" *Washington Examiner*, February 26, 2010, https://www.washingtonexaminer.com/weekly-standard/quote-of-the-day-so-far-421923?_amp=true.
65. Bush, author interview.
66. "Full Interview with Chris Michel," *Buckley Beacon*, September 28, 2015, https://buckleybeacon.com/2015/09/28/full-interview-with-chris-michel/.
67. David Maraniss, "The Bush Bunch," *Washington Post*, January 22, 1989, https://www.washingtonpost.com/archive/lifestyle/magazine/1989/01/22/the-bush-bunch/30638df5-7bde-4bf3-8f54-7d8219ac55ba/.
68. Bush, *Decision Points*, 5.
69. Ibid., 459.
70. Ibid., 477.
71. Dan Merica, "Hillary Clinton in 2001: We Were 'Dead Broke,'" CNN, June 9, 2014, https://www.cnn.com/2014/06/09/politics/clinton-speeches/index.html.
72. "How George W. Bush Scored Big with the Texas Rangers," Center for Public Integrity, January 17, 2000, https://publicintegrity.org/politics/how-george-w-bush-scored-big-with-the-texas-rangers/.
73. Bush, author interview.
74. Mike Allen, "Bush Back in Saddle for Speaking Tour," Politico, February 23, 2009, https://www.politico.com/story/2009/02/bush-back-in-saddle-for-speaking-tour-019212.

75. George W. Bush, *41: A Portrait of My Father* (New York: Crown, 2014), 250.

76. Bush, author interview.

77. Ibid.

78. *New York Times Magazine* (New York: New York Times, 1995), 28.

79. Don Evans, author interview via Zoom, July 14, 2021.

80. Howard Fineman, "Campaign 2000: Words from the Heart," *Newsweek*, December 31, 1999, https://www.newsweek.com/campaign-2000-words-heart -162854.

81. "User Clip: George W. Bush on Why He Admires Christ," C-Span, December 14, 1999, https://www.c-span.org/video/?c4528159/user-clip-george-w -bush-admires-christ.

82. Hanna Rosin, "Bush's 'Christ Moment' Is Put to Political Test by Christians," *Washington Post*, December 16, 1999, https://www.washingtonpost .com/wp-srv/WPcap/1999-12/16/045r-121699-idx.html.

83. Frank Bruni, "The 2000 Campaign: The Texas Governor; Bush Calls on Gore to Denounce Clinton Affair," *New York Times*, August 12, 2000, https:// www.nytimes.com/2000/08/12/us/2000-campaign-texas-governor-bush-calls -gore-denounce-clinton-affair.html.

84. Bush, author interview.

85. Bush, *Decision Points*, 32.

86. Bush, author interview.

87. Ibid.

88. Jenna Bush Hager, author interview by phone, May 5, 2021.

89. Evans, author interview, July 14, 2021.

90. Barbara Bush, author interview.

91. Ibid.

92. Ibid.

93. Ibid.

94. Jenna Bush Hager, author interview.

95. Bush, author interview.

96. Donnie Radcliffe, "Fashioning a 'Ferraro Look,'" *Washington Post,* July 23, 1984, https://www.washingtonpost.com/archive/lifestyle/1984/07/23/fashion ing-a-ferraro-look/788edb10-125c-4f38-88c6-d90afa80a64a/.

97. Margaret Garrard Warner, "George H. W. Bush's Greatest Campaign Challenge: Revisiting *Newsweek's* 1987 Cover Story, 'The Wimp Factor,'" *Newsweek*, December 3, 2018, https://www.newsweek.com/newsweek-1987 -cover-story-george-hw-bush-wimp-factor-1241611.

98. "Bush's Wife Assails Ferraro, but Apologizes," *New York Times*, October 9, 1984, https://www.nytimes.com/1984/10/09/us/bush-s-wife-assails-ferraro -but-apologizes.html.

99. Bush, *Portrait of my Father*, 244.

100. Ibid., 249–50.

101. Bush, author interview.

102. Ibid.

103. Ibid.

104. Ibid.

105. "Presidential Historians Survey 2021," C-Span, https://www.c-span.org/presidentsurvey2021/?page=overall.

106. Bush, author interview.

107. Ibid.

108. Bush, *Portrait of My Father*, 223.

109. Ibid., 229.

110. Peter Baker, "George W. Bush's '41: A Portrait of My Father,'" *New York Times*, November 19, 2014, https://www.nytimes.com/2014/12/28/books/review/george-w-bushs-41-a-portrait-of-my-father.html.

111. Stephen Battaglio, "President George H. W. Bush's Funeral Was Watched by More Than 17 Million TV Viewers," *Los Angeles Times*, December 7, 2018, https://www.latimes.com/business/hollywood/la-fi-ct-bush-funeral-ratings-20181207-story.html.

112. Bush, author interview.

113. Jeff Muskus, "Bush: Jimmy Carter 'Made My Life Miserable,'" *Huffington Post*, April 28, 2010, https://www.huffpost.com/entry/bush-jimmy-carter-made-my_n_478419.

114. Bush, *Decision Points*, 226.

115. Bush, author interview.

116. Eun Kyung Kim, "Barbara Bush on Jeb Run: 'We've Had Enough Bushes in White House,'" *Today*, April 25, 2013, https://www.today.com/news/barbara-bush-jeb-run-weve-had-enough-bushes-white-house-6C9602466.

117. Eli Stokols, "George W. Bush Unleashes on Ted Cruz," Politico, October 19, 2015, https://www.politico.com/story/2015/10/jeb-bush-george-bush-donors-ted-cruz-214933.

118. Bush, author interview.

119. "South Carolina Primary Results," *New York Times*, https://www.nytimes.com/elections/2016/results/primaries/south-carolina.

120. Eli Stokols, "Jeb Bush Drops Out of White House Race," Politico, February 20, 2016, https://www.politico.com/story/2016/02/breaking-news-jeb-bush-is-suspending-his-presidential-campaign-219564.

121. M. J. Lee, "How Donald Trump Blasted George W. Bush in S.C.–and Still Won," CNN, February 21, 2016, https://www.cnn.com/2016/02/20/politics/donald-trump-south-carolina-military.

122. Ashley Parker, "Jeb Bush Sprints to Escape Donald Trump's 'Low Energy' Label," *New York Times*, December 29, 2015, https://www.nytimes.com /2015/12/30/us/politics/jeb-bush-sprints-to-escape-donald-trumps-low-energy -label.html.

123. Shane Goldmacher, "Inside the GOP's Shadow Convention," Politico, July 19, 2016, https://www.politico.com/magazine/story/2016/07/rnc-2016-gop-re publican-party-leaders-future-donald-trump-214065/#ixzz4Ermv50bQ.

124. "2016 Presidential Election Results," *New York Times*, August 8, 2017, https://www.nytimes.com/elections/2016/results/president.

125. Ibid.

126. "RNC 2016 Schedule of Events and Speakers," Politico, July 18, 2016, https://www.politico.com/story/2016/07/rnc-2016-schedule-of-events-and -speakers-225704.

127. Jeremy Diamond, Bob Dole Endorses Trump," CNN, May 6, 2016, https:// www.cnn.com/2016/05/06/politics/bob-dole-endorses-donald-trump.

128. Rick Klein, "Presidents Bush to Skip Obama Inaugural," ABC News, January 18, 2013, https://abcnews.go.com/blogs/politics/2013/01/presidents -bush-to-skip-obama-inaugural.

129. Bush, author interview.

130. Ibid.

131. Hillary Rodham Clinton, *What Happened* (New York: Simon & Schuster, 2017), 11.

132. "President Trump Job Approval," RealClear Politics, https://www.realclear politics.com/epolls/other/president_trump_job_approval-6179.html.

133. Lydia Saad, "George W. Bush and Barack Obama Both Popular in Retirement," Gallup, June 19, 2017, https://news.gallup.com/poll/212633/george -bush-barack-obama-popular-retirement.aspx.

134. Bush, author interview; "Michelle Obama Explains Viral Cough Drop Moment with George W. Bush," *Today*, October 11, 2018, https://www.today .com/video/michelle-obama-explains-viral-cough-drop-moment-with-george -w-bush-1341729859700?v=raila&.

135. Laura Bradley, "Ellen DeGeneres, George W. Bush, and the Limits of Unconditional Kindness," *Vanity Fair*, October 8, 2019, https://www.vanityfair .com/hollywood/2019/10/ellen-degeneres-george-w-bush-football-game.

136. "Number of Active Users at Facebook over the Years," Yahoo Finance, October 23, 2012, https://finance.yahoo.com/news/number-active-users-face book-over-years-214600186--finance.html.

137. Bush, author interview.

138. Joshua Bote, "Former President George W. Bush at John Lewis' Funeral: 'He Will Live Forever in the Hearts of Americans,'" *USA Today*, July 30,

2020, https://www.usatoday.com/story/news/politics/2020/07/30/george-w
-bush-speaks-john-lewis-funeral-full-transcript/5544051002/.

139. Cleve R. Wootson Jr., "Both Bush Presidents Just Spoke Out on Charlottes-ville—and Sound Nothing Like Trump," *Washington Post*, August 16, 2017, https://www.washingtonpost.com/news/politics/wp/2017/08/16/both-bush
-presidents-just-spoke-out-on-charlottesville-and-sound-nothing-like-trump/.

140. "Statement by President George W. Bush," Bush Center, June 2, 2020, https://www.bushcenter.org/about-the-center/newsroom/press-releases
/2020/06/statement-by-president-george-w-bush.html.

141. Bush, author interview.

142. "Statement by President George W. Bush on Insurrection at the Capitol," Bush Center, January 6, 2021, https://www.bushcenter.org/about-the-center
/newsroom/press-releases/2021/statement-by-president-george-w-bush-on
-insurrection-at-the-capitol.html.

143. "Statement by President George W. Bush on Insurrection at the Capitol."

144. "Former Presidents Obama, Bush, and Clinton Ask Americans to Work To-gether," NBC News, January 20, 2021, https://www.youtube.com/watch?v
=8VjSwI3qmA8.

145. "Statement by President and Mrs. Bush on Afghanistan," Bush Center, August 17, 2021, https://www.bushcenter.org/about-the-center/newsroom
/press-releases/2021/08/statement-president-and-mrs-bush-afghanistan
.html.

146. "Statement by President George W. Bush on Ukraine," Bush Center, Feb-ruary 24, 2022, https://www.bushcenter.org/newsroom/statement-by-presi
dent-george-w-bush-on-ukraine.

147. "George W. Bush Presidential Center Dedication Ceremony," Bush Cen-ter, April 26, 2013, https://www.bushcenter.org/events-and-exhibits/george
-w-bush-presidential-center-dedication-ceremony.

148. Bush, *Decision Points*, 294.

149. "Bush Library Fundraising Surpasses $300 Million Goal," NBC DFW, Sep-tember 19, 2011, https://www.nbcdfw.com/news/local/bush-library-fund
raising-surpasses-300-million-goal/1886149/.

150. "Dean at SMU Weighs in on Bush Library," Denny Burk, February 14, 2007, http://www.dennyburk.com/dean-at-smu-weighs-in-on-bush-library/.

151. Ralph Blumenthal, "SMU Faculty Complains about Bush Library," *New York Times*, January 10, 2007, https://www.nytimes.com/2007/01/10/us/politics
/10library.html?ex=1326085200&en=3170689537c4434c&ei=5088&partner
=rssnyt&emc=rss.

152. "George W. Bush Presidential Center," Southern Methodist University, https://www.smu.edu/bushcenter.

153. Ken Hersch, author interview via Zoom, January 15, 2021.

154. "The President's Malaria Initiative," White House, https://georgewbush-whitehouse.archives.gov/infocus/malaria/.

155. "PEPFAR at 20: Remarks from Bono," Bush Center, February 24, 2023, https://www.bushcenter.org/publications/pepfar-at-20-remarks-from-bono.

156. Nicholas Kristof, "When George W. Bush Was a Hero," *New York Times*, April 8, 2023, https://www.nytimes.com/2023/04/08/opinion/aids-pepfar-bush.html.

157. "Go Further: Ending AIDS and Cervical Cancer. Program-Wide Highlights," Bush Center, https://gwbushcenter.imgix.net/wp-content/uploads/GoFurther_GlobalHighlights_FY22Q2_18_JULY_2022.pdf.

158. Bush, author interview.

159. "PEPFAR and the George W. Bush Institute Welcome Merck to the Partnerships to End AIDS and Cervical Cancer among HIV-Positive Women in Africa," Bush Center, June 5, 2019, https://www.bushcenter.org/newsroom/pepfar-and-the-george-w-bush-institute-welcome-merck-to-the-partnership-to-end-aids-and-cervical-cancer-among-hiv-positive-women-in-africa.

160. Bush, *Decision Points*, 340.

161. Bush, author interview.

162. Laura Bush, author interview.

163. Bush, author interview. Corroborated by Barbara Bush, author interview.

164. George W. Bush, "George W. Bush: PEPFAR Saves Millions of Lives in Africa. Keep It Fully Funded," *Washington Post*, August 7, 2017, https://www.washingtonpost.com/opinions/george-w-bush-pepfar-saves-millions-of-lives-in-africa-keep-it-fully-funded/2017/04/07/2089fa46-1ba7-11e7-9887-1a5314b56a08_story.html.

165. "The US President's Emergency Plan for AIDS Relief," KFF, April 18, 2023, https://www.kff.org/global-health-policy/fact-sheet/the-u-s-presidents-emergency-plan-for-aids-relief-pepfar/.

166. Laura Bush, author interview.

167. "How Team 43 Is More Than a Sports Program," Bush Center, July 31, 2019, https://www.bushcenter.org/publications/how-team-43-is-more-than-a-sports-program.

168. Book assembled by veterans for George W. Bush's seventy-fourth birthday, George W. Bush private collection.

169. Bush, author interview.

170. "Changing the Dialogue of PTS," Bush Center, July 29, 2018, https://www.bushcenter.org/publications/changing-the-dialogue-of-pts.

171. Bush, author interview.

172. John Harwood, "An Unforeseen Force Looms Large over the Race," *New York Times*, October 22, 2012, https://www.nytimes.com/2012/10/23/us /politics/unseen-but-looming-over-the-race-george-w-bush.html.

173. "Yale Professor's Advice to Former US President: Paint," *Yale University News*, April 26, 2013, https://history.yale.edu/news/yale-professor-s-advice -former-us-president-paint.

174. Mimi Swartz, "'W.' and the Art of Redemption," *New York Times*, March 21, 2017, https://www.nytimes.com/2017/03/21/opinion/w-and-the-art-of-re demption.html.

175. John Lewis Gaddis, author interview via Zoom, September 20, 2021.

176. "Yale Professor's Advice to Former US President: Paint."

177. Winston S. Churchill, *Painting as a Pastime* (New York: McGraw-Hill, 1950), https://gutenberg.ca/ebooks/churchillws-paintingasapastime/churchillws -paintingasapastime-00-h-dir/churchillws-paintingasapastime-00-h.html.

178. John Lewis Gaddis, author interview by phone, September 20, 2021.

179. Bush, author interview.

180. Laura Bush, author interview.

181. Bush, author interview.

182. Laura Bush, author interview.

183. Rove, author interview.

184. Laura Bush, author interview.

185. Barbara Bush, author interview.

186. Laura Bush, author interview.

187. "The Art of Painting: A Conversation with President Bush's Art Instructors," YouTube, September 6, 2017, https://www.youtube.com/watch?v=Z-Mr4x -rqMU.

188. Ibid.

189. Bush, author interview.

190. "Romanian National 'Gufficer' Extradited to Face Hacking Charges," United States Attorney's Office for the Eastern District of Virginia, April 1, 2016, https://www.justice.gov/usao-edva/pr/romanian-national-guccifer-extradited -face-hacking-charges.

191. "Romanian Hacker 'Guccifer' Sentenced to 52 Months in Prison for Computer Hacking Crimes," Office of Public Affairs, U.S. Department of Justice, September 1, 2016, https://www.justice.gov/opa/pr/romanian-hacker-guccifer -sentenced-52-months-prison-computer-hacking-crimes.

192. Bush, author interview.

193. Ibid.

194. Ibid.

195. "The Art of Leadership," Bush Center, https://www.bushcenter.org/exhibits -and-events/exhibits/2014/the-art-of-leadership-a-presidents-personal-dip lomacy.html.
196. Hamid Karzai, author interview via Zoom, January 31, 2021.
197. Condoleezza Rice, *No Higher Honour* (New York: Simon & Schuster, 2011), xxx.
198. Jason Garago, "George W. Bush's Portraits of World Leaders: Art That Tells Us Nothing at All," *Guardian*, April 4, 2014, https://www.theguardian.com /artanddesign/2014/apr/04/george-bush-portraits-world-leaders.
199. Roberta Smith, "The Faces of Power, from the Portraitist in Chief," *New York Times*, April 6, 2014, https://www.nytimes.com/2014/04/07/arts/design /george-w-bushs-art-exhibition-at-presidential-center.html.
200. Bush, author interview.
201. Laura Bush, author interview; "The Art of Painting: A Conversation with President Bush's Art Instructors."
202. Bush, author interview.
203. Laura Bush, author interview.
204. Bush, author interview.
205. Ibid.
206. Hersch, author interview.
207. Bush, author interview.
208. Saul Martinez, author interview by phone, January 26, 2021.
209. Ibid.
210. Bush, author interview.
211. Nicholas Frank, "Bush's *Portraits of Courage* Project Helps Heal the Wounds of War," *San Antonio Report*, March 25, 2018.
212. Julie Fancher, "Painting Veterans George W. Bush's Way to Give Back: 'I Was Just So Honored to be Their Commander-in-Chief,'" *Dallas Morning News*, February 27, 2017, https://www.dallasnews.com/news/2017/02/28/painting -veterans-george-w-bush-s-way-to-give-back-i-was-just-so-honored-to-be-their -commander-in-chief/.
213. Bush, author interview.
214. David Smith, "Two Years Ago I Stared Down the Barrel of a Shotgun and Nearly Took My Own Life," Task and Purpose, September 10, 2014, https:// taskandpurpose.com/community/two-years-ago-stared-barrel-shotgun/; "Meet Warrior Dave Smith," Bush Center, April 28, 2012, https://www.bushcenter .org/publications/articles/2012/09/meet-warrior-dave-smith.html.
215. Bush, author interview.
216. Katherine Schaeffer, "The Changing Face of America's Veteran Population," Pew Research Center, April 5, 2021, https://www.pewresearch.org/fact-tank /2021/04/05/the-changing-face-of-americas-veteran-population/.

217. J. J. Charlesworth, "George W. Bush's Veteran Portraits Yearn for a Return to Innocence," CNN Style, October 7, 2019, https://www.cnn.com/style /article/george-w-bush-paintings/index.html.

218. "George W. Bush: Snowden Damaged US; Security Programs Protect Civil Liberties," CNN, July 1, 2013, https://cnnpressroom.blogs.cnn.com /2013/07/01/george-w-bush-snowden-damaged-us-security-programs-protect -civil-liberties/.

219. Bush, author interview.

220. "Read Former President George W. Bush's Speech at the Flight 93 Memorial Service," CNN, September 11, 2021, https://www.cnn.com/2021/09/11 /politics/transcript-george-w-bush-speech-09-11-2021/index.html#:~:text =Twenty%20years%20ago%2C%20we%20all,would%20never%20be%20 heard%20again.

221. "Remarks by President George W. Bush at the Flight 93 National Memorial in Shanksville, Pennsylvania," Bush Center, September 11, 2021, https:// www.bushcenter.org/about-the-center/newsroom/press-releases/2021/09 /remarks-president-bush-shanksville-9-11.html.

222. Rajan Menon, "Obama's Afghan Challenge," *Los Angeles Times*, January 9, 2009, https://www.latimes.com/opinion/la-oe-menon9-2009jan09-story.html.

223. "Final Presidential Job Approval Ratings," American Presidency Project, UC Santa Barbara, https://www.presidency.ucsb.edu/statistics/data/final-pres idential-job-approval-ratings.

224. "Presidential Historians Survey 2021."

225. Bush, author interview.

226. Ibid.

227. Ibid.

228. Ibid.

229. Laura Bush, author interview.

230. Ken Mehlman, author interview by phone, February 23, 2021.

231. Mitchell Owens, "Laura and George W. Bush's House in Texas," *Architectural Digest*, December 16, 2016, https://www.architecturaldigest.com /story/laura-and-george-w-bush-prairie-chapel-ranch-texas-article.

232. Bush, author interview.

233. Matthew Kassel, "George W. Bush Paints a New Chapter," *Jewish Insider*, May 3, 2021, https://jewishinsider.com/2021/05/george-w-bush-book-painting -kissinger-powell-mccormick/.

234. George W. Bush, *Out of Many One*, 193.

235. Bush, author interview.

236. Mehlman, author interview.

237. George W. Bush, "George W. Bush: Immigration Is a Defining Asset of the

United States. Here's How to Restore Confidence in Our System," *Washington Post*, April 16, 2021, https://www.washingtonpost.com/opinions/2021/04/16/george-w-bush-immigration-portraits-out-of-many-one/.

238. Bush, author interview.

239. "Waxing Poetic: Expressions with Cold Wax," Bush Center, https://www.bushcenter.org/events-and-exhibits/waxing-poetic-expressions-with-cold-wax.

240. Bush, author interview.

241. "George W. Bush Presidential Center to Open 'Waxing Poetic: Expressions with Cold Wax,'" Bush Center, March 30, 2022, https://www.bushcenter.org/about-the-center/newsroom/press-releases/2022/03/waxing-poetic-expressions-with-cold-wax-press-release.html.

242. Bush, author interview.

243. Barbara Bush, author interview.

244. Bush, author interview.

245. Laura L. Carstensen, et al., "Taking Time Seriously: A Theory of Socioemotional Selectivity," *American Psychologist* 54, no. 3 (April 1999): 165–81, https://www.researchgate.net/publication/13099435_Taking_time_seriously_A_theory_of_socioemotional_selectivity.

246. Bush, author interview.

247. Tom Porter, "George HW Bush Would Have Been 95 Today. He Used to Celebrate Every Fifth Birthday by Going Skydiving," *Insider*, July 12, 2019, https://www.businessinsider.com/george-hw-bush-marked-birthday-with-skydive-2019-6.

248. Bush, author interview.

249. Ibid.

250. "George W. Bush's Favorable Rating Has Pulled a Complete 180."

251. Bush, author interview.

CONCLUSION

1. Alexander Hamilton, "The Federalist Papers: No. 70, March 18, 1788," Avalon Project, Yale Law School, https://avalon.law.yale.edu/18th_century/fed70.asp.

2. Carl Jung and Edward Hoffman, ed., *The Wisdom of Carl Jung* (New York: Citadel Press, 2003), 103.

BIBLIOGRAPHY

BOOKS

Abbott, Lawrence F. ed. *Taft and Roosevelt: The Intimate Letters of Archie Butt, Military Aide*, vol. 1. Garden City, NY: Doubleday, Doran, 1930.

Adams, Henry. *History of the United States during the Administrations of Thomas Jefferson*. New York: Charles Scribner's Sons, 1889.

Adams, John Quincy. *Memoirs of John Quincy Adams: Comprising Portions of His Diary from 1795 to 1848*. Philadelphia: J. B. Lippincott, 1874.

Addis, Cameron. *Jefferson's Vision for Education*. New York: Peter Lang, 2003.

Algeo, Matthew. *The President Is a Sick Man: Wherein the Supposedly Virtuous Grover Cleveland Survives a Secret Surgery at Sea and Vilifies the Courageous Newspaperman Who Dared Expose the Truth*. Chicago: Chicago Review Press, 2011.

Allen, Frederick Lewis. *Only Yesterday: An Informal History of the 1920s*. New York: Open Road Media, 2015.

Alter, Jonathan. *His Very Best: Jimmy Carter, a Life*. New York: Simon & Schuster, 2021.

Anderson, Judith Icke. *William Howard Taft: An Intimate History*. New York: W. W. Norton, 1981.

Anthony, C. S. *Florence Harding: The First Lady, the Jazz Age, and the Death of America's Most Scandalous President*. New York: William Morrow, 1998.

Arnold, Peri E. *Remaking the Presidency: Roosevelt, Taft, and Wilson, 1901–1916*. Lawrence: University Press of Kansas, 2009.

Ayers, Edward L. *The Promise of the New South: Life after Reconstruction*. 15th anniversary ed. New York: Oxford University Press, 2007.

Ayton, Mel. *Hunting the President: Threats, Plots and Assassination Attempts—from FDR to Obama*. Washington, DC: Regnery, 2014.

Baime, A. J. *The Accidental President: Harry S. Truman and the Four Months That Changed the World*. Boston: Houghton Mifflin Harcourt, 2017.

Bain, Richard C., and Judith H. Parris. *Convention Decisions and Voting Records*. Washington, DC: Brookings Institution, 1973.

Bemis, Samuel Flagg. *John Quincy Adams and the Union*, vol. 2. Indexed by Dorothy W. Bridgwater. New York: Alfred A. Knopf, 1956.

Bennett, E. M., and Norman A. Graebner. *The Versailles Treaty and Its Legacy: The Failure of the Wilsonian Vision*. New York: Cambridge University Press, 2011.

Best, Gary Dean. *Herbert Hoover: The Postpresidential Years, 1933–1964, Volume One: 1933–1945*. Stanford, CA: Hoover Institution Press, 1983.

———. *Herbert Hoover: The Postpresidential Years, 1933–1964, Volume Two: 1946–1964*. Stanford, CA: Hoover Institution Press, 1983.

———. *The Life of Herbert Hoover: Keeper of the Torch, 1933–1964*. London: Palgrave Macmillan, 2013.

Beveridge, Albert J. *Abraham Lincoln, 1809–1858*. London: Victor Gollancz, 1928.

Bird, Kai. *The Outlier: The Unfinished Presidency of Jimmy Carter*. New York: Crown, 2021.

Blassingame, John W., ed. *Slave Testimony: Two Centuries of Letters, Speeches, Interviews, and Autobiographies*. Baton Rouge: Louisiana State University Press, 1977.

Blumenthal, Sidney. *A Self Made Man: The Political Life of Abraham Lincoln*. New York: Simon & Schuster, 2017.

Bober, Natalie S. *Abigail Adams: Witness to a Revolution*. New York: Atheneum Books for Young Readers, 2010.

Boller, Paul F., Jr. *Presidential Anecdotes*. New York: Oxford University Press, 1996.

———. *Presidential Campaigns*. New York: Oxford University Press, 1996.

Brands, Hal. *Making the Unipolar Moment: US Foreign Policy and the Rise of the Post–Cold War Order*. Ithaca, NY: Cornell University Press, 2016.

Brinkley, Douglas. *The Unfinished Presidency: Jimmy Carter's Journey to the Nobel Peace Prize*. New York: Penguin Books, 1999.

Brodsky, Alyn. *Grover Cleveland: A Study in Character*. New York: St. Martin's Press, 2000.

Brookhiser, Richard. *Founding Father*. New York: Free Press, 1997.

Brzezinski, Zbigniew. *Power and Principle: Memoirs of the National Security Adviser, 1977–1981*. New York: Farrar, Straus and Giroux, 1983.

Buckley, William F. *Rumbles Left and Right: A Book about Troublesome People and Ideas*. New York: Putnam, 1963.

Burnstein, Andrew. *Madison and Jefferson*. New York: Random House, 2010.

Burton, David Henry. *William Howard Taft: Confident Peacemaker*. Philadelphia: St. Joseph's University Press, 2004.

Bush, George W. *41: A Portrait of My Father*. New York: Crown, 2014.

———. *Decision Points*, enhanced ed. New York: Crown, 2010.

———. *Out of Many, One: Portraits of America's Immigrants*. New York: Crown, 2021.

Carter, Jimmy. *The Blood of Abraham: Insights into the Middle East*. Fayetteville: University of Arkansas Press, 2007.

———. *Everything to Gain: Making the Most of the Rest of Your Life*. Fayetteville: University of Arkansas Press, 1995.

———. *A Full Life: Reflections at Ninety*. New York: Simon & Schuster, 2016.

———. *Keeping Faith*. Fayetteville: University of Arkansas Press, 1995.

———. *Palestine*. New York: Simon & Schuster, 2007.

Carter, Rosalynn. *First Lady from Plains*. Fayetteville: University of Arkansas Press, 1994.

Chace, James. *1912: Wilson, Roosevelt, Taft & Debs—The Election That Changed the Country*. New York: Simon & Schuster, 2009.

Chambers, John Whiteclay, II, ed. *The Oxford Companion to American Military History*. New York: Oxford University Press, 1999.

Chambers, Whittaker. *Witness*. Washington, DC: Regnery, 2014.

Chaplin, Jeremiah, and J. D. Chaplin. *Life of Charles Sumner*. Introduction by Hon. William Claflin. Ann Arbor: Scholarly Publishing Office, University of Michigan Library, 1874.

Chapple, Joe Mitchell. *Life and Times of Warren G. Harding: Our After-War President*. Boston: Chapple, 1924.

Cheney, Lynne. *The Virginia Dynasty: Four Presidents and the Creation of the American Nation*. New York: Penguin Books, 2020.

Chernow, Ron. *Washington: A Life*. New York: Penguin Books, 2011.

Chollet, Derek, and James Goldgeier. *America between the Wars: From 11/9 to 9/11: The Misunderstood Years between the Fall of the Berlin Wall and the Start of the War on Terror*. New York: PublicAffairs, 2008.

Churchill, Winston S. *Fishing and Shooting Sketches*. New York: The Outing Publishing Company, 1906.

———. *Painting as a Pastime*. New York: McGraw-Hill, 1950. https://gutenberg .ca/ebooks/churchillws-paintingasapastime/churchillws-paintingasapastime -00-h-dir/churchillws-paintingasapastime-00-h.html.

———. *Presidential Problems*. New York: Century Company, 1904.

Clifford, J. Garry, and Masako R. Okura. ed. *The Desperate Diplomat: Saburo Kurusu's Memoir of the Weeks before Pearl Harbor*. Columbia: University of Missouri Press, 2019.

Clinton, Hillary Rodham. *What Happened*. New York: Simon & Schuster, 2017.

Cohen, Jared. *Accidental Presidents: Eight Men Who Changed America*. New York: Simon & Schuster, 2019.

Cohen, P. C., et al. *The American Promise, Combined Volume: A History of the United States*. New York: Bedford/St. Martin's, 2012.

Continetti, Matthew. *The Right: The Hundred-Year War for American Conservatism*. New York: Basic Books, 2022.

Cooper, William J. *The Lost Founding Father: John Quincy Adams and the Transformation of American Politics*. New York: W. W. Norton, 2017.

Costanzo, Michael B. *Author in Chief: The Presidents as Writers from Washington to Trump*. Jefferson, NC: McFarland, 2019.

Crawford, Alan Pell. *Twilight at Monticello: The Final Years of Thomas Jefferson*. New York: Random House, 2008.

Crispell, Kenneth R., and Carlos Gomez. *Hidden Illness in the White House*. Durham, NC: Duke University Press, 1988.

Crook, Colonel W. H. *Memories of the White House*. Boston: Little, Brown, 1911.

Crowley, Monica. *Nixon Off the Record*. New York: Random House, 1996.

Currie, David P. *The Constitution in Congress: Democrats and Whigs, 1829–1861*. Chicago: University of Chicago Press, 2005.

Davis, R. J. *The Boys' Life of Grover Cleveland*. New York: Harper & Brothers, 1925.

Dean, John. *Warren G. Harding*. New York: Times Books, 2004.

DeFrank, Thomas M., and James Addison Baker. *The Politics of Diplomacy: Revolution, War, and Peace, 1989–1992*. New York: G. P. Putnam's Sons, 1995.

Dickson, Paul, and William B. Mead. *Baseball: The Presidents' Game*. New York: Walker, 1997.

Dikotter, Frank. *The Tragedy of Liberation*. New York: Bloomsbury, 2013.

Dunlap, Annette. *Frank: The Story of Frances Folsom Cleveland, America's Youngest First Lady*. Albany: State University of New York Press, 2010.

Eaton, Herbert. *Presidential Timber: A History of Nominating Conventions, 1868-1960*. Glencoe, IL: Free Press of Glencoe, 1964.

Ehrenhalt, Lizzie, and Tilly Laskey, ed. *Precious and Adored: The Love Letters of Rose Cleveland and Evangeline Simpson Whipple, 1890–1918*. St. Paul: Minnesota Historical Society Press, 2019.

Ellis, Joseph J. *American Sphinx*. New York: Knopf Doubleday, 1998.

———. *His Excellency: George Washington*. New York: Knopf Doubleday, 2005.

Emerson, Ralph Waldo. *A Year with Emerson: A Daybook*. Boston: D. R. Godine, 2003.

Everett, Edward. *A Eulogy on the Life and Character of John Quincy Adams: Delivered at the Request of the Legislature of Massachusetts, in Faneuil Hall, April 15, 1848*. Boston: Dutton and Wentworth, 1848.

Farber, David. *Taken Hostage: The Iran Hostage Crisis and America's First Encounter with Radical Islam*. Princeton, NJ: Princeton University Press, 2006.

Feerick, John D. *From Failing Hands: The Story of Presidential Succession*. New York: Fordham University Press, 1965.

Ferling, John. *John Adams: A Life*. New York: Oxford University Press, 2010.

Ferrell, Robert H. *American Diplomacy in the Great Depression: Hoover-Stimson Foreign Policy, 1929–1933*. New Haven, CT: Yale University Press, 1957.

_____. *Choosing Truman: The Democratic Convention of 1944*. Columbia: University of Missouri Press, 2013.

Figes, Orlando. *The Story of Russia*. New York: Henry Holt, 2022.

Fischer, David Hackett. *Albion's Seed: Four British Folkways in America (America: A Cultural History, Vol. 1)*. Oxford, UK: Oxford University Press, 1989.

Fish, Carl Russell. *Civil Service and the Patronage*. New York: Longmans, Green & Co, 1904.

Ford, Paul Leicester, ed., and Thomas Jefferson, *The Writings of Thomas Jefferson, Volume IX, 1809–1815*. New York: G. P. Putnam's Sons, 1898.

Fortescue, Sir John, ed. *The Correspondence of King George the Third, from 1760 to December 1783, Volume VI: May 1782 to December 1783*. Oxfordshire, UK: Routledge, 2014.

Freehling, William W. *Prelude to Civil War: the Nullification Controversy in South Carolina, 1816–1836*. Oxford, UK: Oxford University Press, 1992.

_____. *The Road to Disunion: Secessionists at Bay, 1776–1854*. New York: Oxford University Press, 1990.

Freeman, Joanne B. *The Field of Blood: Violence in Congress and the Road to Civil War*. New York: Farrar, Straus and Giroux, 2018.

Fuess, Claude M. *Calvin Coolidge: The Man from Vermont*. Fuess Press, 2007.

Gallucci, Robert L., Daniel B. Poneman, and Joel S. Wit. *Going Critical: The First North Korean Nuclear Crisis*. Washington, DC: Brookings Institution Press, 2004.

Gambler, James. *Dining with Thomas Jefferson and Fascinating Guests*. Palm Beach, FL: Bacchus Press, 2015.

Gay, George I. *Public Relations of the Commission for Relief in Belgium*, vol. 2. Stanford, CA: Stanford University Press, 1929.

Goldsmith, Harry S. *A Conspiracy of Silence: The Health and Death of Franklin Delano Roosevelt*. New York: iUniverse, 2007.

Goodwin, Doris Kearns. *The Bully Pulpit: Theodore Roosevelt, William Howard Taft, and the Golden Age of Journalism*. New York: Simon & Schuster, 2013.

Gould, Lewis L. *Chief Executive to Chief Justice: Taft Betwixt the White House and Supreme Court*. Lawrence: University Press of Kansas, 2014.

_____. *Grand Old Party: A History of the Republicans*. New York: Oxford University Press, 2012.

Graff, Henry Franklin. *Grover Cleveland*. New York: Henry Holt, 2002.

Graham, Katharine. *Katharine Graham's Washington*. New York: Vintage Books, 2003.

Greenberg, David. *Calvin Coolidge: The American Presidents Series: The 30th President, 1923–1929*. New York: Henry Holt, 2006.

Gwynn, Stephen, ed. *The Letters and Friendships of Sir Cecil Spring-Rice, A Record*, vol. 1. Boston: Houghton Mifflin, 1929.

Haig, Alexander. *Caveat: Realism, Reagan, and Foreign Policy*. New York: Scribner, 1984.

Hale, William Bayard. *Woodrow Wilson: The Story of His Life*. Cambridge, MA: Harvard University Press, 1912.

Hammond, Scott J., Valerie A. Sulfaro, and Robert N. Roberts. *Presidential Campaigns, Slogans, Issues, and Platforms: The Complete Encyclopedia*. Westport, CT: Greenwood, 2012.

Harris, David. *The Crisis: The President, the Prophet, and the Shah—1979 and the Coming of Militant Islam*. Boston: Little, Brown, 2004.

Hayes, Kevin J. *Jefferson in His Own Time: A Biographical Chronicle of His Life, Drawn from Recollections, Interviews, and Memoirs by Family, Friends, and Associates*. Iowa City: University of Iowa Press, 2012.

Hecksher, August. *Woodrow Wilson: A Biography*. New York: Scribner, 1993.

Hiltzik, Michael. *The New Deal: A Modern History*. New York: Free Press, 2011.

Hoover, Herbert. *Addresses upon the American Road: World War II, 1941–1945*. New York: D. Van Nostrand, 1946.

——. *America's First Crusade*. New York: C. Scribner's Sons, 1942.

——. *An American Epic: The Relief of Belgium and Northern France, 1914–1930*. Washington, DC: Regnery, 1959.

——. *The Challenge to Liberty*. New York: Charles Scribner's Sons, 1934.

——. *The Crusade Years, 1933–1955: Herbert Hoover's Lost Memoir of the New Deal Era and Its Aftermath*. Stanford, CA: Hoover Institution Press, 2013.

——. *The Memoirs of Herbert Hoover: The Great Depression, 1929–1941*. Redditch, UK: Read Books Limited, 2015.

——. *The Memoirs of Herbert Hoover: Years of Adventure, 1874–1920*. New York: Macmillan, 1957.

——. *The Ordeal of Woodrow Wilson*. Baltimore: Johns Hopkins University Press, 1958.

Horne, Charles F., ed. *Source Records of the Great War*, vol. 5. United States: National Alumni, 1923

Inboden, William. *The Peacemaker: Ronald Reagan, the Cold War, and the World on the Brink*. New York: Dutton, 2022.

Jeansonne, Glenn, and David Luhrssen. *Herbert Hoover: A Life*. New York: New American Library, 2016.

Jefferson, Thomas. *The Writings of Thomas Jefferson: 1807–1815*. New York: G. P. Putnam's Sons, 1892.

Johnson, Charles C. *Why Coolidge Matters: Leadership Lessons from America's Most Underrated President*. New York: Encounter Books, 2013.

Jones, Howard. *Mutiny on the "Amistad."* New York: Oxford University Press, 1987.

Keene, Michael L., and Katherine H. Adams. *Alice Paul and the American Suffrage Campaign*. Champaign: University of Illinois Press, 2010.

Kelly, Jack. *The Edge of Anarchy: The Railroad Barons, the Gilded Age, and the Greatest Labor Uprising in America*. New York: St. Martin's, 2019.

Kennedy, David M. *The American People in the Great Depression: Freedom from Fear, Part One*. New York: Oxford University Press, 2003.

Kennedy, David M., and Lizabeth Cohen. *The American Pageant*, vol 2. Boston: Cengage Learning, 2012.

Kerney, James. *The Political Education of Woodrow Wilson*. New York: Century Company.

Kierner, Cynthia A. *Martha Jefferson Randloph: Daughter of Monticello*. Chapel Hill: University of North Carolina Press, 2012.

Kissinger, Henry. *Leadership: Six Studies in World Strategy*. New York: Penguin Press, 2022.

Klingaman, William K. *1929: The Year of the Great Crash*. New York: Harper & Row, 1989.

Knight, Lucian Lamar. *Woodrow Wilson, the Dreamer and the Dream*. Atlanta: Johnson-Dallis, 1924.

Knock, Thomas. *To End All Wars*. Princeton, NJ: Princeton University Press, 1995.

Kohlsaat, H. H., *From McKinley to Harding: Recollections of Our Presidents*. New York: Charles Scribner's Sons, 1923.

Kraditor, Ailenn. *Up from the Pedestal*. Chicago: Quadrangle, 1970.

Kucera, Major Peter G. *Brigadier General Henry A. Wise, C.S.A. and the Western Virginia Campaign of 1861*. London: Golden Springs, 2014.

Küng-Shankleman, Lucy. *Inside the BBC and CNN: Managing Media Organisations*. London: Routledge, 2000.

Lachman, Charles. *A Secret Life: The Lies and Scandals of President Grover Cleveland*. New York: Skyhorse, 2011.

Larson, E. *In the Garden of Beasts: Love, Terror, and an American Family in Hitler's Berlin*. New York: Crown, 2011.

Lazarus, Richard S., and Susan Folkman. *Stress, Appraisal, and Coping*. New York: Springer, 1984.

Leuchtenburg, William E. *In the Shadow of FDR: From Harry Truman to George W. Bush*. Ithaca, NY: Cornell University Press, 2001.

Link, Arthur S. *Woodrow Wilson and the Progressive Era, 1910–1917*. New York: Harper, 1972.

Lochne, Louis Paul. *Herbert Hoover and Germany*. London: Macmillan, 1960.

Lodge, Henry Cabot, and Theodore Lodge. *Selections from the Correspondence of Theodore Roosevelt and Henry Cabot Lodge, 1884–1918*. New York: C. Scribner's Sons, 1925.

Lomazow, Steven, and Eric Fettman. *FDR's Deadly Secret*. New York: PublicAffairs, 2009.

Longo, James McMurtry. *From Classroom to White House: The Presidents and First Ladies as Students and Teachers*. Jefferson, NC: McFarland, 2011.

Longworth, Alice Roosevelt. *Crowded Hours*. New York: Charles Scribner's Sons, 1933.

Lurie, Jonathan. *William Howard Taft: The Travails of a Progressive Conservative*. New York: Cambridge University Press, 2011.

Lyons, Eugene. *Herbert Hoover: A Biography*. New York: Doubleday, 1964.

MacMahon, Edward B., and Leonard Curry. *Medical Cover-Ups in the White House*. Washington, DC: Farragut, 1987.

Malone, Dumas. *Jefferson and His Time*, 6 vols. Boston: Little, Brown, 1948–1981.

———. *Jefferson and the Ordeal of Liberty*. Charlottesville: University of Virginia Press, 2005.

———. *The Sage of Monticello*. Charlottesville: University of Virginia Press, 2006.

Markel, Rita J. *Grover Cleveland*. Minneapolis: Twenty-First Century Books, 2006.

Marshall, John. *The Life of George Washington*, 5 vols. New York: Derby & Jackson, 1857.

Marsico, Katie. *Women's Right to Vote: America's Suffrage Movement*. Terrytown, NY: Marshall Cavendish Benchmark, 2011.

Martin, Christopher. *The Amistad Affair*. New York: Abelard-Schuman, 1970.

Martinez, J. Michael. *Libertines: American Political Sex Scandals from Alexander Hamilton to Donald Trump*. Lanham, MD: Rowman & Littlefield, 2022.

Mason, Alpheus Thomas. *William Howard Taft, Chief Justice*. New York: Simon & Schuster, 1965.

McElroy, Robert McNutt. *Grover Cleveland, the Man and the Statesman: An Authorized Biography*. 2 vols. New York: Harper & Brothers, 1923.

McWilliams, W. Carey, and Frank X. Gerrity, ed. *The President and His Powers, in the Collected Works of William Howard Taft*, vol. 6. Athens: Ohio University Press, 2003.

Meacham, Jon. *American Lion: Andrew Jackson in the White House*. New York: Random House, 2009.

———. *Thomas Jefferson: The Art of Power*. United States: Random House, 2012.

Mead, Walter Russell. *The Arc of a Covenant: The United States, Israel, and the Fate of the Jewish People*. New York: Knopf Doubleday, 2022.

Mee, Charles L., Jr. *The Ohio Gang: The World of Warren G. Harding—An Historical Entertainment*. Lanham, MD: M. Evans, 2014.

Meltzer, Milton. *Brother, Can You Spare a Dime? The Great Depression, 1929–1933*. New York: New American Library, 1977.

Milkis, Sidney M. "William Howard Taft and the Struggle for the Soul of the Constitution." In *Toward an American Conservatism*. Edited by Joseph W. Postell and Johnathan O'Neill. London: Palgrave MacMillan, 2013.

Miller, Scott. *President and the Assassin*. New York: Random House, 2011.

Miller, William Lee. *Arguing about Slavery: John Quincy Adams and the Great Battle in the United States Congress*. New York: Vintage, 1998.

Moley, Raymond. *The First New Deal*. New York: Harcourt, Brace & World, 1966.

Monkman, Betty C. *The White House: Its Historic Furnishings and First Families*. New York: Abbeville Press, 2000.

Morley, Felix. *For the Record*. South Bend, IN: Gateway Books, 1979.

National Democratic Committee. *The Campaign Text Book of the Democratic Party of the United States; for the Presidential Election of 1888*. New York: Brentanos, 1888.

Nevins, Allan. *Grover Cleveland: A Study in Courage*. Oakland, CA: Ishi Press, 2018.

———. ed. *Letters of Grover Cleveland, 1850–1908*. Boston: Houghton Mifflin, 1933.

Nichter, Luke A. *The Last Brahmin: Henry Cabot Lodge, Jr. and the Making of the Cold War*. New Haven: Yale Universitiy Press, 2020.

Nixon, Richard. *RN: The Memoirs of Richard Nixon*. New York: Simon & Schuster, 2013.

———. *Six Crises*. New York: Simon & Schuster, 2013.

Nordholt, J. W. Schulte. *Woodrow Wilson: A Life for World Peace*. Berkeley: University of California Press, 1991.

O'Shaughnessy, Andrew J. *The Illimitable Freedom of the Human Mind: Thomas Jefferson's Idea of a University*. Charlottesville: University of Virginia Press, 2021.

Oakes, James. *The Crooked Path to Abolition: Abraham Lincoln and the Antislavery Constitution*. New York: W. W. Norton, 2021.

Offner, John L. *An Unwanted War: The Diplomacy of the United States and Spain over Cuba, 1895–1989*. Chapel Hill: University of North Carolina Press, 1992.

Olin, Spencer C. *California's Prodigal Son: Hiram Johnson and the Progressives, 1911–1917*. Berkeley: University of California Press, 1968.

Packer, George. *Our Man: Richard Holbrooke and the End of the American Century.* New York: Knopf, 2020.

Pafford, John M. *Cleveland: The Forgotten Conservative.* Washington, DC: Regnery, 2015.

Parker, George Frederick. *A Life of Grover Cleveland: With a Sketch of Adlai E. Stevenson.* London: Cassell, 1892.

Parsons, Lynn H. *John Quincy Adams.* Lanham, MD: Rowman & Littlefield, 1999.

Patrick, Stewart. *The Best Laid Plans: The Origins of Multilateralism and the Dawn of the Cold War.* New York: Rowman & Littlefield, 2009.

Pérez, Louis A. *Cuba between Reform and Revolution.* Oxford, UK: Oxford University Press, 1988.

Picchi, Blaise. *The Five Weeks of Giuseppe Zangara: The Man Who Tried to Kill FDR.* Chicago: Academy Chicago, 1998.

Pierson, George Wilson. *Tocqueville and Beaumont in America.* Baltimore: Johns Hopkins University Press, 1938.

Pietrusza, David. *1920: The Year of Six Presidents.* New York: Basic Books, 2008.
———. *Roosevelt Sweeps Nation: FDR's 1936 Landslide and the Triumph of the Liberal Ideal.* New York: Diversion Books, 2022.

Pirnie, Bruce R., and Edward O'Connell. *Counterinsurgency in Iraq (2003–2006): RAND Counterinsurgency Study*, vol. 2. Santa Monica, CA: RAND, 2008.

Pringle, Henry Fowles. *William Howard Taft: The Life and Times.* Newtown, CT: American Political Biography Press, 1998.

Pullman, David Lloyd. *The Constitutional Conventions of Virginia from the Foundation of the Commonwealth to the Present Time.* Charleston, SC: Nabu Press, 2010.

Randall, Henry Stephens. *The Life of Thomas Jefferson: In 3 Volumes*, vol. 1. Charleston, SC: BiblioLife, 2013.

Randolph, Sarah N. *The Domestic Life of Thomas Jefferson.* New York: Harper & Brothers, 1871.

Rappleye, Charles. *Herbert Hoover in the White House: The Ordeal of the Presidency.* New York: Simon & Schuster, 2016.

Rauchway, Eric. *Winter War: Hoover, Roosevelt, and the First Clash over the New Deal.* New York: Basic Books, 2018.

Reeves, Thomas C. *Gentleman Boss: The Life of Chester Alan Arthur.* Newtown, CT: American Political Biography Press, 1991.

Remini, Robert V. *John Quincy Adams: The American Presidents Series: The 6th President, 1825–1829.* New York: Henry Holt, 2014.

Rice, Condoleezza. *No Higher Honor.* New York: Simon & Schuster, 2011.

Ritchie, Donald A. *Electing FDR: The New Deal Campaign of 1932.* Lawrence: University Press of Kansas, 2007.

Rosen, Jeffrey. *William Howard Taft: The American Presidents Series: The 27th President, 1909–1913.* New York: Henry Holt, 2018.

Ross, Ishbel. *An American Family: The Tafts, 1678 to 1964.* New York: World Publishing, 1977.

Rove, Karl. *The Triumph of William McKinley: Why the Election of 1896 Still Matters.* New York: Simon & Schuster, 2015.

Rubin, Barry M., and Judith Colp Rubin. *Yasir Arafat: A Political Biography.* New York: Oxford University Press, 2005.

Schake, Kori. *Safe Passage: The Transition from British to American Hegemony.* Cambridge, MA: Harvard University Press, 2017.

Schwartz, Bernard. *A History of the Supreme Court.* New York: Oxford University Press, 1995.

Seager, Robert. *And Tyler Too: A Biography of John and Julia Gardiner Tyler.* Sacramento, CA: Creative Media Partners, 2015.

Seale, William. *President's House.* New York: Harry N. Abrams, 1986.

———. *The President's House: A History.* Baltimore: Johns Hopkins University Press, 2008.

Sellers, Charles. *James K. Polk, Two Volumes.* Easton, CT: Easton Press, 1987.

Senik, Troy. *A Man of Iron: The Turbulent Life and Improbable Presidency of Grover Cleveland.* New York: Threshold Editions, 2022.

Severn, William. *William Howard Taft, the President Who Became Chief Justice.* Philadelphia: McKay, 1970.

Seward, William H. *Life and Public Services of John Quincy Adams.* Scotts Valley, CA: CreateSpace, 2013.

Shlaes, Amity. *The Forgotten Man Graphic Edition: A New History of the Great Depression.* New York: HarperCollins, 2014.

Sigal, Leon. *Disarming Strangers: Nuclear Diplomacy with North Korea.* Princeton, NJ: Princeton University Press, 1999.

Silber, William L. *The Story of Silver: How the White Metal Shapes America and the Modern World.* Princeton, NJ: Princeton University Press, 2019.

Silva, Ruth. *Presidential Succession.* New York: Greenwood Press, 1968.

Smith, Gene. *When the Cheering Stopped: The Last Years of Woodrow Wilson.* New York: William Morrow, 1964.

Smith, James Morton, ed. *The Republic of Letters: The Correspondence between Thomas Jefferson and James Madison 1776–1826,* 3 vols. New York: W. W. Norton, 1995.

Smith, Richard Norton. *An Uncommon Man: The Triumph of Herbert Hoover.* New York: Simon & Schuster, 1984.

Smith, William Henry. *A Political History of Slavery. Being an Account of the Slavery Controversy from the Earliest Agitation in the 18th Century to the Close of the Reconstruction Period in America*. Introduction by Louis Filler. New York: Frederick Ungar, 1966.

Sobel, Robert. *Coolidge: An American Enigma*. Washington, DC: Regnery, 2015.

Sprague, William C. *The Law Student's Helper*. Detroit: Collector Publishing Company, 1914.

Stanwood, Edward. *A History of the Presidency, from 1897 to 1909*. Boston: Houghton Mifflin, 1912.

Steil, Benn. *The Marshall Plan: Dawn of the Cold War*. Oxford, UK: Oxford University Press, 2018.

Striner, Richard. *Woodrow Wilson and World War I: A Burden Too Great to Bear*. Lanham, MD: Rowman & Littlefield, 2014.

Summers, Mark Wahlgren. *Rum, Romanism, and Rebellion: The Making of a President, 1884*. Chapel Hill: University of North Carolina Press, 2003.

Sydenham, Thomas. *The Whole Works of That Excellent Practical Physician, Dr. Thomas Sydenham*, 4th ed. London: Benjamin White, 1705.

Taft, Helen Herron. *Recollections of Full Years*. New York: Dodd, Mead, 1914.

Taft, William Howard. *Popular Government: Its Essence, Its Permanence and Its Perils*. Hartford, CT: Yale University Press, 1914.

———. *Presidential Addresses and State Papers of William Howard Taft, from March 4, 1909, to March 4, 1910*. New York: Doubleday, 1910.

Thomas, Benjamin P. *Abraham Lincoln: A Biography*. Carbondale: Southern Illinois University Press, 2008.

Thomas, Evan. *Being Nixon: A Man Divided*. New York: Random House, 2015.

Todd, Alden L. *Justice on Trial: The Case of Louis D. Brandeis*. New York: McGraw Hill, 1964.

Traub, James. *John Quincy Adams: Militant Spirit*. New York: Basic Books, 2016.

Truman, Harry S. *Memoirs by Harry S. Truman: Year of Decisions*. Old Saybrook, CT: Konecky & Konecky, 1955.

Truman, Margaret. *First Ladies: An Intimate Group Portrait of White House Wives*. New York: Fawcett, 2009.

Trump, Donald J., and Tony Schwartz. *Trump: The Art of the Deal*. New York: Ballentine, 2009.

Tugwell, Rexford Guy. *Grover Cleveland*. London: Macmillan, 1968.

Unger, Harlow G. *John Quincy Adams*. New York: Hachette, 2012.

Urofsky, Melvin I. *Louis D. Brandeis: A Life*. New York: Schocken, 2012.

Valsania, Maurizio. *Limits of Optimism: Thomas Jefferson's Dualistic Enlightenment*. Charlottesville: University of Virginia Press, 2012.

Walch, Timothy, and Dwight M. Miller, ed. *Herbert Hoover and Franklin D. Roosevelt: A Documentary History*. Westport, CT: Greenwood Press, 1998.

_____. *Herbert Hoover and Harry S. Truman: A Documentary History*. Worland, WY: High Plains Publishing company, 1992.

Wall, Joseph Frazier. *Andrew Carnegie*. New York: Oxford University Press, 1970.

Walters, Ryan S. *The Last Jeffersonian: Grover Cleveland and the Path to Restoring the Republic*. New York: WestBow Press, 2012.

Ward, Artemus. *Deciding to Leave: The Politics of Retirement from the United States Supreme Court*. Albany: State University of New York Press, 2012.

Warren, Harris Gaylord. *Herbert Hoover and the Great Depression*. New York: Oxford University Press, 1959.

Weeks, Philip, ed. *Buckeye Presidents: Ohioans in the White House*. Kent, OH: Kent State University Press, 2003.

Weinstein, Edwin. *Woodrow Wilson: A Medical and Psychological Biography*. Princeton, NJ: Princeton University Press, 1981.

Weiss, Ellen, and Mel Friedman. *Jimmy Carter: Champion of Peace*. New York: Aladdin Paperbacks, 2003.

Welch, Richard E. *The Presidencies of Grover Cleveland*. Lawrence: University Press of Kansas, 1988.

Wheelan, Joseph. *Mr. Adams's Last Crusade: John Quincy Adams's Extraordinary Post-Presidential Life in Congress*. New York: PublicAffairs, 2009.

Whisenhunt, Donald W. *President Herbert Hoover*. New York: Nova Science, 2007.

Williams, R. *Realigning America: McKinley, Bryan and the Remarkable Election of 1896*. Lawrence: University Press of Kansas, 2010.

Willis, Resa. *FDR and Lucy: Lovers and Friends*. New York: Routledge, 2004.

Wills, Garry. *Inventing America: Jefferson's Declaration of Independence*. New York: Knopf Doubleday, 2018.

Wilson, Woodrow. *The Papers of Woodrow Wilson*, 68 vols. Edited by Arthur S. Link. Princeton, NJ: Princeton University Press, 1966.

Wilentz, Sean. *Andrew Jackson: The American Presidents Series: The 7th President, 1829–1837*. New York: Times Books, 2005.

Winston, Diane, ed. *The Oxford Handbook of Religion and the American News Media*. New York: Oxford University Press, 2012.

Witcover, Jules. *The American Vice Presidency: From Irrelevance to Power*. Washington, DC: Smithsonian Books, 2014.

Wood, Gordon S. *Friends Divided: John Adams and Thomas Jefferson*. New York: Penguin Books, 2017.

Zimmermann, Warren. *First Great Triumph: How Five Americans Made Their Country a World Power*. New York: Farrar, Straus and Giroux, 2004.

ACADEMIC ARTICLES

"The Antislavery Views of President John Quincy Adams." *Journal of Blacks in Higher Education*, no. 18 (Winter, 1997–98): 102.

Blinder, Alan S. "The Anatomy of Double-Digit Inflation in the 1970s." Chicago: University of Chicago Press, 1982. https://www.nber.org/system/files/chapters/c11462/c11462.pdf.

Bruenn, H. G. "Clinical Notes on the Illness and Death of President Franklin D. Roosevelt." *Annals of Internal Medicine* 72, no. 4 (April 1970): 578–91.

Butterfield, Lyman H. "The Dream of Benjamin Rush: The Reconciliation of John Adams and Thomas Jefferson." *Yale Review* 40 (1950): 297–319.

Carstensen, Laura L., et al. "Taking Time Seriously: A Theory of Socioemotional Selectivity." *American Psychologist* 54, no. 3 (April 1999): 165–81. https://www.researchgate.net/publication/13099435_Taking_time_seriously_A_theory_of_socioemotional_selectivity.

Crackel, Theodore Joseph. "The Founding of West Point: Jefferson and the Politics of Security." *Armed Forces & Society* 7, no. 4 (Summer 1981): 529–43.

Dueck, Colin, and Henry Cabot Lodge. "Hawaii, and the Shift from Continental to Hemispheric Defense." *Orbis* 66, no. 3 (2022): 320–33.

"Economists against Smoot-Hawley." *Econ Journal Watch* 4, no. 3 (September 2007): 345–58. https://econjwatch.org/file_download/162/2007-09-editorsfetter-char_issue.pdf.

Feuer, Lewis. "America's First Jewish Professor: James Joseph Sylvester at the University of Virginia," *American Jewish Archives* 36, no. 2 (1984): 152–201.

Foster E., et al. "Jefferson Fathered Slave's Last Child." *Nature* 396, no. 6706 (November 1998): 27–28.

Garrow, David J. "Mental Decrepitude on the U.S. Supreme Court: The Historical Case for the 28th Amendment." *University of Chicago Law Review* 67, no. 995 (2000): 995–1087. https://chicagounbound.uchicago.edu/cgi/viewcontent.cgi?article=5893&context=uclrev.

Hacker, David J. "Decennial Life Tables for the White Population of the United States, 1790–1900." *Historical Methods* 43, no. 2 (April 2010): 45–79.

Harris, Stanley G., and Robert I. Sutton, "Functions of Parting Ceremonies in Dying Organizations," *Academy of Management Journal* 29, no. 1 (March 1986): 5–30.

Heffron, Paul T. "Theodore Roosevelt and the Appointment of Mr. Justice Moody." *Vanderbilt Law Review* 18, no. 2 (March 1965): 545–68. https://scholarship.law.vanderbilt.edu/cgi/viewcontent.cgi?article=3654&context=vlr.

Hochman, Steven Ha. "Thomas Jefferson: A Personal Financial Biography." PhD diss. University of Virginia, 1987, 235.

Hoxie, Robert F. "The Silver Debate of 1890." *Journal of Political Economy* 1, no. 4 (September 1893): 535–87.

Irwin, Douglas. "The Welfare Cost of Autarky: Evidence from the Jeffersonian Trade Embargo, 1807–09." *Review of International Economics* 13, no. 4 (September 2005): 631–45.

Kolasky, William. "Theodore Roosevelt and William Howard Taft: Marching Toward Armageddon," *Antitrust* 25, no. 2 (Spring 2011): 103–104.

Leavy, R. L. "Social Support and Psychological Disorder: A Review." *Journal of Community Psychology* 11, no. 1 (January 1983): 3–21.

Lebergott, Stanley. "Labor Force, Employment, and Unemployment, 1929–39: Estimating Methods." *Monthly Labor Review* (July 1948): 50–53. https://www .bls.gov/opub/mlr/1948/article/pdf/labor-force-employment-and-unemploy ment-1929-39-estimating-methods.pdf.

Lee, Fiona, and Larissa Z. Tiedens. "Is It Lonely at the Top?: The Independence and Interdependence of Power Holders." *Research in Organizational Behavior* 23 (2001): 43–91.

Lukacs, John. "HISTORY: Herbert Hoover Meets Adolph Hitler." *American Scholar* 62, no. 2 (Spring 1993): 235–38.

Lurie, Jonathan. "Chief Justice Taft and Dissents: Down with Brandeis Briefs!" *Journal of Supreme Court History* 32, no. 2 (2007): https://supremecourthistory .org/assets/schs-journal/pub_journal_2007_vol_2.pdf.

Luthin, Reinhard H. "Waving the Bloody Shirt: Northern Political Tactics in Post-Civil War Times." *Georgia Review* 14, no. 1 (Spring 1960): 64–71.

Mason, Alpheus Thomas. "Taft, William Howard (1857–1930)." *Encyclopedia of the American Constitution*, 2633–37. https://law-journals-books.vlex.com/vid/taft -william-howard-51715611.

McHargue, Daniel S. "President Taft's Appointments to the Supreme Court." *Journal of Politics* 12, no. 3 (August, 1950): 478–510.

McWilliams, Tennant S. "Hames H. Blount, the South, and Hawaiian Annexation." *Pacific Historical Review* 57, no. 1 (February 1988): 25–46.

Miles, Edwin A. "President Adams' Billiard Table." *New England Quarterly* 45, no. 1 (March 1972): 31–43.

Murray, Margaret, et al. "Maxillary Prosthetics, Speech Impairment, and Presidential Politics: How Grover Cleveland Was Able to Speak Normally after His 'Secret' Operation." *Surgery Journal* 6, no. 1 (January 2020): e1–e6. https:// www.ncbi.nlm.nih.gov/pmc/articles/PMC6887570/.

Noyes, John E. "William Howard Taft and the Taft Arbitration Treaties." *Villanova Law Review* 56, no. 3 (2011): 535–58. https://digitalcommons.law.villanova .edu/cgi/viewcontent.cgi?article=1017&context=vlr.

O'Brien, Patrick G., and Philip T. Rosen. "Hoover and the Historians: The Resurrection of a President." *Annals of Iowa* 46, no. 2 (1981): 83–99. https://pubs.lib.uiowa.edu/annals-of-iowa/article/4449/galley/113326/view/.

O'Connell, Kaete M. "Weapon of War, Tool of Peace: U.S. Food Diplomacy in Postwar Germany." Dissertation, August 2019. https://scholarshare.temple.edu/bitstream/handle/20.500.12613/507/680714_pdf_791075_E9E0695C-ACB9-11E9-B0C5-299A4D662D30.pdf?sequence=1&isAllowed=y.

"Oil Dependence and U.S. Foreign Policy: 1850–2022," Council on Foreign Relations. https://www.cfr.org/timeline/oil-dependence-and-us-foreign-policy.

Pappas, Theodore N. "The Assassination of Anton Cermak, Mayor of Chicago: A Review of His Postinjury Medical Care." *Surgery Journal* (New York) 6, no. 2 (June 2020): e105–e111. https://www.ncbi.nlm.nih.gov/pmc/articles/PMC7297642/.

Post, Robert. "The Supreme Court Opinion as Institutional Practice: Dissent, Legal Scholarship, and Decision-Making in the Taft Court." *Minnesota Law Review* 85 (2001): 1267, 1271.

Rable, George C. "Slavery, Politics, and the South: The Gag Rule as a Case Study," *Capitol Studies* 3 (Fall 1975): 69–87.

Richardson, Gary, and Tim Sablik. "Banking Panics of the Gilded Age." Federal Reserve History, 2015. https://www.federalreservehistory.org/essays/banking-panics-of-the-gilded-age.

Schneeberg, Norman G. "The Medical History of Thomas Jefferson." *Journal of Medical Biography* 16, no. 2 (May 2008): 118–25.

Simonton, Dean Keith. "Presidential IQ, Openness, Intellectual Brilliance, and Leadership: Estimates and Correlations for 42 U.S. Chief Executives." *Political Psychology* 27, no. 4 (August 2006): 511–26.

Sotos, John G. "Taft and Pickwick: Sleep Apnea in the White House." *Chest* 124, no. 3 (September 2003): 1133–42.

Spero, Patrick, Abigail Shelton, and John Kenney. "The Other Presidency: Thomas Jefferson and the American Philosophical Society." *Proceedings of the American Philosophical Society* 162, no. 4 (December 2018): 321–60.

Steindl, C., et al. "Understanding Psychological Reactance: New Developments and Findings." *Zeitschrift für Psychologie* 223, no. 4 (2015): 205–14.

Stern, Sheldon M. "Henry Cabot Lodge and Louis A. Coolidge in Defense of American Sovereignty, 1898–1920." *Massachusetts Historical Society* 87 (1975): 118–34.

Stevens, Rosemary. "A Time of Scandal: Charles R. Forbes, Warren G. Harding, and the Making of the Veterans Bureau." *American Historical Review* 124, no. 1 (February 2019): 274–75.

Timberlake, Richard H., Jr. "Repeal of Silver Monetization in the Late Nineteenth Century." *Journal of Money, Credit and Banking* 10, no. 1 (February 1978): 27–45.

Verrastro, Frank A., and Guy Caruso. "The Arab Oil Embargo—40 Years Later." Center for Strategic and International Studies, October 16, 2013. https://www.csis.org/analysis/arab-oil-embargo-40-years-later.

Warren, Earl. "Chief Justice William Howard Taft." *Yale Law Journal* 67, no. 3 (January 1958): 353–62.

Wilson, Gaye. "Monticello Was Among the Prizes in a Lottery for a Ruined Jefferson's Relief," *Colonial Williamsburg Journal* (Winter 2010).

Winter, David. "Why Achievement Motivation Predicts Success in Business but Failure in Politics: The Importance of Personal Control." *Special Issue: Personality and Politics* 78, no. 6 (December 2010): 1637–68.

ONLINE RESOURCES

270 to Win. https://www.270towin.com. Used as a resource for election details.

American Presidency Project. UC Santa Barbara. https://www.presidency.ucsb.edu. Presidential speeches.

"Amistad Committee." National Park Service. https://www.nps.gov/people/the-amistad-committee.htm.

"Annexation Process: 1836–1845: A Summary Timeline." Texas State Library and Archives Commission. https://www.tsl.texas.gov/ref/abouttx/annexation/timeline.html.

Architect of the Capitol. https://www.aoc.gov.

Avalon Project, Yale Law School. https://avalon.law.yale.edu.

Bush Center. https://www.bushcenter.org.

Carter Center. https://www.cartercenter.org.

Chronicling America: Historic American Newspapers, Library of Congress. http://chroniclingamerica.loc.gov.

Congress Project. https://www.thecongressproject.com. References to different congresses.

Encyclopedia Virginia. https://encyclopediavirginia.org.

"Enrollment Act: March 3, 1863." Omeka Virtual Exhibits. https://omeka.hrvh.org/exhibits/show/new-paltz-in-the-civil-war/laws/enrollment-act--march-3--1863.

FDIC. https://www.fdic.gov.

Federal Reserve History. https://www.federalreservehistory.org.

Founders Online, National Archives, https://founders.archives.gov.

Franklin D. Roosevelt Presidential Library & Museum. https://www.fdrlibrary.org.

General Services Administration. https://www.gsa.gov.

HarpWeek. http://elections.harpweek.com. Various articles were referenced from their archive.

Herbert Hoover Presidential Library and Museum. https://hoover.archives.gov.

History, Art & Archives, United States House of Representatives. https://history.house.gov.

"Inauguration Weather." National Weather Service. https://www.weather.gov/lwx/events_Inauguration.

Jefferson Monticello. https://www.monticello.org. Various articles were referenced from this site.

Jimmy Carter Presidential Library and Museum. https://www.jimmycarterlibrary.gov.

John Quincy Adams Digital Diary. Massachusetts Historical Society. https://www.masshist.org.

Joint Congressional Committee on Inaugural Ceremonies. https://www.inaugural.senate.gov. Referenced for inauguration details.

"A Man Who Saved the Lives of Millions." *Zoom in on America* 14, no. 155 (July–August 2018): https://pl.usembassy.gov/wp-content/uploads/sites/23/Zoom-in-on-America-July-August-2018.pdf.

Miller Center, University of Virginia. https://millercenter.org.

National Archives. https://www.archives.gov. Various documents were referenced from the archives.

National Park Service. https://www.nps.gov/articles. Various articles were referenced from their archive.

Office of the Historian. https://history.state.gov/. Copies of treaties.

United States Census Bureau. https://www.census.gov.

United States Courts. https://www.uscourts.gov. References to Supreme Court.

White House. https://www.whitehouse.gov.

INTERVIEWS

Astor, Vincent. Courtesy of the FDR Presidential Library. "Oral History Interview with Harry Easley," interviewed by J. R. Fuchs, August 24, 1967. Harry S. Truman Presidential Library, https://www.trumanlibrary.org/oralhist/easleyh.htm.

Bush, Barbara. Author interview, Kennebunkport, Maine, August 10, 2021.

Bush, George W. Author interview, Kennebunkport, Maine, August 10, 2020.

———. Author interview, Kennebunkport, Maine, August 11, 2020.

Bush, Laura. Author interview, Kennebunkport, Maine, August 10, 2020.

Evans, Don. Author interview via Zoom, July 14, 2021.

Ford, Freddie. Author interview by phone, August 5, 2021.

Gaddis, John Lewis. Author interview via Zoom, September 20, 2021.

Hager, Jenna Bush. Author interview by phone, May 5, 2021.

Hersch, Ken. Author interview via Zoom, January 15, 2021.

Karzai, Hamid. Author interview via Zoom, January 31, 2021.

Martinez, Saul. Author interview by phone, January 26, 2021.

McAdams, Dan. Author interview by phone, September 21, 2020.

Mehlman, Ken. Author interview by phone, February 23, 2021.

Nash, George. Author interview by phone, January 17, 2022.

O'Shaughnessy, Andrew. Author interview by phone, May 3, 2022.

Parker, Mary Louise. Author interview by phone, April 15, 2021.

————. Author interview, New York, NY, December 3, 2021.

Perino, Dana. Author interview via Zoom, July 30, 2020.

Rove, Karl. Author interview via Zoom, July 27, 2021.

Spellings, Margaret. Author interview via Zoom, January 6, 2021.

Tran, Tina. Author interview by phone, January 26, 2021.

Winter, David. Author interview by phone, October 2, 2020.

INDEX